THE PAPERS OF ULYSSES S. GRANT

THE PAPERS OF

ULYSSES S. GRANT

Volume 28:

November 1, 1876–September 30, 1878

Edited by John Y. Simon

ASSISTANT EDITORS

William M. Ferraro
Aaron M. Lisec

TEXTUAL EDITOR

Dawn Vogel

SOUTHERN ILLINOIS UNIVERSITY PRESS

CARBONDALE

Library of Congress Cataloging in Publication Data (Revised)

Grant, Ulysses Simpson, Pres. U.S., 1822–1885.
  The papers of Ulysses S. Grant.

  Prepared under the auspices of the Ulysses S. Grant Association.
  Bibliographical footnotes.
  CONTENTS: v. 1. 1837–1861.—v. 2. April–September 1861.—
v. 3. October 1, 1861–January 7, 1862.—v. 4. January 8–March 31,
1862.—v. 5. April 1–August 31, 1862.—v. 6. September 1–
December 8, 1862.—v. 7. December 9, 1862–March 31, 1863.—
v. 8. April 1–July 6, 1863.—v. 9. July 7–December 31, 1863.—v. 10.
January 1–May 31, 1864.—v. 11. June 1–August 15, 1864.—v. 12.
August 16–November 15, 1864.—v. 13. November 16, 1864–
February 20, 1865.—v. 14. February 21–April 30, 1865.—v. 15.
May 1–December 31, 1865.—v. 16. 1866.—v. 17. January 1–
September 30, 1867.—v. 18. October 1, 1867–June 30, 1868.—
v. 19. July 1, 1868–October 31, 1869.—v. 20. November 1, 1869–
October 31, 1870.—v. 21. November 1, 1870–May 31, 1871.—
v. 22. June 1, 1871–January 31, 1872.—v. 23. February 1–
December 31, 1872.—v. 24. 1873.—v. 25. 1874.—v. 26. 1875.—
v. 27. January 1–October 31, 1876.—v. 28. November 1, 1876–
September 30, 1878.
  1. Grant, Ulysses Simpson, Pres. U.S., 1822–1885. 2. United
States—History—Civil War, 1861–1865—Campaigns and battles—
Sources. 3. United States—Politics and government—1869–1877—
Sources. 4. Presidents—United States—Biography. 5. Generals—
United States—Biography. I. Simon, John Y., ed. II. Ulysses S. Grant
Association.
E660.G756   1967   973.8'2'0924   67-10725
ISBN 0-8093-2632-9 (v. 28)

The paper used in this publication meets the minimum requirements
of American National Standard for Information Sciences—Perma-
nence of Paper for Printed Library Materials, ANSI Z39.48-1992. ∞

Published with the assistance of a grant from the National Historical
Publications and Records Commission.

Ulysses S. Grant Association

Contents

———

Introduction

═══

The 1876 PRESIDENTIAL CAMPAIGN between Republican Rutherford B. Hayes and Democrat Samuel J. Tilden ended in uncertainty. Tilden appeared to have won the popular vote, but the electoral vote could swing either way pending the outcome of disputes in Louisiana, South Carolina, Florida, and Oregon. As partisan passions heated, Ulysses S. Grant took action to avert a constitutional crisis. He responded to reports of fraud and intimidation by ordering army commanders in Louisiana and Florida to protect the canvassing boards. In his telegram transmitting this order, Grant supplied a guiding principle. "Either party can afford to be disappointed in the result but the Country cannot afford to have the result tainted by the suspicion of illegal or false returns."

Both political parties dispatched statesmen and lawyers to assist local election officials, and the activities of these observers, especially those sent by Grant, raised apprehension. Grant attempted to maintain a discreet distance from the complicated process of validating contested ballots, but appeals from distraught politicians and concerned army commanders (particularly Colonel Thomas H. Ruger in South Carolina) involved him in unfolding events. Grant defended his actions in a forthright message to the House of Representatives. "I have not employed troops on slight occasions, nor in any case where it has not been necessary to the enforcement of the laws of the United States."

Tension mounted as inauguration day approached. Many feared the outbreak of violence. Finally, a special electoral commission was devised to pass judgment on the disputed counts. Grant commended legislation creating this commission as "a wise and constitutional means of escape" from an unprecedented predicament. Composed of five senators, five representatives, and five supreme court justices, and dividing along political lines into eight Republicans and seven Democrats, this commission decided in every case for the Republican electors and made Hayes the winner.

Fears of violence lingered because of outrage among some Democrats. Because the usual inauguration day, March 4, 1877, fell on a Sunday, the formal ceremony was postponed until the fifth. To minimize chances for an outbreak, Grant kept troops nearby and persuaded Hayes to take the presidential oath privately at the White House on Saturday evening, March 3. Nothing marred the orderly transition of power.

Reflecting on his presidency in his final annual message, Grant recapitulated the difficulties that he had overcome. Acknowledging mistakes, but not wrongdoing or culpability, he declared "that I have acted in every instance, from a consciencious desire to do what was right, constitutional, within the law, and for the very best interest[s] of the whole people. Failures have been errors of judgement, not of intent." Grant also noted the achievements of his Indian policy and denounced greedy gold prospectors as the source of hostilities still plaguing the Black Hills region. Grant's candid introspection raised eyebrows, as did his pardons of several men notorious for their convictions as "Whiskey Ring" conspirators.

Calling themselves waifs, Grant and his wife Julia left the White House without a settled home, as they prepared for their long-contemplated trip overseas. Months earlier, Grant had notified Adam Badeau, United States consul general in London. "I expect to be in England early in July where I shall hope to see you if my successor has not decapitated you before that." It took Grant a few weeks to arrange his affairs in Washington. He formally thanked his cabinet officers for their service and recommended a few friends—foremost among them Badeau—for patronage positions. Grant had assessed his personal finances and designated his son Ulysses, Jr., to manage his affairs while he traveled with his youngest son, Jesse, a senior at Cornell. The trip would last only as long as income flowed from stock investments. The outlook for a lengthy trip appeared favorable because Grant had put much of his money into western bonanza mines.

A circuit to visit family and friends in the east and midwest included several public appearances. As military hero and former president, it was impossible for Grant to travel quietly. Popular interest in his movements, activities, and thoughts persisted as the time approached for his departure for Europe.

On May 17, Grant and his party boarded a steamer at Philadelphia for their voyage. Festivities during the previous week had taxed Grant's health, but he rarely turned down invitations. His parting telegram to President Hayes expressed his desire to return to a nation "prosperous in business and with cordial feelings restored between all sections." The State Department had issued a circular letter requiring all ministers and consuls to provide every courtesy to the distinguished traveler.

After a stormy voyage, Grant arrived in England to resounding acclaim. Surprised and gratified, Grant spent the entire month of June attending gatherings or celebrations throughout England. The warm reception pleased Grant, who took pride in having settled the *Alabama* Claims through arbitration, thus eliminating a longstanding source of contention. "It has always been my desire to see all jealousy between England and the United States abated, and all sores healed up." Particularly notable was the ceremony in London during which he received the key to that city. The most awkward moment was the evening spent at Windsor Castle as guests of Queen Victoria. Lacking royal lineage or some official position, Grant and his family created protocol problems. Chilliness characterized an abbreviated visit.

Unsettled French politics compelled Grant to postpone his visit to Paris originally planned for July. Instead he toured Belgium, the Rhine valley, Switzerland, and northern Italy. Grant especially enjoyed the Swiss Alps near Lucerne, where he saw "the grandest scenery immaginable from every point."

Grant returned to London in late August and spent the next few weeks sightseeing in Scotland and the northern reaches of England. During his travels he carefully observed agricultural and industrial development. While relaxation and adventure were goals, Grant genuinely wanted to increase his knowledge and understanding of foreign nations and people. Whenever possible, he slipped away from his hosts to mingle with the populace. Grant also tried to keep abreast of news from the United States, and he followed with keen interest the railroad strike that crippled the nation in July, 1877, writing privately that "it should have been put down with a strong hand."

After a short trip to southern England to visit his daughter Nellie and her family, Grant and his wife went to Paris. Unimpressed, Grant expressed disbelief that so many Americans lived there. "I certainly should prefer any of our large cities as a residence." Having arranged with the Navy Department for passage aboard a warship in the Mediterranean, Grant left Paris to sail down the Italian peninsula. Along the way, the party toured the ruins of Pompeii and spent Christmas in Sicily.

This voyage prepared Grant for an even more exotic trip up the Nile that occupied the winter months of 1878. Egyptian ruins exceeded Grant's expectations. "I have seen more in Egypt to interest me than in all my other travels." The people, however, left a less favorable impression. "Innate uglyness, slovenlyness, filth and indolence witnessed here is only equaled, in my experience, by seeing the lowest class of Digger Indians found on the Pacific Coast."

Continuing eastward to Jerusalem, where he encountered bad roads and snow, Grant eventually arrived at Constantinople at the conclusion of a war between Turkey and Russia. Russian forces prevailed and left Grant in an awkward position when he received lavish attentions from Turkish leaders. The plight of refugees moved Grant. "They are fed entirely by charity and mostly by foreigners. What is to become of them is sad to think of." Grant condemned the class separation that he observed in this region. "The people would be industrious if they had encouragement, but they are treated as slaves, and all they produce is taken from them for the benefit of the governing classes and to maintain them in a luxurious and licentious life. Women are degraded even beneath a slave. They have no more rights than the brute. In fact, the donkey is their superior in privileges."

Much of what Americans knew about Grant's travels in Africa and Asia came from accounts written by John Russell Young, a *New York Herald* correspondent assigned to accompany Grant. Young traveled with Grant only sporadically prior to the voyage across the Mediterranean. His firsthand accounts reveal much more than did his earlier columns.

More revealing than Young's travelogues, however, were his presentations of Grant's private views on his military and political career. Young presented Grant's words, distilled from numerous conversations, in the question-and-answer format of an interview that gave them an appealing coherence. These interviews attracted considerable attention in the United States. Key figures publicly disputed Grant's assessments. Speculation grew about Grant's political ambitions. Grant regretted the publicity that Young gave his private views, but the two remained on friendly terms. Despite holding strong opinions on some policies, particularly legislation remonetizing silver that he characterized as the most severe blow to the country "since the attempt of the Southern states to secede," Grant reiterated his delight to be a private citizen after sixteen years of official toil.

During the spring of 1878, Grant traveled briskly through Greece and Italy. His Egyptian experiences dampened his enthusiasm for Rome's wonders. "Here you see modern and comparatively insignificant ruins, not dating back many centuries before the beginning of the Christian era. On the Nile one sees grand ruins, with the inscriptions as plain and distinct as when they were first made, that antedate Moses by many centuries." After another sojourn in Paris, primarily to visit the recently opened exposition, Grant toured Scandinavia, Germany, Russia, and Austria. Meeting Chancellor Otto von Bismarck of Germany in Berlin highlighted this period.

Having covered all of northern Europe, Grant set out for Spain and Portugal. He was unsure whether this trip would complete his overseas travels. Sizing up his wishes and his funds, Grant weighed the proposition to extend his journey to India, China, Japan, and across the Pacific. Both he and Julia longed for home, but such a chance might never come again. Newspapers in the United States speculated that Grant's allies would time his return to maximize his strength at the 1880 Republican presidential convention. Such considerations played no role in Grant's thinking. Curiosity was his principal motivation as he continued around the world.

We are indebted to J. Dane Hartgrove and Howard H. Wehmann for assistance in searching the National Archives; to Harriet F. Simon for proofreading; and to Robyn Rhoads and Kimberly T. Dowd, graduate students at Southern Illinois University, for research assistance.

Financial support for the period during which this volume was prepared came from Southern Illinois University, the National Endowment for the Humanities, and the National Historical Publications and Records Commission.

JOHN Y. SIMON

July 4, 2004

Editorial Procedure

1. Editorial Insertions

A. Words or letters in roman type within brackets represent editorial reconstruction of parts of manuscripts torn, mutilated, or illegible.

B. [. . .] or [— — —] within brackets represent lost material which cannot be reconstructed. The number of dots represents the approximate number of lost letters; dashes represent lost words.

C. Words in *italic* type within brackets represent material such as dates which were not part of the original manuscript.

D. Other material crossed out is indicated by ~~cancelled type~~.

E. Material raised in manuscript, as "4th," has been brought in line, as "4th."

2. Symbols Used to Describe Manuscripts

AD	Autograph Document
ADS	Autograph Document Signed
ADf	Autograph Draft
ADfS	Autograph Draft Signed
AES	Autograph Endorsement Signed
AL	Autograph Letter
ALS	Autograph Letter Signed

ANS	Autograph Note Signed
D	Document
DS	Document Signed
Df	Draft
DfS	Draft Signed
ES	Endorsement Signed
LS	Letter Signed

3. Military Terms and Abbreviations

Act.	Acting
Adjt.	Adjutant
AG	Adjutant General
AGO	Adjutant General's Office
Art.	Artillery
Asst.	Assistant
Bvt.	Brevet
Brig.	Brigadier
Capt.	Captain
Cav.	Cavalry
Col.	Colonel
Co.	Company
C.S.A.	Confederate States of America
Dept.	Department
Div.	Division
Gen.	General
Hd. Qrs.	Headquarters
Inf.	Infantry
Lt.	Lieutenant
Maj.	Major
Q. M.	Quartermaster
Regt.	Regiment or regimental
Sgt.	Sergeant
USMA	United States Military Academy, West Point, N.Y.
Vols.	Volunteers

4. Short Titles and Abbreviations

ABPC	*American Book Prices Current* (New York, 1895–)
Badeau	Adam Badeau, *Grant in Peace. From Appomattox to Mount McGregor* (Hartford, Conn., 1887)
CG	*Congressional Globe.* Numbers following represent the Congress, session, and page.
J. G. Cramer	Jesse Grant Cramer, ed., *Letters of Ulysses S. Grant to his Father and his Youngest Sister, 1857–78* (New York and London, 1912)
DAB	*Dictionary of American Biography* (New York, 1928–36)
Foreign Relations	*Papers Relating to the Foreign Relations of the United States* (Washington, 1869–)
Garland	Hamlin Garland, *Ulysses S. Grant: His Life and Character* (New York, 1898)
Julia Grant	John Y. Simon, ed., *The Personal Memoirs of Julia Dent Grant* (New York, 1975)
HED	*House Executive Documents*
HMD	*House Miscellaneous Documents*
HRC	*House Reports of Committees.* Numbers following *HED, HMD,* or *HRC* represent the number of the Congress, the session, and the document.
Ill. AG Report	J. N. Reece, ed., *Report of the Adjutant General of the State of Illinois* (Springfield, 1900)
Johnson, Papers	LeRoy P. Graf and Ralph W. Haskins, eds., *The Papers of Andrew Johnson* (Knoxville, 1967–2000)
Lewis	Lloyd Lewis, *Captain Sam Grant* (Boston, 1950)
Lincoln, Works	Roy P. Basler, Marion Dolores Pratt, and Lloyd A. Dunlap, eds., *The Collected Works of Abraham Lincoln* (New Brunswick, 1953–55)
Memoirs	*Personal Memoirs of U. S. Grant* (New York, 1885–86)
Nevins, Fish	Allan Nevins, *Hamilton Fish: The Inner History of the Grant Administration* (New York, 1936)

O.R.	*The War of the Rebellion: A Compilation of the Official Records of the Union and Confederate Armies* (Washington, 1880–1901)
O.R. (Navy)	*Official Records of the Union and Confederate Navies in the War of the Rebellion* (Washington, 1894–1927). Roman numerals following *O.R.* or *O.R.* (Navy) represent the series and the volume.
PUSG	John Y. Simon, ed., *The Papers of Ulysses S. Grant* (Carbondale and Edwardsville, 1967–)
Richardson	Albert D. Richardson, *A Personal History of Ulysses S. Grant* (Hartford, Conn., 1868)
SED	*Senate Executive Documents*
SMD	*Senate Miscellaneous Documents*
SRC	*Senate Reports of Committees.* Numbers following *SED, SMD,* or *SRC* represent the number of the Congress, the session, and the document.
USGA Newsletter	*Ulysses S. Grant Association Newsletter*
Young	John Russell Young, *Around the World with General Grant* (New York, 1879)

5. Location Symbols

CLU	University of California at Los Angeles, Los Angeles, Calif.
CoHi	Colorado State Historical Society, Denver, Colo.
CSmH	Henry E. Huntington Library, San Marino, Calif.
CSt	Stanford University, Stanford, Calif.
CtY	Yale University, New Haven, Conn.
CU-B	Bancroft Library, University of California, Berkeley, Calif.
DLC	Library of Congress, Washington, D.C. Numbers following DLC-USG represent the series and volume of military records in the USG papers.
DNA	National Archives, Washington, D.C. Additional numbers identify record groups.

IaHA	Iowa State Department of History and Archives, Des Moines, Iowa.
I-ar	Illinois State Archives, Springfield, Ill.
IC	Chicago Public Library, Chicago, Ill.
ICarbS	Southern Illinois University, Carbondale, Ill.
ICHi	Chicago Historical Society, Chicago, Ill.
ICN	Newberry Library, Chicago, Ill.
ICU	University of Chicago, Chicago, Ill.
IHi	Illinois State Historical Library, Springfield, Ill.
In	Indiana State Library, Indianapolis, Ind.
InFtwL	Lincoln National Life Foundation, Fort Wayne, Ind.
InHi	Indiana Historical Society, Indianapolis, Ind.
InNd	University of Notre Dame, Notre Dame, Ind.
InU	Indiana University, Bloomington, Ind.
KHi	Kansas State Historical Society, Topeka, Kan.
MdAN	United States Naval Academy Museum, Annapolis, Md.
MeB	Bowdoin College, Brunswick, Me.
MH	Harvard University, Cambridge, Mass.
MHi	Massachusetts Historical Society, Boston, Mass.
MiD	Detroit Public Library, Detroit, Mich.
MiU-C	William L. Clements Library, University of Michigan, Ann Arbor, Mich.
MoSHi	Missouri Historical Society, St. Louis, Mo.
NHi	New-York Historical Society, New York, N.Y.
NIC	Cornell University, Ithaca, N.Y.
NjP	Princeton University, Princeton, N.J.
NjR	Rutgers University, New Brunswick, N.J.
NN	New York Public Library, New York, N.Y.
NNP	Pierpont Morgan Library, New York, N.Y.
NRU	University of Rochester, Rochester, N.Y.
OClWHi	Western Reserve Historical Society, Cleveland, Ohio.
OFH	Rutherford B. Hayes Library, Fremont, Ohio.
OHi	Ohio Historical Society, Columbus, Ohio.
OrHi	Oregon Historical Society, Portland, Ore.

PCarlA	U.S. Army Military History Institute, Carlisle Barracks, Pa.
PHi	Historical Society of Pennsylvania, Philadelphia, Pa.
PPRF	Rosenbach Foundation, Philadelphia, Pa.
RPB	Brown University, Providence, R.I.
TxHR	Rice University, Houston, Tex.
USG 3	Maj. Gen. Ulysses S. Grant 3rd, Clinton, N.Y.
USMA	United States Military Academy Library, West Point, N.Y.
ViHi	Virginia Historical Society, Richmond, Va.
ViU	University of Virginia, Charlottesville, Va.
WHi	State Historical Society of Wisconsin, Madison, Wis.
Wy-Ar	Wyoming State Archives and Historical Department, Cheyenne, Wyo.
WyU	University of Wyoming, Laramie, Wyo.

Chronology

November 1, 1876–September 30, 1878

━━━━━

Nov. 7.   Democrat Samuel J. Tilden won the popular vote for president over Republican Rutherford B. Hayes.

Nov. 10.   At Philadelphia, USG declared the Centennial closed. Amid growing uncertainty over electoral totals, USG directed troop movements and requested that Republican leaders witness vote counts at New Orleans.

Nov. 11.   USG ordered Lt. Gen. Philip H. Sheridan to New Orleans "to keep the peace and to protect the legal Canvassing board in the performance of its duties."

Nov. 13.   USG requested that Republican leaders witness vote counts in Fla. and S.C.

Nov. 14.   John S. Mosby warned USG of possible assassination.

Dec. 3.   USG ordered U.S. troops not to interfere in a dispute over rival legislatures in S.C. To U.S. Representative Abram S. Hewitt of N.Y., Democratic national chairman, USG confidentially acknowledged Republican defeat in La.

Dec. 5.   USG's eighth and final annual message opened with a candid assessment of his presidency.

Dec. 6.   USG gave Hewitt "a piece of his mind" concerning Democratic tactics, especially in S.C. Presidential electors cast their ballots, giving Tilden 184 to Hayes 165, with 20 still disputed (Fla., La., Ore., and S.C.).

Dec. 23.   USG ordered troops to Miss. He also announced the resumption of extradition to and from Great Britain after a protracted treaty dispute.

Jan. 1.   In La., Republicans and Democrats set up rival governments.

Jan. 9.   La. Democrats ousted Republican-appointed justices.

Jan. 14.   USG declared that he would not "sit quietly by" and allow La. Democrats to seize power "gradually" and "by illegal means."

Jan. 17.   USG told Secretary of State Hamilton Fish that the Fifteenth Amendment "was a mistake; that it had done the negro no good."

Jan. 19.   USG ordered troops to assist revenue officials facing armed resistance from illicit distillers in N.C., S.C., and Ga.

Jan. 26.   USG pardoned John McDonald, leader of the St. Louis Whiskey Ring.

Jan. 27.   USG told Fish that the La. dispute "had given him a great deal of anxiety and trouble."

Jan. 29.   USG signed an act creating an electoral commission to resolve disputed vote counts in contested states.

Feb. 1.   USG stopped criminal proceedings against former Secretary of War William W. Belknap.

Feb. 3.   USG urged Congress to hasten specie resumption.

Feb. 5.   USG countermanded an order to withdraw troops from the capital.

Feb. 9.   Hayes won the Fla. electoral vote.

Feb. 16.   Hayes won the La. electoral vote.

Feb. 20.   USG wrote to Hayes that his election was "virtually determined" and invited him to stay at the White House before the inauguration.

Feb. 23.   Hayes won the Ore. electoral vote.

Feb. 26.   Republicans and Democrats reportedly met at Wormley's Hotel in Washington, D.C., to discuss a compromise settlement to the electoral crisis.

Feb. 27.   Hayes won the S.C. electoral vote.

Feb. 28.   USG signed into law an agreement by which the Sioux ceded rights to the Black Hills.

Mar. 1.   USG declined to support the Republican contender for La. governor, citing public opposition.

Mar. 2.   At 4:10 a.m., the Senate certified Hayes as president. Hours later, Hayes arrived in the capital and met USG.

Mar. 3.   On the advice of USG and Fish, Hayes was quietly sworn in as president prior to a White House dinner.

Mar. 5.   Hayes was formally inaugurated. USG and Julia Dent Grant left the White House for Fish's home, where they stayed for nearly three weeks.

MAR. 7–8. USG conferred with senators amid rumors that he sought to defeat the nomination of Carl Schurz as secretary of the interior.

MAR. 17. USG's grandson Algernon Edward Sartoris was born.

MAR. 24–APRIL 23. USG and Julia Grant visited family and friends in Cincinnati, St. Louis, Chicago, Galena, and Pa. At Cincinnati, USG said: "I don't suppose I will have any political opponents now, since we are all sovereigns together."

APRIL 2. "There are books enough already," USG told a St. Louis reporter who asked whether he planned to write his memoirs. In the same interview, USG supported Hayes's Southern policy but distanced himself from civil service reform.

APRIL 24. U.S. troops left New Orleans, ending federal occupation of the South.

APRIL 28–MAY 9. USG and Julia Grant visited relatives and friends in Elizabeth, Newark, and Morristown, N.J.

MAY 6. Pursued since the Battle of Little Big Horn, Crazy Horse surrendered.

MAY 9–16. At Philadelphia, USG attended the opening of a permanent Centennial exhibition and was mustered into George G. Meade Post No. 1, Grand Army of the Republic.

MAY 17. USG, Julia Grant, and son Jesse sailed for Liverpool aboard the *Indiana*.

MAY 28. Enthusiastic crowds welcomed USG and party to Liverpool.

MAY 30–31. USG spoke at Manchester and Leicester, en route to London.

JUNE 8. USG attended an agricultural exhibition at Bath.

JUNE 18. USG breakfasted with Matthew Arnold, Robert Browning, and Anthony Trollope. He told a Reform Club dinner that he was "overwhelmed by the kindness" shown to him in England.

JUNE 23. USG dined with the Prince of Wales.

JUNE 26. USG and party dined with Queen Victoria at Windsor Castle, where they spent the night.

JUNE 28. USG told a Liverpool audience: "We are of one kindred, one blood, one language, and one civilization."

JULY 3. To a delegation of British workers, USG saluted "the labourer who is the author of all greatness and wealth."

JULY 5. From Folkestone, USG and party crossed the English Channel to Ostend, Belgium.

JULY 6–8. At Brussels, USG met King Leopold of Belgium.

JULY 9–17.   In Germany, USG stopped at Cologne, Frankfort-am-Main, and Heidelberg, where he met Richard Wagner.

JULY 18–31.   In Switzerland, USG and party visited Lucerne, Interlaken, Bern, and Geneva.

AUG.   The Grants toured northern Italian lakes. At Lake Maggiore, USG said: "There is one Italian whose hand I wish especially to shake, and that man is General Garibaldi."

AUG. 25.   From London, USG inquired about his mining stock, writing that his future travels "will have to depend in some degree upon the length of time it continues to pay dividends."

AUG. 29.   En route to Edinburgh, during a lengthy interview with a *New York Herald* reporter, USG disparaged Charles Sumner.

AUG. 30–SEPT. 20.   Touring Scotland, USG received many civic honors. At Glasgow, he commented: "I find that I am being made so much a citizen of Scotland that it will become a serious question where I shall go to vote."

SEPT. 21–29.   The Grants toured England, from Newcastle to Leamington. USG tired of public ceremonies. "I would rather be kicked—in a friendly way—than to make these replies." At Stratford upon Avon, he received an address "in a Casket made out of Shakespeare's Mulberry Tree."

OCT. 1–8.   USG and Julia Grant visited their daughter, Ellen Grant Sartoris, at Warsash, the Sartoris family home. On Oct. 6, USG toured nearby Southampton.

OCT. 8–15.   At Torquay, USG, Julia Grant, and daughter Ellen were guests of Alfred D. Jessup.

OCT. 16–17.   USG spoke at Birmingham, where he met Joseph Chamberlain.

OCT. 18.   Wendell Phillips defended Sumner in the wake of USG's interview. On Oct. 20, Fish rebutted Phillips.

OCT. 24–NOV. 30.   At Paris, USG met President Maurice de MacMahon, sat for painter George P. A. Healy, and viewed the construction of the Statue of Liberty. He wrote: "I have seen nothing here that would make me want to live in Paris."

DEC. 1.   USG and party left Paris for Nice, by way of Lyons and Marseilles.

DEC. 13–JAN. 5.   The U.S.S. *Vandalia* carried USG and party from Nice to Alexandria, Egypt. Stops included Genoa; Naples, where USG toured Mount Vesuvius and Pompeii; and Palermo, where the party celebrated Christmas.

JAN. 5–8.　At Alexandria, USG met Henry M. Stanley.

JAN. 9.　At Cairo, USG met the khedive.

JAN. 16–FEB. 3.　USG and party explored the Nile by steamer, visiting ruins at Thebes and Memphis.

FEB. 9.　USG boarded the *Vandalia* at Port Said.

FEB. 11–17.　USG and party braved bad roads and weather to tour the Holy Land. At Jerusalem "it rained, blew and snowed all the time."

FEB. 22.　USG arrived at Smyrna, Turkey.

MAR. 1–6.　At Constantinople, Sultan Abdul Hamid II presented USG with two Arabian stallions.

MAR. 8–15.　USG visited Athens, "one of the most beautiful, cleanest and best paved cities in Europe," inhabited by "a very energetic and advancing people."

MAR. 18.　The *Vandalia* arrived at Naples.

MAR. 21–APRIL 14.　In Rome, USG visited the studios of American artists and met Pope Leo XIII.

APRIL 15–21.　At Florence, USG toured the Uffizi Gallery.

APRIL 22–MAY 7.　USG visited Venice, Milan, Turin, and Dijon, before returning to Paris.

MAY 11.　USG toured the Paris Universal Exposition. "It is quite a success, but, I think, no improvement on our Centennial show. The buildings and grounds are far inferior to ours."

MAY 27.　The *New York Herald* published an interview in which USG countered criticism of his Va. campaign by Gideon Welles and former C.S.A. Lt. Gen. Richard Taylor.

JUNE 14.　The Grants left Paris for The Hague, Rotterdam, and Amsterdam. USG called Holland "the most interesting country—and people—that I have yet seen."

JUNE 26–JULY 2.　At Berlin, USG met Chancellor Otto von Bismarck and reviewed Prussian military units.

JULY 4.　Near Hamburg, USG told an Independence Day gathering of Americans: "The humblest soldier who carried a musket is entitled to as much credit for the results of the war as those who were in command."

JULY 6–12.　At Copenhagen, the guest of brother-in-law Michael John Cramer, U.S. chargé d'affaires, USG discounted a presidential run in 1880: "I have had all the honors, and would like to avoid the vexations of political life for the future."

JULY 13–29.　USG toured Scandinavia.

JULY 24. The *New York Herald* published a lengthy interview with USG, who assessed Union and Confederate commanders, described the Appomattox campaign, and defended his Santo Domingo policy.

JULY 30–AUG. 14. USG visited St. Petersburg and Moscow. A conversation with Tsar Alexander II focused on Indian policy.

AUG. 18–22. The Grant party reached Vienna by way of Warsaw. USG met Emperor Francis Joseph I.

AUG.-SEPT. USG and Julia Grant toured the Alps. USG met Emperor William I of Germany at a spa near Salzburg.

SEPT. 23. At Zurich, USG attended a dinner in his honor.

SEPT. 25. John Russell Young and others greeted USG on his return to Paris.

The Papers of Ulysses S. Grant
November 1, 1876–September 30, 1878

To Adam Badeau

———

Nov. 2d /76

DEAR BADEAU:

I have read with great pleasure your chapter on the Cold Harbor Campaign and given it to Babcock to return.[1] I have no criticisms to make, and think it not only very accurate but that it will explain many existing misapprehensions in regard to that Campaign.

I have no time to write further people being in waiting now wishing to come in to see me. By June next I hope to see you, in person, in London. It is my intention by that time to start on a somewhat extended tour, taking Mrs. Grant & Jesse with me. Jesse will then be a Senior in Cornell University and may only remain with me during his vacation. But if he remains with me he will still graduate at the age of twenty-one, quite young enough.

Always taking an interest in your wellfare, I subscribe myself,

Your friend

U. S. GRANT

ALS, Munson-Williams-Proctor Institute, Utica, N. Y. On Sept. 12 and Nov. 11, 1876, Adam Badeau, consul gen., London, wrote to USG. "I send you today the proofs of the concluding chapter of the Wilderness campaign; the summing up, and the arrangement of the figures have cost me months of very close labor, but I consider the hardest and most important part of my task is done. If I have my health, I hope to finish by March. I enclose a letter for Porter, which I beg you to read, and then send to him. If it suggests any remarks to you, or if the perusal of the proof does, I shall be delighted to see them in the hand writing which was once so familiar. I send Porter another copy of the proof, so that if you wish to send me your emendations it can be done. I hope you will note what I say to him about your political papers. Buck ought to care for those, if Porter cannot, and see that all of importance are preserved before it is too late. I see Mr Pierrepont frequently; he is certainly uncommonly well received here. The Queen went out of her usual course to be civil to him and Mrs. Pierrepont. He talks about you with a pwarmth and a personal regard which is refreshing, and makes me thinks of the devotion of your staff, in old times. The sole topic of talk, or of newspaper discussion just now—is Bulgaria. It looks very much as if a grand European war wasere near; but I dont think the present party will go out of power. Neither do I think it will in America. The returns from the Maine election are announced to-

day, and they don't look like defeat. If the democrats *should* get in, there might very easily
be use for you again as a soldier. To me off here, it looks as if there were a good deal of the
wicked old leaven left at the South, and with Tilden at the head of affairs, such things
might be done as the North would not tolerate—and then. Please make my best and kindest wishes to Mrs Grant. Mr. Pierrepont says you talk of coming abroad, when you leave
office You and Mrs Grant would have a princely reception. Mrs Sartoris and her husband
were in town for twenty four hours last week, and I went to see them, but missed them.
They breakfasted with the Minister I hope you will not fail to let me know if you think
any corrections or changes are advisable in the matter which I send. I shall have all but the
last thirty pages stereotyped, before you receive this, but can even then make alterations. . . . P. S. I have determined to send the proof first to Porter, and ask him to forward
it with my letter to him—to you; So that when—you are ready, all you will have to do will
be to direct the proof and any remarks you choose to make to be sent direct to me" "I suppose that Mr. Pierrepont is also sending you a copy of the World from London, as he is so
pleased with it; but you may like or Mrs Grant may, to have another copy. You know that
it is written by Mr. Jennings, late of the N. Y. Times. I also send you a proof of the most
important part of my annual report, in which you will find many valuable items, I am sure.
It has cost me a great deal of labor and time; but I am still at work on my literary matters.
I am trying to arrange for an English edition; to be brought out about the time that you
arrive here. I suppose Mr Pierrepont has told you that he has spoken to two members of
the Govt here, who assure him that your reception would be all that your friends could
wish, and that the Govt would do its best to contribute to that result; or rather that *they
two* would. I begin to doubt however whether you will be able to leave the country very
soon. We are still awaiting here to know the result of the elections; If Tilden is elected, I
think you may be needed at home The country would look only to you in case of serious
trouble; and I think another war not impossible, nor even improbable. With Hayes elected,
and you for the next four months at the White House, the rebellion will 'simmer down.'
The sympathy here with the South and the Democracy is most pronounced—I shall send
Gov. Fish and Mr Morrill printed copies of the slips of my report, and ask for it to be
printed; and I hope you will do me the kindness to recommend this to the State Dept. If a
Democratic President comes in, he will do nothing to show that your friends did good service of any sort, and the report will be smothered; and even in the ordinary course, it would
not be printed under a year, when all its information will be stale. Now it would be of use.
It would also be useful to *me*, and I think not undesirable, just before the appearance of
Vol 2. I have not yet received the proof from you of Chapter IV. I have done Petersburg; I
received your telegram about Smith (Baldy). If he never made a report to the War Office
he allowed Swinton to see one, for that noble historian quotes from it largely. I beg you to
remember me most cordially to Mrs Grant and Mrs Sartoris, and all your children. If there
is another war I want to be at your side; *I beg you to remember this.* Mrs Badeau has been ill,
but is better. She and her sister have instituted five lawsuits against the trustee of their fathers estate; one alone is for $40,000 *interest* due during the last five years—" ALS, USG 3.
On Nov. 1, USG had telegraphed to Badeau in response to a request for Maj. Gen. William
F. Smith's Cold Harbor report. "No report from Smith after June 4th." *Badeau,* p. 477. See
letter to Adam Badeau, Nov. 15, 1876; Badeau to Hamilton Fish, Nov. 11, 1876, DLC-
Hamilton Fish.

On Sept. 27, Henry T. Crosby, chief clerk, War Dept., had written to USG. "I have the
honor to inform you that in accordance wit[h] his cable telegram to you a copy of General
Baldy Smith['s] Petersburg report was sent yesterday in the State Departmen[t] mail to
General Adam Badeau London." Copy, DNA, RG 107, Letters Sent, Military Affairs. On

Nov. 13, Secretary of War James D. Cameron wrote to Badeau. "In accordance with your request of September 12th, I forward herewith, copies of papers asked for, with the exception of the Third Return of the Army of the Potomac for May 10th 1864, which has not been received in the Adjutant Generals office" Copy, *ibid.* On Nov. 16, Cameron wrote to Horace Porter, Chicago. "I have the honor to acknowledge the receipt of your letter of the 7th instant, requesting on behalf of General Badeau a copy of General Lee's, or his Adjutant Generals report dated June 13th 1864, also a rebel return showing the losses of Lee, between May 1st and June 13th 1864. A careful search has been made in the Rebel Archive office of the War Department, for the information desired by General Badeau, but without success. The report of Genl. Lee referred to is not on file, nor is there any return showing the losses sustained by General Lee's Army during the campaign of the Wilderness in 1864, nor data from which an estimate can be made." Copy, *ibid.* See William W. Belknap to Badeau, Oct. 15, 1875, *ibid.*

On Sept. 8, 1876, William H. Doherty, Washington, D. C., wrote to USG. "*Private* . . . I have long desired to communicate with you, on the part of many of my learned Friends in England, & in this, my adopted country, on the subject of your writing a memoir of your life & public services—I think such a labor would honorably occupy your coming years of well-earned repose—and would enable you to refute, & utterly destroy, the many & infamous falsehoods which your enemies, and some of your pretended friends, have circulated—I think also that such a plain & truthful narrative of your eventful, but highly honorable life, would be your best legacy to your promising & talented children, and a great & real boon to our Common Country—Your War record, as it is, perhaps, fairly commenced by Mr Badeau, ought to be Completed, under your own eye & *careful supervision*— but this would not at all answer the purpose which I have in view, in the publication of your own *private & personal* Memoir of your life—What would not the world give to have a Memoir of the life of some of the great men of past times?—Alexander,—Julius Caesar— Hannibal, Marlborough, Frederick of prussia,—Buonaparte Wellington, or Washington! —Now, I have not the least intention of being so rude as to attempt flattery,—And I only feel impelled to write thus because I fear that a natural disgust with the ingratitude & injustice that you have met with, may prevent you from doing as I venture to suggest,—And the near approach of your retirement from your high Office precludes the idea of any selfish aims on my own part.—I most firmly believe that when all your actions, in discharge of your high & all-important duties, are known, that you will stand just as eminent as a Statesman & Politician, as you confessedly do as a Great General.—I am well known to Genl R. C. Schenck, & Genl. Burnside—& was the friend & associate of the late Hon. Horace Mann, with whom I co-operated in founding *Antioch College, Ohio*—of which I was professor—. . ." ALS, USG 3. On Jan. 30, 1873, Robert C. Schenck, U.S. minister, London, had written to USG. "I venture to write to you in behalf of ~~Captain~~ Professor W. H. Doherty who is now, & has been for the past two years or more, a clerk in the Patent Office,— a position, as I think, quite below his qualifications & his deserving. At the beginning of the War, & through the war, circumstances concurred to make me well acquainted with Prof. Doherty's history. He was a clergyman of the church of United Brethren, a man of the highest character & of much learning. He was Principal of a Literary Academy in Newburg in North Carolina, having gone from Ohio to that state. By birth he is an Irishman, although for many years a citizen of the United States. At the breaking out of the rebellion he was threatened & driven away from North Carolina, on account of his bold & avowed loyalty to the Union, his school & means of support broken up, & his school property, in which he had invested all he had, entirely destroyed or taken from him. He had to take refuge in Ohio. The facts coming to the knowledge of Mr Stanton, Secretary of War, he consulted with me what he might do, within his power, for Mr Doherty, & it resulted in his giving him an appointment in Military service as A. Q. M. with the rank of Captain, & assigning him, or having him assigned, to special duty in North Carolina after our troops were in possession there again. At Newburg, & in that neighborhood the Professor as Quarter Master did efficient service, as I have learned, in looking after the clothing of the soldiers, & especially in maintaining his ground & ~~looking after~~ & taking care of them when the yellow fever was prevailing, & when others fled. In this he behaved nobly. . . ." AL (incomplete), DNA, RG 59, Letters of Application and Recommendation.

1. On Oct. 26 and 31, 1876, Orville E. Babcock, Washington, D. C., wrote to Badeau. "I have just returned your proof sheets to the President who asked me to read and criticise them. I have made a few suggestions on the margin and want to add one here. That is, that all you say as to Lee's failure to take advantage of Grants movements, and Grants superior generalship, are all true, but would they not be better at the end of the campaign— rather than in the middle, for you must treat the Va campaign as an entirety, and wont people construe so much in connection with Cold Harbor, as a sort of dust thrown to hide that one days work. I merely mention this as a suggestion—I want to thank you for your good letter and to say that it should have been acknowledged long ago, but when I was out of one difficulty, they sprung a meaner charge and I resolved to wait until I had wiped that out also. I assure you we appreciated your letter, and all have come (even the President and Mrs Grant) to look as you do on the Wilsons—especially Harry—the ingrate. . . ." ALS, DLC-Adam Badeau. "I send you herewith proofsheets 217 to 330. The President has read it and says he has no comments to make. He handed me also to day your letter of the 7th. I am now hunting the matter up and will send the report of Smith about Petersburg, soon as I can. Your telegram to him called, as he supposed for his (Grants) reports commencing June 4th ~~764~~. . . ." ALS, MH.

Endorsement

———

Referred to the sec. of the Navy. Gen. McCawley[1] has removed this applicant and appointed in his stead a man removed from the Treas. as a democrat. This at least can not be allowed.

U. S. GRANT

NOV. 3D /76

AES, DNA, RG 45, Letters Received from the President. Written on a letter of Nov. 2, 1876, from Samuel A. H. Marks, Washington, D. C., to USG. "My Son, S. A. H. Marks Jr, has been the clerk to the Commandant of the Marine Corps since the 1st Jany 1864, and has filled the position acceptably under the late Col John Harris and the recently retired Brig Genl Zeilin—He served as a Captain during the late rebellion, in the Union Army in the District of Columbia, and has ever when opportunity offered voted the Republican ticket. I respectfully ask under these circumstances that he may be permitted to retain the position held by him, under the new Commandant of the Corps." ALS, *ibid.* On Nov. 6, Commodore John C. Howell, act. secretary of the navy, wrote to USG. ". . . It has been the custom of the Navy Department, so far as my memory serves me, to permit Commanding Officers to appoint or dismiss their Confidential Secretaries or clerks—the position of Confidential Secretary or clerk being held to be entirely outside of politics—The dismissal of Mr. Marks and the appointment of Mr Colgate were approved as mere matters of routine. At the time, I had no personal knowledge of either gentleman—and knew nothing of their condition or politics. I have the honor to inform you that a copy of the endorsement upon Mr Marks' letter, will be transmitted to Colonel McCawley, and that he will be directed to conform to its conditions." LS, *ibid.* On the same day, Col. Charles G. McCawley, commandant, U.S. Marine Corps, wrote to USG. "I am informed by Commodore Howell, Acting Sec. of the Navy, that you have some objection to the appointment of Mr J. Colegate as my clerk, on the ground that he had been dismissed from the Treasury as a democrat. I respectfully beg leave to inform you that Mr. Colegate is the father of my deceased Wife—that he has been many years in the Treasury Department—& was one of those dismissed in Oct. for lack of appropriation to pay them. In an acquaintance of thirteen years—I have never heard Mr Colegate express an opinion as a democrat, & I know he has always been a loyal man & an efficient clerk. He has a large family dependent upon him & is without private means. I therefore respectfully beg that you will allow his appointment. I regret that a severe attack of sciatica has prevented me from calling upon you in person to return my sincere thanks for my promotion." LS, *ibid.* James Colegate continued as chief clerk, commandant; Marks, Jr., served as chief clerk, Marine Corps q. m.

1. Born in 1827 in Philadelphia, Charles McCawley joined the Marine Corps as 2nd lt. in 1847 and fought with distinction during the Mexican War and the Civil War. On Dec. 12, 1876, USG nominated McCawley as col. and commandant, Marine Corps, to date from Nov. 1.

On Oct. 16, Ulysses S. Grant, Jr., had written to Secretary of the Navy George M. Robeson. "The President directs me to say that you may inform Genl. Zeland that he will be retired, to take effect at the end of this month" ALS, *ibid.* On Oct. 25, Brig. Gen. Jacob Zeilin, commandant, Marine Corps, wrote to USG. "After your generous kindness to me, in the past—I would not presume to impose any further request for favor upon you, were I not actuated by motives of deepest interest, in one, who for years, has been my firm friend, and faithful assistant. I refer to Lieut. George C. Reid, my Aide, whom of all men, next to my own son, I am most attached to, and whose future welfare I am most deeply interested in On the last of the present month, I am to close my official life by retirement, and I can do so after forty five years service without regret, except that it more than likely to work to the disadvantage, and discomfort to Lieut. Reid, on account of his service to me as Aide, and devotion—and if I may ask a last favor of you Mr. President, it is, that you will give Lieut. Reid an appointment, either in the Staff of the Marine Corps, or Army, upon the first vacancy—a position which he is in every respect, qualified to fill properly. He has been over twelve years in the service, and my Aide, since my promotion to Brig. General." LS, *ibid.* No appointment followed.

Also on Oct. 25, Governor Alexander H. Rice of Mass. wrote to USG. "I have known Major Wm B. Slack of the Marine Corps many years, and especially during my connection with the Com. on Naval Affairs of the House of Representatives during the War. His fidelity and efficiency have never been questioned, to my knowledge, and he has had, as you know, a very long experience in connection with that Corps. I am informed that a vacancy or change, in the head of the Marine Corps is likely soon to be made; and the purpose of this letter is respectfully to invite your consideration of the claims of Major Slack and his eminent qualifications for that position." ALS, *ibid.*

To George W. Childs

Nov. 5th /76

MY DEAR MR. CHILDS:

Mrs. Grant & I will accept yours & Mrs. Childs kind invitation to stay with you on the occasion of our visit to Phila to witness the close of the exposition. We will leave here on the afternoon train Wednesday[1] and expect to return friday evening.[2] There will be no one but Mrs. Grant & myself of the party. Gov. Fish & Buck will be in New York City, to vote, on tuesday and will meet me in Phila on thursday. It is probable that all the members of the Cabinet will be there at that time.[3]

My kindest regards to Mrs. Childs and all our Phila friends.

Yours Truly

U. S. GRANT

ALS, Haverford College Library, Haverford, Pa.

On Oct. 25, 1876, Ulysses S. Grant, Jr., wrote to Joseph R. Hawley, chairman, Centennial Commission, Philadelphia. "The President directs me to acknowledge the receipt of your favor of the 21st inst—requesting his attendance at the ceremonies on the closing of the International Exhibition, and say that it will afford him much pleasure to be present, and make the formal announcement of closing, in accordance with your courteous invitation.—He also wishes me to say, that, whatever arrangements the Commission may be pleased to make for holding the reception proposed in your further communication of the 21st, will be agreeable to him—" Copy, DLC-USG, II, 3. On Oct. 30, Culver C. Sniffen wrote to Hawley. "The President directs me to acknowledge the receipt of your letter of the 28th instant, and to say that the change proposed therein is agreeable to him—If, however, M. Du Sommerard is to be present at the dinner as the Representative of the French Government, the President must decline being there—" Copy, *ibid.* On Oct. 28, Elihu B. Washburne, Paris, had telegraphed to Secretary of State Hamilton Fish. "Paper publishes monstrous libel of Mr. Du Sommerard, French commissioner, on exhibition and American people. Intense indignation among Americans. . . ." *Foreign Relations, 1877,* p. 129. On the same day, Washburne wrote to Louis duc Decazes, French foreign minister. "I have read with amazement the extraordinary letter published in the Figaro of yesterday over the signature of Du Sommerard, who is the general commissioner of France *près les Expositions Universelles.* Were this a letter from a private individual, I should deem it utterly unworthy of notice; but being from a high functionary of the French Government, having official connection with the American Centennial Exposition, I should be forgetful of my duty and all the obligations I owe to my government and to the people of the United States did I not hasten to denounce to you the charges contained in the letter touching the exposition, against my country, its magistracy, and even its women, as the most monstrous calumnies. . . ." *Ibid.* On Oct. 29, Edmond Du Sommerard, Paris, wrote official letters denying authorship. *Ibid.,* pp. 130–31. A published letter, dated Oct. 1, had derided the "cursed exhibition at Philadelphia" and judged American women as "not worth a charge of powder." *Ibid.*, pp. 131–32.

On Nov. 1, Sniffen wrote to Fish. "The President directs me to ask whether you have seen the complaints of Capt. Aufrye of the French Centennial Commission, published in the N. Y. Herald of yesterday—7th page, especially the third column?" ALS, DLC-Hamilton Fish. On the same day, Fish recorded in his diary. ". . . I had just previously received from Mr Washburn a copy of the Duc Des Cazes's reply to his letter with regard to the alleged letter of Mr de Sommerard containing severe charges and reflections on the Officers of the Centennial Exhibition I took it together with Washburns letter to the President who thinks they had better both be published. He suggests that Captain Aufrye be immediately dismissed, as however he is not accredited to the Government and is an under Secretary we cannot dismiss him but I suggest to the President the proper course would be in conversation with the French Chargé to say that Captain Aufryes further presence is not acceptable." *Ibid.* On Nov. 3, Fish reported to the cabinet conversations with Francisque de Vaugelas, French chargé d'affaires, who "at first insisted that Aufrye should be publicly dismissed but on the representation of the difficulty which might arise between the two governments he assented to let him remain on the assurance that he should be quietly withdrawn and that he should not be allowed to appear in Washington publicly as connected with the Legation nor officially at the closing ceremonials of the Centennial at which he was to be present. . . ." Fish diary, *ibid.* See *ibid.*, Nov. 2, 4, 1876. On Nov. 4, Fish wrote to Washburne. "While you & the Duc DeCazes were so successfully engaged in removing the unpleasant effects of the calumnious publication in the 'Figaro,' you will have observed, from a publication in the NY Herald of a few days since that Capt. Aufrye, Military Attaché to the French Legation here, has allowed himself to become the author of similar charges—possibly the Vienna publication, reproduced in the Figaro, proceeded originally from him, & may have been transmitted (perhaps *through* M. De Sommerard) & found its way into print—However, Du Sommerard disclaims, & we have to accept the disclaimer. On the appearance of the publication in the Herald the indignation which the calumnious charges had excited, were naturally transferred from Du Sommerard to Aufrye, who, in addition to the Authorship or repetition of the Charges, was guilty of the undiplomatic & inadmissable act, while attached to the Legation, & enjoying Diplomatic privileges & immunities of appearing in print as the Author, or circulator of grave calumnies against the members of the Centennial Board, & generally against the order, & good character of our people. . . . The President goes to Philadelphia within a few days, to close the Centennial Exposition at which Aufrye is in some position as Commissioner or otherwise in behalf of his Government—Here again seems to be an embarassment, as the President could not consent to his presence on the occasion—Mr Vaugelas thereupon undertook to say that Aufrye should not be there, but should go to NewYork while the President shall be in Philadelphia, which was accepted as satisfactory—I trust that thus, the second & last Chapter of this very disagreeable incident is disposed of—. . . Long before this reaches you, the telegraph will have informed you the result of the Election I *hope* that it may be satisfactory—but my hopes are very far from being free of grave fears—" ALS (press), *ibid.* The arrest of Aufrye and other French officials at the Centennial Exhibition caused further diplomatic complications. See Fish diary, Dec. 8, 21, 28, 1876.

On Nov. 10, USG concluded ceremonies marking the last day of the Centennial Exhibition by saying "I now declare the Centennial International Exhibition of 1876 closed." *Philadelphia Public Ledger*, Nov. 11, 1876. See James D. McCabe, *The Illustrated History of the Centennial Exhibition,* . . . (Philadelphia, 1876), pp. 819–44.

On [*Nov.*] 15, Yoshida Kiyonari, Japanese minister, presented to USG a letter from

Emperor Mutsuhito. "Now that the great exposition in honor of the one-hundredth of your Excellency's National Government [h]as been eminently successful, I write to congratulate you and the people over whom you preside. From my subjects in the United States I have heard nothing but words of kindness in the manner in which they have been treated, and as I believ[e], th[e] recent intercourse between our countries will have a tendency to strengthen the friendship already existing   And I would here express the sincere hope that the incoming century will not only witness the continued progress and prosperity of your nation in all branches of industry, but also prove to be an era of peace. [T]his will be handed to you in person by my Minister, resi[d]ing near your government, who has been directed to emphasize my very friendly c[o]ngratulations." Undated newspaper clipping, DLC-Myrtilla Miner.

On Nov. 24, Ernesto Oldendorff, Philadelphia, wrote to USG. "The undersigned Comissioner-General of the Argentine Republic at the Centennial Exhibition of the United States, begs leave to hand to Your Excellency inclosed herein,—an embroidered handkerchief, which was sent to the Exhibition by Miss Gregoria Etchevehre, of Diamante, province of Entre-Rios, Argentine Republic and respectfully dedicated to Your Excellency.—Hoping that Your Excellency will kindly accept this gift a South american young lady" ALS, USG 3.

On Feb. 9, 1877, USG wrote to Congress transmitting the report of the board on behalf of executive depts. at the exhibition, recommended that it be printed, and backed a national museum to house Centennial collections. Copy, DNA, RG 130, Messages to Congress. *HMD*, 47-2-20, part 1.

1. Nov. 8, 1876.
2. On Friday, Nov. 10, USG, Philadelphia, wrote to Bishop Henry B. Whipple. "I have accepted an invitation to dinner this evening, but it will be convenient for me to meet Bishop Whipple, at Mr. Childs house, at any hour from Nine thirty to twelve m tomorrow." ALS, Minnesota Historical Society, St. Paul, Minn. That evening, USG attended the opera. On Nov. 11, noon, USG left for Washington, D. C. See *Washington Evening Star*, Nov. 11, 1876.
3. On Nov. 8, Hawley had telegraphed to Fish. "Pray oblige us by telegraphing the number and names cabinet officers who will attend dinner" Copy, DNA, RG 59, Miscellaneous Letters. Sniffen endorsed this telegram. "The President thinks all the Cabinet will be present." AES (undated), *ibid.*

To Edward Y. Goldsborough

November 6th, 1876.—

U. S. MARSHAL—
BALTIMORE—MD
DEAR SIR:

In the absence of the Secretary of War—no instructio[ns] have been given the Commanding Officer at Fort McHenry to give assistance in case of riot at the election to-morrow—But should their services be needed a telegram to me, to that effect, will insure their speedy co-operation in securing peace and quiet.—

Yours Truly.—
U. S. Grant

Copy, DLC-USG, II, 3.

On Nov. 6, 1876, George Bliss, U.S. attorney, New York City, twice wrote to USG. "In view of the excitement accompanying the approaching election, I deem it my duty, solely as a matter of precaution and with both the hope and the belief that no necessity for further action will arise, to make the following recommendations; *First.* That an order be issued to the General Commanding this Department, upon the call of the Marshal of the Southern or Eastern District of New York, to furnish him all the aid in his power in enforcing the laws of the United States upon election day, and, to that end, to use such troops as may be under his command. If the Companies on Governor's Island or any of them are not under the command of the General Commanding the Department, then that they be either temporarily placed under his command or that their commanding officer be directed to respond to the Marshal's call. *Second.* That a similar order be issued to the proper officer commanding the Marines at the Brooklyn Navy Yard or on vessels of war. The several officers should be directed to provide boats or other speedy means of transport. *Third* That an order be issued by you similar to that issued in 1870 on the application of the then Marshal and Hon. Caleb Cushing to the Major General Commanding the National Guard in the City of New York, directing him to respond with his command to the call of the Marshal. This Major General is Alexander Shaler. This latter order to be confided to the Marshal or such other person in this City as you may deem proper and to be used only in case a great emergency should arise. I respectfully suggest that all these orders and this application be not made public, as it is desirable to avoid all excitement and not to raise or encourage fears which I believe are groundless." "The application which my Chief Assistant, Gen. H. E. Tremain will hand you, is made after a consultation with Marshal Fiske, Gen. C. A. Arthur, Hon. Thurlow Weed, Hon. Zachariah Chandler, Commr Davenport, Hon W. E. Chandler and Police Commissioners Wheeler and Erhardt, all of whom are of the opinion that these precautions should be taken, though we all expect a quiet election. If the orders to Gen. Hancock and the Commandant at the Navy Yard would be exposed to publicity by going through the usual channels in the War and Navy Departments, I would suggest if possible that some other course be adopted. Publicity would be most injurious and by exciting apprehension and feeling might precipitate the very Condition of matters which we desire to avoid. The special order—the third one named in my letter—is proper under Section 1642 of the Revised Statutes which is a reenactment of the Act of 1795. It is desirable that Gen. Tremain should return by the 1. P. M. train Monday, if possible, and that the telegraph should *not* be used about this business" ALS, DNA, RG 60, Letters from the President. Secretary of the Interior Zachariah Chandler endorsed the first letter. "I concur with Mr Bliss & others and deem the orders of great importance" AES, *ibid.* See *PUSG*, 21, 4.

To Alphonso Taft

Nov. 7th /76

Hon. A. Taft,
Atty. Gn.
Dear Sir:

Enclosed I send you dispatches rec'd from the Governor & Marshal of La. and letter of instructions to the Act. Sec. of the Navy. If you approve the latter please send it to the officer to whom addressed, and telegraph the Marshal that his request has been complied with.

Respectfully &c.
U. S. Grant

ALS, DNA, RG 60, Letters from the President. On Nov. 6, 1876, Governor William P. Kellogg of La. telegraphed to USG. "I respectfully request if Consistent that the Commanders of the osseppee and Canonicus be instructed to Cooperate with Genl Augur in Case he desires the aid of their Marine forces" Telegram received (at 9:40 P.M.), *ibid.* On the same day, John R. G. Pitkin, U.S. marshal, New Orleans, telegraphed to USG. "The democratic criminal sheriff is swearing in hundreds of white league deputies in violation of law which requires consent metropolitian police Board   armed men gathering in different parts of the city   I urgently ask that orders may be sent to naval captains Breese & Kells to act with me in conjunction with Genl Augur" Telegram received (on Nov. 7, at 1:33 A.M.), *ibid.* *HMD*, 44-2-34, part 2, p. 829. On Jan. 29, 1877, Pitkin, Washington, D. C., testified on the response to this telegram. "I received a reply, I think the same night, or the next morning, from the Attorney-General giving a warrant to make requisition upon Captain Breese in case it became necessary. I don't recollect the precise terms of the commission to make requisition, and I think it was coupled with a caution to be very careful not to impress this force into service unless necessary." *Ibid.* For Pitkin's related testimony, see *ibid.*, pp. 797–803, 823–30.

To Alphonso Taft

Nov. 8th /76

Hon. A. Taft, Atty. Gen.

Dear Sir:

If the pardons of McKee & Avery are to be signed this week they had better be sent over this forenoon as I leave for Phila by the onethirty train.

Yours &c

U. S. Grant

ALS, DLC-William H. Taft. On Nov. 13, 1876, USG pardoned William O. Avery, former chief clerk, Internal Revenue bureau, convicted of conspiracy to defraud the U.S. of whiskey tax revenues and sentenced in April to two years in the Mo. penitentiary and a $1,000 fine. Copy, DNA, RG 59, General Records. See John McDonald, *Secrets of the Great Whiskey Ring* . . . (Chicago, 1880), pp. 285, 297–300. On Nov. 18, USG pardoned William McKee, St. Louis newspaper publisher, also convicted of conspiracy in the whiskey ring and sentenced in May to two years in the St. Louis County jail and a $10,000 fine. Copy, DNA, RG 59, General Records. See Hamilton Fish diary, Nov. 18, 1876, DLC-Hamilton Fish. On Oct. 31, Secretary of State Hamilton Fish had recorded in his diary. "The Attorney General brought up the question of the application of pardons of Avery & McKee convicted of connection with the Whiskey Frauds in St Louis. A letter from Mr Broadhead Consul for the United States in some of these prosecutions dated St Louis Nov—5th and says that that date completes six months of McKees imprisonment argues from various causes that this amount of confinement is sufficient and recommends his pardon. The Attorney General inclines to the pardon of both Avery & McKee and lays stress on Mr Broadheads letter . . ." *Ibid.*
    On May 6, Saturday, Silas Reed, Washington, D. C., had written to USG. "Please pardon ~~the~~ my intrusion ~~of my opinions~~ upon you at this time—I am & always have been your devoted & unwavering frien[d]—~~Also of~~ Mr McKee whom I have known for 30 years. I gave my time to hear all his trial last winter as I did to Genl. Babcock's—and also scrutinized all the witnesses against him, & their testimony—In the light of all the testimony & surrounding influences, I became ~~to the~~ firmly convinced of the awful conspiracy at work to overthrow Mr McKee . . . Next wednesday is his last day out of jail, if you do not ~~come to his try to~~ save him—You know him well—He never before had trouble, & he is so sensitive about this & feels the wrong so keenly that I greatly fear the worst consequences to him if relief is not obtained—My faith is stronger in the triumph of your name at the Convention near at hand, than any other—the Globe democrat is the strongest & most widely circuted paper in the west. It has now its 100,000 readers weekly—Our friends need its influence in the coming campaign, in all its vigor & power—not weakened by the stigma of its chief proprietor in jail—It & its friends can & will defend thoroughly your clemency in to Mr McKees' behalf—. . ." ADf (2), CtY. On May 8, George Bain, St. Louis, telegraphed to U.S. Senator Oliver P. Morton of Ind. "When I left Washington it was understood that immediately on return of att'y General the president would examine Maguires case Since then the Judges and District Att'y have reported to Mr Pierrepont their in-

tention to to ignore his request as to recommending executive clemency or otherwise
Maguire must suffer Wednesday unless prompt action is had   I must request you to lay
this before the President & request him to consider it   please answer" Telegram received,
DLC-USG, IB. On May 15, USG wrote. "Send word to Sec. of the Treas I would like to
see him about half past eleven   The Atty. Gn. at 12" AN, OHi. "The Attorney General had
a long interview with the President to day regarding the pardon of McKee and Maguire,
and the case was referred to the Attorney General. After his return from the White House
Hon. D. W. Vorhees, counsel for Maguire, had a short interview with him, Maguire remaining in the anteroom. Mr. Knox, of Wisconsin, counsel for McKee, also saw him. He
will recommend that the law shall take its course without executive intervention." *Washington Evening Star*, May 15, 1876. Constantine Maguire, former collector of Internal Revenue, St. Louis, had been convicted of conspiracy in the whiskey ring.

On July 28, Mary McDonald, Dartford, Wis., telegraphed to USG. "General John
McDonalds father is dying & asks the favor of his sons presence to see him die. will you
grant it? Please answer at once to Dartford Wis" Telegram received (at 12:10 P.M.), DNA,
RG 60, Letters from the President. On Oct. 28, Gen. William T. Sherman telegraphed
to McDonald, Jefferson City, Mo. "Your despatch this moment received. Have just seen the
President who has also received your despatch. He kept mine and has referred both to the
Attorney General. Accept my assurances of heartfelt sympathy and I hope and pray that
your husband's life may be spared. I know the President's heart is moved by your appeal
and that he will do all that is possible under the circumstances" Copy, *ibid.*, RG 94, Letters
Sent. On Oct. 2, John A. Joyce, Jefferson City, had written to Orville E. Babcock, Washington, D. C. "I see by the dispatches that you have been once more triumphantly acquitted
of the develish charges trumped up against you by copperhead hate, rebel vengeance and
political persecution. Let me extend to you my most hearty congratulations for the brave
manner in which you have withstood the terrible storm started for your ruin. Now that
you are perfectly free, I trust you will think of your friends that hold the fort, and come to
their relief. McDonald and myself have stood like rocks in mid ocean to break the waves
that raged high and fearful against yourself and the President; and even *proffered* liberty
and cash in hand could not induce us to turn against those who had been our friends in the
sunshine of prosperity. Will such pluck and fortitude as ours be ignored while the con-
fessed thieves & perjurers go scot free? We hope not, and look now for a *speedy* relief from
this hell hole of fraud and rebel persecution! McDonald sends warm congratulation—
. . . P. S. I wish you would drop a line to Chester Krum or Gov. Fletcher and tell them to
get up my papers for pardon!" ALS, ICN. See letter to Alphonso Taft, Sept. 16, 1876. On
Dec. 15, USG pardoned John A. Mead, John E. Howard, Richard B. Jones, and Henry Alm-
stead, all conspirators in the St. Louis whiskey ring. Copies, DNA, RG 59, General
Records. On Dec. 29, John McDonald, Jefferson City, wrote to Chester Krum. ". . . I Have
ben in Pison nearly forteen months & am nearly dead—one Hand I cannot use attall & my
Hed is all broke out & I blead all the time from the bowles & Have ben given up by the doctor two or three times—Now in all candor How am I to keep my Patience—especily when
you know I was assured by Grant through Babcock that as sune as his trile was over & He
got Back to Washington I would be Pardoned—. . . I must Have such assurances as will
satisfy me beyond mear Promases or I will go to congress & see what relief I can get by
fighting within the next twelve days—I fulley appricate what you say about showing ill
feelings But you know me Better   I Have got sufficent in my Hands to convince the world
that it is not mear feelings or spite & I say once for all I must Have Liberty or a fite—I am
as Low down as it is posable for them to sink me & every act of mine as you well know has
ben to Protect those that should have Long since came to my assistance   Have they done
it—no—But every time I have said anything to Help them they Have dumped another

Lode on me; . . ." ALS, Babcock Papers, ICN. On Jan. 1, 1877, Joyce wrote to Babcock. "*Personal . . .* Here is the New Year & yet McDonald and myself are in prison when all the whiskey men have been pardoned by the President—You know that before your trial Chester Krum, Governor Fletcher and your brother from Lawrence Kans. as well as yourself made promises to McD, & myself that just as soon as your trial was over, if we gave up certain letters, that the President would pardon McDonald and myself—Chester Krum showed me your promise and I have a copy of it—You know that we gave up many of the letters in our possession in order that you might go clear, and to keep great scandal off the President & his household—Well, you were set at liberty, then there was a halt for the Belknap case, and the cincinnati convention—then we were asked to wait until 'after the election', when we should surely be pardoned—But those promises proves to be down right falsehoods—McDonald now believes that it was never intended to pardon him and that you and the President really intend to keep him in to the last, and bury him deeper—Feeling this way he has written in his own hand writing to Chester Krum, and perhaps by the time this reaches you, the news of his ultimatum will be in your hands. McD has arranged all his secret letters, notes, telegrams, papers—the Team business—Lindell Hotel bills, talks, and names that will corroberate all his political & personal confidences for the past seven years and he will on the 10th inst, make arrangements with Stilson Hutchins of the St. Louis Times to put the whole trunk load before Proctor Knot, Hewett & Sam Randall—and then every man can 'scratch gravel' in his own way—Mc. feels that he has been played for a fool & treated like a dog! He knows that he is down as low as his so-called friends can get him—but he is aware that other people deserve the criminal bed he suffers upon. Genl, I trust you will take this in all seriousness and kindness—and for Gods sake get poor Mc, out—There is nothing can stop him but a *pardon or death*. I shall hold my course to the end, & if dragged in, I shall be true as possible—. . . P. S. I send this letter by my wife—in order that it shall not fall into strange hands—" ALS, *ibid.* On Jan. 26, USG pardoned McDonald, convicted of conspiracy in the whiskey ring and sentenced to three years in prison and a $5,000 fine, citing concerns "that he is suffering from a complication of painful and dangerous maladies which will probably terminate his life in a short time hence, should he be detained in prison, being such as can only be properly treated outside of prison; . . ." Copy, DNA, RG 59, General Records. Joyce remained in prison. See McDonald, *Secrets of the Great Whiskey Ring*, pp. 282–85, 305–26; Fish diary, Feb. 27, 1877, DLC-Hamilton Fish.

On March 2, USG pardoned Alfred Bevis and Edward B. Frazier, convicted of whiskey fraud in St. Louis and sentenced to one day in prison and a $1,000 fine, on grounds that "their means of paying the said fine has been exhausted by settlement of their liabilities under civil proceedings . . . and inasmuch as they were used as witnesses for the Government upon the trials of others . . ." Copy, DNA, RG 59, General Records. Earlier, USG had written. "Ask the Sec. of the Treas. to enquire of the Com. of Int. Rev. about the compromise in Bevis & Frazier case and to do what is equitable & just to the parties & to the Govt." AN (undated), Goodspeed's Book Shop, Inc., Boston, Mass.

Also on March 2, Attorney Gen. Alphonso Taft wrote to USG. "In the matter of the petition of John F. Long, Esq., of St. Louis, Mo, for the relief of the bondsmen of certain distillers, a request was immediately made to Wm H. Bliss, Esq, U S Atty. in that City for a report upon the subject, but no response has been received, although the reference was made Aug 3. 1876. The petition will therefore be considered upon the Statement of facts made therein, which it is respectfully submitted do not make out a case for executive interference. . . ." Copy, DNA, RG 60, Letters Sent to Executive Officers. *HED*, 49-1-360, 3. In [*Aug., 1876*], John F. Long had written to USG for bondsmen of John Busby, a deceased distiller connected with St. Louis whiskey frauds. ". . . I wish to God your Excellency could give them some assurance of relief; their confidence was betrayed; they were deceived by the man they thought honest; he died long ere the facts were developed of his crookedness. With confidence in your kindness of motives, . . ." *Ibid.*, pp. 13–14.

On Dec. 4, 1875, Alfred H. Edwards "and many others," Evansville, Ind., had telegraphed to USG. "Believing that the Whiskey Ring is forever broken, the law fully vindicated & the parties allready sorely punished we the people of southern Indiana would ever feel grateful if you would interpose & save our Erring citizens from the great dishonor of the States prison." Telegram received, DNA, RG 60, Letters from the President. On June 27, 1876, USG pardoned Philip C. Eberwine and five others convicted in Ind. of violating internal revenue laws. Copy, *ibid.*, RG 59, General Records. On July 8, Taft wrote to U.S. Senator George F. Edmunds of Vt., chairman, judiciary committee. "I have your favor of the 7th inst., referring to the charge made by Hon. E. J. Phelps 'that the President immediately after the retirement of Mr. Bristow from his Cabinet had pardoned some six of the whiskey thieves that had been convicted at the West,' and inquiring what, if any foundation exists for the charge. I find on examination of the files of this Department, what I suppose to be the origin of this statement. There were six persons who had been convicted of offences against the revenue laws in Indiana, to wit: Phillips, Eberwine, Simonson, Snyder, Miller and Lewis,—and imprisoned five or six months. The district attorneys who prosecuted and the judge who presided at the trial, recommended their pardon on the ground that they had received sufficient punishment, . . . On receiving this evidence I recommended to the President the pardon of these men, and the pardon was granted. I am not aware that the President had any other knowledge or agency in the matter than to act on the recommendation of this Department; and I am satisfied that it was a clear case for pardon. I presume that this was the only ground of the charge made by Mr Phelps; but he was undoubtedly under a misapprehension in regard to the facts of the case." Copy, *ibid.*, RG 60, Letters Sent to Executive Officers. USG also pardoned Alfred M. McGriff (June 27) and Thomas J. Robb (July 10), convicted in Ind. of violating internal revenue laws. Copies, *ibid.*, RG 59, General Records.

On May 20, U.S. Senator John J. Ingalls of Kan. had telegraphed to USG. "I very respectfully Concur in the request that the sentence of John L Bittinger of St Joseph Mo. lately convicted at Jefferson City may be commuted to imprisonment in the County Jail" Telegram received, *ibid.*, RG 107, Telegrams Collected (Bound). On June 5, USG wrote. "The Atty. Gen. is authorized to direct the Marshal of Mo. to retain _____ Bittengerr in jail until further notice from here, and to give time to receive papers understood to be on the way here in his behalf." ANS, *ibid.*, RG 60, Letters from the President. On June 12, USG granted a conditional pardon to John L. Bittinger, convicted of whiskey fraud in western Mo., allowing him to serve his two year term in the Buchanan County, Mo., jail, instead of the Mo. penitentiary. Copy, *ibid.*, RG 59, General Records. On Dec. 23, USG granted Bittinger a full pardon. Copy, *ibid.* On Jan. 3 and Feb. 24, 1877, USG pardoned Henry R. W. Hartwig, Ernst F. Hartwig, and Edward Sheehan, also convicted in western Mo. Copies, *ibid.*

On June 5, 1876, Culver C. Sniffen had written to Secretary of the Treasury Benjamin H. Bristow. "The President directs me to say, that he suggests that Sedgwick, Collector of Internal Revenue—District of California, be ordered on to Washington to answer the charges made against him—One of the charges, distroying records, is of such a nature, that, unless satisfactorily explained, should lead, the President thinks, to prosecution in addition to removal.—" Copy, DLC-USG, II, 3. On Dec. 13, USG nominated William Higby as collector of Internal Revenue, 1st District, Calif., to replace John Sedgwick.

On June 26, USG had written. "The Atty. Gen. may, if he thinks advisable, direct the continunce of Ed Fehrenbach in jail until the question of pardon is considered" AN, OHi.

On July 15, USG pardoned Edward Fehrenbach, convicted in La. of conspiracy in whiskey frauds. Copy, DNA, RG 59, General Records. On Jan. 10, 1877, USG pardoned John Henderson and William G. James, also convicted of conspiracy in La. whiskey frauds. Copies, *ibid.*

On Sept. 20, 1876, Taft had written to USG. "The bearer of this is Geo. B. Goodwin Esqr, a member of the bar of Millwaukie who has presented the cases of of Wirth & others for pardon. I have recommended the pardon of the four men whom he represents, & he carries to you the recommendation" ALS, Free Library of Philadelphia, Philadelphia, Pa. On Sept. 19, Taft had written to USG. "I am preparing a paper with the grounds of our action, to forward to you in the four cases." *The Collector*, No. 890 (1983), q285. On Sept. 22, USG pardoned Leopold Wirth and three others convicted of whiskey fraud in Milwaukee. Copy, DNA, RG 59, General Records. Between April and Nov., USG pardoned eight other conspirators in the Milwaukee whiskey frauds. Copies, *ibid.* Alfred Waterman (Nov. 9) and James N. Hildreth (March 3, 1877), former gaugers, were pardoned for similar offenses in Ill. Copies, *ibid.*

To Gen. William T. Sherman

Nov. 10th [*1876*]

GEN. SHERMAN, WASHINGTON, D. C.

Send all the troops to Gen. Augur he may [deem necessar]y to insure entire quiet and a peaceable [count] of the ballots actually cast. They may be taken from South Carolina unless there is reason to suspect an outbreak there.[1] The presence of Citi[zens] from other states I understand, is requested in La. to see that the Board of Canvassers make a fair [count] of the vote actually cast.[2] It is to be hoped that representative and fair men of both parties will go.

U. S. GRANT

ALS (telegram sent), Mrs. Paul E. Ruestow, Jacksonville, Fla.; telegram received, DNA, RG 94, Letters Received, 4788 1876. *HED*, 44-2-30, 26. Secretary of State Hamilton Fish recorded an undated diary entry (across from the page dated Oct. 28, 1876) explaining why USG sent this telegram. "While at the dinner given on the evening of the 9th nov just before the closing of the Exposition we heard rumors of trouble in the South and afterwards went to the telegraph office and heard of the wrecking of trains, tearing up to telegraph wires and general disturbances. That night he ordered Genl Ruger and troops down to Florida without giving him any specific instructions. Coming home in the carriage I suggested that it might be well to give explicit orders with regard to the use to be made of the troops. . . ." DLC-Hamilton Fish. On Nov. 10, 1876, 1:30 P.M., Gen. William T. Sherman telegraphed to USG, Philadelphia. "Your despatch is received and has been repeated verbatim to Generals Sheridan and Hancock who will do the Same to Generals Augur and Ruger." ALS (telegram sent), DNA, RG 94, Letters Received, 4788 1876; telegram sent, *ibid.*, RG 107, Telegrams Collected (Bound); telegram received, DLC-USG, IB. *HED*, 44-2-30, 25. See next telegram.

On Nov. 8, Sherman had written to Lt. Gen. Philip H. Sheridan, Chicago. "Yours of Novr 6 about the Reynolds matter is received. I would act promptly on the case, being sure that nothing but a Court Martial can reach the root of ~~the case~~ it, but I know that the President promised Reynolds to provide it by a Court of Inquiry. Genl Grant starts this morning for the Centennial. I saw him last night, and he said in answer to certain other matters of which I spoke that neither he or the Secretary would be back till after the 10th. So that I must defer action till their return. Every thing thus far reported indicates the Election of Mr Tilden. This will give us a four years struggle for existence, and makes our positions insecure—As soon as the President comes back I will advise that a Court Martial of 13 members be ordered to meet at Cheyenne or Laramie, to try Reynolds, and I will endeavor to get the Artillery Companies now in S. C. back to their posts, & probably the 16th to Leavenworth—The presence of the troops South has probably ensured a quiet Election, but has not materially Changed Results. I need your annual Report to enable me to make mine which ought to be in, by Novr 10th at furthest." ALS, DLC-Philip H. Sheridan. See *Calendar*, March 8, 1877. On Nov. 9, Sherman telegraphed to Maj. Gen. Winfield S. Hancock, New York City. "Despatch of eight (8th) received—consulted the President yesterday about the withdrawal of troops from the South, He has gone to Philadelphia and on his return will endeavor to fix the date for calling back Breckenridges Company as also others" ALS (telegram sent), DNA, RG 94, Letters Received, 4788 1876. See message to Senate, Dec. 14, 1876.

For election evening, Nov. 7, the Western Union Telegraph Co. ran wires into the White House. *Washington Evening Star*, Nov. 8, 1876. On Nov. 7, William L. Burt, postmaster, Boston, telegraphed to USG. "Claflin Butler Loring Banks Elected frost Rep Defeated by Morse Chapin Dem Defeated by Robinson in springfield we gain four Congressional Districts and lose two" Telegram received, DLC-USG, IB. On Nov. 8, Chauncey I. Filley, postmaster, St. Louis, telegraphed to USG. "Carried two Congressmen in St Louis and County ticket" Telegram received (at 9:36 P.M.), *ibid.* On the same day, a telegram was sent from Milwaukee, probably to USG. "The Republican Ex. Com. figure that the republicans have carried the State by from 2000 to 3000 majority" Telegram received, *ibid.* On Nov. 10, Jesse Root Grant, Ithaca, N. Y., telegraphed to USG. "Will you let me know by telegraph what you think the final result is" Telegram received, *ibid.*

On Nov. 8, Oscar Rierson, Charlottesville, Va., had telegraphed to USG. "Give me the most cheering news. When will you vacate." Telegram received (at 1:05 P.M.), *ibid.*

1. On Nov. 10, 3:50 P.M., Sherman telegraphed to Sheridan, Chicago, transmitting USG's instructions and adding that "General Ruger has taken to Tallahassee the bulk of his troops, but if you Call for more than you now have in NewOrleans, I will do all that is possible." ALS (telegram sent), DNA, RG 94, Letters Received, 4788 1876. On the same day, 3:54 P.M., Sherman telegraphed to Hancock. "Please order all detachments in South Carolina to assemble at Columbia, and Charleston to be ready for NewOrleans or wherever they may be wanted." ALS (telegram sent), *ibid.* Also on Nov. 10, Secretary of War James D. Cameron, Philadelphia, telegraphed to Sherman. "I have telegram from South Carolina expressing desire to have troops retained at Columbia Nine Companies ought to be sufficient for Florida The commanding officer in South Carolina Should be personally at Columbia and should communicate with Governor Chamberlain as to the disposition of troops in the same manner that General Ruger has I shall probably return to Washington tomorrow afternoon" Telegram received, *ibid.* On the same day, USG, Philadelphia, telegraphed to Sherman. "Unless further advised you need not make further order

of troops" Telegram received (at 9:30 P.M.), *ibid. HED*, 44-2-30, 28. On Nov. 11, 10:30 A.M., Sherman telegraphed to Hancock to check the concentration of troops at Charleston and Columbia, S. C. ALS (telegram sent), DNA, RG 94, Letters Received, 4788 1876. *HED*, 44-2-30, 28. On the same day, Sheridan telegraphed to Sherman. "Augur says three regiments are sufficient. They are all now *en route* to New Orleans." Telegram received (in cipher), DNA, RG 94, Letters Received, 4788 1876.

On [*Nov.*] 7 and 8, "Justice," Hamburg, S. C., and Augusta, Ga., had written to USG. "on the 7 of November in Georgia and South Carolina the Election was not a fair one. Some places We Poor Colord were treated Very Wrong. in augusta Half of the Colored was not Allow'd to. Except voting for Tilden and Hendricks the Polls was Crowded with Whites and ½ of the Blacks could not vote. pistoles were Drawed on us for nothing if we had of had men to mind the Polls we could not have Been Beat so. In Hamburg white men Came from Augusta and voted the Democrat Ticket and in Augusta too. And the best way is to do is to Know How many Votes ech State always Carry or always had Carried. that is the only way we Sutherners will be treted Right. Look at Augusta! on the 7th White Men voted in Augusta and went over to Hamburg and voted again. Police Mans were Stationed at the Bridge To not Let any Colored Man Cross what could not vote in Augusta. . . . We would d[e]spatched to you on the 7 but they would not Despatch for" L, *ibid.*, RG 60, Letters from the President. *SMD*, 44-2-48, III, 98–99.

2. On Nov. 10, Secretary of the Interior Zachariah Chandler, New York City, telegraphed to USG, Centennial Grounds, Philadelphia. "I sent the Secretary of War a long dispatch at two this Morning from U. S. Marshal in New Orleans giving account of destruction of ballot boxes by Democrats. at three Oclock I sent another from Gov. Kellogg giving account of further destruction of boxes I asked the Secretary to order all available troops to New Orleans City to protect the returning board in the making of a fair count. Have heard nothing from him—Kellogg asks that Prominent Men from Different parts of the Country may be sent there observe the work of Canvassing and see that is fairly done. claiming the State to be largely republican I have requested Senator Logan to go there I fear blood-shed there during the Count unless we guard against it and I urge that Lieut. General Sheridan be directed to proceed to New Orleans at once—" Telegram received, DLC-USG, IB.

To Gen. William T. Sherman

[*Dated* PHILADA Nov 10 *1876*.
To GEN W T SHERMAN WASHN D C
Instruct Gen Augur in La and Gen. Ruger in Fla[1] to be vigilant with the force at their Command to preserve peace & good order and to see that the proper & legal boards of Canvassers are unmolested in the performance of thereir duties should there be any grounds of suspicion of fraudulent] counting on either side it should be reported and denounced at once. No man worthy of the office of President would be willing to hold it if "counted in" or placed there by any

fraud. Either party can afford to be disappointed in the result but the Country cannot afford to have the result tainted by the suspicion of ~~fa~~ illegal or false returns.[2]

U. S. GRANT

ALS (telegram sent, partial facsimile), Christie's Sale No. 1032, March 27, 2002, no. 114; telegram received (at 2:16 P.M.), DNA, RG 94, Letters Received, 4788 1876; copy, USG 3. *HED*, 44-2-30, 24–25. USG endorsed the autograph letter. "Given to C. C. Sniffen, Private Secretary." AES (undated), Christie's Sale No. 1032, March 27, 2002, no. 114. In an undated diary entry (across from the page dated Oct. 28, 1876), Secretary of State Hamilton Fish described the composition of this telegram on the morning of Nov. 10, 1876. ". . . the President wrote a telegram and after reading it I read the following which I had written. Either political party can afford to be disappointed in the results of the Elections—but, the Country cannot afford to have the result ~~questioned~~ tainted by the suspicion of illegal or false returns   He said I would like to put that in which he does and sends the telegram" DLC-Hamilton Fish. On Nov. 10, 3:54 P.M., Gen. William T. Sherman telegraphed to USG, Philadelphia. "Your second (2) despatch is received, and I have sent it to General Sheridan to Know if he wants the troops from South Carolina. Genl Ruger has taken thirteen (13) companies to Tallahassee which leaves but a Small force in South Carolina   Gen Augur has three (3) Regments of Infantry ordered to Assemble in NewOrleans for the very purpose indicated in your dispatch. I will notify Genl Hancock however to hold the troops in South Carolinins ready" ALS (telegram sent), DNA, RG 94, Letters Received, 4788 1876; telegram sent, *ibid.*, RG 107, Telegrams Collected (Bound); telegrams received (2), DLC-USG, IB. *HED*, 44-2-30, 26. On the same day, Secretary of War James D. Cameron, Centennial Grounds, Philadelphia, telegraphed to Sherman. "The President thinks and I agree with him that it will be well for you to give to the Associated Press his telegram and mine to you referring to affairs now in the south—" Telegram received, DNA, RG 94, Letters Received, 4788 1876. *HED*, 44-2-30, 26. Also on Nov. 10, 2:35 P.M., Sherman telegraphed to Cameron. "Glad to receive your despatch this momt, thought as much but felt a delicacy about publicity without your Consent—. . ." ALS (telegram sent), DNA, RG 94, Letters Received, 4788 1876. *HED*, 44-2-30, 26. See previous telegram.

On Nov. 11, two Bostonians, J. A. Sevy and S. C. Fay, Philadelphia, telegraphed to USG and "officials of Louisiana or Florida Washn DC." "Our lives and fortune are at your service if we can assist in maintaining peace." Telegram received (at 9:00 A.M.), DLC-USG, IB. On the same day, D. W. Wright, New York City, telegraphed to USG. "Your order is not the least of your great acts" Telegram received, *ibid.* Also on Nov. 11, J. C. Briggs, St. Joseph, Mo., wrote to USG. "Although no politition yet I am not without deep anxiety as to the consequences to the country in the event of what seems now a probable Democratic victory. If this was the result of a majority of northern votes, or even of Southern votes in the exercise of a free use of the Ballot I would not write you: but as the colored vote of the south is only democratic through intimidation, Shall the Government be turned over to Rebels who have *thus gained* what they lost in Battle?!! . . ." ALS, USG 3.

On [*Nov.*] 12, Governor Alexander H. Rice of Mass., New York City, telegraphed to USG. "The entire republican and independent press in Massachusetts heartily sustains you in ordering troops to preserve order in the disturbed States and the people will as loyally abide by the result of the election when honestly determined" Telegram received, DLC-USG, IB. On the same day, William B. Stage, former asst. surgeon, 35th Ky., Vienna, Ind., wrote to USG, "President & Generalissimo of the. U. S. After our profound regard." "A large majority of the Democrats of Indiana greet You, And assure You, that You will find them as You did in 1861, & -65 True to the Union, And all they ask in this the 2d Crisis of our Country, is, Should it turn out, that Gov Tilden has been legally elected President of the U S. that he gets his seat as such. But on the other hand Should it be that Gov Hayes is the Man, We Will Stand by You until *Hell freezes over. . . .*" ALS, USG 3.

On Nov. 13, a correspondent reported from Washington, D. C. "Secretary Chandler had an interview with the President today. He expressed his confidence that Florida, Louisiana and South Carolina had gone for Hayes. . . ." *New York Times,* Nov. 14, 1876. On the same day, Ward H. Lamon, Martinsburg, West Va., wrote to USG. "From the intolerant spirit, manifested here, since the election, by the dominant party—little security is felt by the Republicans. For three days after the election the most intense feeling prevailed; since then there seems to be a lull, and at the same time a fearful suspense—at no hour have we been secure from an outbreak—and should it occur; it will be terrible.—Both parties are determined and desperate—The suspense attending the issue between the two national parties only intensifies the bitterness and partizan spirit here, which is far greater and more desperate than during the war—If hostilities are once commenced here there is no telling where the thing will end—There is an element of lawlessness in this portion of this state, prevailing in the Democratic party, that is not only desperate but dangerous—It will be met! but be not surprised, if Troops will not be required, to quell disturbances even among the chivalry of West Virginia before the vote is counted. . . . P. S. I had hoped for three days—there w'd be no necessity for sending this letter—but I have been mistaken— There are, sir, men good and true, in the Democratic party ǫf in West Va as lives—but there are a class of persons here who, in their blind ignorant devotion to party—would renounce, if necessary, for success, the teachings of the Saviour of the World! and at the command of a Traitor to his country, would stand sentinel under cover of some convenient tree, on the day of Judgement if he could have the imaginary honor of wearing a confederate uniform and be armed with a Rebel shot Gun, ready to assassinate the *Holy Trinity,* so as to avert the just judgement of an Offended God against the Democratic Leaders whose infamous Servants he and his confreers are—have been, and ever will be, as long as they are permitted to live" ALS, USG 3. Also on Nov. 13, Benjamin F. Sawyer, editor, *Rome Courier,* Rome, Ga., wrote to USG. "Permit me, as an humble American Citizen, an exconfederate and a zealous democrat, to thank you for the golden words of patriotism you have spoken, touching the sanctity of the electoral vote, They come as came the words of our blessed Savior when he stood amid the wrath of the storm and said to the troubled waters 'Peace be still' They touch the heart of every true patriot in the land—Again I thank you—and may God bless you—" ALS, *ibid.*

On Nov. 14, James F. Rusling, pension agent, Trenton, N. J., wrote to USG. "In behalf of all patriotic and right thinking people here, pray allow me to thank you for your recent timely & just orders to Gen. Sherman, relating to Florida & Louisiana. They were right in the nick of time, and were so just and fair in every respect, that only the foolish & the perverse can take exception to them. There was an ugly feeling brewing, born of hunger & desperation, and if you have not extinguished, you have at least largely suppressed it. The crisis was certainly a very grave one, and still continues, nor will it end until your successor is duly inaugurated. I think all good citisens are deeply impressed with the gravity of the situation; but the country looks to you to save it, as you did at Appomattox, and again by your veto of Inflation, and confidently believes it will not look in vain. Great responsibilities are again upon you, but you will face them with calmness & wisdom, as heretofore. If the worst comes, of course, we shall not have 1860–61 over again. President Grant, all may depend, is *not* President Buchanan! Better fight from the start, and let traitors know, that we have a Government, and mean to defend it. We are not Mexico, nor South America, but Anglo Saxon Yankees, and (God willing) we don't mean the Republic to perish yet awhile. If we are to fight again, let us fight it thoroughly out, and leave no fuel this time for another conflagration. Men's minds, here and everywhere, are pondering these things, and the country will sustain you, in the most vigorous measures, come what may. I send you these words, as the quiet conclusions of public sentiment here, as I believe they are of all good citisens everywhere, . . ." ALS, *ibid.* On the same day, James G. Shields, New Albany, Ind., wrote to USG. "Should the Democrats get up another 'Civil War' as treasonable talk indicates at this time (in this portion of Indiana where the 'Knights of the Golden Circle' flourished during the late war, please make 'Treason odious' and use abundance of hemp at the final and that will make this the strongest governmt on the face of the Globe twas our *leniency towards rebels* that has *weakened our governmt*—With best wishes for our Whole Country & the election of Hays as President . . ." ALS, *ibid.*

On Nov. 15, Norwood Mitchell, Richmond, wrote to USG. "Your Excellency: Will I trust pardon me for requesting a few moments of your valuable time. As a citizen of Virginia, and one who remembers with pride and pleasure the courtesy extended to him by your Excellency, sometime since, upon my introduction to you by Col. James F. Casey, I have presumed to address you in reference to your course in Southern affairs. Your Excellency will I trust allow me, as a citizen of the South, to offer my humble congratulations to you upon the prompt and wise course you have adopted towards the disputed states, expressing the belief that my sentiments have the sincere concurrence of all true Republicans, and will also be shared in by the leaders of the Democratic Party when the present excited feeling has worn away. With the sincere hope that the administration of the affairs of the Government, under Gov Hayes, may be conducted with the same wisdom and success attendant upon your own administration; . . ." ALS, *ibid.*

On Nov. 16, John W. De Forest, New Haven, Conn., wrote to USG. "Pardon me, a simple and insignificant citizen, for venturing to express to you my profound admiration for your management of the election difficulties in the contested states. It is my belief that your action was absolutely necessary; that without it there would have been fraud, intimidation, bloodshed and, in a certain sense, revolution; that no other course could have given the Legal majority of the electoral college to that candidate, whichsoever he may be, whose right it is. You will doubtless arouse enmity. Denunciations, threats & entreaties will be freely used to turn you from your purpose of seeing the laws executed. Hungry candidates, timid capitalists, political imposers & born alarmists will all unite in a selfish or cowardly outcry against you. There will be a seemingly monstrous storm of opposition & of censure. But this uproar will be largely fictitous, & is sure to have but a brief duration. Once the honest return of the electoral college established, the defeated party will soon submit to an accomplished fact founded on justice, and our national life will resume a tranquillity which it could not draw from concessions to artifice & turbulence. More than that, criticism will be followed by admiration, and anxiety by gratitude. Within a year it will be admitted that never, not even on your fields of victory, have you done a wiser & braver deed, or more effectually served the public interests, than when you intervened to prevent local demagogues from illegally deciding the character of our government." ALS, *ibid.* See "An Independent's Glance at the South," *The Nation,* XXIII (Sept. 28, 1876), 196–97.

On Nov. 18, Thomas B. Swann, Charleston, West Va., wrote to USG. "A large number of gentlemen called to see me last night, & requested me to express to you the views of the Republicans of West Va. We desire to thank you for your efforts to keep the peace in the Southern States, & to have fair elections, & an impartial count. In view of impending complications, we desire you to know you can count upon the Republicans of WVa We feel confident you will Stand by the country in the approaching storm, & we desire you to know we will stand by you. Hoping for peace & impartial right, we further hope the vexed question of Nationality and State Sovreignty may be settled & ended while you are at the head of affairs. We only s[erve] our own feelings, in assuring you of confidence, with a firm purpose to sustain you." ALS, USG 3.

On Nov. 25, Frederick H. Wines, secretary, Board of Public Charities, Springfield, Ill., wrote to USG. "By the advice of the Hon. C. E. Lippincott, Auditor of Public Accounts, I have the honor to communicate to you the substance of certain statements made yesterday, in conversation with myself, by a knot of representative members of the Democratic party, from Several counties of this State, in the office of the Register, a Democratic newspaper published in this city. 1st. These gentlemen all predict the election of Gov. Hayes, by frauds to be perpetrated in the States of Louisiana, Florida & South Carolina. 2nd. They were divided in opinion as to the policy of war to prevent his inauguration—one part contending that four years of Hayes would be better than four years of war; the other part urging that unless resistance to usurpation is made now, four years from now it will be too late. 3rd. They all agreed that the decision of this question rests upon the orders of Gov. Tilden; that if he decides a war to be necessary for the preservation of constitutional liberty, they will follow him into the field. If he opposes war, they will submit. 4th. The point of law, on which they base their denial of Gov. Hayes' right to the Presidency, is the right of both Houses to participate in the counting of the electoral vote. In case the House refuses to count the vote of Louisiana, they argue that there will be no election, & in that event, the election will be thrown into the House. They declare that the House will never consent to count the vote of Louisiana for Hayes. 5th. They predict that the action of the House will be followed by its dispersion by military force, & the arrest of its members. They say that if the members can make their escape from Washington, they will reassemble in New York, where they will defy the power of the government to capture or dislodge them. 6th. It was argued by some of those present, that the safest policy for the Democratic party would be for the House to determine in advance that it would take no part in the count, & leave Washington for New York, before that event, in order to prevent the arrest which they fear. 7th. One gentleman remarked that Gen Grant is now 'the biggest man' (to use his expression), in the United States; that he has silenced the opposition to himself in his own party, & has the Democratic party at his feet, through fear of his power. To this another replied that 'the events of twenty-four hours might deprive Grant of all his power.' Gen. Lippincott & myself both interpret this remark as a suggestion of assassination. I had the honor of an introduction to you last spring, by Senator Oglesby. You may not remember me. I do not communicate this information because I overestimate its importance, but because it appears to be the fullest revelation of the feeling & plans of the Democrats in this section that any of us have been able to obtain from an authentic source—" ALS, DNA, RG 60, Letters from the President. Governor John L. Beveridge of Ill. favorably endorsed this letter. AES (undated), *ibid.* Also on Nov. 25, Governor John L. Pennington of Dakota Territory wrote to USG. "Come what will the great heart of the West is with you, and will be with you and stand by you in the defence of the right. Your recent utterances and Acts have captured the popular heart, and I have never known so many Grant men in the West before. We all pray for peace, but if trouble is to come we are thankful that there is one at the helm in whom we can trust—one who we know will not allow traitors to seize the forts and arsenals and steal the Property of the Government. If it turn out that Hayes is elected I do not think the Southern rebels will be guilty of the overt Act of treason, as before, but they are working with the Northern Democrats to arouse the mob with the hope that rebellion will commence in the North. We hope for the election and peaceable inauguration of Hayes, but if our ticket is elected and War is attempted as in 1861, I have only to say that the West will not fail you." ALS, USG 3. Supportive letters to USG from Charles Burrows, Paterson, N. J. (Nov. 13), Francis A. Fogg,

New York City (Nov. 14), "Republican & old Soldier," Indianapolis (Nov. 15), Daniel Clark, Edgehill, Pa. (Nov. 20, Dec. 18), Albert L. Child, Plattsmouth, Neb. (Nov. 22), J. R. Smith *et al.*, Paducah (Nov. 24), Charles Scott, Washington, D. C. (Nov. 24), "A republican," Hartford (Nov. 26), John J. Hooker, Cincinnati (Nov. 27), Samuel McKee, Louisville (Nov. 28), Calvin Phelps, Lockport, N. Y. (Nov. 30), and Julie R. Seaver, San Francisco (Nov. 30), are *ibid.*

On Nov. 14, Fish recorded in his diary. "Cabinet—All present the condition of the Election was discussed and the possibility of violence and disturbance was considered with reference to the adoption of precautionary measures Various reports of threats of violence were mentioned among others Colonel Mosbys had advised the President to be careful of his own person as from the tenor of conversations which he had heard he was led to fear that in case of violence an effort would be made to assassinate him. I met Mosby on my way to the President's and he told me that the language of the Democrats now was more desperate and more threatening and violent than that of the Southern men on the Election of Lincoln in 1860 That he feared there would be blood shed in case it was ascertained that Hayes was elected. He himself has left his home and reports great excitement and violence of feeling against every Republican that they had worn out a warrant of arrest against him simply because he prevented a Democrat at the Poles from clubbing a colored voter and had insisted on the right of the negro to vote. He had told the President of the threatening language of the Democrats who in indicating their intention of violence were accustomed to say that the President must be the first man to be gotten out of the way." DLC-Hamilton Fish.

On Nov. 20, A. M. B., Washington, D. C., wrote to USG. "There is no passage in past life to remind you of so humble a person as the writer—But I beg you to read these lines for the information concerns you personally. I overheard a conversation between two men who were plotting your *assassination.* Said the first man, 'do you think the plan will work' 'Admirally' replied the second, 'he is in the habit of walking alone, we can be on the watch and some dark evening when he enters either of the gates of the White House, we can conveniently post ourselves, and then the dagger must do the rest. The first blow must do the work for he is brave and will defend himself.' I hesitated to impart the above, but the more I thought over it, the more convinced I became that you should know that bad men seek your life. You have rendered great service to my race, and we owe you a debt of gratitude we can never cancel. I know not what amount of importance you will attach to the above, but like myself you remember the saying, viz, 'A man forewarned, is a man forearmed,' and will govern yourself accordingly." L, OFH. On Nov. 22, "United Order of Bush Rangers," Boston, wrote to USG, adorning the letter with drawings of a skeleton in a casket, a skull and crossbones, a rifle, a dagger, and a pistol. "you are a doomed man You and your assistant thieves will soon be assasinated I kindly advise you not to be out on dark nights one of your men is one of our sworn Friends even half your soldiers are on our side I give you fair warning beware We have got an Association of 10.000 ~~sworn~~ sworn men all over the states beware you sneak thief Your Doom Blood Blood your Blood Family KKK Your Bitter Enimies" L, USG 3. On Nov. 24, J. Pelton, Long Point, Ark., wrote to USG. "I write to informe you of a conversation I overherd last week in De Witt arkansas co ark there ware three men in conversation about the election one man said President Grant is trying to have louisiana South Carolina and Colorado all returned for Hayes and he knows damd well that Tilden carried all three of them, and if he does there will be war as sure as hell, and if there is, I am there, and the first thing I do will be to Put a ball through old grants head if I can hold a rifle straight enough it is no murder to kill a man in war I will play Lincoln with him dam him, now if it should so happen that we should have a little trouble you had better take care of yourself for that man means just what he said" ALS, DNA, RG 60, Letters from the President. On Nov. 25, F. A. Lewis, Rippon, West Va., wrote to USG. "I warned President Lincoln of the Pollicy he was pursueing & if he did not change it some terrible clamity would befall him. I now warn you in the name of the living God whose servant I am, that thus saith Lord that those who do things without Law shall perish without Law. Hoping that you may see the error of your ways, & that you will repent & turn & serve the living God . . ." ALS, USG 3. On Nov. 26, Anonymous, Atlanta, wrote to USG. "There is a plot hatched up in Virginia to *assisnate* you it is to be done by a federal solger now in your city who is to do it by accident to stumble down and let his gun go off or run a baynott throgh you this much is all the writer knows cant find out name of soldier or when but look out for there is a plot on foot . . ." L, *ibid.* On Nov. 27, "A farmer of 'Virginia'" wrote to USG. "In that *Supreme,* and *Extreme* hour, you 'would rather be *right,* than *President'* 'All men must die'— . . . N. B. 'Mene, Mene, Tekel Upharsin'" L, *ibid.* On the same day, Jonathan Cory, Westfield, N. J., wrote to Cameron. "We Presbyterians thank God that U. S. Grant, and not James Buchanan, is president of the U. S. You are now fighting a battle foretold by the apostle John 1780 years ago; and by Daniel the prophet 2410 ago. Pres. U. S Grant is the Michael of whom both prophets speak in the 12th chapter of each. There is no dodging the conflict and there is no middle fortune between death and victory. The Roman papers and bishops S. J. Tilden, the Copperheads and the Devil are all combined, not merely to murder some hundred thousand black and white Republicans, but to murder Pres. U. S. Grant Gov. R. B. Hayes and Wheeler and you J. D. Cameron, and the whole Republican party. This is a war which has been foretold more than 2000 years. The Pope and the Devil mean business. A Roman Catholic priest in speaking of it, said, 'We have the South and will soon have the West then you Damned Presbyterians will wade up to your knees in blood.' With great respect your teacher in 1841." ALS, *ibid.* On Nov. 28, Pope Gibbs, Walkerton, Ind., wrote to USG reporting a conversation between two potential assassins. ALS, DNA, RG 60, Letters from the President. In Nov., "a True friend and a republican also an Old soldier of the rebelling" wrote to USG. "i wish to warn you against danger which i fear you are to be in before long about the time of the inaguration i heard that your fate was to be the same as our late president Mr Lincolns. act wisely and be on your Gard" L, USG 3. In the same month, Anonymous, Petersburg, Va., warned USG about an assassination threat. L, *ibid.* Probably near this date, Anonymous wrote to [*USG*]. "If you do not look to a honest count of votes honestly cast for Mr Tilden you will be shot down like a dog. You Kellogg Packard Stearns Chamberlin—Look out Beware" L (undated), *ibid.* On Dec. 4, E. H. Stafford, Stony Point, Va., wrote to USG threateningly, adding that an assassin was ready to act for $1,000. ALS, *ibid.* On Dec. 12, Nelson Gillam, Methodist pastor, Bluffton, Ind., wrote to USG. "I do not intend to trouble you with a long letter, for I know you receive many such; but being a firm friend of my Country and its Chief Magistrate I wish to say to you that there is a determination on the part of the Democrats to assassinate you as they did the lamented Lincoln. They think if they can put you out of the way they can inaugurate Tilden by force. Leading Democrats here say Grant will not live until the 4th of March. I am impressed to say this to you fearing you are not as fully apprised of your critical situation as you should be. They also threaten Hayes. This of course is *strictly private* . . . P. S. Be careful how you go out, and whom you admit." ALS, DNA, RG 60, Letters from the President. On Dec. 16, Benjamin Harding, Ainsworth, Iowa, wrote to USG. "I have the honor of herewith saying to you again that your life is in danger again and it behoves you to keep a strong body guard around you to prevent the aproach of our enemies . . ." ALS, *ibid.*

1. On Nov. 9, Secretary of the Interior Zachariah Chandler, New York City, had telegraphed to USG, care of George W. Childs, Philadelphia. "Gov. Stearns of Florida

telegraphs from Tallahasse this day as follows to me: 'There is no doubt of our majority if we can secure an honest canvass, but the indications are that violence is to be freely resorted *to, to* prevent any returns from remote points in the interior. We shall need an army to protect us. Our special train leaving here last night for the Chattahoochie to despatch couriers to verify & secure intact the returns from Western counties was Kukluxed a few miles west of here & the train thrown from the track, which was torn up and blockaded in several places. Give us all the protection possible. M. L. STEARNS Gov. Please have this attended to immed'y." Copy, DLC-Zachariah Chandler. *HMD*, 45-3-31, IV, 342–43. On the same day, Cameron telegraphed to Governor Marcellus L. Stearns of Fla. "In answer to your request to the President, a sufficient number of troops have been ordered to Tallahassee to give the aid you desire." *Ibid.*, 44-2-42, 436. Also on Nov. 9, Cameron telegraphed to Sherman. "Telegraph Genl Ruger to proceed at once in person to Tallahassee Florida and upon his arrival there to communicate with Gov Stearns   Say to him to leave affairs in So Carolina in hands of an entirely discreet and reliable office" Telegram received, DNA, RG 94, Letters Received, 4788 1876. *HED*, 44-2-30, 23. On the same day, Sherman telegraphed to Col. Thomas H. Ruger, Columbia, S. C., transmitting "this third despatch within an hour" received from Cameron. ALS (telegram sent), DNA, RG 94, Letters Received, 4788 1876. *HED*, 44-2-30, 24. On Nov. 13, Ruger, Tallahassee, telegraphed to AG Edward D. Townsend. "Have arrived here & had Conference with the Govr of Florida relative to subject of my orders" Telegram received, *ibid. HED*, 44-2-30, 24. See Cameron to Sherman (2), Nov. 9, 1876, DNA, RG 94, Letters Received, 4788 1876; Ruger to Sherman, Nov. 9, 10, 1876, *ibid.*; Sherman to Maj. Gen. Winfield S. Hancock, Nov. 10, 1876, *ibid.*; telegram to William E. Chandler, Nov. 20, 1876.

2. In a letter docketed Oct. 31, and another dated Nov. 7, C. W. B. Moab had written to USG. "thire is about from 500 to to 1500 men that Cant vote   they have left Ga this year and the Whites Democrtic Party wants to Tax them $3 dollar and Braging how they intend to do the Colord and the Poor People did not no When to Give in they taxs   Please allow us achance to Vote for our Party" "this is to Certify the votes Which the oxford White People Wouted let them vote hear   Sixteen of them Coloded men and old Citizens to and Said they had already Paid tax in this County. and at the same time When thire Was White men Who had the Colod men hier to Cut Wood for them. the White men Voteed hear and then they Would not let the Poor Colorded People Vote hear When all of them stays at the same place in Calhoun Co ala. . . ." ALS, DNA, RG 60, Letters from the President. On Nov. 8, B. Z. Stone, Marion County, Ala., wrote to USG. "thare is sump thing rong hur   the people has not got to vote in the presidential election for haze becose the tickets never cumto the balitbox for them to be voted and they was a great many never voted on that acount . . ." ALS, *ibid.*

On Nov. 7, Anderson Low, Americus, Ga., had telegraphed to USG. "We cant do anything today   the democrats are tearing up our ticket   answer immediately" Telegram received (at 1:01 P.M.), DLC-USG, IB. On Nov. 24, C. B. Barnes, Cuthbert, Ga., wrote to USG. "I now drop you a few lines To inform you about the Election held here on the 7th day of Nov 1876 Mr. R. H. Whiteley was the ɪRepublican Candidate for Congress in this Second Congressional District. And no dout but what he would of been Elected by a handsome majority in this County. If the Republicans had of had a half chance to cast their ballard. The Colared people was Push away from the Polls and they could not get a chance to vote   The whites taken the window whare the votes was cast and when the Colored men come up to vote they would take thire ticket and exchange and give them a Democratic ticket because they could not read. This was all done againts thire will. hence Several hundred voted the Democrat that did not desired to do so. The Republican leader[s] was intimidated and thiarten so they was afraid to go to the window to see justice done. I was one of the Supervisor's of the Election in this place and when I would Seak to them a bout doing the colored people So bad they would curse me. The Democrats had five managers and the Republicans did not have any manager at all. . . ." ALS, DNA, RG 60, Letters to the President. *HED*, 44-2-30, 150. On Nov. 28, George Thomas, Atlanta, wrote to USG. "I take this chance to write to you to let you know that the democrats of Atlanta says the negros belongs to them for Tilton is the rightful and the supreme ruler in America and he will change things around 'tor Grant said they' will soon leave the White-house with the greatest regret as ever an ex-President has   Some counties here that a colord vote was prohibited making them vote a democrat ticket or none at all. I heard two white fellows say the other night that he voted at every pole in the City and put in some countrymen the same. They ought to beat us at this rate. We want to remain on free Columbias ground and are willing to come at your call if needed for the rebs say they can get ut a million of men before Hays shall get in power. They says we are dead now under they power They say we voted a ginst our freind for copit beggers Use ous as gack's then kick ous out of doors A gack can eat at leasure but we have but little a hard time. One drew his pistole on me as I wass tilling him the ~~enfmy~~ opeenion I do not say surender tho I half of my eagerness I will not give not give give up They say we are dus well are dum ~~cheep~~ sheepe and they are the leders. and they will showit. They want you out of the way. They said if Hays did get it they would carry him out out like Linclon I can not tell you half Answer soon   to you person'aly" ALS, DNA, RG 60, Letters from the President.

On Nov. 8, a person in Buffalo had written to USG. "It is an outrage, that this Government, should be given over to the late Rebels. It is plain, that many of the Southern States, are really Republican, if a fair Election was had. Constitutional, or not Constitutional, the fraud ought to be resisted, and you can do it. As it is, Mr Tilden, by the aid of his New York Irish blackguards, is disposing of the interests of a great Nation of forty millions of enlightened people, a thing which ought to be prevented. Is there any way of preventing this great fraud from succeeding if there is, the man who once saved this Nation, is the one to do do it. . . . There ought to a new and a fair Election, held in the late Slave states   that is the thing to do." ALS (signature illegible), USG 3. On Nov. 14, Ensley Moore, Jacksonville, Ill., wrote to USG. "PRIVATE. . . . Republicans here, generally, think New York city counting cheated us out of the Empire State majority. Cannot the government compel a right count there? With wishes for long life and happy rest to You, . . ." ALS, *ibid.* On Nov. 18, Attorney Gen. Alphonso Taft wrote to USG recommending an $8,055.62 payment to Oliver Fiske, U.S. marshal, Southern District, N. Y., "for extra[or]dinary expenses of the Presidential and Congressional Election in November, 1876, for his District." Copy, DNA, RG 60, Letters Sent to Executive Officers.

On Nov. 11, William R. Moore, Memphis, had written to USG. "STRICTLY *Confidential.* . . . Nothing but a deep sense of duty induces me to address to you this letter: But the imperilled condition of the liberty of not only the entire Black but also the white population of this country seems to me to demand that *every* friend of the Nation should speak out. The Elections south of us, particularly in Mississippi, have been *worse* than a hollow mockery and *wicked* crime. Whole communities, and counties (as I hear) of Republicans have *not cast a single vote*, or if they have done so, cast them *under stress* for Democrats. The state has been one continuous scene of 'Red shirted troopers' shooting and yelling over the country until the poor negroes are almost frantic with fear, dread and terror. It is sad to see the pitiable horror with ~~with~~ which they whisper to those whom they know to be in harmony with the national idea; and the reasonable though *timid* portion of honest *whites* are not much better off. Talk about slavery! That which enchains the whole people of the southern section of the U. S. *today* is *freedom* compared to the 'negro slavery' of 1860. If the Govt is prepared to surrender *now* the liberties of ~~the~~ its loyal subjects, It had been better to have surrendered them at appomatox, and saved all the subsequent strife and turmoil. God grant you grace to continue for the *right*." ALS, *ibid.*, Letters from the President. On Nov. 12, R. O. Harris, Aberdeen, Miss., wrote to USG. "As an humble individual of the state of Mississippi. expressing the sentiments of all Miss republicans. I must say *To Arms To Arms*—we know the conflict is inevitable and let it come, and when Miss republicans fail to do their duty on the field of battle turn them over to the tender mercy of rebel democrats. You are cheated out of 94 Votes—and we earnestly hope the backbone will not be wanting to deal with rebels as they should be. And in taking a new start in Government affairs place them where they belong" ALS, USG 3. On the same day, H. R. Ware, chairman, Republican State Central Committee, Jackson, Miss., wrote to USG. "From Telegramms in the morning Papers I notice, that your attention has been called to the recent election in Louisianna, and you have taken some action toward securing a fair and just expression of the will of the people in that state; Can nothing be done to affect that Consumation, so devoutly to be wished in this state. I assure you Mr. President that the late Election in this state, was but a medley of tragedy, Commedy and force, the most shameless and unblushing outrage, ever enacted in a free Country. The proof of this can be made ample and overwhelming. The 'Investigation held by the Senate Committee last Summer bad as was that development will pale into insignificance before the so called election a few days since. . . ." ALS, DNA, RG 60, Letters from the President. *HED*, 44-2-30, 131. On Nov. 15, L. W. B., Jr., Washington, Miss., wrote to USG. "Alas, alas, at this present hour I will seat my self to drop you a few lines to let you know how I live. I has been a speaker in the canvass for Hayes & Wheeler & our congressman Jno. R. Lynch now the election is over and I can not stay in my house at night last night I heard an echoe and I was out in my barn, and I look out and what was my surprise 50. armed KluKlux came from adjonin county Jefferson to destroy me now I have to quit my family and go away I wander is we Colored friend compell to live under such cruel laws is this. Seven men was found dead in fayette last week 9 of nov they was at church and the armed men came and surround the church and fired on us. we are afraid to own our name radical, if If you can do us any good try it I will not sign all of my name" L, DNA, RG 60, Letters from the President. *HED*, 44-2-30, 131–32.

On Nov. 14, William Bassett, Jarratt, Va., had written to USG. "I ask your Hon as I am in great trouble first about some land which I bought and the last payment is due the 1st of December, and I have not the money and can't get it. I have one Church and a small congregation that cannot pay me a support, and was teaching Public School here also under Conservative Trustees. and because I was a colored man and also a Republican, they took the school from me, and gave it to a one legged ex Rebel Soldier, who is a Conservative yet. They also heard that I would be Supervisor of the past Election and was one truly. So that made them very mad, and they took the school from me. now make their threat that they will take my home from me, after the time is out. if I had kept the school, every dollar would have been in hand. or if I could have gotten the money which I lost in the Freedmen's Bank $200, in Washington just across the street from you, and $16. in Norfolk Branch and have only gotten 20 per cent the 1st of Nov. last. if I had that money it would make me all right. if you think this is not true look on the Bank Book. for my name (William Bassett) Now I ask you in the Name of the Lord to please give, I pray the $74.45 cts to me. that I may save my save home. I have a family and I am not able to lose my home, if I can save it. The Democrats want to get me away from here. in order that they may do the Republicans as they please. I caught the Judges in their trick of stuffing the Ballot Box and reported them to Attorney L. L. Lewis of Richmond Va. this was done in the 2nd District as far as I hear. where the Conservative Papers say that John Goode is Elected. I do say that if Republicans are to be cheated like that: there is no use of us voting. Such as Conservatives taken the ballot Boxes at recess under their arms, and carring them every where they went, in other houses too, putting as many ballots in as they want. and then taken out Republican which were voted single every one. in the place of them is too much to bear. The Conservative tickets were in bunches of six and ten. I told them that it was stelling in the high way. and there was in the joining Co. a Precinct where the Judges would not qualify because so many Republicans were there. and not one could vote. and at another place they (Conservatives) took the ballot Box in a room, and would not let a single Republican be with them. even the Supervisor. while they counted. are these things right? and should they stand?. . . I dont want you, nor any other man to pay me for being a Republican, no! if I be so poor that I could not get bread to eat. I should be a Republican still from principle. I could be a Democrat for money. but I will die first—yes if needs be, over and again. . . . Please write soon. to the above named place." ALS, DNA, RG 60, Letters from the President.

On Nov. 16, C. M. Thompson, Waco, Tex., wrote to USG describing Democratic intimidation of black voters. ALS, _ibid. HED,_ 44-2-30, 144.

On Nov. 17, Alfred V. Dockery, Rockingham, N. C., wrote to USG. "The election South must convince everybody that universal suffrage is a mistake and the ballot a fraud. The north ought be made understand the meaning of theseis election & take precautionary steps. Tildens great majorities are in the 'Solid South'. Sectionalism will be revived. This is the Critical period & all depends upon the action of those _now_ in power—Southern Republicans, as such, are not longer to be permitted to exist. Then let the north manage gov't on sectional grounds if necessary. My _faith,_ as well as that of _very many_ others, in Republican Institutions is becoming _very_ weak & we are ready to help make the nation strong enough not to be shaken by elections.—No one else is better qualified than yourself to manage the nation—" ALS, USG 3. On Nov. 18, Mary P. Glover, Swan Quarter, N. C., wrote to USG. "Their was a party of Democrats that took my husband Dr. A. J. Glover and murdered him on the night before the election, he was the most prominent Republican in Hyde County. The civil authorities will not notice it at all, they say it was only an accident, their is a plenty of men in the county that know of the whole plot and say they will sware to the truth if they are called upon to do so. I hope you will do what you can to have the parties arrested and brought to justice. Their is one Dr Edward Jones sais he will advance five hundred dollars to have Mr. E. H. Guirken a Republican put in the same fix that Dr. Glover is in. The Republicans of this county are very much frightened. . . . P. S. Dr. Glover was supervisor of the ellection a commisioned officer I think the U. S. authorities will attend to his murderers." ALS, DNA, RG 60, Letters from the President.

On Nov. 17, Josiah Deloach, postmaster, Memphis, had written to USG. "I wrote you that we could Elect our Member to Congress and ten Members to the Legislature provided Judge Lewis was out the way, our Election was done Great damage by the obstinacy of Judge Lewis, well done all I wrote you we would do, But the Most awful stuffing the ballot Boxes never known before, Mr Randolph was Elected to Congress by from 600 to 1000 votes, our whole ten Members were Elected but lost all but two by fraud, The basest Frauds that ever was known in this County and Fayette—Mr Randolph a _fine Lawyer,_ was our Candidate, and our Legislative ticket was the very best ticket ever offered in this County since 1837, I pray to god that Hays is Elected—I write this for the reason I wrote you the letter I refer too, about Judge Lewis I am proud that I can say to you that my _office_ is _right to a cent._" ALS, _ibid._

On Nov. 21, Charles Munger, Methodist pastor, Farmington, Maine, wrote to USG. "Are you aware of the existence of an organization called 'The Veterans' whose [av]owed purpose is to fight if the Democracy do not succeed in obtaining the Government by the election of Tilden? A prominent Democrat in Maine told me yesterday that there was such

an organization in the North West numbering a hundred thousands & showed me a letter
from a Major Corse urging similar organizations in Maine . . ." ALS, *ibid.* On Nov. 23, Edward H. Lively, postmaster, Williamsburg, Va., wrote to USG. "I Saw a letter yesterday
written by one Allcote of New York City who is Extensively Engaged ~~Extensively~~ through
native Agents here in the wood business to the effect that all wood chopping business here
must stop forthwith—He further states that private money has been subscribed to the Extent of one and a half millions of dollars & more than 100-000 men are ready to made a
raid on Washington at the first tocsin of trouble—This man was your Supporter in you
1st & 2d election—He is now a Tilden man To be forewarned is to be forearmed" ALS,
ibid. On the same day, J. W. D., Chicago, wrote to USG. "I Halve Ben Aprised Of a Plot of
the Rebels & Democrats If Defeated In the Presidential Alection to Burn Washington
City Pleas Be Ware ~~as it~~ & Receive this as from a Friend to the united States & freedom Be of good Chear. God Bless you In Preserving Peace" L, *ibid.* On Nov. 26, James A.
Van Fleet, National Soldiers' Home, Dayton, wrote to USG. "Will You excuse a greate liberty from a verry humble source. Sir do You not believe the Capitol is in great danger of
capture by the enemy. Please hear these reasons for believing that it is in danger. If You
have read the Tribune of N. Y. You have probbably read a letter from S. Carolina, showing
that the Rebbles have, in the last year procured no less than Twelve Batteries of Artilery.
But You have undoubtedly a better oppertunty for obtaining information, than any other.
Would it not be wisdom to act on it. . . . Do You not think it behooves Your Excellency to
take greate care of Yourself? Do not forget the fate of Our martyred President. . . ." ALS,
USG 3. In a letter docketed Dec. 2, "Friend" wrote to USG. "An army *secretly* organizing
by Tildenites in N. Y. City, and in Virginia, N. Carolina, S. Carolina, Ga., Ala., Miss., Louisiana, and all through Rebeldom—They say, '*Tilden or blood,*' and boast of it. *They mean it.*
The writer has just been in *four* of those States, *and is not mistaken.*" L, DNA, RG 60, Letters from the President.

On Nov. 15, Gouverneur Carr, secretary, Republican Reform Club, and former lt.
col., 165th N. Y., New York City, had written confidentially to USG suggesting that
army pensioners be enlisted "for defense against the sudden uprising which is more than
possible within the next 100 days." ALS, DLC-USG, IB. See *New York Times,* Sept. 24,
1889. On Nov. 20, Charles G. Otis, former maj., 21st N. Y. Cav., New York City, wrote to
USG. "Should the Country require the Services of her Sons Count me in. I am ready to
change my clothes" ALS, USG 3. Three similar letters to USG, dated Nov. 13, 29, and 30,
are *ibid.*

To James A. Garfield

———

[C]ENTENNIAL GROUNDS PHILA NOV 10 [*1876*]
[GEN]L. J A GARFIELD WASHN D. C.
[I w]ould be gratified if you would go to [New] Orleans to remain
until the vote of Louisia[na is] Counted. Gov. Kellogg requests that
reliable [wit]nesses be sent to see that the Canvass of the [vote i]s a
fair one   Answer

U S GRANT

Telegram received, DLC-James A. Garfield. *HMD*, 45-3-31, I, 789. On Nov. 10, 1876, 9:15 P.M., Culver C. Sniffen telegraphed to USG, care of George W. Childs, Philadelphia. "When will you be here. Genl. Garfield waits to know." ALS (telegram sent), DLC-USG, IB; telegram received, *ibid*. On the same day, USG telegraphed to Sniffen. "Will return by limited express tomorrow" Telegram received (at 10:40 P.M.), *ibid*. Also on Nov. 10, 10:18 P.M., Sniffen had written to U.S. Representative James A. Garfield of Ohio. "Have been waiting until this time for a reply from the President. Am now going home, having ordered the Western Union people to send anything from the President to my house & I will send it to you from there" ANS, DLC-James A. Garfield. On Nov. 11, Garfield wrote to Burke A. Hinsdale concerning his meeting with USG late that afternoon. ". . . I have concluded to go, and shall leave at midnight. I go with great reluctance; but feel it to be a duty from which I cannot shrink. . . ." Mary L. Hinsdale, ed., *Garfield-Hinsdale Letters: Correspondence Between James Abram Garfield and Burke Aaron Hinsdale* (1949; reprinted, New York, 1969), pp. 339–42. See *ibid*., pp. 343–45; *HMD*, 45-3-31, I, 789–806, 843; Harry James Brown and Frederick D. Williams, eds., *The Diary of James A. Garfield* (East Lansing, Mich., 1967–81), III, 379–92; Allan Peskin, *Garfield* (Kent, Ohio, 1978), pp. 407–11.

Also on Nov. 11, USG, Wilmington, Del., telegraphed to Benjamin Harrison, Indianapolis. "I would be gratified if you would visit New orleans to witness Count of the vote" Telegram received, DLC-Benjamin Harrison. On Nov. 13, Harrison telegraphed to USG. "Find it impossible to go to NewOrleans" Telegram received (at 3:00 P.M.), DLC-USG, IB.

On Nov. 11, USG, Wilmington, had telegraphed to J. Cortlandt Parker. "I would be gratified if you would visit New Orleans to witness count of votes." *HMD*, 45-3-31, I, 725. On [*Nov.*] 12, Parker, Newark, N. J., telegraphed to USG. "Telegram received too late for answer yesterday Hope to leave tonight or tomorrow" Telegram received, DLC-USG, IB. On Nov. 29, Parker, New Orleans, wrote to USG. "I am compelled to leave this city without waiting for the close of the Session of the returning officers—When your telegram reached me I was actually engaged in the trial of an important cause. The Vice Chancellor before whom it was pending agreed with me that I ought to go—and said that he would postpone the case till my return. He did put it off till the 28th—But I learn by telegraph that it was then ordered on, and is now proceeding. My client acceded to my coming on condition of this postponement but now demands my return. The action taken by the Returning Board makes my stay here now comparatively unprofitable. The testimony on the subject of intimidation and irregularities is but partially taken before them, and it is expected to close to-day, but several officers are engaged examining witnesses before Commissioners in different quarters of the City. This evidence when finished goes to the board with written arguments, if any, and their deliberations are, of course, private—I have been a regular and attentive observer at all the sittings of the Board. I have seen nothing inconsistent with the utmost fairness in conduct and intent. I have witnessed much that impressed me with their judicial impartiality. I have examined a good deal of the testimony presented with the returns and therefore already before the Board—If I should stay I could know little, if anything, more than I now do. It is proposed, as I understand, that the persons honored with by your request to witness this count, should make a formal report on the subject. I reserve till then any further observations respecting our mission." ALS, DNA, RG 60, Letters from the President. See *HMD*, 45-3-31, I, 725–41.

On Nov. 11, Saturday, William M. Evarts, Windsor, Vt., had telegraphed to USG. "HAVE JUST RECEIVED THE TELEGRAM YOU DID ME THE HONOR TO SEND ME AT NEWYORK. I SHALL RETURN TO THAT CITY ON MONDAY AND GIVE THE SUBJECT MY IMMEDIATE ATTENTION." Telegram received, DLC-USG, IB.

On the same day, Stanley Matthews, Cincinnati, telegraphed to USG. "As requested will leave for New Orleans tonight" Telegram received (at 2:42 P.M.), *ibid*.

Also on Nov. 11, Edwin W. Stoughton, New York City, twice telegraphed to USG. "I shall obey your request, leaving NewYork nine oclock tonight will pass through Washington tomorrow morning where I will be glad to receive any suggestion which you desire to make" "WAS MISTAKEN ABOUT TRAINS   FIRST TRAIN WHICH WILL TAKE ME THROUGH LEAVES NEW YORK SIX O.CLOCK SUNDAY MORNING REACHING NEW ORLEANS WEDNESDAY NOON WILL THIS BE IN TIME FOR ME TO BE OF SERVICE. PLEASE ANSWER." Telegrams received (at 3:33 and 6:55 P.M.), *ibid.*

On Nov. 12, James H. Van Alen, New York City, telegraphed to USG. "Leave tonight   my new-orleans address St-Charles Hotel." Telegram received, *ibid.* See *New York Times*, Jan. 4, 1877, July 26, 1886. On June 8, 1872, U.S. Senator Roscoe Conkling of N. Y. had written to USG. "I have the honor of enclosing a letter from Mr James H Van Alen, and would respectfully call your attention to the wish therein expressed." LS, Anthony Collection, NN.

On Nov. 12, 1876, U.S. Senators Oliver P. Morton of Ind. and Aaron A. Sargent of Calif., San Francisco, telegraphed to USG. "We recommend following men be ~~to~~ invited to go south to insure fair count senators Cameron Cragin Howe, McMillan Boutwell Congressmen Conger Freye Rusk Congressmen Elect Hanna and [same] should be sent to south, Carolina—" Telegram received (at 6:25 P.M.), DLC-USG, IB.

Probably on Nov. 13, John A. Dix, New York City, telegraphed to USG. "I would most cheerfully comply with your request but it is impossible for me to leave home" Telegram received (at 2:51 P.M.), *ibid.*

On July 24, 1878, U.S. Representative Eugene Hale of Maine, Atlantic City, N. J., testified concerning USG's request to witness the vote count in New Orleans. "I was at home in Maine when I received the summons to go to Washington, and there I saw President Grant. . . . It was stated that other gentlemen were going on both sides. . . . I left Washington alone. On striking the Pennsylvania Central Railroad I found Mr. Stoughton, Mr. Van Allen, and, I think, Mr. Kasson. At Cincinnati I found Mr. Sherman, and together we all traveled to New Orleans. . . ." *HMD*, 45-3-31, I, 742. See *ibid.*, pp. 742–49; message to Congress, Dec. 6, 1876.

To John A. Logan

Nov. 210th *1876.*

To GEN. LOGAN, CHICAGO, ILL.

I hope you will comply with the request to go to New Orleans to witness the count of the vote of La. I have requested Judge Kelley,[1] Mr. Ditty[2] of Balt. and ~~Judge Kelley~~ Gen. Garfield to go also.

U. S. GRANT

ALS (telegram sent), Mrs. Paul E. Ruestow, Jacksonville, Fla.; telegram received (at 2:10 P.M.), DLC-Logan Family Papers. On Nov. 10, 1876, U.S. Senator John A. Logan of Ill., Chicago, twice telegraphed to USG, Philadelphia. "I can not go but will see that some prominent men go." "The matter is attended to good men will go to witness Count" Telegrams received (forwarded from Washington, D. C.), DLC-USG, IB. On the same day,

USG telegraphed to Logan. "Your arrangement satisfactory" Telegram received, DLC-Logan Family Papers. See James Pickett Jones, *John A. Logan: Stalwart Republican from Illinois* (Tallahassee, 1982), p. 94.

1. Born in 1814, William D. Kelley practiced law in Philadelphia, served as common pleas judge (1846–56), and participated in the 1860 Republican National Convention. In 1861, he started an unbroken tenure in the U.S. House of Representatives. On July 24, 1878, Kelley, Atlantic City, N. J., testified concerning USG's request to witness the vote count in New Orleans. "I went at the request of President Grant, who, on the 10th of November in that year was in Philadelphia for the purpose of participating in the closing ceremonies of the Centennial Exhibition. I was there with friends when inquiry was made in the auditorium to know whether I was there, and it was suggested that the President desired to see me. I found him surrounded by a number of distinguished gentlemen, among whom was General Robert Patterson, of Philadelphia, and the President then proposed that I should visit New Orleans to witness the action of the returning-board. At first I declined. The President said that a number of prominent gentlemen of the other party had gone there and that it was deemed advisable that some of our political friends should be there, and suggested that as my conduct had been a little independent on some questions, as I had kicked the traces sometimes, as the phrase goes, it was thought important that I should go to New Orleans, and so I was prevailed upon to consent, and I went there. Q. The President asked you to go to New Orleans to witness the count?—. . . A. *To witness the count.* He said, 'We want you to do nothing but be a looker on, and note any thing that you may think extraordinary, and especially anything improper, if any such thing should occur.'. . . I had no conference on the subject of my going with anybody but President Grant, except that one or two of the gentlemen who were present at the time, markedly General Patterson, concurred in the suggestion that my position in the party at that time was such as made it important, in their judgment, that I should go. . . ." *HMD*, 45-3-31, I, 715–16. See *ibid.*, pp. 715–25.

2. C. Irving Ditty, Baltimore lawyer, had served as cav. officer, C.S. Army. On Feb. 9, 1877, Ditty, Washington, D. C., testified on his activities in La., especially his contacts with Joseph H. Maddox. See *ibid.*, 44-2-42, 271–78, 341–44; telegram to John Sherman, Nov. 11, 1876.

To Edward Wilkins

Nov. 10th 1876.

To Collector Wilkins, Baltimore, Md.

Gov. Kellogg, in fear of violence and misstatment in regard to the count, of the vote of the state by the returning board has requested that [r]eliable persons be sent from other states to witness the count. I have requested Judge Kelley and Gen. Garfield to go and would be glad to have Ditty of Baltimore to go also. Will you ask him for me?

U. S. Grant

ALS (telegram sent), Mrs. Paul E. Ruestow, Jacksonville, Fla. On Nov. 10, 1876, Edward
Wilkins, collector of customs, Baltimore, telegraphed to USG, Philadelphia. "Evening papers here publish hewitts request to democrats to go to neworleans Am I authorized to
publish your dispatch asking [D]itty to go" Telegram received, DLC-USG, IB. On the
same day, USG endorsed this telegram to Gen. William T. Sherman. "Answer Yes to within
dispatch." AES, *ibid.*

On Nov. 13, Pere Wilmer, Baltimore, wrote to USG. "Permit me to congratulate you
that you have sent additional troops to Florida, and Louisiana; and after it is confirmed—
as it undoubtedly will be—that Hayes has 185 electoral votes:—permit me to suggest that
you order an investigation in some other states—which would have had Republican majorities—had not intimidation, violence, and fraud been used. I take the liberty of calling
your attention to the fact—that one of the persons (J. L. Carroll) sent to N. Orleans by
Hewitte was elected by fraud, and must know that he is only a bogus Governor." ALS,
DNA, RG 60, Letters from the President.

On Nov. 18, "An Outlaw of the west," Baltimore, wrote to USG. "I know that you are
not prepared to die I want to give you notice that your days are. short in this wourld, I
have been Paid a large sum of money to take your life we find that the country will be
ruened if you reman in this wourld much longer I will give you about three weeks to live
so prepair for death I am bound under oath to take your life I have been Paid 10,000 dollars to do the work you will not be the first one that I have put out of this wourld, you
may think this nothing but remember that the mony is easley made by takeing the life of
a feith and the man who has ruined our courntry there is threee of us to do the Job you
must and shall die we can afford to hang to Save the Country. So do not be surprised if you
find your Self a corfes there is no hope for you" L, OFH. On Nov. 21, "A Member of Peeler
Club," Baltimore, wrote to USG. "I as a friend to you advise you to be careful as their is
going to be an Assassination, and you are the Victim . . . You *are damned* thief. You shall be
murdered, you cannot hold the White House. *New York & Balto. are Solid*" L, *ibid.*

On Nov. 24, James M. Deems, Baltimore, wrote to USG. "In view of the threatening
aspect of affairs, I ask permission, should there be a necessity, to raise a Regt. of Cavalry
in this state—Several officers and many men of my old Regiment (1st Md Cav.) reside
here. We have two Regiments of 'Boys in Blue' here—the 2nd of which I am Lieut Col—
will be glad to respond to your call." ALS, USG 3.

On Nov. 27, S. B. J., Boston, for "(*Ten Boston* MERCHANTS)," wrote to USG. "As a good
republican and friend of the Adminstration, I feel bound to report to you the result of my
observations during a recent visit to Baltimore & N. Y. City. In the former City a secret
conclave is forming & strengthning every day: for the avowd purpose of protecting their
rights. & similar bodies are forming in other large Cities. for the acknowledged purpose of
securing & safely placing *Gov Tilden* in the White House, when the proper time shall arrive: The 'Dead Rabbits,' of Baltimore & Plug uglies of N. Y. City are developing strength
at a furious rate, and the general public are quieted by assurances of the Democratic press
that force will be the last (instead of the first) thing they will resort to, under any circumstances!! The general feeling here among the Merchants of this City is, that you will *not* be
deluded by such assurances, but will be at all times (in a quiet way) in a Condition to meet
any plot or wicked attempt to do wrong, in a manner & way it may deserve. To be forewarned, is to be fore armed, and we can but feel that any attempt to take possession of the
'*White House*,' by the Democrats, unless it is clear that they have a right to, will be met &
punished with a severity it deserves." L, DNA, RG 60, Letters from the President. On the
same day, 10:00 P.M., Henry F. Moring, Baltimore, wrote to USG. "It is quite evident that
there is some mischief brewing among the Democratic roughs in this City, as certain dis-
reputable characters who are known to be the henchmen and tools of the ring leaders here,

are quite loud in their boastings on the streets tonight of what fun they will have in Washington in a few days. They seem to be cognizant of some preconcerted movement against certain high officials in Washington, which is to be put into operation in a very few days— probably on the 29th, and from remarks overheard by me it looks very much like assassination & bloodshed were the programme of these gentlemen. Whatever their plot may be it is certain that they are in league with certain democratic roughs in Washington, and that mischief will be attempted there—*What better could the Democrats wish just now than the death of our present President?* I think it would be worth while therefore not only to be on the alert, but to send a few shrewd detectives here to watch proceedings among the known roughs of this City. The lateness of the hour prevents my giving you fuller details." ALS, *ibid.*

On Nov. 30, W. H. Oliver, Baltimore, wrote to USG. "Please allow me to thank you. for the *firm* yet impartial manner displayed. in the management of the *most difficult problem* that has ever fallen to the Executive of the United States. Tho' we have differed on political matters in the past, yet I am *strong* in *Support* of *your views* & stand with Stoughton, Ditty (an old personl friend) Mosby—& others who can recognize *honest* administrative abilities, as well as a Sincere devotion to *true Constitutinal liberty*" ALS, USG 3.

On Dec. 11, John M. Freshour, former sgt., 1st Md., Frederick, wrote to USG. "for sometime Since the Ellections, men who I can name if neaded, have used such Threats as the folering, That in the Event of Hayes being President, they would rais companes to provent him from being President, and menny such to numorus to mention I ask your opinion in regards to the above. hopeing that I shall here from you . . ." ALS, DNA, RG 60, Letters from the President. On the same day, "Balto Secret Government," Baltimore, wrote to USG. "At meeting of our Society resolutions passd our lodge, of two hundred & fifteen members, to send you a warning, The course which you have pursued dose not meet the approbation of our members, and you are hereby ordered to resign the office of President, by the 1st Jany or you will assasinated, It will be put into iffect at once, if praticable, but in the event it is not so that it can be done descreatly, we will do it on first opportunity, ~~and~~ you can rely on us we will do it if we have to wait twelve months for an opportunity Your adminsitration has brought the laboring class to want & misery, & unless you vacate, your blood shall flow, to avenge ~~tour~~ wrong, . . ." L, *ibid.*

On Dec. 16, L. W. Johnston, Baltimore, wrote to USG. "I write this in strict confidence and solemnly promising to say nothing to any one, myself, about it. You have, and all of your party have an enemy, who will cause intense trouble, if he can to all of you. I allude to John Young Brown, the Kentucky representative. He is, as you know out of Congress after this session, and he desires to bring himself prominently to Tilden's notice in such a way, as to be able to obtain, a certain office, under his Administration, should he be inaugurated. Although apparently now very quiet, and inactive, he is only waiting until he thinks a good time to act has arrived. . . . He is artful and vindictive, and says he would like to see you and Hayes both murdered, and [that] you are the greatest villain this side of Hell, and he would think no more of helping to send you there than he would of drinking a glass of water. These are his very words. . . . In all his plans he is in the habit of communicating to a young woman living here, and with whom I can prove he is criminally intimate, and who is the embodiment of spite and mischief, and really puts him on to doing a good deal of it. This girl has been in the habit of going to Washington to meet Brown, and he has during the last session been here with her several times, and is perfectly infatuated. . . ." ALS, *ibid.*

On Dec. 19, D. Royce, Reading, Pa., wrote to USG concerning a plan to concentrate a Democratic force at Baltimore. "My Office is next dore to 8 ward democratic Head Quarters of this place I Have herd many thing said hardly lawfull to be said almost Evry day for the last three months, and since the Election I have herd many of them say that if Tilden was not declaired to be Elected & Inaugerated there would be a fight. I have herd them say not unfrequently that if Hays was declaird Elected then the democrats would withdraw from both hous of Congress & Elect Tilden & Hendrecks & Install them in office & Establesh a Sepperate government when there would be a fight. . . ." ALS, *ibid.*

On Jan. 9, 1877, "A Colored man, 1st 2nd 3rd Key which I will produce when I come," Baltimore, wrote to USG. "I at last conclude to write and inform you of what I know to be going on in Balt. in Democratic Circles regarding Tilden, and plans to be carried out to secure his Inauguration on the 4th of March. I hope you will not regard this as mere sensasional because I have not signed my name, every word is facts which you will soon see, however you will please keep this as I hope soon to appear before your Excellency and recognze this letter by the Key which is 1st 2nd 3. 1st. In Balt there is a deep laid plot amongst the Demcracy to capture Gov. Hayes, sometime previous to Inauguration, and conseal him untill Tilden is Inaugurated, in New York, or Wash. this whole thing seem to come from New York, but the captureing part is to be done by men from Indiana and Balt. Tilden is to take up his abode in Wash as soon as posible, so as not to excite susspisions. on that day there will be thousands of Democrats, who will understand the matter, will take him to the Capital &c &c and them to the Mansion During all this time Gov. Hayes will not be found. Mr President, these are all facts as I over heard the parties relating them, and why I think there is something in it, is because they made much ado about the Press publishing the report, about Tildens going to Washington, they seem to think there was traitors in there ranks, why and how it should get out. Genl. French was spoken of but I could not get any thing reliable, also the 5th and 6th Regiments, and the answer was that the 6th was Devided &cc. Now Mr President, I do earnestly hope and pray God, that all our great men will Stick to the party as you have done, also Hon. O. P. Morton, Z. Chandler, and others. Please give this your attention." L, *ibid.*

On Jan. 13, Joseph F. Carter, Howard County, Md., wrote to USG. "I enclose you an extract from to-days paper. showing the animus of the '*Unarmed men*' business it being very clear that they wish to intimidate you and the U. S Senate. they have let the cat out of the Bag, and we should prepare to meet them with force as that is their game. the force of Regulars is very small. and cannot be relied upon to fight such a Mob. we have 5000 men that we could muster in Maryland, who have seen service and could be relied upon to fight. quite a number living in the counties adjacent Washington. who could be on hand to support you. until the Troops from Pennsylvania under Hartranft could reach the District" ALS (misdated 1876), USG 3. The enclosure is *ibid.*

To Lt. Gen. Philip H. Sheridan

Washington, D. C.
Nov. 11th /76

GEN. P. H. SHERIDAN,
CHICAGO, ILL.

There is such apprehension of violence in New Orleans during the Canvassing of the vote of the state of La. that I think you should go in person.[1]

The Military have nothing to do with the counting of the vote. Its province is to keep the peace and to protect the legal Canvassing board in the performance of its duties. The gentlemen of both polit-ical parties who will be there ~~will~~ will observe the conduct of the Canvassers.

U. S. GRANT

ADfS, DNA, RG 94, Letters Received, 4788 1876. On Nov. 16, 1876, Lt. Gen. Philip H. Sheridan, New Orleans, telegraphed in cipher to Gen. William T. Sherman. "There is nothing new here; very little excitement no appearance of any trouble Twenty six com-panies now here judiciously stationed. Number of troops deemed sufficient." Copies (2), *ibid. HED*, 44-2-30, 41. See following telegram.

Also on Nov. 16, Sherman wrote a memorandum entitled "Projet a la General Scott" outlining plans for troop redeployment to safeguard the capital. AD, DNA, RG 94, Letters Received, 4788 1876. On Nov. 15 and 16, Sherman confidentially wrote to Col. William F. Barry, Fort Monroe, Va., detailing troop movements to the capital. AL (ini-tialed) and copy, *ibid.* On Nov. 21, Sherman wrote to Maj. Gen. Winfield S. Hancock. ". . . Eight Companies of Artillery are now here at the Arsenal—Commanded at pres-ent by Capt. Loder. I expect Colonel Barry here tomorrow when I will instruct him to take Command and report to you. Their object is to make safe the the most important personages and property necessarily here at the Capitol. The Four Companies of the 1st Artillery now at Fort Sill will soon come here. . . ." Copy, *ibid.* See Sheridan to Sher-man, Nov. 16, 1876 (2), Sherman to Col. Richard C. Drum, Nov. 16, 1876, Sherman to Han-cock, Nov. 16, 1876, Barry to Sherman, Nov. 17, 1876, Sherman to Col. Joseph C. Auden-ried, Nov. 18, 1876, *ibid.*; *New York Times*, Nov. 20–23, 26, 1876.

On Dec. 1, Samuel Yorke AtLee, Washington, D. C., wrote to USG. "I was told to day by a citizen who is in daily intercourse with the soldiers at the arsenal, that they were gen-erally Tilden men; that one of the companies were, with the exception of two men, all dem-ocrats. He tells me that he was informed by one of the Sergeants of a company lately in So. Ca., that the illiterate negroes would show the tickets in their hands to the soldiers saying that as the Union Soldiers would not deceive them they wanted to know whether the tick-ets they held were Hayes tickets? These tickets were Tilden tickets, but the soldiers as-sured them that *it was all right.* In this way at least 200 votes were given, in a certain pre-cinct, for Tilden Electors which ought to have been and were intended to be deposited for the Republican Electors. As a citizen and a Republican, I thought it my duty to acquaint you with these facts: ~~which~~, whether they of any importance you can best judge." ALS, DNA, RG 60, Letters from the President. A related testimonial is *ibid.*

On Dec. 11 and 21, Sherman wrote to Sheridan. "Confidential. . . . Where ever you can, collect your troops into as large garrisons as possible, convenient for moving. The President intimated that he might want as many as 4000 men here, and that is impossible without drawing from you." ". . . The President does not seem now as anxious as he was about troops for Washington, so I doubt if you will be called on for more—. . ." ALS, DLC-Philip H. Sheridan.

1. On Nov. 1, Governor William P. Kellogg of La. had written to Secretary of War James D. Cameron requesting that Sheridan take personal command in New Orleans prior to the election because "his presence in the City will go very far towards preserving the public peace, averting violence and bloodshed, and securing to all Citizens protection in the exercise of the right to vote as guaranteed by the Fifteenth Amendment to the Con-

stitution of the U. S." LS, DNA, RG 94, Letters Received, 4788 1876. *HED*, 44-2-30, 40. On Nov. 6, Sherman telegraphed in cipher to Brig. Gen. Christopher C. Augur, New Orleans. "Governor Kellogg writes to the Secretary of War, asking that General Sheridan be in New Orleans on Election day. Notify him that General Sheridan was here a few days ago, in conference with the President and Secretary, and the programme agreed on. General Sheridan will not come to NewOrleans unless in a case of extreme urgency." ALS (telegram sent), DNA, RG 94, Letters Received, 4788 1876. *HED*, 44-2-30, 40.

To John Sherman

Dated PHILADA PA 11 NOV *1876*

To SENATOR JOHN SHERMAN.

I would be much pleased if you would join other parties who have already accepted same invitation to go to New Orleans to witness the Canvassing of the vote of La.

U. S. GRANT

Telegram received (at 8:35 P.M.), DLC-John Sherman; copy, OFH. On Sunday, Nov. 12, 1876, U.S. Senator John Sherman of Ohio, Mansfield, telegraphed to USG. "Am detained by legal business pending in court until wednesday Could go then if not too late—" Telegram received (at 1:05 P.M.), DLC-USG, IB. On the same day, 2:00 P.M., USG telegraphed to Sherman. "Unless you can reach there by Friday morning it will be too late" Copies, *ibid.*; OFH. On Nov. 13, Sherman telegraphed to USG. "Will go, reaching NewOrleans thursday morning." Telegram received (at 9:37 A.M.), DLC-USG, IB. See *HMD*, 45-3-31, I, 760–88; message to Congress, Dec. 6, 1876; *John Sherman's Recollections of Forty Years . . .* (Chicago, 1895), I, 553–60.

On Nov. 11, William Dennison, D. C. commissioner, Columbus, Ohio, had telegraphed to USG. "Your invitation to Senator Sherman to go to New Orleans I am sure would gratify our friends here. I leave for Washington noon train today" Telegram received, DLC-USG, IB.

On Nov. 22, Lt. Gen. Philip H. Sheridan, New Orleans, telegraphed in cipher to Gen. William T. Sherman. "There does not seem to be any necessity for my remaining here. If however I am to remain until after vote is canvassed? Please let me know." Telegram received, DNA, RG 94, Letters Received, 4788 1876. *HED*, 44-2-30, 41. On the same day, 2:15 P.M., Sherman telegraphed in cipher to Sheridan. "Have read your cypher telegram to Secretary of war, who says he and President will feel more Comfortable if you will remain till the Canvas is Concluded." ALS (telegram sent), DNA, RG 94, Letters Received, 4788 1876. *HED*, 44-2-30, 42.

On Nov. 24, USG had written a note. "I wish the Sec. of the Int. would see Mr. Maddox Spl. Agt of the Treas. who has just returned from New Orleans and has valuable information" ANS (facsimile), A. M. Gibson, *A Political Crime: The History of the Great Fraud* (New York, 1885), p. 360. Joseph H. Maddox allegedly communicated messages from La. returning board members to Democratic and Republican leaders that the state's electoral votes could be bought for a large sum of cash. Congressional investigators decided not to probe Maddox's conversation with USG. On Feb. 5, 1877, U.S. Representative William Lawrence of Ohio telegraphed to USG. "Governor Wells says Maddox had a letter to you signed by Wells dated about November 20th. If proper to do so will you Examine and send letter to me by Messenger at once for [exa]mination by Committee [of] House." Telegram received, OFH; DNA, RG 107, Telegrams Collected (Bound). On the same day, Culver C. Sniffen replied to Lawrence. "The President has no recollection of receiving such a letter nor do our records or files show the letter—" AE, OFH; ALS (telegram sent), DNA, RG 107, Telegrams Collected (Bound). See *HMD*, 44-2-42, 131–40, 143–62, 178–83, 191–97; *SED*, 50-1-277, 51-1-101; *SRC*, 50-2-2656; *New York Times*, Feb. 10, 1877.

On Nov. 29, 1876, J. Y. Payne, Boston, had written to USG. "I send you a slip that I cut from Evening Herald of this city of this date, thinking that else it may not meet your eye. It looks as if the United States government was too weak to protect its citizens. What has been done about punishing those who led out the 98 republicans who about 1870 or 71 were led out to the edge of the town of Opelousas, La. and shot dead. See the evidence obtained by Cap't. F. M. Coxe, 25th U. S. Infantry who went there after the outrage. What has been done about bringing those men to punishment who shot the judge and Sheriff at Franklin La. at about the same time? I have lived in Louisiana for ten years, and know wherof I speak. Do not be afraid of the Confederat Congress. Be bold brave and strong *now* and all will be well." ALS, DNA, RG 60, Letters from the President. The enclosure is *ibid.*

To Gen. William T. Sherman

Nov. 12th /76

DEAR GENERAL:

If you receive this in time come up and take a social dinner with us, at 6 O'clock—if not otherwise engaged. If engaged come after dinner, or in the morning soon after ten.

Yours Truly

U. S. GRANT

GEN. W. T. SHERMAN,

P. S. Nothing in relation to movement of troops or election matters.

ALS, Madigan Collection, NN.

To Abel R. Corbin

————

Washington,
Nov. 14th '76.

MY DEAR MR. CORBIN:

Jennie's and your letter is just received. I shall not be in New York, nor away from Washington, until after the meeting of Congress. But I will gladly give you the hour or two you speak of if you come to Washington. If you and Jennie could come this week we could make a spare room without inconvenience. Mrs. Smith—of Washington, Pa., with her two children—are with us, but they can be put in the room with their mother.

The alarm about the removal of Holden as Collector of Internal Revenue for the Covington district is premature.[1] There was a *raid* made upon him by a person in whom I take no *stock*, and a statement made in regard to him which I said—if proved true—would mean that he must go out. But I think that rumor was entirely dispelled.

My Message is not "blocked out," nor scarcely thought of. So many other exciting matters preoccupy my time and thoughts that I do not bother myself about the other. I shall trust to the inspiration of the moment for what I shall say. Will be brief, but to the point if I can.

Yours truly,
U. S. GRANT.

J. G. Cramer, pp. 125–26.

1. On Dec. 8, 1875, USG nominated Winfield S. Holden as collector of Internal Revenue, 6th District, Ky. He remained in office.

To Adam Badeau

————

Nov. 15th /76

DEAR BADEAU:

I received from Chicago on last Sunday[1] your sixth chapter of "Grant & his Campaigns" and read ~~them~~ it over hastily at once, intending to give a more careful perusal. I have not had time however since to do so; but as I gave it to Sherman to read, the same evening and as he read the most of it aloud, it is not necessary for me to retain it any longer. I send you Porter's letter. It indicates that he had some criticisms to make! I certainly have none to make myself, nor had Sherman further than to make two or three small correction of distances in the field of his campaigns.[2]

I hope you will be able to get out the second volume by May or June. I expect to be in England early in July where I shall hope to see you if my successor has not decapitated you before that. The question of successor is not yet fully determined nor can it be until we get the official canvass of the states of La. S. C. & Fla.

With best wishes for your wellfare,

Yours Truly

U. S. Grant

ALS, Munson-Williams-Proctor Institute, Utica, N. Y. See letter to Adam Badeau, Nov. 2, 1876.

On Dec. 4, 1876, Adam Badeau, consul gen., London, wrote to USG. "Will you please have a list of the corps, division, and brigade commanders, Army of the Potomac May 1, 1864, made out for me, with the changes up to April 9th 1865,—in fact an 'organization' of the Army, including the cavalry. Also I beg you to have copies sent me of two despatches from Gen Forrest, about Fort Pillow, dated April 15th and 19th 1864. I think they are in the form of *Reports* of the capture of Fort Pillow; but I cannot say who was Forrest's immediate superior officer, to whom they were addressed. I had copies of them once, so I know they are in the Rebel Archive office. I shall be greatly obliged if these papers can be sent me *immediately.*" ALS, USG 3. On Feb. 3, 1877, Secretary of War James D. Cameron wrote to USG. "In reply to your verbal request of the 2d instant, to push the preparation of information for General Badeau's history, I beg leave to inform you that on the 8th ultimo, I forwarded to you two reports of Major General Forrest, dated April 15th 1864. and stated that no dispatch of April 19th 1864 was found on file; and on the 26th ultimo, I forwarded to General Badeau a list prepared in the Adjutant Generals office, of Corps, Division and Brigade Commanders in the Army of the Potomac, from May 1st 1864 to April 9th 1865. The only remaining paper asked for by General Badeau viz: the organization of the Army of the Potomac by Corps and Divisions of date May 1, 1864, and the organization of the 9th Corps, is being prepared, as rapidly as possible and will be ready in a few days." Copy, DNA, RG 107, Letters Sent, Military Affairs. On Feb. 10, Cameron wrote to Badeau. "I have the honor to transmit a statement of the Adjutant General, showing the organization of the Army of the Potomac May 1st 1864, and giving the number present for duty, and present equipped for duty" Copy, *ibid.*

1. Nov. 12, 1876.
2. On Feb. 28, 1877, Badeau wrote to Gen. William T. Sherman. "[Co]*nfidential* . . . I have recently opened a letter from you to Gen Grant of May [*March*] 10th 1864, which, by his direction, I sealed up immediately after it was received; and which I do not think has

ever been seen by any one besides himself, Gen Horace Porter, and me. I do not know whether you kept a copy, and therefore send you one. I should like your permission to use, if I find it desirable, some of the passages *marked*. I think they will add to the interest and fidelity of the picture I am striving to make, of your and Gen Grants relations—which seem to me among the most beautiful and remarkable in history. Your own Memoirs show very plainly your feeling about Mr Stanton's Memorandum, so that the *marked* passages will betray nothing hitherto unknown. I was with Grant, when he first saw the memorandum; indeed I took him the copy; and I well remember his excitement and indignation. He was absolutely enraged, and you know how rare that is with him. He said it was 'infamous' that four years of such services as yours should be so rewarded. All this I mean to tell, and to show that the confidence your letter shows in him—was not without foundation. . . . I noted the corrections you were good enough to make on some proofs which I sent to Gen Grant and made my text conform to them . . ." ALS, DLC-William T. Sherman. See *PUSG*, 10, 187–88; *ibid.*, 15, 12–15.

To Hamilton Fish

Nov. 18th /76

Hon. Hamilton Fish;
Sec. of State;
Dear Sir;

If it is not to late to do so I suggest that the record in the case of R. M. Johnson,[1] late Consul to Hankow, China, be changed from suspension to resignation. I understand that his report in response to certain charges that had been preferred against him was received within a few days after action had been taken upon them, and that the report shows the matter in a more favorable light.

Respectfully &c.
U. S. Grant

ALS, DLC-Hamilton Fish. On Nov. 18, 1876, Secretary of State Hamilton Fish wrote to USG. "The Commission to Mr Shepard as Consul at Hankow in place of Mr Johnson 'suspended' was signed on the 3d inst. and has passed the Great Seal, & been recorded, & notice thereof forwarded to China—No resignation has been received from Mr Johnson—He sent a communication to the Department, received four days after his suspension had been signed, in relation to the charges against him—I do not think his reply satisfactory, though, to some extent it may relieve him—I told him this morn'g that I would endeavour in acknowledging the receipt of his explanation, to make it as favourable to him, as the circumstances will justify. I do not think however that the actual record can be altered—" ALS (press), *ibid.* On Oct. 20, John L. Cadwalader, asst. secretary of state, had attended a cabinet meeting. "While there telegram came from Shepard, Consul at Swatow, asking to be appointed at Hankow.—President said he had no objection if a vacancy. I said there was no vacancy but there were serious charges of certain money affairs agst Johnson, who was here, which he had evaded replying to, for months, and that he had been written to, that he *must* reply and at once.—He said, Johnson came to see him when in town, and said he must not believe the charges, and that he meant to resign." Fish diary, *ibid.* See *ibid.*, Nov. 1, 1876. Also on Oct. 20, Isaac F. Shepard telegraphed to USG. "Will you appoint me to Hankow Please answer at my cost" Telegram received, DNA, RG 59, Letters of Application and Recommendation. On Dec. 7, USG nominated Shepard.

On April 11, John C. S. Colby, consul, Chin Kiang, had written to Orville E. Babcock. "... if I am legislated out, which you will know much sooner than I, do all you consistently can to induce the President to give me some other place either in China or Japan, or else where for the matter of that. It is rumored that Mr Johnson at Hankow is going home, and that he will not return, that he will either resign or be removed, as he is supposed to be in some trouble at the Dept. If that place should become vacant, I would like it very much, ..." ALS, ICN. On Sept. 12, 1874, U.S. Representative Isaac C. Parker of Mo., St. Joseph, had written to USG recommending Colby in place of Weston Flint. ALS, DNA, RG 59, Letters of Application and Recommendation. On Sept. 17, USG endorsed this letter. "Respectfully referred to the Secretary of State. Mr Colby [is recommended] by the republican delegation from Missouri. More than sufficient time has been given Mr Flint to report. Mr Colby's appointment may now be made." ES, *ibid.* Related papers are *ibid.* See *PUSG*, 20, 284–85. On Dec. 8, USG nominated Colby. On Jan. 5, 1875, USG wrote to the Senate. "In answer to the resolution of the Senate of the 21st of December last requesting the return of its resolution of the 17th of the same month, advising and consenting to the appointment of J. C. S. Colby to be Consul of the United States at Chin Kiang; I have the honor to state that Mr Colby's commission was signed on the 17th of December and upon inquiry at the Department of State it was found that it had been forwarded to him by mail before the receipt of the resolution of recall." Copy, DNA, RG 130, Messages to Congress.

On Sept. 30, 1874, Babcock had written to Cadwalader. "The President directs me to ask you if there is not a vacant consulship in China—with compensation of $4000. per year? If so he desires you to make out an appointment of Isaac F. Shepard of St. Louis, Mo. for the place." LS, *ibid.*, RG 59, Letters of Application and Recommendation. On the same day, Cadwalader telegraphed to Babcock. "There is no vacant consulship in China, with a salary of four thousand dollars per year. The President within a few days past forwarded to the Dep't a direction for the appointment of J C S Colby of St Louis Mo. place of Western Flint of Mo. as Consul at Chin Kang. this was forwarded to secretary of State" Telegram received, *ibid.*, RG 107, Telegrams Collected (Bound). On Dec. 8, USG nominated Shepard as consul, Swatow.

1. On Feb. 23, 1869, McKee, Fishback & Co., St. Louis, had written to USG. "The bearer, Richard Johnson Esq, informs us that he is an applicant for office under your administration. He has been known to us from boyhood, as a most capable, energetic & deserving person—His application is accompanied by the best testimonials. You are personally familiar with many of his friends & relatives—. . ." L, *ibid.*, RG 59, Letters of Application and Recommendation. Related papers are *ibid.* On April 12, USG nominated Richard M. Johnson, former q. m. clerk in USG's hd. qrs., as consul, Hankow.

To William E. Chandler

WASHINGTON, *November* 20. [*1876*]

WM. E. CHANDLER, *Tallahassee, Florida:*

I hope you will remain in Florida until the count of the vote of the State is decided.

U. S. GRANT.

HMD, 45-3-31, I, 528. William E. Chandler graduated from Harvard Law School (1854), was N. H. speaker of the house (1863–64), and served as 1st asst. secretary, Treasury Dept. (1865–67). As secretary, Republican National Committee, he played significant roles in the 1868 and 1872 presidential campaigns. On Nov. 21, 1876, Chandler, Tallahassee, telegraphed to Edward H. Rollins, Boston. "Baker understands condition of proofs and McCammon what we want, President and Attorney General have just stopped me from giving North and will facilitate the matter." Copy, New Hampshire Historical Society, Concord, N. H.

On Nov. 13, Governor Marcellus L. Stearns of Fla. had telegraphed to USG. "Eminent democratic politicians are gathering rapidly here from adjoining States, and are expected from the North. I feel that I should have the counsel of men eminent in our own party." *HMD*, 44-2-42, 438. On the same day, U.S. Representative Jacob M. Thornburgh of Tenn., Knoxville, telegraphed to USG. "In response to your telegram I will start to Tallahassee tonight" Telegram received (at 9:00 P.M.), DLC-USG, IB. Also on Nov. 13, Jonas M. Bundy, New York City, telegraphed to USG. "OUR FRIENDS HERE THINK IT WOULD BE WELL TO SEND DAVENPORT AND SAMUEL BARLOW TO LOUISIANA." Telegram received, *ibid.* On Nov. 14, Tuesday, Francis C. Barlow, New York City, wrote to Thomas L. James, postmaster, New York City. "I go to Tallahassee, Fla—tonight with D. G. Rollins & shall reach there on Friday A. M. It may be that before, (or after) that things may so turn that we shan't be needed in Florida & may be in South Carolina. If it shld. turn out so, will you have me telegraphed to (by the Prest.) to go to South Car—as it is right on my way & I am ready for any service—" ALS, USG 3. Barlow provoked controversy when he questioned the final determination of a Republican majority in Fla. See Barlow to USG (docketed Dec. 19, 1876), DNA, RG 60, Letters from the President; *HMD*, 45-3-31, I, 1361–79, 1382–410.

On Nov. 13, Williams C. Wickham, Richmond, had telegraphed to USG. "Impossible for me to go as you request" Telegram received (at 4:37 P.M.), DLC-USG, IB. On the same day, U.S. Senator Frederick T. Frelinghuysen of N. J., Newark, telegraphed to USG. "I am sorry not to comply with your request but I am not well enough to go" Telegram received, *ibid.* On Nov. 14, John A. J. Creswell, Elkton, Md., telegraphed to USG. "Your telegram just recd Will go to Washn by next train & will see you immediately on my arrival Cannot go to Florida Send members of the Senate & House from the North" Telegram received (at 9:58 A.M.), *ibid.* On the same day, Governor John F. Hartranft of Pa. telegraphed to USG. "Despatch recd. Regret that I could not personally comply with your request. My attorney General started for Wash'n last night & will comply with your wishes" Telegram received (at 10:00 A.M.), *ibid.*

On Nov. 15, John Tyler, Jr., Raleigh, wrote to USG. "With the 'Solid South', fifteen States in number, backed up in the North by a 'Solid' Catholic support, constituting not less than three fifths of the entire Democratic vote cast there in the recent election, thus assuring an *united South* and a *divided North*, the National Situation will be precisely reversed with Tilden as President, from that it occupied with Buchanan as President, and the results of the Civil War that *must* inevitably follow will be, most likely, the reverse also of that which has afflicted the Country. The Politico-Philosophical analysis of the election makes plain the fact that the recent Democratic movement originated in and was conducted by and through a Roman Catholic policy, in view of the situation of the Church throughout the world. Taking advantage of the passions and prejudices of the South, and the general tendency to a political reaction, they at once conceived the policy of a Solid and reunited South together with their force in the North, to grasp the Government of the United States out of the hands of the Republican Party and the Evangelical Protestant Societies sustaining that Party, thus strengthening their position in the world as against Bismarck and Germany in the lead of Protestantism and in alliance with Russia upon the Eastern question. In view of the whole I need not say that the National necessity is either Governor Hayes as President, or yourself as Dictator which I would prefer. Believe me in all sincerity . . ." ALS, USG 3. Filed with this letter is an undated note from Tyler, Jr., written on White House stationery. "A perfectly reliable Republican, just from Tallahassee, now at the Ebbitt House, says that the Republican Majority in Florida, rightfully 3500, was neutralized by the defection of the Cuban Catholic vote from the Republican Party to the Democracy, and that the appointment of Mr Goven as Postmaster at Jacksonville, at the instance & through the treachery of Senator Conover, only supplied them 'with powder & ball' to fire upon the Republican ranks. This I was satisfied of at the time, but no one would listen to me in the business. I believe, however, that Govr Stearns will secure the Electoral vote to Hayes—" ANS, *ibid.* On Nov. 19, Tyler, Jr., Washington, D. C., wrote to USG. "I have just arrived from North-Carolina. The conclusions forced upon my mind may be briefly expressed as follows—The recent so-called Democratic movement was the result of an understanding between the Catholic Hierarchy and Samuel J Tilden, in concert with the Democratic Leaders of the South, to secure the possession of the Government in their mutual interest. In other words it was a Concerted combination between the Catholics and the Democrats—*the Jesuits and the Ku-Klux*—Jesuitically planned with all the subtle deviltry of the Serpent, and attempted to be executed through the instrumentality of an all-pervading secret political organization, alike remorseless and inexorable, in view of the object. How near to success they have come you are fully aware. A more damnable Conspiracy in my Judgement never was Concocted, nor one more hellishly executed in the attempt to achieve success. I have no doubt whatever of that which I assert, and it does seem to me that steps should be taken and agencies employed, to ferret out and expose to the country the whole infernal plot. It may be safely said that from one end of the Country to the other the Catholic Priests were in the movement heart and soul with all their influences; and I have no doubt that from that source money was poured into the coffers of Mr Tilden like Water. I wrote you from Raleigh something as to this, and please revert to what I then said in connection with what I now say; . . ." Copy, OFH. Other Nov. letters from Tyler, Jr., to USG, Attorney Gen. Alphonso Taft, or Governor Rutherford B. Hayes of Ohio on the disputed election are *ibid.*; Tyler Papers, College of William and Mary, Williamsburg, Va.; DLC-Rutherford B. Hayes; DNA, RG 60, Letters Received, D. C. On Dec. 5, Tyler wrote a "*Memorandum for the President.*" "While Senator Jones of Florida, An Irish Roman Catholic, during the late Presidential and state election in Florida, devoted himself *in person* to securing for the Democracy and Mr Tilden the Roman Catholics of Key-West among the Cubans and others there, Senator Conover made it quite convenient for himself *in person* to be away at the North, leaving the field entirely to Senator Jones, never visiting Key-West atall, notwithstanding all of his assertions that this vote at Key-West held the balance-of-power in the popular vote of the State between the two Parties, and notwithstanding the further fact that the appointment of the Non-American Citizen, Goven, had been yielded to him as Postmaster at Jacksonville to the end of Securing that vote for Mr Hayes and the Republican Party. It were well for Mr Hanibal Hamlin to know this fact, . . . And furthermore, Mr President, let it be remembered that the Man of you choice as Postmaster at Jacksonville whose confirmation by the Senate was reconsidered at the instance of Senator Conover in favour of the Cuban Traitor to his own Government, and whose only Status in the United-States was that of a Refugee from Justice, to escape being shot, or hung, was a man who stood in this Centennial year the Representative of an unbroken line of the most distinguished services to the Country covering the whole Century from the year 1776 to the year 1876, with one hundred and fifty years of distinguished services added to that century, and who in his own person had braved much for the Republican Party and for the Union *as a Nation supreme in sovereignty*—And let Mr Hannibal Hamlin furthermore consider this fact in reviewing his own part in the business." ADS, Tyler Papers, College of William and Mary, Williamsburg, Va. On Dec. 7, Ezra N. Hill, Washington, D. C., wrote to USG. "As President of the Southern Republican Association, I am directed by it to present to you the accompanying Resolution, a duty which I take great pleasure in discharging, as I conceive that the Hon: John Tyler Jr is one of the best and ablest Representatives of that class of Southern Republicans who will, in the near future, draw to the Republican Party in the Southern States an element that will make the Party Self-protecting in those states,—and in most of them put it in the majority—" Copy, *ibid.* The enclosure is a resolution adopted on Dec. 5. ". . . That it is the Sentiment of the Southern Republican Association, that, as a graceful acknowledgement of the Success of the Republicans of Florida in polling its Electoral vote for Hayes and Wheeler, and in preventing that State from being Captured by Democratic Banditti, And as a fitting recognition, not only of his Stirling ability and historic name, but also of his distinguished services during the late Campaign, the President of the United States is respectfully requested to confer on the Honourable John Tyler Jr the office of United-States District Judge for the District of Florida made vacant by the death of the late Judge Frazer. . . ." Copy, *ibid.* On Jan. 3, 1877, Taft wrote to USG. "I have the honor to transmit herewith a communication received by me on the 22nd ult. from Hon. John Tyler, Jr., in the perusal of which I think you may be interested." Copy, DNA, RG 60, Letters Sent to Executive Officers. See *PUSG*, 26, 452–54.

On Nov. 20, 1876, Edmund C. Weeks, Tallahassee, had written to USG. "Permit an old soldier to thank you for your prompt and proper action in Florida. I but express the sentiments of all the Loyal men in this state   Should circumstances arise requiring you to retain the reins of Government you may rely on our earnest support and cooperation" ALS, USG 3.

On Nov. 24, Myron L. Mickles, Washington, D. C., wrote to USG. "Permit me, a private citizen, without unnecessary preface to offer you a few suggestions on the state of political affairs in the state of Florida. That we, the Union Party, have nearly met with a total defeat in my state and the nation I need not repeat to you. Perhaps a word as to the causes in my own state may save us something in the future. Our enemies are cunning and unscrupulous. The same spirit animates them as before and during the war. It is well dissembled and many strong Union men from the north have been led to look upon them as martyrs. It is not to be denied that this impression has been created in part by corruption in the Republican party. We have bad men in the party holding positions of influence. They are a load which it is impossible for us to carry. There are not a few northern Union men in the state of Florida who voted the Democratic ticket at the last election, whom a reasonably fair administration would lead back into the Republican fold: and in this we should be aided very materially by the spirit of hate which is exhibited by the rebels quite too prominently when they feel that they are again about to resume the control of affairs. A fruitful source of trouble among us has been the inexorable rule of the U. S. Senate that they will not confirm the nominations of the Executive unless supported by at least one Senator—if republican—from the state in which the appointments are to be made. And in defence of that rule they say they can know the state only through its representatives. If they are not good ones we must send better. The gentlemen are not ignorant of the fact that by this course they enable these corrupt men to control our republican nominations and thus compel us to choose between them and Bourbons. I have taken the liberty of addressing a line to the Hon. Chairman of the National Ex. Committe on the same subject in the hope that the Senate may be able to see that that the interests of the country demand that their power in this particular should be used with discretion. Another serious mistake in our general policy has been that of 'concilliating' by appointments that class of southern rebels who will never under any circumstances become Union men. To admit such men into the Republican fold 'through bye' and forbiden paths' as has been repeatedly done in consequence of the rule of the Senate before refered to, instead of ~~first~~ demanding that they shall first take public position in support of the Republican party and National Administration is like supplying the enemy with bread and amunition. If the balls we give them return hurtling amongst us we may thank our own stupidity. I do not wish to be understood by this as saying that there are not in our ranks good and true southern men who may have participated in the rebellion, because there are some such who are reliable but all these have had the courage to assume before the world Republican position and stand firmly arrayed with us in support of the National authority. Again—Republicans should not find it necessary to go to Florida to learn that Cubans are subjects of the Pope. True, the Cubans get their orders from the 'Junta,' but the 'Junta' receive their instructions from ~~the~~ Rome. We may fight, the Romish Church; but if we attempt to trade with her we shall be pretty sure to be overreached. It seems to me that our true policy is a very plain one. Put on guard those who harmonize with the policy of the Administration: not those whom we hope to convert by purchase. To borrow a little wisdom from our enemies let us give evil disposed men purgatory until they are purified. If we admit them to Heaven with all their iniquity our garments become soiled and theirs not improved. One word more. The 'Old line Whigs' are still 'Old line Whigs.' They are in the camp of the enemy, but are not of them, and if properly encouraged would harmonize with Republicans. Florida is at heart Republican, and there never need be the necessity for a suspicion of false counting to 'save the state.' The fact is she has been 'saved' too much. I feel that I have a right, which few men of my state have, to be heard upon this subject. Many of the best of our northern citizens have settled in Florida through my influence. They have taken their money and goods and I am in a measure responsible for their well being. I ask for no office for myself or my friends, but I do ask that we may be permitted in peace and security to attend to our groves and vineyards, without being compelled periodically to 'save the state' from the Rebel element only to leave it in the hands of questionable Republicans. Hoping that I have not trespassed upon your time to no profit . . ." ALS, *ibid.*

On Dec. 6, [*Secretary of the Interior Zachariah Chandler*] telegraphed to USG. "The following telegram has just been recd 'Tallahassee Fla. Dec. 6th to Hon Z Chandler Washn D. C. Hayes' majority nine hundred & three. Storrs majority three hundred less Both Congressmen Elected W. E Chandler" Telegram received, DLC-USG, IB; DNA, RG 107, Telegrams Collected (Bound). On the same day, U.S. Senator Simon B. Conover of Fla.

telegraphed to USG. "I have just recd the following telegram from the governor of Florida, Tallahassee Fla Dec. 6th Hon S. B. Conover Washn. Official canvass nine hundred thirty majority for Hayes, State ticket five hundred forty—both congressmen elected Board unanimous. M. L. Stearns." Telegram received, *ibid.* Also on Dec. 6, Lewis Wallace, Tallahassee, telegraphed to USG. "Count just finished Hayes majority nine hundred & thirty republicans elect governor Lieut governor & both members of Congress. all quiet" Telegram received (at 10:00 A.M.), DLC-USG, IB. See *SRC*, 44-2-611; *HMD*, 44-2-35, parts 1–3, 44-2-42, 1–39, 70–85, 299–304, 311–15, 438–40, 45-3-31, I, 468–77, 509–16, 525–39; Leon Burr Richardson, *William E. Chandler: Republican* (New York, 1940), pp. 184–200; George T. McJimsey, *Genteel Partisan: Manton Marble, 1834–1917* (Ames, Iowa, 1971), pp. 190–96; Jerrell H. Shofner, *Nor Is It Over Yet: Florida in the Era of Reconstruction 1863–1877* (Gainesville, 1974), pp. 314–27; Robert E. Morsberger and Katharine M. Morsberger, *Lew Wallace: Militant Romantic* (New York, 1980), pp. 247–51.

To Zachariah Chandler

[*Nov. 22, 1876*]

Dear Mr. Secretary;

I am about through with my duties preparitory to receiving Congress. Two members of the Cabinet have been in and said they would be here again about seven p. m. If you will come full one half the Administration will be present, and we will discuss matters until twelve at night, when all "good people" should retire.

Yours

U. S. Grant

Hon. Zacheria Chandler,
Sec. of the Int.

Please send Answer by bearer.

U. S. G.

ALS, DLC-Zachariah Chandler.

To James D. Cameron

November 26.—1876.—

HON: J. D. CAMERON—SECRETARY OF WAR.—

SIR:

D. H. Chamberlain is now Governor of the State of South Carolina beyond any controversy, and remains so until a new Governor shall be duly and legally inaugurated—Under the constitution the Government has been called upon to aid with the Military and Naval forces of the United States to maintain republican government in the State against resistance too formidable to be overcome by the State authorities—You are therefore directed to sustain Governor Chamberlain in his authority against domestic violence until otherwise directed.

U. S. GRANT.—

Copy, DLC-USG, II, 3. On Saturday, Nov. 25, 1876, Governor Daniel H. Chamberlain of S. C. telegraphed in cipher to USG. "The legislature meets on Tuesday next I have satisfactory evidence that armed and violent men will attempt to prevent its assemblage and to interfere with it in the lawful discharge of its duties Will you please have the U. S. military commander here instructed to so place his troops as to give the legislature protection against unlawful force." Telegram received (at 7:47 P.M.) and copy, OFH. On Nov. 26, Secretary of State Hamilton Fish recorded in his diary. ". . . I drove to the White House and found the Secretaries of War, Interior & Treasury & the Attorney General. Information had reached the President that the rifle companies in South Carolina were to be present in force on Tuesday at the seat of government to the number of some 7 or 8,000 armed men with the intent of overawing or taking possession of the legislature and the Governor wishes protection against violence, before I reached there the President had drafted a paper the substance of which was subsequently adopted as an instruction to the Secretary of War some changes were made in the draft and the Secretary of War then submitted the draft of an order which he should issue to the commander of the forces in South Carolina. They will both appear in tomorrows papers." DLC-Hamilton Fish. On Nov. 27, Secretary of War James D. Cameron wrote to USG. "I have just recd the following from Govr Chamberlain—. . . Ruger not here, Expected tonight. Black says he will act with me. signed D. H. CHAMBERLAIN" ALS, OFH. See HED, 44-2-30, 31–32; Alphonso Taft to Fish, Nov. 26, 1876, DLC-Hamilton Fish.

Also on Nov. 27, U.S. Senator John B. Gordon of Ga., Va. Senator Bradley T. Johnson, Wade Hampton, and many others, Columbia, S. C., telegraphed to USG. "We the undersigned visitors from a distance, committee of the Democratic Members elect of the South Carolina legislature, The democratic Executive committee and citizens having just seen by Associated press despatch that Gov Chamberlain has applied for U. S troops to be placed under his orders at the assembling of the the legislature tomorrow, send this our solemn protest against the troops being placed under Command of gov Chamberlain. We have no objection to the presence of troops, and will cooperate with them in preserving the peace, but we protest against the use of U. S. Army in Controlling org organization of legislature and enforcing the inauguration of Gov Chamberlain who has been defeated by the white and colored voters at the ballot box. There is not the remotest danger of disturbance of the peace by democrats. If it occurs it will be at the instigation of Gov Chamberlain, whose partizans have taken the only lives lost in the late exciting canvass in this state, not one drop of blood has been shed in any political disturbance except by republicans. It is literally true that the democrats received their greatest majorities in the counties where the U. S. Soldiers were stationed. What pretence, therefore, is there for Gov Chamberlains demand for troops to keep the peace? We refer for confirmation of these statements to the Commander of U. S. forces at this place and elsewhere in the state" Telegram received (at 7:00 P.M.), OFH. On the same day, Fish recorded in his diary. "At a little after eight oclock Mr Sartoris the Presidents son in law called at my house saying the President wished the Members of the Cabinet to meet him immediatly. I attended as did all except the Secretary of the Treasury & Navy, the the President read a very long telegraph despatch from John B. Gordon, Bradley Johnson and others from Columbia referring to the orders supposed to be given by the Military and protesting against the troops being under the protection of Gov Chamberlain when I entered the room the President was preparing an answer, but handing me the telegram said he thought it was a question whether any answer should or should not be sent. Chandler Cameron & Tyner thought none should be sent. I differed and thought a reply should be sent denouncing the correctness of the statements which were evidently as I contended calculated for popular effect and the letter would be published putting its misrepresentations before the public, which should not be allowed to go uncontradicted. Taft expressed no decided opinion either way and after an hour and a half's discussion it was concluded not to make any reply, at least none tonight." DLC-Hamilton Fish. See *HMD*, 44-2-31, part 1, pp. 305–37; *SMD*, 44-2-48, I, 984–92; Ralph Lowell Eckert, *John Brown Gordon: Soldier, Southerner, American* (Baton Rouge, 1989), pp. 175–82.

On Nov. 13, Cameron had written to Lt. Col. Henry M. Black. "Fearing that the order of Gen. Sherman of this date (a copy of which is enclosed) might not reach you by the regular channel I send this by special messenger. It is the desire of the President that the Board of Canvassers in South Carolina have complete and absolute protection in the discharge of their legal duties; and that all interference with them be prevented. With this end in view you will consult fully with the Board and so dispose your forces as to preclude the possibility of their being in any way interfered with or disturbed." Copy, DNA, RG 107, Letters Sent, Military Affairs. *HED*, 44-2-30, 30–31. Troop movements in S. C. raised concerns that insufficient force remained at Aiken and Edgefield Court House to ensure prosecution of those on trial for the Hamburg massacre. See David T. Corbin and Chamberlain to Taft, Nov. 12, 1876, Gen. William T. Sherman to Maj. Gen. Winfield S. Hancock, Nov. 13, 1876, AG Edward D. Townsend to Black, Nov. 13, 1876, Chamberlain to John J. Patterson, Nov. 15, 1876, Sherman to Black, Nov. 16, 1876, DNA, RG 94, Letters Received, 4788 1876. On Jan. 18, 1877, Attorney General Alphonso Taft wrote to USG. "I have the honor to transmit herewith for your information a copy of a letter of the 13th instant, addressed to me by the United States Attorney for the District of South Carolina, in which statements are made relative to the witnesses for the government in the case of the Hamburg and Ellenton murders; and desire to call your attention specially to the suggestion of Mr. Corbin as to the furnishing of rations by the War Department to the witnesses referred to, who are in a state of great suffering." Copy, *ibid.*, RG 60, Letters Sent to Executive Officers.

On Nov. 13, 1876, U.S. Representative John B. Packer of Pa., Sunbury, had telegraphed to USG. "I will go down by first through train today" Telegram received (at 2:38 P.M.), DLC-USG, IB. On the same day, USG requested Judge David K. Cartter, D. C. Supreme Court, "to be present at the canvass of the votes in South Carolina," and he departed that evening. *Washington Evening Star*, Nov. 14, 1876. On Nov. 14, William H. Armstrong, Pittsburgh, telegraphed to USG. "your telegram forwarded & received here am engaged in U. s. court regret I cannot go" Telegram received (at 12.52 P.M.), DLC-USG, IB. On Nov. 15, Armstrong wrote to USG. "Permit me to thank you for the honor of being named by you as one of the persons selected to be present at the counting of the vote in S. C. Nothing but the impossibility of leaving here at this time prevented my going— I am in the midst of a law suit in the U. S. Circuit Court—for clients in Boston involving nearly $80.000—They were entirely unwilling I should go—and ~~thought~~ I did not feel at liberty to leave the case—Your whole course in this matter is very much talked of and cordially approved by the better class of men of both parties—The rigorous defence of the rights of suffrage, and your determination to enforce a fair count of a fair vote—and that no fraud shall triumph in the defeat of the peoples will, which fair means can prevent, will fittingly crown your long & successful administration—You have done the right thing at the right time & I beg leave to commend your action & to congratulate you with warmest satisfaction—With kindest personal regard and pride in your administration as it approaches its conclusion . . ." ALS, USG 3.

On Nov. 17, John C. Winsmith, Spartanburg, S. C., wrote to USG. "I take the liberty of again addressing your Excellency upon the condition of affairs in South Carolina. At the outset I would freely say that you deserve the thanks of every good citizen of the Nation for your prompt and decisive action in securing a fair return of the votes cast in S. C., La., and Fla. As far as S. C. is concerned, I am sure the Republican Electors are legally elected. My Father—Hon. John Winsmith—is one of the Electors, and having been actively engaged in the canvass, he declares unequivocally that that the spirit of rebellion among the Ku Klux Democracy is far greater than it was prior to secession, particularly in the upper portion of the State. The truth is, Hampton, Butler and Gary inaugurated their military and rebellious campaign with the massare at 'Hamburg.' I think Gov. Chamberlain erred in not declaring martial law over the entire State. He will be declared elected Gov. and must be inaugurated. The same condition of things which existed in upper La. and in the upper counties of S. C. will again exist. Even now the Ku Klux Democracy are preparing for the murder of Republicans in the upper counties. Hence I implore you to send a military force along the line of the Air Line R. R. in S. C. Let the force consist of Artillery, Infantry and Cavalry, and let it come *before* the Inauguration of Gov. Chamberlain. Let the officers be *stern*, of unswerving *fidelity* to the Nation, and elevated above the blandishments of the Ku Klux Democracy." ALS, DNA, RG 60, Letters from the President. *HED*, 44-2-30, 111. See *SMD*, 44-2-48, I, 718–19. On the same day, Anonymous, Aiken, wrote to USG. ". . . at this moment the investigation that is going on in Columbia demands from Truth and justice the *facts* of '*frauds in votes*' To be brief my dear Sir, what do you call it but *Robbery* for car Loads of *Giorgians to come over to Aiken from Augusta city and* the sorrounding country *and vote* and then disperce & hire houses—*and go to any & all the Polls far* & near in *Aiken County &* VOTE *over* & *over again with thier own names* & with *fictitious names.* out in some of the country *cracker White* towns where Federal Soldiers were in Nos to protect the Polls, they voted the entire day over & over & it is a pure fraud without one atom of justice to allow such a majority in Aiken Co *especially* and all over the State of South Carolina it is a cheat! a contrived & concocted trick to make the one party of Politics entirely *a crash Democratic!* by allowing Boys 12 & 14 years of age to vote, & by intim-

idating & promising to pay the ignorant Negro to vote and by killing the Negroes . . . For
the Sake of Peace 'Let us have Peace' & get justice in the Votes cast for Gov Chamberlain
in South Carolina & for Hayes *for President*" L, DNA, RG 60, Letters from the President.

On Nov. 18, Cartter and Packer, Columbia, telegraphed to USG. "In accordance
with your request we have attended and witnessed the Canvass of the Electoral vote of
South Carolina by the State board of Canvassers who report the following as the Official
Count upon the returns of the County Commissioners of Elections. Republican Bowen
91786 Winsmith 91870—Johnston 91852 Harley 91136 Nashn 91804. Cook 91432—
Myers 91830. Democratic Barker 90896. McGowan 90737. Harrington 90895. Ingraham
90798 Wallace 90905 Irwin 90906 Aldrich 90860. The Canvass has been Conducted
peacefably and fairly in the presence of Representatives of both parties—" Telegram received (at 1:50 P.M.), DLC-USG, IB. On the same day, Secretary of the Interior Zachariah
Chandler telegraphed to USG. "The dispatch from Columbia S C announcing the vote of
that State was signed B S L Hoge who is a member of Congress from S. C." Telegram received, OFH.

On Nov. 23, L. Cass Carpenter, collector of Internal Revenue, Columbia, wrote to
USG. "If there is any reliance at all to be placed upon appearances, the republicans of this
state stand upon the very brink of a precipice. The action of the Board of State Canvassers
of this state, which adjourned yesterday *sine die*, has exasperated the democrats so much,
that they openly threaten to exterminate the leading republicans unless Wade Hampton is
permitted to take his seat quietly. It is in evidence, that the most glaring and outrageous
frauds were perpetrated by the democrats on the 7th inst., frauds upon which the returns
of the County Canvassers were based, and upon which the followers of Hampton base their
claim to the governor's chair. The Board of State Canvassers threw out only two counties,
Edgefield & Laurens, two counties in which intimidation and repeating were the rule and
not the exception. In Edgefield county 2000 more votes were polled than there are votes
in the county, as shown by the census of 1870, and the state census of 1875; and yet at least
1200 republicans did not vote at all. The rifle clubs surrounded the polls at many places
and would allow only democrats to approach them. In Laurens county the republicans
were driven away openly by armed men, and where the republicans should have had a majority of 1000, the democrats have, or rather claim, a majority of 1200. The Supreme Court
of the state is believed to be under pay from the democrats, for all its actions thus far point
strongly in that direction. What it will now do in view of the action of the Board of Canvassers no one can predict. The democrats openly threaten, that if Hampton is not seated
there will be war. The railroad lines leading into Georgia have advertised excursion tickets for less than half fare, and it is openly asserted on the streets here, that at least 20.000
Georgians will be in the city the day of the inauguration. If they come, there *may* be
trouble. Senator J. B. Gordon has been here for several days, apparently deeply interested
in our affairs, and his Georgia friends claim that he represents the fighting element of that
state. At all events he displays more zeal than prudence in meddling with affairs not his
own. We hope for the best, but shall try to be prepared for the worst. Judge Bond was yesterday publicly insulted in front of the Court House where he holds his court. I also received by express, a Coffin, from one of the counties in my Congressional district, one of
the worst places in the state, Newberry. Such mementoes however do not frighten us in
the least." ALS, DNA, RG 60, Letters from the President. *HED*, 44-2-30, 111. See *HMD*,
44-2-31, part 1, pp. 246–59. On the same day, "Detective," Charleston, wrote to USG. "I
write you something in the Cause of Humanity & peace, I am the same as wrote you Concerning the election &c I also wrote the Govr but hereafter will write only to you & beg
you to keep Strictly private, as regards the election if Hampton is elected we must believe
it is by fraud, now it is evident that we are to have trouble here no matter who is elected,

there are those who will resist Chamberlain & also others who will resist Hampton. I have been told they intend to put Hampton in, I have been told there are Men here who will fight U. S. Soldiers, I believe there are Twenty thousand rampant rebels not so many of the old School but many hot headed Young men who know what they are about to engage in, that something is onfoot I believe & I believe something is to be done about the 15th Decr what I do not know yet, now as I engaged in the cause of Humanity I Continue & you as chief magistrate & believer in god & christ should assist me in this, the two parties stand ready at any moment to pitch [i]n to each other, & I believe the colored people are only waiting for sufficient to saddle the blame on the democrats & they will fire the city & commence a general massacre there are many of these we know would not engage in this horrible work but many who would both in the city & surrounding it, now the only thing which can keep the Democrats down are Soldiers so let us have them, . . ." L, DNA, RG 60, Letters from the President.

On Nov. 29, Anonymous, Charleston, wrote to USG. "this Letter Is from a Poor freedman I write to Let you no about times down this way the rebels are outragous In our City they Have about fifteen Haundred Riffles Scartered about In difrent Houses & they Sit up evry night to watch them they Sey the first chance they get they are going to kill the dam Leaders of the republican party & all the dam yankeis & niggers & that Is Just what they are doing they tried to kill mr mackey the day after the election & they are Shooting the negroes evry night from Secred places In the city & most evry night Some poor Collord man Is Shoot by Some unkown Person we Collord citziens are Suffering dreadfull from the democrats my god President Stand by us & protect us . . . Look out for the rebles they after rising on another War a Ship came In this port a few days ago with twenty Boxess of rifles the Boxs marked oil Cloth they were So Hevy that I were compeled to Se them And there were rifles marked oil cloth Please give us Strong Protection And we Will Stand By the republican party untill Gudgment day" L, *ibid. SMD,* 44-2-48, III, 99. See *HMD,* 44-2-31, part 1, pp. 294–305, 369–78; *SMD,* 44-2-48, I, 837–43, II, 232–36.

To Alphonso Taft

———

Nov. 30th 1876.

HON. A. TAFT, ATTY. GN.

DEAR SIR:

The enclosed dispatch from Gov. Chamberlain is just received. I am somewhat at a loss as to the instruction that should be given. If the members claiming seats from Edgefield, and counties to whom the returning board refused to give certificates, were excluded until the legislature is organized and passes upon their claims, it seems to me about all we can do. The democrats who hold certificates have the same rights in the state building that the republicans have, and right to a voice in the organization of the legislature if they choose to use

it. Any order therefore for the exclusion of any member pretending
to be a part of the legislature of the state should apply only to those
who do not hold certificates. of the kind named.

No action should be positively taken until after consideration by
the full Cabinet to-morrow. Would it not be well to request of Gn.
Ruger a full statement of the situation in the mean time? Gn. Sherman could telegraph to-night and his answer could be received before Cabinet meeting to-morrow.

Respectfully Yours

U. S. GRANT

ALS, DNA, RG 60, Letters from the President. On Nov. 28 and 30, 1876, Governor Daniel
H. Chamberlain of S. C. telegraphed to USG. "The House and Senate organized to-day.
Th[e] Democrats, on the refusal to admit the members from Edgefield and Laurens Counties, withdrew, leaving sixty members in the House, a quorum of all the members chosen.
The House then proceeded to business. The Senate organized without delay. Gen. Ruger
has preserved the peace, and acted with perfect impartiality and great goo[d] judgment."
New York Times, Nov. 30, 1876. "The House of representatives presided over by Mr. Mackey in the State house adjourned yesterday to twelve M. today. At half past eleven today
the Democrats who had organized outside went to house of representatives in State house
and forced their way in & their so-called speaker & clerk usurped the speakers chair &
clerks desk and have refused to yield them to the lawful speaker and clerk. Mackey and his
house has been formally recognized by the Senate and both houses have exchanged messages with each other and with me. I have recognized the Mackey house and regard it as
unquestionably the legal house and the only legal house. I have called as Governor upon
General Ruger to enforce the authority of Mackey as speaker and to enforce his orders as
speaker. Gen. Ruger hesitates & doubts the validity of Mackeys election & the organization of the house on the ground that perhaps no quorum was present when he was elected
and under the circumstances my authority as governor to enforce Mr. Mackeys orders.
Both bodies are now occupying the Hall of representatives in the State house—Mr. Wallace is presiding over the Democrats and Mr. Mackey over the regular house. My authority to enforce Mr. Mackeys orders if I had the power could not be questioned   As I have
not the power I respectfully request that orders be given to Gen. Ruger to enforce the
authority of the officers of the house presided over by Mr. Mackey and recognized by
the Senate and by me as Governor. Against domestic violence" Telegram received (at
3:45 P.M.), DNA, RG 60, Letters from the President. On Nov. 30, Chamberlain telegraphed
to Attorney Gen. Alphonso Taft. "I have telegraphed situation here to President & secy
of war Please see their dispatches immediately—we need orders to enforce authority of
speaker of House forthwith . . . I trust orders will be sent tonight to protect our house
against all interference & to enforce its powers & orders in doing its regular business   at
this moment our speaker is excluded by force from his Chair & members from Edgefield
& Laurens who have not been declared elected by Canvassers are on the floor. this is domestic violence & will soon be revolution." Telegram received (at 4:40 P.M.), *ibid.*

On the same day, Wade Hampton, Columbia, S. C., telegraphed to USG. "The democratic members of lower House sixty five in number met quietly in Hall today with their
speaker in Chair republicans fifty nine also assembled there & placed their speaker on
desk Genl Ruger proposes to take out of House eight members duly elected holding cer-

tificates from supreme court, the House is sole Judge of the qualifications of its members we propose to leave question to House these members will remain until expelled by force but we earnestly desire peaceful solution the legislature will not interfere with the presidential electoral vote. we seek only a constitutional legislature peaceably assembled for the good of the state." Telegram received (at 11:00 P.M.), OFH.

Also on Nov. 30, Col. Thomas H. Ruger, Columbia, telegraphed to Gen. William T. Sherman. "a new state of circumstances as to the Legislature has taken place today The governor calls on me to eject certain persons claiming to be entitled to places which persons are those claiming to have been and those who were elected as democrats Both parties are now in the assembly room In the absence of any riot or violence I have not at once acted for reasons stated in a message which will follow this. I request delay of action until my full message & that this be brought to the attention of the Secretary of war and President as soon as possible I will send my full dispatch as soon as possible" Telegram received (at 2:56 P.M.), DNA, RG 94, Letters Received, 4788 1876. HED, 44-2-30, 33–34. On the same Thursday, Ruger again telegraphed to Sherman, "or in absence of Gen Sherman to The Hon Sec'y of War or the President." "On Tuesday last at the meeting of the legislature on refusal of admission to persons who held certificates of election from the clerk of the Supreme Court and who were democrats those democrats who held certificates from the Secretary of State based upon the report of the State board of Canvassers did not enter the hall of the house of representatives The republican members to the number of fifty nine organized as the house. The democrats including those who held certificates from the clerk of the supreme court of the State also organized but at another place. Today at the time of meeting of the assembly both bodies, the democratic body somewhat before the regular hour, entered the hall of representatives and have been going through the forms of preserving order and other business. The Governor of the State on the report of the speaker elected by the body recognized by him as the house of the facts and that he could not enforce his authority as Speaker called upon me to enforce the authority of the speaker. [I did not decline to do this eventually but in the absence of any riot or physical conflict in the house did as I had and have doubts as to the authority of the Governor under the circumstances to act at once act in the premises and the fact that of those present in the democratic body were present those having certificates from the State board of canvassers as to whose right to places. Tthere is no question]—I took time to consider—it is my opinion that the reason why the democratic member elect who held certificates from the State canvassers did not take their places the first day after the refusal to admit those of their party who held the certificates of the clerk of the court was because they could not in that case control the organization of the house. The fifty nine members republicans who did organize as the house did not as I have no doubt constitute a quorum under the constitution of the State and could only adjourn from day to day. The democratic body was also in the same condition without a quorum. I believe that the question is essentially a struggle for the control of the house and that the only way which will be fair to both parties to which no sound legal objection can be taken and which will secure future quiet in the State should be based on the fact of the legality and conclusiveness of the certificates of election issued by the Secretary of State on the report of the State board of canvassers on the sufficiency of which certificates depends action of the presidential electors as well as the right of members to seats in the house of representatives of the State. My present view is that unless otherwise instructed I shall at the next meeting of the house so far comply with the application of the Governor as to require that no person shall be admitted to the floor of the house except those having certificates of the Secretary of State based on the report of the board of State Canvassers—The question of organization if still open can then be determined by those who undoubtedly have a right to Seats and all doubts about the legality the acts of the legislature bee ended and also I believe the Ggenerally unsettled state of things in the State as all will accept the decision as final. As a party question no injustice would be done as the two parties would stand as after action by the State board of canvassers. The question of presidential election I understand not to be involved at all" Telegram received (at 4:40 P.M.; brackets in original), DNA, RG 94, Letters Received, 4788 1876. *HED*, 44-2-30, 34. Another rendering of this telegram received (at 6:00 P.M.), addressed to USG, is in DNA, RG 60, Letters from the President. Also on Nov. 30, 10:30 P.M., Sherman telegraphed to Ruger. "Both of your despatches of today were placed in the hands of the Secretary of War, who has gone to the President with the Attorney General, for consultation. I will give you the Earliest possible answer, tonight if possible." ALS (telegram sent), *ibid.*, RG 94, Letters Received, 4788 1876. *HED*, 44-2-30, 34. On the same day, Ruger telegraphed to Sherman. "Despatch recd the status remains the same. on further reflection I should somewhat modify my former dispatch. I will send a despatch as early as possible in the morning based on the then condition of things & stating exactly what has been heretofore done by the troops relative to the meeting of the legislature" Telegram received, DNA, RG 94, Letters Received, 4788 1876. *HED*, 44-2-30, 33.

Also on Nov. 30, Secretary of State Hamilton Fish recorded in his diary. "While at dinner Secretary Cameron called and wished me to accompany him at dinner. He had a telegram from Gov Chamberlain and Genl Ruger stating that the Democrats had gotten possession of the Assembly Hall in that State and had organized with their Speaker and Clerk and in possession of their respective chairs. Chamberlain wishes instructions to the military to expel them, Ruger has hesitated to comply with such request but wishes orders. Cameron proposes to instruct Ruger to remove the Democratic Speaker and Clerk to put the Republicans in their place and to expel and exclude from the State House the Democrats from Edgefield & Lawrence Counties. I object strenuously to any such orders or to any force being employed by the Military other than in the repression of violence. He urges that unless this be done the republicans in Florida and Louisianna will loose heart and abandon their States. I regret that if such should be the result but earnestly insist that no erring step should be taken on the part of the Federal Government and that the Military shall not be employed to control the organization of a State Legislature. He leaves me promising to send his carriage shortly. Going after dinner to the Presidents I found Cameron & Taft there with him. Cameron repeats the same views he had presented to me and Taft supports him. I remonstrate and protest against improper & unlawful employment of the Military in any interference with the organization or any other purpose and to suppress violence and preserve the peace—The President is of the same opinion . . . In reply to my remark to the precedents cited by Taft during war and Revolution Cameron said this is war and Revolution the President interrupted him by saying decidedly no! no! it is no such thing. Cameron proposed an order to Ruger to support Chamberlain and to exclude the Edgefield & Laurence members who were certified to by the Supreme Court. The President objected saying that the troops were not there to act under the orders of Chamberlain but were there to preserve peace and order and he did not think that he (the President) had any right to say who should or should not be excluded from the Chamber Taft also hesitated to assent to the order proposed by Cameron but said he would be willing to go so far as to telegraph to Ruger and Chamberlain that the government here thought the Republican House presided over by Mackey was duly and regularly elected and organized, to which I objected saying that this was the very question involved, that it was for the house itself to determine who were its members and that the President and Cabinet are not competent to pass on the question and if competent that we have not evidence on which we should be justified in acting The President took the same view and added that the Executive of South Carolina in that State occupies the same position that the Executive of the United States does here, that the question of organization of the Legislature belongs to the State to settle and not to the general government The question of what answer should be sent in reply to the telegram of Ruger & Chamberlain was considered and Cameron prepared telegrams under direction of the President acknowledging their receipt and saying that the subject would be considered by the President & Cabinet tomorrow." DLC-Hamilton Fish. See Nevins, *Fish*, pp. 846–47.

On Dec. 1, Ruger telegraphed to Sherman or Cameron. "The status as to the Legislature remains as at time of my despatch last evening. On further reflection I am of opinion that the wisest course will be to permit the two bodies claiming to be the House to worry the contest out so long as the public peace is preserved or at least for the present. I think the result will be as satisfactory a Conclusion as can be attained by interference. I have carefully abstained from interference with the organization of the House from the first . . ." Telegram received (at 10:40 A.M.), DNA, RG 94, Letters Received, 4788 1876. *HED*, 44-2-30, 35. On the same day, Fish recorded a cabinet discussion in his diary. "The telegram from Ruger was read giving an account of his own proceedings differing materially from the course attributed to him by the Journals and also giving a statement furnished by some person not named but described by him as a disinterested person of the proceedings of the State Court on the application for a mandamus against the board of canvassers. The publication of so much of the telegram as refers to Rugers proceedings was deemed advisable and the Secretary of War was directed to telegraph to him the approval of his course thus far. . . . The President has a telegram from Wade Hampton stating that the returns of the Presidential Electors are not involved in the question. Cameron also had a telegram from Bradley Johnson to the same effect but stated that he would not believe them and that they intended to violate their pledges and that as soon as Hampton should be inaugurated Governor a law would be passed changing the mode of appointment of Electors and giving them to Tilden. I asked how that could be done while there was a Republican Senate—The President remarked 'thats a fact it ca'nt be done' Cameron replied they will do it nevertheless. 'they will buy somebody', the discussion then turned on the organization of the house. Taft repeated what he had said last night, that he would be willing to say to them, that we recognized the organization of a Republican House I replied arguing as I did last night. . . . Robeson counsels great care and moderation in what may be done, Tyner inclines, but without decided expression of opinion, that a majority of the returned members although not a majority of all entitled to be in the House is sufficient. The precedents in the Senate and House of Representatives in 1862 & 3 were referred to by Robeson asking the question whether any precedents can be found when less than a majority of the whole number constituting the body has declared less than that body a quorum—Taft does not know. . . . The President declines to telegraph any opinion in favor of either house but confines it simply to an approval of the course taken by General Ruger. Cameron expressed a wish and Chandler silently nodded assent that the troops be authorized to eject the Edgefield and Laurence members. The President rejected the idea saying that the federal government had no right to interfere in the organization of a State Legislature that the country had been much excited with regard to what occurred in Louisianna and that Republicans and Democrats both condemned such interference. That the authorities of South Carolina must settle the organization of their Legislature—that Chamberlain is the governor of that state and must be so regarded until a successor is duly elected and inaugurated and as the Executive of that state he has the same power there that he (the President) has in the general government that the United States troops can only be used for the suppression of domestic violence. Cameron wishes a telegram to Chamberlain of encouragement and reads a draft to that effect he had prepared, the President objects but states what he would be willing to say which after some modification is put into form to the effect that the President does not think that the exigency of the case is such as to call for any affirmative action on his part at present but wishes to be kept advised of whatever may happen." DLC-Hamilton Fish. See *HED*, 44-2-30, 37–38.

To Col. Thomas H. Ruger

———

Washington, D. C. [Dec. 3, 1876]

GEN. RUGER, COLUMBIA, S. C.

Fearing your instructions may be conflicting and leave you in doubt as to your duties in the present unhappy condition of affairs existing in S. C. I wish to say this.

Governor Chamberlain is the legaly constitutional Governor of the State and remains so until the legislature canvasses the vote and instals his successor, and he is entiled as such to your support and protection. It is a civil duty to organize the legislature devolving on State Authorities. The Military or the general government have nothing to do with it. ~~In purging the legislature — if such a thing is attempted — you can not interfere.~~ [It is not your duty to purge the Legislature] All you can do is to prevent unauthorized persons from interfering with the governor and other authorized state officers in the performance of their duties. The question of recognition of a legislature may become incumbent upon me. I hope it will not, but if it does I shall not shirk the responsibility. ~~As at present advised I do not believe any legal house has been organized, such a house as could decide upon claims of cotestants for seat. I do not believe such a house will exist until at least sixty-three members holding certificates from the returning boad get together and organize. But these are only immature views and are given to guide you in your action until other instructions can be sent you if found advisable.~~

~~The two~~ To be plain I want to avoid any thing like an unlawful use of the Military and I believe it would be regarded with disfavor if they were used in taking men claiming seats out of the legislative hall. [but] It would be entirely right to protect the Governor, or any of his agents, being interfered with by unauthorized persons in the performance of their duties.

ADf (bracketed material not in USG's hand), OFH. *HED*, 44-2-30, 38; *SD*, 57-2-209, 186.

To Col. Thomas H. Ruger

Washington, D. C. Dec 3 1876

GENL RUGER COLUMBIA S. C—

Your despatch of this date is received. I do not think you would be justified in taking U. S. troops into the legislative hall to resist opposition made by persons claiming to have a right to be there either under the certificate of election from the board of canvassers or from the Supreme Court of the State or who have since been admitted by either of the pretended legislatures. Unless further advised you will confine your action to preventing unauthorized outside parties from resisting the action of the legal Governor of the State. Tomorrow on consultation I may be able to further advise you

U. S. GRANT

Copy, OFH. On Dec. 3, 1876, Col. Thomas H. Ruger, Columbia, S. C., twice telegraphed to USG. "your despatch of this date rec'd. the present state of the Case is this. persons claiming to be members of the lower house of the legislature who the Supreme Court of the State had decided were entitled to have the usual Certificate of Election & Consequently authorized to be present at its organization were refused admission to the chamber of at the time of organization they with Enough others as to whom there was no question in all sufficient as to number to form an undoubted qurorum organized if the decision of the Supreme Court of the State was valid or should be regarded then this body is the legal house gov chamberlain recognized the other body. both organizations are now in the hall of rep's in the state house. today gov chamberlain decided to attempt tomorrow by the use of a small force to Eject the persons who claim the right to seats by virtue of the decision of the Supreme Court & Calls on me to aid in case resistance is Made. I have no doubt resistance will be made by those persons & others belonging to the same body in the hall itself & that the only way to avoid bloodshed & possibly a horrible calamity is Either to consider that a slight resistance will justify the bringing of the troops into the room to Eject the persons or that the troops shall go in with the force of the gov & act. the gov will not make the attempt unless supported by the troops. will you please acknowledge this" "I Intended to have closed my dispatch just sent with the words 'Will you please answer.'" Telegrams received (at 11:22 and 11:50 P.M.), *ibid.*

Also on Dec. 3, USG telegraphed to Governor Daniel H. Chamberlain of S. C. "Your despatch received For present answer see despatch just sent to Genl Ruger." Copy, *ibid.*

On Dec. 4, 1:30 A.M., Secretary of State Hamilton Fish wrote to USG. "I have been awakened to receive the accompanying telegrams from Wade Hampton which I bring to you In case you think any immediate action necessary I await your suggestion." ALS (press), DLC-Hamilton Fish. On Dec. 3, Wade Hampton, Columbia, had twice telegraphed to Fish. "Information Just received makes your action necessary before eight o'clock tomorrow morning, has first despatch reached you." "A plot was laid yesterday by state officials which would have resulted in attack on and possible murder of the democrats in the House had it not been discovered. A number of roughs brought from abroad were to be introduced into the hall by the conspirators. The colored members of the Mackey house were to withdraw gradually giving their seats to the roughs. Mackey was then to order arrest of Democratic Speaker and expulsion of Edgefield and Laurence delegations, if they resisted, as was known they would do, they were to be attacked by U. S. troops then called in, the roughs were to be brought in as State Constables by order of Chamberlain. The plot was revealed by a Republican Official and details given in letter which follows also. I have no doubt of its existance I notified General Ruger and gave all plans assured him that under no circumstances would resistance be made to U. S troops but that if Chamberlain persisted in plot bloodshed and murder would follow for which Chamberlain would be responsible. Information tonight leads to fear attempt to carry out plan tomorrow and Gen Ruger has been so informed—we deprecate resort to violence and desire to abide decission of lawful authorities. Chamberlain will precipitate conflict here unlss restrained by orders from Washington In the interest of peace in the name of the Constitution I invoke such orders" Copies (marked 11:52 P.M. and 12:05 A.M.), Fish diary, Dec. 4, 1876, *ibid.* An undated letter from "A Hayes Republican of the Stripe of Evarts & Bryant" to Hampton and two others, outlining the purported plot, is *ibid.* On Dec. 4, Fish recorded in his diary. "I took them at once to the President He had received a telegram shortly before from General Ruger anticipating in some respects an interference in the organization of the House. The President had replied substantially that the Military were not to interfere with either 'pretended house'; he had subsequently received a telegram from Chamberlain to which he rather curtly replied referring him to the telegram he had sent to Gen Ruger. He did not think any notice necessary of Hamptons despatch which I left with him returning home at about three o'clock. On my way to the Department at about 9½ o'clk this morning I stopped at the Executive Mansion to speak to the President about his message and suggested that it be delayed until tomorrow and saying that if he so desired it could be delayed until Wednesday. I found Cameron & Chandler there each had telegrams from South Carolina and each was urgent for authority for the troops to eject the Edgefield & Laurence Members or in some other way to intervene forceably—The President decidedly resisted this suggestion." *Ibid.* At a special cabinet meeting held the same day to discuss the situation in S. C., USG decided "that he will not at present recognize either house." *Ibid.*

Also on Dec. 4, Chamberlain telegraphed to USG. "I am prepared to act in purging legislature but Gen Rugers construction of his orders makes violence and bloodshed probable I cannot think he correctly interprets his orders as telegraphed me by the Attorney Genl all I ask is that his forces be so desposed as to prevent outsiders from joining in the struggle & to instantly aid in case violent resistance to my force this alone will prevent deplorable consequences" Telegram received (at 1:10 A.M.), OFH.

To Col. Thomas H. Ruger

————

Dec 4. 76

To GENL RUGER COLUMBIA S. C.

Are any steps being taken by either branch of the legislature of South Carolina to canvass the vote for Governor? What is the condition of the vote for the presidential electors? Is an effort being made to deprive the electors holding certificates of election from casting their votes?

U. S. GRANT.

Copy (marked "sent 2 P. M."), OFH. On Dec. 4, 1876, Col. Thomas H. Ruger, Columbia, S. C., twice telegraphed to USG. "I did not state in former despatch that troops still occupy lower part of State house. Such is the fact & has I think prevented in Some degree an agreement of the two bodies—The republican members expecting that the troops would sooner or later expel from the hall certain of the other body & the democratic members waiting with intent TO ALL REMAIN unless expelled by the troops" "Action to Canvass the returns for Governor will I am informed be had tomorrow by the Senate & house Recognized by Governor Chamberlain provided there shall be a quorum of the house. A mandamus against the speaker of that house to turn over the returns to the Speaker of the other body was argued today before the supreme Court & a decision will probably be had tomorrow   as to presidential Electors there is a mandamus to correct Elector returns begun some time since & a few days ago a quo warranto be fore the Supreme Court   these may come up for argument tomorrow but it is not probable a decision could be reached, as to Electors by the sixth,   no other efforts so far as I know is being made as to Electors   I will telegraph further tomorrow" Telegrams received (at 11:00 A.M. and 11:06 P.M.), *ibid.*

Also on Dec. 4, Monday, Governor Daniel H. Chamberlain of S. C. twice telegraphed to USG. "Dispatch received—the Situation is this—Gen Ruger has one company on duty at State house—both the mackey & Wallace house have been in session night & day since thursday   the edgefield & Laurens men with no credentials persist in taking part. I have recognized Mackey & his house and am prepared to enforce his authority in purging his house of unauthorized person—at this point Gen Ruger & I expect riot & bloodshed to indefinite extent   we are unwilling to begin this—If as Judge Tafts despatch Stated Ruger were to enforce my authority when resisted we Could go forward but unless we are willing to precipitate a bloody Conflict no progress Can be made except by having Ruger allow me to proceed to the point of actual resistance in the hall to my force and thereupon he Come in & enforce my authority. It is necessary also that Ruger should prevent partisans from either side entering the Statehouse during the Struggle as this will add fuel to flames. we are ready to do our full duty but we hesitate to Sacrifice lives   the U S troops under Specific orders Such as I have indicated Can enforce My Authority without bloodshed" "The Democratic members of the House withdrew this forenoon on announcement of my purpose to Eject Edgefield & Laurens men by state Constabulary   it is now reported that democrats will inaugurate Hampton today or tomorrow & he will then proceed to declare me no longer governor or legislature will proceed to declare election of governor as rapidly as possible   Meantime I deem it prudent to ask that Gen Ruger may have clear orders to permit no violence on Either my part or Hamptons till the whole situation is known to you. An attempt may be made today to gain possession of State house under Hampton as pretended Governor   I think this should be provided for—" Telegrams received (at 10:55 A.M. and 3:15 P.M.), *ibid.*

Draft Annual Message

To the Senate and House of Representatives

In submitting my eighth, and last, Annual Message to Congress it seems proper that I should refer to—and in some degree recapitulate—the events ~~and and history of~~ [*my*] ~~entire occupancy of the office of Executive of the Nation.~~ official acts of the past eight years.

It was my fortune or misfortune, to be called to the office of Chief Executive without any previous political training. From the age of seventeen I had never even witnessed the excitement attending a Presidential Campaign, but twice, ~~previous~~ [antecedent] to my own candidacy, and at but one of them was I elegible as a voter. Under such circumstances it is but [re]asonable to suppose that errors of judgement must have occurred. Even had they not, differences of opinion between the Executive, bound by an oath to the strict performance of his duties, and writers and debaters must have arisen. It is not ~~always certain that the Executive has blundered because of these different views.~~ necessarily evidence of blunder on the part of the Executive because there are these differences of views. ~~But m~~Mistakes have been made as all can see, and I admit, but it seems to me oftener in the selections made of the assistants appointed to aid in carrying out the various duties of Administering the govt. —in nearly every case selected without a personal acquaintance with the appointee ~~but who have been strongly~~ [but upon] recommend~~ed,~~[ation] ~~and urged, by~~ [of] the representatives chosen directly by the people. It is impossible that where so many trusts are to be ~~filled~~ allotted that ~~all should be filled by the very best men for the places.~~ the right parties should be chosen in every instance. ~~A comparison between~~ History shows that no administration, from [the time of] Washingtons ~~time~~ to the present, has ~~any administration~~ been free from thi~~s~~[ese] mistake[s]. ~~Washington had even in his Cabinet — a position supposed to be filled wholly on the confidence of the President in the appointee either from a personal acquaintance or the public record of the man — a Randolph. Why should it be expected that with a greatly extended territory, a population fifteen~~

~~times greater, and public officers increased in a larger ratio, should be more exempt.~~ But I leave comparisons to history, claiming only that I have acted in every instance, from a consciencious desire to do what was right, constitutional, within the law, and for the very best interest[s] of the whole people. Failures have been errors of judgement, not of intent.[1]

My civil career commenced too at a most critical and difficult time. ~~for any Executive. The~~ Less than four years before, the country had emerged ~~but four years before~~ from a conflict such as no other Nation had ever ~~before~~ survived.[2] Nearly one half [of] the states had revolted against the Govt. and of those ~~states~~ remaining ~~true~~ faithful to the Union a large percentage of the population sympathized with the rebellion and made an "enemy in the rear" almost as dangerous as the more honorable enemy in the front. The latter ~~if they~~ committed ~~an~~ errors of judgement, ~~at least they maintained their~~ judgement but they maintained ~~it~~ [them] openly and courageously. The former received the protection of the Govt. they would see destroyed, and reaped all the pecuniary advantage to be gained out of the then existing state of affairs; many of them by obtaining contracts and by swindling the govt. in the delivery of their goods. ~~The four years intervening Almost~~ Immediately on the cessation of hostilities the then Noble President, who had carried the country so far through its perils fell a Martyr to his patriotism, ~~by~~ at the hands of an assassin, and in the interest of the rebellion.[3] The intervening time, to my first inauguration, was filled up with [in] wranglings between Congress and the new Executive as to the best mode of "reconstruction" or, to speak plainly, as to whether the controll of the government should be thrown immediately into the hands of those who had so recently and persistently tried to destroy it or whether the victors should continue to have an equal voice with them in this controll. Reconstruction, as finally agreed upon, means this and only this except that the ~~enfran~~ late slave was enfranchised, giving an increase—as was supposed—to the Union loving and Union supporting votes. If *free*, in the full sense of the word, they would not disappoint this expectation. Hence, at the begining of my first Administration the work of reconstruction—much embarrassed by the

long delay—virtually commenced. It was the work of the legislative branch of the govt. My province was wholly in approving their
acts, which I did most heartily, Urging ~~upon~~ the legislatures of
States that had not yet done so to ratify the Fifteenth Amendment to
the Constitution.

~~With~~ tThe country was laboring under an an enormous debt
contracted in the suppression of rebellion, and taxation was so oppressive as to discourage production. aAnother danger also threatened; us;—a foreign war. ~~This has been adjusted satisfactorily and a
foreign war thus averted~~. The last difficulty had to be adjusted and
was ~~done~~ adjusted without a war and in a manner highly honorable
to all parties concerned Taxes have been reduced within the last
seven years ~~about~~ nearly ~~$3~~ three hundred Million[s] pr. annum, and
the national debt has been reduced in the same time over four hundred & thirty-five Millions. of dollars By refunding the six pr cent
bonded debt ~~and issuing~~ for bonds bearing five, and four & one half
pr. ct [interest], respectively, the annual interest has been reduced
from over One hundred & thirty Million[s of] dollars in 1869 to, but
little over One hundred Millions [of dollars] in 1876. ;tThe balance
of trade has been changed from over one hundred & thirty ~~Millions~~
Millions against the U. S. in 1869 ~~the United States~~ to more than one
hundred & twenty millions [of dollars] in our favor, ~~with a reduction
of Million of gold included in our exports~~. in 1876

It is confidently believed that the balance of trade in favor of the
U. S. will increase, not diminish, and that the pledge of Congress to
resume specie payments in 1877[9] will be easily accomplished even
in the absence of much desired further legislation. ~~which however is
much~~ on the subject

A policy has been adopted towards the indian tribes inhabiting a
large portion of the territor~~ies~~y of the U. S. which has been humane
and has substantially ended indian hostilities in the whole land except in a portion of Nebrask, [and] Dakotah Wyoming and Mon-
tanna [Territories]—the Black Hills region & approaches thereto.
Hostilities there have grown out of the averice of the white man who
has violated our treaty stipulation[s] in his search for gold. The
question might be asked: Why the govt. has not enforced obedience

to the terms of the treaty prohibiting the occupation of the Black Hills region by Whites? The answer is simple. The first emigrants [immigrants] to the Black Hills were removed, by troops. But rumors of rich discoveries of gold took into that region increased numbers. Gold has actually been found, in paying quantity, and an effort to remove the miners would only result in the desertion of the bulk of the troops that might be sent there to remove them. All difficulty in this matter has however been removed—subject to the approval of Congress—by a treaty ceding the Black Hills, and approaches to settlement by the U. S. white citizens.

The subject of Indian policy and treatment is so fully set forth by the Sec. of the Int. and [the] Commissioner of Indian Affairs, and my views so fully expressed therein that I refer to his report and recommendations as my own.

The report of the Commissioner of Agriculture, accompanying this Message, will be found one of great interest, marking as it does, the great progress of the last century in the variety of products of the soil produced, increased knowledge & skill in the labor of producing, saving,—and manipulating [manipulating] the same to prepare [prepare] them for the use of man; in the improvements in machinery to aid the agriculturist in his pursuits labors; and in a knowledge of those scientific subjects necessary to a thorough system of economy in pr agricultural production; namely, Chemistry, Botany, Entomology [etc.] the A study of their repport this by those interested in agriculture, and deriving their support from it, will find it of value in pointing out those articles which are raised in greater quantiy than the needs of the country world require—and must sell therefore for less than the cost of production—and those which command a a profit over cost of production because there is not an over-production.

[I call especial notice attention to the Depts need of need of the Department for a new gallery for the reception of the exhibits returned from the Centennial Exposition Exhibition, including the donated exhibits from by Japan, Sweden, Spain Portugal &c, very many foreign countries nations also] and to the recommendations of the Com. of Agriculture generally

The report[s] of the District Commissioners and ~~of~~ the "Board of Health" are just received—too late to read them [&] to make recommendations thereon—and are herewith submitted.

The international exhibition held in Phila this year in commemoration of the [one] hundredth anaversary of American independence has proven a great success, and will no doubt be of enduring advantage to the country. It has shown the great progress in the Arts, sciences & Mechanical skill made in a single century, and demonstrated that we are but little behind older nations in any one branch, while in some we scarsely have a rival. It has served too not only to bring peoples and products of skill & labor from all parts of the world together but in bringing together people from all sections of ~~the~~ our own country, ~~sharing their views and giving them a more exalted opinion of the grandure of their native land~~ which must prove a great benefit in the information imparted and pride of country engendered

It has been suggested by scientists interested in and connected with the Smithsonian Institution,—in a communication[4] herewith ~~attached~~—that the govt. exhibit be removed to the Capital, and a suitable building be erected or purchased for its accomodation as a permanent exhibit. I earnestly recommend this, and believing that Congress would second this view I directed that all govt. exhibits at the Centennial ~~exposition~~ Exhibition should remain where they are—except such as might be injured by remaining in a building not intended as a protection in inclement weather, or such as may be wanted by the dept. furnishing them—until the question of permanent exhibition is acted on

~~The subject of our indian affairs is so fully discussed in the reports of the Sec. of Indian Aff the Int. and the Supt. of Indian Affairs that I refer Congress to their reports, concurring entirely in their recommendations.~~

Many nations have voluntarily contributed their exhibits to the United States to increase the interest in any permanent exhibition Congress may provide for. For this act of generosity they should receive the thanks of the people and I respectfully suggest that a resolution of Congress to that effect be adopted.

The attention of Congress cannot be to [too] earnestly called to the necessity of throwing some greater safeguard over the method of choosing and ~~counting~~ declaring the ~~vote~~ election of a President. Under the present system there seems to be no provided remedy for contesting the election in any one state. The singular spectacle is presented of nearly a solid section of the country supporting one candidate when it is clear that with an untrammeled, protected freedom of franchise to all the legal voters the result would have been far different. Intimidation and assassination ~~has~~ [have] not only produced the result alluded to,—~~and may select the chief President~~—but ~~it has~~ [have] captured one house of Congress and changed the majority in the other. A continuation of such methods of getting controll of the govt. must lead to dangerous results sooner or later[5]

The remedy is [partially] no doubt in the enlightenment of electors. The compulsory support of the free school, and the disfranchisement of all who cannot read and write the english language—after a fixed probation—would meet my hearty approval. I would not make this apply however to those already voters but I would to all becoming so after the expiration of the probation fixed upon. Foreigners coming to the country to become citizens who are educated in their own language would acquire the requisite knowledge of ours during the necessary residence to obtain naturalization. If they did not take sufficient interest in our language to enable them to study the institutions and laws of the country intelligibly, I would not confer upon them the right to make ~~those~~ such laws, nor to select those who do. ~~So far I am unhesitatingly a Native American.~~

~~An further remedy would be to exclude immediate benefit might obtained by excluding from Congress all doubtfully elected members. When violence and intimidation, or any other form of fraud, is unquestioned resorted to—either in selecting the legislature which chooses a senator or in the district choosing a Congressman—refer them back to their constitutents and only admit them after a fair election has been secured.~~

I append to this message, [for convenient reference] a synopsis of [administrative events & of] all recommendations to Congress [made] by me during the last seven years. ~~for convenient reference.~~

Time may show some of ~~them~~ [these recommendations] not to have been wisely conceived, but I believe the ~~average~~ [larger part] will do no discredit to the Administration. ~~There is o~~One ~~of these~~ [of these] recommendations ~~which made by me~~ met with ~~the entire~~ the united opposition of one political party ~~entire~~ in the Senate, and with a strong opposition from the other, namely: ~~for~~ The treaty for the Annexation of Santo Domingo[6] to the U. S., to which I will specially refer, ~~and~~ maintaining as I do that if my views had been concurred in the Country would be in a more prosperous condition to-day both politically and financially. Santo Domingo is fertile and ~~produces~~ [upon its soil may be] grows[n] just those tropical products of which the United States use so ~~much~~ many ~~of~~ and which are produced ~~now~~ or prepared for market now by slave labor, almost exclusively: namely Sugar, coffee, dye woods, Mahogany, tropical fruits, tobacco ~~&c~~[etc]. About seventy-five per cent of the exports of Cuba are consumed in the United States. A large percentage of the exports of Brazil also find the same market. These are paid for almost exclusively in coin, legislation, particularly in Cuba, being unfavorable to ~~all~~ a mutual exchange of the products of each country. Flour shipped from the Mississippi river to Havanna can pass by the very entrance to the city on its way to a port in Spain; there pay[s] a duty fixed upon articles to be re-exported; transfered to a Spanish vessel and brought back almost to the point of starting, pay[s] a second duty and still leave[s] a profit over what would be received by a direct shipment.

All that is produced in Cuba could be produced ~~by~~ [in] Santo Domingo. Being a part of the United States, commerce between the ~~i~~Island and ~~the~~ Main land would be free. There would be no export duties on her shipments nor import duties on those coming here. There would be no import duties upon the supplies, machinery ~~&c.~~ [etc] going from the States. The effect that would have been ~~had~~ produced upon Cuban commerce, with these advantages to a rival, is observable at a glance. The Cuban question would have been settled long ago in favor of "Free Cuba." Hundreds of American vessels would now be ~~p~~advantageously ~~in use~~ used in transporting the valuable woods, and other products of the soil of the ~~i~~Island, to a market, and in carrying supplies and emmigrants to it. The Island is but sparsely settled alth while it has an area sufficient for the profitable employment of several Millions of people. The soil would have soon fallen into the hands of United States capitalist. The products are so valuable in commerce that emigration there would have been encouraged: the emancipated race of the South would have found there a congenial home where his [their] civil rights would not be disputed; and his [their] labor would be so much sought after that the poorest among them could have found the means to go there. Thus, in cases of great oppression and cruelty, such as has been practiced upon them in many places within the last eleven years, whole communities would have sought refuge in Santo Domingo. I do not suppose the whole race would have gone, nor is it desirable that they should do so [go]. Their labor is desirable—indispensable almost—where they now are. But the possession of this territory would have left the negro "Master of the Situation," and by enabling him to demand his rights at home on pain of finding them elswhere.

I do not present these views now as a recommendation for a renewel of the subject of Anexation. But I do refer to it as a to vindicatione in a matter where much abuse, and I think a gooddeal of mis of my course in a matter where I think the subject has not been understood and hence ignorant abuse has been heaped upon the Administration my previous action in regard to it.

With the present term of Congress my official life terminates. It is not probable that public affairs will ever again receive attention of from me further than as a citizen of the republic, always taking a deep interest in the general welfare, honor, integrity and prosperity of the whole land.

[EXECUTIVE MANSION DEC 5 1876—]

ADf (bracketed material in another hand), ICarbS. *Foreign Relations, 1876*, pp. III–XVI. As printed, the message included substantial passages on foreign relations and immigration, and synopses of departmental reports.

On Dec. 4 and 5, 1876, Secretary of State Hamilton Fish recorded in his diary concerning USG's message. "At about two o'clock he began reading his message. At two different points in the message he discusses the recent Presidential Election reviewing in very severe terms the course attributed to the Democrats especially in the Southern States   I suggest the impolicy of such reference and especially of the use of some severe terms of denunciation of any large body of the citizens   Cameron thinks it all right   I admit that the statements of the President may be fully justified by the facts but that a communication of the nature of the Presidents Message to Congress was of a high character and should be of a high tone and free from partizanship or imputations upon a large body of citizens. Chandler thinks it the best part of the message and that it will do good. I reply that I differ from him that far from doing good I think it will do harm, that the public mind is already sufficiently excited without such imputations from such a source which would be resented by the whole of one party and a large portion of the other would disapprove   Some questions were raised by Morrill as to the accuracy of the Presidents statement of the extent of the annual reduction of the public taxation. The President caused a little laugh by saying it might be inaccurate but he had taken it from Morrill's own figures. The figures are to be examined and if incorrect are to be altered." "Enquire of the President whether he has his message ready to transmit today. I ask whether he has retained the passage relating to the Southern Elections   He replies that he has not that he is satisfied they will produce no good and might a good deal of harm and that he confined himself to a recommendation of provisions for the future to guard against irregularities in the counting of the Electoral Votes" DLC-Hamilton Fish.

On Dec. 2, U.S. Senator George F. Edmunds of Vt. had written to Fish. "I beg to suggest the great importance of having the President's Message state the fact of the compliance by Colorado with the terms of the Act of Congress authorizing her admission into the Union, and the President's proclamation announcing that fact according to the provisions of law, and that he submit a copy of the proclamation with his message." LS, *ibid.* See *Foreign Relations, 1876,* p. x.

On Dec. 6, Ansell A. Terrell, Sterling, Ill., wrote to USG. "I was one of those 'Liberal' chaps who did not vote for you the last time, but I confess my error, & if I have ever prayed earnestly, it has been to be forgiven for that act, & I praise God that you were elected, & now piloting the old ship thro— a fearfull storm. Again you have saved all we hold dear as a people & may God bless you for it—" ALS, USG 3.

On the same day, U.S. Representative J. Ambler Smith of Va. telegraphed to USG. "Every man with a national sentiment in the South will be greatful for your noble message   May God bless you, is my prayer" Telegram received, DNA, RG 107, Telegrams Collected (Bound).

Also on Dec. 6, Daniel E. Sickles, New York City, wrote to USG. "Your message is admirably received by leading Democrats as well as Republicans of all shades of opinion. A better feeling seems to prevail in this city. Enclosed I send you some views expressed by me to the Editors of the *Tribune* and which they thought fit to publish. I have seen the Editors of Several of our papers since my return and have conversed with our friends in the Union League Club & elsewhere. I am satisfied you will be sustained in firm and positive measures should the emergency demand them. . . . P. S. I am glad to see Senator Edmunds is pushing the Investigation based on the penal clause in the 14th Amendment to which I called your and his attention. I am sure it will have excellent results in the North on men of all parties." ALS, USG 3. On Nov. 23, Sickles had written to USG. "Permit me to call your attention to the second clause of the 14th Amendment to the Constitution, which provides a practical remedy for the wholesale disfranchisement of voters in many of the Southern States. I respectfully suggest that this provision of the Constitution be brought to the notice of Congress in your Annual Message, with the recommendation that measures be taken to ascertain how far such disfranchisement has deprived these States of the representation they have heretofore been allowed in the Electoral College and in Congress. This investigation would plainly show to the people that several of the Southern States have forfeited all right to the enlarged representation given to them since the rebellion, because they have permitted a large portion of their population to be disfranchised by force in violation of a plain provision of the Constitution. This would be the best answer to the outcry that we are electing Hayes by one vote obtained through technical means. It would refute the allegation that Tilden has a majority of the popular vote. And it would convince all fair minded persons of the perfidy of the Southern Democrats in profiting by their Amnesty whilst repudiating impartial suffrage,—the condition on which Amnesty was granted to them. Such an enquiry ought to be pushed energetically by the Senate, and testimony taken by the Supervisors of election & otherwise, in time for publication & use before the electoral vote is finally declared. It seems to me our position would be thereby greatly strengthened." ALS, *ibid.* On Nov. 15, Sickles had written to USG offering his services in the electoral crisis. Parke-Bernet Sale No. 2235, Dec. 3, 1963, no. 212. USG received letters concerning his message from James H. Ela, Albany, N. Y. (Dec. 7); George K. Gilmer, Richmond (Dec. 7); J. N. Davis, Elkridge Landing, Md. (Dec. 7); Robert A. Griffith *et al.*, Baltimore (Dec. 8); David B. Goewey, Lyons, N. Y. (Dec. 8); Ambrose N. Cole, Wellsville, N. Y. (Dec. 8); George W. Sayler, Kaolin, Pa. (Dec. 8); Governor John L. Beveridge of Ill. (Dec. 9); Samuel A. Foot, Geneva, N. Y. (Dec. 9); Leverett Griggs, Bristol, Conn. (Dec. 11); James S. Hallowell, Brookeville, Md. (Dec. 18); and Thomas J. Wood, Dayton (Dec. 27), all in USG 3.

     1. "In concluding this subject I will say that no official act of my life would I conceal. Go back to my entrance into the Military Academy; the eleven years of service thereafter; and now nearly sixteen years of public service since, no official act of mine has ever been conceived except, as I though[t], in the interest of the govt. It never occurred to me that I was singular in this particular. My thought was—like the sentinel—'orders must be obeyed,' and the Constitution, and laws were these orders." ADf, ICarbS. This paragraph was written on a separate sheet and marked "*Excluded.*"

     2. A related fragment of USG's message is marked "*Excluded.*" "If either should be found oppressive abundance of means—of a pacific character—were provided for by the Const & laws. Evasion of regulations, or laws was only to conceal their defect, and prevent outbreak until revolution become inevitable. The observance would point ~~these out~~ out defect, and lead to the proper remedy them peacefully. Had the same rule been observed by 'Statesm[en]' our late conflict never would have been entered into. Slavery the holding of human beings as chattells, is a condition of society revolting to civilization; it is a condition of affairs that could not exist long with a high civilization, and could not be inaugurated at all in such civilization. The only toleration it had was from ~~in~~ its inheritance among us: it contributing to individual wealth and ease: and an indifference on the part of those not observably effected by it. But leaders ~~say~~id that it was obnoxious to ~~the~~ civilized, and christian ideas. Unless the area over which the institution might spread should be increased and the domination of the holders of property in man be secured over the whole territory within which the institution exists all would be ~~gone with~~ lost to them. Temporizing and compromising on this subject continued for many years, and the conflict came. I believe not in compromise with ~~n~~known evils, but in a prompt suppression of them" ADf, *ibid.*

     3. The words following "assassin" were marked "Excluded."

     4. On Nov. 13, Joseph Henry, Smithsonian Institution, had written to USG conveying resolutions, adopted at the Oct. meeting of the National Academy of Sciences, urging USG to support the preservation of Centennial collections for permanent display at Washington, D. C. ". . . I beg leave in favor of the proposition to suggest *First*—that the exhibit would form a fitting Memorial of the centennial condition of the country. *Second,* that it

would illustrate in a striking manner the appliances used by the Government in carrying on its various and complex operations. *Third*, that it would be a repository in which the natural resources of each State would be exhibited. *Fourth*, that it would give information in one view, of importance to the statesman, legislator, scientist, educator and the capitalist of our own and of foreign countries. *Fifth*—it would be of interest to the intelligent public at large, and would meet the approbation of all who regard the prosperity of the country, and take pride in the condition of the National Capital. . . ." LS (press), Smithsonian Institution Archives. *HED*, 44-2-1, part 8, pp. 1–2; *HRC*, 44-2-144, 9. On Nov. 20, Col. Stephen C. Lyford, Washington, D. C., wrote to USG. "I have the honor to report that in obedience to instructions received through the War Department, copy herein inclosed, I gave directions on the 17th inst., that the Government Building at the International Exhibition be maintained for the present *in statu quo*, and that all packing and work for breaking up the collection be stopped at once, except of such articles as are immediately needed in the Departments here. . . ." LS, DNA, RG 56, Expositions. On the same day, Culver C. Sniffen endorsed this letter to Lyford, "who will, at his discretion, allow such articles as may be liable to injury, by remaining in the Government Building at Philadelphia, to be removed to Washington, and there to be held by the Representatives of the Executive Departments, subject to future orders—" ES, *ibid.* Related papers are *ibid.* On the same day, Henry wrote to USG. "I have been informed that great detriment may accrue to the specimens at the Centennial, belonging to the Smithsonian Institution and the several Departments of the Government, if the packing up for transportation is suspended until Congress shall have an opportunity of acting on the proposition of the transfer of the whole Government exhibit to Washington; and therefore I would respectfully suggest that permission be granted for all the articles to be packed and made ready for shipment. Unless they are packed they are liable to injury from the present damp and unventilated condition of the building, and the work can be better done now than before the setting in of the inclement weather of winter. . . ." LS (press), Smithsonian Institution Archives.

5. The three sentences beginning "The singular spectacle" were marked "Excluded in copy to Congress."

6. On Dec. 6, Henry O. Wagoner, Denver, wrote to USG. "I have just read your late and last Annual Message to Congress with deep interest and thoughtful attention. I note many impressive passages; and, not least among them, to the Colored man, is St. Domingo, which includes Hayti. On this subject, how pained I was at the Course of my dear Sumner. Then, as now, I felt sure that I Could discern your honest intent and pure purpose; and I think time will bear you out in your views on the subject. Myself and Son have interchanged many thoughts on this subject. He has fully recognised the wisdom of your views. I am rather sad at the thought of your leaving the Presidential Chair so Soon. But I presume you feel an inward relief from overwhelming Cares. But I will not dwell. With best wishes for your health, happiness and prosperity, . . ." ALS, USG 3.

On Dec. 7, George K. Gilmer, Richmond, wrote to USG. "Allow me to thank you for your very able and excellent message to Congress. And especially allow me to thank you for that part of it that reminds the country of your policy in reference to the Annexation of Santo Domingo to this country. I cordially approved of this policy at the time, as wise and judicious, and so said to Senator Lewis and other Senators, but the country failed to respond to the suggestion, and the Senate unfortunately failed to perceive its wisdom, and consequently it failed. But it was right and wise, and the country will yet come to so regard it. I might add a word as to the general outlook of the present political situation to the loyal southerner, but I have no heart to speak of it. Suffice it to say, I have an abiding faith in the virtue, intelligence and loyalty of the American people, and cannot believe that they will allow the present rebellious, anarchical spirit that now holds high carnival in many sections of the country, and especially in many sections of the South, to achieve by finesse and *force* what secession and war failed to accomplish." ALS, *ibid.*

On Dec. 8, George W. Sayler, Kaolin, Pa., wrote to USG. "It is not without hesitation that I venture again, to take up any of thy valuable time. But after reading thy late message to Congress, I wanted to say to thee in the first place that I am greatly pleased with its contents; and particularly with what thou hast said on the St. Domingo subject. I very much approved at the time of thy treaty for its annexation to the United States, and think the opposition to it proceeded from stupidity, not to say malevolence. My long years of arduous labor and sacrifices of many years of the prime of my life and thousands of dollars in opposition to Slavery prepared me for cheerful accordance with that very interesting and important measure—and it seems to me unaccountable how any enlightened citizen of the United States solicitous for her prosperity can be indifferent to its importance. It would have been the death blow to Slavery on the Western Hemisphere; and would inevitably have composed the principal waves of trouble which now so seriously threaten our beloved country...." ALS, *ibid.* See *PUSG,* 26, 422–23.

To Daniel H. Chamberlain

Washington, D. C. Dec. 5th *1876*

To GOVERNOR CHAMBERLAIN, ~~CHARLESTON~~ COLUMBIA, S. C.

Your dispt this date rec'd.

If Mr. Hewitt [1] has sent, or authorized to be sent, to Columbia the statement that when sixty-three of the members of the legislature holding certificates from the returning board meet, and organize, I ~~would~~ will recognize them he has misstated, or authorized to be misstated, the facts, and has violated a confidence and his subsequent statements. to me I did have a pleasant—as I thought—conversation with him in which many subjects were talked over, and as then advised, my opinion was that sixty-three was the least legal number to constitute a quorum to transact business. But I never authorized the chairman of the democratic ~~house~~ national committee to give forth my views to determine the political action of any state. With the assurances Mr. Hewitt has given me I do not credit for a moment that he ever authorized the statements you say are attributed to him. I am not a lawyer and my judgement as to whether a quorum consists of a majority of all possible members of the lower house of the South Carolina legislature, or only of a majority of those chosen, is open to argument, and to the advise of my ~~law~~ legal law advisor, with such other advice as may be at my command.

ADf, OFH. On Dec. 5, 1876, Tuesday, Governor Daniel H. Chamberlain of S. C. twice telegraphed to USG. "In view of Reports reaching here from Washington I deem it my duty
to state the legal position of the Legislature now, on Tuesday of last week the House was
organized & mr mackey was elected speaker. Fifty nine persons holding certificates of the
secretary of state Being present & voting. This we regard as a constitutional quorum
beigng a majority of all the members chosen. Since then the House has acted on contested
seats & has seated fourteen additional Republican members who have been sworn in & are
now acting as Members. This gives the House presided over by Mr Mackey a membership
of seventy three meantime five of the original fifty nine have also been sworn in to the
house organized by the Democrats but if the organization of the mackey house at first was
constitutional no withdrawals subsequently can destroy its validity unless the whole number including the additional members seated is reduced below fifty nine. The mackey
House now has a membership of sixty eight. The House & Senate are now engaged in
counting the votes for Govr & Lt Govr & will probably declare the result today we regard our legal position as impregnable & intend to stand upon it. we have a senate and
House each regularly organized Our opponents have neither It is positively asserted here
that you have informed Mr Hewitt that you will recognize any House which has sixty three
persons holding certificates of secty. of state we do not for one moment credit the report
& we respectfully submit that no change of action on the part of those who originally
formed part of the mackey House can affect its validity unless the whole number now
seated is reduced below a quorum" "Legislature in joint convention declared me elected to-
day by majority of three thousand one hundred & forty five—" Telegrams received (at 6:20
and 8:22 P.M.), *ibid.*

Also on Dec. 5, 3:10 P.M., Secretary of War James D. Cameron telegraphed to Col.
Thomas H. Ruger, Columbia, S. C. "At the request of Governor Chamberlain the President
directs me to repeat his instructions to you to prevent all outsiders from interfering with
the Legislature." Copies, DNA, RG 94, Letters Received, 4788 1876; *ibid.*, RG 107, Letters
Sent, Military Affairs. On the same day, Ruger twice telegraphed to USG. "The republican members of the Senate the Democratic taking no part and the House recognized
by Governor Chamberlain including members from two Counties admitted Since day of
meeting in place of Democratic members holding certificates from the Secy of State but
Sixty three including such Substituted members are now Engaged in canvassing the vote
for Governor." "I had no intention to allow outsiders to interfere with the legislature. Did
not consider it necessary to keep some control of state House. Told Governor Chamberlain would leave a guard & he could provide for police duty on his alarm I kept a Company
in state House with special Orders as to disturbance & remained near myself during day
until both Houses adjourned Have now two companies in state House as formerly—"
Telegrams received (at 2:25 and 7:24 P.M.), OFH.

1. Born in 1822 in N. Y., a protegé of Peter Cooper, Abram S. Hewitt prospered as an
iron manufacturer, entered Congress in 1874, and served as chairman, Democratic National Committee, during the 1876 campaign. See letter to Hamilton Fish, Dec. 6, 1876.

To Congress

To the Senate and House of Representatives—
I have the honor to transmit herewith a letter accompanied by testimony, addressed to me, by Hon: John Sherman and other distinguished citizens in regard to the canvass of the Vote for electors in the State of Louisiana—[1]

U. S. Grant.

Executive Mansion—December 6. 1876.

Copy, DNA, RG 130, Messages to Congress. *SED*, 44-2-2. On Dec. 6, 1876, U.S. Senator John Sherman of Ohio and ten others wrote to USG. "In pursuance of your request that several of the undersigned should proceed to New Orleans, and there witness the canvass, by the returning-board of the State of Louisiana, of the votes cast in that State for electors for President and Vice-President of the United States, we have performed that duty, and now most respectfully report: That on our arrival in that city we found several gentlemen from other States, who had proceeded there at the request of the chairman of the National Democratic Committee, and we also found there several gentlemen who came representing republican State organizations who have throughout co-operated with those who went at your request, and whose names are also appended to this communication. Between the gentlemen representing the democratic party and ourselves a correspondence in writing ensued, a copy of which is appended hereto. Reference to it will disclose that a conference with us for the purpose of exercising an influence upon the returning-board was declined, upon the ground that the only duty devolved upon us was to attend before the board, carefully note its proceedings, and finally to report a faithful history thereof, with such opinions concerning the same as truth and justice should demand. Such report we are now able to present, and we take pleasure in stating that our ability so to do is due to the exercise of a courtesy and kindness by the returning-board which entitle its members not only to our thanks, but to that confidence which a just public extends toward every tribunal which desires that all its proceedings should be daily presented to public scrutiny.... Having thus presented a statement of the means accorded of witnessing the canvass, it may be well to state briefly the causes which led to the creation of such a board in Louisiana, and to call attention to the statute which devolves upon it powers and duties of great public importance. The white people of that and other Southern States had by their rebellion forfeited all right to representation in Congress or to any participation in the Government of the Union, and had been compelled, as a condition of resuming their former political rights, to assent to the constitutional amendments by which, in hostility to their will, those who had been but lately their slaves were made citizens; and although it was their duty to submit to this political re-organization, the annals of the South, and especially of Louisiana, disclose a wide-spread and persistent determination of its ruling white people to prevent the exercise of the elective franchise by the colored race, except subject to their will.... Until a radical change could be effected in the nature and purposes of those who had been their owners, and who repudiated the idea of being placed upon terms of civil equality with them, it was evident that a fair election could not be held in parishes containing any considerable majority of colored voters, and hence the act of 1870, acquiesced in by both political parties, and amended in 1872, was passed, creating a returning-board, authorized to sit in New Orleans, having supreme authority to canvass the votes cast throughout the entire State, and authorized, if convinced that riot, tumult, acts of violence, intimidation, armed disturbance, bribery, or corrupt influences had prevented voters from registering, or had materially interfered with the purity or freedom of election at any poll or voting-place, or had materially changed the result of the election, to exclude votes cast at such polls or voting-places from the final count. This law, with some amendments, not materially changing its nature, is that under which the present returning-board of Louisiana is now organized and sits. That some such independent tribunal was necessary for the protection of the legal voter, and as a check upon the violence and intimidation which had before prevailed throughout the State, no one can deny. It will be seen, when the statute organizing this board and defining its duties is examined, how inadequate are its provisions to afford full relief against the wrongs it was designed to prevent. Thus the powers of the board are limited to the rejection of votes polled for the causes stated, while it cannot in any case add to the returns votes which would have been polled but for the intimidation, violence, &c., mentioned. . . . It will, therefore, readily occur to any one, that a careful selection by political managers of certain parishes, known to have large republican majorities, for scenes of intimidation and violence, in the belief that other parishes within the State would enable them to carry it for their party even should their majorities in parishes thus selected be rejected might well be a favorite method for achieving success; and as we proceed, it will be apparent that such was the mode adopted to carry Louisiana for the democratic party. While from the very nature of the mischief to be remedied the law could but partially repair it, the statute under which the board acts is so framed as to prohibit the rejection of votes cast at any poll or voting-place unless certain solemn formalities are first complied with, which must be supplemented by the testimony of witnesses. . . . There were in the State of Louisiana on the day of the election 92,996 white registered voters, and 115,310 colored, a majority of the latter of 22,314. It was well known that if left free to vote uninfluenced by violence or intimidation, the blacks would be almost unanimously republican, and that with the white republican vote its majority would be about equal to that above indicated. The plan appears to have been to select for purposes of intimidation and violence as few parishes as possible, (for in forty of fifty-seven parishes where these were not employed the republican majority was 6,000,) but to select those in which the colored vote, as compared with the white, would be large unless unlawfully prevented; for in so doing it might be expected that should any majority they could thus obtain in such parishes be rejected, they would nevertheless attain their purpose by the suppression of a large republican vote. In pursuance of this plan, five of the parishes selected in which the greatest violence and intimidation were practiced were East and West Feliciana, which border upon that portion of Mississippi in which murder and outrage so prevailed, during and preceding the election, as substantially to prevent any republican vote; East Baton Rouge, which borders upon the southern portion of East Feliciana; Morehouse, which adjoins the State of Arkansas; and Ouachita, which adjoins and lies directly south of Morehouse. The geographical position of these five parishes was well suited to the purpose to be attained; for it was easy for the members of the clubs to be formed therein, and who usually perpetrated their outrages with masked faces, to pretend that they were committed by border-ruffians from Mississippi and Arkansas, where like outrages had been perpetrated. The location of these five parishes was not, however, better suited to the plan to be accomplished than was the great disproportion existing therein between the number of white and colored voters. The former numbered but 5,134; the latter, 13,244; a majority of the latter equal to more than one-third of the entire majority of colored voters in the fifty-seven parishes of the State. The returns of votes actually cast in these five parishes suggest that the clubs to whom was assigned the task of securing democratic majorities therein had performed their work of violence and intimidation effectually; while the proof discloses (brief summaries of portions of which are hereto annexed) that where violence and intimidation were inefficient, murder, maiming, mutilation, and whipping were resorted to. Instead of a majority of six or seven thousand which the republicans should have had in these parishes upon a fair election, there was actually returned to the returning-board a democratic majority, for the parishes of East and West Feliciana, Morehouse, and Ouachita, of 3 878; and in East Feliciana, where the registered colored voters number 2,127, not a republican vote for electors was cast. In East Baton Rouge, containing 3,552 colored registered voters and but 1,801 whites, the democrats claim a majority of 617, which, but for the rejection of several polls by the commissioners and supervisors of election, would have been returned to the returning-board as votes actually cast. If, to the democratic majority from the five parishes as above stated, we add the 617 thus claimed and insisted upon before the returning-board, a democratic majority of 4,495 is the result of an election in five parishes containing 13,244 colored republicans and but 5,134 white democratic voters. The conclusion that intimidation and violence alone could have produced this is almost irresistible; and that such influences were employed, and were supplemented by murder when that was thought necessary, is established by the proofs already referred to. It but confirms this conclusion to refer to the vote cast in these five parishes in 1874, when no special motives existed for the use of cruel means to influence the election. The republican majority therein was then 3,979. A result so suggestive of violence and intimidation was obtained by means the most terrible and revolting. Organized clubs of masked armed men, formed as recommended by the central democratic committee, rode through the country at night, marking their course by the whipping, shooting, wounding, maiming, mutilation, and murder of women, children, and defenseless men, whose houses were forcibly entered while they slept, and, as their inmates fled through fear, the pistol, the rifle, the knife, and the rope were employed to do their horrid work. Crimes like these, testified to by scores of witnesses, were the means employed in Louisiana to elect a President of the United States. And when they shall succeed, the glories of the republic will have departed, and shame and horror will supplant in the hearts of our people that love and veneration with which they have hitherto regarded the institutions of their country. . . . To guard the purity of the ballot; to protect the citizen in the free and peaceful exercise of his right to vote; to secure him against violence, intimidation, outrage, and especially murder, when he attempts to perform this duty, should be the desire of all men, and the aim of every representative government. If political success shall be attained by such violent and terrible means as were resorted to in many parishes in Louisiana, complaint should not be made if the votes thus obtained are denounced by judicial tribunals and all honest men illegal and void." *Ibid.*, pp. 1–9. On the same day, U.S. Representative James A. Garfield of Ohio wrote in his diary that he and "other gentlemen who went to New Orleans" delivered this report to USG. "In the partisan fashion of this period I have no doubt it will be bitterly assailed. Doubtless we are ourselves partisan in making it, but we have sought to exhibit the truth." Harry James Brown and Frederick D. Williams, eds., *The Diary of James A. Garfield* (East Lansing, Mich., 1967–81), III, 391. See *CR*, 44–2, 54–64, 68 90; *HMD*, 44-2-42, 40–52, 85–88, 126–30, 162–77, 184–91, 197–218, 246–53, 376–87; *SMD*, 44-2-14; John M. Palmer, *Personal Recollections of John M. Palmer: The Story of an Earnest Life* (Cincinnati, 1901), pp. 396–429; Henry Watterson, *"Marse Henry" An Autobiography* (New York, 1919), I, 296–99; Ralph J. Roske, "'Visiting Statesman' in Louisiana 1876," *Mid-America*, 33, 2 (April, 1951), 89–102.

On Dec. 13, USG wrote a note. "The Sec. of War I think should have Gen. Augur instructed to give such protection in the interior of La. during Congressional investigation as he may deem advisable. To this end any troops in Miss. or Tenn. may be withdrawn for that purpose." ANS, NN. On the same day, Secretary of War James D. Cameron wrote to Gen. William T. Sherman transmitting USG's instructions. ". . . It is alleged that in the interior parishes the witnesses are being murdered and frightened to prevent their testifying before the Committee. Will you please instruct Gen. Augur to examine this at once and to protect these witnesses if necessary with the troops under his command. He should however keep enough troops in New Orleans to meet any emergency, and if he needs an increased force to accomplish both purposes he should ask for it at once" LS, DNA, RG 94, Letters Received, 4788 1876. See Gen. Sherman to Lt. Gen. Philip H. Sheridan, Dec. 13, 1876, Sheridan to Sherman, Dec. 14, 1876, *ibid.*; *HMD*, 44-2-34, parts 1–6.

1. On Dec. 4, Secretary of State Hamilton Fish had recorded in his diary. "The President expresses the opinion from what has been reported to him and what he gathers that at least a part of the Tilden Electors will be returned from Louisianna and his regret that the necessity of sustaining Hayes Election should rest upon returns coming from a board whose passed character has deprived of any claims to confidence." DLC-Hamilton Fish.
On Dec. 6, Stephen B. Packard, New Orleans, telegraphed to USG. "Eight votes for Hayes & wheeler have just been cast by electors of Louisiana" Telegram received (at 7:00 P.M.), DNA, RG 60, Letters Received, La.

To Hamilton Fish

Dec. 6th /76

DEAR GOVR

I send you two dispatches just received from Mr. Hewitt, with the sketch of about what I propose to say[1] if any answer is given atall. Will you be kind enough to read and return this evening or to-morrow morning your thought on the subject.

Yours Truly

U. S. GRANT

ALS, DLC-Hamilton Fish. On Dec. 6, 1876, U.S. Representative Abram S. Hewitt of N. Y. twice telegraphed to USG. "I have received a reliable telegram from Columbia stating that the sixty third member holding a certificate from the Secretary of State has been sworn into the House presided over by Speaker Wallace which is therefore organized in accordance with the requirements of law as stated by you" "I have just received a later dispatch saying that the Supreme Court of South Carolina has pronounced its judgement & declared the House presided over by W. H. Wallace to be the legally constituted House of Representatives, that Mackey is a private person not speaker or in any respect an Officer of the legislative body" Telegrams received, DNA, RG 107, Telegrams Collected (Bound).
On Dec. 3, Hewitt had written a memorandum of a conversation with USG. "After a few commonplace remarks, the President said that he longed for the day when he should be able to retire from office; That he counted the hours just as when he completed his terms

at WestPoint during the last three months of his term he looked forward for the freedom which was in store for him: That for sixteen years he had consecrated his life to the public service without any interval of rest or any possibility of being free from great responsibility;—That while he was in the army, during the war, he was in the picket line, so to speak, for four years, and that if in any of the engagements where he had gained a victory, he had lost a battle, the whole cause of the Union would have been lost; That during Johnson's administration, he was the bulwark between Congress on the one hand, and the President on the other, and had been compelled to exercise greater powers, and discharge more complicated duties than any ~~other~~ previous General-in-chief; That during his eight years of the Presidency, the most difficult questions had been presented, and had to be solved.—: That he was aware that at times, he had been misunderstood, but he believed that the great mass of the people were disposed to do him and his motives full justice, To which I remarked that I had no question of that fact; That his career formed the most memorable part of American history; That his fame was the property of the American people; That we all had a jealous regard for him, and, speaking for the Democratic party, I could assure him that they were disposed to do him full justice; and that they had a confidence that now, at the close of his administration, no act of his would tarnish the glory of his past achievements.—The President replied that the present House of Representatives had not given evidence of a desire to do him justice; That they had raked up petty accusations against him, and had brought back from Ireland a lunatic, who for a long time had followed him about, threatening vengeance, so that for six months, he had carried a heavy cane for protection.—I said to him that this matter had made so little impression on the public mind that I was not aware of such an investigation, and I begged that he would not attribute to a great party, the malice or blunders of a few individuals; That he was recognized by both parties, as the General who had brought the war to a close, and who had assured the continuance of the Union.—I then remarked that the present crisis was one in which he could render to the country even a greater service than any he had heretofore rendered, and that it seemed to me that it rested wholly with him whether the present complication should result in war, or in a peaceful solution.—He replied that if there was to be any fighting, he certainly would not begin it; That he would maintain order, as he was bound to do, but that he would not provoke any collision by the use of mere power, where it was not his duty to employ it.—I then referred to the recent use of troops in South Carolina.—He said that his orders to General Ruger directed him simply to preserve the peace, and that he had not been authorized to interfere in the organization of the legislature;—That General Ruger's report showed he issued orders in accordance with these instructions, but that the orders had been misconstrued by a young officer, and that members had been refused admission to the hall, but as soon as this fact had been brought to the notice of General Ruger, this obstruction was removed.—He referred to the statement signed by General Gordon and Wade Hampton, that notice had been sent by General Ruger to the members from Laurens and Edgefield counties, that they would be removed from the hall, unless they absented themselves, and he stated that this was an error; that General Ruger had not directed any such notice to be given, though it was probable that Governor Chamberlain had sent such notice.—As to the organization of the two houses, the President, after a conversation of some length, laid down this proposition.—That neither house had a quorum for the transaction of business, and was therefore, not properly constituted; That it required sixty-three members to make a quorum; That, the Republican house had fifty-nine members with certificates, and that the Democratic house had fifty-six members with certificates; That in case he should be called upon, as he might be, to recognize one or other of the houses; he should not recognize either, unless it had sixty-three members holding the original certificates of election, I called his attention to the fact that four members holding these original certificates of election, had been unseated by the Republican house, and other persons, having no certificates of election, had been put in their place, The President thought that this could not be the case, and I promised to inquire, and let him know the fact.—I have since inquired, and am told positively, that the four members from Barnwell, having regular certificates, have thus been unseated by the Republican house.—The President said if this was so, it could not be justified.—Then, coming to the Presidential question, he said he thought he had sufficient information to justify him in forming a judgment as to the situation, and he repeated a remark previously made, that he did not think any man could afford to take the place of President, unless the general judgment concurred in the belief that he was fairly elected; That so far as South-Carolina was concerned, he believed that the state had gone, on the face of the returns, for Hayes & Wheeler, throwing out entirely the counties of Edgefield and Laurens; that in these counties there had been really no election; that they had been overridden by companies of armed men from Georgia, and that the black population had been deterred from voting, and although he, the President, had nothing officially to do with the matter, as it was confined to the returning board alone, he thought that these counties had been properly thrown out, and that the state of South-Carolina should justly be counted for Hayes & Wheeler.—As to Florida, he said that the result was very close, but that on the face of the returns, he believed that Hayes & Wheeler had a majority of about forty, and that this was independent of the question of frauds, which, if allowed a fair weight, would probably increase the majority, as he was credibly informed.—I asked him from whom he got his information, and he said from Mr. Kasson, who had gone South at his request.—Up to this point, the President had enjoined no confidence, but coming to Louisiana, he remarked that what he should say to me must be in confidence.—He said that on the face of the returns, Tilden & Hendricks unquestionably had a majority of six to eight thousand votes: That there were six parishes in which there had been intimidation to such an extent, that he did not think there had been a fair election, and that they had to be thrown out; That he believed that when thrown out, there was still a majority for Tilden & Hendricks, to which I remarked that it was somewheres about two thousand,—and that this majority could only be overcome by assuming that the votes of five thousand naturalized citizens of New-Orleans were all Democratic, and that by throwing them out on account of some defect in the naturalization papers.— The President remarked that the returning-board in Louisiana was in very bad odor with the public; that the people had no confidence in it, and even if it did right, it would not be credited with honest intentions.—He believed that there had been no honest election in Louisiana since Slidell got control of its politics.—I suggested to him that, as a matter of fact, it was not possible to have a fair election in that state, and that it was a most serious blow to Republican government, that a state in which a fair election could not be had, should decide a Presidential contest.—The President replied that this was true, and that it would not be unreasonable that the vote of Louisiana should be thrown out, as it was in 1872, on account of irregularities of election, and the peculiar functions of the returning-board.—I remarked that this would give the election to Tilden; that he would then have a clear majority of all the electors appointed.—He said, 'no'; that it had been held in Lincoln's time that the President must have a majority of all the votes to which the states are legally entitled.—I replied that it had been so asserted, but that no tribunal had ever considered the question. The President answered 'certainly not, because Lincoln had the necessary majority.'—Whereupon I remarked that if a majority had belonged to the states in rebellion, it would not be held that the loyal states should go without a President, and he said; 'certainly not, they would have to do the best they could.'—However, assuming that Louisiana were thrown out, and that it was still necessary to have one hundred and eighty-five votes, this would throw the election into the House, who would then elect the President, and the Senate would elect the Vice President, which was one solution of the problem.—However, he said he did not expect there would be any serious trouble; that a solution would be reached, that would, in the main, be satisfactory to the people; That if one of the doubtful states should cast all or any part of its votes for Tilden, that would settle the question.—He would be inaugurated as quietly as he, General Grant, had been.—It was not, however, for him to decide the question, but it was the duty of Congress under the Constitution: That his duty would be to see that their decision was carried into effect.—I asked the President whether in the event of the two houses getting into conflict, and coming to blows, he would feel it his duty to use the military force of the Goverment to restore order.—To which he replied; 'certainly not,' but that if either side should call up an armed force or a mob, to its support, he would feel bound to protect the public property from its attack, and to repel them from the Capitol,—In conclusion, he said that his great desire was to retire from office with the country at peace, and generally satisfied with the conclusion which might be arrived at; and that he thought it rather hard that any one should suspect him, who had given his best years to preserve the country, of any design upon its liberties.—I assured the President of the great gratification I experienced in hearing such sentiments expressed; That I was confirmed in my faith in his patriotism, and that it should not be long before the whole country, and both parties, would do him and his motives full justice.—I omitted to say, in the proper place above, that, speaking of the Presidential election, the President said that it was a matter of substance, and not of technicalities; That any attempt to appropriate a vote in Vermont, or Rhode Island or Oregon, which had given a Republican majority, would be regarded only as a trick, just as any attempt to get a vote of Louisiana by fraud would be regarded as indefensible.—I assured the President that I heartily concurred in this view, and that if a vote from Oregon was really certified to the Democrats, I did not believe that any other use would be made of it than to get a fair hearing in the case of the other states, which, in the judgment of the Democratic party, might be improperly certified to Hayes; That neither Governor Tilden or his friends desired to have him succeed to the Presidency unless he had been honestly elected, and that in the event of there being so much doubt in regard to the real result, as to make it difficult for fair-minded men to say who was elected, I felt justified in saying that Governor Tilden and his friends, would cheerfully assent to a new election; That while he and they felt that they had a duty to perform, that they were not disposed to press an extreme issue in the face of a reasonable doubt. Incidentally, I mentioned to the President that the House would probably appoint committees to investigate and report upon the facts developed in the elections of South-Carolina, Florida and Louisiana.—He replied that he expected that they would do so, and thought it very proper, and that it would be a very desirable thing to get reports from committees properly constituted.—Incidentally, the President said that Mr. Anderson, on the Louisiana returning board, was a brother of Major Robert Anderson of Fort Sumter fame, and of Lars Anderson of Cincinnatti; He must, therefore, be an honest man, and that he would be inclined to believe any certificate he might sign, and to discredit any certificate he did not sign.—I since learn that the gentleman is not a brother of the gentleman named.—" D, Columbia University, New York, N. Y. On Dec. 5, Secretary of State Hamilton Fish recorded in his diary a cabinet discussion of Hewitt's memorandum. ". . . The President thinks that in the main Hewett has fairly recorded the Conversation although in some points the statement needs correction. A part of the conversation including that with regard to the Louisianna election was under confidence. . . ." DLC-Hamilton Fish.

On the night of Dec. 6, Hewitt and U.S. Senator Theodore F. Randolph of N. J., both

Democrats, visited the White House to discuss the situation in S. C. "All are reticent as to what occurred, but it is certain that the President departed from his habitual reserve, and gave his visitors what might be called 'a piece of his mind.' He talked in a manner exceedingly vigorous and pointed in regard to the present situation and on the efforts of the Democrats to capture the Government, and was not at all solicitous of the feelings of his listeners. Wade Hampton's dispatch was an assurance that if the United States troops were withdrawn there would be no trouble. The President in hearing it read is understood to have retorted with tremendous earnestness that the rifle clubs in Columbia indicated the character of the peace that would prevail if the troops were withdrawn, and that they would not be withdrawn until assurances were received from proper authorities that they were no longer needed. Mr. Hewitt says that Gen. Grant spoke for nearly an hour. The President himself told a Republican Congressman this morning that he made the longest speech he had ever made in his life. . . ." *New York Tribune*, Dec. 8, 1876. See *ibid.*, Dec. 11, 1876; *CR*, 46–1, 542–43. On Dec. 9, John A. Durkee, New York City, wrote to USG. "Having Read in yestardays Tribune the account of Hewitts visit to you The Writer said that you gave him 'a piece of your *mind*' my heart felt much gratitude to *you* for so doing. The people Sir will Honor and love you for sustaining Govr chamberlain in his trying *ordeal*, and now It having been declared that Gov Hayes has a majority of the Electoral votes for Presdt The people Will depend upon *you Sir* to see that at the proper time he is inaugurated If necissary at the point of the Bayonett I suppose you get all necissary Encouragement from men of prominence. but I thought you might not hear much from men like me down among the commoners. I have worked for the Republican party Since Its organization believing Its principles the best for the country. Having been unfortunate in recent years I besought my former friends Hon Geo. W. McCrary of Iowa and Register John Allison to assist me to place under Govt but they have not been able to do anything for me yet." ALS, USG 3.

On Dec. 11, E. J. More, Allentown, Pa., wrote to USG. "I desire to thank you for the words which you have spoken to Mr Hewit, as published in todays paper. I am one of those who in 1872 fell away from you, and though I have frequently regretted having done so, I never did more so than today. Feel assured that this country is with you, in the course you are pursuing. I am taking perhaps an unwarrantable liberty in addressing you, but you are the Chief Magistrate of my country, and I want to say to you that so far as my observation goes, thousands stand up and call you blessed, and say all honor to President Grant." ALS, *ibid.*

1. See following Memorandum.

Memorandum

————

[*Dec. 6, 1876*]

In South Carolina a condition of affairs exist that threaten a "new rebellion," apparently designedly so. There is a Governor in the state who was elected, and installed, legally beyond any controversy, or claim to the contrary. His term of office has not yet expired, nor is it

claimed that it has. An election has been held to elect his successor—
with all other elective state officers, Congressmen and presidential
electors—and by ~~const~~ the state laws, constitutionally enacted, he
remains Govr until the legislature meets, organizes and canvasses
the vote for Govr and other officers. The legal board of canvassers
have given certificates to one hundred and sixteen of the candidates
for the lower house of the legislature, and refused certificates to
all the candidates of two counties—Edgefield & Lawrens—on the
ground of fraud, intimidation &c. preventing a fair expression of
~~their~~ the will of the legal voters of those counties. In the assembling
of the legislature chosen candidates from the excluded counties
claimed the right to meet as a part of the legislature to organize,—
and to determine upon their own right to seats among other duties—which was resisted to the extent of excluding them. The Clerk
of the old house, the legal and constitutional officer to swear in and
admit the new house, decided, as it was his right and duty to do, that
members about whos claims to seats there was a dispute should not
be seated until the legislature, composed entirely of members about
whos right to seats there was no question, had met, organized and
determined the claims of contestants. Under these circumstances—
there being sixty republicans and fiftysix democrats holding recognized certificates—the democrats withdrew, admitted the eight
excluded democrats, and proceeded to organize. The republicans
having sixty out of a possible one hundred & twenty four, assumed
that they were a majority of the house because of these eight vacancies. The Governor has recognized the act of this branch of the legislature and of the legality of the Senate about which there seems
to be no dispute. In opposition to this organization there is the
claimant to ~~new Guber~~ the Governorship, backed by other influences—behind all those influences which made the result in the
state doubtful. Should they withdraw these doubtful members and
permit the organization of the house without them, there would be
no further contest. If Hampton has a majority of the votes of the
state—so determined by the legislature—he would be installed.
Chamberlain would receive the same consideration. The democratic
plan proposes a compromise which recognizes no chance for the re-

publican party to remain in controll no matter what the result. The republican plan proposes to determine the actual result of the election and to give the victors the benefit of success.

ADf, USG 3. See preceding letter.

On Dec. 6, 1876, Secretary of the Interior Zachariah Chandler telegraphed to USG. "Telegrams received announce the electoral vote of South Carolina Illinois & Wisconsin cast solid for Hayes and Wheeler" Telegram received, DNA, RG 107, Telegrams Collected (Bound).

To Col. Thomas H. Ruger

Washington, D. C. Dec. 7th *1876*

To GEN. RUGER, COLUMBIA, S. C.

Do not recognize in any manner any person as Governor of South Carolina other than D. H. Chamberlain until you hear further from me.

It is understood that there are armed bodies of men in Columbia, probably a part of those who were commanded by proclamation to disband, threatening the peace of the present authorities. Is this so?

U. S. GRANT

Copy (telegram sent), OFH. On Dec. 7, 1876, Col. Thomas H. Ruger, Columbia, S. C., telegraphed twice and wrote to USG. "The Supreme Court of the State decided yesterday in the matter of the Speaker of the Mackey House, recognized by Governor Chamberlain that the Wallace house is the Constitutional house. The Wallace house now claims Sixty three members holding the original Certificates of the Secretary of State. No other change since Canvass of votes by the Senate and the House. recognized by Govr Chamberlain." "Knew I have no authority, have not thought of so doing & have neither said nor done anything that could be so construed. Much excitement for few days & quite large number of men in place some attending state fair but most Came on account of political Situation. greater part have gone. No doubt Members of rifle clubs Came did not appear on st as organization or armed. Have learned that arms were brought into city. No open demonstration has been made against state authorities threatening talk by individuals on street & about hotels. will send letter more in detail" "I have the honor to say in addition to my statement by telegraph of this date, as to reports that armed bodies of men are here, probably a part of those who were commanded by Proclamation to disband, threatening the peace of the present authorities' that, for the past few days there have been quite a large number of men here, not residents of the city, who for the greater part, have left. The State Fair opened on the 6th and some, no doubt came to attend that but the greater part I think because of the political situation, and particularly because of the expected attempt by the State constabulary to remove certain persons, Democrats, claiming right to seats, from the Hall of the House of Representatives. How many of these men belonged to the 'Rifle clubs' I do not know, quite a number probably and as I have no doubt, but the greater part I think did not. No Clubs have appeared on the Streets as orgaisizations or armed, No demonstration has been made by any apparent organization, or any open demonstrations against the State Authorities. There has been talk of a threatening character by individuals about the streets and hotels. Many probably most of the men had pistols, which however is a common custom in the State, or sonearly so. I have learned that some arms were brought into the city but how many or whether belonging to members of Rifle clubs or others I have not been able to learn. My opinion is that most of these men came for the purpose of resisting the action of the State Constabulary or else under a belief that a riot would occur. The rumor as to the action of the Constabulary produced great excitement in the State. Whatever may have been the purpose, the special occasion passed and no disturbance took place. The presence of the troops and the knowledge that they would be used if necessary has had a controlling influence for the preservation of the peace; and there is a general intention I think to avoid collision in any way with them." Telegrams received and ALS, *ibid.* See Hamilton Fish diary, Dec. 8, 1876, DLC-Hamilton Fish; "President Grant's Use of the Troops," *The Nation,* XXIII, 597 (Dec. 7, 1876), 337–38.

Also on Dec. 7, "Detective," Charleston, S. C., wrote to USG. "All goverments do or should protect their loyal citizens therefore if the Howling Mobs, Ku Klux, & crowds & Robbers cannot be made to retire when night comes I say there should be put on (2000) Two Thousand extra policemen with 16 shooter Rifles to fire length-Wise the streets if necessary & not so as to endanger the lives of Woman & children. . . . I say soldiers should be placed here with extra policemen and at every place of any importance in the state, every care possible should be taken to prevent something We are not ready for that is a negro massacre of the whites, knowing they are largely in the majority in this state & I believe would soon whip the fight if arristocracy did not receive help from other states & foreigners & if this should take place it would be the end of the negro, in my opinion & what I can hear the negro plan is not a fair fight but take the bush burn & kill the white race as they come, . . ." L, DNA, RG 60, Letters from the President.

On the same day, Mason H. Abbey, Hillsdale, Mich., wrote to USG. "For myself, & the great body of the Clery of the North, I wish to express to you our profound sense of gratitude for your recent Military Orders. On the whole we have indorsed your Administration as one of impatial justice; but these Orders are its crowning glory. We are not technically politicians; still it may not be arrogant in us to say that no class of men are better posted in current events, & we believe that events that have transpired in the South have justified your course. . . ." ALS, USG 3.

On Dec. 15, W. W. Heath, Edgefield Court House, S. C., wrote to USG. "I congratulate you, as the President of this great nation,—I send you a thousand thanks for the stand you have taken, for the down trodden Colored people of this State, and for the Republican cause here, had it not been for the presence of the United States Soldiers here during the present election, not a Republican would have dared to have said their souls were their own, The Democratic Clubs would have cut to the right, and left, and any man *white* or colored who would have dared to cheer Hayes and Wheeler, would have had his head taken off. There has been fraud enough committed in Edgefield County alone to damn the whole State, I am on the Republican ticket for Probate Judge of Edgefield County, and the only white Republican in the County, and I have been warned, not to take the Office, should I get a certificate of election, But I shall pay no heed to their threats, but shall enter at once on my duties as Probate Judge when I receive my commission, Again I say a thousand cheers for the President of these United States . . . I must say a few words more about the election, in South Carolina, and what I say is Gods truth, If there had been a fair election, on the 7th November last, Chamberlain, and Hayes, and Wheeler, would have carried the

State, by *20000*, majority at least, and to hear Wade Hampton talk about his getting 75000, of the white votes and *17000* of the Colored votes, is all the meerrest bosh and he well knows it too, as well as any *man* in South Carolina. Mr President you need no person to dictate to you what to do in the premises,   But I must say stick to the Hon D H Chamberlain, and the poor people of the State both white and Colored   God Bless you Mr President" ALS (misdated 1877), *ibid.*

On Dec. 18 and 19, Henry L. Newfville, Jr., wrote to USG. "I' am a poor Laboring colored man with a family & with out children, Expect Soon to have. I' am compelled, to work for the Enemies of my welfare, and progress—I' have always voted and done Every thing in my power, to forward the cause of Republicanism. the past Election, I' were told by the agent of my Employers, that unless, I'—and the Rest of us voted, for Hampton, that we would be—discharged. I' did not do as was Requested, and the day after the Election, I' went to work, all of the white Employees, together with the agent, were pointing out who voted, for hampton, and who did not. they done their best to make me Quit. I' would not. Every merchant, and factor had for Sworn to Employ those that did vote for hampton and them only, Spies—were sent to Every precinct to watch how we voted.—and Report the Same, Since that time I' have been placed on the parlor car as porter, a position in which I' have filled with Satisfaction the past. year: until now: I' am brow beaten Every opportunity. the conductors or Engineers has about my polotics. I' am almost afraid. to Run on the Car. armed Bodies of men—do congregate at Every station along the Line of the Road,—Huzzahing for hampton, and Damnation to Every Negro, Grant, chamberlain and Company—for God Sake, General, Help Help me, to Come out of this Country of assassins. . . . From florence to Charleston in, the dead hours of night, any Quantity of Klu Kluxes, from there to Kingstree. they openly declare their intention. Help us—for God Sake," ". . . I' am a citizen and a Native of Charleston So Ca. Were born free, but my freedom was not worth a fig. until. Mr Lincolns Proclamation were passed and Ratified. . . . there is to my certain and positive knowledge, a Conspiracy in the State of So. Ca. to kill Every Colored & white man that do not assist, in denounceing—your self—and the Republicans—Generally a conductor on the N. E. R. R. Pass-Train, E. G. Cain, by name, told me. Last week. that so soon as Hampton, occupied the Gubernatorial chair and the troops—were Removed that they intended to give Whittimoore, Chamberlain and the Damn Negro thieves Hell. I' am in great dread. Dear General, for God Sake do all you Can, to prevent, the Lion Democrats—from Anhilliateing us—put the State in Martial Law. Rather than we Killed for our Political Principles. . . . I' were at 3—different times, teacher of public Schools—My Salary was Very Good but Seldom paid, caused my wife, and I' to Seperate. Well to obtain her favor, I' Gave up Teaching—and Return to work on the Rail Road, . . . Space for bids further mention of the out Rages we now Endure I' observed a burial casket. shortly after the Election filled, I' think with arms, consigned to Edgefield, from New York—I' am certain there must have been arms—as four of us— Could Scarce Lift it. marked in Small Stencils from Burial case Depot, from New York, and any Quantity of Gun powder—. . . ." ALS, DNA, RG 60, Letters from the President.

On Dec. 29, Thomas J. Jones, Benjamin Durham, and William Jenkins, Plain, S. C., petitioned USG. "Whereas information have reached us from his Excellency ~~the~~ Ulysses. S. Grant President of the U. States of America to kno[w] whether or not that we desire to be seperated from the white people of the South or not Whereas we have tried to live in peace and harmony with the white people of South Carolina before and since the rebellion and we find it impossible to live together any longer under the scorging whippings, murderings, and many other things which we have been made to groan under. Many of us have suffered martyrdom for the republican cause and we earnestly solicit you to help us to obtain relief. Many a weeping mother and a fatherless child are at this time without a home or a morsel of bread to eat save those who (havent) the sympathy and generosity to divide the last morsel of bread that they possess: those who have been fortunate enough among the colored people to have a few bushels of corn left them We deem it absolutly essential that there shold be immediate steps taken to bring the matter to a close. We have heared that it have been reported by the the democratic party that we the colord people of South Carolina dont desire to be seperated. We hereby denounce it to be a malicous falshood in every particular And that we hereby certify that this letter gives the true senti ments of the republican party of Austin and Fair View Townships Greenville County South Carolina. And if our names are needed or if there is a vote to be cast we are ready to give our names or cast our votes . . . We are ready to cast our votes in Favor of a seperation. Peace and, harmony will never come among us until every man woman and child is allowed to sit under their own vine and fig tree and none to molest or make afread. We would be glad for you to return us an answer as soon as practicibl" DS, *ibid.*

On Feb. 1, 1877, Governor Daniel H. Chamberlain of S. C. wrote to USG. "*Personal* . . . A few kind words spoken of me by you, as reported in the N. Y. *Tribune* of Jan 30, leads me to say, what I hope you have believed before, that I fully appreciate and approve your careful and prudent course towards me and our party here in our present troubles. While these troubles involve more personal sacrifice and danger than any one knows who is not here, I do not allow myself to think that greater interests must be imperilled in order to aid us. I would give almost anything to be relieved of my position here, but I must hold on till the Presidential question is settled, and then I trust our fate will soon be settled. In any event, or whatever the result, I wish you to know that I could not have received better treatment or juster consideration than you have given me in all these troubles of the last five months." ALS, USG 3. On Jan. 29, a correspondent had reported USG's views on the S. C. political situation and his opinion that Chamberlain was "a man of superior education, ability, and purity of character." *New York Tribune*, Jan. 30, 1877. See Chamberlain, "Reconstruction in South Carolina," *Atlantic Monthly*, LXXXVII, DXXII (April, 1901), 473–84; Edward L. Wells, *Hampton and Reconstruction* (Columbia, S. C., 1907), pp. 148–88; Alfred B. Williams, *Hampton and His Red Shirts: South Carolina's Deliverance in 1876* (1935; reprinted, Freeport, N. Y., 1970), pp. 375–441.

On Feb. 15, Chamberlain again wrote to USG. "I feel constrained to call your attention to a matter affecting the public peace and order of this state. On the 7th of October last I issued my proclamation as Governor ordering the 'Rifle Clubs' of this state,—illegal organizations existing for unlawful purposes,—to disband and cease to exist. On the 17th of the same month you as President issued your proclamation ordering the same Clubs to disband and retire to their homes and 'hereafter abandon such organizations' &C. The Rifle Clubs have never done more than yield an outward obedience to these proclamations, and have remained as fully organized as before. Now, however, Wade Hampton has undertaken to Commission the officers of some of these clubs, especially here in Columbia, and a public parade of such clubs is announced to take place in Columbia on the 22d inst. Such action is plainly in bold defiance of your proclamation, as well as mine, and a menace to the public peace of this state. I have in all possible ways sought to avoid any occasion for asking federal intervention here pending the settlement of the Presidential Election, and to preserve the *status quo* as far as possible, but I do not feel that I should be doing my official duty if I failed to inform you of this action on the part of Wade Hampton and the 'Rifle Clubs.' I have no powers to enforce any orders in this matter, and whatever is done must be done by you, through the military officers here. My judgment is that a peremptory order should be given forbidding the parade of these Clubs on the 22d inst., or on any other day and that the military officers in command should be instructed to enforce it." L (press), South Carolina Archives, Columbia, S. C. See Fish diary, Feb. 20, 1877, DLC-Hamilton

Fish. On Feb. 21, John C. Winsmith, Spartanburg, S. C., wrote to USG. "I would respectfully call the attention of Your Excellency to the fact that Hampton is organizing 'Rifle
Clubs' all over South Carolina. Your proclamation ordering the revolutionary Clubs to disband has been treated with contempt, and anarchy now prevails in South Carolina. Hampton organized the Ku Klux in 1868 and 1869, and set on foot the movement to collect funds
to defend those tried in the U. S. Courts. Long impunity has emboldened him in crime, and
now he not only openly sets at defiance the President's Proclamation, but he is collecting
the money to equip his military force. His object is to set himself and Butler and Gary and
other conspirators and murderers in command of the State of South Carolina. Will the National Government allow these murderers to carry out their hellish purposes? The Republican Party is not *organized for murder*, and hence such scoundrels as Hampton, Butler
and others have concluded they can accomplish all their purposes. Though I respectfully
suggested to you, years ago, that under your proclamation of martial law over the upper
counties of S. C., General Sheridan should be sent here, and ordered to try *these leaders*
by Military commission, yet as that was not considered proper, I do trust your Excellency,
in the closing of your Administration, will summarily arrest the course of these bandits
to whom I have referred. If the murderers in S. C. and La. are not *now* checked the *War*
will have been a failure and *Reconstruction* worse than folly. May Heaven bless you." ALS,
DNA, RG 60, Letters from the President. See *PUSG*, 25, 339–41; *Washington Evening Star*,
Feb. 26, 1877.
    On Feb. 18, a correspondent had reported from Washington, D. C. ". . . In speaking
of the political status of South Carolina and Louisiana, the President said that the cases
were very dissimilar and could hardly be treated under one general line of action. In South
Carolina the contest had assumed such a phase that the whole army of the United States
would be inadequate to enforce the authority of Gov. Chamberlain. The people of that State
had resolved not to resort to violence, but adopted a mode of resistance much more formidable and effective than armed demonstration. They have refused to pay their State
taxes to Gov. Chamberlain, and it would be useless to sell out their property, as no one
would buy it. Unless Gov. Chamberlain could compel the collection of taxes it would be
utterly useless for him to expect to maintain his authority for any length of time. This
state of affairs must inevitably result in the abandonment of all efforts by Gov. Chamberlain to maintain himself in the exercise of the gubernatorial functions of the State of South
Carolina. . . ." *New York Tribune*, Feb. 19, 1877.

To *Abel R. Corbin*

————

Dec. 13th /76

MY DEAR MR. CORBIN:

    I wish you and Jennie would come down and make us a visit. We
now have room, and will have until Fred. returns with his *extensive
family*, which will probably be a few days before Christmas.—Some
time before my term of office expires I want mother to make us a
visit. If she would like to come down during the holidays we would
make room by sending one of the boys out o'nights. The children

will all be at home during that week; possibly the last time we will have them all at home together. At all events it may be the last opportunity mother may have of seeing them together.

I rec'd your kind letter of the 11th this a. m. This year, owing to election excitement, department reports only come in a few days before the meeting of Congress. When they did come the situation in South Carolina was so critical that dispatches were coming to me, or to members of my cabinet, and brought from them to me, in such rapid succession that I do not think I had one single half hour—without interruption—all the time I was preparing my message. I am sure I did not have four hours in its preparation all told, exclusive of the time consumed in reading the departmental reports. I left out necessarily topics I should liked to have talked about, but would not mention without being sure I was right.

Yours Truly
U. S. GRANT

My love to all.

ALS, NNP.

To Senate

To the ~~Senate of~~ United States Senate.

In ~~obedience~~ answer to the resolution of the Senate of the 6th of Dec. "requesting information whether troops of the United States were stationed at the city of Petersburg, in the State of Virginia, on the 7th of Nov. 1876, and if so, under what authority, and for what purpose," ~~I submit the following report of the General of the Army, with all the papers accompanying said report~~. I submit the enclosed letter from the Sec. of War—to whom the Senate resolution was referred—to-gether with the report of the General of the Army, and accompanying papers. These enclosures will give all the information called for by the resolution, and I confidantly believe will justify the action taken.—It is well understood that the presence of United States troops, at polling places, never prevented the free exercise of the franchise by any citizen, of whatever political faith. If then they

have had any effect whatever upon the ballot cast, it has been to insure protection to the ~~elector~~ [citizen] casting it in giving it to the
candidate of his unbiassed choise, without fear and thus securing the
very ese[s]ence of liberty. It may be the presence of [24] United
States Soldiers, under [the comd of Capt &] a Lieut. ~~in the Army~~,
quartered in the Custom House ~~of~~ [at] Petersburg, Va on the 7th of
Nov. at a considerable distance from any polling place, without any
interference in their part whatever, and without going near the polls
during the election, *may have secured a different result* from *what would
have been obtained if they had not been there*—to maintain the peace in
case of riot—~~but if~~ *on the face of the returns.* But if such is the case it
is only proof that in this one Congressional district, in the State of
Va the legal and constitutional voters have ~~had~~ been able to return,
as elected, the candidates of their choice.

[U. S. G.

Ex Man
Dec 14, 76]

ADf (bracketed material in another hand), ViU. *SED*, 44-2-5. On Dec. 14, 1876, Secretary
of War James D. Cameron wrote to USG. "In reply to the note of your Secretary just received, I beg leave to inform you that the troops sent to Petersburg were Foot Battery "B"
2d Artillery Capt. Joseph C. Breckenridge, 1st Lt. R. G. Howell and (24) twenty four enlisted men. Capt. Breckenridge's Report and all the correspondence on the subject appear
among the documents which I am having prepared in response to your note of 9th inst. I
hope to send these papers to you this afternoon" Copy, DNA, RG 107, Letters Sent, Military Affairs. See *ibid.*, RG 94, Letters Received, 4788 1876.

On Nov. 3, Benjamin W. Hoxsey, asst. U.S. attorney, Richmond, had written to Attorney Gen. Alphonso Taft. "Mr Joseph Jorgenson Republican candidate for Congress for
the 4th District of Va. will call upon you with this letter & will ask that you advise the
President to direct the Judge, Marshall & District Attorney to attend at Petersburg on
Election day under Sec 1988. of the Rev Statutes—I am of opinion that the measure is a
wise one and that the President has, or will have after seeing Dr Jorgenson, abundant reason to beleive that offences are likely to be committed against the provisions of Chapter 7
of Tittle Crimes, at Petersburg. From what I can learn I judge that it is intended to arrest
the supervisors and that during their absence the ballot boxes are to be stuffed. We should
be prepared to arrest under Sec 5522 any person who interferes with the supervisors. I beg
of you, referring to our conversation yesterday, to send us if possible the Company at Old
Point or even a detachment of it if not more than 30 men—I do not beleive that if the Pres't
should make the order above requested that those who are likely to make the trouble
will do so if the U. S. Officers are supported by troops—otherwise I fear much fraud and
violence—" ALS, *ibid.*, RG 60, Letters from the President. On Nov. 4, USG endorsed this
letter. "Let an order be prepared addressed to Judge Hugh L. Bond, C. P. Ramsdell, Marshall, & L. L. Lewis, atty., directing them to attend at Petersburg, Va., Nov. 6th 7 & [8] &
[9]th /76 for the purpose named in the provisions of the law within referred to." ES, *ibid.*

On the same day, USG signed such an order to Judge Robert W. Hughes, Eastern District, Va. DS, College of William and Mary, Williamsburg, Va. Voters in the 4th Congressional District of Va. elected Joseph Jorgenson. See *PUSG*, 24, 371.

On June 11, 1874, Samuel B. Paul, Petersburg, had written to USG. "Twelve Citizens of Petersburg Judges of a late Election which was purely municipal are arrested this morning by united States marshalls and are to be Carried to Richmond instead of being taken before the Commissioner here where they can give ample bail Great Excitement exists and this people would feel grateful to have the executive intervene to prevent Citizens from being taken from their homes The universal belief is that the prosecution is partisan and without foundation and all ask you for Justice," Telegram received (at 2:00 P.M.), DNA, RG 60, Letters from the President. Appended to this telegram is one from George F. Doggett, "Late Republican Candidate for Commonwealth Atty in Petersburg." "I know of no reason why this prosecution should be instituted and certainly none why these citizens should be carried to Richmond there being a u, S. Commissioner here," *Ibid.* On the same day, Charles P. Ramsdell, U.S. marshal, Richmond, telegraphed to Attorney Gen. George H. Williams. "Writs issued by Commissioner pleasants directing me to bring prisoners before him at Richmond" Telegram received (at 7:00 P.M.), *ibid.* Also on June 11, Rosen G. Greene, postmaster, Petersburg, wrote to Postmaster Gen. John A. J. Creswell. "I have the honor to report that owing to a great political excitement that now exists here I am in great danger of personal violence and obstruction in the discharge of my duties as Postmaster . . . The immediate cause of the excitement is the arrest of certain Judges of Election by the U. S. Marshall for violations of the Enforcement Act and every U. S. Officer in the city is freely threatened and in danger. . . . Men armed with concealed weapons are marching about the streets and in the vicinity of this office. The Mayor of the city does not feel that he can depend upon his police force in this emergency if a riot should take place, and as this is a U. S. Government Affair he thinks the government should send a military force. . . ." ALS, *ibid.* USG had earlier written. "Reappoint Rosen G. Greene postmaster of ~~Richmond~~ Va [Petersburg, Va]" AN (undated, bracketed material not in USG's hand), Wayde Chrismer, Bel Air, Md.

On June 12, U.S. Representative J. Ambler Smith of Va. and five others telegraphed to USG from the capitol. "We the undersigned representatives in Congress from Va. respectfully ask that you will not order soldiers to Petersburg, we believe that under the able men now marshall & district attorney the laws of our country will be enforced and if any one has committed an offence he will be punished. Ordering U. S. Soldiers there at this time will in our opinion ~~will~~ injure our state and do no earthly good With sentiments of high regard, . . ." Telegram received, DLC-USG, IB. On the same day, a correspondent reported from Petersburg. ". . . For the first time since the war the Conservative Party have succeeded in getting control of the city government. The city election held on the 28th ult. resulted in a Conservative triumph. When it is known that the Radicals have a clear majority on an honest count of at least 700, and in one instance the Republican ticket was elected by over one thousand majority, it may be imagined how its defeat was effected on this occasion. Of course the Republican Party is made up largely of the colored element, and, as might be expected, the Conservatives used every available means to deprive the colored men of their rights of citizenship. Ballot-box stuffing, false returns, the refusal of colored men's votes on the slightest pretexts, intimidation, threats, and even personal violence—all of these, and more, were used on election day to carry the Conservative ticket. The election laws, both State and Federal, are only obeyed as a matter of convenience, or when it best suits the purpose of the Conservatives. . . . In consequence of these frauds, which the Republicans very justly considered an infamous outrage upon their rights, twelve warrants were issued yesterday by United States Commissioner Pleasants, of Richmond, for the arrest of twelve of the election judges on charges preferred by voters who had been denied their right. Ten of the twelve was arrested by Deputy United States Marshals Coldwell and Burke yesterday afternoon without serious difficulty, and were immediately taken before United States Commissioner Waterman, of this city, who, by order of Commissioner Pleasants, bailed them in the sum of $1,500 each to appear at Richmond today. Of the two who were not arrested, one had fled the town and the other was away on business. When it became generally known that arrests were being made yesterday, the wildest excitement prevailed, . . . The most bitter Conservatives are bent upon spilling blood, and nothing but the fear of a higher power—the United States Government— deters them. . . ." *New York Times,* June 21, 1874. On June 13, a correspondent reported from Washington, D. C., on Petersburg. ". . . Owing to statements to Representatives Platt and Stowell of Virginia, they yesterday made application to the President to send troops there to preserve the peace. Judge Harris, Representative from Virginia, called on the President to-day for the purpose of protesting in the name of the people against military interference in that State, and to assure him that as good order prevailed in Petersburg as in any other city of the Union. But the President being absent from the city, he went to the office of the Attorney General, who furnished him with a copy of a telegram addressed by Attorney General Williams to United States Marshal Ramsdell, Petersburg, as follows: 'You are instructed to take the necessary steps to protect the property of the United States from injury and the officers of the Government in Petersburg from any violent interference with them in the performance of their official duties, and to that end, if you think proper, you may summon a posse of the citizens to aid you, but if these men are found inadequate for the purpose, you will be furnished upon a call made by you upon me with troops from Fortress Monroe. It is desirable not to use troops if possible.'" *Ibid.,* June 14, 1874.

On June 17, Governor James L. Kemper of Va. wrote to USG. "With respectful deference, I invoke your attention to the instructions very recently delivered by the Attorney General of the United States to the Marshal of the eastern District of Virginia, in relation to alleged disorders in Petersburg. I cannot suppose that those instructions were issued either with your approval or your cognizance. They appear to have been dispatched directly from the Department of Justice to an inferior officer of a Federal District Court in Virginia, but without communication with any of the authorities of this State; and in directing that officer to resist the alleged disorders, they assure him that, upon his requisition, a military force of the United States would be forwarded to his assistance. They assume that disorders existed in Petersburg, although no breach of the peace or disturbance whatever had in fact occurred or been attempted or threatened or was likely to arise in that city. They completely ignored the existance of this Commonwealth and its constituted authorities; or, at the least, they assume that the Government of Virginia is unable or unwilling to maintain the peace within the just jurisdiction of the State. They imply that a federal department may exercise immediate and discretionary control, within this State, over vital interests which are distinctively local and domestic. They empower a subordinate ministerial agent of the general government, at its discretion, to subject a peaceful community together with all its authorities to the domination of an armed federal force. Such instructions if carried into execution, wrest from the people the right of self-government and convert the State itself into a province or a military division of a central and virtually imperial power. They erect the dominion of the federal sword, in time of peace, over the civil authority of the State. It was but a few days before the date of these instructions, that other wrongs were inflicted by federal authority upon citizens of Petersburg.—Certain Judges of a local election were charged with rejecting legal votes—an offence at all times cognizable and punishable by the State tribunals by virtue of State laws, due evidence of the offence being shewn either on the complaint of any person aggrived or without such complaint. These causes were not permitted to be heard by a State Court, nor yet by the appointed federal authority located for such investigations at Petersburg—the residence of all the parties and their witnesses; but the accused were forced under arrest to Richmond and here tried by a United States Commissioner who, although as is confidently believed no probable cause was shewn, held the parties for indictment and trial in a federal court, and in so doing he announced the monstrous doctrine that in such case it devolved upon the accused to prove their own innocence. If it be claimed that the exercise of such arbitrary and despotic powers, in time of peace, is permitted by the letter of the federal statute, commonly known as the enforcement act—a statute which sprung from the exigencies and passions resulting from war, and the provisions of which are abhorrent to all the traditions of free government and to the principles of all its founders—let it suffice to answer that the violent remedies sought to be provided by that act were never intended to be employed within a State, except to repress actual and serious infractions of law and order, and then only in case the authorities of the State should fail efficiently to meet the emergency. Desiring to cultivate peaceful, beneficial and cordial relations with the common government and with each of its departments: cheerfully yielding to that government the full measure of its delegated authorities: I oppose with all the constitutional means at my command these acts of invasion of the rights of the States and the liberties of the people. I affirm the inalienable right of this Commonwealth to self-government, its authority to rule its internal and municipal affairs—in accordance with supreme organic law and without undue restraint or hinderance from any power whatever: I point to the yet recent past for proof that this government has the capacity and the will to protect personal right and to enforce Justice, order and law: and I solemnly protest against the late action of the Attorney General of the United States as a flagrant wrong and indignity to State authority, as subversive of the principles of free-government and destructive of the organism of American Constitutional liberty. In the name and behalf of the injured government and people of Virginia, I charge that officer with a usurpation of power which imperils the safety of both and of all. I confront him before the justice and authority of your great office, and I appeal to you for action which will at once redress the wrongs of the past and guard the principles of the government against a like infraction in the future." LS, DNA, RG 60, Letters from the President; (press), James L. Kemper Letterbooks, ViU.

On July 27, "VINDEX," the pseudonym of John M. Gordon, Norfolk, wrote "POSTAL CARD, No. 152," addressed to USG. "You have not yet publicly replied to the letter of the Governor of Virginia, making complaint against the outrage threatened the rights and dignity of the State, in the affair of the Petersburg fiasco, by your minion and subaltern the senate-stigmatized Williams, Attorney General of the Rebel Government and your cabinet minister and legal adviser. Your neglect so to do, and to make an ample apology, is viewed by myself and all my fellow citizen as a personal insult. . . . The spirit of the South is still alive! It has not been quenched as you and your aiders and abettors may yet find to your dismay, and to the delight of every friend of the Constitution both north and south of the Potomac." Pamphlet, DNA, RG 59, Miscellaneous Letters.

To House of Representatives

To the House of Representatives.—

In answer to the resolution of the 7th instant of the House of Representatives asking to be informed "whether any and what negotiations have been, or are being made with the Sioux Indians for their removal to the Indian Territory, and under what authority the same has been or is being done," I submit herewith a report received from the Secretary of the Interior, which contains, it is believed, all the information in possession of his department touching the matter of the resolution—

U. S. Grant.—

Executive Mansion—December 14. 1876.

Copy, DNA, RG 130, Messages to Congress. *HED*, 44-2-10. See message to Congress, Dec. 22, 1876.

To J. Russell Jones

Washington, D. C. Dec. 17th *1876*

Dear Jones:

Your letter containing a slip from the Chicago Tribune,[1] speaking of me for the place of Sec. of War, under Hayes, or the sSenate, to replace Logan, was received two or three days ago. I want to say that there is no place within the gift of the President, foreign mission, Cabinet position or any other, which I would accept. I would not accept the Senatorship for three reasons. The first is that I have had Sixteen years of constant responsibility and care and want to play the "Sovereign" now for a little while to rest and recuperate. Second: although a resident of Ill, and of no other State or Territory, I have not lived there enough to feel entitled to a position belonging so exclusively to the state as that of Senator. Third: the present incumbent—who is a candidate for re-election—has made a good Senator. During the rebellion he rendered distinguished services, and at the begining of it he left his seat in Congress—to which he had been

elected by a democratic constituency, by an overwhelmning majority—to raise troops for the war. Had Logan stuck to the democracy,
and been a Copperhead, the section of the state he represented
would, in all probability, have been as bad as any portion of Ky. It
certainly would have been so for a time after the breaking out of
hostilities. The course he pursued changed all that and gave us from
his district all the volunteers ever called for from there, and as brave
and good soldiers as went to the field from any section. It is my recollection that the draft was never resorted to in that district, but on
the contrary that at every call for more troops there were always
enough volunteers to more than fill their quota.—I am most decidedly in favor of the re-election of Logan for his fidelity to the Union
in the hour of its need, first, and for his fidelity to the principles for
which he fought in the second place.

It is impossible to conjecture what the next two months is to
bring forth, but I have an abiding faith that no alarming occurrence
is to take place. There is too much interest at stake, and the scenes
of twelve-sixteen years ago are too vividly in the recollections of the
people to allow any such thing. I shall at least hope for the best.

Yours Truly

U. S. GRANT

ALS, George Jones, Chicago, Ill. USG publicized this letter, and the following letter to
John A. Logan, to a correspondent. See *Chicago Inter-Ocean,* Dec. 21, 1876.

On Jan. 11, 187[7], J. Russell Jones, collector of customs, Chicago, wrote to USG.
"*Personal* . . . I could'nt get rid of promising Genl Hammond—on Genl Sherman's staff
during the war, to write you in his behalf for Govr of Huron. He showed me a letter from
Genl Sherman, saying he would favor his appointment. The Senatorial question waxes hot.
Logan—largely ahead, but I cannot see how he can pull through—He claims to have some
Democratic votes which he can count on. A Desperate effort is being made to create the
impression that I am heading the opposition to Logan, but it is false—many of his opponents are men I never saw or heard of. Logan offered one of the *Evening Journal* men the
Pension Agency here if the *Journal* would support him, and he told a man day before yesterday that both Geo Bangs and Harvey had resigned. The appraiser's resignation it is said
is being witheld for L. to trade upon—Everything here in the market but the collectorship, but I dont beleive you will let him trade me out of that until the 4th Mch. . . . This is
a specimen of the letters I am getting every day—dozens of them" ALS (misdated), USG 3.
The enclosure is a letter of Jan. 8 from George A. Fitch, Springfield, Ill., to Jones. "Permit
me, through the medium of this note, to introduce to your favorable acquaintance S. M.
Smith, Esq., of Kewanee, who will lay before you all of the facts relative to the present *status* of the Senatorial question. The re-election of John A. Logan is a matter of impossibility. Even if the Independents were to support Logan, he could not succeed, on account of
the disaffection in the ranks of the Republicans. What, then, is to be done? Are we to be

compelled to sit quietly by and witness the election of some 'reminiscence of the rebellion'—some relict of Bourbonism? in a crisis like the present, simply on account of the obstinacy of Mr. Logan and a few of his friends? The Independents will unite with the Republicans in support of some gentleman in whom they have confidence, and of unquestioned Republican antecedents and principles. Isn't this better than to have Trumbull, Palmer, or Fuller elected? There can be no doubt of it. Come here *at once*, therefore, with as strong a delegation as you can obtain, and help us out in this object. Pray, dont hesitate." ALS, *ibid.*

On [*Jan.*] 26, Ferdinand McDonough, Cincinnati, wrote to USG. "Allow me to suggest the appointment of Gen. John A. Logan as Judge of the Supreme Court in place of Judge Davis just elected to the Senate from Illinois. By so doing you would please a large number of citizens and ex-soldiers and confer a just compliment upon a brave officer and efficient Statesman." ALS (misdated Feb. 26), DNA, RG 60, Applications and Recommendations. See letter to J. Russell Jones, Aug. 13, 1876; James Pickett Jones, *John A. Logan: Stalwart Republican from Illinois* (Tallahassee, 1982), pp. 93–98.

1. "The St. Louis *Globe* proposes Gen. Grant as Secretary of War in President Hayes' Cabinet, and thinks he would be the right kind of a man for the office in case there is to be any war, foreign or domestic, during the next four years. The *Evening Post*, of this city, believing there will be no war, suggests that the Illinois Legislature this winter should elect him United States Senator. Not a bad idea. It is at least worth turning over and thinking about." *Chicago Tribune*, Dec. 14, 1876.

To John A. Logan

———

Dec. 17th /76

DEAR GENERAL:

I enclose you a note which I have just written to J. R. Jones, of Chicago, in answer to one received from him a few days ago containing a slip from the Chicago Tribune. I send it for your perusal before sending it off, and to say further that if you think there is any thing further that I can do to aid you I will be glad to hear your suggestion. I have many times stated, in conversation, that the services you rendered at the begining of the rebellion in shaping the course of the citizens of the Southern part of the state had never been fully appreciated.

Yours Truly
U. S. GRANT

HON. JOHN A. LOGAN, U. S. S.

ALS, DLC-Logan Family Papers. See preceding letter.

To Congress

To the Senate and House of Representatives—

I have the honor to transmit herewith a letter, submitted by the Secretary of the Interior, from the Commissioner of Indian Affairs accompanied by the report and journal of proceedings of the Commission appointed on the 24th day of August last to obtain certain concessions from the Sioux Indians in accordance with the provisions contained in the Indian Appropriation Act for the current fiscal year.—

I ask your special consideration of these Articles of Agreement, as among other advantages to be gained by them, is the clear right of citizens to go into a country of which they have taken possession[1] and from which they cannot be excluded.—

U. S. Grant.

Executive Mansion—December 22. 1876—

Copy, DNA, RG 130, Messages to Congress. *SED*, 44-2-9. On Dec. 19, 1876, John Q. Smith, commissioner of Indian Affairs, wrote to Secretary of the Interior Zachariah Chandler. ". . . By the terms of the agreement, the Sioux surrender all claim to any country lying outside the boundaries of their permanent reserve, as defined by the treaty of 1868, and to so much of said reserve as lies west of the one hundred and third meridian of longitude and as is included between the North and South Forks of the Cheyenne River east of said meridian. The Government thereby secures full possession of a tract of country which includes the Black Hills and is defined by natural boundaries. The Indians grant a right of way over their reservation for three roads from the Missouri River to the ceded territory—the routes to be designated by the President. They also agree to receive all subsistence and other supplies, which may hereafter be furnished, at such points on or near the Missouri River as the President may designate. In consideration of these concessions, the commissioners, on behalf of the United States, agree to furnish subsistence to the Sioux until such time as they shall become self-supporting—. . ." *Ibid.*, p. 2. Smith recommended the purchase of land from the Cherokee and other tribes in the Indian Territory for a future Sioux reservation. ". . . I am led to hope that such cession might be obtained on fair and equitable terms, for two reasons: 1st. It must be obvious to every intelligent man in the so-called civilized tribes, that land in excess of the amount which can be profitably used is of little or no value. 2d. They must be aware that so long as they hold vast areas of valuable land, lying, and destined to lie as long as they hold it, an unprofitable and unimproved waste, the cupidity of tens of thousands of white men is thereby excited—a cupidity which, already almost uncontrollable, will increase in intensity from year to year till it becomes irresistible. It is vain and idle to expect or hope that 55,000 Indians shall exclusively hold for a great length of time more than twenty millions of acres of the most desirable uncultivated lands now in the United States. . . ." *Ibid.*, p. 3.

On Aug. 15, USG had signed legislation appropriating $1,000,000 for Sioux subsistence, "*Provided,* That none of said sums appropriated for said Sioux Indians shall be paid to any band thereof while said band is engaged in hostilities against the white people; . . . *And provided also,* That no further appropriation for said Sioux Indians for subsistence shall hereafter be made until some stipulation, agreement, or arrangement shall have been entered into by said Indians with the President of the United States, which is calculated and designed to enable said Indians to become self-supporting: . . ." *U.S. Statutes at Large,* XIX, 192. On Aug. 16, Wednesday, Culver C. Sniffen wrote to Secretary of the Interior Zachariah Chandler. "The President directs me to say that he thinks the names herein given would make a good Commission to treat with the Sioux—He is of the impression though, that, Daniels should be left out—Any other name that pleases you will suit him, if you think there should be five members of the Commission—. . . P. S.—The President will not leave Washington until Saturday Morning—" Copy, DLC-USG, II, 3. USG proposed Henry C. Bulis, Henry H. Sibley, Albert G. Boone, and Newton Edmunds as commissioners, and John S. Collins as secretary. Collins did not serve; Sibley did not accompany the commission because of ill health. The commission also included George W. Manypenny as chairman, Henry B. Whipple and Jared W. Daniels as commissioners, Augustine S. Gaylord, asst. attorney gen., as legal adviser, Samuel D. Hinman as interpreter, and Charles M. Hendley as secretary.

On Dec. 18, Manypenny *et al.,* Washington, D. C., wrote to Smith. "The commissioners appointed by the President to negotiate an agreement with the Sioux Indians, parties to the treaty of 1868, pursuant to the following provisions of an act of Congress passed August 15, 1876, . . . respectfully report: . . . While the Indians received us as friends, and listened with kind attention to our propositions, we were painfully impressed with their lack of confidence in the pledges of the Government. At times they told their story of wrongs with such impassioned earnestness that our cheeks crimsoned with shame. In their speeches, the recital of the wrongs which their people had suffered at the hands of the whites, the arraignment of the Government for gross acts of injustice and fraud, the description of treaties made only to be broken, the doubts and distrusts of present professions of friendship and good-will were portrayed in colors so vivid and language so terse, that admiration and surprise would have kept us silent had not shame and humiliation done so. . . . From the information received the commission believe that, if the Indians are to be made self-supporting as speedily as possible, they ought to be removed to the Indian Territory at as early a day as practicable. We are unanimous in the opinion that these Indians can, for the present, find homes on the Missouri River; but we do not think they will ever become a self-sustaining people there. We do not think that it would be advisable at this time to remove the large proportion of the Sioux to the Indian Territory; but in view of the fact that it is the only valuable country upon which Indians can be located, that this country has been set apart by the most solemn guarantees as the future home of the Indians, that to open any part of this Territory to white settlers would be a violation of the nation's plighted faith, and that here the Indians can become a self-supporting people, we believe that it is just and humane to remove to this Territory, from time to time, bodies of the Sioux who are ready and prepared to live by labor. . . . After long and careful examination we have no hesitation in recommending that it is wise to continue the humane policy inaugurated by President Grant. We believe that the facts will prove that under this policy more has been done in the work of civilization than in any period of our history. It has accomplished this one thing, that those who were placed in trust of the national honor did not receive their appointment as a reward for political service. The great obstacle to its complete success is that no change has been made in the laws for the care of Indians. The Indian is left without the protection of law in person, property, or life. He has no personal rights. He has no redress for wrongs inflicted by lawless violence. He may see his crops destroyed, his wife or child killed. His only redress is personal revenge. There is not a member of either house of Congress who does not know that, even with all the influences of Christian civilization, schools, churches, and social restraints, there is not a community of whites which could protect itself from lawless violence under the same conditions; and yet we take it for granted that the superior virtue of a savage race will enable it to achieve civilization under circumstances which would wreck our own. . . ." *SED*, 44-2-9, 5–6, 8–9, 16. On Feb. 28, 1877, USG signed an act ratifying the agreement with the Sioux, amended to prohibit the removal of the Sioux to the Indian Territory without congressional approval. See *U.S. Statutes at Large*, XIX, 254–64; *CR*, 44–2, 1055–58, 1615–17; Manypenny, *Our Indian Wards* (Cincinnati, 1880), pp. 342–72; Richmond L. Clow, "The Sioux Nation and Indian Territory: The Attempted Removal of 1876," *South Dakota History*, 6, 4 (Fall, 1976), 456–73; Edward Lazarus, *Black Hills White Justice: The Sioux Nation Versus the United States, 1775 to the Present* (New York, 1991), pp. 90–93.

Probably in Feb., Smith drafted a proposed order. "Civil Agents at all the Sioux Agencies except Spotted Tail and Red Cloud will hereafter be allowed to exercise entire control of the distribution of all goods and supplies to the Indians at their respective Agencies, with the understanding that no supplies of rations shall be issued to any Indians who have been engaged in hostilities against the Government until they shall have been arrested and dismounted. As far as lies in their power agents will assist the military in the discovery arrest and dismounting of Indians who after taking part in hostilities have returned to agencies, and in preventing Indians at Agencies from joining or giving relief or information to the hostiles. The above regulation will take effect at the Spotted Tail and Red Cloud Agencies as soon as Civil Agents shall have been appointed thereto." Copies (press, undated), DLC-Philip H. Sheridan. On Feb. 12, Gen. William T. Sherman endorsed this document. "The enclosed rough draft of the desire of the Commissioner of Indian Affairs is handed me in pursuance of an agreement made at an extended conference of the Indian Peace Commissioners, the Interior and War Department and President. The President seemed disposed to order peremptorily the restoration of the Indian Agents to the full powers of their office: But I begged that the military authorities be consulted I wish General Sheridan to examine this carefully. If he approve he may order accordingly, and return this with a copy of his order—but if he object return this rough draft with the memorandum of what will in his opinion give the Indian Agents the necessary powers and yet leave the military situation undamaged." Copy (press), *ibid.* On Feb. 15, Lt. Gen. Philip H. Sheridan, Chicago, wrote to Sherman. "I have the honor to ack the receipt of the draft of an order on the subject of the control of issues of goods & supplies by the civil Agents at the Sioux Agencies along the Missouri river, and to enclose for your examination one which differs only in a word or two from the draft you sent out The troubles at the Agency did not arise from any desire on the part of the military to control issues to India[ns] present and friendly or to those who had made their peace, but it was to prevent issues to more Indians than were present which substantially amounted to issuing to the hostiles, as the supplies of goods were carried out to them I will cheerfully agree to the promulgation of the order revised by myself or even to your draft if the Commissioner insists on it as I have the greatest desire to comply with the wishes of the Hon. Commissioner of Indian affairs whose course has been conservative and courteous" Copy (press), *ibid.*

Possibly in 1875 or 1876, USG had written a note. "Letter to 'Blue Teeth' Spotted Tail Agency, Neb. acknowledging receipt of pipe with his kind message." AN (undated), Mrs. Paul E. Ruestow, Jacksonville, Fla. See *HED*, 44-1-1, part 5, I, 681; *SED*, 44-2-9, 23.

1. On Dec. 1, 1876, Mayor E. B. Farnum of Deadwood, Dakota Territory, telegraphed to USG. "My Telegraph this day Completed to our city the People of the Black

Hills Send GREETS and Trust that this Little may form the Link necessary not only to Unites us with But to make the richest mineral country of the Continent a part of the U. S" Telegram received (via Cheyenne, at 1:00 A.M.), DLC-USG, IB.

To Congress

———

To THE SENATE AND HOUSE OF REPRESENTATIVES—
When Congress adjourned in August last, the Execution of the Extradition Article of the Treaty of 1842, between the United States and Great Britain, had been interrupted.—

The United States had demanded of Her Majesty's Government the surrender of certain fugitives from justice, charged with crimes committed within the jurisdiction of the United States, who had sought asylum and were found within the territories of Her British Majesty, and had, in due compliance with the requirements of the Treaty, furnished the evidence of the criminality of the fugitives which had been found sufficient to justify their apprehension and commitment for trial as required by the Treaty, and the fugitives were held and committed for Extradition.—

Her Majestys Government, however, demanded from the United States certain assurances or stipulations, as a condition for the surrender of these fugitives.—

As the Treaty contemplated no such conditions to the performce of the obligations which each Government had assumed, the demand for stipulations on the part of this Government was repelled.—

Her Majesty's Government thereupon, in June last, released two of the fugitives, (Ezra D. Winslow and Charles J. Brent,) and subsequently released a third, (One William E. Gray,) and refusing to surrender, set them at liberty—

In a Message to the two Houses of Congress on the 20th day of June last, in view of the condition of facts as above referred to, I said "The position thus taken by the British Government, if adhered to, cannot but be regarded as the abrogation and annulment of the Article of the Treaty on Extradition—

Under these circumstances it will not, in my judgment, comport with the dignity or self-respect of this Government to make demands upon that Government for the surrender of fugitive criminals, nor to entertain any requisition of that character from that Government under the treaty."—

Article XI of the Treaty of 1842, provided that, "the tenth article, (that relating to Extradition) should continue in force, until one or the other of the parties should signify its wish to terminate it, and no longer"—

In view, however, of the great importance of an Extradition Treaty, especially between two States as intimately connected in Commercial and social relations as are the United States and Great Britain, and in the hope that Her Majesty's Government might yet reach a different decision from that then attained, I abstained from recommending any action by Congress terminating the Extradition Article of the Treaty—I have, however, declined to take any steps under the Treaty toward Extradition.—

It is with great satisfaction that I am able now to announce to Congress and to the Country, that by the voluntary act of Her Majesty's Government the obstacles which had been interposed to the Execution of the Extradition Article of the Treaty have been removed.—

On the 27th of October last, Her Majesty's representative at this Capital, under instructions from Lord Derby, informed this Government that Her Majesty's Government would be prepared as a temporary measure, until a new Extradition Treaty can be concluded, to put in force all powers vested in it for the surrender of accused persons to the Government of the United States, under the Treaty of 1842, without asking for any engagement as to such persons not being tried in the United States for other than the offences for which Extradition had been demanded—

I was happy to greet this announcement as the removal of the obstacles which had arrested the execution of the Extradition treaty between the two Countries—

In reply to the note of Her Majesty's representative, after referring to the applications heretofore made by the United States for the surrender of the fugitives referred to in the Correspondence which was laid before Congress at its last Session, it was stated that on an indication of readiness to surrender these persons, an agent would be authorized to receive them, and I would be ready to respond to requisitions which may be made on the part of Her Majestys Government under the Xth Article of the Treaty of 1842, which I would then regard as in full force, until such time as either Government shall avail itself of the right to terminate it, provided by the XIth Article, or until a more comprehensive arrangement can be reached between the two Governments in regard to the Extradition of Criminals—an object to which the attention of this Government would gladly be given with an earnest desire for a mutually satisfactory result.—

A copy of the correspondence between Her Majesty's representative at this Capital and the Secretary of State on the subject, is transmitted herewith.—

It is with great satisfaction that I have now to announce that Her Majesty's Government, while expressing its desire not to be understood to recede from the interpretation which in its previous correspondence it has put upon the treaty, but having regard to the prospect of a new treaty, and the power possessed by either party of spontaneously denouncing the old one, caused the re-arrest on the 4th instant of Brent, one of the fugitives who had been previously discharged, and after awaiting the requisite time within which the fugitive is entitled to appeal, or to apply for his discharge, on the 21st instant, surrendered him to the Agent appointed on behalf of this Government to receive and to convey him to the United States.—

Her Majestys Government has expressed an earnest desire to re-arrest, and to deliver up Winslow and Gray, the other fugitives who had been arrested and committed on the requisition of the United States, but were released because of the refusal of the United States to give the assurances and stipulations then required by Great Britain—These persons, however, are believed to have escaped from British jurisdiction; a diligent search has failed to discover them.—

As the surrender of Brent without condition or stipulation of any kind being asked, removes the obstacle which interrupted the execution of the Treaty, I shall no longer abstain from making demands upon Her Majestys Government for the surrender of fugitive criminals,[1] nor from entertaining requisitions of that character from that Government under the Treaty of 1842—but will again regard the Treaty as operative, hoping to be able before long, to conclude with her Majesty's Government a new treaty, of a broader and more comprehensive nature—

U S. GRANT—

WASHINGTON. D. C. DEC 23D, 1876.—

Copies, DNA, RG 59, Reports to the President and Congress; *ibid.*, RG 130, Messages to Congress. *HED*, 44-2-15; *SMD*, 49-1-162, part 2, II, 792–94; *Foreign Relations, 1877*, pp. 271–73. See message to Congress, June 20, 1876.

On Sept. 4, 1876, Monday, Secretary of State Hamilton Fish, Garrison, N. Y., wrote to USG, Long Branch. "Sir Edward Thornton passed Saturday with me. He came to submit a proposition in behalf of his Government, to negotiate a new Extradition treaty. he read to me a note written by instruction of Lord Derby, expressing the wish of the British Government, in that direction, and proposing as a temporary arrangement for a limited time to renew the surrender of fugitives under the Treaty of 1842, agreeing, on the part of the British Government, not to attach any stipulations or conditions to the surrender. The note stated however, that if a surrendered fugitive should be tried for other than the offence for which he was surrendered that Great Britain would feel constrained to terminate the Treaty: it contained also some other reference, & agreements which would call for a reply on our part—He said that he wished not to deliver a note which could not be acceptably received, & therefore had come to see me and to submit the note, & the proposition, before a formal presentation. I pointed out wherein I thought the note was open to exception,—that the limit of duration proposed for the temporary arrangement was insufficient—that the declaration that they would terminate the Treaty, in a contingency, which really involved the fundamental difference between the two Governments, had a minatory appearance, and can not be accepted as a basis of an arrangement— that it implied also a suspicion, as well as the assertion of a point of Construction of the Treaty which we should be compelled, probably, to controvert,—and that other references &c in the note, would, as I thought, require a reply from us, and might lead to a correspondence, rather than a settlement. His object, he said, had been in coming, precisely to ascertain how the note would appear to us, and he impliedly at least, assented to my criticism, and asked me whether a modification which was suggested would be satisfactory. It would remove my objection to the form & contents of the note—and I so replied, but said that the United States would expect as a condition to the renewal of surrender, on its part, that Winslow should be given up by Great Britain. His instructions did not authorise him to say that he would be delivered, but notwithstanding my decided statement that such must be done, he continued, and seemed to manifest the greatest confidence in being able to bring about the arrangement. The note which he had prepared, he [t]old me, followed the language of his instructions—that he had thought best to do so, in view of the past correspondence between the Governments, & so that the Foreign Office, should be represented as nearly as possible in its own language— he would therefore telegraph home, asking further instructions, and suggesting the modification of the note as had been proposed—With regard to a new treaty, they are willing to agree that the surrendered fugitive may be tried for other than the offence [—] on the application for surrender, provided the consent of the surrendering State, be obtained, & full information of the case be given. I think that they may be willing to advance a little further, as it is, it is a near approach to our position. They will agree to endeavour to obtain a modification by Parliament, of the Act of 1870. I declined discussing the terms of a new treaty further than to state the two points on which we had differed. I. the right to try for other than the single offence for which surrender had been made. II the responsibility of the Government to determine the political character of an alleged offence. I have thus given you I think, the substance of a conversation and interview which extended over several hours, on Saturday, and which Thornton again briefly opened yesterday, in a manner that impressed me with the belief that they are ready to yield *substantially*, all that we have contended for, wanting only to be allowed some means of saving their pride and their feelings. Thornton returned last evening to Washington, expecting to receive very shortly a reply to his telegraph request (sent from here on Saturday) for further instructions, on the receipt of which he will probably, formally, send me a note. Shall I, if the note be such as I have intimated, agree to the proposal to renew operations under the existing treaty of 1842, on Great Britains agreeing not to ask any stipulation in making surrenders, and agreeing to surrender Winslow? I endeavoured to impress upon Thornton the importance of the actual surrender of Winslow—he does not know that he is still in England, & said that he supposed would [—] the demand for his surrender. I advised him to let Lord Derby know, that we should expect the surrender, & to ask that he be watched, so as to detain in case the arrangement be made. he promised to do so—would it not be advisable that I telegraph to Pierrepont, to employ a trusty detective to keep sight of him. The whole business must be [—] with great care to prevent any suspicion on the part of Winslow, or his friends, & I have urged Thornton to exercise the utmost reticence, & not to allow any suspicion to get abroad as to the pendency of any discussions respecting Extradition. If you approve of the proposed arrangement, will you have the goodness to let me know, either by telegraph or by letter. I will then telegraph to Pierrepont to have Winslow kept in sight. I will understand any telegram expressing approval, without its reference to ~~any~~ the particular question, as authorising me to endeavour to make the arrangement proposed—" ALS (press), DLC-Hamilton Fish. On Sept. 7, USG telegraphed to Fish. "Your letter of fourth 4th rec'd—It's Contents are approved—" Telegram received, *ibid.* See Fish diary, Aug. 30, Sept. 2, 1876, *ibid.*

On Oct. 31, Nov. 17, and Dec. 21, Fish recorded in his diary. ". . . The President approved the draft note to Thornton and authorized the negotiation of a new Treaty saying that it must provide that surrendered criminals may be tried for any of the Extradition crimes. I stated that the British Government were prepared as I had reason to believe for such an arrangement provided the consent of the surrendering country is asked and given and the necessary information furnished by the country receiving the criminal. He said he thought that probably might be sufficient." "After Cabinet I mention to the president a communication made yesterday to me by Thornton and the note subsequently received from him I also read Pierreponts private letter of the 4th Nov stating that he thinks Winslow is either in the United States or Canada and that General Butler knows where he is" "British Minister Sir Edward Thornton has no information of the surrender of Brent. He refers to the newspaper statements that he had been yesterday surrendered and sent to Queenstown today. He asks whether on receiving tidings of Brents surrender we should be prepared immediatly to demand Maraine Smith and whether he may telegraph to London that I am prepared to begin the negotiation of a New Treaty. I tell him no but that I should propose to him a draft as the basis of negotiation, that this draft will contain what he calls the amendments that I propose that the President shall communicate to Congress the fact of Brents surrender and that he is prepared to put the Treaty into execution and that I will inform him officially to the same effect, that there are large numbers of persons addressing me and I don't really know whether they are all in the favor of justice or to effect something in aiding the escape of some of the parties." *Ibid.* See *ibid.*, Oct. 27, Nov. 13, 24, Dec. 13, 1876, Feb. 1, 1877. On Jan. 2, 1877, USG authorized the extradition of Charles J. Brent, wanted for forgery in Ky. Copy, DNA, RG 60, General Records.

1. Beginning on Dec. 23, 1876, USG authorized extradition from British jurisdiction for Maraine Smith, wanted for murder in Mich.; Thomas R. Lewis (Dec. 27), charged with forgery in N. Y.; Charles Jones (Dec. 30), wanted in Ohio for arson; and Thomas D. Conyngham (Jan. 2, 1877), charged with forgery in Pa. Copies, *ibid.*; DS (Lewis case), *ibid.*, Extradition Case Files.

Endorsement

Referred to the Sec. of War. I think it advisable to send a company of troops from N. Orleans to Port Gibson at once.

U. S. GRANT

DEC. 23D /76

AES, DNA, RG 94, Letters Received, 4788 1876. Written on a letter of Dec. 23, 1876, from U.S. Representative John R. Lynch of Miss. to USG. "From information received by me I am satisfied that Claiborne County Mississippi is in a lawless condition   mob-law and violence reigns supreme throughout the county. The lives of leading Republicans are being threatened daily and it is seriously apprehended that, unless something is done for the protection of these people that many lives will be lost. In consequence of these facts I respectfully ask that a company of Federal troops be sent to Port Gibson as soon as possible." ALS, *ibid.*

On Dec. 19, William H. Garland, Summit, Miss., had written to USG concerning intimidation of Republicans. ". . . To such an extent has this fear gone, that at the recent Presidential election my son & myself were the only whites who *openly* dared to vote the Republican ticket at this Box.—I presume that no sane man doubts that if this terrorism was removed & a fair expression of the popular voice allowed that this State is overwhelming Republican—As evidence—in Madison County at the election in the Fall of 1875—for State Treasurer—The Democratic Candidate received 1488 votes, the Republican 2587   at the Presidential election last fall, the Democratic elector received 1478 votes, the Republican 13 votes—What became of the 2500 Republican votes?—the Democratic candidate did not get them—Comment is unnecessary. . . ." ALS, DNA, RG 60, Letters from the President. *HED*, 44-2-30, 133.

To George W. Childs

Washington, D. C. Dec. 31st *1876*

MY DEAR MR. CHILDS;

Suppose you invite Gov. Hayes to attend your next "Saturday Evening"? If he should happen to accept I will be there also, though with some inconvenience.

If you should invite the Governor say nothing about my having written to you on the subject, nor nothing about my intention of being there if he is.

Yours Truly
U. S. GRANT

ALS, DLC-USG. On Dec. 25, 1876, Governor Rutherford B. Hayes of Ohio wrote to USG. "I had a long and very satisfactory interview yesterday with Judge Taft, and was glad to find that our views on the situation were in perfect accord, and especially on the subject in which he seemed chiefly interested. I have no doubt whatever that if you and I could meet and talk over present affairs it would be found that we were equally agreed on the same topic. I have thought it best to remain uncommitted on Cabinet &c &c until after the count is declared. While I am satisfied that the Republican candidates are equitably as well as legally entitled to a declaration in their favor I, of course, recognize the possibility of an adverse result. I know that a fair Election would have given us at least 10,000 majority in Louisiana. But whatever the Event I shall never cease to regard with admiration and gratitude the course you have taken before and since the Election in relation to it." ALS, USG 3. Hayes remained in Ohio during the electoral crisis. See Charles Richard Williams, ed., *Diary and Letters of Rutherford Birchard Hayes* (Columbus, 1922–26), III, 393–95; Ross A. Webb, *Benjamin Helm Bristow: Border State Politician* (Lexington, Ky., 1969), pp. 262–65.

To William P. Kellogg

Dated WASHINGTON D. C. 7 JANY *1877*
To GOVERNOR WM P KELLOGG NEW ORLEANS LA
I am constrained to decline your request for the aid of troops to inaugurate the new state government tomorrow   To do so would be to recognize one of two rival governments for the state executive & legislative at the very time when a committee of each House of Congress is in the state capitol of La investigating all the facts connected

with the late election at which each of the contestants claim to have
been legally elected   All the troops can be called upon to do will be
to suppress violence if any should take place & leave constitutional
authority & means to settle which is the rightful governor, & which
the legal legislature, This done, troops may be used to uphold the
rightful government in the state if called upon in ac[cor]dance with
the spirit and meaning of the constitution

U. S. GRANT

Telegram received (at 6:10 P.M.), Gilder Lehrman Collection, NNP. *HMD*, 45-3-1, III, 603.
On Jan. 5, 187[7], Friday, Governor William P. Kellogg of La. telegraphed to USG. "Grave
apprehensions felt that upon Nicholls inauguration Monday he will forthwith appoint a
Supreme court also a police board for this metropolitan district assuming to be governor
This board will supply a police force to capture the police stations and dispute the beats.
If this be done it will be reinforced by the White League in strong force pretending to be
Nicholls militia   The conflict thus precipitated may be avoided by prompt recognition on
Monday of authority of incoming administration of Packard to be inaugurated that day and
if directions be given to Gen. Augur to support it as the legal government." Copy (received
at 4:00 A.M.), DNA, RG 60, Letters Received, La. On Jan. 7, Secretary of State Hamilton
Fish attended a cabinet meeting. "Being the first to arrive I enquire the object of the meeting, and the President answered that it was 'again the Louisianna trouble', adding with
some manifestation of impatience, 'they are always in trouble there and always wanting the
U. S to send troops' 'They want me to inaugurate their governor and legislature'. He
handed me a paper which he said was the answer he intended to give them—It was a
peremptory refusal to comply with their request. Shortly after, all the Members of the Cabinet appeared and the President then stated the object he had for convening the meeting
and referred to the applications made to him, one of which was that read in Cabinet on
Tuesday last from Kellogg, the the other one received, as I understood, either the passed
night, or this morning both from Govr Kellogg besides two received by the Attorney General from Pitkin, the Marshall of the District,—The Presidents proposed reply was then
read which I thought might imply doubt as to the right of the Executive without the concurrence of Congress to decide between two contending parties each claiming to be the
political power of one of the States, with these alterations which the President readily accepted, his draft answer was agreed to without dissent, but the Secretary of War manifested some impatience, and in reply to a question of his when the Federal Government
could interfere, the President answered not unless there be actual resistance or conflict.
Cameron remarked to me in an undertone, I am afraid that won't come for our fellows
down there won't fight. The President sent off his reply by telegraph and instructed the
Attorney General to reply to the Marshalls. I requested that he should confine his reply to
these points. 1st that the emergency in which alone the United States can interfere has not
yet arisen 2d that the request forwarded is not verified or sufficient to call for action; and
the President approved all of these suggestions." Fish diary, DLC-Hamilton Fish.

On Jan. 1, Republicans and Democrats in La. had organized rival legislatures. On the
same day, Kellogg telegraphed to USG conveying resolutions of the Republican legislature that "certain evil disposed persons are forming combinations to disturb the public
peace and defy the lawful authorities" and requesting USG "to afford the protection guaranteed Each state by the constitution of the united states when threatened with domestic

Violence." Telegram received (on Jan. 2, 10:00 A.M.), DNA, RG 60, Letters from the President. On Jan. 2, Henry D. Ogden and Louis Bush, president *pro tem* and speaker of the Democratic legislature, telegraphed to USG that "owing to the armed occupation of the state house under orders issued by the governor of the state & owing to the refusal of armed bodies under instructions of the Executive to admit into the State house legally Elected members of the General Assembly in order to avoid a Conflict with the Said armed bodies a Constitutional quorum of both Houses of the general assembly went to St Patricks Hall & that at that place the two Houses of the general Assembly of the state of Louisiana were permanently organized & that the body claiming to have organized as the general assembly at the state house has never had a legal quorum in either house & is an illegal unconstitutional & usurping Body of individuals," Telegram received (at 8:00 A.M.), *ibid.*

On Jan. 8, Kellogg and Pierre G. Deslonde, La. secretary of state, telegraphed to USG. "The two houses of the General assembly convened last monday The house had sixty eight members out of one hundred seventeen returned elected The Senate had nineteen out of thirty six members elected and holding over a quorum of both houses The Second day is fixed by the Constitution to count the vote for Governor and Lieutenant Governor by legislature. There were present that day twenty one members of the Senate and seventy members of the House assembled in Joint Convention more than a quorum of both Houses and counted the vote and declared Packard and Antoine. They take the oath of office and enter upon the discharge of their respective offices in half an hour." Telegram received (at 3:30 P.M.), *ibid.* On the same day, Stephen B. Packard telegraphed to USG. "Having been declared by the legislature of the State as Provided by the Constitution duly elected Govr of Louisiana I have this day taken the oath of office & entered upon the duties of the position there have been each day fully sixty eight of the legally returned members of the House & nineteen Members of the Senate in attendance more than a quorum of both houses every department of the Govt is in full operation" Telegram received (at 6:00 P.M.), *ibid.* Also on Jan. 8, Francis T. Nicholls telegraphed to USG. "I have the honor to announce to you that I have this day been inaugurated Governor of the State of Louisiana under the Constitution and laws thereof and have entered upon the discharge of my duties as such" Telegram received (at 1:50 A.M.), *ibid.*

On Jan. 9, James Longstreet, New Orleans, telegraphed to USG. "Gen Nichols was yesterday inaugurated Governor of the State amid enthusiastic demonstrations of patriotism that should be gratifying to Every American Citizens I believe him fairly elected to the office to which he has been inducted and that he will maintain peace & good order throughout the state I beg there fore that you will maturely consider the premises notwithstanding adverse sensational dispatches that may reach you—" Telegram received (at 11:36 A.M.), *ibid.* Also on Jan. 9, Packard telegraphed thrice to USG. "I respectfully request a reconsideration of your determination not to recognize the legal existing Govt of the state I am Governor by virtue of the vote of the State as shown by the legal returns & counted by the General assembly with more than a quorum present as provided by the constitution of the State The democratic Candidate for Gov has no other title than a certificate of election from the Democratic Committee & the count of a Socalled legislature without a quorum only forty two in house & seventeen in Senate Nicholls will appoint another Supreme Court he has appointed police board & placed a police force on the streets an-archy & perhaps bloodshed will follow the lawful outgoing state Govt recognized & has commissioned all officers of my Gov't. The opposite party holds from McEnery." "The white league are assembling in large numbers with muskets and are moving under orders of their Chiefs attack in force upon the constituted authorities of the state is imminent. I respectfully request that the concurrent resolution of the general as-

sembly calling upon the Government of the United States to protect the state from domestic violence be complied with. There is an insurrection against the state and domestic
violence which the state authorities are unable to suppress" "A quorum of the Supreme
Court confirmed by the senate & commissioned by Govr Kellogg met this morning & under laws of state removed Civil sheriff Handy for cause appointing Alfred Bourges sheriff
in his stead The White League subsequently took forcible possession of court building
and installed as judges Persons holding commissions from Nicholls handy the deposed
Sheriff still assumes to act It is probable process will issue from this pretended supreme
court which will greatly complicate matters White leaguers several thousands in number
under Arms have taken possession of Central police station & carried the third precinct
station and made prisoner of the forces there State forces are concentrated at capital both
Houses of General assembly in session." Telegrams received (at 11:30 A.M., 11:48 A.M., and
3:41 P.M.), *ibid.* On the same day, Caesar C. Antoine and Michael Hahn, lt. governor and
speaker of the Republican legislature, telegraphed to USG "to afford immediately such aid
as may be necessary to suppress the insurrection against the state." Telegram received (at
4:27 P.M.), *ibid.* Also on Jan. 9, Nicholls telegraphed to USG. "Information having reached
me that Jno. T. Ludeling has telegraphed you that he as holding over Chief Justice had
been dispossessed of his seat on the supreme court bench and asking for the armed assistance of the united states to reinstate him I respectfully inform you that John T Ludelings
commission as well as the commissions of all his associates on the bench expired by constitutional limitation in august last that he was reappointed a few days ago by mr Kellogg
and confirmed by that body known as the packard senate mr Ludelings title to the office
of chief justice therefore rests upon the same basis as mr Packards title to the office of Governor the civil sheriff of this parish whose title to office is independent either of my government or of mr Packards government refused this morning to recognize mr Ludeling
and recognized and placed my appointees in possession of the court room of which the
sheriff is by law the custodian" Telegram received (at 12:24 A.M.), *ibid.*

On Jan. 9, in cabinet, USG drafted a telegram for Secretary of War James D. Cameron
to Brig. Gen. Christopher C. Augur, New Orleans. "Dispatch just received from [the U. S.
Marshall] New Orleans indicate that unauthorized Armed bodies of men are organized
and assembling in a manner to threaten the peace and safety of the city. If this be so notify
the leaders of such organizations that they must desist on pain of coming in conflict with
United States authority sustained by the military power of the government. Report at once
the situation and your action, [keeping in mind the fact that this order has no reference to
a recognition of either of the claimants for the Governorship or either Legislature]" ADf
(bracketed material not in USG's hand), *ibid.*, RG 94, Letters Received, 4788 1876. See
Fish diary, Jan. 9, 1877, DLC-Hamilton Fish.

Also on Jan. 9, John R. G. Pitkin, U.S. marshal, New Orleans, telegraphed to Attorney Gen. Alphonso Taft. "The state House is in state of siege & environed by armed white
legue—Lt Com Kells U. S Navy officially reports loud threats to shell or burn the state
House to night—The whole City is in terror—for gods sake act packard will hold state
House till death" Telegram received (at 5:35 P.M.), DNA, RG 60, Letters Received, La.
USG endorsed this telegram. "Packard will do right if he holds out. No doubt, under the
instructions already given, any attempt to destroy the building occupied by Packard Govt.
will be resisted by Govt. Mil force." AE (initialed, undated), *ibid.*

On Jan. 10, Packard telegraphed to USG that justices appointed by Kellogg and confirmed by the Republican senate had met on Jan. 9. ". . . Later in same day white league several thousand strong with Cannon unlimbered & trained on building took forcible possession of Court house & records ejected sheriff pro tempore & installed as judges persons

holding Commissions from general Nicholls professedly Confirmed by Body claiming to be senate acting with nicholls. That body has never at any time had legal quorum The legal senate which confirmed reappointment of Holding over judges organized with eight holding over Senators & eleven declared elected Senators making full quorum & Subsequently & previous to confirmation of judges was reinforced by presence of one holding over democratic Senator making twenty out of thirty six If even confirmation of these three judges by legal senate be informal their title as judges holding over under Constitution Cannot be questioned Those who have superseded them have no title in law or in fact The pretended Court installed by white league remains in possession of Court house & records. State authorities have exhausted all means at command to dispossess them. I have today applied to Commanding officer U. S forces for detail of troops to act as posse to aid sheriff pro tempore in enforcing written order of Supreme court requiring him to place the court in possession of court room & records." Telegram received (at 1:29 A.M.), *ibid.*, Letters from the President. On Jan. 10, U.S. Senator Timothy O. Howe of Wis. and three others, New Orleans, telegraphed to USG. "If you Consult Genl Auger he will probably advise you that the Same armed force which today under the orders of the War office he removed from the State house Yesterday took possession of the Rooms & records of the Supreme Court excluding therefrom five judges . . . In their Stead are seated by the Same force five judges whose only title rests upon a nomination by Mr Nicholls & a Confirmation by the body known as his Senate" Telegram received (at 1:31 A.M.), *ibid.* See Pitkin to Taft, Jan. 10, 1876, *ibid.*

On Jan. 11, Thursday, Fish recorded in his diary. "At Cabinet on Tuesday last while discussing the Louisianna question Cameron, & Chandler, ~~having~~ evinced some little impatience at the Presidents decision not to interfere in the Louisianna trouble, & Cameron had remarked 'we must wait then until a shot is fired and then we can act,' and Chandler, apparently without any special thought, had said to Cameron 'if you telegraph to Genl Augur "consult Gov Kellogg and place your troops as he shall direct" would'nt that settle it'?—the reply was made generally 'yes! that would settle it'—The President remarked 'we will not settle it that way yet at least.' These remarks did not strike me as peculiar at the time, but the appearing last night in the 'star' of the annexed telegram looks at though they were gaining ground in the direction of recognition." DLC-Hamilton Fish. The clipping includes a telegram of Jan. 10 from Cameron to Augur. "It is reported that the state house in New Orleans is surrounded by a mob. If this is so notify all persons to disperse, and compel compliance with your order. It is the determination of the President to see that the legislature is not molested. When he has full knowledge of all the facts in the premises he will decide which should be recognized." *Ibid.*; ADfS, DNA, RG 94, Letters Received, 4788 1876.

On Jan. 11, Pitkin twice telegraphed to USG. "Published report here of Nicholls dispatch and louisiana Delegations statement to you that Ludeling was reappointed by Packard Such dispatch if sent and statement if made are lies. Ludeling Leonard & King were appointed by Kellogg and alone competent to act till a recognized Senate shall confirm or reject before end of session March fourth ~~all~~ although Packard Senate has already confirmed now an armed mob hold the court and have installed five men appointed and confirmed by a governor and senate which you have not recognized ~~theiry~~ supplant the appointees of a Governor whom you have recognized" "The lawless armed bodies still remain in possession of supreme Court & police stations the leaders do not desist despite Secretary Wars order of tuesday transmitted by Gen Auger to Nicholls. the armed mob appeared under orders early yesterday and Squads were all day about the city several hundred men yesterday captured and robbed the state arsenal dragging thence three brass

pieces & two gatlins through the streets Police Sergeant Ancoin was last night shot by
one of Nicholls police who disputed his authority McEnery a Nicholls appointee accompanied by McGloins armed white league band which captured city hall Sept 14th 1874 has
just captured important office recorder of mortgages Judge Staes first municipal court
has just been violently expelled by mob two hundred armed men occupy Court house the
mob asserts itself only by arms as militia & police & obstructs legal methods to Secure
peace & administration of justice   the Commanding Genl should not be content with
Nicholls dishonored promises to disband unless Nicholls regime is to be suffered to acquire title by tacit recognition   to require the retirement of the mob from posts invaded
& to leave them as prior to inauguration of two claimants will alone relieve this city of present terror yet will not imply recognition of Packard" Telegrams received (at 4:12 and 4:44
P.M.), *ibid.*, RG 60, Letters from the President.

Also on Jan. 11, Samuel Bard, New Orleans, telegraphed to USG. "Genl Longstreets
dispatch to you dated Jany Eighth regarding the political situation here contains the truth
the whole truth & nothing but the truth. I believe you will act upon his sound counsel &
maturely consider the situation the people are for law & order and if Gov Nicholls is not
interfered with the constitution as amended will be honored & your administration exalted. Justice wisdom & moderation will cover the entire ground & obviate all trouble"
Telegram received, *ibid.*

On Jan. 12, Packard telegraphed and wrote to USG. "unauthorized armed bodies have
today arrested & imprisoned assistant sergeants at arms of the senate, whilst in the execution of their duty I have laid full statement of facts before General Augur requesting
him to enforce instructions of secretary of war of date Jany nine & ten" "The critical condition of affairs in this state constrains me to address you I write, not to plead my own
case, but that of an aggrieved loyal people, who after having been subjected to exceeding
hardship in the late campaign, now see, upon the ascertainment by a legal and ultimate tribunal of the election of myself and a republican legislative majority, the installation of the
State government interrupted, the courts, arsenals, & police stations in New Orleans captured & held by an armed mob, details of which styling themselves 'militia' or 'police' still
occupy the streets and public places of the capital & make arrests without warrant or authority in law. Official data have already been forwarded to the Attorney General, in relation to the organization of the Legislature, the counting by them of the official vote for
Governor, &c, in accordance with the Constitution together with other documents. The
republican case is this: The Board of Returning Officers is final in its finding The Legislature in determining the qualification of its members has confirmed that finding. The
democratic claimants to the Governorship, and his partizans, in his so-called legislature
stand accredited by no official return of the only body known to the laws of Louisiana by
whom returns of the results of elections are authorised to be made. A pretended return, by
a partizan committee, clothed with no official authority is the sole basis on which the assembly which disputes the authority of the legislature now convened at the State House
rests its claims. A recognition by you of the laws which prevail in Louisiana, and consequently of the binding judicial determination by the Board of Returning Officers (attested
by all the distinguished republicans who came here, at your instance, during the session of
that Board) is all that we ask The testimony taken by the Comtees of both Senate and
House now in this city during the searching investigations now drawing to a close will I
am emboldened to say justify this course and show to the country that the decision of the
Returning Officers is not only binding in law but was abundantly justified by the facts I
forwarded by telegraph a statement in relation to the forcible overthrow of the Supreme
Court of the State By the Constitution of this State the outgoing Governor and Secretary

of State remain in office one week after the declaration by the Legislature of the election of their successors incoming Governor. On the sixth of January two days before the expiration of this term Governor Kellogg recommissioned Chief Justice Ludeling to succeed himself. Associate Justices Leonard and King were likewise appointed by Governor Kellogg whom all departments of the National Government recognized as Governor. These Judges were, it is true, confirmed by the new Republican Senate, but even admitting for sake of argument the illegality of that body, their titles as appointees were not impaired. They are alone competent to Act until the end of the Session of whichever Senate shall yet be recognized. If this appointment be not sustained they have yet their old titles, as have the remaining two Judges who hold over under the Constitution until their successors shall be appointed   Mr Nicholls, in violently ejecting these Judges, and installing others of his own choice, leaps over an authority unquestionably competent to appoint, and asserts his own authority and that of a Senate likewise which you decline as yet to recognize; and thus in defiance of law violently seizes upon the last legal recourse of the Citizen   The revolutionary character of the Court thus attempted to be set up will be better understood when I state that one of the Judges selected by General Nicholls is R H Marr who made demand on Governor Kellogg to abdicate September 14 1874, and on refusal bade the mob go home and get their rifles; and that another is Alcibiades De Blanc who in 1873 headed an armed White League insurrection in St Martins parish, and is still on bail under charge of conspiracy under the Enforcement Act. . . . Throughout the 10th and 11th inst and to day (the 12th) men have been moving about the city with rifles upon their shoulders and the police beats are occupied by men furnished with pistols   When it is known to you that the 'Adjutant General' of this military mob is D B Penn, who as a claimant to the Lieut Governorship under McEnery headed the assault upon the Government in Septr /74 that F N Ogden still leads the White League and has the same regimental commanders as then the temper of the new revolution will be fully seen. I copy from one of the City newspapers this suggestive paragraph: 'To facilitate the assembly and concentration of troops Genl Behan La State Militia issued an order last evening that in case of an alarm requiring the presence of troops "No 22" would be sounded from the fire alarm bells as signals to assemble in Jackson Square and "No 33" as signal for concentration in Lafayette Square. This order was published to the various commands last evening'   Without seeking to anticipate your ultimate action I have respectfully and earnestly to ask that the Supreme Court and Police Stations be recommitted to the hands in which they were prior to the assembling of the armed bands, and that the declaration of the only legal body competent to adjudicate upon the returns be considered as conferring a *prima facie* title until a final determination shall be reached, which I confidently believe will be a recognition of the Administrat[ion] of which I am the elected he[ad]   If such recognition cannot be at once assured I respectfully urge that the Commanding General be furnished instructions to see the public posts restored" Telegram received (at 12:30 A.M.) and LS, *ibid.* Also on Jan. 12, Fish recorded in his diary. "The Attorney General referred to the Louisiana difficulties and a general conversation took place as to the present position. Cameron expressed himself in concurrence, with others of the desirability of quiet, and the inexpediency of any present recognition of either government. A general coincidence of opinion seemed to exist, that whenever it became necessary to recognize one or the other, that the Packard one, was the one that which must be recognized. The President remarked however while the committee of Congress were examining the question, he thought it better to defer any opinion, in which Cameron expressed concurrence, Chandler for once was quiet" DLC-Hamilton Fish. See Joseph G. Dawson III, *Army Generals and Reconstruction: Louisiana, 1862–1877* (Baton Rouge, 1982), pp. 243–48; telegram to Brig. Gen. Christopher C. Augur, Jan. 14, 1877.

To Gen. William T. Sherman

Jan.y 8th 1877.

DEAR GENERAL:

I wish you would write a private note to Prof. Kendrick saying that I have been informed that he would like to retire. If this is so, and vacancies should occur or the retired list between this and March 4th to enable me to do so; I will retire him and appoint his successor. But there is no argument that could induce me to retire Prof. Kendrick against his his will. The Academy will never see his superior over the department he now has charge of, and I have no doubt but his qualifications will serv[e] him for many years yet if he chooses to hold his position. My desire in this matter is to accommodate my old teacher in whatever he may wish in the matter.

Yours Truly

U. S. GRANT

GN. W. T. SHERMAN U. S. A.

ALS, USMA. Henry L. Kendrick, USMA 1835, served as asst. professor of Chemistry, Mineralogy, and Geology at USMA (1835–47), received bvt. maj. for service in the Mexican War, and returned to USMA as professor in 1857. On Jan. 9, 1877, Kendrick wrote to Gen. William T. Sherman. "Your note of yesterday has just now come to hand—too late for answer by this day's mail. I have NO *desire to retire.* You do not know how much I feel obliged to you for your very kind note, & for the good opinion you express of my usefulness here; & I beg that you will take an occasion to convey to the President my grateful appreciation of his friendly & most valued remembrance of me." ALS, DLC-William T. Sherman. See Sherman to Kendrick, Jan. 8, 1877, *ibid.*

On Jan. 27, Maj. Gen. John M. Schofield, superintendent, USMA, wrote to Sherman. "I observe that a Bill has been introduced in the House of Representatives to provide for the appointment of a Professor of Law at the Military Academy. No doubt this has been done at the instance of some person who expects to get the appointment, rather than from any well considered opinion regarding the best interests of the Academy. I hope the measure will be defeated, either in Congress or by the President. The Academy does not want a *Professor* of Law, who would more likely be a political theorist than a sound Constitutional and military lawyer. It is much safer to have such a subject taught by an Army officer detailed for the purpose. Then if a mistake is made in the selection it can readily be remedied, while if a bad appointment is made the evil must be endured for a generation. . . ." ALS, *ibid.* On Jan. 31, Sherman wrote to Schofield. ". . . It seems that Maj Gardner applied for the creation of a Professorship of Law, with the approval of the President, and with the understanding that he was to be appointed Professor. The President after hearing your letter answered, I guess Schofield is right, and without committing himself to any promise consented that I should check, in Committee if possible, any steps actually taken to Establish such a Professorship. This I will do, and I am sure Either Committee of the Senate or House will be glad to prevent any Increase in the number of Professorships at West Point. . . ." ALS, CSmH.

To Brig. Gen. Christopher C. Augur

Washington, D. C
Jan. 14th. 1877.

To. Gen. C. C. Augur. New Orleans. La.

It has been the policy of the Administration to take no part in the settlement of the question of rightful Gov't. in the State of La. at least not until the Congressional Committees now there have made their report. But it is not proper to sit quietly by and see the State government gradually taken possession of by one of the claimants for Gubernatorial honors by illegal means. The Supreme Court set up by Mr. Nichols[1] can receive no more recognition than any other equal number of lawyers convened on the call of any other citizen of the State. A returning board existing in accordance with law, and having judicial as well as ministerial powers over the count of the votes, and in declaring the result of the late election have given certificates of election to the legislature of the State. A legal quorum of each house holding such certificates met and declared Mr. Packard Governor. Should there be a necessity for the recognition of either it must be Packard.

You may furnish a copy of this dispatch to Packard & Nichols.

U. S. Grant.

Copy, DNA, RG 60, Letters Received, La. *HMD*, 45-3-31, I, 962, III, 604; *SRC*, 46-2-388, 158–59. See telegram to William P. Kellogg, Jan. 7, 1877.

On Jan. 14, 1877, Francis T. Nicholls, New Orleans, telegraphed to USG. "It has been represented to me that an effort has been made to convey the idea that a recount of the electoral vote of Louisiana will be made either through the instrumentality of the Supreme Court or the Legislature or myself and others   Such reports are utterly false   Such is not and has never been our intention   The time has passed for the meeting of the electoral college and that matter is now beyond our control and can only be decided by Congress" Telegram received (at 1:50 A.M.), DNA, RG 60, Letters from the President. *HMD*, 45-3-31, III, 604.

On Jan. 15, U.S. Senator J. Rodman West of La. telegraphed to USG. "A number of senators desire to know if the rumor now current here is true that you have recognized

Packard's government" Telegram received, DLC-USG, IB; DNA, RG 107, Telegrams Collected (Bound). On the same day, Culver C. Sniffen telegraphed to West. "It is not true that there has been any formal recognition—" ALS (telegram sent), *ibid.*

On the same day, Samuel H. Kennedy and three others, bank presidents, New Orleans, telegraphed to USG. "That you may not act in error as to the real situation here we desire to inform you that the senate recognizing Nicholls is composed of twenty two members twenty of whom hold certificates from returning board nineteen constitute a quorum this body is therefore the senate of Louisiana The Packard body is without a quorum the House of Representatives recognizing Nicholls and recognized by the legal senate contains sixty two more than a quorum of members shown to have been elected by the precinct returns we are not connected with Politics but citizens anxious to see good Government restored in this state." Telegram received (at 5:38 P.M.), *ibid.*, RG 60, Letters from the President.

Also on Jan. 15, Brig. Gen. Christopher C. Augur, New Orleans, telegraphed in cipher to AG Edward D. Townsend. "It is claimed that the dispatch from the President to me yesterday authorized me to judge of the necessity under which the Packard Government is to be recognized and to use the troops to reinstate its courts, arsenals, &c. I do not so regard it, or as changing my orders in any respect. I am strengthened in this view by a despatch from the Attorney General to Marshal here on Tuesday last, saying substantially the troops could not be used until the President had issued a proclamation under the call of the Packard Legislature for assistance. I have so informed Packard." Copy (received at 5:00 P.M.), *ibid.*, RG 94, Letters Received, 4788 1876.

On the same day, Stephen B. Packard, New Orleans, telegraphed to USG. "After receipt of copy of your order sent General Augur I issued temperate proclamation ordering armed bodies to disperse &c Instead of complying white league immediately assembled in force at their various rendezvous and are prepared to resist any attempt to compel obdience to state authorities a demand made by acting Civil sheriff for possession of the rooms of supreme court was refused and the Judges denied admittance. Supreme Court have again today called upon me to furnish military force under the law ~~and~~ to enforc[e] possession of the records &c. I have transmitted the same with a letter to Genl Augur in view of inability of state force to dislodge insurgents the excitement attending the assembling of armed men constantly tending to violence the Rabble openly discuss their ability with eight to ten thousand armed men organized into infantry & atillery to successfully resist u s forces if they attempt any support unfortunate results will ensue if this insurgent rebellious organization is not promptly crushed by the federal government they have seven pieces of atillery & all the small arms belonging to the state except those in hands of the small force in state house besides their own." Telegram received (on Jan. 16, 1:10 A.M.), *ibid.*, RG 60, Letters from the President.

On Jan. 16, John R. G. Pitkin, U.S. marshal, La., Washington, D. C., wrote to USG. "In addition to the communication sent in to you this morning from my hands, I have respectfully to enclose a telegram sent me at midnight by my deputy. The 'Democrat' is the official organ of Nicholls." ALS, *ibid.* On Jan. 15, Job B. Stockton, New Orleans, had telegraphed to Pitkin. "In speaking of Governor Packard's proclamation evening Democrat says 'we advise our friends to let the full weight of their vengence fall upon the leaders of this iniquitous murderous and most damnable scheme and to follow Packard into the hotel and if need be into the Custom House itself and hang him from highest window.' mounted Orderlies with sabres & yellow Saddle skirts are on streets tonight" Telegram received (on Jan. 16, 1:00 A.M.), *ibid.* Pitkin endorsed this telegram. "The term 'hotel' means the State House, formerly the St Louis Hotel." AES, *ibid.*

On Jan. 16, 2:00 P.M., Secretary of War James D. Cameron telegraphed to Augur. "Your understanding of the Presidents telegram of the 14th is entirely correct He desires me ~~to say~~ to repeat to you that he wishes the present status ~~to be~~ throughout the state maintained until the Congressional Committees now in Louisiana return—" Df, *ibid.*, RG 94, Letters Received, 4788 1876. See Hamilton Fish diary, Jan. 16, 1877, DLC-Hamilton Fish.

Also on Jan. 16, Packard twice telegraphed to USG. "The following extract from the Picayune of this morning gives a Correct statement of the condition of affairs at the supreme Court building and shows the force of white league present   at midnight the court buildings and the third precinct station were in a state of preparation to resist any attack which might have been made However large   Cols. Angel Allen and Landry were in charge of the regiments of militia posted in the buildings and genl Behand Chief In command of the post   the number of men occupying the buildings was between six hundred & one thousand" "I desire respectfully to represent that the status of today not only works Great injury to the claims of my Govt which has prima facia right to recognition but the usurpation of the supreme & other courts is calculated to work delay & damage to delegations & business interest. Would it not be simply justice to restore the status as it existed at the close of Gov Kelloggs adminstration   The just claim of either party could be injured by this course   Aggression is extending at this writing to the country parishes" Telegrams received (at 12:55 and 11:50 P.M.), DNA, RG 60, Letters from the President.

On Jan. 17, Secretary of State Hamilton Fish recorded in his diary a conversation in which USG "remarked that he rarely lost his sleep, but that lately he had been much disturbed by the Louisianna difficulty and the importunities, of what he called, 'some of the rabid Republicans' to induce him to take extreme measures, he named John Sherman & Hale as having frequently urged him to such measures; that having been there, they seemed to have gotten themselves more excited—I suggest that possibly they have committed themselves and wish to draw him into the same views; he spoke with a good deal of warmth of the extreme incapacity of the men attempting to rule Louisianna that they had no interests there, but had simply gone there to hold office and so soon as they should lose it, intended to come away. He says he is opposed to the XV amendment and thinks it was a mistake; that it had done the negro no good, and had been a hindrance to the South, and by no means a political advantage to the North. He read a letter of Longstreet, addressed to himself, which he said seemed to be proposing a political bargain, to which of course he could not be a party; the letter in substance stated that the Nichols Government would be content to recognize the 'Hayes electors' if their government could be established, and invited a reply from the President; which he said he should not make. He expressed great anxiety for the solution of this question, and for relief from the pressure brought to bear on him. He said he had thought of sending to Congress all the information he had received by letter or telegram (and while as at present advised he believed the 'Packard Government' to be legally) ~~and~~ to submit the question for the decision of Congress. He commented with some earnestness on the embarrassments of the position of the Republicans as to Louisianna from the fact, that admittedly from 6000 to 9000 majority was cast for the Tilden electors; that a returning board had taken out or rejected sufficient votes to change the majority into from 2000 to 4000 for the Republicans. He commented on the fact that the returning board had failed to fill up the vacancy in its body and that the whole subject was surrounded with difficulty & suspicion. Asking my opinion as to the advisability of such message, I was not prepared to advise sending it without further consideration; that it would probably have a very marked bearing on the counting of the Electoral votes, and I thought there was a serious constitutional question, raised whether the decision of the question as to which was the legitimate government of a State rested with the President or with Congress." DLC-Hamilton Fish.

On Jan. 19, Packard telegraphed to USG. "I have this a m Sent Gen Augur information of the capture during last night by the nichols party of the State library and arrest of officers guarding Same Gen Nichols is also appointing officers who are taking possession of the offices in the parishes which seems to be in violation of your orders to have the Statu quo preserved" Telegram received (at 3:50 P.M.), DNA, RG 60, Letters from the President.

On Jan. 21, Pitkin wrote to USG. "I have respectfully to call your attention to a new and serious project of the Nicholls party to interrupt the *statu quo* in Louisiana, despite the telegram of the Secretary of War on the 16th inst. conveying to Gen. Augur the wish of the President to maintain the present status until the La. Congressional committees shall have reported. A telegram received by me from Mr Packard reads as follows; 'New Orleans Jan. 20th 6.30 P. M. Houston, one of the Nicholls Gov't. seated by the White League, has enjoined tax-collector Lanier of Carroll parish and other tax-collectors from paying or settling with the Auditor of the State, Johnson. These tax-collectors are now in the city with their monies. The Auditor is a part of the government and the injunction against recognizing him is ruinous. The monies are needed for Schools, Charity Hospital and other purposes, and such proceedings by a government of armed force are equal to the use of arms as a means of disintegration, if permitted to go on.' Auditor Johnson is the old Auditor and was returned Elected. He is, moreover, in possession of the Auditor's office and under new and heavy bonds. The old Kellogg tax-collectors, now making their fiscal returns, are enjoined by a Nicholls partisan on the Bench. The sacred needs to which the revenues have promptly to be applied, impel me to ask that as in the case of the old State Librarian deposed on the 19th by Nicholls and restored on the 20th by Gen Augur, the Auditor be left unembarrassed in his duty to receive and hold in custody the public monies now held by the tax-collectors of the numerous parishes, who are in New Orleans seeking to be relieved of their responsibility. This, I conceive, will be but in discharge of the intent, expressed in Secretary Cameron's telegram of the 16th, to maintain the *statu quo* and will aid the proper conservation of monies absolutely needful to subsist whichever government may be ultimately recognized." ALS, *ibid.*

On Jan. 25, Packard telegraphed to USG. "January twenty D Pierson defeated Candidate district Judge Natchitoches Parish took possesion Court under Commission of Nicholls & same day suspended Republican sheriff & Coroner unquestionably elected for not recognizing him is now threatenig to imprison President of Police Jury unless he approves Bond of his Piersons appointee as sheriff in Parish ouchata number of officers were displaced in similar way Jany seventeen Nicholls in letter Gen Augur today claims this not violation Status Quo Because he had Commissioned these men before Jany sixteen when your order issued I respectfully ask that Genl Commandig be directed either to reinstate supreme court of state illegally Ousted so that dispossessed officials may enforce their rights through Court or that Genl Augur be instructed to eject all officers who have illegally seized possession under pretended Commissions of Nicholls since Jany sixteen in violation of Status Quo" Telegram received (at 11:00 P.M.), *ibid.* On the same day, Augur telegraphed to Townsend on the same subject. ". . . I send all the papers by mail, General Nicholls states if the President after seeing them decides that status has been violated, he will advise officers installed to conform to his wish." Copy (received on Jan. 26, 1:00 A.M.), *ibid.*, RG 94, Letters Received, 4788 1876. On Jan. 26, Cameron telegraphed to Augur. "Your telegram of yesterday is received and shown to the President who says that he has heard both sides of the question to which you refer and thinks that in the case of Ouachita the status has not been changed but in the case of Natchitoches it has been and that it should be restored to same status as previous to the sixteenth—" Copies, *ibid.*; *ibid.*, RG 107, Letters Sent, Military Affairs.

On Jan. 27, Fish recorded in his diary a conversation with USG. "He spoke with a great deal of feeling of the Louisianna troubles, and of the importunity with which they were pressing him to recognize the Packard Government; said that with the information now before him, were he obliged to decide between the two he should be forced to recognize the Packard Government, in as much as it appeared that a majority of the Members of the Legislature received the certificates of the Returning Board; that this board was organized by a law of the state, but was in his Judgment an outrageous contrivance, and had in its whole history been tainted with suspicion, if not ~~of~~ with actual fraud; that he was convinced that it would be for the interest of the people of Louisianna, both white and black, that the Nichols Government should be in power; that as a political question, he thought any action at this time looking to the recognition of either government, would be injurious to the Republican Party, and to the ultimate success of Gov Hayes; that this whole question had given him a great deal of anxiety and trouble; that he had been importuned, in season, and out of season, to an extent which was indelicate if not indecent; that ~~on recognition~~ a recommendation from this City had been made that Packard and his friend ~~would~~ should force a collission, so as to force the necessity of a recognition; that he had abstained from bringing up the question for discussion by the Cabinet, in as much as he believed that there would be about six members against him, and only one with him. I told him I thought Robeson would not be against him, and I was not sure that Morrill would favor present action—'Well,' he said 'at best it would be one with me one or two half & half and four or five against me but I will not, unless forced by circumstances take any action at present or until the full reports of the Louisianna Investigating committee are before me, and the Presidential question decided'" DLC-Hamilton Fish.

On Feb. 5, Packard telegraphed to USG. "I respectfully urge that so soon as the facts of the election in this State shall have been officially reported to Congress by the Committees appointed for that purpose Recognition be immediately accorded to the legally organized state Govt for the following among other pressing reasons   the faith of the state pledged by constitutional amendment to its Creditors at Home & abroad for Prompt payment of interest on its Bonded debt is in danger of being violated by the enforced suspension of tax collection   The levees which protect the state from overflow are in a critical condition   the state engineers are without funds to proceed to their relief   The inmates of the State Charitable Institution specially the unfortunates in the Insane asylum are suffering cruel provations from Cold & insufficient food & Clothing   relief can only be afforded by legislative appropriation which Cannot be passed without a quorum which cannot be obtained without recognition   The commerce of N. Orleans is paralized   every material interest of the state suffers & the public peace is gravely menaced by the continuance of the present uncertainty" Telegram received (at 9:00 P.M.), DNA, RG 60, Letters from the President. On Feb. 6, Fish recorded in his diary. "The President read a telegram from Packard, of New Orleans, assigning reasons why one or other of the State Governments should be speedily recognized. The President stated he would not recognize either until the Congressional decision on the Electral vote; and that his present opinion is, that he will be governed by their action unless it be that they should admit the Hayes electral votes *solely* on the ground that they cannot go behind the certificates" DLC-Hamilton Fish.

On [*Feb. 14*], USG drafted a telegram for Townsend to Augur. "The President directs me to say that information is received from New Orleans, purporting to be correct, that dispairing of a favorable result ~~to~~ from the Commission chosen to settle disputed points in the Electoral count, for the democratic candidate, it is the determinations of the friends of

Nichols to seize, by force, the State House immediately on the declaration of an adverse ~~declaration~~ decission. Also to murder certain prominent republicans to compel Martial law. He is loth to believe that murder & assassination can be resorted to for such a purpose, but deems it his duty to call your attention to these rumors in order that you may inform yourself of the foundation for them and to prepare for an effectual prevention" ADf, DNA, RG 94, Letters Received, 4788 1876. On Feb. 15, Augur telegraphed in cipher to Townsend, who handed a copy to USG at 7:25 P.M. "I have received your cipher despatch of yesterday. There has been and is undoubtedly a good deal of talk here of the character referred to therein. There seems from what I can learn a fixed determination on the part of a large majority of people here to resist in every possible way the establishment of the Packard Government. They prefer a military one—in what manner and to what extent they will proceed cannot be told. I do not think murder or assassination are contemplated, certainly not by nicholls. But they may result from such loose talk. Packards opponents are numerous, united and aggressive, his friends few, unorganized and furnish no moral or material support. From present appearances his Government can only be maintained by use of United States troops. I do not understand that they care so much who is President." Telegram received, *ibid.*

On Feb. 15, Stockton telegraphed to Pitkin. "An attempt to assassinate Gov Packard was made at twelve oclock the assassin shot Packard in leg & Packard returned fire mortally wounding the assassin more in a few minutes" Telegram received (at 2:02 P.M.), *ibid.*, RG 60, Letters from the President. Related telegrams are *ibid.*

On [*Feb. 16*], USG drafted a telegram for Townsend to Augur. "[I am directed by the President to say] Reported from New Orleans that wires will be cut to-night and an Attack made upon ~~Kel~~ Packard party to-morrow. The rumor may be idle, but every precaution should be taken to preserve peace. Should there be no communication with you to-morrow the gravest apprehension will be felt here. [Report tomorrow by telegraph]" ADf (bracketed material not in USG's hand), *ibid.*, RG 94, Letters Received, 4788 1876. USG endorsed this draft. "The Adj. Gen. will please send dispatch of the above substance, in syher, to be delivered at once." AES, *ibid.* On Feb. 17, Augur telegraphed in cipher to Townsend. "Everything quiet this morning. Newspapers counsel resistance to Packard Government should it be recognized If it should be I think it advisable to precede such action by sending a light battery here." Telegram received, *ibid.*

Also on Feb. 17, Thomas F. Oliver, deputy tax collector, Richland Parish, Rayville, wrote to USG. "Although I am but an humble citizen of the United States and State of Louisiana I nevertheless feel it to be my right and privilege to place before you, the in true condition which Political Excitements have brought Society to in the State of Louisiana Having resided in this State since AD 1837 I know the temper and character of her citizens We are a people of no fixed Principles beyond Pecuniary covetousness and envy. the party in possession of Official Positions is invariably a Target at whom the most denunciating Poisonous attacks of both the press and tongue are fired which not unfrequently results in having encouraged the lower and less informed part of our community Secretly resort to use Firearms and other Deadly weapons against the persons and the torch against the combustible property of the envied to avenge their malicious animosities. These acts sometimes occur between enemies of the same Political creed who avail the Political Fever as a cover for the Deed. Within the last (30) thirty days Congress has enacted the Electoral commission Law which was heartily accepted by our Democratic Element as a true and Satisfactory means of arriving at who properly is entitled to the Presidential Chair of these United States after 4th of next march the same element proclaimed both by Tonge & press that any awards made by the Electoral commission Should be a Satisfactory Settlement of that Subject. To the Law Some Republican Journals made considerable opposition Now Since the commission's judgement is contrary to the wishes of the first named element they impugn it with Partisanship and are using all the denunciatory Poisonous languages both by press ('Vicksburg Herald' and 'N. O. Democrat' being) prominent) and tongue at their command to arouse the most inflamatory feelings in the minds of the weaker Intellect and Evil Doers of their party which will result (under civil Government) in the loss of life to many good citizens who are isolatedly located in this state—If Genl Nichols should receive the Recognition of the Federal Government as Governor he cannot Controll and Govern this people in harmony and tranquility. fFor as soon as he will have filled his appointive Offices (for each of which there is an average of Five applicants from his own party) The disappointed applicants in their Averice and envy return to their respective Influences and denounce his administration as foul and teach their followers not to obey his Mandates and comes the Same reversion of bitter feeling (which will be as hard to overcome as ever was the prejudices against Gov Kellogg) and as now exists against the Electoral commission Should Capt Packard be recognized by the Federal Government, as Govenor of Louisiana he has the weight of prejudices against former Govenor's—Warmoth and Kellogg in addition to the bitter feeling which exists at present against an administration to be directed by him and I do not think he can even hold possession of the Executive offices unless backed up by the U. S. Army and while he might be thus far in that way be sustained every Intilligent citizen who would indorse his Government in the interior Parishes remote from U. S. Troops would be in Peril of loosing his life in a way that the offenders would never be overtaken. as in the 'Colfax' and 'Cushatta' cases and should they be overtaken and corrected (I now speak for Personal safety) what consolation or relief would it afford me after my life has been taken to have the laws enforced and the offender punished that will not not bring me back into existance That rule Imitates too much locking the stable Door after the horse was stolen I disire some plan of Goverment for Louisiana adopted by which my own and many others (like me) lives will be protected. as well as Mr Packard's Government and life The Elictive system here has run into of making the Officers the instruments of their constituents (in Many instances) instead of Law and the result is that not much law is enforced and I look upon Elections in Louisiana as being destructive of all harmony and tranquility in Society besides a great drawback upon all the pursuits of the Country for there are but few of our intelligent Citizens who do not devote as much of their time in Political planning as they do to all other pursuits. It is therefore obvious to you that if so much of the time of the talent of the country is thrown away for discordant purposes—That Agriculture and other industrial pursuits must necessarily seriously suffer. Hence it is my conviction that if Louisiana could be deprived of Elective priveleges for Ten years to come her people would become a Happy, harmonious and prosperous. I am a very conservative Republican and supported the last State & National Rep Ticket I have conversed with conservative Democrats who inform me that that Party have resolved not to Submit to the Packard Government And desiring a Military Government in preference. I trust in God to direct you in your action with La in such a way as may make us amicably Social at least It must be clear to your mind that the publicity of this letter would imperil my personal safety. I therefore do not give you the privilege of using my name publicly in connexion with it Very Resp Pardon my long espistle, as I have made it as conscise as I could to cover the Subject" ALS, *ibid.*, RG 60, Letters from the President.

On the same day, James Longstreet, New Orleans, wrote to USG. "I wrote you about a month ago trying to explain the solution of the political embrolio in Louisiana according to my judgment. My interest in your good name, and the affairs of the country, will I trust be sufficient excuse for this further trespass upon your valuable time. In my former letter I tried to show that the many republican votes that were cast for the democratic ticket were freely given for the Nichols ticket, but that none of them were intentionally given to the democratic electors. That therefore whilst the Hayes electors were entitled in equity to these votes, the Nichols State ticket is also entitled to them, and that therefore the Nichols government should be recognised. I beg leave further to state that it will be better for the republican party south, if this idea can be adopted. For if the Packard government is forced upon this State, the greater part, if not all, of the southern men who have been identified with the republican party; in the hope that some day the party might be put upon a basis that might justify their efforts, in giving it permanent organisation, will be obliged to abandon their hopes and await some more favorable opportunity. Mr Packard is not, I think, in condition, to maintain himself and the party in such manner as to warrant any of us in attempting to maintain our identity with it, and without some stronger element in the party in this section it must fail of success here. Whilst with Gov Hayes as President the party can be so organised, as to divide the white and colored vote, not only in Louisiana but throughout the South, and make the party strong. This can be more readily accomplished under Nichols as governor, simply because the forcing of Packard upon the people as governor, will at once arouse all of the former prejudice and opposition of the whites, and render the party more objectionable with them than it has ever been." ALS, OFH. USG endorsed this letter. "Call attention of the President to this" AE (undated), *ibid.*

On Feb. 19, Fish recorded in his diary a conversation with USG. "I then spoke of the condition of affairs in Louisiana, asking if he had come to any conclusion, in his own mind, as to the course he was to pursue. He had not definitely; but said he was very much ~~embarrassed~~ embarassed by the importunities brought to bear on him, and expressed the same opinion he had heretofore done. I urge upon him that unless there be an absolute necessity of his recognizing one government or the other, he should leave it for his successor, as otherwise he might be imposing on Gov Hayes a policy adverse to his own views, and thus embarrass and jeopard the success of the Administration for the next 4 years. He admitted the force of this, saying he did not think he should be called on to make any decision; and not justified unless an imperative necessity required it. I asked if he had seen the Capital of yesterday, he had not, as he does not allow the paper in his house, but is aware of the nature of an article it has published suggesting assassination and insurrection. I told him I thought it would be advisable to have a prosecution instituted against the Editor, to which he immediatly assented; and sent for the Attorney General who shortly came and the President requested him to have a complaint and arrest made today and an indictment found as soon as possible" DLC-Hamilton Fish. See Fish diary, Feb. 18, 1877, *ibid.*

On Feb. 20, Thomas Lynne, New Orleans, wrote to USG. "I fear our Louisiana case is not ended—the old spirit dominates here. I am not at all surprised at any thing that Mike Hahn touches—Poison—look out   he happened to be appointed as my Successor as State Registrar of Voters for this State. . . . I wish you would direct Genl. P. H. Sheridan to come here—the old Rebels are afraid of Him as soon as he comes   Little Phil as the Rebels call him—Peace—Peace or War." ALS, DNA, RG 60, Letters from the President.

On Feb. 23, Fish recorded in his diary. "The President has received an application from Packard of Louisiana asking for an increase of Military force, on the 6th of March when the Legislature is to adjourn. With a good deal of emphasis, he remarked I shall do no such thing; we will not sustain Legislatures with Military force." DLC-Hamilton Fish.

On Feb. 28, Armistead Burwell wrote to USG. "I write a few words to you earnestly, and ask you to read and consider what I say. Ours is a government of Law and constitution, founded in the consent of the governed and sustained by public and enlightened opinion   It is vain to strive for the mere theory. That is working against an impossibility. Sentimentality never governed well and I apprehend never will. The wealth, intelligence & business energies of a state will strive for and in the end gain the ascendancy in the conduct of affairs; and it merely delays, & increases the difficulty, to make the endeavour by mere points of doubtful Law and by the points of the bayonets of armed men, to put off the day of the recognition of such ascendancy. Waste and ruin may be made, but nothing will be gained in the end by the party resorting to such means to defeat the true will of the people. This mere party view does not influence me so much as my concern for the whole country. The counting of the Electoral vote for Hayes & Wheeler under the decision of the commission, does not settle the right, nor exclude the claim of the people of Louisiana, to the local self government elected by the large majority of her people. It is not according to my idea of our system to use the Army as a constabulary force: to make the Military the central planet: to make state governments revolve around it. If this be done, then we have the form of free & Republican goverment; the dead carcass, but the soul will have fled forever. It is not the province of the United States to dictate in the matter of erecting a state Goverment, or to supervise the election of state offices. Still less is it the duty of the goverment of U. S to impose an imbecile and corrupt administration of state affairs on an unwilling people. The imbecility of the Packard concern is apparent. The public good demands that it be swept from existence. This can be done without the shedding of one drop of blood. Remove all the extraneous and illegal support, and it will fade from existence. Either find a way through the subtle quibbles invented to defeat the will of the people, or make one. The public good demands this. It is right and just to relieve the incoming administration of all embarrassment. Place the people of Louisiana under the state Government of their own choice: withdraw all support to what that people denounce, as usurpation, & revile as the result of fraud perjury and forgery, and which in every way the people of Louisiana, refuse to sustain. For this great act closing your administration, forty millions will bless & honor you. It may be difficult, but it is not impossible to give greater brilliancy to the diamond. Your illustrious career will be fitly closd by this act, more than all others contributing to the Union peace & prosperity of the whole country." Copy, OFH. See letter to James D. Cameron, March 3, 1877; Joseph G. Dawson III, *Army Generals and Reconstruction: Louisiana, 1862–1877* (Baton Rouge, 1982), pp. 248–52.

1. Born in 1834 in La., Nicholls graduated USMA in 1855, left the army in 1856, and served as brig. gen., C.S. Army, before resuming law practice.

To House of Representatives

To THE HOUSE OF REPRESENTATIVES—

The "Joint Resolution authorizing the Secretary of War to supply blankets to the Reform School in the District of Columbia" is before me—

I am in entire sympathy with the purpose of the Resolution, but before taking any action upon it I deem it my duty to submit for your consideration the accompanying letter received from the Secretary of War, embodying a report (Made in anticipation of the passage of the Resolution) by the Quartermaster General of the Army, in which, among other facts, it is stated that "the appropriation for clothing for the Army for this fiscal year is much smaller than usual, and the supply of blankets which it will allow us to purchase is so small that none can properly be spared for other purposes than the supply of the Army.—

If it be thought by Congress worth while to cause the supply of blankets for the institution referred to, to be procured through the War Department, it is respectfully suggested that provision to meet the expense be made by special appropriation".—

U. S. GRANT—

EXECUTIVE MANSION—

JANUARY 15. 1877.

Copy, DNA, RG 130, Messages to Congress. *SMD,* 49-2-53, 404–5. On Jan. 11, 1877, Secretary of War James D. Cameron wrote to USG. "I have the honor to state that it appears from the Congressional Record of January 10th 1877, page 2, that House Resolution No. 169, authorizing the Secretary of War to supply blankets to the Reform School in the District of Columbia, was passed by the Senate on the 9th instant. The Quartermaster General reports on this resolution, as follows:—'There are about seven hundred blankets of the old style in the depots of the Quartermaster's Department. They are not so good as those made lately, and they are reserved for issue to Military prisoners. Some have lately been sent to the Indian prisoners at St. Augustine. The Military prison at Fort Leavenworth makes constant requisition upon this stock which will not last long. . . . The Army blanket under present contract costs $4 25. It weighs five pounds, is of pure wool, and measures 7 feet by 5 feet 6 inches. If appropriation be made early it will be possible to procure in addition to the army supply, those needed for the school under the existing contract.'" Copy, DNA, RG 107, Letters Sent, Military Affairs. On Jan. 26, USG approved a resolution authorizing the secretary of war "to deliver, for use of the Reform School of the District of Columbia, two hundred Army blankets, from any in his custody belonging to the United States." *U.S. Statutes at Large,* XIX, 409. See *CR,* 44–2, 492–93.

To House of Representatives

————

To the House of Representatives:

On the 9th day of December, 1876, the following resolution of the House of Representatives was received, namely:

"*Resolved,* That the President be requested, if not incompatible with the public interest, to transmit to this House copies of any and all orders or directions emanating from him or from either of the Executive Departments of the Government to any military commander or civil officer, with reference to the service of the Army, or any portion thereof, in the States of Virginia, South Carolina, Louisiana, and Florida, since the 1st of August last, together with reports by telegraph or otherwise from either or any of said military commanders or civil officers."[1]

It was immediately or soon thereafter referred to the Secretary of War and the Attorney-General, the custodians of all retained copies of "orders or directions" given by the executive department of the Government covered by the above inquiry, together with all information upon which such "orders or directions" were given.

The information, it will be observed, is voluminous, and, with the limited clerical force in the Department of Justice, has consumed the time up to the present. Many of the communications accompanying this have been already made public in connection with messages heretofore sent to Congress. This class of information includes the important documents received from the governor of South Carolina, and sent to Congress with my message on the subject of the Hamburgh massacre;[2] also the documents accompanying my response to the resolution of the House of Representatives in regard to the soldiers stationed at Petersburgh.[3]

There have also come to me and to the Department of Justice, from time to time, other earnest written communications from persons holding public trusts and from others residing in the South, some of which I append hereto as bearing upon the precarious condition of the public peace in those States. These communications I have reason to regard as made by respectable and responsible men. Many of them deprecate the publication of their names as involving danger to them personally.

The reports heretofore made by committees of Congress of the results of their inquiries in Mississippi and in Louisiana, and the newspapers of several States recommending "the Mississippi plan," have also furnished important data for estimating the danger to the public peace and order in those States.

It is enough to say that these different kinds and sources of evidence have left no doubt whatever in my mind that intimidation has been used, and actual violence, to an extent requiring the aid of the

United States Government, where it was practicable to furnish such aid, in South Carolina, in Florida, and in Louisiana, as well as in Mississippi, in Alabama, and in Georgia.

The troops of the United States have been but sparingly used, and in no case so as to interfere with the free exercise of the right of suffrage. Very few troops were available for the purpose of preventing or suppressing the violence and intimidation existing in the States above named. In no case, except that of South Carolina, was the number of soldiers in any State increased in anticipation of the election, saving that twenty-four men and an officer were sent from Fort Foote to Petersburgh, Virginia, where disturbances were threatened prior to the election.

No troops were stationed at the voting-places. In Florida and in Louisiana, respectively, the small number of soldiers already in the said States were stationed at such points in each State as were most threatened with violence, where they might be available as a posse for the officer whose duty it was to preserve the peace and prevent intimidation of voters. Such a disposition of the troops seemed to me reasonable and justified by law and precedent, while its omission would have been inconsistent with the constitutional duty of the President of the United States "to take care that the laws be faithfully executed." The statute expressly forbids the bringing of troops to the polls, "except where it is necessary to keep the peace," implying that to keep the peace it may be done. But this even, so far as I am advised, has not in any case been done. The stationing of a company or part of a company in the vicinity, where they would be available to prevent riot, has been the only use made of troops prior to and at the time of the elections. Where so stationed, they could be called in an emergency requiring it by a marshal or deputy marshal as a posse to aid in suppressing unlawful violence. The evidence which has come to me has left me no ground to doubt that if there had been more military force available it would have been my duty to have disposed of it in several States with a view to the prevention of the violence and intimidation which have undoubtedly contributed to the defeat of the election law in Mississippi, Alabama, and Georgia, as well as in South Carolina, Louisiana, and Florida.

By article 4, section 4, of the Constitution, "The United States shall guarantee to every State in this Union a republican form of goverment, and shall protect each of them against invasion, and on application of the Legislature, or of the executive, (when the Legislature cannot be convened,) against domestic violence."

By act of Congress (R. S. U. S., sections 1034-'5,) the President, in case of "insurrection in any State," or of "unlawful obstruction to the enforcement of the laws of the United States by the ordinary course of judicial proceedings," or whenever "domestic violence in any State so obstructs the execution of the laws thereof and of the United States as to deprive any portion of the people of such State" of their civil or political rights, is authorized to employ such parts of the land and naval forces as he may deem necessary to enforce the execution of the laws and preserve the peace, and sustain the authority of the State and of the United States. Acting under this title (69) of the Revised Statutes, United States, I accompanied the sending of troops to South Carolina with a proclamation such as is therein prescribed.[4]

The President is also authorized by act of Congress "to employ such part of the land or naval forces of the United States" . . . "as shall be necessary to prevent the violation and to enforce the due execution of the provisions" of title 24 of the Revised Statutes of the United States, for the protection of the civil rights of citize[ns], among which is the provision against conspiracies "to prevent by force, intimidation, or threat, any citizen who is lawfully entitled to vote from giving his support or advocacy in a legal manner toward or in favor of the election of any lawfully qualified person as an elector for President or Vice-President, or as a member of Congress of the United States." (United States Revised Statutes, 1989.)

In cases falling under this title, I have not considered it necessary to issue a proclamation to precede or accompany the employment of such part of the Army as seemed to be necessary.

In case of insurrection against a State government or against the Government of the United States, a proclamation is appropriate. But in keeping the peace of the United States at an election at which members of Congress are elected, no such call from the State or proclamation by the President is prescribed by statute or required by precedent.

In the case of South Carolina, insurrection and domestic violence against the State government were clearly shown, and the application of the governor founded thereon was duly presented, and I could not deny his constitutional request without abandoning my duty as the Executive of the National Government.

The companies stationed in the other States have been employed to secure the better execution of the laws of the United States and to preserve the peace of the United States.

After the election had been had, and where violence was apprehended by which the returns from the counties and precincts might be destroyed, troops were ordered to the State of Florida, and those already in Louisiana were ordered to the points in greatest danger of violence.

I have not employed troops on slight occasions, nor in any case where it has not been necessary to the enforcement of the laws of the United States. In this I have been guided by the Constitution and the laws which have been enacted and the precedents which have been formed under it.

It has been necessary to employ troops occasionally to overcome resistance to the internal-revenue laws from the time of the resistance to the collection of the whisky tax in Pennsylvania, under Washington, to the present time.

In 1854, when it was apprehended that resistance would be made in Boston to the seizure and return to his master of a fugitive slave, the troops there stationed were employed to enforce the master's right under the Constitution, and troops stationed at New York were ordered to be in readiness to go to Boston if it should prove to be necessary.

In 1859, when John Brown, with a small number of men, made his attack upon Harper's Ferry, the President ordered United States troops to assist in the apprehension and suppression of him and his party without a formal call of the Legislature or governor of Virginia and without proclamation of the President.

Without citing further instances in which the Executive has exercised his power as Commander of the Army and Navy to prevent or suppress resistance to the laws of the United States or where he has exercised like authority in obedience to a call from a State to suppress insurrection, I desire to assure both Congress and the country that it has been my purpose to administer the executive powers of the Government fairly, and in no instance to disregard or transcend the limits of the Constitution.

U. S. GRANT.

EXECUTIVE MANSION, *January* 22, 1877.

Printed (with ellipsis), DNA, RG 130, Messages to Congress. *HED,* 44-2-30; *HRC,* 44-2-175, part 2, pp. 21–23. On Dec. 14, 1876, Secretary of War James D. Cameron wrote to USG. "In response to your note of December 9th 1876, I beg leave to submit, herewith, copies of papers, on file in this Department, upon the general subject of political outrages, and the use of the Army in the South, from 1865 to the present date. . . ." Copy, DNA, RG 107, Letters Sent, Military Affairs. *HED,* 44-2-30, 4. On Dec. 16, Attorney Gen. Alphonso Taft wrote to USG. "The papers relating to the military orders, and to the Precedents, and to the grounds of the action of the President in the Southern states, have not been completed. I have requested the War department to furnish the military orders in sundry cases, for instance, in the case of John Brown's raid, the Dorr Rebellion, the rescuing a fugitive slave in Boston & others, which have just come over; and we are having the letters of marshals & others in the Southern States copied & abstracted so as to be accessible, but the work takes more time than I supposed. It may require several day yet. But if you regard it as important, it must be hurred up." ALS, PHi.

On Dec. 1, Joseph J. Bartlett, New York City, had written to USG. "I have since the election strongly desired to address you upon the situation of Affairs connected with the succession to your Office of President of the United States. The Public Press can give no positive information to you as to the state of feeling of those who were with you in saving the Union, and they cant themselves, as I see, unless they do so personally. I therefore desire to state that my sympathies are entirely with you in what you are doing to preserve the peace. And I believe the entire responsibility will finally rest with you alone to give the country a stable government during the next four years. What I desire most especially to accomplish through this personal letter is to recall myself to your mind and beg you to put me down for future use, in any capacity,—amongst the first of your old Vol Generals to be called upon in case of necessity. I believe the Country is with you, and I should very much regret to see a News Paper howl frighten the government from doing its whole duty" ALS, USG 3.

On Dec. 2, John Brown, Jr., Put in Bay, Ohio, wrote to USG. "(*Private*) . . . Be assured, my dear sir, of my full sympathy with you, and that this sympathy is not of a new-fledged kind. If you have within eight years past, made some few mistakes, (who is there who has not made them,) I ought certainly to be advised of them for I have been a suscriber to the New York Sun for several years; yet I have steadily voted for you. Have been, and still am an unflinching Republican, as in Principle my Father was, and his Fathers before him. On this morning of the 17th Anniversary of the execution of my Father at Charlestown Va, I give my first hour in this tribute of my esteem for you as a worthy President,—a great General; and for what is more,—a *Man.*—During the Kansas troubles, and while I could, during the War of the Rebellion, I tried to do my duty. Am 55 years of age, yet better fitted for another Campaign should one come; than at any former period of my life. If there comes again a struggle at arms, Pplease consider me as enlisted during the war in *any* capacity which I can fill, even the humblest; so I may serve the *cause* of humanity, which it rejoices me to believe you Mr President have so dear to your heart. I would have you know that you can depend on me and on what little influence I might be able to bring in such an emergency. That an emergency of that kind will arise, seems to me only a question of time, whoever may be, by our late election, declared President. . . ." ALS, *ibid.* See *New York Times*, Sept. 23, 1872.

On Dec. 3, William F. Goodman *et al.*, Elmira, N. Y., petitioned USG. "we the Colored Citizens of this city and State with other Colored Citizens of the United States of America Send—Greeting—to Ulysees. S. Grant. Cheif magistrate of the Government—as natural born citizens as Honorable discharged Solders of United States Service, as Sailors upon your high Seas—as bonafide citizens. &. Supporter of Every work in arts. &. of Science in America—hereby do Faithfully and Hopefully Petition you the President of these. United. States. and Pray your direct intervention and. Powerfull Protection in behalf and for the life of our Suffering Brothers throughout the Southern States of America—and Especially in their Civil and Religious Rights and may *Almighty. God* aid you to listen meditate. &. Grant our Earnest Appeal and Relieve us from Annialation. &. the utter destruction of our Greatest Talented men among us as A Race of People—and we will Ever Pray yours Ever. &. Ever Citizens. &. Americans forever &c" DS (55 signatures), DNA, RG 60, Letters from the President.

On Dec. 4, W. L. Lawrence, "Formerly of Sacketts Harbor NY," Marysville, Calif., telegraphed to USG. "Who is elected President   Please answer" Telegram received, DLC-USG, IB.

In a letter docketed on Dec. 4, J. P. McRae, postmaster, Wadesborough, N. C., wrote to USG. "I hope you will Excuse an humble servant who has Twice helped to place you in the Highest position within the gift of the American people for Taking the Liberty of writing you. The Republicans of this State seems to be about to lose there rights by fraudeulent Manipulation of The Democrats. our only Hope is now to look to the General Goverment for protection. the Democrats have been very violent here since the Election. mal Treating the colored Republicans & in some instances the Whites and using Threatening Language Generally. Govr Vance & Jas. M. Leach spoke here last night. the Spirit of 1860 is in full Blast here. the Democrats are just waiting for their Northern friends to make a move then they will go into any thing. Republicans can not get protection here now from the local officers. I will give an instance of a colord man who was assaulted by a croud one night. he made complaint to a Democratic justice, who issued a warrent for the parties, the shff and others went to the justice and told him if He prosecuted the case He would be impeached and throwed out of office. consiquently he stoped the case. there are from fifteen Hundred to Two Thousand Republicans in this county who are *Loyal* to the *Government*—who look to the Same for protection, and who will do all they can to sustain the governmnt I feel it my duty as a citsven who has the wellfare of the country at Heart to make these Statemts to you and Hope you will pardon me for Taking this liberty. I do this because I belive you feel an interest in the *humblest citizen* as well as the Highest. . . . This place is the Home of *Hon. T. S. Ashe M. C.*" ALS (undated), DNA, RG 60, Letters from the President.

On Dec. 6, Samuel E. Bish, Adrian, Pa., wrote to USG. "i have Been thinking this Long time of writing to you and Now i am resolved to do So Since this trouble about the Election   i have heard it for years that the Catholicks wer prepparing for and out Brake And was filling ther churches With fire arms and amunition And it is a Serious matter and Should be Seen to By Som one and Since the Election Some of them have Said that if tilden

Was Elected it would be the last president that would Ever Set in Washington they Said if S. J. tilden was Elected the Religious War Would begin And popery Would Be Established And if S J tilden is not a Catholict he is working for them for all the catholicks here ar very afeared hayse will be Elected and tilden Defeated now this ar the felings of the catholicks in this place and they could make bad work of it if let runn On So i hope and trust that thes things may be Envestigated in time to Save Blood Shed For they ar Bound to try to Brake down Cristianity and the prodistant religion they have been Seen taking heavy Boxes from the Depot and taking them to ther churches and Som hav made ther Braggs What they will do and if Eveyr they do Brake out it will Be in the knight So they can do all they can when people is Sleeping now i will Leave this matter in you Care and if it is worth you thought and thinck it deserves notic then act acording hoping you will do all that is fair and honorable i now will close hoping you will not take anny insult from this as i mean no harme only i rite this for the Safty of our Country nothing more at present" ALS, *ibid.*

On Dec. 7, J. N. Davis, "Baltimore Conference M. E. Church," Elkridge Landing, Md., wrote to USG. "*Private* . . . My acquaintance with Southern men, having been born and raised in Virginia, warrants me in saying that I do not believe that the white leaders in the South intend to be reconciled, nor will they for a long time to come consent to live in peace with those they do not rule, whether it be ~~in~~ among the plantations, or in the halls of legislation, state or national. For the South is still full of latent treason, and should an opportunity present itself the scenes of 1861 will be reenacted by her leading spirits. When a boy I read that, 'wolves lose their teeth, but not their nature.' And be assured that Rome, the eternal enemy of civil and religious liberty, is the inspiration of the present democratic party, which is just now so bitter and defiant, a party the component parts of which are represented by three *Rs*, which stand for *Rome, Rum* and *Rebellion.* And yet I doubt not but that the success of of the Republican party in the election of Governor Hayse will tend greatly to cripple and kill these three giant enemies of the Republic. . . ." ALS, USG 3. On Feb. 23, 1875, Davis, "an itinerant minister of the M. E. Church for more than twenty years consecutively," Washington, D. C., had written to USG applying for a consulship. ALS, DNA, RG 59, Letters of Application and Recommendation. Related papers are *ibid.* No appointment followed.

On Dec. 8, 1876, J. E. Kelley, Cincinnati, wrote to USG. "I need not stat you the condision of the colard pepol of the South you no as well as I But not with standieng Mr Preidente I no this Repoblican form of govimente ar now in Geit trubial . . . we no that the Repoblican party in the north ar the colard man friend But I can not say mutch of the white Repoblica[n] of the south if thay wer true friend to the colard man thar wolde not have Bin so mutch secante murders co mited By thaes d— traters of the south it is moste horiubel to think of it may God all mity stetch foth his arm and sink thoes Barbriains in to Ever lastien eturnity I say it is a dis grace a pom the holde in tier american pepol to sufer sutch Barbarious murders to Bea carmitied in this sivelis lande. I. will now turn,— the surpote of the Republician Party the colard man standes By the Republican party if thay will oneley stand;—them they ar. a. greite meney colard mene ar going a round thru the ~~the~~ cuntry saying that the Republicans have not don nothing for them but they ar the onthorteful colard men thus speake theas senturments But I mouste say to you and to all the leadeing R. P—the oneley way to ReGen the Republican party is to giv the colar man imploiment in all Brachies of Bisnis in this govrimente if he Be capribiel of eny Bisnis then I say the colard,—will then prve faith,—to his party I mouste say that this pedvies mouste ~~wiped~~ Bea wiped out I exsperienc this grite, prevdis evry day righte her in Hamilton county   the Re. P—, will not imploy a colard man for nothing if theay can gut oute of it that has geite tendisey to a rise prgudies . . ." ALS, *ibid.*, RG 60, Letters from the President.

On Dec. 9, John Krausler, Philadelphia, wrote to USG. "Before me, in my room, I have the portraits of 'Lincoln and Grant' whom I look upon as the Saviours, under God, of our country. Were it not that you are at helm, those old rebels, who never gave you a chance to whip them, but who did every thing in their power to frustrate your plans, while they run no risk, would have inaugurated civil war ere this. Nothing keeps them in check but the Knowledge that the Invincible is at the head and when it comes to fighting, he never makes mistakes 'Hold the fort' and don't let them get inside. Whilst we are assured that you will do nothing unfair, do not give one inch to the old blustering rebels, Tilden, Wood and their cursed crew. You can't imagine how secure & safe your old friends felt just because you have command of the Army & Navy. Hold on!" ALS, USG 3.

Also on Dec. 9, William L. Helfenstein, Mott Haven, N. Y., wrote to USG. "*Personal* . . . I wrote you several times from my former home in Pottsville Penn. I feel constraind now to write to you to say that the firmness & wisdom of your measures in the South have saved the Country—We all owe a renewed debt of gratitude to you—I am [s]ure the American People will sustain you in the most rigorous measures to prevent & suppress *treason*. . . . If the leading Rebels had been shot & hung, as they ought to hav[e b]een & been conquered, the whole Country North & South would have [b]een prosperous long ago—Mercy, false mercy to them has cost the nation ten of thousands of valuable lives & millions of treasure—I rejoice that such courageous men as yourself & Sect. Cameron & others now hold power at Washington—" ALS, *ibid.*

On Dec. 10, Angelo Vizzolo, Monkton, Md., wrote to USG offering "his services, if they are required, in defense of the American Union. He is an old campaigner, having seen much service in Europe and Africa." ALS (in Italian), *ibid.*; summary translation, *ibid.*

On Dec. 14, C. S. Brown, Houston, wrote to USG. "I take great Enerest in law biding Citizens of Western D. C. of texas and want peace reserve all over the land everywhere and we have no such goverment here as that our state is ffull of desperadoes the killing of the poor Colored Peoples up to date of this letter and we as legal Citizen do earnesty ask protection from your Strong arm of goverment to suppress this great outrage on us one White man A. Briant have not slept in his own house for (6) weeks an account off fear an other Colored man name Jackson also had to flee from his own home entirily and quit living there and we as citizen of Texas pray that this outrage may cease to continue any more When this letter reaches your Cabenet—from 19—of august has been (33) or 34 killed—Since that date . . . Please publish the Same" ALS, DNA, RG 60, Letters from the President.

On Dec. 15, Secretary of State Hamilton Fish recorded in his diary. "a good deal of conversation with regard to the possibility of trouble and disorder to arrise from the Presidential contest; various letters have been received by different Members of the Cabinet indicating an intention of violence on the part of the Democrats and others suggesting precautionary measures against suspected or apprehended designs in most if not all instances they appear to be the results of frights or of restless dispositions. A body of some 12 or more men a deputation as they said from the Stars & Stripes Association headed by a Mr C. C. Adams called on the President and read him a resolution tendering their services in case of any disturbance. The President replied—that he had no apprehension of any disturbance when one of them enquired from whom they should receive their orders in case they were needed. The President laughingly replied that that was a question he had not begun to think of." DLC-Hamilton Fish. On Dec. 13, Crawford C. Adams, president, and Edwin D. Tracy, secretary, "Order of the Stars & Stripes," Washington, D. C., had written to USG offering their services "for any emergency that may arise out of the present political complications, in which it may be necessary to protect by Arms the Archives and Treasures of the Government." LS, USG 3.

On Dec. 16, S. D. Smith, Hartford, wrote to USG. "Permit a humble citizen and friend (tho' a stranger) to express his gratitude to yourself for the honorable and manly course you have pursued during the political campaign just closed. Although misrepresented and maligned by democrats—and even by *some* republicans—you hold firmly the great, intelligent body of the people as firmly as 12 years ago—when your deeds in War were making you a record that can *never* be forgotten by patriots. I hope no such verbiage as the 'Herald' of N. Y. gives out from time to time will be allowed to irritate you, or turn you from the path of duty, and I have no idea that it will. I wish I could express a fraction of the esteem all my family—brothers and sisters—hold you in—but we can only say to you we are your well-wishers and hope you may live long to enjoy the blessings of a country you did so much to make great and to preserve. This isn't written in the hope that an office will be given me,—not at all.—If I wanted *that* I should write to Gov. Hayes—but as this is my first letter to a president—I think it likely to be my last. . . . A private letter to the president of the United States—from a citizen who voted for him twice and would again if he could—" ALS, *ibid.*

On Dec. 18, John Adams, Jersey City, wrote to USG. "Charles the 1st had his Cromwell & Ceaser had his Brutus and there is 200,000 men in Jersey who are ready to sustain Tilden in his claim to the Presidency of the united states—If you *should* rise above Party and the demegouges who are advising you—againt your own Judgement, and come out for the *right*, you would stamp upon your person the Seal of immortality I voted for you twice and I know you will stand by the conservetive frends of our Common Country" ALS, *ibid.* On the same day, Asbury F. Haynes, Brooklyn, wrote to USG. "Some little time ago I wrote you for an apointment under the Goverment, stating I had been a soldier all through the McClellan and Grant campaighns before Richmond, and in the latter campaighn I captured a battleflag from the 21st North Carolina Regt. &c. I received no repley to the aplication so far. At that date I felt in my necessity for a livelihood for myself and family that I had some groud for requesting an opportunity to get an honest susport, for an honest days work to the Republic I helped to *maintain*. Mr President today I am not so solicitoes as to my own well being as I am for the well being off our Country. In my daily intercourse with men which brings me largley with the rank and file I hear threats of an uprising in the great Citys of New York & Brooklyn I not only hear it in New York state, but in New Jersey, and it is not confined to the lower classes alone, but to the influential, and men in good social standing. I am as satisfied in my own mind that mischief is brewing as that I am writing this letter. . . ." ALS, DNA, RG 60, Letters from the President. Haynes, former corporal, 17th Maine, had received the Congressional Medal of Honor for his exploit at Sayler's Creek, Va., on April 6, 1865.

On Dec. 20, 1876, J. R. Burns, asst. U.S. attorney, Galveston, Tex., wrote to USG. "This is to say, first, that in the difficulties surrounding you, you have the warm, earnest sympathy of the Republicans of this state, and will, if necessary, receive their united support *vi et armis*. They will cheerfully come to your assistance in securing the peace of the nation if it have to be fought for. sSecond, the southern idea is that the North will become involved in a presidential clash of arms, and *then* the 'lost cause' will be revived, and the independence of the south secured. A state democratic senator, W. H. Ledbetter, said to me a few days ago, that a division of the country was only a question of time—that Texas was big enough for a separate nationality—that the North might as well let the South go at once &c. This sentiment is almost universal among the democracy. Third, I have information that the democrat planters in Louisiana very generally impose the payment of taxes upon their negro tenants, in addition to the customary rent—telling them that the radicals put on the taxes But that the democrats will take them off if elected—that the way to get rid of taxes is to vote the democratic ticket &c. This information I have from Capt. I. G. Killough, a leading democrat of Fayette County, who stated it publicly—saying he had been in La. among the people and got it from them. It might be well for the Senate Committee now in La. to inquire into this matter. Killough said the plan of making the negroes pay the land taxes helped to make many of them vote the democratic ticket. If the fact be true, as I doubt not it is, for Killough is a responsible man, it is the revelation of a terrible engine of political oppression that ought to be stopped in some way. A reconstruction seems to be the only effectual remedy for the existing condition of things in some of the states south. If Tilden were elected thousands and tens of thousands of Republicans would immediately move North—men whose whole lives have been spent in the south—their lives would be as valu[e]less as a pinch of snuff. Thank God, however, fraud violence will not be permitted to cheat Hayes out of his election." ALS, USG 3. See Burns to James A. Garfield, Sept. 30, 1880, DLC-James A. Garfield.

On Dec. 22, William S. Cheatham, Nashville, wrote to USG. "The object of this epistle to ask you to give me the position of Gauger of liquors or Some good position in one of the Goverment Departments—If I Should get the appointment of Gauger I would like to be appointed to Stay here—I am a Republican and have always been—I never was any thing but a union man—I refer you to Hon Horace H Harrison who is a Republican and who but a Short Time ago represented this Congressional District in Congress and Hon Horace Maynard and W G Brownlow—The feeling here a mongst the Rebels is in Tensely bitter—The Rebels here have ~~have~~ organized an Artillery Company to go on to Washington to See that Tilden is in Augurated President of the united States—The Rebels Say they will kill all the Colored people here and throughout the South if the war Should break out—A few nights after the Presidential election here they went the Democrats to the Republican Head Quarters and broke out the windows and took a large Eagle they had Down that was over the Door and Destroyed it and then Took Down the American Flag and broke the Staff and Carried the Flag off and Said they were going to burn it but Some men came a cross them and got the Flag a way from them—The Rebels here are more bitter now than they were in 1861 when the war broke out—I hope you will See that Hayes will be in augurated President of the united States—If you want any men to fight you Can get a good many from here—I Trust you will Do me the favor to give me the position I ask for or Some good position here or up North—" ALS, DNA, RG 56, Applications. On Nov. 24, 1872, Cheatham had written to USG. "I rejoice from the bottom of my heart that you have been chosen by a majority of the American people as their chief Representative for four years more as President of the United States over Horace Greeley by a pleurality of over Seven hundred Thousand votes—Andrew Johnson and the Rebel General Frank Cheatham were both beaten for Congress for the State at large from this State by the Hon Horace Maynard as True a Republican as walks on the American Continent—. . . One of the leading Rebels in this State by the name of John House who resides in the County Williamson Says the colored people in that County Shall not vote any more in that County because they vote the Republican Ticket and if they Should try it he will get his Ku-Klux and have all the Colored people killed—That man John House was one of Andrew Johnsons warmest Supporters in Johnsons recent election—. . ." ALS, *ibid.* Related papers are *ibid.* No appointment followed.

On Dec. 23, 1876, John D. Banks, Cincinnati, wrote to USG. "I have the honor to transmit herewith a copy of resolutions adopted at a meeting of Citizens, held in this city on the 20th Inst, at which the Hon, Henry Stanbery presided." ALS, USG 3. On Dec. 20, citizens meeting at Pike's Opera House had adopted a preamble and resolutions. "The public mind is filled with apprehension and alarm at the course of the recent events in our political history. This course seems to tend to the dreadest of all issues which can be presented to a civilized and free people—to the alternative between violence on the one hand and conscious submission to a wrong subversive of the very foundation of civil liberty on the other. We believe that this fatal course can be arrested, if all good citizens will at once come to an understanding as to a few simple principles without which that union of liberty and order which constitute the basis of our national life is a manifest impossibility. To this end be it—Resolved, That the Government of the United States is founded upon universal suffrage, the free and fair exercise of which under the Constitution and laws of the respective States is the most sacred right of the citizen. Resolved, That all attempts arbitrarily to abridge or interfere with this right of necessity tend to anarchy and revolution; that the deprivation of this right upon the allegation of violence or fraud in its exercise is the severest penalty which can be visited upon American freemen; that such a penalty ought, therefore, never to be inflicted, except upon clear proof before a competent and impartial tribunal. . . . Resolved, That the most dangerous of all usurpations in a free country is that of the functions of civil authority by the military power, and that the use of this power, not in the service of the country, but in the furtherance of the interests of a party, and the employment of National troops in times of peace to control or influence elections in States or Territories which are not threatened either by invasion or by domestic violence, is an outrage upon the rights and liberties of the people. . . . Resolved, That until the two houses of Congress, either by concurrent or joint action, shall declare who is constitutionally elected President, it is the duty of Republicans and Democrats alike to frown down any declaration by the excited partisans of either party that their candidate is elected and shall be inaugurated, such declarations by the citizens or the press being calculated to rouse passions which may lead to civil war. . . ." Copy, *ibid.*

On Dec. 26, John D. McAdoo, Jefferson, Tex., wrote to USG. "*Personal.* . . . A Southern man, and a Republican from the first organization of the Republican Party in Texas, I feel that I cannot permit the present occasion to pass without an expression of my profound personal approval of your Administration of the affairs of the Nation, and of your course in the recent and present exciting aspect of the times. You have grasped and comprehended the real situation. In your public expressions, and in your public acts, with the Military arm of the Government directed to the preservation of the peace, and to the protection of the weak (, in fact, though not in numbers) in an honest expression of their choice of rulers through the ballot-box, in these Southern States, you have doubly enshrined yourself in the hearts of all truly patriotic citizens of the country. At no period of your life—eventful and valuable as it has been for nearly a score of years—have your services at the head of affairs been so much needed as now. Men like my self *know* that Gen. Hayes, and not Samuel J. Tilden, received the nearly unanimous vote of the colored people, wherever they were *permitted* to exercise a free ballot. A democratic negro at heart is an anomoly; a democratic negro in fact is one through fear and fear alone. The *free* ballot of this country elected Hayes by an enormous popular majority; he *is* elected President of the United States; the public interest demands a continuance of Republican National Administration, and it cannot stand a democratic administration. You hold the key to the situation; your sound judgment can, and your patriotism and manhood will save this country from ruin—a ruin far worse than secession and separtion. You may feel assured that Southern Republicans, who have an opportunity to know and do know the real truth of the situation, will gratefully remember ~~the~~ him, whose strong arm and patriotic devotion to the whole nation, will be in the future regarded by the whole country as twice its savior from ruin." ALS, *ibid.* Three others endorsed this letter, including Adam G. Malloy, "late Col. 17th Wis. Vol. Infty and 1st Lieut 35th U. S. Infty." "I have been a resident of Texas for ten years and have closely observed the political conduct of colored voters.—They never vote other than the Republican ticket, but when intimidated by fear of personal violence, I heartily concur with Judge McAdoo in all he has stated in his letter" AES (undated), *ibid.* On Dec. 13, 1875, USG had nominated McAdoo, former Tex. Supreme Court justice, as postmaster, Marshall.

On Dec. 29, 1876, Wells W. Leggett, Cleveland, wrote to USG. "Although from my standpoint I can see no immediate prospects of an outbreak requiring other than U. S. Troops: Yet, as a graduate of West Point, I here tender my services, in case I can be of any use in any capacity. I served as a staff officer during the war, & during the latter years of the war as Capt. A. D. C. & Engineer in the 17th Army Corps,—After the war entered, & graduated in 1869 from, West Point, since which time I have been practicing at Law in the United States Circuit Courts. I took an active part for Hayes in the last Campaign, & filled several appointments to speak in this state, and in Michigan. I state the above, as it may indicate in what capacity, if any, I may be of service." ALS, *ibid.*

On Dec. 30, P. Brown and many others, Charlotte, N. C., petitioned USG. "being othorized by A. Ban~~t~~d of Col. People on. Last Night Dec ~~30~~29 to Address ~~in~~ you in the most oppropeate maner, in Regardes to Colonization Sir owing to the Disadvantig Afforded us, by our White People. South We feel it our Dieuty to flee from them if Posible We have Served Hear A. Long times and it Appears that the White People South and Col. People are more Anmity to Each other to Day then 10 years. hence first because We are Compelled to voate With them or Suffer Second because~~d~~ we Are not Regarded As. People in Whose Body is Liveing Soulds. third because it Keeps the North Working night And Day All most to Keep the Col People in the Chanall of Liberty 4th because We think it Rite before God. that We Should Go to our Selfs. fifth and Last because it Will Bring Some of our White Ememys South to under Stand the importance of Paying for Labor after it is Dun and not try to Starve the Pore Col. People out for Voateing to Suit thare offeations And as A. Col. People. Who Desiar Justice We Deem it Nescsary that We Should if there be Aney Posible Chance Sent to our own Selfs not Left With the White People of the South Any Longer then We can get. A. Way from them And We are Willing to Go to Ainy territorry that We can Live At . . ." DS, DNA, RG 60, Letters from the President. Related papers are *ibid.*

On Jan. 4, 1877, E. Finney, Leighton, Ala., wrote to USG. "as i have got in to trouble i waunt your advice for [one] of my principals is run over and abbused in this country last november was a year a go their is certain classes of men that taken a too horse wagon loaded with double barrel Shot gunes an naveys an went to the ballet box to keep men of my principals from voting and ever Since they hav ben burning up Schoolhousses an Shooting in to peoples housses on the 27 of june they Shot about thirteen guns in my house So Said my neighbors that counted thegm wee was so excited that wee did not count thegn they Shot in among my woman an children o[ne] got a slite wound in the lip i received a Sli[te] wound on the hand i then moved to Ala Co[lb]ert Co wee was forsed when wee went to move to sell our littel Stock and then In august i was in tupelo Missisip and was going down to my old place to go get up Some hogs and my friends advised me not go untill this croud was removed and my wife made a sale dew the first of november of my Stock and wee have never ben able to get a dollar on it . . ." ALS, *ibid.*

In an undated letter, "Your Brutus & Booth" wrote to USG. "Take *warning* in time, or you shall *go down* like Benedict Arnold & Jeff Davis, in the history of the contry. The writer of this *knows well* your *secret* wish And measures *sure and swift*, has been *so!* arranged, that you will be *stopped* without forewarning, the moment you *imagine* yourself well seated." L, USG 3. A clipping criticizing USG's use of the military in southern states is *ibid.*

    1. U.S. Representative Fernando Wood of N. Y. had presented this resolution to gain political advantage for the Democrats and to fulfill a personal desire to find grounds to impeach USG. See *CR*, 44–2, 925–28; *New York Times* and *New York Tribune*, Jan. 23, 25, 1877; Jerome Mushkat, *Fernando Wood: A Political Biography* (Kent, Ohio, 1990), p. 216.
    2. See message to Senate, July 31, 1876.
    3. See message to Senate, Dec. 14, 1876.
    4. See Proclamation, Oct. 17, 1876.

To House of Representatives

To THE HOUSE OF REPRESENTATIVES—

    In answer to the Resolution of the House of Representatives of the 8th of December last inquiring "whether any increase in the Cavalry force of the Army on the Mexican frontier of Texas has been made, as authorized by Act of July 24. 1876 and whether any troops have been removed from the frontier of Texas, and from the Post of Fort Sill on the Kiowa and Comanche reservation and whether, if so, their places have been supplied by other forces"—I have the honor to transmit herewith a report received from the Secretary of War.—

                    U. S. GRANT—

EXECUTIVE MANSION. JANUARY 22D 1877—

Copy, DNA, RG 130, Messages to Congress. *HED*, 44-2-33. The report from Gen. William T. Sherman to Secretary of War James D. Cameron, dated Dec. 15, 1876, is *ibid.*, pp. 2–3; DNA, RG 94, Letters Sent.
    On Oct. 24, Thomas L. Kane, San Antonio, had written to USG. "I shall not probably get to Mexico. All the way down to San Antonio, I have been receiving reports of the outrages committed on the Rio Grande; from and on reaching here, find them in such a degree confirmed, that I feel as if it were my duty as a citizen to examine into the truth for myself. I cannot inform you how many men are butchered monthly—how many head of cattle stolen: but this much seems certain, that, (miserably driven in as we have suffered the national frontier to be), the women and children along a line miles in length are now flying in terror from their homes. I am accordingly going over to Eagle Pass, and thence probably down the River, and trust you will not consider it a liberty if I shd. communicate with you by telegraph." ALS, *ibid.*, RG 60, Letters from the President. See Hamilton Fish diary, Nov. 21, 1876, DLC-Hamilton Fish; Sherman to Brig. Gen. Edward O. C. Ord, Nov. 22, 1876, DNA, RG 94, Letters Sent; Ord to Sherman, June 27, Aug. 8, 1876, Jan. 15, 1877, DLC-William T. Sherman; Lt. Col. William R. Shafter to Ord, Jan. 8, 1877, *ibid.*

On Dec. 22, William L. Helfenstein, Philadelphia, wrote to USG. "Sojourning here a few days I notice the capture at Chihuahua Mexico by the revolutionist bandits, Mr Miller of that City—& his probable execution—A native of Germany, came to U. S. a boy, lived at St. Louis, learned & pursued his trade as a Machinist & was naturalised—removed to Chihuahu by his industry & frugality amassed a large fortune—is President of the Bank & owns immensely large Ranchs & much real estate—Has a large circle of friend & much influence, & much esteemd Can a Telegram be sent to Ft. Davis to make all efforts to res cue him—There are many Germans & Americans there who will be plunderd & then murdered—I am largely interested in the old Spanish Silver Mines there, self & frends invested larg amont—several hundred thousand Dolls These revolutionst robbers are [—] our Mines & levying enormous taxes & by this time have probably broken up our works. There is no Goverment in Mexico—Five thousand of our Troops would sustain a Protecterate there & restore peace & ensure safety—Our Goverment will be obliged to interfere at last & why not now?—before those robbers murder all our frends & Countrymen & destroy all their property—I am sure you feel a deep interest in this sad subject & I beg that you can give it your attentn" ALS, DNA, RG 59, Miscellaneous Letters. See Louis H. Scott to Fish, Jan. 23, 1877, *ibid.*, Consular Despatches, Chihuahua.

On Jan. 22, 1877, USG wrote to the House of Representatives. "I have the honor to transmit herewith reports and accompanying papers received from the Secretaries of State and War in answer to the resolution of the House of Representatives of the 9th instant relative 'to the imprisonment and detention by the Mexican authorities at Matamoras of John J. Smith an American citizen, and also of the wounding and robbing by Mexican Soldiers at New Laredo of Doctor Samuel Huggins, an American citizen—" Copy, *ibid.*, RG 130, Messages to Congress. *HED*, 44-2-31. On the same day, Secretary of State Hamilton Fish had written to USG transmitting papers from the State Dept. Copy, DNA, RG 59, Reports to the President and Congress. *HED*, 44-2-31. See Cameron to USG, Jan. 15, 1877, *ibid.*, p. 42; DNA, RG 107, Letters Sent, Military Affairs. By early Jan., the Mexican government had released John Jay Smith, an alleged spy.

Veto

To The House of Representatives.

I return herewith House Bill No 4350. to abolish the Board of Commissioners of Metropolitan Police of the District of Columbia and to transfer its duties to the Commissioners of the District of Columbia, without my approval—

It is my judgment that the Police Commissioners—while appointed by the Executive—should report to, and receive instructions from the District Commissioners—Under other circumstances than those existing at present, I would have no objection to the entire abolition of the Board, and seeing the duties devolved directly upon the District Commissioners—The latter should, in

my opinion, have supervision and control over the Acts of the Police
Commissioners under any circumstances—But as recent events
have shown that gross violations of law have existed in this District
for years directly under the eyes of the Police, it is highly desirable
that the Board of Police Commissioners should be continued, in
some form, until the evil complained of is eradicated, and until the
Police force is put on a footing to prevent, if possible a recurrence of
the evil—

The Board of Police Commissioners have recently been changed
with the direct object of accomplishing this end.—

U. S. GRANT

JANUARY 23D 1877. EXECUTIVE MANSION.

Copy, DNA, RG 130, Messages to Congress. *SMD,* 49-2-53, 405–6. A bill to abolish the
D. C. police commission passed the House of Representatives on Jan. 8, 1877, and the Senate on Jan. 9. On [*Jan. 10*], USG wrote to [*Culver C. Sniffen*]. "Write the Atty. Gen. that I
would like to get appointments and commissions to the new Police commissioners to-day
if possible. I want them to take action before approving the bill passed yesterday—not yet
presented—which I will hold for some days, probably ten, before signing." AN (undated),
Wayde Chrismer, Bel Air, Md. On Jan. 30, the House voted to override USG's veto. On
Feb. 3, USG wrote to U.S. Senator John J. Ingalls of Kan. "Since seeing you this A. M. I
have had a consultation with two of the new police commissioners and after hearing their
statements, I am satisfied that it is advisable that the board should not be abolished—The
board should, in my judgment, be required to report to the District Commissioners, and
to receive instructions from them—But as a new District Government must be organized
within the next year it may not be necessary to make this change of the board until the
whole re-organization of the District Government takes place.—" Copy, DLC-USG, II, 3.
On Feb. 6, the Senate sustained USG's veto. See *CR,* 44–2, 1111–12, 1284–89.
On Jan. 3, Ulysses S. Grant, Jr., had written to Attorney Gen. Alphonso Taft. "The
President directs me to say that he will be pleased to have you address a note to the Board
of Police Commissioners—by his direction—that he would like to have the immediate res-
ignation of the entire Board." LS, DNA, RG 60, Letters from the President. On Jan. 5,
William J. Murtagh, Peter F. Bacon, James G. Berret, Henry M. Sweeney, and William H.
Smith each wrote to USG resigning as D. C. police commissioners. ALS and LS, *ibid.* On
Jan. 6, Saturday, 11:30 A.M., Sniffen wrote to Taft. "The President directs me to say that
when the last member of the Board of Police Commissioners was appointed you decided
that it was not necessary that they should reside—3 in the City; one in Georgetown and
one in the County. Of the present Commissioners four reside in the City. Of those proposed
four live in the City and one in Georgetown as before. If the resignations come in before
two o'clock to day it would be well to announce the appointments so that they might be
published in the evening and Sunday papers. They are as follows: John C. Harkness, vice
Berret, John T. Mitchell vice Georgetown Member Matthew G. Emory vice Washington
City Member (not Murtagh) Frederick Douglass vice Colored Member." ALS (misdated,
tabular material expanded), *ibid.*; copy, DLC-USG, II, 3. On the same day, Taft wrote to
USG. "Having been with the Secretary of State this morning on the Nicaragua Treaty, I

have just received your note relating to the Board of Police. I think that the phrase 'one
from the county of Washington at large,' does not exclude the cities of Washington and
Georgetown. One may be appointed from the county at large therefore, who resides in the
city." Copy, DNA, RG 60, Letters Sent to Executive Officers. Also on Jan. 6, a correspondent reported from Washington, D. C. "The President stated this morning that he had a
list of names made out for nomination as Police Commissioners in place of the board whose
resignations he had demanded. This list he would not change, and the nominations will be
made on Monday. The President said they were good men of the District, and when appointed the investigation into the conduct of the Police with respect to the gambling-
houses and of all other charges would be carried forward, and the busines would be probed
to the bottom. The President spoke of the insinuations against himself, which had been allowed to go into the testimony heretofore taken, to the effect that he had bet at horse races
and had pardoned a gambler immediately after his conviction, and thus discouraged other
prosecutions. He said he had been to but two horse races since he was President, and at
one of those his family was with him. He had no personal recollection of the pardon referred to, and only knew that he must have acted on the recommendation of the Attorney
General, as he never pardoned any one without that recommendation. The statements
about the President were maliciously interjected by witnesses, and admitted by the board
without shadow of reason. The President, by making a new Police Board of good citizens,
will gain great approbation. The question with which the public are most interested is that
pertaining to the immunity enjoyed by the gambling fraternity, and the reason the business had been allowed to prosper. It is understood that ex-Mayor Matthew G. Emery; John
T. Mitchell, a well-known merchant; John C. Harkness, a prominent architect, and Frederick W. Douglass are the gentlemen selected. The resignation of Mr. William J. Murtagh, the President of the old board, has not yet been accepted, and it is thought probable
that he will be retained as a member of the new board." *New York Times,* Jan. 7, 1877. On
Jan. 15, George W. McElfresh, D. C. detective, testified before a House committee. "On the
morning after the President had requested the resignation of the board of police, myself
and Mr. McDevitt went to the President's House and sent in our cards; and after a short
lapse of time the President admitted us. We stated to the President that we supposed he
had heard of our little trouble in the investigation. He said he had read it in the paper. I
said to the President that we had come up to see him to lay the facts before him, so that we
could not be misrepresented, if we had not already been. I think then Mr. McDevitt mentioned to him the Whitthorne matter. . . . About Mr. Murtagh calling upon the major and
requesting Miller and McDevitt to follow Mr. Whitthorne and catch him in a house of ill-
repute, or inveigle him into one and have the house raided, and to hold this thing over him
as chairman of the Naval Committee. He also remarked at the time to the President that
he did not think Mr. Robeson knew anything about the matter. . . . The President said: 'No,
no; I do not think he did. The President then said, 'Well, gentlemen, I do not know of any
suggestions that I can make to you.' I repeated again, 'Mr. President, we do not come up
for that purpose. We just want to lay the facts as they exist before you, so that we could
not be misrepresented, if we have not already been.' The President said that Mr. Murtagh
had not spoken to him about the matter, nor no one else, I think he said, but that he had
got tired of seeing this stuff in the paper, and acted upon his own responsibility. . . . I think
the President remarked that he had got tired of seeing this stuff in the paper, where folks
had testified before the police commissioners that he had gambled, and none of the board
had stopped them, or asked them when or where. . . . I was detailed to do duty at the President's house for pretty nearly two years in his first term of office." *HMD,* 44-2-40, 45–46.
See *HRC,* 44-2-189. On April 8, 1875, Orville E. Babcock had written to Murtagh. "The

President requests me to say that in the reorganization of your force he hopes—unless there are good reasons to the contrary—that Mr Sargeant and Mr. McElfresh may be retained in their positions." Copy, DLC-USG, II, 2.

On Jan. 5, 1877, Alexander R. Shepherd wrote to USG. *"Personal . . .* I have been requested by Genl Bacon to enclose his resignatn as a member of the Police Board and desire to call your attention to the fact that he was appointed less than sixty day's ago. & has not yet been confirmd   That he is one of our oldest & best citizens whose character is without reproach   That he was the only member who openly rebuked the gambler[s] Clagett [& Williams] when he charged you with attending horse races and betting   That he is a true noble man and the peer of any one in worth and qualificatns for the place   I make these statements Mr President as a friend who. loves & esteems you above all men living and has perfect confidence in your justness and nobleness" ALS (bracketed material in another hand), USG 3. On Nov. 13, 1876, Sniffen had written to Murtagh. "The President directs me to ask you how Peter F. Bacon would do for police commissioner?" Copy, DLC-USG, II, 3. Bacon replaced Charles H. Nichols, who had resigned on Nov. 4.

On Jan. 13, 1877, Sniffen wrote to Taft. "If Mr John C. Harkness has declined to accept one of the Police Commissionerships, The President directs me to say that a commission may issue at once to Theodore F. Gatchel." ALS, DNA, RG 60, Letters from the President.

On Jan. 15, USG wrote to Taft. "I am just in receipt of the declention of [John T] Mitchel & [Matthew G] Emery as members of the police board. I send you the name of Geo. W. Sissell, of Georgetown, in place of the former, and Thos. Summerville in place of the latter." ALS (bracketed material in another hand), *ibid.* The declinations are *ibid.*

On Jan. 18, USG wrote to [*Sniffen*]. "Send note to Atty. Gn. to please appoint I G. Kimball, of Washn Police Com. vice Murtagh resigned," AN, Wayde Chrismer, Bel Air, Md. On Jan. 29, Sniffen wrote to Murtagh. "The President directs me to say that he wishes to commission Kimball today as one of the Police Commissioners, and unless he hears from you by 2 P. M. to day, he shall do so.—" Copy, DLC-USG, II, 3. On the same day, Murtagh wrote to USG. "I respectfully request that my resignation as a member of the Board of Metropolitan Police which was tendered to you at the time of the removal of the Board may be accepted from this date. For your kindness and confidence please accept my heartfelt thanks" ALS, DNA, RG 60, Letters from the President.

Also on Jan. 29, Sniffen wrote to Taft. "The President directs me to request that a commission issue to date from to-day, for Alexander T. Britton, as a Police Commissioner for the District of Columbia." ALS, *ibid.*

On Feb. 7, Sniffen wrote to Taft. "The President directs me to say that he will be pleased to have a commission prepared and sent for his signature today for A. H. Herr of Georgetown to be Commissioner of Police for Dist. of Columbia in the place of Frederick Douglass." LS, *ibid.* On Feb. 11, a correspondent reported from Washington, D. C. "Frederick Douglass has resigned as a member of the Police Board of Commissioners, President Grant requesting his resignation in order that he might comply with the law which requires the appointment of one member of the board from Georgetown." *New York Times,* Feb. 12, 1877. Alexander T. Britton, Theodore F. Gatchell, George W. Cissell, Abraham H. Herr, and Thomas Somerville served as police commissioners at the close of USG's administration.

On Jan. 20, 1876, Levi P. Luckey had written to Attorney Gen. Edwards Pierrepont. "The President directs me to say that, he thinks the present Commissioners of Police for the District of Columbia had better be re-appointed, without change" Copy, DLC-USG, II, 3. On Feb. 1, USG nominated Murtagh, Sweeney, Berret, Nichols, and Smith.

In [*Feb.*], Owen Dawson and ten others petitioned USG. "The undersigned Petitioners represent directly a very large and intelligent meeting of the Colored people of the District of Columbia held at Lyceum Hall on the 15th inst, and indirectly a much larger number of said class of our fellow citizens. The object of the meeting was to protest against the reappointment of Mr. W. H. Smith as a member of the Board of Metropolitan Police Commissioners. We were appointed and authorized by the meeting, to condense a statement of facts having a bearing upon the case, and to bring the subject to your notice, by an appeal to your Excellency for the withdrawal of the name of Mr. Smith, and to use any other reasonable means necessary to the accomplishment of the end desired. . . . The Board of Police Commisioners as at present constituted is emphatically a sectarian Board; and while it is neither prudent or essential at this time to discuss the means by which this sectarian majority was first obtained, and the duplicity and misrepresentation resorted to in order to perpetuate it, we feel Mr. President, that it is our imperative duty to say to you that out of the forty thousand colored people of the District there is not one thousand who are Roman Catholics, and that Mr. Smith aside from this fact, and except in the matter of his complexion has not, and cannot, in any sense, represent any considerable number of the colored people, not even those of his own religious faith. We believe it therefore entirely inconsistent with the ends of justice and fairness that the Board of Police Commissioners should be made a sectarian Board in order to give the colored people representation thereon. As to the evidences of injustice and wrong growing out of the fact that Messrs. Smith, Berrett, and Sweeney, are the representatives of one religious sect on this Board, we feel that we can submit the most convincing circumstantial evidence in abundance, and we believe in more than one instance direct and positive evidence of this fact. In this view of the case whatever may be said of other members of the board we ask in all earnestness that the name of Mr. Smith be withdrawn from the list now before the Senate for confirmation. We do not believe all the other members of the board are as imaculate as they are represented to be by some of those who have been specially benefited by their good offices, and who indulge the hope of a continuance of this personal special benefit from the board. But as this is a matter of general interest while that of the representation of that of the colored race is one of special and peculiar interest to us, we are willing to waive our opposition to others to some extent; but we cannot allow so glaring an inconsistency, and so great an injustice to be longer practiced in the name, and ostensibly in the interest of those, who are in reality made sufferers instead of being benefited thereby. In the hope that this petition may receive an immediate and favorable response we subscribe ourselves in behalf of those who sent us to you Mr. President, . . ." DS (docketed March 6), DNA, RG 60, Letters from the President. On [*March 3*], USG wrote. "Withdraw nomination of Wm H. Smith and nominate John A Gray as a Commissioner of Police of the Dist. of Columbia." AN, OHi. In a letter docketed March 7, John F. Cook, D. C. collector, and four others, wrote to USG. "The undersigned most respectfully call your attention to the circumstances connected with the withdrawal of the name of Wm H. Smith which was before the U. S. Senate for confirmation as Police Commissioner for the D. C. Previous to the withdrawal of the name of Mr. Smith charges had been preferred against him by certain persons residents of the District, seriously reflecting on his course as a public officer, and on this complaint the Senate Committee on D. C. suspended action on the nomination and referred Mr Smith's name, in connection with two others to a special committee for investigation into the charges preferred. Pending this action the name was withdrawn. Mr. Smith is not willing to rest under the suspicion, that naturally attach its is itself to his name, and is anxious that an opportunity be given to have these charges either sustained or disproven, and to that end we ask if it be possible that action in the case of Mr. Gray be stayed in order that Mr. Smith may have the opportunity desired." LS, DNA, RG 60, Letters from the President. See *Washington Evening Star*, March 6, 1876. On March 23, USG withdrew John A. Gray and nominated Smith as D. C. police commissioner.

To John F. Long

———

Jan.y 28th /77

DEAR JUDGE.

After the expiration of my term of office I propose to remain some place in the United States until Jesse's examination, in June, when he with Mrs Grant and myself will sail for Europe. I have no plans laid either as to where we will go, or how long remain absent. We will not return however until the party becomes homesick which may be in six months, and may not be for two years. I may get to St. Louis before starting, but if I do not I wish to say that I would like you to continue in charge of my St. Louis property until my return. U. S. Grant Jr.—now a member of a law firm in New York City—will have a power of atty. to act for me during my absence,[1] and can receipt for, and do all other things that I could do if here. I shall not care to sell any real estate however before my return. My means will be sufficient—owing to a fortunate purchase of paying Bonanza mining stock—to keep me for a few years, by which time it is to be hoped real estate will have some value which it has not now.

I have scarcely thought of where I will make my home on my return. I am free to go whereever it seems to be the most agreeable. Having gone from the Army into my present place I have neither business nor attachments [——] to take me to any [— lo]cality. My last residence before entering the Army was Galena. But I lived there less than a year, and nearly every one I knew there have either left the place or died. My acquaintanc[e] here has been exclusively among officials, and they are ever changing. You see I am in that happy condition but few people reach—of being able to select the home of their choice. Generally circumstances over which we seem to have no controll governes both our residence and our occupation.

Please present my kindest regards to Mrs. Long and the family.

JUDGE J. F LONG

AL (signature clipped), MoSHi.
On Jan. 25, 1877, USG wrote to George W. Childs concerning the "sale of my bonds at 54 & 54½ per share, leaving about $19,000 with what I deposited of my money in banks.

The stock has fallen about $10 per share since the sale and may fall still more. If it should go below $40 per share I would like to repurchase again because I am sure the stock will go up to about sixty when it begins to pay dividends . . . Will you speak to Mr. Drexel for me about this matter?" Swann Galleries, Sale No. 1615, Jan. 28, 1993, no. 118.

1. On March 2, USG wrote to J. E. Cussans, secretary, Anglo-Californian Bank, that business matters should be directed to Ulysses S. Grant, Jr., who held his power of attorney. Sotheby Parke Bernet, Sale No. 4652E, June 22, 1981, no. 196.

To Senate

To the Senate of the United States:

I follow the example heretofore occasionally permitted of communicating in this mode my approval of the act to provide for and regulate the counting of votes for President and Vice-President, and the decision of questions arising thereon, for the term commencing March 4, A. D. 1877, because of my appreciation of the imminent peril to the institutions of the country from which, in my judgment, the act affords a wise and constitutional means of escape.

For the first time in the history of our country, under the Constitution as it now is, a dispute exists with regard to the result of the election of the Chief Magistrate of the nation.

It is understood that upon the disposition of disputes touching the electoral votes cast at the late election by one or more of the States depends the question whether one or the other of the candidates for the Presidency is to be the lawful Chief Magistrate. The importance of having clearly ascertained by a procedure regulated by law which of the two citizens has been elected and of having the right to this high office recognized and cheerfully agreed in by all the people of the Republic cannot be overestimated, and leads me to express to Congress and to the nation my great satisfaction at the adoption of a measure that affords an orderly means of decision of a gravely exciting question.

While the history of our country in its earlier periods shows that the President of the Senate has counted the votes and declared their standing, our whole history shows that in no instance of doubt or dispute has he exercised the power of deciding, and that the two

Houses of Congress have disposed of all such doubts and disputes, although in no instance hitherto have they been such that their decision could essentially have affected the result.

For the first time then [the] Government of the United States is now brought to meet the question as one vital to the result, and this under conditions not the best calculated to produce an agreement or to induce calm feeling in the several branches of the Government or among the people of the country. In a case where as now the result is involved, it is the highest duty of the law-making power to provide in advance a constitutional, orderly, and just method of executing the Constitution in this most interesting and critical of its provisions. The doing so, far from being a compromise of right, is an enforcement of right and an execution of powers conferred by the Constitution on Congress.

I think that this orderly method has been secured by the bill, which, appealing to the Constitution and the law as the guide in ascertaining rights, provides a means of deciding questions of single returns through the direct action of Congress, and in respect to double returns, by a tribunal of inquiry, whose decisions stand unless both Houses of Congress shall concur in determining otherwise; thus securing a definite disposition of all questions of dispute in whatever aspect they may arise. With or without this law, as all of the States have voted, and as a tie vote is impossible, it must be that one of the two candidates has been elected; and it would be deplorable to witness an irregular controversy as to which of the two should receive or which should continue to hold the office. In all periods of history controversies have arisen as to the succession or choice of the chiefs of states; and no party or citizens loving their country and its free institutions can sacrifice too much of mere feeling in preserving through the upright course of law their country from the smallest danger to its peace on such an occasion, and it cannot be impressed too firmly in the heart of all the people that true liberty and real progress can exist only through a cheerful adherence to constitutional law.

The bill purports to provide only for the settlement of questions arising from the recent elections. The fact that such questions can arise demonstrates the necessity, which I cannot doubt will before long be supplied, of permanent general legislation to meet cases which have not been contemplated in the Constitution or laws of the country.

The bill may not be perfect, and its provisions may not be such as would be best applicable to all future occasions; but it is calculated to meet the present condition of the question and of the country.

The country is agitated. [and excited.] It needs and it desires peace and quiet and harmony between all parties and all sections; its industries are arrested, labor unemployed, capital idle, and enterprise paralyzed by reason of the doubt and anxiety attending the uncertainty of a double claim to the Chief Magistracy of the nation. It wants to be assured that the result of the election will be accepted without resistance from the supporters of the disappointed candidate, and that its highest officer shall not hold his place with a questioned title of right. Believing that the bill will secure these ends, I give it my signature.

U. S. GRANT.

EXECUTIVE MANSION, *January* 29, 1877.

Printed copy (bracketed material added by hand), DNA, RG 130, Messages to Congress. *SED*, 44-2-25. The electoral act created a commission of five representatives, five senators, and five justices, to decide all cases of double returns. See *U.S. Statutes at Large*, XIX, 227–29. On Jan. 27 and 28, 1877, Secretary of State Hamilton Fish recorded in his diary. "In the course of the morning, Senators Edmunds & Frelinghuysen called to see me, and said they were anxious for the President to announce his approval of the Electral Bill by Special Message—I advised them to go and see him, on the subject, they assign reasons for preferring not to do so at present. I ask them to indicate the points which they thought should be brought out, in such message, which they did not; and they urge me to prepare one, which I decline to do; but told them if they would prepare one, I would endeavor to bring it to the Presidents notice; this they decline; they finally agree to put on paper some 'head notes', or 'points', which they wish covered; and in the afternoon they sent me such memorandum." "I took the memorandum which Edmunds & Frelinghuysen had sent me, and put in the form of a message; calling with it, on the President on his return from church; and asked him if he had made up his mind on the subject of a Special Message. He replied that he had returned from Baltimore late, and had not had the time; but should he not be interupted this afternoon, would endeavor to prepare one. I told him I had supposed he could do nothing yesterday, and might be prevented today; and had therefore taken the liberty of preparing a draft, which might be of assistance to him; but that should he not like it, the fire-place would be a good ~~receptacle~~ receptacle. Having asked me to read it, he took it, saying it would save him any further trouble, and that he would adopt it, as written, saying with a smile 'it was a great deal better than he would have done it, and somewhat longer.'" DLC-Hamilton Fish. An undated draft of USG's message, partly in Fish's hand, is *ibid.*

On Jan. 6, John Tyler, Jr., Washington, D. C., had written to USG. "*Personal.* . . . The following information I have gained this morning. Upon consultation with Judge Edmunds he advises that it be communicated to you, and to Senator Morton, at once. There is in the course of preparation, *for the use of a Senator,* a new constitutional view as to *the count*—a view which has been pronounced by Jeremiah Black to be unanswerable, I understand; and upon which, I further understand, the Tildenites will plant themselves with the public, and proceed to act accordingly. It is about as follows—First—that, under the provision of the Constitution specifying that all the Certificates &c of the Electoral votes shall be opened and counted in the presence of the two Houses of Congress, no provision is made, or direction given, as to the manner in which the count shall be made; nor as to who shall exercise a supervisory control over the count; nor as to who is empowered to Judge of the correctness and Sufficiency of the Returns. All this, it is contended, depends upon another provision—that in reference to the duty imposed upon the House of Representatives to proceed to elect a President in the *contingency* that there is no election, and requiring that the House in voting shall vote *by states.* Second—the positions assumed, '*quo ad hoc,*' are, that inasmuch as the responsibility under the contingency is solely with the House, the House is necessarily empowered to Judge and determine whether the contingency has arisen; that, consequently, it is the imperative duty of the House to exercise a Supervisory control over the count, in order that it may understandingly ascertain if the contingency thus provided for by the constitution has, or has not, arisen; that, therefore, the House is enjoined to examine and to Scrutinize all the Returns made to the President of the Senate; that the House must do this in order to Judge of the correctness and Sufficiency of the Returns; that, *the contingency* thus being made to appear, the House is commanded to proceed to an election, *voting by states.* Third—that, by the requirement that the House in proceeding to an election s*hall vote by states,* the House is made to stand, in respect to *the contingency,* as the Representative of *both the People and the States,* to the exclusion of the Senate, and, therefore, the conclusion is again drawn that with the House resides absolute Jurisdiction over *the Count.* Fourth—taking these positions, I further understand it to be the intention of the Tildenites, through and by the House, to declare Samuel J Tilden the duly elected President of the United States, or otherwise so to elect him, and to proceed to his Inauguration accordingly. The argument now in preparation on the above points has been partly read to me voluntarily, and the conversation that followed leads me to add the fourth paragraph. Suffice it for me to add, in conclusion, that I have confidence in the relations occupied by my Informant, and in himself as a man of character in the Democratic Party. You are standing, Mr President, in view of the pending issue, as the Representative of Peace, order, and the Industrial and Property-interests of the Country, as against a Jacobin Oligarchy representing agrarianism and anarchy—politics philosophically speaking. In this issue believe me, in all sincerity, . . ." Copy, OFH.

On Jan. 8, C. C. Merritt, "Springfield," wrote to USG. "I will not forbear an expression of my respect and endorsement of you the Executive of my Country I believe in and most ardently esteem the Constitution and Government of the United States. The manner in which you have discharged the executive functions meets the approval of your Countrymen. Especial do I concede the great honor which I think is due you for the tranquillity and confidence that the people have felt since the indecisive result of the late election Trusting that you will not consider this as any intrusion upon your notice and duty . . ." ALS, USG 3.

On Jan. 10, Samuel Walker, maj. gen., Kan. militia, Lawrence, wrote to USG. "Twenty five thousand good Men can be riazed here in ten Days to Sustain you" ALS, *ibid.*

Also on Jan. 10, James W. Green, Culpeper, Va., wrote to USG. "Sometime ago in the month of November last I called on you being introduced by a card from Col: John S. Mosby and presented you a plan in the form of proposed Amendments to the Constitution of the United States for a peaceful and permanent solution of the present disturbed condition of the country. To day by the same mail with this I send you a pamplet which gives the philosophy of the proposed plan. You will on reading it at once see that that the question of who is to be the President on and after the 4th of March next becomes quite immaterial to the Country should the Amendments be proposed by Congress and adopted by three-fourths of the States. I think I may say with certainty they would be at once adopted by all the Southern States. OnIn thelike other hand manner manner, it would be quite immaterial who should become the Governor-General. This plan would not only give us peace for the present but permanently and under it we should have a Union of peace and harmony, in which the people of all the States would be secure against sectional or oppressive action on the part of their common government. On the other hand, it matters not which of the recent candidates for the Presidency is inaugurated without these amendments the strife continues and must necessarily at no distant day result in civil war with all its horrors. These being my earnest convictions I beg you will read this pamplet carefully, weigh well itsthe truths therein stated and if convinced as I am there is no other mode of permanently averting civil war that you will make these truths the basis of your official action. Should you be able to carry out this plan it will be the crowning act of your career and you will have done the country a service not surpassed by the Father of his Country. I can speak thus of the plan with modesty for you will observe I am not its author. I only suggest an application of its truths to the present disturbed condition of the country." ALS, OFH. Green's pamphlet, "The Present Disturbed Condition of the Country: Its Cause and the Remedy. . . ." (New York, 1876), incorporated John C. Calhoun's "Disquisition on Government" and advocated the formal division of the government into northern and southern sections, each empowered to block legislation, and each to select alternately a joint president and governor-gen., beginning with Rutherford B. Hayes and Samuel J. Tilden.

On Jan. 12, L. A. Dunham, Cohoes, N. Y., wrote to USG. "We are Praying for you, for our Beloved Country, & for the United States Goverment & we thank the Grate Ruler of all for his kindness & mercy to us as a Nation, in, as we believe Placeing the *right* men in the Right Place, & to day we thank him for *your* Firmness and Persaverance in the Right. God Bless, & keep you, & give you Grace, Wisdom, Strength & Firmness to do your duty wholey, & when the time comes to Inaugurate Gov. Hayes as your Faithfull Successor, we do believe that God will not suffer the Raines of our Goverment to be turned over to so vile a party and so Base & wicked a Man as Tilden & the presant so called Democratic Party, from all such rule we Pray Good Lord deliver us, forgive us for tresspasing on your time and Patience, but altho we are obscure we can appreciate the right, but we do hate the vile. We Prayed for you, when you went on the Battle Field, we have Prayed for you since, & still we Pray God Bless & keep you Firmly to the Right," ALS, USG 3.

Also on Jan. 12, T. G. Maquier, Philadelphia, wrote to USG. "You will excuse me, for takeing this liberty, in addressing thease few lines to you; but it is, in justice to you, the Country, and to myself, where I live, that I take thease steps, I was born and raised a strict Roman-Catholic, and shall die one, but there is a plan on foot, for the Roman-Catholicts to take the Country; the Catholicts are hibernians, the hibernians are all Molly-Maguires. With McClosky of New York at their head, the Preists have established, their force at the South, among the Negros. They owe no elegence to the Country, but only to the Pope, and McClosky of New York will be the pope here; Every Catholic Church is an Arsnel, and the

Bludy work will soon begin, I have now give you notice, to Rise and defend the writes of America, that Washington, so nobely won, the glittering sword of Justice, will prevale though the heavens fall. all there Movements you shall know at the shortest Notice" ALS, DNA, RG 60, Letters from the President.

On Jan. 15, James J. Brady, St. Louis, wrote to USG. "I have noticed the demonstration and listened to the threats that are being made through the Country by the Democratic Party until I feel anxious to do Something for the Party I have Clung to Since I was (16) Sixteen years of age I was Born in Menard County Illinois and Enlisted In Company "C" 6th Illinis, Cav Sept 20th 1861 and Remained with the Regiment through out the entire War, was with Colonel B. H. Grierson on his famous Raid through Mississippi in 63 and was Private Orderlie for Colonel M. H. Starr until he was Killed at the time of Forrest Raid on Memphis Tenn. I Served my Country (4) four years and (2) two months before I (21) was twenty one years of age after the war, I Enguaged In Hotel Keeping for Some time and In 1868 was threatened by a mob, In Mason City Illinois Because I named my house the Grant House and Employed Colerd Servants and finally had to leave the place on account of my Radical principals I have waited patiently for years hopeing that Old Rebel Spirit would Die out and wee could have Peace. only to See them become more aggressive and Insulting if the Republican Party cannot administer the affairs of this Goverment with out threats of war and Deeds of blood by the Democratic party I hope the Republicans will give them all they wish I would freely Sacrifice my own life Rather than See them attain to Power with the principals they now adhere to I am confident from observations I have made that the Irish Catholic Societys through out the United States are fully armed and ready to Strike with the democrats if they have a chance If I can be of any Service to your Self or the Republican Party as a Private detective I am at your Service as I desire to work for the Good of my Country and my party hopeing you will pardon me for the Liberty I take In addressing the Chief Magistrate of our Country as I assure you I am only promted by honesty and fidelity to my party and my Country" ALS, *ibid.*

On Jan. 16, W. W. Heath, "only white Republican in Edgefeld County," Edgefield Court House, S. C., wrote to USG. "Every day of your administration, as your motives, ability and honesty, are developed, shows most conclusively, that you are the President for the times, If you were as weak, as James Buchanan was in 1861, we should have had another Rebellion, as sure as fate; There has been fraud enough committed in Edgefield County alone, during the past Election, to damn the whole State, I congratulate you on your success as President of these United States for the last 8 years, . . . Mr, President, I must say a few words more, in your praise, as President, and it comes from my heart of harts, I say to you now, that I belive your prompt action in the matter of responding, to the call of Governor Chamberlan for troops, to assist him in carrying out the civil authority of the State of South Carolina, saved the State from a great calamity, and I tell you still further if those 2 companes of U, S, Soldiers, were taken away from Edgefeld C H there would be plenty of trouble, yet, for the Democrats would knock down and drag out, and kick up Hell generly. they come *right* out and *say so* OPENLY, please excuse me for using the word Hades, for know of no more appropriate term to use" ALS, OFH.

On Jan. 17, Fish discussed with USG whether Congress or the President could determine the legitimacy of electoral votes from disputed states, notably La. "He requested me to examine the question; and then proceeded to remark on the counting of the votes, saying that he felt sure that the right of the President of the Senate to count them would not be sustained He named Conkling, Robertson, Conover West and others, including as he thought Edmunds & Frelinghuysen, who disavowed the right of the President of the Senate, that he felt sure there was a sufficient number of Republican Senators of that opinion with the Democrats to make a majority in opposition to the right. Throughout the conversation he expressed the greatest anxiety for a peaceful solution of the question, adding that while he most earnestly desired the declaration of Gov Hayes as President, he thought that should he come into power with his administration embarrassed with the question of the votes of two or three states he would be much crippled in power; on the other hand if Tilden were elected he would be unable to satisfy the expectations of the South, and with the commitment of his party against the use of the Military for any purpose of the government, he would be unable to collect the Internal Revenue in the South,— that already, since the doubts as to the elections, the Whiskey Distillers are running their Stills, paying no tax, and that the running down of receipts, has been very great; and that heretofore it would have been impossible to have collected the revenue (from Distiller &c. at the South) had it not been for the Military. He thinks that Tilden will be unable to reduce the debt, probably not to pay the running expenses of the government, without an increase of taxation, and that four years of his administration will satisfy the country with the Democrats and make a better chance for the Republicans coming into power." Fish diary, DLC-Hamilton Fish.

On Jan. 19, Gen. William T. Sherman wrote to Maj. Gen. John M. Schofield. ". . . You have seen the Bill & Report of the Joint Committee of 14—signed by 13—a strong vote I saw Mr Conkling last night, also General Grant—The former will be its advocate in the Senate, and General Grant said it met his approval—and removed all fear of violence, obviating any necessity for the doubtful use of Troops &c. . . ." ALS, CSmH. On Jan. 29, Sherman wrote to Lt. Gen. Philip H. Sheridan, Chicago. "The President has today approved the Bill for ascertaining and declaring the vote for President & Vice President of the U. S. leaving Congress to complete the details. This by universal Consent terminates the dead lock which has so long Existed and which made Military precautions necessary. The probabilities are that you will not be called on for any troops, and you had better arrange for the further prosecution of active operations against the hostile Sioux as early as your judgmt may approve—. . ." ALS, DLC-Philip H. Sheridan. See A. M. Gibson, *A Political Crime: The History of the Great Fraud* (1885; reprinted, New York, 1969), pp. 24–29.

On Jan. 20, Fish had recorded in his diary. "Called on the President, with reference to the question he had asked me to examine as to the power of the President to examine and determine which of two was the legal government of a State; and I read to him Chief-Justice Taney's opinion in the case of Luther vs Borden 7 Howard pages 42 & 43. He spoke of the compromise bill for the counting of the votes, saying that yesterday he had avoided speaking of it in Cabinet, not knowing what might be the opinion of some of the members; but that for his own part he was highly in favor of it; that as a proposition to apply to all cases, he would not like it but in the present condition of the question, there must be some mode of settlement, and some tribunal whose decision both political parties would accept; or else we would have anarchy and possibly blood shed; that he had expressed himself to this effect to Members of Congress, and several others whom he had seen during the day; that the only member of the Cabinet he had seen was Cameron, who at first had been disposed to object, but he thought that after the conversation he had had with him, he had modified his views. He said that he would use what influence he had, and could exert to aid in the passage of the measure." DLC-Hamilton Fish.

On [*Jan. 21*], "A Philadelphia Lawyer" addressed an open letter to USG, titled "Our Country's Salvation." ". . . The Republic can only be saved by a coup de 'etat and by your consecrating your life to the task of regenerating the political, commercial, industrial and social life of the people. The wealth, the brains, the patriotism of the United States will rejoice in your determination to be equal to the emergency in which you are placed. declare

YOURSELF TO BE PRESIDENT FOR LIFE. Let the peoples' representatives return to their homes. Appoint Senators for life. Form a National Council, and commit to it the task of preparing a new Constitution. . . . Let it be repeated—we want no counting of electoral votes, because no count can be fair, square and honest. Both parties practiced dishonesty and corruption in the late election and no earthly means can now discover which candidate would have been elected on a fair election. . . ." Printed (for the *Philadelphia Sunday Press,* Jan. 21, 1877), DNA, RG 60, Letters Received, Pa.

In [*Jan.*], George Hoyl, "Nite watch at this place for the lumber co," Loudon, Tenn., wrote to USG that on Jan. 16 he had overheard a plot to kill USG for $10,000. ALS (docketed Jan. 24), *ibid.,* Letters from the President.

On Feb. 2, Justice Nathan Clifford, president, Electoral Commission, wrote to USG. "You are invited, together with any member of your family, to attend the sittings of the Electoral Commission held at the Supreme Court Room U. S." LS, USG 3.

On Feb. 3, Judge Alexander Rives, Western District, Va., Charlottesville, wrote to USG. "I cannot refrain from expressing to you my hearty approval of the views of your admirable message accompanying the return to the Senate of the Bill for the Electoral Count. I have been equally gratified at your reported purpose to recommend and urge instant measures of Specie resumption. These two measures will reflect the greatest credit upon the close of your administration; and will, in some measure, compensate your friends for the painful sense they have been called to endure, of the cruel and unmerited abuse cast upon you. I can scarcely express the indignation with which I see the Tribune still pursuing you with the most malignant clamor from day to day. But I am sure, all this will soon pass away, and give way to the hearty plaudits of the People upon the great and beneficent results of your administration. None in my opinion will stand higher in our history. I avail of this occasion, upon your retirement from office, to assure you of the sentiments of gratitude and admiration, with which I am inspired by your eminent public services, and of the cordial warmth and attachment, with which my best wishes shall ever attend you." ALS, *ibid.*

On Feb. 5, Culver C. Sniffen wrote to Secretary of War James D. Cameron. "The President directs me to request of you that the order for the removal of troops from Washington be countermanded, for the present—" Copy, DLC-USG, II, 3.

To Congress

To the Senate and House of Representatives:

I desire to call the attention of Congress to the importance of providing for the continuance of the board for testing iron, steel, and other metals, which by the sundry civil appropriation act of last year, was ordered to be discontinued at the end of the present fiscal year. This board, consisting of engineers and other scientific experts from the Army, the Navy, and from civil life, (all of whom, except the secretary, give their time and labors to this object without compensation,) was organized by authority of Congress in the spring of

1875, and immediately drafted a comprehensive plan for its investigations, and contracted for a testing machine of four hundred tons capacity, which would enable it to properly conduct the experiments. Meanwhile the subcommittees of the board have devoted their time to such experiments as could be made with the smaller testing machines already available. This large machine is just now completed and ready for erection at the Watertown arsenal, and the real labors of the board are therefore just about to be commenced. If the board is to be discontinued at the end of the present fiscal year, the money already appropriated and the services of the gentlemen who have given so much time to the subject will be unproductive of any results.

The importance of these experiments can hardly be overestimated when we consider the almost endless variety of purposes for which iron and steel are employed in this country, and the many thousands of lives which daily depend on the soundness of iron structures. I need hardly refer to the recent disaster at the Ashtabula bridge in Ohio,[1] and the conflicting theories of experts as to the cause of it, as an instance of what might have been averted by a more thorough knowledge of the properties of iron and the best modes of construction. These experiments cannot properly be conducted by private firms, not only on account of the expense, but because the results must rest upon the authority of disinterested persons. They must, therefore, be undertaken under the sanction of the Government. Compared with their great value to the industrial interests of the country, the expense is very slight.

The board recommend an appropriation of $40,000 for the next fiscal year, and I earnestly commend their request to the favorable consideration of Congress. I also recommend that the board be required to conduct their investigations under the direction of the Secretary of War and to make full report of their progress to that officer in time to be incorporated in his annual report.

U. S. Grant.

Executive Mansion, *January* 30, 1877.

Printed, DNA, RG 130, Messages to Congress. *SED*, 44-2-28. On Dec. 22, 1876, William Sooy Smith, chairman, Committee on Tests, American Society of Civil Engineers, Maywood, Ill., wrote to USG. "The testing machine for the use of the Board appointed to test American iron, steel and other metals will, it is now thought, be completed and ready for use by the 1st of February next. It will be as we believe by far the most accurate machine ever employed in testing metals. . . ." Copy, DNA, RG 45, Subject File, Div. XV. On Feb. 3, 1877, Secretary of War James D. Cameron wrote to USG transmitting reports that Smith had requested. Copy, *ibid.*, RG 107, Letters Sent, Military Affairs. On Feb. 27, Charles F. Conant, act. secretary of the treasury, wrote to USG transmitting reports from treasury bureaus. Copy, *ibid.*, RG 56, Letters Sent to the President. Congress withheld support. See *PUSG*, 26, 91–93; *U.S. Statutes at Large*, XX, 223.

1. On Dec. 29, 1876, an iron bridge in Ohio over the Ashtabula River had collapsed under a Lake Shore & Michigan Southern Railroad train, killing nearly one hundred people. See Stephen D. Peet, *The Ashtabula Disaster Illustrated* (Chicago, 1877); T. Harry Williams, ed., *Hayes: The Diary of a President 1875–1881* (New York, 1964), 67.

To Edward Atkinson

February [2],[1] 1877

DEAR SIR:

After our conversation on the subject of specie resumption on the occasion of your recent visit to this city, I made inquiries[2] of the Secretary of the Treasury as to his views upon the subject of his power under all existing acts of Congress to do what I believed would practically bring legal tender notes to par; or near par, with gold. I found that there was a positive prohibition to any diminution of the issue of legal tenders except as provided for in the Act authorizing an unlimited increase of National bank circulation. Under these circumstances, I believed some legislation to be necessary authorizing the retirement of a portion of these notes, to accomplish a result so essential to the public good as I believe specie resumption to be. I have accordingly embodied my views on this subject in a short message to Congress, which will be delivered tomorrow.

I am much obliged to you for your kind note of the 30th inst. and hope that you, and all who desire to see sound currency take the place of our present fluctuating medium of exchange will give the subject such attention as will be likely to lead Congress to feel the necessity of action on their part. I feel anxious only as to the result, not as to the means by which it is accomplished. Any member of

Congress who will devise a measure that will cure the present currency evil—be he Democrat or Republican—will receive my hearty co-operation.

> With my best regards
> Your obedient servant
> U. S. GRANT

EDWARD ATKINSON, ESQ.

Harold Francis Williamson, *Edward Atkinson: The Biography of an American Liberal 1827–1905* (Boston, 1934), pp. 96–97. Edward Atkinson, a prosperous Boston textile merchant, championed reform politics, advocating free labor, free trade, and the gold standard. In Jan., 1877, Atkinson visited USG to promote accelerated specie resumption. Late in Jan., Atkinson wrote privately to USG. "Since my return from Washington, I have made a more complete examination of the acts passed subsequently to the legal-tender acts and I can find nothing to conflict with what I hold to be the essence of the Acts of 1862 and 1863. I hope the law officers of the Government may confirm my views. I am the more solicitous in this matter because I know that very prominent Democrats take my view, that a note paid in for taxes is dead, and I desire earnestly that it shall be buried under Republican administration. I hope nothing may be left for a possible Democratic administration to do that it may be claimed that a Republican administration might have done. I have caused my argument to be printed and I send herewith twenty copies. I retain a number of copies, but shall not allow them to be issued unless I learn that you have permitted the suggestions to be made public. In such event, I should be glad to have your authority to distribute some of them among my friends whose support of the measure might be of great value, and I shall be much gratified to have your permission to distribute them. . . . I have been much honored and gratified by the attention you have given to my suggestions, and a letter from you would be a valuable bequest to my descendants." *Ibid.* (ellipsis in original), p. 96. See Atkinson to Elihu B. Washburne, Dec. 27, 1867, DLC-Elihu B. Washburne; Atkinson, "Veto of the Inflation Bill of 1874," *Journal of Political Economy*, I, 1 (Dec. 1892), 117–19.

On Feb. 9, Atkinson, Boston, wrote a "Memorandum in regard to the Resumption Act of 1875 and the power granted to the Executive thereunder." "1st All provisions of law inconsistent therewith are repealed . . . The act of 1870 authorized the sale of bonds only *for* coin, the resumption act authorized sale at 'not less than par, *in* coin,' The evident construction of the change in the substitution of the word *in* for the word *for*, is that it enables the Secretary to sell the bonds for notes at such price as shall not represent less than par in coin. Any other construction of the act as a mode of preparation for specie payment is absurd—The other alternative would be to sell the bonds *for* coin and to pile up this coin in mass until Jan 1. 1879 and then to pay it out in one sum of $300.000.000—more or less It follows that it is now not only the right but the duty of the Secy of the Treasury to sell bonds for notes at a price not less than par in coin and to cancel and retire the notes in order 'to prepare for specie payment Jan 1. 1879 The clause in the Revised Statutes suspending the power of the Secy to retire and cancel said notes is repealed by the Resumption Act because it is inconsistent with it in substance and in form 9th It follows that Congress should at once pass the act for the issue of a 40 year 4 per cent bond not because such act is necessary as a preparation for resumption but because it is a more expedient bond to issue for the purpose than a 30 year 4½ per cent bond" ADS, USG 3. See message to Congress, Feb. 3, 1877.

1. Misdated Feb. 7.
2. On Jan. 22, Ulysses S. Grant, Jr., had written to Attorney Gen. Alphonso Taft. "The President asks that you will examine the two legal tender acts of 1862 and the act of 1869 pledging the Government to specie resumption to see if authority does not exist to resume specie payments without waiting until the 1st of Jany 18679." ALS, DLC-William H. Taft. On Jan. 23, Secretary of State Hamilton Fish recorded in his diary. "A long conversation as to the possibility of specie payments, reaching however the conclusion that without further legislation immediate resumption would be impracticable." DLC-Hamilton Fish.

To Congress

To the Senate and House of Representatives:

By the act of Congress approved January 14, 1875, "to provide for the resumption of specie payments," the 1st of January, 1879, is fixed as the date when such resumption is to begin. It may not be desirable to fix an earlier date when it shall actually become obligatory upon the Government to redeem its outstanding legal-tender notes in coin on presentation, but it is certainly most desirable and will prove most beneficial to every pecuniary interest of the country to hasten the day when the paper circulation of the country and the gold coin shall have equal values.

At a later day if currency and coin should retain equal values it might become advisable to authorize or direct resumption. I believe the time has come when by a simple act of the legislative branch of the Government this most desirable result can be attained. I am strengthened in this view by the course trade has taken in the last two years, and by the strength of the credit of the United States at home and abroad.

For the fiscal year ending June 30, 1876, the exports of the United States exceeded the imports by $120,213,102; but our exports include $40,569,621 of specie and bullion in excess of imports of the same commodities. For the six months of the present fiscal year, from July 1, 1876, to January 1, 1877, the excess of exports over imports amounted to $107,544,869, and the import of specie and bullion exceeded the export of the precious metals by $6,192,147 in the same time. The actual excess of exports over imports for the six months, exclusive of specie and bullion, amounted to $113,737,040, showing for the time being the accumulation of specie and bullion in the country amounting to more than $6,000,000 in addition to the national product of these metals for the same period, a total increase of gold and silver for the six months not far short of $60,000,000. It is very evident that unless this great increase of the precious metals can be utilized at home in such a way as to make it in some manner remunerative to the holders, it must seek a foreign market as surely as would any other product of the soil or the manufactory. Any legislation which will keep coin and bullion at home will, in my judgment, soon bring about practical resumption and will add the coin of the country to the circulating medium, thus securing a healthy "inflation" of a sound currency to the great advantage of every legitimate business interest.

The act to provide for the resumption of specie payments authorizes the Secretary of the Treasury to issue bonds of either of the descriptions named in the act of Congress approved July 14, 1870, entitled "An act to authorize the refunding of the national debt," for not less than par in gold. With the present value of the 4½ per cent. bonds in the markets of the world, they could be exchanged at par for gold, thus strengthening the Treasury to meet final resumption and to keep the excess of coin over demand, pending its pemanent use as a circulating medium, at home. All that would be further required would be to reduce the volume of legal-tender notes in circulation. To accomplish this I would suggest an act authorizing the Secretary of the Treasury to issue 4 per cent. bonds, with forty years to run before maturity, to be exchanged for legal-tender notes whenever presented in sums of $50, or any multiple thereof, the whole amount of such bonds, however, not to exceed $150,000,000. To increase the home demand for such bonds I would recommend that they be available for deposit in the United States Treasury for banking purposes under the various provisions of law relating to national banks.

I would suggest further, that national banks be required to retain a certain percentage of the coin interest received by them from the bonds deposited with the Treasury to secure their circulation.

I would also recommend the repeal of the third section of the joint resolution "for the issue of silver coin," approved July 22, 1876, limiting the subsidiary coin and fractional currency to $50,000,000.

I am satisfied that if Congress will enact some such law as will accomplish the end suggested, they will give a relief to the country instant in its effects, and for which they will receive the gratitude of the whole people.

U. S. GRANT.

EXECUTIVE MANSION, *February* 3, 1877.

Printed copy, DNA, RG 130, Messages to Congress. *HED*, 44-2-37. On Feb. 2, 1877, Secretary of State Hamilton Fish recorded in his diary. "The subject of the resumption of specie payments was discussed, and the President read a rough draft of a Message which he proposed to send to Congress authorizing the issue of $150.000.000 of the .04% 40 year bonds, to be exchanged for greenbacks and to be made receivable from Banks, as security for circulation. Some suggestions were made in addition, to the Presidents recommendation, but substantially, it met the approval of all present." DLC-Hamilton Fish. On Feb. 3, Culver C. Sniffen telegraphed to USG. "Senate adjourned, Shall I put Message into the House or bring both back?" Telegram received, DNA, RG 107, Telegrams Collected (Bound). On March 2, USG telegraphed to Abel R. Corbin, Elizabeth, N. J. "I go to the Capitol to-night to urge passage of bill to aid resumption." ALS (telegram sent), *ibid.* Congress took no action. See *CR*, 44–2, 2163–66.

To Congress

TO THE SENATE AND HOUSE OF REPRESENTATIVES—

The accompanying "Memorial" is transmitted to Congress at the request of a Committee composed of many distinguished citizens of New York recently appointed to co-operate with a generous body of French citizens who design to erect in the harbor of New York a colossal statue of "Liberty enlightening the World"—

Very little is asked of us to do, and I hope that the wishes of the memorialists may receive your very favorable consideration.—

U. S. GRANT—

EXECUTIVE MANSION—FEBRUARY 9. 1877—

Copy, DNA, RG 130, Messages to Congress. *SED*, 44-2-36. On Feb. 1, 1877, William M. Evarts, Edwin D. Morgan, William Cullen Bryant, and seventeen others, New York City, wrote to USG asking him to transmit an undated memorial to Congress. *Ibid.* Evarts *et al.*

asked Congress for "passage of a law authorizing the proper Department to set off sufficient ground for the purpose on either Bedloe or Governor's Island, and to provide for its future maintenance as a beacon." *Ibid.*, p. 2. On March 3, USG approved a joint resolution authorizing the President to choose a site for the statue, intended to commemorate the Centennial. See *U.S. Statutes at Large*, XIX, 410; *HRC*, 48-2-2259.

On Oct. 26, 1875, Édouard Laboulaye, president, French American Union Committee, Paris, had written to USG. "On the solemn occasion of the Centennial anniversary of the Independance of the United States, we thought that France would be happy to participate in the joy of her américan friends, and to show how much she remains faithful in her old traditions. We long thought of offering our américan friends at the time of that festivity, a mark of our feelings worthy of the genius of France. Our idea has been splendidly formed by our friend the celebrated sculptor Aug. Bartholdi member of our Committee. He went to América to study the question, he saw and came to an understanding with a great number of our friends. Our project would be; to build in the middle of the New-York harbour on a little Island belonging tho the Union, facing Long-Island where the first blood has been shed for Liberty a gigantic statue of the Indépendance. The colosse would show her grand figure in the space, horizoned by the large cities of New-York, Jersey-City, and Brooklyn. At the entrance of that vast continent full of a new life, where ships meet from all point[s] of the world, it will look as it were raising u[p] from the bosom of the deep; representing 'Liberty enlightning the world.' At night a luminous aureola, projected from the head, will radiate on the far flowing waves of the Ocean[.] This project has been laid before your Excellency, three years ago by Mr Barthol[di] who has been introduced to you by our frien[d] the colonel J. W. Forney. Mr Bartholdi had the honour to infor[m] your Excellency of our desire to erect th[is] monument on Beddloe's Island, where a small fort belonging to the Union is situated[;] your Excellency Kindly told him that th[e] subject required to be submitted to the Congre[ss.] Consequently Sir, we have the honour to pr[esent] our request about the matter to your Excellency. Bedloe's Island is a wonderful situation for the projected purpose. Our monument erected in the middle of the central court, would occupy a square of about 40 feet on each side. It is to be supposed that it would not be prejudicial to the use of the fort. For the scenery of the entrance to the New-York harbour, that situation of the monument of Independance would be magnificent; it would present a prospect unique in the world and worthy of the glorious events which it will record. We offer the statue to our american friends; they on their side will take charge of organising a subscription to build up the piedestal and erect the statue. Both nations will be associated in that pious hommage rendered to the glorious past time, as they have been tho conquer the Independance. We wish in France to warmly show our enthusiasm for that noble Liberty, which represents the glory of the United States and which enlightens modern people by its exemple. The echoe of our appeal has been listened to with fervour. we shall feel happy on that exchange of sympathy with the American nation and still more, as our manifestation will fortify us in the work of regeneration which we endeavour to accomplish in our own country. We hope Sir, your Excellency will Kind[ly] maintain our request with the Congress and authorities on which it dépends." LS and copy, DNA, RG 59, Diplomatic Despatches, France. During a dinner in Paris to raise funds on Nov. 6, "telegrams were sent to General Grant and Marshal MacMahon, conveying to the two Presidents the expression of the feelings which animated the gathering." *The Times* (London), Nov. 8, 1875. See *Union Franco-Américaine . . . Banquet du 6 Novembre 1875* (Paris, n. d.); letter to Édouard Laboulaye, Nov. 21, 1877; Elihu B. Washburne to Hamilton Fish, Nov. 10, 1875, March 16, 1876, DNA, RG 59, Diplomatic Despatches, France.

To John P. Newman

Feby 10th /77

DEAR DR.

When Bishop Ames was last here I promised him to nominate his son for reentrance into the Army as a 2d Lt. The order was given to the Sec. of War the first time I met him after the promise was made. Delay was intentional because of the great number of applications for these appointments, and the persistincy with which they would be urged if new nominations were announced. For this reason it was determined not to send it in until the last week of my officia[l] life. Yesterday the Secretary reported to me that Capt. Ames stood charged at the department with deficiencies to the amount of $19.284 00, $13.820.00 of it to the Indian Department, & $5.464.00 to the Quartermaster[s] Department. If there is not a satisfactory settlement, or explanation, of this I can not of course appoint him. The Sec. however told me that he would examine the matter himself, and if it did not disbar Capt. Ames, in his judgement, he would so report in time to make the appointment.

I did not like to write this to the Bishop, but write to you so that if his son should not be appointed you can explain the reason. I will yet make the appointment if it should prove proper to do so.

Very Truly Yours,
U. S. GRANT

DR. J. P. NEWMAN.

ALS, John M. Taylor, McLean, Va. On Feb. 27, 1877, USG nominated Edward R. Ames, former capt., as 2nd lt., 6th Inf. See *PUSG*, 19, 347–48.

To Edwards Pierrepont

Feby 11th /77

DEAR JUDGE;

But three weeks remain until I close my official career. Although so short a time it appears to me interminable, my anxiety to be free from care is so great. As yet the question of "who is to succeed me" is not definitely settled; but the chances seem to be much in favor of the republican candidate. But he must gain every point to succeed, while his opponent requires but one. Even this he can forego—the majority of the states being democratic in their House representation—if he can deprive the republican of one electoral vote on any technicality. I believe quiet will be preserved in any event, though it seems possible now that the democrats in the house may prevent any count unless they get their candidate declared elected.

I shall remain in Washington until April. After that I shall visit the West—St. Louis, Galena & Chicago—to see my friends in that section, and to arrange for the care of my property during my proposed absence. I will not take my departure for Europe until about the 20th of June. I propose to take Jesse with me but will wait until he is through with his examination, which will close about the middle of June. I shall not embarrass myself by plans in advance of where to go, how long to stay at any one place, or when to return, but will move as circumstances may direct, and return when I get homesick or funds fail. It will be my effort to move about as quietly as possible and to see all that is to be seen.—Mrs. Grant & I hope to meet you and Mrs Pierrepont in London, but if Tilden should happen to be our President it is hardly to be expected that it will be as the representative of the United States. A clean sweep of all officials in that event may be expected. That is the meaning of "Tilden & Reform."

Please present Mrs. Grant's & my kindest regards to Mrs. Pierrepont, and accept my thanks for your kind notes received since your absence.

Very Truly Yours
U. S. GRANT

HON. EDWARDS PIERREPONT U. S. MIN. PLEN.

ALS, CtY. On April 3, 1877, Edwards Pierrepont, U.S. minister, London, wrote to Hamilton Fish. ". . . I received a long letter from General Grant written just three weeks before his term of office closed—It is charming in its truth and naturalness—I will keep it & show it to you some future day—He was heartily glad to lay down official responsibilities as I am sure you are—. . ." ALS, DLC-Hamilton Fish.

To Rutherford B. Hayes

———

Feby 20th 1877

DEAR GOVERNOR;

I take it the question of the "count" to determine who is to be my successor is now virtually determined,[1] and that you will be in this city on or before the 3d of March! I write to invite you and your family to come directly to the Executive Mansion to be my guests until the inauguration. On Saturday, the 3d, I would like to entertain you & Mrs Hayes, and such of your party as you may suggest, at dinner. The capacity of our table is Thirty-eight. My own family to be present would number sieven. The Cabinet, whom I should like to be present, with the ladies, number fourteen more; twenty-one in all. If you will signify your acceptance, and the names of any gentlemen or ladies, in or out of Congress, whom you would like to fill the vacant places I will be pleased to invite them.

Very Truly Yours
U. S. GRANT

GOV. R. B. HAYES,

ALS, OFH. On Feb. 23, 1877, Governor Rutherford B. Hayes of Ohio wrote to USG. "I am in receipt of your very kind note of the 20th. Sinister rumors from W. leave us in doubt as to the final issue. In case of success I expect to be in Washington next Thursday, 29th, and to go directly to Senator Shermans. If after seeing you it seems best, I will be glad to accept your hospitality on Saturday for myself and family. I will also be pleased to dine with you as proposed on that day. I can not name all or perhaps any of my party except my own family, but I suppose that besides Mrs Hayes and myself and Son, Webb C, there will also be Genl & Mrs Mitchell and possibly four others. If you wish to invite others, may I suggest Mr Wheeler Senator and Mrs Sherman. I noticed an item saying that you would on leaving the Ex. Mansion go to Mr Fish's. I will be *particularly* gratified if you will remain where you are as long as it may be convenient for you to do so, and until your own residence is ready. Mrs Hayes is now absent, but you may assure Mrs Grant that my wife will feel obliged to her if she will remain at least a few days with us after the 5th of March. As to my family coming to your house on Saturday it occurs to me that with your dinner &c &c this may be inconvenient, and that it is best for me to remain at Senator Shermans until after inauguration. All this on the supposition that we are finally declared successful. . . . P. S. It is perhaps best that the date of my expected arrival in W. should not be made public." ALS, USG 3. Hayes arrived in Washington, D. C., on March 2, and attended USG's dinner the next evening. See *Washington Evening Star,* March 5, 1877.

On Feb. 20, Hayes had written to USG. "I am informed that an Officer of the army is to be detailed to take charge of the Soldiers Home near Washington, and that Gen J. H.

Potter wants the place. I write to say that I am acquainted with Gen P. and his family; and would be particularly gratified if he can be appointed consistently with usage, justice to others, and the interests of the service." ALS, OFH. On July 1, Col. Joseph H. Potter was detailed as governor, Soldiers' Home.

1. On Feb. 16, the Electoral Commission had voted to count the La. electoral vote for Hayes; on Feb. 19, the Senate upheld this decision.

Endorsement

Miss Van Lew was appointed by me Postmaster of Richmond, Va soon after my entrance upon the duties of President from a knowledge of her entire loyalty during the rebellion and her services to the cause. She has filled the office since with capacity and fidelity and is very deserving of continued confidence by a republican administration.

U. S. GRANT

FEB.Y 26TH /77

AES (facsimile), William Gilmore Beymer, "Miss Van Lew," *Harper's Monthly*, CXXIII, DCCXXXIII (June, 1911), 97. No appointment followed. See Endorsement, Feb. 3, 1881; *PUSG*, 19, 337–39; Elizabeth R. Varon, *Southern Lady, Yankee Spy: The True Story of Elizabeth Van Lew, A Union Agent in the Heart of the Confederacy* (Oxford, 2003), pp. 231–38.

On April 6 and Oct. 2, 1869, Elizabeth Van Lew, postmaster, Richmond, wrote to USG. "I write to you not as the president but as a dear friend—How I thank you for the position you have given me God only knows—for your faith & trust in me I thank you and will try & prove worthy. I am not responsible for the many things the papers say of me and I am not responsible for things wh: I sometimes hear I have said but never heard of until I am surprised by their coming to me—I do not think you would wish to humiliate my only sensible & beloved brother by overlooking him—I earnestly entreat you will give him a position wh: will enable him to make his living, something which our community has *refused to permit him to do*—He is an earnest & faithful Republican—and if he obtains the position he desires will be enabled to put into office faithful and honest Virginians who will be the men to support your measures and administration—but who will never otherwise be heard of, having suffered all things for loyalty—and who would die for a principle—I have but a moment to close for the mail—I leave my brother in yr. hands with full trust that you will do what you can for him—and me—" "It gives me pleasure to introduce to you the bearer of this Mr. William S—Rowley—The bravest of the brave—and truest of the true. At his house have I seen spies secreted, and deserters harbored, ready and willing for the most daring service was he ever found—even to perilling his own family—The body of poor Col. Dahlgren was carried to his house watched over by him—and by him alone driven through our strongest pickets to a friendly grave   I hope you may be able to talk with Mr. Rowley—you will find him *a character*—he is a man of rare perception—and wonderful intuition—understood here both Mr. Lincoln and yourself long before other people did—Were Mr. Botts living he would commend him to you—as a person to be honored by all loyal people—Pardon my writing so much my subject must be my apology— I think it will gratify you to know him—" ALS, NN. John N. Van Lew later clerked in the Richmond post office. See *PUSG*, 11, 434; Meriwether Stuart, "Colonel Ulric Dahlgren and Richmond's Union Underground April 1864," *Virginia Magazine of History and Biography*, 72, 2 (April, 1964), 162–66, 171–82.

On March 25, 1876, Louis Ganbin, Washington, D. C., wrote to USG. "Your welcome message, was on Wednesday the 15th inst, joyfully and thankfully received by me and my family, and, according to your kind directions, I at once called on Mr Jewell, Supt of the Bureau of Printing and Engraving, who at first, hesitated in giving me employment, but, on further consideration, concluded to assign me to the post of Watchman. . . ." L, DNA, RG 56, Applications. On April 24, 1877, Ganbin wrote to Secretary of the Treasury John Sherman seeking reinstatement as watchman. ". . . Having, during the late War, had occasion to render the Govt some very valuable services in connection with Miss E. Van Lew, the present Post-Mistress of Richmond Va; I formed the resolution to address a letter to Ex Prest Grant, stating the case in regard to said services as well as my circumstances, and enclosing some of my Testimonials with an endorsement from Senator O. P. Morton of Indiana.—On the 15th of said month (March /76), the President having kindly taken my circumstances into consideration, returned me my letter with an endorsement to Mr Jewell, . . ." L, *ibid.* No appointment followed for Ganbin, former hospital steward, C.S. Army.

To Senate

———

To The Senate of the United States—

In answer to the Resolution of the Senate of the 27th instant, I transmit, herewith, a report of the Secretary of State, together with the paper which accompanied it—

U S Grant—

Washington February 28th 1877.

Copies, DNA, RG 59, Reports to the President and Congress; *ibid.*, RG 130, Messages to Congress. On Feb. 28, 1877, Secretary of State Hamilton Fish wrote to USG. "The Secretary of State having received a Resolution of the Senate that he transmit to that body any communication received by him demanding the payment of moneys claimed to be now due the Dominican Government, from the government of the United States has the honor to communicate herewith to the President a copy of a note addressed to him purporting to be from the late Minister of Foreign Affairs of San Domingo bearing date the 21st day of June 1876, which was received on the 31st day of January last." Copy, *ibid.*, RG 59, Reports to the President and Congress. On June 21, 1876, Manuel de J. Galvan, "Department of State of Foreign Relations," Santo Domingo, had written to [Fish] demanding payment past due from the U.S. under an 1869 agreement to lease Samana Bay. LS (in Spanish), *ibid.*, Notes from Foreign Legations; translation, *ibid.*

On Jan. 27, 1875, USG had spoken with Fish concerning "the amount due to St Domingo for the lease of Samana Bay for the second year He said that Murphy was nearly ruined and had advanced some $40.000 or $50.000 on account of the rent and that some others, without naming them, had also made advances, that the money ought to be paid; and that Conkling had spoken with him and suggested that I should bring the matter to the notice of the Committee on Foreign Relations. . . . He asked if it could not be paid out of the contingent fund of foreign intercourse—I explained to him that the appropriation only amounted to about $100.000 and with the strictest economy the expendatures could only be kept $2.000 below it. He suggested that an appropriation for $150.000 might be made without indicating its object. I thought that it would be impossible and he asked whether I could not suggest such an appropriation informing the Administration Senators of its object—I replied that I could not, that the present temper of Congress and the public was such that no appropriation of the kind could be expected and that it would be very damaging to him and to the Republican Party for the administration to propose an appropriation for the St. Domingo Treaty The President admitted that he was precluded from asking but thought that I might. . . . He finally remarked that he supposed that the only thing would be for the party to make application to Congress to which I replied that I could suggest nothing but that the Administration should take no part in it" Fish diary, DLC-Hamilton Fish.

On July 18, 1876, Ulysses S. Grant, Jr., wrote to Fish. "The following is a dispatch to the President at Deer Park which reached there too late to be received yesterday. 'July 17. '76 THE PRESIDENT. Deer Park W. Va. Committees of both houses have agreed to the payment of one years rent for Samana, if the Secretary of State will telegraph Senator Windom today that such rent is passed due and unpaid. Tomorrow will be too late. (Signed) T. M.' Mr Murphy says that it is most important to have this matter attended to at once. and the President has directed me to send you a copy of the despatch and ask you to consider it at once." ALS, *ibid.* See Fish diary, July 14, 18, 19, Nov. 28, 1876, *ibid.*; Nevins, *Fish*, pp. 834–36.

On Feb. 13 and 28, 1877, Fish recorded in his diary. "After Cabinet I remained and spoke with the President about Tom Murphys effort to get an appropriation nominally for Samana Bay; . . . He agreed with me that there was no possibility of the appropriation, but Murphy was very poor, and he ~~thought~~ he could get the money. I told him that Conkling, though twice requested, had not come to look at the papers; and that I thought he wished the President and myself to bear the responsibility, of either bringing up the question, or of declining to do so; and that he was encouraging Murphy while he would not, himself, give him active open support." "Received a Resolution from the Senate calling for a copy of the application of San Domingo for rent for Samana Bay. I caused a copy of it to be made and took it to the President telling him that but for his interest in Tom Murphy the resolution should not be answered; that the whole subject was a fraud, of which I wished to wash my hands; that if, at the time, (as Tom Murphy says) he had advanced the money to San Domingo, then it is no longer an international claim, but merely the effort of Mr Murphy an American Citizen to be repaid a speculative, and very improper investment of his own; that the paper of which I now send a copy is in my Judgment fraudulent; that it bears date on 21 June last, and was not delivered until 31st January; that the party who signed it, as Minister of Foreign Affairs, was out of office months before the letter was delivered; and that the administration of which he was a member, had been overthrown and expelled from power, and that I doubted whether the paper had been signed by him while in Office; that my reluctance at having anything to do with it, arose from my conviction that it was a swindle from beginning to end, and that I did not wish, in the last days of the Administration, that either he or my Department, should be smirched by connection with such a transaction. He said that the Senator (alluding as I supposed to Conkling who has been the sneeking advocate of this Job without taking any personal responsibility for it) said that the appropriation would pass beyond doubt as the Senators generally were in favor of it. I handed him the paper, and he signed the message transmitting ~~the message~~ it to the Senate." DLC-Hamilton Fish. See Fish to Roscoe Conkling, Feb. 9, 11, 1877, *ibid.*; *CR*, 44–2, 1960, 2103–4.

Order

Executive Mansion
Washington, D. C
March 1st 1877

Brevet Brig. Gen. O. E. Babcock, U. S. Engs. is hereby relieved from the opperation of Special Orders No 75, dated March 3d 1869.

For faithful and efficient service as private Sec. for more than six years of my two terms of office he has my acknowledgement and thanks, and the assurance of my confidence in his integrity and great efficiency.

U. S. GRANT

ADS, Babcock Papers, ICN. See *PUSG*, 19, 143. Relieved as superintendent of public buildings, Washington, D. C., Maj. Orville E. Babcock was ordered to "report to the Hon. Secretary of the Treasury for duty as engineer of the fifth light-house district." *Washington Evening Star*, March 1, 1877.

To James D. Cameron

March 3d 1877.

DEAR SIR:

In my dispatch to Mr. Packard of La. I intended to convey the idea that all obligations to require him or General Nichols to observe the status in quo, commanded by the instructions to General Augur in his orders of the 16th of January was at an end. In having this dispatch communicated to General Augur my idea was, that, he would construe it as instructions to him to limit his orders to the mere preservation of peace in case of riot—I would let the two Governors work out their own precedence for Executive recognition in the same manner as any Northern state would have to do under like circumstances—

Very respectfully—
U S. GRANT—

HON: J D CAMERON. SECRETARY OF WAR—

Copy, DLC-USG, II, 3. See telegram to Christopher C. Augur, Jan. 14, 1877.

On March 1, 1877, Stephen B. Packard, New Orleans, telegraphed to USG. "Statements are authoritatively made here that you have announced your purpose to withdraw the U S forces from the various positions to which they have been assigned in the interests of peace & public order in this City & State So Soon as the electoral vote shall have been declared it is further stated that assurances have been given on the part of Mr Nicholls & his armed supporters who I may State are identically the Same organization that under the name of the White League rose insurrection against the State government in eighteen Seventy four & were Suppressed by your orders. that if the Support of the U S troops should be with drawn the government of which I am the head would disintegrate & Mr Nicholls would be installed without violence or bloodshed. it is Currently reported & believed here on the other hand that the White League are under orders & will attack the State house so soon as the troops are withdrawn from the City & that it is their purpose by the annihilation of the officers of the government to leave no republican State government for your Successor to recognize the validity of my title as governor having been passed upon by the only tribunal known to the State laws & being now Confirmed by the decision of the national electoral tribunal I deem it my duty to maintain the government by all the means at my Command I therefore most respectfully but earnestly request to be informed whether any changes are contemplated by you in the orders heretofore given to the general Commanding the U S forces in this State in order that I may be able to take Such Measures as the Circumstances & my duty as chief executive of the State may seem to require & I again most respectfully request at your hands the recognition of the legal State government of Louisiana" Telegram received (at 12:10 P.M.), OFH. On the same day, Culver C. Sniffen telegraphed to Packard. "In answer to your dispatch of this date the President directs me to say that he feels it his duty to state frankly that he does not believe public opinion will longer support the maintenance of state government in Louisiana by the use of the military and that he must concur in this manifest feeling. The troops will hereafter as in the past protect life and property from mob violence when the State authorities fail, but under the remaining days of his official life they will not be used to establish or to pull down either claimant for control of the state. It is not his purpose to recognize either claimant." Copy, DNA, RG 94, Letters Received, 4788 1876. *HMD*, 45-3-31, I, 537, 961, 1041, III, 33. Also on March 1, Secretary of State Hamilton Fish recorded in his diary that USG sent him a draft of this telegram, with an initialed endorsement. "Will the Secretary of State please read the enclosed despatch, and my proposed answer and note his views" Copy, DLC-Hamilton Fish. Fish wrote to USG. "The position taken in your proposed reply to Gov Packard is perfectly right. I approve from beginning to end—it cannot be improved." Copy, *ibid.*

On March 2, 5:00 A.M., Edward A. Burke, Washington, D. C., wrote to USG. "I am just in receipt of the following Telegram from New Orleans, viz: 'Republicans here say that

Presidents order removing troops intended in their interest, that they may make sudden dash and take court buildings and stations before we could rally or bring troops from Barracks, seems reason to believe Packard is trying to recruit his force so as to make effort to capture buildings. I have not guarded them heavily relying on Status quo, could place sufficient force to render attack folly and were they even taken by surprise could retake in short order unless restrained by federal relations. State these facts to President and ask him in event Packard should make dash and take buildings by reason my unwillingness to garrison as on war footing, whether my retaking would not be Justifiable if not, whether Packard would be ordered to replace matters as formerly. Needs scarcely say can easily dispose of his attempts if not interfered with—signed, F. T. NICHOLLS.'" ALS, OFH. On the same day, Burke and three others telegraphed to Francis T. Nicholls, New Orleans. "The President says he sent a despatch to Packard yesterday, notifying him that troops could no longer be employed to uphold either claimant, and that he does not believe that Packard would attempt any offensive operations. The President sent the despatch so that he might have time to retire his pretensions if disposed. The President says instructions have been issued which cancel all orders for the preservation of the *status quo*, and that neither you nor Packard are longer bound to observe it; that he means the people of Louisiana are as free in their affairs from Federal interference as the people of Connecticut, and that there will be no disposition to interfere with them any more than with the people of New York. The President concurs with us that you immediately issue a proclamation urging protection, amnesty, and peace. Being asked if posse executing process of Nicholls' court would be interfered with by military, he replied, 'no more than in any other State.' Being asked if Nicholls' officers should take possession of the offices in the State without mob violence would there be military interference, he replied there would be none; that the military would only be used as it had been once in New York, and would be in any of the States, to overcome mobs too formidable for the civil power or State authorities. . . . We have submitted the foregoing despatch of yesterday to the President, who has revised it with his own hand, and authorizes us to state that in its present form it is absolutely correct." *HMD*, 45-3-1, I, 1041, III, 626–27. Burke later testified. "The correction made was this: As stated in the original despatch sent to Governor Nicholls, General Grant used the language: 'Assuming that the Packard government will disappear.' When the despatch was read over to him he said, 'It is true I said that, but it would only be wounding my party friends, and I would prefer to strike it out.'. . ." *Ibid.*, p. 627. Also on March 2, Burke wrote twice more to USG. "Enclosed please find telegram from Gov. Nicholls, New Orleans, 6 p. m., saying, 'No demonstration here; no danger of any violence by our people. Proclamation will be issued soon as Augur notifies of reception orders.' It is reported that the orders referred to have not been transmitted." "Telegram from Governor Nicholls received 7.55 p. m. 'Parties from Army headquarters here say no orders regarding withdrawal of troops received up to this hour. How is this? Answer quick.' Can you advise me what to answer to send?" *Ibid.*, p. 628. On the same day, Nicholls telegraphed to Burke. "Augur has received copy telegram & sent it to us since last dispatch. Proclamation as suggested issued." *Ibid.*

On March 3, Gen. William T. Sherman telegraphed to Brig. Gen. Christopher C. Augur, New Orleans. "I cannot undertake to interpret the Presidents letter to Mr Packard— Of course you will keep the Peace if possible, and by you Counsels I believe you can prevent any material changes in the attitude of the Contending parties till the new Administration can be fairly installed, and give the Subject mature reflection. The question of the attitude of the State of Louisiana to the National Goverment is too important, to be hastily decided. Every Citizen is interested that this question be settled right—" ALS (telegram sent), DNA, RG 94, Letters Received, 4788 1876. See Joseph G. Dawson III, *Army Generals and Reconstruction: Louisiana, 1862–1877* (Baton Rouge, 1982), pp. 252–60; Ari Hoogenboom, *The Presidency of Rutherford B. Hayes* (Lawrence, Kan., 1988), pp. 43, 47–50.

To Simon Wolf

March 3, 1877.

MY DEAR MR. WOLF:

Your letter of yesterday has given me a great deal of pleasure. You have during the eight years of our official intercourse shown the true spirit of an American citizen, and our personal relations have at all times endeared you to me.

I thank you sincerely and hope that your future years may bring you still greater honors, health and happiness.

Sincerely yours,

U. S. GRANT.

Simon Wolf, *The Presidents I Have Known from 1860–1918* (Washington, [1918]), pp. 96–97. On March 2, 1877, Simon Wolf wrote to USG. "Day after tomorrow you will, by virtue of law, retire from the Presidency which you have so splendidly adorned. Our intercourse personally and officially has been of such a pleasant character that I can not help but congratulate myself for the high privilege and distinction which this intimacy has conferred. You have at all times been most considerate and cordial. Time and again you have given evidence of your good-will, and indeed your forbearance. Although you will retire to private life, I will ever have the highest esteem of your character as soldier, patriot and citizen. May the years yet in store for you, bring you health and happiness and good cheer." *Ibid.*, p. 96.

On Nov. 4, 1876, Peter B. Starke, former C.S.A. brig. gen., Lawrenceville, Va., had written to USG. "Some four years ago Just before the Presidential Election I wrote what might seeme an intrusive Letter to you, In which I made some suggestions. on my return from Miss I found a polite answer. And now Just before an other Election I suggest that it matters not which of the Candidates are Elected President. he will have the most dificult Task to perform that ever a man encounterd except the one that devolved on you in taking charge of this vast Empire after the the most stupendous civil war that ever occured When every thing was upset society upturned constitutions overthrown a new civilisation four millions of People Lying loose without any plan dvised to care for and manage them. With a wide spread demorilazation that was never witnessed before. That you should have held together this immense Empire for 8 years and hand it over in tact is one of the performances of the age. To mention all the dificulties you have had to encounter would take Books. I stop for the present by simply predicting that at the end of the next Administration if it should hold together that the task of reforming the reformers will open the Eyes of the Nation and the question will be who can save the country The answer will almost embrace all the good men of all parties that he who saved the country in War and in the Cabinet is the only man equal to such an immegency. As before Either party will be to glad to Get the use of your name. If you should read this Letter mark the predicton" ALS, USG 3.

On Feb. 10, 1877, Manning F. Force, Cincinnati, wrote to USG. "Your term of office is drawing to a close, and while you are congratulating yourself upon the approaching release from its burden and cares, I desire to congratulate you on some of your achievments in civil life that may fairly rank with your successes in war. The foreign relations of the country have never been handled with greater ability, success or brilliancy, than during the past eight years The constant improvement of the public credit and your veto of the inflation bill, will always be monuments of your administration. The serious effort to apply to the treatment of the Indians, the rules of humanity and christianity, make an epoch in the history of the government. The attempt to improve the methods of the civil service, though it failed through the hostility of congress and the indifference of the people, is a pioneer in the road that must save the government from destruction. Your conduct in relation to the southern states has been vehemently decried. But when the clouds roll away, recognition will be given to its justice, generosity and firmness. Your patriotic course in the troubles growing out of the late presidential election, is already gratefully recognized. Your prompt and cogent declarations in public emergencies, words that stayed trouble and preserved peace, will remain memorable Your retirement will be sweetened, with the thought that your public life had but the single aim, to save the country; and with the assurance that history will do justice to your administration Allow me to say that the respect for your character, and the regard for you personally, which I formed early in the war, have never wavered, . . ." ALS, *ibid.*

On Feb. 13, Governor Mason Brayman of Idaho Territory wrote to USG to congratulate him on achievements in war and peace. ALS, *ibid.*

On Feb. 26, Peter P. Pitchlynn, Choctaw delegate, and eight other Chickasaws, Cherokees, and Creeks, Washington, D. C., wrote to USG. "On the eve of your retirement from Office, we desire to express our appreciation of the course you have pursued towards our people while President of the United States—At all times just and humane you have not failed to manifest an earnest wish for their advancement in the arts and pursuits of civilized life, a conscientious regard for their rights and the full purpose to enforce in their behalf, the obligations of the United States. The results have been peace among themselves and among others so far as their influence reached, increased confidence in the pledges of protection given them and steady progress in knowledge and industry—For these things, we thank you, and trust that the merited gratitude of the weak and friendless will be not least of the honors, which this and future generations will associate with your name—" LS, *ibid.*

On March 3, Col. Albert J. Myer, chief signal officer, Washington, D. C., wrote to USG. "When you became President you gave me as a memento the last signature signed by you as 'General of the Army' on a sheet like this—If it is not seeking too great a favor may I ask that tomorrow March 4th before noon you will write for me on the opposite sheet your autograph as President—I wish to keep it as a memento" ALS, DLC-Albert J. Myer. USG's autograph, dated the same day, is *ibid.*

On March 12, T. Jefferson Martin, Dowagiac, Mich., wrote to USG. "As a colored Man I feel in duty bound to return you my greatful and heart felt thanks, for your firm stedfast and successful administrations of our country, both as Millitary chieftain and civil Ruler of this nation. More then any other military cheiftain while acting as such you contended for the unqualified liberty and protection of all Men under our jurisdiction. When four millions of our people was weighed in the scale of Battle and their liberty was made contingent upon your success, you never faultered but was successful though many generals before you had failed For this success I Thank you Especially you have Restored to the people of this country, the government intact—and fully upon the basis upon which the founders laid it but failed to carry out to completion. To the effect that 'All men are created equal, and indowed by their creator with certain inaleinable Right (first) among which are life, liberty and the persuits of happiness' My Dear friend to humanity. Without the cooperation of yourself in harmony with the good men of the Republican Party the 14th and 15th amendments to our national constitution, those just principles would not of been adopted and made the law and practice at this time and age. For your persistant and firm support of these amendments I especially Return My sincere thanks When we look back and consider, that you Took up arms in defence of this government 16 years ago. That colored people by our laws was mere chattles and that our liberty was contingent upon your success in sustaining the government against its foes. And that as late as eight years ago. When you Took poscession of the civil Reigns of government, ~~The~~ We were hardly qualifiedly free. And that we to day by the laws of land injoy unqualified liberty in common with all the citizens of the united states. And in the greatest measure it is owing to your persistant and stedy perpose of head and heart to carry into law and practice during your administrations these rightious and just principles as declared at the inception of this government a hundred years ago. for the consumation of this not only me—but mankingd of all Races will *Ever* thank you. And now you have just Turned the government over to the people of the united states and to your successor upon firm basis I hope. in peace with all the nations of the Earth, and not one slaves under the jurisdiction of our common country you have adopted and carried into practice the ancient amphictyonic council which your successer indorses. which is an assurance of continued peace with the nations of the world and our country My kind and noble friend your national administrations in my estemation shows the grandest and truest career Recorded either in ancient or modern history. your acts public acts cannot be weighed in the scales of Material wealth Your Taking your position to day on a level with the common citizens Truly personifies the greatest and best man god ever give the world as an example of how we should walk through this life I Return you my congratulation for all your succeses in life. It is all that I have to give you, and I Thank you a hundred times over. The Ruler of all things will bear witnes to my cincerety both now and forever May god especially bless you and yours now and forever" ALS, OFH.

On March 17, John A. Logan wrote to USG. "I intended calling this morning prior to leaving for home, that I might pay my respects to yourself and family, but am suffering with rheumatism so that I fear to go out in the storm. I can not leave however without expressing to you my thanks and grateful acknowledgemts, for your many kind acts to me. Be assured that you have my best wishes, and earnest hopes that prosperity and happiness may attend yourself and family in all the future." ALS, USG 3.

USG also received congratulatory letters dated Jan. 5 from James H. Warren, San Francisco; dated Feb. 2 from Frederick A. Aiken, Philadelphia; dated March 3 from George H. Crosby, Leavenworth, Kan., E. O. Orr, West Galway, N. Y.; dated March 4 from William W. Mason *et al.*, Decatur, Ill.; dated March 5 from E. Purcell, New York City, Charles C. Parker, Parsippany, N. J. *Ibid.*

To Rutherford B. Hayes

Washington, D. C.
March 6th /77

DEAR SIR:

I take great pleasure in commending Judge Rayner, recently of the Alabama Claims Commission,[1] to the pPresident as a most worthy and capable gentleman, well qualified for any judicial position. If a vacancy should occur on the bench of the Court of Claims I know of no person better suited to the position. The Judge is a Southern unionest, now residing in ~~South~~ Mississippi, though formerly from North Carolina which state he represented in Congress for six years prior to the late rebellion.

Very respectfully
your obt. svt.
U. S. GRANT

THE PRESIDENT.

ALS, Kenneth Rayner Papers, Southern Historical Collection, University of North Carolina, Chapel Hill, N. C. USG also addressed an undated envelope to "The President Introducing Hon. K. Rayner." AD, *ibid.* On Oct. 16, 1877, President Rutherford B. Hayes nominated Kenneth Rayner, former U.S. Representative from N. C. (1839–45), as solicitor of the treasury.

On July 21, 1876, U.S. Representatives Clinton D. MacDougall and Thomas C. Platt of N. Y. had telegraphed to USG. "We believe the appointment of Kenneth Rayner as Commissioner of Internal Revenue would strengthen the party in North Carolina and the South, and that he would make an excellent Officer" Telegram received, DNA, RG 56, Appointment Div., Letters Received; *ibid.*, RG 107, Telegrams Collected (Bound). No appointment followed.

On Feb. 26, 1877, Rayner wrote to USG. "There is a Bill pending before Congress, and which, I think, has passed both Houses,—'To provide for the preparation and publication of a new edition of the Revised Statutes of the United States.'—This Bill provides for the appointment of a commissioner for the purpose of preparing and publishing this new edition of the revised statutes—such appointment to be made by the President of the United States, by and with the advice and consent of the Senate. You will please allow me, Mr President, to request of you, that you will confer this appointment on myself. I can only assure your Excellency, that if I should recieve this appointment, my convictions of ~~pride~~ duty, and my sense of ~~du~~ pride, will stimulate me to do the work entrusted to me, in such way, as will give satisfaction, to the Bench and the Bar, throughout the country. At the same time, my grateful appreciation of your kindness and confidence, will induce me, so to perform my duty, that you shall not have cause to regret having conferred this favor upon me." ALS, *ibid.*, RG 60, Letters from the President. On Feb. 27, USG endorsed this letter.

"Referred to the Atty. Gn. In case the apt. suggested within has to be made I know no more competant man for the place than Judge Rayner. I approve his appointment." AES, *ibid.* On March 2, USG nominated Rayner for the position; the Senate took no action. See *U.S. Statutes at Large*, XIX, 268–69; Rayner to Hamilton Fish, March 7, 1877, DLC-Hamilton Fish; Gregg Cantrell, *Kenneth and John B. Rayner and the Limits of Southern Dissent* (Urbana, 1993), p. 163.

On Feb. 28, USG had endorsed a Feb. 24 letter from Rayner to Secretary of the Treasury Lot M. Morrill requesting the reconsideration of a long-standing claim. "Referred to the Secretary of the Treasury for his action in accordance with the merits of the claim." *HRC*, 47-1-1637, 18.

1. See *PUSG*, 24, 275–76.

To Stanley Matthews

Washington, D. C.
March 8th /77

HON. STANLEY MATHEWS:
DEAR SIR:

This will introduce Mr. J. L. Chapman, of Balt. an original Union man of that city, and Mayor from /61 to /67. He has ever been faithful & true both to the Union & to the republican party.

Very Truly Yours,
U. S. GRANT

ALS, DNA, RG 56, Naval Officer Applications. Stanley Matthews, former Ohio judge, had acted in behalf of Rutherford B. Hayes during the electoral controversy. On March 12, 1877, John L. Chapman, Baltimore, wrote to Matthews. "I called on Genl Grant asking his influence with President Hayes—He declined being placed in that position. I then asked for a letter to you, and he gave me the enclosed—I am an antire stranger to you, but would ask a letter of introduction to President Hayes, with your influence, if you would be so kind as to favor me. In 1861 when Massachusetts Soldiers were shot down in our streets, and the Mayor of Baltimore was sent to 'Fort Warren' I was chosen to fill the position, by the City Council, and from that time, was elected Mayor for three successive terms, of two years each, and until 1867, when the emmigration of Southern Men into Maryland gave it a Democratic majority. I was at that time offered the Mayoralty for a fourth term, and the Gubanatorial chair to join them, which I indignantly refused I filled the Naval Office during General Grants first term, being placed there through his personal recognition of my record, and left out was not re-appointed the second term, General Grant promising me a similar place. I feel convinced that he has always regretted this action, and that politicians induced him to take this step. I have been a *Clay Whig* and *Republican* all my life—I have never used intoxicating drinks, or tobacco, in any form. I was born in Baltimore, and have resided here all my life. I have incured, during the Rebellion, an immense number of risks of life, any any ammount of slander, Baltimore being the key to Washington, in a Millitary sense, has been the pandemonium of Union Men I have lost a fortune in my devotion to the Union, and would solicit your influence for *Naval Officer of the Port of Baltimore as the present incumbent, it is said, will certainly be left out on account of his bad habits*" ALS, *ibid.* Matthews forwarded this letter to Hayes. AES (undated), *ibid.* As of Sept. 30, Chapman worked as a superintendent, Baltimore Customhouse.

On May 29, 1873, Chapman had written to USG. "I would most respectfully ask for the position of a Consulate or second class Ministry—. . ." ALS, *ibid.*, RG 59, Letters of Application and Recommendation. Related papers are *ibid.* On Jan. 15, 1874, Chapman wrote to USG. "I am informed through public rumor that the office of 'Commissioner of Pensions' will probably become vacant—I should feel greatly indebted if circumstances would permit you to place me in *this*, or a *similar position*. . . ." ALS, *ibid.*, RG 48, Appointment Div., Letters Received. On May 27, 1875, Chapman, Washington, D. C., wrote to USG. "It is rumored that the position of Sixth Auditor of the Treasury in the Post Office Department will be vacant I would ask for this position . . ." ALS, *ibid.*, RG 56, Appointment Div., Letters Received. A related letter is *ibid.* On Feb. 14, 1876, William F. Keirle, Baltimore, wrote to USG criticizing Republican leadership in Md. and urging Chapman's appointment as marshal. ALS, *ibid.*, RG 60, Records Relating to Appointments. On Aug. 17, Chapman, Baltimore, wrote to USG. "Rumor says that you have determined not to appoint Gen Tyler U S Marsall If this be true I would suggest my name for this position feeling certain that it would give general satisfaction" ALS, *ibid.*

To Hamilton Fish

———

Washington, D. C.
March 9, 1877.

HON. HAMILTON FISH,
SEC. OF STATE
DEAR SIR:

In severing our official connection, of nearly eight years duration, allow me to express my appreciation of your valuable and distinguished services to our common country, by the able and efficient manner in which you have discharged the laborious duties of your office. During your term of office new and complicated diplomatic questions have arisen which might readily have produced costly & bloody wars, which the country was illy prepared to meet. Through your statesmanship more than through any individual these questions have been peacibly settled, and in a manner highly creditable to the nation and without wounding the sensibilities of other nations in such degree as to create jealousy likely to produce difficultes or sought for pretexts. Our relations have at all times been so pleasant that I shall carry the remembrance of them through life.

With sincere wishes for your continued health and prosperity, I subscribe myself,

Yours Faithfully,
U. S. GRANT

ALS, The Scriptorium, Beverly Hills, Calif.

On March 9, 1877, USG wrote to Secretary of the Interior Zachariah Chandler. "With the hope for many years of the same warm personal relations between us as has existed during our official relations, allow me to thank you for your eminent public services as a member of the Cabinet,—now that we sever these connection—and to hope that the good work which you have done may be faithfully continued. I wish for you many years of health, prosperity & happiness, and years of usefulness in public as well as in a private capacity." ALS, DLC-Zachariah Chandler. On March 10, Chandler wrote to USG. "Permit me to thank you for your very kind and complimentary letter of yesterday. I wish to express to you my sincere and heartfelt thanks for your many acts of kindness and confidence not only during my brief services in your Cabinet, but during the past 8 years. The country owes you a debt of gratitude which it can never repay   Impartial history will accord to you an administration of its Civil affairs second to none, in purity and ability since the foundation of the Government. again thanking you for your generous confidence and invariable kindness, with the hope that your life may be prolonged & that our present & past friendly relations may be continued . . ." ALS, USG 3.

On March 9, USG wrote to Postmaster Gen. James N. Tyner. "In parting company as officials permit me to express my appreciation of your public service during the time we have been together, and to express the hope the unbroken friendship between us during our remaing life may continue as it now exists. Hoping for you and yours health, prosperity & happiness, . . ." ALS, Earl G. Marhanka, Dowagiac, Mich. On [*March*] 12, Tyner wrote to USG. "I thank you for the kind and graceful manner in which you refer, in your note of the 9th. *instant*, to my services as Postmaster General during a portion of your late Administration, and especially for the assurance of your continued confidence and friendship. Our official intercourse was of short duration, but it was long enough to enable me now to bear testimony to your patient, careful and successful management of the affairs of the Government. In thus joining you in an official leave-taking, I desire to express my deep sense of personal gratitude for the honor of a seat in your Cabinet, and for your uniform courtesy and kindness; and, also, to assure you that my warmest friendship, and most earnest wishes for your uninterrupted prosperity, will accompany you through life." ALS (misdated Feb.), USG 3; ADfS, MH.

On March 9, Secretary of War James D. Cameron had written to USG. "I have your letter of this date and hasten to reply and thank you for it. For your kind words in reference to my official life I thank you. Whatever may occur in the future, I shall always remember with pride that I was connected with your administration, for I am confidant that your cause as President will grow more and more illustrious as time passes. The manner in which you speak of our personal relations, is most gratifying and I can assure you that I do most earnestly trust that we may be so situated that I may continue to enjoy the pleasant social relations with you which have given me so much pleasure in the past. Please accept my best wishes in whatever position you may occupy in the future and I desire to say the same for each and every member of your family from each and all of whom I have received so many evidences of kindness—" ALS, USG 3. On March 20, USG visited the War Dept. "and bade good bye to the army officers stationed there." *Washington Evening Star,* March 20, 1877.

On March 10, Secretary of the Navy George M. Robeson had written to USG. "I hardly know how to thank you for your letter of yesterday. It adds one more to the obligations which have been renewed each day for nearly eight years of close association, & which I can never repay, except by continued affection & respect. You, will remain, in the affections of your countrymen & in the memory of the world, long after Enemies & friends are alike forgotten, and, for your unvarying kindness, your steady confidence & support & your unfailing sympathy, I shall be your constant debtor while I live, happy if I can retain your personal friendship & association—Hoping that you will give me some chance to serve you in the future & assuring you that I shall be always at your service, & again thanking you, . . ." ALS, USG 3.

On March 17, Alphonso Taft, Cincinnati, wrote to USG. "I was touched by your very kind letter, of a recent date, assuring me of your confidence and friendship. It is impossible for me to tell you, how much I appreciate this generous expression from you, who called me from private life, and have given me a year of most interesting experience in the public service; a year, made memorable and happy by your uniform kindness & support. My confidence in your integrity, and admiration for your ability, with which I accepted your call to office, have grown stronger and stronger by our official and social intercourse. That you life may hereafter, be as happy as it has hitherto been useful and glorious, is the best wish of your sincere friend." ALS, *ibid.*

On April 26, Lot M. Morrill, Washington, D. C., wrote to USG. "Allow me at this late day, with my first returning strength, thankfully to acknowledge the receipt of your greatly esteemed letter of the 9th ultimo. Your words of confidence encouraged my acceptance of the important office, to which you invited me, and now I am rejoiced at your words of assurance that you found that confidence not misplaced. It would indeed have been difficult for me, near the close of an administration, to have left the Senate for its service had I entertained a less exalted opinion of its executive head. Now that our official relations are severed, I may be allowed in this personal and friendly note to give brief expression to my convictions of your public career. As was the period of your military service, so was that of your Presidency; both were, and both will continue to be epochs of universal interest in American history. In the former, no one of our countrymen, since Washington, has rendered such transcendent service; while the individual characteristics which made that successful reappear in, and will be accredited to, the civil administration. I beg to add the most cordial reciprocation of friendly expressions, and the hope that these pleasant relations may ever endure." LS, ICarbS.

To Ulysses S. Grant, Jr.

———

March 12th /77

DEAR BUCK:

I do not understand you about having given a check to Barnett, of Jacksonville, Fla. for $56 00 and of obtaining a receipt for $84 00.

I am not aware of any the existence of any such person nor of owing any person in the state of Fla.

It is not probable that I shall be in New York much before May unless my presence should be required. I could go any day if necessary. It makes but little difference to me what line of Steamers I sail upon so that should I receive an invitation to go by the Inman line[1] I should accept it.

Of course I said nothing in the Senate, or elsewhere, about the rejection of any of President Hayes nominations.[2]

All are very well.

Yours Truly
U. S. GRANT

ALS, USG 3. Papers related to the payment of a $56 bill to A. C. Barnett for eight dinners, liquors and wine, coaches, and cigars, dated March 8 and 16, 1877, are *ibid.*

1. The popular name for the Liverpool, New York, and Philadelphia Steamship Co., a British concern established by William Inman in 1857.

2. On March 7, 1877, USG visited the Senate chamber, "where he received much attention from Senators. He remained for some time, occupying a seat next to that of Senator Conkling, with whom he carried on an animated conversation." *Washington Evening Star*, March 7, 1877. On March 8, USG conferred with U.S. Senator Henry B. Anthony of R. I. at the capitol. "It is reported that he is using his best efforts to defeat the confirmation of Schurz as Secretary of the Interior." *Ibid.*, March 8, 1877. Republican senators opposed to the cabinet nominations delayed confirmation proceedings. See *New York Times*, March 8, 11, 1877; Ari Hoogenboom, *Rutherford B. Hayes: Warrior and President* (Lawrence, Kan., 1995), pp. 295–97, 301–2.

Endorsement

Referred to the Sec. of the Treas. Mrs. Doll was a young lady of strong loyalty during the rebellion, from the "Blue Grass" region of Ky. She was then Miss Letcher. From her letter I suppose she has married since, and been left a widow, without means.

U. S. GRANT

MARCH 17TH /77

AES, DNA, RG 56, Applications. Written on a letter of March 15, 1877, from Nelly Letcher Doll, Lexington, Ky., to USG. "Just before your term of office expired—knowing how difficult it was to reach you—I sent a letter to you under cover to Gov. McCormick, which he tells me he delivered in person; but it being too late for you to take any action you promised to refer it to Pres. Hayes. My necessities being *very* great, may I hope you will not only see him, but *urge* the matter *to a speedy consummation.* If there is no recompense *here* for you—the God of the widow & orphan will shower blessings upon you for your kindness of heart in assisting the needy." ALS, *ibid.* On June 1, Doll wrote to Secretary of the Treasury John Sherman seeking an appointment. ALS, *ibid.* Related papers are *ibid.* As of Sept. 30, Doll worked as a counter in the Treasury Dept.

To John Sherman

Washington, D. C.
March 23. 1877

HON JOHN SHERMAN
SECRETARY OF THE TREASURY
DEAR SIR.

This will present Colonel Hawkes who was discharged from a 3d class Clerkship in the Treasury, while he was on the stump for the republican ticket last fall.

I believe nothing can be said against the integrity or efficiency of Col Hawkes. who has been a Soldier and in the Civil Service

He was a Classmate of mine at West Point. though did not graduate. I have known him therefore for many years back, our second acquaintance commencing in Cairo at the beginning of the rebellion.

If he can be placed in the service again I shall be pleased.

Very Truly Yours
U. S. GRANT

Copy, DNA, RG 56, Applications. Born in Salem, Mass., Benjamin F. Hawkes spent two years at USMA and became lt. col., 78th Ohio, after extensive staff service. On Oct. 19, 1876, Governor John F. Hartranft of Pa., Philadelphia, wrote to USG urging Hawkes's reinstatement. Copies (2), *ibid.* On April 10, 1877, Hawkes, Washington, D. C., wrote to Secretary of the Treasury John Sherman drawing attention to USG's advocacy. "To day it is six months since my name was dropped from the Rolls, and I feel a necessity to urge a reinstation or appointment. . . ." ALS, *ibid.* Related papers are *ibid.* Hawkes later clerked in the Pension Office.

To Adolph E. Borie

———

Washington D. C.
March 23d /77

MY DEAR MR. BORIE:

I have taken the privilege of sending two boxes of Champagne to your house for the use of my party in crossing the ocean. We expect to go by the American line,[1] from Phila in mMay, before the 20th. We will be in Phila & Elizabeth probably two weeks before sailing. The interval we will spend in traveling over some of your old stamping ground in the West.

Please give Mrs. Grant's and my love to Mrs. Borie.

Yours Truly
U. S. GRANT

ALS, PHi.

1. The American Steamship Co. provided service between Philadelphia and Liverpool. See H. W. Schotter, *The Growth and Development of the Pennsylvania Railroad Company* (Philadelphia, 1927), pp. 92–93, 179, 211.

To Charles A. Boutelle

———

WASHINGTON, D. C.,
March 23, 1877.

C. A. BOUTELLE, ESQ., Bangor:

The BANGOR WHIG AND COURIER'S account is strictly correct except in this: Nothing was said about swords, side-arms, baggage, or private horses, until I wrote the terms of surrender, in which I gave them, at which General Lee was much affected and said those terms would have a good effect upon his army.

He had on apparently an entirely new uniform and a magnificent sword—such as is not usually worn in the field—and it certainly left the impression that the expectation was to surrender it.

Nothing was said in the preliminary conversation to warrant the assumption that anything more was to be granted to the rebel army than that they were to be permitted to return to their homes on laying down their arms, and not to be molested in their persons so long as they remained there and obeyed the laws in force thereat.

U. S. GRANT.

Bangor Whig and Courier, March 27, 1877. In 1874, Charles A. Boutelle became principal owner of the *Bangor Whig and Courier*. An assertion that Gen. Robert E. Lee "surrendered his blood-stained sword" to Joshua L. Chamberlain precipitated first a correction by the *Bangor Whig and Courier* that USG had declined Lee's sword and then a letter of March 15, 1877, from "J. W. J.," Richmond, to the *Richmond Dispatch*. "I am sorry that you allow to pass unchallenged the item in your paper of this morning from the BANGOR (ME.) WHIG about Grant's magnanimity in declining to receive Lee's sword, &c. Several years ago you published a letter from your correspondent, 'Viator,' giving Gen. Lee's own account of the surrender, in which he denied most emphatically that he ever tendered his sword to Gen. Grant, or had any idea of doing so. . . ." *Ibid.* On March 20, the *Bangor Whig and Courier* wrote to USG "requesting him to settle this interesting matter of history concerning that memorable interview at Appomattox." *Ibid.*

To Sophia C. Page

Washington, D. C.
March 23d /77

MRS. S. E. PAGE:
DEAR MADAM.

Mrs. Grant has given me your letter of the 21st to answer. It will be very difficult for me to give the time you request to sittings for the portrait Mr. Page proposes to paint. I go West to-morrow and will not probably reach the East until a few days before I sail, and may not be in New York City atall as I shall take the Phila line of steamers. If I do visit New York however I will be glad to meet Mr. Page.

In regard to sittings now there is one objection. The proposed picture is to represent me as a soldier. Twelve very hard and eventful years have passed since I had the honor to render service, in the field, as such. I have grown much older and some forty pounds larger in that time all of which would detract very much from such a portrait. However, as I have said, I will be very glad to see Mr. Page if I get to New York City, and to consult him about the matter.

Very Truly Yours

U. S. GRANT

ALS, ICarbS. Born in 1827 in Vt., Sophia C. Stevens was widowed at age 25, traveled to Europe, and married William Page in 1857 in Rome. Page painted a portrait of USG in the late 1870s by consulting photographs. See *PUSG*, 16, 80; Joshua C. Taylor, *William Page: The American Titian* (Chicago, 1957), pp. 208–9.

On Feb. 15, 1877, Sophia Page, Staten Island, wrote to USG. "I have the honor to submit to you, for appointment to the U. S. Military Academy—the name of my Son— William Stevens Page of Staten Island, New York, nephew of your class mate at West Point—George Stevens of Vermont—. . ." ALS, DNA, RG 94, Correspondence, USMA. No appointment followed. 2nd Lt. George Stevens had drowned in 1846.

To Ulysses S. Grant, Jr.

———

Cin. O. March 26th /77

DEAR BUCK:

Your dispatch rec'd. I immediately telegraphed Drexel to purchase for me One Thousand shares of Consolidated Va, and to Seligman to purchase me Five Hundred, the former without limit, the latter at not to exceed 38.[1] I will write to both of them to-day to sell whenever you dictate should ~~you~~ they make the purchase. I will not be where I can watch the markets for the next few weeks. Should there be great fluctuation, or a dividend declared telegraph me. I will be here—with Washington McLain[2]—until Saturday[3] morning. The[n] in St. Louis until the following Thursday; thence we go to Chicag, possibly stopping a day at Galena, thence to Harrisburg. The papers will keep you advised of my where-a-bouts.

Yours Truly

U. S. GRANT

ALS, USG 3.

1. On April 10, 1877, J. & W. Seligman & Co., New York City, wrote to Ulysses S. Grant, Jr., concerning 500 shares of Consolidated Virginia Mining Co. purchased at $37¼. ". . . Sorry to see the stock since declined" L, *ibid.* In Jan., when Consolidated Virginia

stopped paying dividends, stock prices declined. See Grant H. Smith, *The History of the Comstock Lode 1850–1920* (Reno, Nev., 1943), pp. 200–204, 207–9; letter to Ulysses S. Grant, Jr., April 1, 1877.

Before departing for Europe, USG "let both of his cottages at Long Branch for the Summer season. The one he occupied for the past six seasons, next to the cottage of George W. Childs, has been taken by Mr. Henry McAuliff, of Brooklyn; Gen. Grant's cottage on the opposite side of the road, near to Mr. Murphy's, will be occupied by a member of the banking firm of Seligman Brothers." *Newark Advertiser*, May 7, 1877.

2. Washington McLean, a leading Ohio Democrat, edited the *Cincinnati Enquirer*.

3. March 31.

To Douglas Campbell

————

St. Louis, Mo.
Apl. 1st /77

DEAR SIR:

Your favor of the 24th of March asking me to preside at a meeting to be held in New York City on the 17th of Apl. to raise funds for the benefit of destitute soldiers of the rebellion I find in my pocket, probably having been received just as I was leaving Washington City.[1] The object of the meeting is a most commendible one and it would gratify me exceedingly to contribute in any way to its success. But it would be impossible for me to say now that I would attend. In five weeks from Wednesday next I expect to sail for Europe. In the mean time I have business of a private nature here, in Galena, Chicago and Washington which must be attended to before my departure and it is not probable that I will be through by the time specified. Should I do so I will attend the meeting, but ask that some other person be called upon to preside who can perform such duties much better than I can.

Again desiring that the greatest success should attend your meeting, for so worthy an object, I subscribe myself a sincere well-wisher of its cause.

Very Truly Yours
U. S. GRANT

DOUGLAS CAMPBELL, ESQ
CH. OF COM. ON AR.

ALS, NHi. Douglas Campbell, former capt., 121st N. Y., belonged to a group raising funds for a state soldiers' home. USG did not attend the event on April 17, 1877. See *New York Times*, April 18, 1877, March 8, 15, 1893.

1. USG left Washington, D. C., on March 24.

To Hamilton Fish

St. Louis, Mo.
Apl. 1st 1877,

DEAR GOVERNOR:

Since leaving the kind hospitalities of Mrs. Fish & yourself we have had quite a pleasant visit to Cincinnati, from which place Com. Ammen and I visited the scenes and acquaintances of our boy-hood where we had not met for forty-one years before.[1] The people seemed glad to see us, and realized no doubt more fully than we did the changes that had taken place with us. The changes that I saw in others is so great that I felt no desire to tarry long.

Mrs. Grant and I will always remember the kindness of Mrs. Fish and yourself, and will some day hope to return it when we are established in a home of our own. It will more probably be in Wash-ington City than elsewhere, and it may be you will enjoy a few weeks there in the Winter, free from ~~the cares of~~ official cares which have heretofore beset your life in the Capital. Had you accepted the office of Chief Justice when it was tendered, after the death of Chief Justice Chase, I would have hoped to have you for a neighbor, as I now hope to have you always for a friend.—Mrs. Grant was so affected at part-ing that she did not recover until exhausted to sleepiness.

We will leave here about the middle of the week and be in Harris-burg in about two weeks,[2] spending a few days on the way at Galena & Chicago. With kind regards of Mrs. Grant & myself to Mrs. Fish, I am

Faithfully yours
U. S. GRANT

HON. HAMILTON FISH.

P. S. When we left Washington Mrs. Grant left a fan and I left an umbrella. If the servants should find them will you be kind enough to have them sent to Harrisburg, care of Ex. Sec. Cameron.

ALS, ICarbS.

On Thursday, March 22, 1877, Hamilton Fish, Washington, D. C., wrote to J. C. Bancroft Davis, U.S. minister, Berlin. ". . . Genl & Mrs Grant have been stopping with us, since the inauguration. Mrs Sartoris was confined last Saturday, & Genl & Mrs G. leave us day after tomorrow for the West, preparatory f to their trip to Europe—. . ." ALS (press), DLC-Hamilton Fish.

1. On March 26, USG spoke at the Cincinnati Chamber of Commerce. "GENTLEMEN: This reception was entirely unexpected by me. But I assure you I am very glad to meet you all, and feel very thankful to you for this kind reception. I have no doubt but I will be a great deal better fellow now than I was six months ago. I don't suppose I will have any political opponents now, since we are all sovereigns together, as I hope we will continue to be for a great many years yet. I feel that I have considerable life, health and strength left, notwithstanding the past sixteen years of labor and toil I have undergone, which, perhaps is not surpassed by any other sixteen years of my life." *Cincinnati Enquirer*, March 27, 1877. Benjamin Eggleston had introduced USG as "a gentleman who, when the history of this country is fully made up, will stand before it as the second Washington of the nation." *Ibid.*

On March 27, USG left Cincinnati early in the morning "for Brown County. He went by the Georgetown pike, characteristically behind a pair of fine trotters, and accompanied by Commodore Ammen. . . . Mrs. Grant remains during the General's absence the guest of Mrs. Washington McLean." *Ibid.*, March 28, 1877. USG returned to Cincinnati to attend an evening reception at the Queen City Club on March 29. See *ibid.*, March 30, 1877.

On [*March 30*], Alphonso Taft addressed USG and other dinner guests at his home in Cincinnati. ". . . I was curious to observe something of the operations of that mind which had so long shaped the destinies of the country. I am satisfied that it was not chance or any mere use of superior military forces which gave him success, but a self-poised mind that combined facts into practical plans, with courage to carry them out without hesitation. But I rise now, to say to you, my friends, that in the eighth year of his administration, during which I was associated with him in public affairs, I have experienced at his hands nothing but uniform kindness and friendship, and a steady and cordial support in the responsible duties of my position; not fitful and uncertain, but constant and reliable. Allow me to close by saying, that among the memories which shall make pleasant the future of my life, none will be more cherished than that of the confidence and friendship of President Grant." *Chicago Inter-Ocean*, April 4, 1877.

On the same day, USG spoke at the home of Washington McLean. "I thank you heartily for the compliment paid me, and for the enjoyment you have afforded not only to myself but to my host and his fair guests. In the absence which is to follow my visit here, and which will be of three or four years' duration, I shall cherish as one of the pleasantest memories of life this evening's serenade. Gentlemen, good-night." *Cincinnati Enquirer*, March 31, 1877.

2. On April 13 and 16, James D. Cameron, Harrisburg, Pa., wrote to Fish. "I have a Telegram from General Grant saying that they would leave Chicago today for Washington Penna en route to Harrisburg, he does not say when they will reach here, but, I presume it will be next tuesday or Wednesday. My daughter and myself will be very glad to have Mrs. Fish and you pay us a visit while the General and Mrs Grant are with us. As soon as I learn just when they will arrive I will telegraph you." "I have your letter of yes-

terday and regret very much that Mrs. Fish cannot pay us a visit. Genl Grant telegraphs
that they will arrive here on Wednesday afternoon the 18th inst—and will remain a week.
We will be much pleased to have you come while he is here, say Friday. We will go to Lan-
caster Co trout fishing on Saturday & I promise to take you to church on Sunday. Be kind
enough to remember me to Mrs Fish & your daughte[r.]" ALS, DLC-Hamilton Fish. See
letter to William W. Smith, April 22, 1877.

To Ulysses S. Grant, Jr.

St Louis, Apl. 1st *1877*

DEAR BUCK,

We got in here last night about nine o'clock, all well. Will remain
here until Wednesday[1] and then go to Chicago from which place we
will visit Galena for a couple of days. We will then go to Washington, Pa for two or three days, and then to Harrisburg. This will give
you an idea of about how to address letters or dispatches.

Con: Va having gone up above 40 has prevented any purchase for
me.[2] If there is no dividend declared this week I have no doubt but
the stock will go down to 35, or below. You may say to Mr. Drexel
and Mr. Seligman that they need not purchase unless you tell them
to. In regard to purchase you may exercise your judgement, or may
advise with me by telegraph. You have so much to do as my Agt. that
I want you to draw fifty dollars pr. month, commencing March 1st,
for your services.

I enclose with this the Iron stock transfered to you by your Ma.

Yours Truly
U. S. GRANT

ALS, USG 3. On March 31, 1877, USG arrived in St. Louis. "From the Union Depot he
was driven to the ladies' entrance of the Lindell, . . . There were no attendants present, the
ex-President and his lady being quite alone." *St. Louis Globe-Democrat*, April 1, 1877.

On April 2, a reporter interviewed USG. "'After sixteen years of public life I feel a
need of rest from official duty and a desire to have a little quiet time. And now I can have
it. . . . I shall spend a few days here and at Galena and Cleveland, and the East. Then go to
Europe; travel around. May stay as long as two years; may not stay so long; perhaps only
stay a short time; it depends on the news I receive from the East, and come back to settle
down with my family. . . . I shall spend a good deal, a great part of my time at Galena. I
want to enjoy myself with my family at home; may go here and go there, but have no plans
laid out. I can not tell now just what I shall do. Have no idea.' 'But when are you going to
write that book, those memoirs, that are being told of?'. . . 'Oh, I'm not going to write any

book. There are books enough already. . . . Anybody can write a book. I could myself, for that matter, perhaps; but I assure you I haven't had the least thought about such a thing. Can't tell what may be in the future.'. . . 'What do you think of Mr. Hayes' Southern policy?' 'I think it is good policy. I am very anxious to see this color line divided, so that the question becomes more one of parties, and less of color, or race. . . . Break up the distinction of color, so that a party is not composed of all whites or all colored people.'. . . 'Do you think Mr. Hayes will withdraw the troops from South Carolina and Louisiana?' 'I expect him to. I should have done so had I staid in office. Not take the troops all away probably, but relieve them of their present duty. For neither the Chamberlain nor Packard Government can be sustained without the show of military authority, and in this free country, and so long after quiet has been restored everywhere else, the exercise of military authority in civil matters is repugnant to the people, and so, when the troops are gone, the Nicholls and Hampton Governments will rule as matter of acquiescence on the part of the people of those two States. . . . I should believe in the use of troops if there were any outrages calling for it, and, as you know, I believe in using them with a vim at such times; but I think with a reasonable degree of moderation, the Nicholls and Hampton Governments ought to get along without any trouble from the other side.' 'The difficulties in South Carolina and Louisiana are about all of the old war trouble that is left, are they not?' 'Yes, that's about all.' 'How is it that Alabama and Georgia, and one or two other Southern States, get along so well compared to the rest?' 'They are manufacturing, busy States. Northern skilled labor and capital are invited in. Labor is respected, and all goes right. Make labor respected in Louisiana and South Carolina, and the political field will soon be clear of trouble.' 'Speaking of labor, the idea of civil service reform seems to have come up again— the attempt to pick out the best men by competitive examination. You had all that once in your time, didn't you?' 'Yes, but that isn't civil service reform. It's only a means to place the appointments in the hands of those who wish to have them made according to their ideas of fitness—to reform this man out and the other man into office. . . . Our mode of appointment is good enough. The people elect the Senators and Representatives, and they principally appoint, or suggest the appointment, of the various public servants. I think, though, each Senator or Representative ought to hold himself responsible for the conduct of his wards in office. I think that would be a good thing.'" *Ibid.,* April 3, 1877. See *ibid.,* April 4, 1877.

    1. April 4.
    2. On April 12, Anthony J. Drexel, Philadelphia, wrote to USG. "upon receipt of your order a short time ago to buy 1.000 shares Consolidated Virginia at 40 I telegraphed to Sather & Co to execute it & was very much surprised when I saw by the papers it had not been executed at least that we had not received any telegraph that it had been bought and as it had declined to 34¾ I was very glad, & telegraphed to Buck to that effect; But I am now sorry to say the stock was bought on the 6th 300 at 39¾ and 700 @ 40. & duly telegraphed by Sather & Co, but the telegraph was received after close of business & handed to a clerk who mislaid it putting it under some papers & it was only discovered this morning I at once telegraphed to Sather & Co countermanding the order we sent yesterday to buy 1000 at 36. of course it would have been pleasanter if the stock had gone up after the purchase & in which case we would have censured Sather if he had not have executed the order, had he not bought as he did—we have reprimanded the clerk for his Carelessness which has given me of course a great deal of trouble. I could not understand why Sather & Co did not (apparently) telegraph & we telegraphed on monday to know & received no answer as he no doubt supposed we had received his telegraph afterwards—I enclose the mislaid telegraph and can only say I regret the error. I hope the purchase will turn out well.

with Kindest regards to Mrs Grant, . . ." Copy, USG 3. On the same day, Drexel wrote to
Ulysses S. Grant, Jr. "I enclose a copy of a letter which I have sent to your Father about the
Consolidated Virginia purchase which will explain the whole affair   I also enclose a copy
of the telegram of Sather & Co which reached here on the evening of the 6th & was mis-
laid   of course it is a great disappointment but it cant be helped as we would have blamed
Sather very much had he not bought & the stock had gone up instead of down" ALS, *ibid.*
A copy of the telegram, dated April 0, is *ibid.* See letters to Ulysses S. Grant, Jr., March 26,
April 11, 1877.

On May 21, Drexel wrote to Grant, Jr. "Yours of 19th recd   I will execute your message to Mr & Mrs Childs   The cost of the £50 is $262 50   The only stock that I hold for
your Fathers account is the 1000 Consolidated Virginia Mining Co costing *about* $40000
Gold which we advance & will appropriate any dividends to reducing the cost your Father
having instructed me to do so   I will keep you posted on anything interesting   Your Father told me you were depositing with Drexel Morgan & Co his income or receipts. I think
as we will pay all his drawings in Europe you had better close the account with them and
keep it solely with us, remitting us the money as it comes in for his credit   this will save
him interest & save trouble   I hope you will be able to get over to see us before long" ALS,
USG 3.

To Ulysses S. Grant, Jr.

Chicago, Ill.
Apl. 5th /77

DEAR BUCK,

In my last note to you I forgot to make reply to Mr. Seligman's
request for me to give him an evening when I get to New York City.
It is not probable that we will be in New York City to remain before
sailing to Europe. But your Ma and I will visit your Aunt Jennie &
Grand Ma for a few days, and I will be over to the city probably every
day while there and will see Mr. Seligman then. It will probably be
as late as the 1st of May before we go.

Before leaving Washington I authorized Mr. Fitch to rent my
house on P Street Circle at $1800 00 pr. Annum if he could get no
more. I want it rented on the best terms he can make if it is not more
than $1200 00   If he could get a first rate tenant in the house on a
three years lease at $1500 00 I think he would be doing well, and I
would give a ten years lease at that price to any one who would pay
the taxes & repairs in addition.[1]

We run over to Galena on Saturday[2] to be there over Sunday
& Monday. About Thursday evening following—this day week—we

will go to Washington, Pa for a few days, and then to Harrisburg to remain for the balance of this month. While there we will run down to Washington, D. C. for a day or two.

All well.

Yours Truly
U. S. GRANT.

ALS, USG 3.

On April 6, 1877, USG visited the Chicago Customhouse "and spent a half-hour with the Hon. J. Russell Jones, in whose private office he received, . . . In the afternoon he dined with a friend, and spent the evening at his son's, Fred Grant's, residence on Indiana avenue. . . ." *Chicago Tribune*, April 7, 1877. On the same day, USG visited Lt. Gen. Philip H. Sheridan's hd. qrs. *New York Times*, April 7, 1877.

1. Later in April, Fitch, Fox & Co., real estate brokers, ran an advertisement. "FOR RENT.—We are instructed to offer the RESIDENCE of ex-President Grant, located at the intersection of Vermont and Rhode Island avenues, and fronting on the 13th street Park, at a very low rental to a careful and responsible tenant. The house is entirely new, has all modern improvements, and is handsomely frescoed. A fine suite of three rooms on first floor, four rooms on second floor, four rooms on third floor, and billiard or office room, laundry, furnace room, and kitchen in basement. For terms and permit to inspe[c]t the property, apply to FITCH, FOX & CO., 1509 Pa ave." *Washington Evening Star*, April 23, 1877. This house sold for $17,500. See *ibid.*, Dec. 19, 1878; *PUSG*, 21, 499.

On July 7, 20, Aug. 17, and Nov. 14, Fitch, Fox & Co. wrote to Ulysses S. Grant, Jr., concerning Grant properties under its management. L, USG 3.

2. April 7.

To Ulysses S. Grant, Jr.

———

Chicago, Ill,
Apl. 11th /77

DEAR BUCK,

We returned from Galena last evening where we spent a couple of days very pleasantly.[1] The Felts feel their loss most greviously,[2] but our visit seemed to do them a great deal of good. They were very pressing in their invitation to have any of the family when visiting Galena to make their house a home[.] On our return I find a couple of letters from you which I will answer.

In regard to the Bank of America I have never felt than anything was to come of it. I feel but little interest in the matter though you need not say so to Mr. Norville[3] who seems very disinterested so far as concerns himself but much interested in my behalf. When I go east I will talk about the matter. If you deem it advisable you may purchase me fifty shares of the stock. I suppose that amount will be sufficient for all practical purposes, and if I do not wish to retain it it will always sell.

When we go east your Ma and I will stay at your Aunt Jennie's, but I will be able to give Mr. Seligman an evening. I can not now fix the time, but it will be about the first of May. If my dispatch of last evening does not lead to the purchase of Con. Va. stock you might see Mr. Drexel & Mr. Seligman and get authority to draw on the former for the purchase of One thousand shares, and from the latter for five hundred, and authorize Mr. Fair[4] to purchase that amount for me, at his discretion.

I have no doubt but the elevated rail-road stock will ultimately be good paying stock. But having so little of it I do not care to hold on to it. If you can sell therefore at what I paid, with seven percent added, you may sell and deposit with Drexel.[5]

We leave here friday morning[6] for Will Smith's, and will be in Harrisburg about the last of next week.—All well.

Affectionately yours

U. S. GRANT

ALS, USG 3. On April 11, 1877, USG visited friends in "J. Russell Jones' office for an hour or so, and where his time was pleasantly passed in smoking and chatting with those around him. Among the party were the Hon. E. B. Wasburne, Mr. Hempstead Washburne, Col. Fred Grant, Ben H. Campbell, Judge Drummond, Messrs. Robert T. Lincoln, W. H. Bradley, and George L. Dunlap. . . ." *Chicago Tribune*, April 12, 1877.

On May 8, William N. Roach, cashier, Citizens' National Bank, Washington, D. C., wrote to Ulysses S. Grant, Jr., New York City. "Yours of 7th inst: to hand Agreeable to your request, I hand you herewith, 3 Coupons from each of 7 Bonds of Denver & Rio Grande R. R. for $1000 each left with us by your father—These coupons are for May 1 /77 Nov 1 /77 & May 1 /78—as stated in your letter—You will please acknowledge receipt of same & oblige" ALS, USG 3. On Aug. 2, C. Ford Stevens, Denver & Rio Grande Railway Co., New York City, wrote to Grant, Jr., acknowledging redemption of two coupons for $105 each. DS, *ibid.* On Oct. 24, 1878, Roach wrote to Grant, Jr. "Yours of 23d just to hand. I send you herewith (per Express) the Bonds &c of the Denver & Rio Grande R R Co. These are the only papers of any kind we hold, belonging to your father Please acknowledge receipt" ALS, *ibid.*

1. On April 7, USG and Julia Dent Grant had arrived in Galena. See *Galena Weekly Gazette*, April 13, 1877. On April 8, USG and Julia Grant had attended revival services.

Chicago Tribune, April 10, 1877. On April 9, USG spoke at Augustus Estey's residence. "FELLOW CITIZENS: I am obliged to you for this serenade and manifestation of esteem. All I have to remark is that it affords me gratification to make periodical visits to my home, and to come back to you, again after sixteen years of official life, like yourselves one of the sovereigns of this great republic. Good-night." *Galena Weekly Gazette*, April 13, 1877.

2. Lucius S. Felt had died on Aug. 5, 1876. See *ibid.*, Aug. 11, 18, 1876; *PUSG*, 23, 232–33.

On May 2, 1877, Benjamin F. Felt, Galena, wrote to Grant, Jr., New York City. "I send you enclosed tax receipts as pr request of your Father amt paid $66.53 . . ." ALS, USG 3.

3. Possibly Caleb C. Norvell. See *New York Times*, Feb. 4, 1891.

4. James G. Fair, a mining engineer and financier, superintended the Consolidated Virginia mine. See letter to Adolph E. Borie, Jan. 27, 1876.

5. Probably a reference to New York Elevated Railroad Co. stock. See *New York Times*, Dec. 27, 1877, Jan. 9, 1878.

On Dec. 5, 1877, Horace Porter, New York City, wrote to Grant, Jr. "Our Board has called an instalment of 10% on the present stock of the Tran and Improvement Co. payable on the 10th inst. This will be $1000 on your father's one hundred shares. Can you send a check at that time for this payment?" ALS, USG 3. On Dec. 7, Grant, Jr., endorsed this letter. "*Elevated RR.* Genl Porter. Sent cheque for $1000" AE, *ibid.* See Elsie Porter Mende, *An American Soldier and Diplomat: Horace Porter* (New York, 1927), pp. 130–31.

6. April 13.

To Abel R. Corbin

Chicago, Ill.,
April 12th, 1877.

DEAR MR. CORBIN:

To-morrow evening Mrs. Grant and I start for Washington, Pa., where we will spend a few days, then go to Harrisburgh, Washington, D. C., and toward the last of the month get around to Elizabeth to spend a few days with you before taking our departure for Europe. We have not entirely decided whether to take the American line from Philadelphia or the Inman line from New York City. Both have tendered pressing invitations, and both present good accommodations. If we take the former we will sail on the 9th or 16th of May, if the latter on the 19th.[1]

We had a very pleasant trip West but a little hurried. There is much complaint of dull times but really appearances do not justify it. Kindest regards of Mrs. Grant and myself to Mother and Jennie.

Yours truly,
U. S. GRANT.

J. G. Cramer, p. 129.

1. See Speech, [*May 17, 1877*].

To *William W. Smith*

———

Harrisburgh, Pa
Apl. 22d /77

DEAR SMITH,

This evening we leave for Washington, D. C. to remain until about the last of the week.[1] We will then go to Elizabeth, N. J.[2] where my mother is, and pass about a week there and seeing New York City friends, after which we will return to Phila to remain until the day of sailing,—now fixed, definitely—for the 17th of May. I wish you & Emsy could be over to see us start, and go down the Delaware with us. A special steamer will accompany us to the mouth of the river to bring back the party that will accompany us that far.

Don Cameron goes to the Western part of the state on Wednesday—day after to-morrow—to be absent some ten days. If you should send him an invitation to go over to Washington, Pa when you hear of him being in Pittsburgh I know he will be glad to go.

All send love to you, Emsy, Miss Tilly & the children.

Yours Truly
U. S. GRANT

ALS, Washington County Historical Society, Washington, Pa. On April 6, 1877, USG, Chicago, wrote to William W. Smith. "Mrs. Grant & I will be in Pittsburgh the last of next week on our way east, and will stop over to pay you a visit of a few days. I cannot tell just what day, but will telegraph you when we start." ALS, *ibid.* On April 13, USG telegraphed to Smith, Washington, Pa. "Will be in Pittsburgh tomorrow noon fort-Wayne Road" Telegram received (at 11:50 A.M.), *ibid.*

On April 20, Zachariah Chandler and Adolph E. Borie joined USG at Harrisburg, Pa. *Washington Evening Star*, April 21, 1877.

1. On April 23, USG and Julia Dent Grant arrived in Washington, D. C., "and joined Mr. and Mrs. Sartoris at Willard's Hotel." *Ibid.*, April 24, 1877.

On April 26, John P. Newman hosted a reception for USG and Julia Grant. *Ibid.*, April 27, 1877.

2. On April 28, USG, Julia Grant, "and several members of their family, accompanied by ex-Secretary Fish," left for Elizabeth, N. J. *Ibid.*, April 28, 1877.

To Adam Badeau

———

Washington, D. C.
Apl. 23d /77

DEAR GENERAL:

I have just read your letter of the 24th of March, and have before me the chapter on the Petersburgh Mine explosion which I will read so soon as I finish this letter.—I am much obliged for the kind expressions in your letter and shall only be too happy to serve you when ever it may be in my power. I spoke to Mr. Hayes in your behalf in the only interview I ever had with him when the subject of retention of any of my appointees was mentioned. Mrs. Grant & I have been west for the past three weeks, and over, which accounts for the lateness of this letter, and the delay in returning your manuscript.

I wrote Judge Pierrepont that we would arrive in England late in June.[1] Jesse goes with us and as his college examination does not take place until the middle of June that time was fixed upon for starting. But subsequently to writing that letter Jesse was home during a few days vacation—at the end of a term—and said that by dilligent study he could get through his course much earlyer. He finished last friday[2] and is now with us, practically a senior two months in advance of his class. We will sail earlyer therefore, most likely on the 17th of May, and by the American line of Steamers from Phila   I wish you would explain this matter to Judge Pierrepont, and present my kindest regards to him and Mrs. Pierrepont.

Yours faithfully
U. S. GRANT

GEN. A. BADEAU

ALS, Munson-Williams-Proctor Institute, Utica, N. Y.; *Badeau*, pp. 479–80.

On March 5 and 8, 1877, Orville E. Babcock, Washington, D. C., wrote to Adam Badeau, consul gen., London. "I am in receipt of your favors—appreciate them all, and will answer them fully one of these days, but will to day content myself with a note, so as to get your proof sheets back to you. I had not read Chapter VI, but have and think it fine, I venture to make one suggestion as you will see. The President has read both before. Chapt VII I read and he sent it back to you so I have not submitted it to him. Your box which was at the White House is in the storeroom in my house. I spoke to the President and Mrs Grant both about your having access to his records, and they said they would not forget the order. They are stored at the Navy Yard. I was at the Presidents room at the Senate yesterday and told him I had received another letter from you. I did this to refresh his mind as to you, and your letter to him which I sent to him in due time. I do not think he has any positive plans for the future. If I can find out in any way your status, I shall post you by cable. . . . I appreciate my dear fellow all you say about the persecutions I have borne, and the perfidy of those who should have been my best friends. And Pierrepont served me about the meanest little trick of them all, by insinuating that I had stolen a paper from the White House which he himself had placed on my desk and for me, a copy of his letter. Instead of being a man and standing up to his letter, as he should have done, and had plenty of evidence to support him, he became afraid of the Bristow click and made the insinuation that I had purloined a confidential letter. I shall make him eat his words or put him into a fine place. He allowed the Democrats to use him in the Safe Burglary matter, and I will show you one of these days what he did. Don't you trust him any more than you would Harry Wilson. I gave up my place (detail) here and take the Light House duty, thanks to Secty Cameron. My family remains here. . . ." "Your note enclosing letter to Genl Grant reached me yesterday. He is at Gov Fishes—I delivered the letter this am. I found him like all true republicans very blue, and much disgusted with the idea of putting Shurz, & Evarts into the Cabinet. . . . Next I expect Bristow will be put onto the Supreme bench, and if he is nominated for that place there will be a devil of a row. Hayes told Genl Grant that if there were any persons in whom he took a personal interest and he would name them they should not be disturbed, and he intended to give him such list about a half dozen, and yours will be on the list, provided he does not nominate Bristow. if he does he will make no such list, for this reason I did not telegraph you, though I do believe you will not be disturbed nothing but a positive rupture with Hayes will prevent his sending list. . . ." ALS and AL, MH. See letter to Alphonso Taft, Sept. 16, 1876. On March 17 and 18, Babcock wrote to Badeau. "I am just in receipt of the enclosed proofs from the President (Grant). I sent him your letter and asked him if I could say anything about the Torbert rumor, and he sends me no information whatever. He may have written to you direct. I am afraid that unless Evarts or Fred Sewards isare your friends some one will want and get the place. The Civil Service matter will play out soon, and most of the Greely sore heads will receive appointments. I am in receipt of your favor of the 1st just at home will send it to the President (Grant). Glad to hear Porter is having such a nice time, wish I could be with you both—all well," "I send you herewith last proof sheets. I read them and sent them to Genl Grant—who returned them last night without remark. I suppose he writes to you. I think you do not quote too much from dispatches—one great charm to me in your book is the fact that you do quote, so that if one reads he can form his own opinion if it does not agree with yours—. . . Between us I doubt the Grants making the trip to Europe, though they may. Nellie gave birth yesterday to a boy all doing well. . . ." ALS and AL (initialed), DLC-Adam Badeau. See Babcock to Badeau, March 20, 1877, *ibid.*

On April 13, Badeau wrote to Gen. William T. Sherman. ". . . It will indeed be most interesting to know the impressions Gen Grant receives from the Old World. I am very sure that he will return more convinced than ever of the superiority of American institutions, and more American himself than ever in feeling and character. That is the effect that either a transient visit, or a prolonged life here has on every true man coming from the Western republic. . . ." ALS, DLC-William T. Sherman.

1. See letters to Edwards Pierrepont, Feb. 11, May 11, 1877.
2. April 20.

To Ulysses S. Grant, Jr.

Washington, D. C.
Apl. 23d /77

Dear Buck,

About next Saturday[1] your Ma & I will go to Elizabeth and will stay there and about New York for a week or more. We will then return as far as Phila and remain until the time of sailing,—May 17th

I enclose you a letter for Capt Doll[2] & Mr. Nicholson which I wish you would put in an envelope and address to one of them. Capt. Doll I used to know very well. He commanded a steamer plying between Portland, Oregon, and San Francisco. I made several trips on his steamer. If you should meet him give him my special regards.

Affectionately yours
U. S. Grant

U. S. Grant Jr.

ALS, USG 3.

1. April 28, 1877.
2. William Dall. See Joseph Gaston, *Portland, Oregon: Its History and Builders* . . . (Chicago, 1911), I, 256–57.

To Basil Norris

Washington, D. C., April 25th, 1877.

Dr. BASIL NORRIS,
Surgeon, U. S. A.
Dear Doctor:

Before leaving the United States to be absent, possibly, for some years, allow me to express my gratitude and that of my family for your many acts of kindness and professional attendance in every case occurring with us for the past eight years. It seems more like the breaking up of a family to part from you, who have been a welcome visitor for so many years, than a mere separation from Government officials. I wish you were to accompany us. But as it is, I hope to find you still in Washington on my return to the country.

Wishing you evesy happiness and success in life, I subscribe myself,

Your friend,

U. S. GRANT.

Copy (printed), DLC-Hamilton Fish. See *PUSG*, 24, 293–94.

To Samuel Worthington

Washington, D. C.
Apl. 25th 1877.

SAM.L WORTHINGTON, ESQ.

POST ADJ.

DEAR SIR.

Your letter of the 11th of Apl. recommending me for membership of the G A. R reached me some place on my recent travels, but I have postponed answering until now   I will keep the recommendation until I visit Phila which will probably be about the 8th of May. From the time of my arrival in your city until the sailing of the vessel in which my passage is secured—the 17th of May—I will be with friends there and will be glad to see you, or any representative of the organization, in person, relative to this matter.

Very Truly Yours

U. S. GRANT

ALS, Candace Scott, Victorville, Calif. On May 16, 1877, George W. Devinney, post commander, and Samuel Worthington, adjt., issued congratulatory orders announcing USG's mustering into "George G. Meade Post, No. 1, G. A. R." *Philadelphia Public Ledger*, May 17, 1877. See Robert B. Beath, *History of the Grand Army of the Republic* (New York, 1889), p. 474; George W. Childs, *Recollections of General Grant* (Philadelphia, 1890), pp. 59–60; Frank H. Taylor, *Philadelphia in the Civil War 1861–1865* (Philadelphia, 1913), pp. 324–27.

To Rutherford B. Hayes

————

Washington, D. C.
Apl. 27th /77

HIS EXCELLENCY,
THE PRESIDENT:

Being about to leave the country, possibly to remain some years, I want to recommend—in case of vacancy—my old classmate, Gen. R. Ingalls, for the position of Qr. Mr. General. General Ingalls is third on the list of quartermasters, below the Chief of the Corps,[1] but his seniors in the Dept. are older men than the chief chief himself.[2] This promotion for immediate retirement might be regarded as a just reward for long & meritorious service, but for executive ability to control the department to the interest of the Govt. Gen. Ingalls has no equal in it. No officer in that Dept. rendered so great or so constant service as did Gen. Ingalls during the rebellion. But very few are possessed of the executive capacity to do so.

His advancement I would regard as a reward for extraordinary services and merit.

With great respect,
your obt. svt.
U. S. GRANT

ALS, OFH. On May 29, 1877, Col. Rufus Ingalls, asst. q. m. gen., San Francisco, endorsed a copy of USG's letter to Gen. William T. Sherman. ". . . Personally, I do not wish to have my Station changed to the East until between June 1st and September 1st 1878." AES, DLC-William T. Sherman. On May 8, 1878, Ingalls, Omaha, wrote to Sherman. ". . . Genl Grant voluntarily called on you in person on my behalf just before sailing for Europe. the written evidence of which I left in your hands the 11th of last June. He also wrote to the President of the United States. A copy of his letter is appended hereto. He was desirous, first, that I should be appointed Quartermaster General when the present incumbent should arrive at 62 years of age, and second, failing of such appointment, I should be stationed in New York City where I have a house and other property, and where I expect to live after retirement from active service. . . ." LS, DNA, RG 94, ACP, 2163 1878. Related papers are *ibid.* See *PUSG*, 25, 144–48; Ingalls to James A. Garfield, March 21, 1879, DLC-James A. Garfield; Russell F. Weigley, *Quartermaster General of the Union Army: A Biography of M. C. Meigs* (New York, 1959), pp. 356–58.

1. Brig. Gen. Montgomery C. Meigs, q. m. gen.
2. Cols. Robert Allen and Daniel H. Rucker, asst. q. m. gens., ranked Ingalls.

To Orville E. Babcock

[*April-May, 1877*]

DEAR GENERAL,

The enclosed chapter of Badeaus book was handed to me just before leaving Chicago.[1] Having a large mail before me at the time—
which I was then engaged in reading and answering I put the chapter & letter in my overcoat pocket and forgot all about it until after
coming east when I was asked by some one "when Badeau's second
volume would be out." For the first time then since receiving it it
flashed upon my mind that I had rec. a chapter to review. I was about
to write back to Fred. to look and see if he could find the missing paper. Before doing so however I made a search of all my pockets and
found it as stated. I have written to B but said nothing about the contents of the chapter under review. In fact wrote my letter before
reading it. It is all right except I would like to see Burnside let off a
little easier.

Yours
U. S. G.

ALS, Munson-Williams-Proctor Institute, Utica, N. Y.; *Badeau*, p. 587. On April 11 and
26, 1877, Orville E. Babcock wrote to Adam Badeau, consul gen., London. "I received your
letter last night and hasten to answer. I am unable to be very positive, for Genl Grant is
in Galena, and I am unable to give a positive answer. . . . I am still of the opinion that he
does not know for certain that he will go; though it looks as though he would. I do not see
where he is to get the means to travel with. He has no income on which to do it. He has
some little principal but I doubt if they want to spend it travelling still they may go. The
Bories will not go with them. I have read the last chapter think it first rate, would not
change it. I have sent it to Mr Campbell in Chicago to give to Genl Grant when he arrives
there. I am very glad you are pushing the book. . . ." "I received the Enclosed sheets from
Gen Grant last night. Those from 52 to 55 inclusive I have seen before, the others I have
not and do not take time this am to read them, for I suppose they may reach you too late
any way to be of any use. I send you his note which will Explain all. I wrote to him about
time of sailing and you will see he says he has written you. I have to be off this am, or I
would venture to hold the Mine matter. I believe in placing the responsibility for the mine
failure just where it belongs, though it may not be pleasant. Goodbye. Good luck to you.
All well here. In haste. . . . P. S. Will you send me a copy of my note to Meade at Appomattox, the day of the Surrender. . . ." ALS, DLC-Adam Badeau. See letter to Adam Badeau,
April 23, 1877.

1. USG left Chicago on April 13.

To George W. Childs

Elizabeth, N. J.
May 1st /77

MY DEAR MR. CHILDS:

Your favor of the 27th of Apl. enclosing an invitation to a reception to be given by the Penn Club,[1] is just received. Mrs Grant and I will leave here on Tuesday next[2] for Phila to remain until the the 17th—the day of sailing for Europe. Any time during that stay that you will fix will be agreeable to me. The citizens of Phila have always been so kind and courtious to me that I do not know how it will ever be in my power to reciprocate only by always bearing them in grateful remembrance. . . .

AL (incomplete facsimile), Swann Public Auction Sale 1952, Nov. 14, 2002, no. 144.
    On March 5, 1877, George W. Childs, Philadelphia, wrote to USG. "Mrs. Childs desires me to write and say we shall be most happy to have you and Mrs. Grant to spend some time with us before you leave on your foreign travels. Any time will suit us. I enclose our leading editorial of to day, wherein we have tried to be just. I regret to say your friend General Patterson is dangerously ill. He never ceased talking of the great kindness shown him by you and Mrs. Grant during his last visit. Anything we can do for you or yours, at any time, you have only to command *us*, this includes Borie Drexel and myself. Remember us all very kindly to Mrs. Grant and believe me ever your sincere friend" ALS, USG 3.

    1. See J. Thomas Scharf and Thompson Westcott, *History of Philadelphia* (Philadelphia, 1884), II, 1094–95.
    2. See following letter.

To Charles T. Jones

Elizabeth, N. J.
May 2d /77

DEAR SIR:

Your favor of yesterday informing me of the courticy extended by the city council of Phila to me during my stay there is just rec'd. I feel very grateful for this marked kindness and shall ever appreciate it. I will be in Philadelphia next tuesday evening,[1] to remain until the 17th of May, the day of my sailing for Europe, during which time I will be at your service.

For the first few days after my arrival in Phila I will be the guest of Mr. J. W. Paul[2] and after that of Mr. G. W. Childs up to day of sailing.

Very Truly yours,
U. S. Grant

Chas. Thompson Jones, Esq,
Ch. of Com.

ALS, Catherine Barnes, Philadelphia, Pa. On April 30, 1877, Charles T. Jones presided over a "Special Committee of Councils, appointed to extend the hospitalities of the city to ex-President Grant, and to offer him the use of Independence Hall for the purpose of receiving the citizens, . . ." *Philadelphia Public Ledger*, May 1, 1877. See *ibid.*, May 8, 1877.

1. May 8. See following note.
2. James W. Paul was a lawyer and member of the Philadelphia Union League. On May 8, a correspondent reported from Philadelphia. "This afternoon J. W. Paul, of No. 2,027 Chestnut-street, with whom ex-President Grant will stop, received a telegram from Elizabeth, N. J., stating that he would not arrive until noon to-morrow." *New York Times*, May 9, 1877. See *ibid.*, Aug. 24, 1897.

To John Jay

Elizabeth, N. J.
May 3d /77

Hon. John Jay,
Pres. Union League Club,
Sir.

Your favor of the 27th of Apl. conveying an invitation from the Union League Club for a reception before my departure for Europe was only received last evening,[1] to late to be answered until this morning. I thank the Club for their tendered courtisy but must decline for want of time. I have engagements which take me from New York City on tuesday next,[2] and I have engagements here for each evening, except this, until that time.[3]

Please accept assurances of my high regard for the members of the Union League Club, and my appreciation of the many courticies extended me by them.

With great respect,
your obt. svt.
U. S. Grant

ALS, Columbia University, New York, N. Y. On April 27, 1877, John Jay, New York City, wrote to USG. "The Executive Committee of the Union League Club having been informed that you are about sailing for Europe have instructed me to tender you a reception by the club before your departure. The committee trust that your convenience will permit you to accept this tribute to the illustrious services which you have rendered to the Republic, and that the members of the club may have the pleasure of expressing to you in person their best wishes for your health and happiness." *New York Herald*, May 5, 1877.

On May 4, USG, Elizabeth, N. J., wrote to John M. Forbes. "I regret that I cannot accept your very kind invitation for me to visit the boys of Grammar School No 35, N. Y. during my stay here. But my time for each day during the remainder of my stay in this vicinity is already engaged." ALS, NIC.

1. On May 1, USG, Abel R. Corbin, and Amos Clark, Jr., had visited U.S. Representative Thomas B. Peddie of N. J. and George A. Halsey in Newark. *Newark Advertiser*, May 2, 1877. In the evening, Elizabeth officials serenaded USG at Corbin's home. *New York Times*, May 2, 1877. On May 2, USG visited Thomas Nast in Morristown. *New York Tribune*, May 3, 1877.

2. May 8.

3. On May 4, USG, Corbin, and Clark, Jr., attended a reception at the Essex Club in Newark. *Newark Advertiser*, May 5, 1877.

On May 8, USG and Clark, Jr., "visited Theo. P. Howell & Co.'s patent leather factory." *Ibid.*, May 10, 1877.

To John Sherman

———

Elizabeth, N. J.
May 4th /77

HON. JOHN SHERMAN
SEC. OF THE TREAS.
DEAR SIR:

In the changes in the New York city Custom House which I see from the papers are likly to occur I want to say a word in behalf of ~~Hone~~—H. H. Smith—a weigher.[1] If Mr. Smith lacked either competancy or faithfullness to duties I would not say a word in his behalf. But I believe his record has always been good in every respect. He is the brother of the first Mrs. Rawlins—the mother of Gen.l Rawlins children—and since the death of the stepmother has had the charge of them. In this charge he has been very faithful and as their Executor I feel an interest in whatever may be for their interest. If their uncle should be removed it might lead to a breaking up of present arrangements for the care of these children—two of whom are girls—that would be quite inconvenient at this time just as I am about leaving the country.

> Very Truly yours
>
> U. S. GRANT

ALS, Gilder Lehrman Collection, NNP. See *PUSG*, 24, 144–48; letter to Levi P. Luckey, July 11, 1874. On May 9, 1877, Secretary of the Treasury John Sherman wrote to Chester A. Arthur, collector of customs, New York City. "*Personal.* . . . I have so much respect for Gen. Grant that I wish to comply with his request. I will thank you, therefore, to protect Mr. Smith from removal, except for cause to be reported to me." LS (press), DLC-John Sherman. H. Horton Smith continued as an employee in the New York City Customhouse.

1. The New York City Customhouse was then under investigation. A headline on May 4 reflected testimony that the weigher's dept. could be reduced significantly. See *New York Times*, April 18, May 1–4, 29, Aug. 22, Sept. 1, 1877.

To Jesse Root Grant, Jr.

———

You young worthless I expected to see you at your grand mas. You will not now get to see her before sailing for Europe. You know we sail on the 17th and if you should not be here you will be left without visible means of support. I shall make no arrangement for you in our absence.

> Yours Affectionately
>
> U. S. GRANT

PHILA PA
MAY 9TH /77

ANS, MoSHi. USG endorsed this note. "Please give this to Jesse." AE (initialed), *ibid.* On May 15, 1877, Tuesday, Jesse Root Grant, Jr., Philadelphia, telegraphed to Culver C. Sniffen, Washington, D. C. "We start on Thursday at 1 Oclock A M" Copy, OFH. See Jesse R. Grant, *In the Days of My Father General Grant* (New York, 1925), pp. 197, 207–11.

To C. Randolph Gardiner

Mr C. R. Gardner
Dear Sir—

Your polite letter extending to me the freedom of the Arch St. theatre during my stay in the city has been received. I regret to say that all my evenings are engaged

It will give me much pleasure if arrangements can be made for Mrs Grant & some friends to visit the theatre—Saturday ev'ing. Thanking you for your courtesy

Very Respectfully
U. S. Grant

May 10th [*1877*]
No 27 Chesnut St.

LS (facsimile), eBay, March 15, 1999; partial facsimile, Nate's Autographs, Los Angeles, Catalog 19, no. 14527. C. Randolph Gardiner was a theatrical agent. See *New York Mirror*, Jan. 25, 1879, March 6, April 10, 1880; Alfred L. Bernheim, *The Business of the Theatre: An Economic History of the American Theatre, 1750–1932* (New York, 1932), p. 42. USG reportedly planned to attend *A Heroine in Rags* at the Arch Street Theatre on Saturday, May 12. See *Philadelphia Evening Bulletin*, May 11–12, 1877; Bartley Campbell, *The White Slave & Other Plays*, ed., Napier Wilt (Princeton, 1941), pp. xxxiv–xxxviii.

To Edwards Pierrepont

Phila Pa
May 11th /77

Dear Judge.

When I wrote to you last it was my expectation to remain here until the latter part of June before sailing for Europe. That time was set because Jesse accompanies me and I desired that he should pass his examination for entrance into the Senior class before leaving. Finding that I prefered an earlier departure he proposed to study up his Junior course as rapidly as possible to give us an earlyer start. He got through three weeks ago. We are now prepared to leave and have taken passage on the Steamer Indiana, which will leave Phila on the 17th inst.

Please present Mrs. Grants & my kindest regards to Mrs. Pierrepont.

Very Truly Yours

U. S. GRANT

JUDGE EDWARDS PIERREPONT
MINISTER PLEN. &c

ALS (facsimile), RWA Inc. Auction Catalog No. 46, July 10, 1999, no. 267. See letter to Edwards Pierrepont, Feb. 11, 1877.

To Frederick Dent Grant

———

Phila Pa

May 12th /77

DEAR FRED.

I am just in receipt of your letter of the 10th of May. The letter you spoke of in which you expressed the desire to be one of the officers detailed to visit the scene of the European War—should any be detailed—was also received. I said nothing about it to President Hayes because I did not like to ask favors for any of my own family. But should Gn. Sheridan approve the idea of your going it would be proper enough for you to address the Sec. of War making such an application should any officers be so detailed. I would advise you to do nothing however without consulting Sheridan.

We sail from here on thursday next.[1] We would be very glad if you and Ida could be here to see us off. But it is a long trip for so little.

Yours Affectionately

U. S. GRANT

ALS, USG 3. On May 17, 1877, Frederick Dent Grant was in Philadelphia to see his parents depart for England.

On May 10, Frederick Grant, Chicago, had written to Ulysses S. Grant, Jr. "yours of May 8th just received. I think as it is mother's property she is the one to decide who shall have ~~the~~ which house. . . . I have with my usual luck been buying Con Vir at 37 I have only lost a $1000. on the last deal. I am sorry you have lost ~~somu~~ much on it Give my love to mother &c. . . . P. S. Let me know how you are getting along in your profession. Write to me often" ALS, *ibid.* See letter to Ulysses S. Grant, Jr., March 26, 1877.

On May 15, Julia Dent Grant, Philadelphia, wrote to Emma Dent Casey. "I received your letter only a few days ago & learned that you had left Washington only when I arrived there. I saw the picture of your southern home whilst I was in W. It is a lovely place indeed. I learn that some one has been appointed in Jims place. I think if J. wanted to retain the position he should have said as much to Mr H—. We sail on Thursday the 17th are to have a grand send off you will see all about it in the papers—Is it not too bad that Nellie dose not go with us. I or rather *We* have had a perfectly love ly time ever since we left the W. House. Have not had time to be home sick yet. We had a lovely visit to Fred & Ida in Chicago. They are keeping house very simply & delightfully Julia is Queen of the house hold, I assure you. I had letters from my Nellie & sister Anne. Annies affairs are still unsettled but with prospects of an early settlement Nellie leaves on 17th also. But Nellie & family sail from Baltimore & we from Philad. I think it is a better arrangement for us all—Hoping to find you & yours all well & prosperous on our return I will close with affectionate love to you all & Wishing Gods blessing on you my dear sister Emma. I am your loving sister . . . Kiss the darling children for Aunt Jule" ALS, Ulysses S. Grant National Historic Site (White Haven), St. Louis, Mo.

1. May 17.

Speech

———

[*Philadelphia, May 16, 1877*]

Mr. Mayor and Gentlemen: It is impossible that I should be heard by the whole of this great assembly, but I desire to say to you, and through you to the people of Philadelphia, that I am profoundly thankful for all the kindness which they have shown me every day and every hour since I have b[e]en in their city, this time, and always when I have been here. I shall carry away an impression of it which neither distance nor time can destroy. So long as I live and wherever I am, I shall remember your kindness. I do not claim to have deserved it, but I shall never forget it, and shall always appreciate it. Hoping your city may continue to advance in all the elements of greatness in the future, as in the past, and thanking all of you personally for your great kindness, I can find no other words except to say God bless you all and good night, and for the present good bye.

Philadelphia Public Ledger, May 17, 1877. USG spoke in response to a serenade at the home of George W. Childs. *Ibid.* See Childs, *Recollections of General Grant* (Philadelphia, 1890), pp. 15, 48. For USG in Philadelphia, May 9–16, 1877, see *Philadelphia Public Ledger*, May 10–17, 1877.

Speech

[*May 17, 1877*]

MR. MAYOR AND GENTLEMEN: I feel very much overcome with what I have heard. When the first toast was offered I supposed the last words here for me had been spoken,[1] and I feel overcome at the sentiments to which I have listened, and to which I feel altogether inadequate to respond. I don't think that the compliments ought all be paid to me or any one man in either of the positions which I was called upon to fill. That which I accomplished—which I was able to accomplish—I owe to the assistance of able lieutenants. I was so fortunate as to be called to the first position in the Army of the nation, and I had the good fortune to select lieutenants who could have filled, had it been necessary—I believe some of these lieutenants could have filled my place, maybe better than I did. I do not, therefore, regard myself as entitled to all the praise. I believe that my friend Sherman could have taken my place as a soldier, as well as I could then have hoped to do, and the same will apply to Sheridan. And I believe, finally, that if our country ever comes into trial again, young men will spring up equal to the occasion, and if one falls, there will be another to take his place. Just as there was if I had failed. I thank you again and again, gentlemen for the hearty and generous reception I have had in your great city of Philadelphia.

New York Times, May 18, 1877. USG spoke on the *Twilight* in reply to farewells by Gen William T. Sherman, Hamilton Fish, Zachariah Chandler, George M. Robeson, Simon Cameron, Isaac H. Bailey, Governor John F. Hartranft of Pa., and Mayor William S. Stokley of Philadelphia. *Ibid.*

1. After Stokley's toast wishing "God-speed to our honored guest, Ulysses S. Grant," USG responded. "MR. MAYOR AND GENTLEMEN: I am very grateful. I am overcome with feeling. I need hardly say how deeply I appreciate your kindness on this occasion." *New York Times*, May 18, 1877.

To Rutherford B. Hayes

———

Steamer Twilight
11 a. m. May 17th /77

PRESIDENT HAYES, EX. MANSION
WASHINGTON D. C.

Mrs Grant joins me in thanks to you and Mrs Hayes for your kind message rec'd on board this boat after pushing out from the wharf. We unite in returning our cordial greeting and in expressing our best wishes for your health, happiness and success in your most responsible position. Hoping to return to my country ~~finding~~ to find it prosperous in business and with cordial feelings restored between all sections, I subscribe myself

Truly Yours
U. S. GRANT

ALS (telegram sent), OFH. On May 17, 1877, President Rutherford B. Hayes, New York City, telegraphed to USG. "Mrs Hayes joins me in heartiest wishes that you and Mrs Grant may have a prosperous voyage, and after a happy visit abroad, a safe return to your friends and Country—" ALS (telegram sent), *ibid.* See *New York Tribune*, May 18, 1877.

Also on May 17, Col. Albert J. Myer, chief signal officer, Washington, D. C., telegraphed to USG, Philadelphia. "Good weather at sea strong westerly winds. Good bye!" *New York Times*, May 18, 1877.

To Ulysses S. Grant, Jr.

———

May 26th *1877*.

DEAR BUCK,

By one to-morrow afternoon we will be in Queenstown.[1] So far we have done well, neither your Ma, Jesse or I having been sea sick for a moment though the weather has been unusually rough. For two days,—Saturday[2] noon to Monday noon—we had a regular February storm. There has been no moment when I felt the slightest nausea.—Jess has made himself a regular "Boy-hoy" among the passengers, singing with the ladies, reading and reciting poetry to them

&c. With the men he passes for a full grown youth who has cut his eyeteeth.

We will go direct to Liverpool[3] where I understand a special car will be in waiting to take us to London.[4] After that I make no plans for the present.

Your Ma wants me to say to you that if you receive her money from your Aunt Anna[5] you need not spend it in Mining stocks if you have not already done so. If you can buy Anglo-Cal. Bank[6] stock without paying much premium you may buy it. Otherwise put the money in bank and await further directions. Write to us often and some one one will keep you advised of our movements. The Cub is writing for the Chicago Inter-Ocean.[7] See his letters.

Yours Affectionately
U. S. GRANT

ALS, USG 3. Written on stationery of the *Indiana.* On May 26, 1877, USG and other passengers presented Capt. R. W. Sargent with a testimonial. "We, the cabin passengers of the steamship 'Indiana,' before departing on our different ways, at the end of a voyage attended with unusually stormy weather and rough seas for the month of May, beg to express our admiration of the staunchness, speed and comfort of the 'Indiana,' . . ." *Philadelphia Inquirer,* June 11, 1877.

On May 26, Secretary of State William M. Evarts wrote to Hamilton Fish, Garrison, N. Y. "Unofficial. . . . I have received your letter of the 19th instant, in which you inform me that General Grant did not provide himself with a passport, prior to his departure for Europe, and suggesting that in view of the disturbed condition of affair[s] there, it may be necessary for him to have one. I thank you very much for calling my attention to this oversight on the part of the General, and I have hastened to have a set of special passports, covering his entire party, made out and forwarded to him, care of Messrs. J. S. Morgan & Co, London, with a copy of a circular letter addressed to our Diplomatic and Consular Officers abroad, inviting their aid to make his journey a pleasant one should he visit their posts. This letter has been forwarded direct from the Department to all our representatives at posts, which it is thought no unlikely the distinguished party may visit, and a copy is enclosed herewith for your information." LS, DLC-Hamilton Fish. The enclosure, dated May 23, is *ibid. Foreign Relations, 1877,* p. 1. On May 22, Evarts had issued a passport for USG. "*Know Ye, that the bearer hereof,* General Ulysses S. Grant, ex-President of the United States, is proceeding abroad, accompanied by his family. *These are therefore to request all whom it may concern to permit* him *to pass freely, without let or molestation, and to extend to* him *all such friendly aid and protection, as would be extended to like* citizens *of Foreign Governments resorting to the United States.*" DS, USG 3. Similar passports for Julia Dent Grant and Jesse Root Grant, Jr., are *ibid.*

1. On [*May 28*], Monday, USG, Queenstown, Ireland, telegraphed to Edwards Pierrepont, U.S. minister, London. "We have arrived safely Sunday and will remain in Liverpool until Wednesday thirteenth will then start for London" Telegram received (stamped

May 28), OHi. See Pierrepont to Fish, May 25, 1877, DLC-Hamilton Fish. On May 27, John Russell Young had written in his diary. ". . . Finally about seven, the Indiana with Grant on board was signalled. . . . Grant with a cloth cap on was leaning over the taffrail and smoking. He was very cordial, and we talked a couple of hours as we sat in the smoking room mainly about the war,—no politics." DLC-John Russell Young.

On May 29, Lord Beaconsfield (Prime Minister Benjamin Disraeli) wrote to USG. "I am sorry, that I am not in town to welcome you to England. I hope, however, soon personally to have that gratification. This is to ask you to do me a great favor, & a greater honor. It is, that you would dine with me on the Queen's birthday, Saturday next, June the 2nd, & meet some of Her Majestys most distinguished subjects, who will give you a hearty welcome." ALS, DLC-John Russell Young. See William Flavelle Monypenny and George Earle Buckle, *The Life of Benjamin Disraeli Earl of Beaconsfield* (London, 1910–20), VI, 168.

2. May 19.

3. On May 25, Charles Hastings Doyle, Portsmouth, wrote to USG. "Our newspapers announce that you are expected to arrive at Liverpool tomorrow I therefore take up my pen to say I hope you will do me the honor to pay me a visit here as soon as convenient after your arrival in England, to enable me, in some small degree, to repay the great kindness you shewed me during your campaigning days, and afterward, when President, at Washington—I hope you will kindly fix upon some *early day* to visit me, as I shall have to break up my establishment about the 15th of June, as the period of my Command will cease about that time, in consequence of my Promotion to the rank of full General. I trust that all your party who have accompanied you from the United State[s] will accompany you—This is one of our most interesting Ports to visit, and I shall be delighted to shew you all that is worth looking at here—. . . P. S. I beg to be kindly remembered to Mrs Grant if with you." ALS, DLC-USG, IB. Doyle, Chichester, again wrote to USG. "I wrote to you a few days ago to express a hope that you and Mrs Grant and any members of your Family who may have accompanied you from the United States, would honor me with a visit to Portsmouth as early as convenient after your arrival as I am obliged to break up my establishment about the middle of June when the period of my command will have nearly expired! If you should have no other engagement will you allow me to propose that you should come to me on the 2nd of June, when we are to keep the Queen's Birth Day, and I should have a good opportunity of parading my Garrison for your inspection. I am *very* anxious you should see them thus early as several of my Regiments are to leave me for the Summer Drills at the Camp at Aldershot. I beg to be very kindly remembered to Mrs Grant, . . . I return to Portsmouth tomorrow" ALS (undated), *ibid.* On May 31, Doyle wrote to Adam Badeau, consul gen. "I was not a little surprised on receiving your telegram to find that General Grant had not received the *two* letters I wrote to him, . . ." ALS, *ibid.* See *PUSG*, 15, 291–93.

4. On May 23, John Walter, *The Times* (London), Wokingham, had written to USG. "I beg to offer you my own & Mrs Walter's hearty congratulations on your arrival in England; the more so, as I fear, judging from the weather that has lately prevailed, that your voyage must have been any thing but agreeable. I regret that our engagements in the country, during the Whitsuntide holiday prevent us from paying our respects to Mrs Grant & yourself as soon as we could wish; but we hope it will be in your power to honour us with your company and that of any members of your family who may be with you, during the week of the Ascot races—i. e. between the 11th & 15th of June, and see a little of English country life. We are only 10 miles from Ascot, and within an hour & a half of London by Rail, our best Station, during Ascot week, being Reading, on the Gt Western Railway, to which there are trains from London nearly every hour—We hope however to see you in Town before that time, as we return on the 31st inst. With our best compliments

to Mrs Grant, . . ." ALS, DLC-USG, IB. On Aug. 29, Walter, Saltburn on Sea, wrote to Badeau extending another invitation to USG. ALS, *ibid.*

    5. Anna E. Dent, widow of Julia Grant's brother Lewis.

    6. Anglo-Californian Bank, organized in 1873. See Ira B. Cross, *Financing an Empire: History of Banking in California* (Chicago, 1927), I, 389–90.

    7. Jesse Root Grant, Jr., dispatched his first letter from Liverpool on May 29. See *Chicago Inter Ocean*, June 13, 1877.

Speech

[*Manchester, May 30, 1877*]

MR. MAYOR AND GENTLEMEN OF THE COMMON COUNCIL OF MAN-
CHESTER, AND LADIES AND GENTLEMEN OF THE CITY OF MANCHESTER,—
It is scarcely possible for me to give utterance to the feelings which have been evoked by the receptions which I have had upon your soil from the moment of my arrival [1] In Liverpool, where I spent a couple of days,[2] I witnessed continually about the same scenes that I have witnessed here in the streets and the public buildings of your city to-day. It would be impossible for any person to have that attention paid to him which has been paid to me without feeling it, and it is impossible that I should give expression to the sentiments which, as I said, were evoked by what I have witnessed in your midst. I had intended, on my arrival in Liverpool, to hasten through to London, and from that point to visit the various points of interest in your country. Among many others I had set down Manchester as one of the most important.—I am aware—and have for a great number of years been aware—of the large number of manufactures you have here, many of which find a market in my own country. I was very well aware during the war which you have mentioned in your address of the sentiments of the great mass of the people of Manchester towards the country to which I have the honour to belong, and of your sentiments with regard to the struggle in which it fell to my lot to take a humble part. For that, and for further expressions of the kind which took place during our great trial, there has been on the part of my countrymen a feeling of friendship towards the people of Manchester, distinct and separate from that which they feel for all the rest of England.—I therefore accept, on the part of my country, the com-

pliments which have been paid to me as one of its representatives, and thank you for them.—

Manchester Guardian, May 31, 1877. On May 30, 1877, Mayor Abel Heywood of Manchester presented a testimonial to USG and recalled "the circumstance that when 14 years ago he previously held the office of Mayor it had been his grateful duty to welcome the Captain of the George Griswold relief ship, which had come from the United States laden with provisions for Lancashire during the Cotton Famine." *The Times* (London), May 31, 1877. Later that day at a luncheon, USG returned thanks for a toast and "said that the observations about his usual reticence which had fallen from the Mayor made it seem the more remarkable that he should be called to his feet twice within so short a time. He might say very truly that Englishmen had drawn from him more speeches than ever were drawn from him in his own country, and he was afraid they were very much poorer ones, because they were longer. If he were to be betrayed into making a long speech, it would become poor in proportion to the length. He must, therefore, again return his thanks for the kindness with which he had been received, and conclude by proposing 'The Health of the Mayoress, Mrs. Heywood.'" *Ibid.* See George W. Childs, *Recollections of General Grant* (Philadelphia, 1890), p. 21.

1. A British editorial had assessed USG's career and predicted his reception. ". . . Here he will find that his eminent services to the cause of international peace are not forgotten. He will be welcomed, not only as an illustrious soldier, but as a statesman who has always been friendly to England, and his political errors on the other side of the Atlantic need not survive in the memories of Englishmen." *The Times* (London), May 23, 1877. For other editorials, see *Daily Telegraph* (London), May 28, 1877, and *Manchester Guardian,* May 30, 1877.

2. On May 28, Mayor A. Barclay Walker of Liverpool welcomed USG. *The Times* (London), May 29, 1877. USG replied. "I thank you very much for the kind welcome you have given me, a welcome which is all the more agreeable because unexpected." *Ibid.* On the same day, John Russell Young, Liverpool, telegraphed to Edwards Pierrepont, U.S. minister, London. "General Grant and party arrived at three all well   propose coming London tomorrow   gave him your letter   great reception here" Telegram received (stamped May 28), William J. Kaland, New York, N. Y. On [*May 29*], Tuesday, Adam Badeau, consul gen., London, Liverpool, telegraphed to Pierrepont. "General Grant will go to Manchester Wednesday morning leave for London same afternoon at five   if any change in plan will telegraph you immediately" Telegram received (stamped May 29), OHi. See *The Times* (London), May 30, 1877.

To Adelaide Kemble Sartoris

June 2d /77

My Dear Mrs. Sartoris,

Mrs. Grant wishes me to thank you for your very kind note and invitation for us to visit you whenever we can. It will afford both

Mrs. Grant & myself the greatest pleasure to do so at as early a date as possible. At present there seems to be engagements for us up to the 28th of June.

[But I hope there will be a short respite between the 15th & 20th . . . which will enable us to run down . . . if only for a day to see Nellie and her new relations. [*Jesse*] certainly will be able to avail himself . . . whether his Ma & I can go or not . . . Since our arrival in England we have seen nothing but the greatest kindness towards our country and ourselves personally. The demonstrations have taken me entirely by surprise but it has been an agreeable surprise . . .]

Mrs. Grant joins me in love to Nellie, Algie & the babe,[1] and in kindest regards to Mrs Sartoris and yourself.

Very Truly yours,

U. S. GRANT

ALS (incomplete facsimile), Charles Hamilton, *American Autographs* (1983), p. 486; RWA Inc., Catalog 45 (1999) no. 1639; *The Collector*, No. 934 (1989), W-503. Written on stationery headed "17. Cavendish Square" [*London*]. Adelaide Kemble Sartoris, sister of the author Fanny Kemble, had been an acclaimed opera singer before her marriage. She also wrote *A Week in a French Country House* (London, 1867) and *Medusa, and other Tales* (London, 1868). See Leon Edel, ed., *Henry James Letters* (Cambridge, Mass., 1974–84), II, 233–34; J. C. Furnas, *Fanny Kemble: Leading Lady of the Nineteenth-Century Stage* (New York, 1982), pp. 366–73.

On June 18, [*1877*], Ellen Grant Sartoris, Southampton, wrote to Ulysses S. Grant, Jr. ". . . You must do just as you think best with my money and then if it is all lost I shall not break my heart over it for I shall have the consolation of knowing that it was in the hands of a lawyer . . . The Dad has gone to Paris he left this a. m. to spend a week and Algy has gone to Kettering to look after his iron jiggers, so Mammy & I are left two 'love lorne widdows' but we start off on a spree to London tomorrow where we expect to have a lovely time in our different ways, Mammy is going to be with Mary and I am going to be with Mamma & Papa & Jesse and I am going also for the pleasure of going out to parties—Algy will join me there the day after we arrive—Papa & Mamma & Jesse are still at the Pierreponts but next week they are to be with Genl. Badeau. I had a letter from the Genl. this a. m. asking me to stay with Mamma at his house during his absence, he is going with Papa & Jesse to Liverpool and Ma will be left alone I am so sorry I cannot manage it this time as Mammy has hasked some friends down here whom she is very anxious I should meet, however perhaps we may persuade Mama to come down here. They all did come last week and seemed to like the place & people ever so much . . ." ALS, USG 3. See *Julia Grant*, pp. 203.

1. Algernon Edward Sartoris was born March 17, 1877.

To George W. Childs

———

London, Eng.
June 6th /77

MY DEAR MR. CHILDS,

After an unusually stormy passage for any season of the year, and continuous seasickness generally, among the passengers after the second day out, we reached Liverpool Monday afternoon the 28th ult. Jesse & I proved to be among the few good sailors. Neither of us felt a moment of quamishness during the voyage. I had proposed to leave Liverpool immediately on arrival and proceed immediately for London where I knew our Minister had made arrangements for a formal reception, and had accepted for me a few invitations of courticy. But what was my surprise to find nearly all the shipping in port decorated to the last flag, and from the Mainmast of each ship the flag of the Union was most conspicuous. The docks were lined with as many of the population as could find standing room, and the streets to the hotel where it was understood my party would stop, were packed. The demonstration was to all appearances as hearty and as enthusiastic as in Phild on our departure. The Mayor was present with his state carriage to convey us to the hotel, and after some chang of toilet to his beautiful country residence some six miles out where we were entertained at dinner with a small party of gentlemen, and remained over night. The following day a large lunch party was given at the official residence of the Mayor, in th[e] city, at which there were some one hundred & fifty of the distinguished citizens and officials of the corporation present. Pressing invitations were sent from most of the cities in the kingdom to have me visit them. I accepted for a day at Manchester and stopped a few moments at Leicester[1] and at one other place.[2] The same hearty welcome was shown at each place, and as you have no doubt seen, the press of the country has been exceedingly kind and courtious in its comments. So far I have not been permitted to travel in a regular train, much less in a common car. The Midland road, which penetrates a great portion of the Island, including Wales & Scotland, haves extended to me the courticy of their road and a Pullman car to take me whereever I wish to go during the whole of my stay in England.[3] We arrived in London Monday evening, the 30th of June [4] ~~and~~ where I found our Minister had accepted engagements for me up to the 27th of June, leaving but few spare days in the interval. On Saturday last we dined with the Duke of Wellington [5] and last night the formal reception at Judge Pierreponts was held. It was a great success, most brilliant in the ~~att~~ number, rank and attire of the audience and was graced by the presence of every American now in the City who had called on the Minister or left a card for me. I doubt whether London has ever seen a private house so elaborately or so tastefully decorated as was our American Ministers last night.[6] I am deeply indebted to him for the pains he has take to make my stay pleasant and the attentions creditable to our country. I appreciate th[e] fact,—and am proud of it—that the attentions which I am receiving are intended more for our country than than for me personally. I love to see our country honored & respected abroad and I am proud to believe that it is by most all nations, and by some even loved. It has always been my desire to see all jealousy between England and the United States abated, and all sores healed up. Together they are more powerful for the spread of Commerce and civilization than all others combined, and can do more to remove cause of Wars by creating mutual interests that would be so much disturbed by war, than all other nations. I have written very hastily and a gooddeal at length but I trust this will not bore you. Had I written for publication I should have taken some pains. As it is you are at liberty to read this to our friends, Borie, Drexel, Geo. H. Stewart Col. Forney and such others as you choose to bore in that way, and to all of whom please present my compliments and respects. To Mrs. Childs and the wives and families of all included in the above category, please remember me also.

Very Truly Yours
U. S. Grant

ALS, deCoppet Collection, NjP. See *The Times* (London), June 20, 1877; George W. Childs, *Recollections of General Grant* (Philadelphia, 1890), pp. 26–28.

On June 6, 1877, James Johnstone, *The Standard* (London), wrote to USG. "Will you kindly let me know when I may have the honor of seeing you when you are not much engaged as I am an invalid and am only in London for for three or four days . . . P. S. I am stopping at the Grosvenor Hotel Victoria Station" ALS, DLC-USG, IB.

1. On May 31, USG had spoken at Leicester. "Allow me, on behalf of my country and myself, to return you our thanks for the honour which you have done us, and for the kind reception I have just had here, as well as for the other kind receptions which I have had since the time that I first landed on the soil of Great Britain. As children of this great commonwealth, we feel that you must have some reason to be proud of the advancement that we have made since our separation from our mother country. I can assure you of our heartfelt goodwill, and express to you our thanks on behalf of the American people." *The Times* (London), June 1, 1877. Mayor William Winterton of Leicester had presented to USG a testimonial. DS (undated), Smithsonian Institution. USG again spoke briefly to acknowledge a gift of "carefully prepared photographs of four unpublished letters from General Washington which are in the Leicester Museum." *The Times* (London), June 1, 1877.

2. Also on May 31, prior to speaking in Leicester, USG spoke at Salford. "Mr. Mayor and Gentlemen,—The reception I have had since my arrival in England has been to me very expressive, and one for which I have to return thanks on behalf of my country, for I feel that it is my country that is being received through me. It is the affection which the people of this island have for their children on the other side of the Atlantic which they express to me as a humble representative of their offspring. The time I have is so limited that I will make no further remarks, but ask you to drink the health of the Mayor and Mayoress." *Ibid.*

3. Edward S. Ellis, chairman, Midland Railway Co., had accompanied USG on the train from Manchester to London. *Ibid.* See Clement E. Stretton, *The History of the Midland Railway* (London, 1901).

On June 2, H. S. Roberts, superintendent, Pullman Palace Car Co., wrote to Adam Badeau, consul gen., London. "Referring to our conversation the other day in the car, I now send for your perusal & at convenience a map, on which I have marked in blue pencil the different routes in England and Scotland over which the Pullman cars have already travelled, and can do so again without any difficulty As I said to you the other day, whenever you are ready to take the trip, one of our cars will be at the disposal of General Grant and yourself with our compliments. I was over the whole of Scotland last summer with one of our cars and shall be glad to give you any information as to the routes &c." LS, DLC-USG, IB.

On May 30, Badeau had telegraphed to Gen. William T. Sherman, Washington, D. C. "Please issue formal order placing me in attendance as army officer on General Grant during stay in England without pay answer" Telegram received (at 5:45 A.M.), DNA, RG 94, ACP, 362 1876. On May 31, Sherman telegraphed to Badeau. "Secretary willing you attend General Grant, but regards you as Consul General—not subject to formal army orders" Telegram sent, *ibid.* On June 13, Badeau, London, wrote to Sherman. "Your kind answer to my telegram was duly received, and I am much obliged for the permission given. You know how highly I value the privilege, and I believe I am not altogether unserviceable to General Grant—in attendance. My request was of course made with his sanction. I have written to the State Department explaining that the application was only intended for social and ceremonial purposes, and not as a request to be relieved temporarily from Consular General duties. . . ." ALS, DLC-William T. Sherman. On June 27, Sherman wrote to Badeau. ". . . Now that he is untrammeled by the personal contests of partisans, all men look upon him as *the* General Grant, who had the courage, with Lee at his front and Washington at his rear, to undertake to command the Army of the Potomac in 1864, to guide, direct, and push it through sunshine and storm, through praise and denunciation, steadily, surely, and finally to victory and peace; and *afterwards, though unused to the ways and machinery of civil government, to risk all in undertaking to maintain that peace by the Constitution and civil forms of government.* There have been plenty of people trying to sow dissensions between us personally, and I feel my conscience clear that, though sometimes differing on minor points, I never doubted his patriotism, firmness, and personal friendship. If the General and family be still with you, give them the assurance of my best love, . . ." *Badeau*, 122–23.

On June 17, J. C. Bancroft Davis, U.S. minister, Berlin, had written to Hamilton Fish. ". . . I am sorry to see that Gen. Grant has let Badeau fasten himself to him. The Gen. wrote me that B. had turned in to help him in his correspondence. By means of it he gets to Come as 'Aid de Camp in Waiting' and he gives the General a party in which he styles him self the same on his card of invitation. It is a pity. It gives the General's enemies, among whom Washburn seems to put himself, a chance to abuse him. I hear that Washburne is abusive of both the General and of you. He took goo[d] care to get all he could out of both of you before he quarrelled . . ." ALS, DLC-Hamilton Fish.

4. USG actually arrived in London on Thursday, May 31. *The Times* (London), June 1, 1877.

5. On June 2, Arthur Richard Wellesley, Duke of Wellington, hosted a banquet for USG. "During the general conversation which followed the supper General Grant was asked what was the comparison between English racing, as he had seen it on the day of the Oaks at Epsom, and the races in America. He said, with a smile, 'There is an impression abroad that I am a great horse racer, fond of horses and know all about races; but, on the contrary, I really know nothing of racing, having seen only two races—one at Cincinnati in 1865 and at the opening of Jerome Park in 1867. I feel, therefore, that I am not qualified to judge of the comparison. Thus far I like London very much. I have, however, accepted so many engagements that I shall be compelled to alter my plans and remain here until the 27th, when I shall visit Ireland.'" *New York Herald*, June 3, 1877.

On June 4, Wellington wrote to Julia Dent Grant. "The enclosed is from the Dean of Windsor the Queens Chaplain   Angeli is the best painter I know of. You see I have kept my promise to enquire. I should think that the best mode of applying to him is by a letter, addressed Herr *von* Angeli.   I underline the Von that you may not omit it. . . . I hope the General is well under the fatigues of ovation." ALS, DLC-USG, IB. A related note is *ibid.* On June 7, Buckingham Palace wrote to Edwards Pierrepont, U.S. minister, London, inviting USG to have his portrait painted by Heinrich von Angeli. Cohasco, Inc., Catalogue No. 26, March 28, 1985, no. 234. See Lawrence H. Francis, ed., *Recent European Art: Selections from the Portfolios of Breton, Dupré, Kaulbach, Max, Conti, Hagborg, and Von Angeli* (Boston, 1890).

6. On May 28, W. Jennings Demorest, London, had written to Pierrepont. "If in accordance with the provisions of the proposed reception to General and Mrs Grant I would be pleased to receive invitations for Self and party which consists of Mme Demorest Mrs J. C. Croly (Jenny June) Miss Demorest Mr Will Demorest" ALS, William J. Kaland, New York, N. Y. See *New York Herald* and *New York Times*, June 6, 1877.

On June 5, William E. Gladstone attended Pierrepont's reception and commented on USG. "He fulfils his ideal as a taciturn, self-possessed, not discourteous, substantial kind of man. Mrs Grant kind but alas 'dowdy'." M. R. D. Foot and H. C. G. Matthew, eds., *The Gladstone Diaries* (Oxford, 1968–94), IX, 224.

To Elihu B. Washburne

—————

June 9th /77

MY DEAR MR. WASHBURNE:

My stay in London has been more protracted than I had intended, or will be before my accepted engagements are fulfilled. I have accepted invitations for every day up to, and including, the 26th of this month. On the 28th of June I will be at a banquet to be given in Liverpool. Within a few of that time—most likely on the 1st day of July—I will be in pParis on my way to Switzerland. My stay will probably not reach more than a day or two beyond the 4th of July in Paris.

The reception I have had in England so far has been very gratifying and I think very complimentary to our country. I recognize the fact that it is more the country all the compliments I am receiving are intended for than for me personally.

I will send my Courier to Paris to secure quarters for our short stay, or will get Gen. Torbert [1] to do this for me. I will be compelled to be very moderate in my expenditures to correspond with my means. In fact the extent of my visit abroad will depend entirely on how long I can stay upon the limited capital I have brought with me.

Please present Mrs Grants & my complements to Mrs. Washburne, and accept the same for yourself.

Very Truly Yours
U. S. GRANT

ALS, IHi. On June 10, 1877, Elihu B. Washburne wrote to USG. "I have your favor of yesterday. Badeau had written me about your coming here in July and I answered him yesterday. He will shew you my letter. I have since conferred with many of our friends on the subject and they all confirm what I wrote, and even more strongly. They are surprised that any [*people*] without any [*invitation*] should have attempted to appropriate you on the 4th of July. I explained this fully in my letter to Badeau. As I wrote him, you could pass through here on your way to Switzerland and stay a day, to get a glance of the city, and then pass on.—You could come *unannounced* to the public and it would not be taken as a visit. A stay of three of four days, as I wrote Badeau, and in the language of Torbert, would *botch* everything for the future. Please let me know what you think of this, but pray dont intimate to Hayes that you have heard from me, because I dont want to be considered as interfering with his arrangements. You might, for instance, leave London in the morning, reach here at night, spend the next day and night here and leave on the second morning for Switzerland. Nothing would be thought of that as you would be deemed to be here simply *in transit*. In such an event you need not send your courier in advance or trouble Torbert, for I can do everything without any inconvenience. We are all pleased at your reception in England, but it is no more than we had a right to expect. I am sorry to say that Mrs. W. is suffering from [*ache*] and cold and loss of voice, but we hope she [*will*] soon be well again. —She desires to join me in kind regards to Mrs. Grant and yourself." ALS (press), DLC-Elihu B. Washburne. See following letter.

On June 8, Adam Badeau, consul gen., London, had written to Washburne, Paris. "I suppose General Grant will write and tell you himself, but I thought you might like to know earlier that he proposes to be in Paris about the 1st of July, and to stay several days on his way to Switzerland. He has directed me to accept an invitation for the 4th to a garden party given by Mr & Mrs Hargies. You will be glad to know that he has been the recipient here, of popular ovations like those which you witnessed after the close of the war. In Liverpool & Manchester the demonstrations were most enthusiastic: and *en route* to London the train was stopped again for Mayors to present addresses &c. When he enters a theatre the play stops, and the people rise and cheer. Here in London he takes precedence in society of ambassadors and Dukes; the ministers all called on him first, and the Prince of Wales came into his box at the Oaks to make his acquaintance   Please make my best complements to Mrs Washburne . . . The General will have something to tell you about one who has pretended to be a friend of his, of yours, and of mine, and has slandered *each* of us, not only to the others, but to the world." ALS, *ibid*. On June 9, Washburne wrote to Badeau. "I have just received your note of yesterday. The Americans here, as well as the French people who are in sympathy with our Government are very anxious to see Genl Grant in Paris, but I have very serious doubts whether it will be policy for him to come at the time you mention, and only to stay three or four days. When he does come, the French officials will want to give him a recognition commensurate with his distinguished reputation, but if he only is to stay four or five days there will be no sufficient time for anything. Arrangements and plans can only be half carried out and just enough will be accomplished to take all the edge off from a later reception. If the General could give us *three weeks* in July for his *regular visit*, it would give us more than time to do all we want to do for him. But even the time indicated is not very favorable, particularly this year for independently of the ordinary heat of that season, there is now raging here an intense political excitement, unfavorable to official and social festivities and attentions. I think it would be more satisfactory to our country men generally, as well as to official circles, if his visit were to be made later, say in September or October. By that time we hope the present extraordinary crisis will be over, and if it should terminate in bringing in a Republican ministry, the reception of the General will be vastly more cordial than it will be now. I think both the General and yourself will appreciate the situation and judge it correctly. . . ." ALS (press), *ibid*.

1. Alfred T. A. Torbert, consul gen., Paris.

To Elihu B. Washburne

June 11th /77

MY DEAR MR. WASHBURNE

Your letter of yesterday came to hand this morning, and also Badeau's. I have written, as Badeau has, to Mr Harjis[1] declining invitation to garden party on the ground that I cannot quite fix the day for being in Paris. As soon as my plans are definitely fixed I will let you know. It is most likely now that I will either visit Scotland & Ireland before going on the Continent or that I will visit Denmark, Norway & Sweden and back to Switzerland without going to Paris until I can stop for some time. If any chang of plan takes place I will keep you informed. Thanks for your kind letter.

Very Truly yours
U. S. GRANT

ALS, IHi.

1. A banker associated with Anthony J. Drexel, John H. Harjes had moved from Philadelphia to Paris in 1868. See *New York Times*, Feb. 16, 1914.

Speech

[*London, June 15, 1877*]

It is a matter of some regret to me that I have never cultivated that art of public speaking which might have enabled me to express in suitable terms my gratitude for the compliment which has been paid to my countrymen and myself on this occasion. Were I in the habit of speaking in public, I should claim the right to express my opinion, and what I believe will be the opinion of my countrymen, when the proceedings of this day shall have been telegraphed to them. For myself, I have been very much surprised at the reception I have had at all places since the day I landed at Liverpool up to my appearance in the greatest city in the world. It was entirely unexpected, and it is particularly gratifying to me. I believe that this honour is intended, quite as much for the country which I have had the opportunity of serving in different capacities as for myself, and I am glad that this is so, because I want to see the happiest relations existing, not only between the United States and Great Britain, but also between the United States and all other nations. Although a soldier by education and profession, I have never felt any sort of fondness for war and I have never advocated it except as a means for peace. I hope that we shall always settle our differences in all future negotiations as amicably as we did in a recent instance. I believe that settlement has had a happy effect on both countries, and that from month to month and year to year the tie of common civilization and common blood is getting stronger between the two countries. My Lord Mayor, Ladies, and Gentlemen, I again thank you for the honour you have done me and my country to-day.[1]

The Times (London), June 16, 1877; variant text in Daily Telegraph (London), June 16, 1877. USG had received the freedom of the city and replied to a speech praising his military and presidential achievements by Benjamin Scott, Chamberlain of London. The Times (London), June 16, 1877. A resolution from the Common Council of London, dated May 31, accompanied the key to the city. D, Smithsonian Institution. See New York Herald, June 16, 1877.

On June 6, James W. Benson, "Jeweller & Silversmith," London, wrote to USG. "Having received instructions from the Corporation of the City of London to send in designs of Casket to be made for you I should esteem it a favor if you will kindly oblige me with your crest, & motto, & initials for a monogram so as to enable me to carry out a good design—" ALS, DLC-USG, IB. On June 7 and 14, William Corrie, Remembrancer of London, wrote to Edwards Pierrepont, U.S. minister, London. "Will you have the kindness to send me the names of the Ladies and Gentlemen who will accompany General Grant on the 15th? I want this information that Cards admitting to Guildhall may be sent to them, and also to enable me to place them near the General at the time of the Ceremony and afterwards at the Dejeuner. Are there any distinguished Americans in London to whom invitations can be sent? The Presentation of the Freedom is fixed for one o'clock, & perhaps General Grant will arrive a short time before that hour." "The Card for Mr Hoppin was sent by post yesterday evening to 25 Westbourne Place S. W. The Lord Mayor will to-morrow propose the Toasts   1 The Queen   2 General Grant   3 His Excellency the Minister for the United States of America   I think that the General or you should then, as the last Toast propose the health of the Lord Mayor   Will you determine this?" LS and ALS, OHi. Other items related to the ceremony are ibid.

1. At a reception following the freedom of the city ceremony, Lord Mayor Thomas White of London toasted USG. The Times (London), June 16, 1877. USG responded. "My Lord Mayor, Ladies and Gentlemen: Habits formed in early life and early education press upon us as we grow older. I was brought up a soldier—not to talking. I am not aware that I ever fought two battles on the same day in the same place, and that I should be called

upon to make two speeches on the same day under the same roof is beyond my understanding. What I do understand is, that I am much indebted to all of you for the compliment you have paid me. All I can do is to thank the Lord Mayor for his kind words, and to thank the citizens of Great Britain here present in the name of my country and for myself." *Young,* I, 26–27.

On June 20, White, Halliford on Thames, wrote to USG. "As I had the honor of proposing that you should be made a Citizen of London may I have the further honor of a visit some afternoon before you leave England at my residence as above accompanied by Mrs Grant & your Son. I would leave the appointment wholly with you. July 4th 11th & 24th I am engaged out and Saturdays, for Citizens of London, are generally most convenient for making holiday with friends." ALS, DLC-USG, IB.

To Elihu B. Washburne

July [*June*] 16th /77

MY DEAR MR. WASHBURNE:

I shall follow your advice in regard to my visit to Paris. I will pass through on my way to Switzerland, possibly staying over two or three days in the city, but having it understood that I am only passing now but will visit there again about the last of October— middle to last—when I will stay some six weeks. I have written to Mr. Harjis who was kind enough to invite me to a Garden party on my arrival, to the same effect, saying however that I should be guided entirely by your judgement as to whether I should accept any invitation until my return in the fall.

I will probably go over to Paris on the 6th of July, but will telegraph or write you the exact time of my departure. The rail-road company here haves been kind enough to ask me to accept a special train to Dover and from Calais to Paris, which will probably put me in advance of the regular train.

I hope Mrs. Washburne has improved since your letter was written, and that we will find her and the children quite well on our arrival.

With kindest regards to yourself and family,

I am, very Truly
your obt. svt.
U. S. GRANT

ALS, IHi. On June 18, 1877, Elihu B. Washburne wrote to USG. "That will be a good time to come—after the 4th of July, say about the 6th. I think it should be understood that you are here briefly *en passant* and that it would be unwise to receive any demonstrations but to keep as quiet as possible. If it were known that you wa[s] here having public or *quasi* public entertainments by your countrymen before your presence should be officially announced to the Government, it would create a false impression. But I will write hereafter more particularly in respect of this matter before [*that time comes.*] I am only anxious that nothing should be done during this transient visit which will take off the edge of your reception when you come to make your longer stay in October. If Gov. Noyes do not come out till after his confirmation, I will be here at that time. He may, however, not be willing to wait so long and he may come before. He will find lively times when he does come. I hardly dare to speak out all I think in regard to the situation here, and I do not write anything to be quoted. I was at the chamber on Saturday and it seems to me that the scenes enacted there can but be the prelude of the most fearful events in France—No man not present can have an idea of the violence, the madness and the ruffianism of the opposition to the Republicans. It was in organized disorder by that faction which feels itself assured of the support of the supreme power of the Government, backed by half a million of armed men obedient to its behests. The assembly is certain to be dissolved and for their demands the country [*might*] be convulsed by the most terrible excitement. The new election must be within three months from the date of the dissolution. I am glad to say that Mrs. W. is much better of her cold, but her voice is not yet entirely restored. She will be so glad to see you and Mrs. Grant, not to say anything about my old friend, 'Uncle Jesse Dubois,' who perhaps has outgrown his old designation. She unites with me in kindest regards." ALS (press), DLC-Elihu B. Washburne. See letters to Elihu B. Washburne, June 9, 22, 1877.

To Ulysses S. Grant, Jr.

June 17th /77

Dear Buck,

It has been now more than a month since we left Phila and yet we have received but one letter from you—that written a day or two after we sailed—and not a line from any other member of the family. I wish you would all write as often as once a week even if you have but little to say. Your Ma is always anxious to hear. And just now she is anxious to learn whether your Aunt Anna has rec'd her money, and if she has paid over to you what she was to. That you were to invest in Anglo Cal. Bank stock if not to high.

As you will see by the papers we are having most enthusiastic receptions. At Liverpool, Manchester and Bath[1] there was about the the same sort of enthusiasm as was displayed at Phila on our departure. All the members of the govt. have invited us to dinner, and we have accepted up to the 3d of June. Invitations have also been received from all the cities in the Kingdom, and from a great many country houses through England & Scotland.[2]—We will go directly after the 4th of July to the Continent and visit Switzerland and run North to Denmark, Norway, Sweden, and to St. Petersburgh, and return here about the last of August. We will then do up Scotland, Ireland, Wales and the principle cities in England and go to Paris about the middle of Oct. We will visit Mr. Borie's friends there.[3] I would write to Mr. B. to-day if I had time, but we go to the country in the course of an hour or two to spend the afternoon—and to dine—with J. S. Morgan.[4] say to Mr. B. that I will write to him as soon as I get an hour or two when I can.—The *Cub* is able to hold his own in society.

Affectionately,

U. S. GRANT

ALS, USG 3.

1. On May 28, Nathan Smith, Bath, had written to USG. "As an American, I have feelings of intense satisfaction in hearing of your arrival in England, and that you are receiving a welcome, so nobly won for long and distinguished services to our country. My voice is but a feeble one, but I wish to do something to testify my debt of gratitude for all you have done for us. I live on account of my health in the quiet provincial town of Bath— It's a place of many attractions, and preserves some of its quaint old customs, handed down from the time of Beau Nash. Now will you, Mrs Grant, and your son come down and make us a little visit—My wife, who is an English lady joins most heartily in the request—I leave the time to you, merely stating that July and August finds our city deserted on account of the heat—June is delightful here. Rail Road time by Express is a little over two hours. I am sure Mrs Grant will be delighted with this part of England. Please excuse the liberty I have taken, . . ." ALS, DLC-John Russell Young. Smith had conducted a hardware business in New York City before retiring to England. See *New York Times*, April 26, 1878. On May 30, Wednesday, Mayor Jerom Murch of Bath wrote to USG. "As Mayor of Bath I hope I may be allowed to express a strong hope that you may be able to honour this city with a visit. I am sure you would be interested at any time in seeing our beautiful neighbourhood and that next week especially you would see it to great advantage. We are to have the hundreth anniversary of a very fine agricultural society. The exhibition will cover forty acres of ground and will be unusually good in horses, other animals of all kinds, machinery, pictures and flowers. I venture to inclose a card of invitation to an official banquet at which I expect many distinguished visitors. My friend and neighbour Mr. Cossham informs me that he would be happy to see you and your family at his house. The President of the Society (the Marquis of Lansdowne) and the Lord Lieutenant of Somersetshire (the Earl of Cork) are to be with me, and I trust I may have the honour of seeing you to meet them here if only for a short visit. By kindly favouring me with an early answer you will confer an additional obligation . . ." ALS, DLC-USG, IB. On the same day, Handel

Cossham, Bath, wrote to USG. "There is a very strong wish in our old City of Bath that you & Mrs Grant and your son should pay us a visit next Week at our Agricultural Show—and I write to support his Worship the Mayor in the official invitation you will receive with this—if you can come I hope you will allow me to show you hospitality I have a very vivid recolection of your kindness to me when we met at St Louis in 1865 (Sept)—I was then one of a party with Sir Morton Peto visiting your great country & you have since done me the honor to send me your valued and valuable reports on the late War—Bath is one of the most beautiful Cities in England and you wd see it in great perfection next Week—we are only 2½ hours run from London—What we should greatly like wd be for you to come down next Tuesday and at any rate stay with us till Wednesday—we will try to make your visit as agreeable as possible—and I hope leave on your mind Sunny recolections of Bath—" ALS, *ibid.* On the same day, Cossham wrote to Edwards Pierrepont, U.S. minister, London, on the same subject. ALS, *ibid.* See *PUSG*, 15, 319. On June 4, John W. N. Hervey wrote to USG. "I hear this morning from Bath that the good people there are most anxious to have the honor of welcoming you one day this week, and that there will be great grief if you should be unable to come. I am going down to Bath tomorrow morning, and it would be a real pleasure if I could carry with me the assurance that your engagements will not prevent you from giving the citizens of Bath and the agriculture of the West of England the gratification which they so much desire of seeing you and paying respect to you, and through you to the great country to which you belong. I feel that I have no right to trouble you with another personal interview on this subject, but a favourable answer would greatly oblige . . ." ALS, DLC-USG, IB. For Hervey, see *The Times* (London), Feb. 26, 1902.

On June 8, USG "expressed the great pleasure it gave him to visit Bath. He was greatly pained at the catastrophe which had happened the day before yesterday, and which had induced him to think that another occasion would have been more agreeable for his visit. He therefore telegraphed to that effect. He had, however, prepared to come that day. He was gratified to be there, and was much obliged for the reception accorded him." *Ibid.,* June 9, 1877. For the railroad bridge collapse in Bath, see *ibid.,* June 7, 1877.

On June 16, Cossham wrote to USG. "His Worship the Mayor of Bristol will call upon you next week with a view of trying to get you to pay the ancient City of Bristol a visit at your Earliest convenience—Bristol lies about 15 miles West of Bath and I can barely say how pleased we shall be to see you down here again Bristol is a great Commercial City—with four times the population of Bath—and she has lately built Iron Cars and Coaches with a view of competing with Liverpool for a share of the trade with your great Country my object in writing is two fold 1st To beg you to look favourably on the request of the Mayor that you should visit Bristol—and 2 To say that if you could do me the honor, of Coming to stay at Weston York Bath the night before your visit to Bristol I wd take care that you should have a quiet rest and an easy ride to Bristol the next day—so as to make your visit less fatigueing—if Mrs Grant & your Son can come with you it will be an additional pleasure to Mrs Cossham . . ." ALS, DLC-USG, IB.

2. On May 29, the directors of Alexandra Palace had invited USG. "Sir Edward Lee is directed by the Lessees of the Alexandra Palace to ask General Grant if it would be agreeable to him to accept an invitation to be present at a Great American Fête which the Lessees would like to organize in General Grant's honour during his stay in the Metropolis. Should General Grant be able to accept such an invitation Sir Edward Lee would be glad to be informed which day say in about a week or 10 days time would be most convenient." D, *ibid.* USG visited a horse show at Alexandra Palace on June 19. See *Daily Telegraph* (London), June 20, 1877; Ron Carrington, *Alexandra Park & Palace: A History* (London, 1975).

Probably in June, Windham Thomas Wyndham-Quin and his wife (Earl and Countess of Dunraven) invited USG and Julia Dent Grant for dinner on June 16. D (undated), DLC-John Russell Young. See Earl of Dunraven, *The Great Divide: Travels in the Upper Yellowstone in the Summer of 1874* (London, 1876).

On June 1, Joseph Dalton Hooker, president, Royal Society, London, invited USG to view new scientific instruments on June 13. D, DLC-USG, IB. USG did not attend. See *The Times* (London), June 14, 1877.

On June 2, H. Astley Hardinge, secretary, wrote to USG. "By direction of the Committee of the Army and Navy Club, I have the honor to invite you, and the gentlemen of your Staff, to become Honorary Visitors of the Club during your residence in London." ALS, DLC-John Russell Young. On the same day, Hardinge enclosed this "amended invitation" to Adam Badeau, consul gen., London, and requested the names of the gentlemen on USG's staff. ALS, DLC-USG, IB.

On June 4, Sydney Webb, Twickenham, wrote to USG. "By Command of H R. H the Prince of Wales a card of invitation has been forwarded to you, for the dinner at the Trinity House on the 23rd inst. This recalls to my mind, the very courteous & hospitable manner in which my late colleague Sir Fredk Arrow & myself, were received by you Sir, at the White House, on our official visit to America to report on the system of lighting that Coast, & more particularly the Fog signals. I feel sure that had my late valued friend Sir F. Arrow been alive, he would not have lost an opportunity of saying a word of welcome to you on your arrival in this Country. His successor Adml Sir Richd Collinson K. C. B our present Deputy Master, asks me to assure you what gratification it will afford all the Members of that Ancient Corporation to welcome you, within their walls, as they most fully appreciated the honor done to their Colleagues not only by yourself but by all the Authorities, with whom it was their good fortune to be thrown in Contact. Personally I hope to have the pleasure of thanking you again. And that it may be on the occasion on which you will honor us with your Company at Trinity House on the 23rd inst" ALS, *ibid.* On June 23, the Prince of Wales presided over "a grand banquet" at Trinity House. *The Times* (London), June 25, 1877. USG responded to speeches and toasts "in such a low voice as not to be heard distinctly, but he was understood to say that he felt more impressed than possibly he had ever felt before on any occasion. He came there under the impression that this was the Trinity House, and that the trinity consisted of the Army, the Navy, and Peace. He therefore thought it was a place of quietude, where there would be no talk or toasts. He had been therefore naturally surprised at hearing both one and the other. He had heard some remarks from his Royal Highness the president of the evening which compelled him to say one word in response to them. The remarks he referred to were complimentary to him. He begged to thank his Royal Highness for those remarks. There had been other things said during the evening highly gratifying to him. Not the least gratifying among them was to hear that there were occasionally in this country party fights as well as in America. He had seen before now as much as a war between the three departments of the State—the executive, the judicial, and the legislative departments. He had not seen the political parties of England go so far as that since he had come to this country. He would imitate their Chairman, who had set the good example of oratory—that was brevity—and say no more than simply to thank his Royal Highness and the company for the visitors." *Ibid.* See *New York Herald*, June 25, 1877.

On June 5, Thomas Hughes, London, had written to Badeau. "I enclose the reply to the invitation I sent last month on behalf of the Crystal Palace Co to await General Grant's arrival—Our Board were anxious to show him the same respect which we should to the representative of any friendly nation, & I need not say that my own sympathies would naturally make me prefer welcoming the surviving leader of your people in their great struggle to any other function of a like kind—I am sorry therefore that the matter shd have been overlooked. Should General Grant be inclined to visit the Crystal Palace we shall be glad to make any arrangements for his reception which may be suggested as agreeable to him, & I would see you as to details—Our next firework day is the 19th but we would gladly arrange for any other day which may suit him   " ALS, DLC-John Russell Young. On June 12, S. Flood Page, "Secretary & Manager" of the Crystal Palace, Sydenham, wrote to USG. "I have the honour, in accordance with the instructions which I have received from the Chairman, Mr Thomas Hughes, and the Directors, to request that you, Mrs Grant and Mr J. Grant will honour them with your company at an entertainment and dinner on Friday next 15th instant. There will be a short Concert and Fireworks." LS, DLC-USG, IB. On June 12 and 13, Page wrote to Badeau concerning the visit to Crystal Palace. LS, *ibid.* On June 15, Hughes toasted USG, who replied. "I think it is I who ought to propose the health of one who is well known in America, the author of 'Tom Brown.'" *The Times* (London), June 16, 1877. See *Young*, I, 27–28; *Julia Grant*, p. 205.

On June 9, USG had lunched with Lord Granville and John Bright. Bright wrote about USG on this occasion. "Pleasant chat with him, being next him at table. Talk on Mormon settlement and its industry, and beauty of Salt Lake City, 'The most beautiful city in the world,' said Gen. Grant." R. A. J. Walling, ed., *The Diaries of John Bright* (New York, 1931), p. 395.

On June 10, USG dined with Charles W. Dilke and others, including Isaac Butt, Irish party leader. See Stephen Gwynn and Gertrude M. Tuckwell, *The Life of the Rt. Hon. Sir Charles W. Dilke* (New York, 1917), I, 228.

On June 11, Marcus B. Huish, managing director, The Fine Art Society, London, invited USG "to view Miss Thompsons four Battle Pieces," assuring that with proper notice "his privacy should not be intruded on." ALS, DLC-USG, IB. Elizabeth Thompson was acclaimed for her military and equestrian paintings. An unrelated invitation, dated June 12, requested USG to meet Italian artists and other dignitaries on June 13. L (in French), *ibid.*

On June 15, Mayor Joseph Cook of St. Helens wrote to USG. "Being informed your Excellency purposes visiting Lancashire shortly it has occurred to me that having regard to the important trade in Glass and Chemicals carried on between this Town and the United States of America an inspection of some of the large Glass and other manufactories here might interest your Excellency. If so and it will suit your Excellency's Convenience to visit St. Helens (distant only Twelve miles from Liverpool) I should deem it an honour to be permitted to arrange for the inspection, and entertain your Excellency at Luncheon on any day your Excellency may appoint." ALS, *ibid.*

On June 16, Robert W. Fyers, secretary, Junior Army & Navy Club, wrote to USG. "I have the honor to inform you that the Committee have unanimously Elected you an Honorary Member of this Club—and I am directed to express a hope that you will accept the Invitation, and afford them the pleasure of making use of the Club." ALS, DLC-John Russell Young.

On June 20, James E. Sewell, vice chancellor, Oxford University, wrote to "Sir," possibly Badeau. "Professor H. J. Smith has today allowed me to see your letter to him; and I hasten to assure you, on my own part, that no such impression as that which you refer to has existed for a moment in my own mind, or, so far as I am aware, in the mind of any other Members of the University who had the opportunity of knowing the precise terms in which General Grant's regret at being unable to visit Oxford at the late Commemoration was most courteously expressed." ALS, *ibid.* On June 13, a correspondent had alluded to reports that USG "somewhat bluntly refused" an invitation to attend the commemoration at Oxford. *The Times* (London), June 14, 1877.

    3. Probably the family of John H. Harjes. See previous letter.

    4. Junius S. Morgan. See Vincent P. Carosso, *The Morgans: Private International Bankers 1854–1913* (Cambridge, Mass., 1987), especially p. 72.

To Richard W. Thompson

June 17th /77

My Dear Mr. Sec.

I am just in receipt of your very kind letter of the 28th of May informing me of the instructions given by the Department to the Commanders of the European, Asiatic and North Pacific Squadrons to facilitate and make pleasant my travels when appearing upon the waters embraced within their respective commands. I sincerely thank you for this courtecy and think it most probable that I will avail myself of it this coming winter while visiting ports upon the Medeteranien. Whether I do or not the obligation will be the same, and I will continue to recollect with feelings of gratitude your very kind action in this matter.

With kindest remembrances to your Chief, your Cabinet associates, and to yourself, I am,

        Very respectfully,
        your obt. svt.
        U. S. Grant

Hon. R. W. Thompson,
Sec. of the Navy

ALS, InFtwL. Secretary of the Navy Richard W. Thompson had been active in Ind. politics for several decades. See Mark E. Neely, Jr., "Richard W. Thompson: The Persistent Know Nothing," *Indiana Magazine of History*, LXXII, 2 (June, 1976), 95–122.

Speech

[*London, June 18, 1877*]

I am overwhelmed by the kindness shown to me in England, and not only to me, but to my country. I regret that I am unable adequately to express—even with the aid in doing so of the omnipresent enterprise of the New York *Herald*—to express my thanks for the courtesy I have received. I hope the opportunity may be afforded me, in calmer and more deliberate moments, to put on record my hearty recognition of the fraternal sentiments of the English people and the desire of America to render an adequate return. The speech of Lord Granville[1] has inspired thoughts which it is impossible for me adequately to present. Never have I lamented so much as now my poverty in phrases—my inability to give due expression of my affection for the mother country.

Young, I, 30; variant text in *New York Herald*, June 19, 1877. On June 19, 1877, a correspondent reported from London. "General Grant spoke under the pressure of unusual feeling and continued with unusual eloquence to express the hope that his words, so far as they had any value, would be heard in both countries and lead to the union of the English speaking peoples and the fraternity of the human race." *Ibid.* On June 5, W. Fraser Rae had invited USG to a dinner at the Reform Club, London, "on a day to be named by yourself, at 8 o'Clock, P. M." ALS, DLC-USG, IB. On the same day, Rae wrote to Adam Badeau, consul gen., London. ". . . I may add that the entertainment will be the most select, as well as notable & representative that has ever been given in the Club. The number present will not exceed about 30; no reporters will be present & everything will be done, to render the guests at home, which can be done in this country by those who have a sincere respect & admiration for their native land. I hope that you will help in persuading General Grant to accept the invitation for the day suggested, the 20th, & that you will endeavour to be present also. May I hint that General Grant's *autograph* acceptance would specially please the important body in whose name I write. As an unusual matter of this kind necessitates many arrangements, an early reply will be as pleasant as the acceptance of the invitation. . . ." ALS, *ibid.*

1. Lord George Granville, British foreign secretary during the later *Alabama* Claims negotiations and a Liberal Party leader, presided over the Reform Club dinner. See John Russell Young diary, June 18, 1877, DLC-John Russell Young; *New York Herald*, June 19, 1877.

To Hamilton Fish

June 22d /77

My Dear Governor.

I have been intending for the last two weeks to drop you & Mrs. Fish a line to say how we have passed our time since arriving in England but have been kept from doing so, until now, by constant engagements and a little by a disposition to procrastinate. The ~~American~~ papers have kept the public very well acquainted with all the receptions and invitations I am offered so that it is not necessary that I should give any description. But my reception has been remarkable in two respects: first by invitations from all authorities connected with the Govt. from the Queen down to the Mayors & City Councils of almost every City in the United Kingdom;[1] and second by the hearty responces of the citizens of all the cities I have visited, or at which trains upon which I have been traveling have stoped even for a few minuest. It has been very much as it was in the United States in /65, directly after the war. I take this as indicative of a present very good feeling towards the U. S. Many persons say to me quietly that they personally were our good friends in the day of our countries trial but they witness now many who were the reverse then that outdo their neighbors in respect and kindness of feeling for us now. Of course I know this is so, but I can understand that the south was purely Agricultural before the war, paid no attenti[on] to manufacturies, and were free traders. Self interest taught them that with separation they would reap large benefits from trade—almost exclusive—with the Southern Confederacy. I believe now the real feeling of the majority is that it i[s] much better that the result should have been in favo[r] of the Union.

My engagements will keep me here until the 5th of July. I then go to Switzerland for a few weeks, thence to Norway, Sweeden & Denmark and back here to see Scotland, Ireland and parts of England not yet visited. I shall endeavor to avoid demonstrations—even if they are offered—as much as possible hereafter.

I received a letter from Mr. Davis[2] and one from Mr. Nicholas

Fish soon after my arrival here welcoming me and asking me to visit them before they leave, the tone of both indicating an expectation of leaving where they are in the fall. I see however, to-day, that Nicholas has been appointed to Switzerland.[3] I hope this may be so and that I may meet him there.

I will be very glad to hear from you at any time you find leasure to write.

Mrs. Grant joins me in kindest regards to Mrs. Fish, Miss Edith and your family generally, and believe me,

Faithfully Yours

U. S. GRANT

HON. HAMILTON FISH.

ALS, DLC-Hamilton Fish. Written on stationery of "16, Beaufort Gardens. S. W.," Adam Badeau's London residence. See letter to Hamilton Fish, Sept. 9, 1877.

On Aug. 7, 1877, Hamilton Fish wrote to Edwards Pierrepont, U.S. minister, London. ". . . Well—you have had General Grant with you—no doubt you had troublous points of etiquette & ceremony to arrange—but you seem to have used your accustomed prudence & tact & disposed of them—The General's reception in Europe is highly gratifying to his friends. Even those who did not love him over much that is, not more than did some of the Liberal Republicans, take to themselves comfort, from his reception, in the idea that it is all meant as a tribute to the 'American people' of which they are part, ergo, the compliment is to them & therefore proper—. . ." ALS (press), DLC-Hamilton Fish.

1. On June 18, when USG breakfasted as the guest of George W. Smalley, *New York Tribune* correspondent, others in attendance included Thomas H. Huxley, Matthew Arnold, Robert Browning, and Anthony Trollope. See *New York Herald*, June 19, 1877.

On June 19, John Russell Young had written in his diary. ". . . I made the arrangement for General Grant to visit the *Times* office. I went to the office, and Grant came in about 11.30 with Badeau. We drove to the office and we were received by Mr MacDonald. We went through the various parts of the building and saw the press at work. Gen Grant much pleased and said he himself had been a printer as a lad. Made fun of me about my foot and gave me a message for Mr Bennett which I sent him." DLC-John Russell Young.

Also on June 19, Albert Chancellor wrote to USG. "As the Honorary Secretary of the Richmond Horticultural Society I am directed by the Committee respectfully to ask permission to present to yourself, and Mrs Grant, an invitation to visit their forthcoming show of Plants, Flowers, Fruit, Table Decorations and Cottagers Productions, which is to be held on Thursday the 28th instant in the Old Deer Park Richmond Surrey. . . ." ALS, USG 3.

On June 21, George Fox, Lichfield, wrote to USG. "On two occasions of my visits to Washington you did me the honor to receive me on the introductions of my late chief and partner Mr A. T. Stewart of New York and of my friends Mr George Childs and Mr George Stuart of Philadelphia I dont imagine you will recollect me, but I remember with much pleasure the courtesy and honor you did to the introductions. On the 5th July I am holding a public sale of Short Horn Cattle including Some of my American importations, and of the most celebrated American Blood,   on the 4th July the Duke of Manchester and Lords Dunmore, Bective &c honor me as guests.   the object of this is you to accept the hospitality of my House for the 4th & 5th July—the 4th in time for Dinner, and to be present at the Sale on the 5th   I have on the other side the Atlantic many friends favorably known to you, and, if you honor me with your company I am sure it will be accepted as a graceful compliment to them. Mrs Fox, herself an American, will be highly honor'd to receive you." ALS, DLC-USG, IB. See *New York Times*, June 1, 1894.

Also on June 21, Maj. Gen. Julius Raines, British Army, and chairman, Wanderers' Club, wrote to USG. "The Committee of the Wanderers Club trust that you & your Staff will do them the honor of considering yourselves Honorary Members of this Club during your Stay in Engand" ALS, DLC-USG, IB. See *Dickens's Dictionary of London, 1879* (1879; reprinted, London, 1972), p. 269.

On June 22, S. Lockhart, honorary secretary, Clerks Club, London, wrote to USG. "You will not be surprised to learn that the Clerks of London (75,000 in number) have followed your career throughout with keen interest   The young Gentlemen of America, who followed your Standard personally, can alone feel more than the Gentlemen I have the honour to represent. We are desirous of obtaining the privilege of expressing our admiration of the General, whose leadership crushed slavery, whose Presidentship re-united your great Country. If you will allow us to say so much personally, and present you with a Ticket of Honorary Membership, we shall be very proud of the opportunity at any date convenient to yourself.—We intend to have appropriate Music and Martial Readings.— the whole ceremony occupying about one evening hour." LS (on a printed "Honorary Member's Ticket"), DLC-John Russell Young.

2. J. C. Bancroft Davis, minister to Germany, spent part of the summer away from Berlin on leave as he prepared to resign his position. See letter to Elihu B. Washburne, July 13, 1877; Davis to William B. Evarts, June 11 (twice), July 1, 25, Aug. 1, 13, Sept. 24, 1877, DNA, RG 59, Diplomatic Despatches, Germany.

3. On July 5, Nicholas Fish, Berlin, wrote to his father concerning his appointment as chargé d'affaires to Switzerland. "Personal & Unofficial. . . . Beyond your letters and what I read in the newspapers I know nothing of my appointment to Berne or when I am expected to go there. . . ." ALS, DLC-Hamilton Fish. On Aug. 2, Davis, Berlin, wrote to Secretary of State William M. Evarts concerning Fish's departure for Bern that evening. ALS, DNA, RG 59, Diplomatic Despatches, Germany. See Nicholas Fish to Evarts, May 25, July 24, 30, 1877, *ibid.*; Evarts to Hamilton Fish, June 15, 1877, DLC-Hamilton Fish.

To Elihu B. Washburne

———

June 22d /77

My Dear Mr. Washburne.

I have determined to leave here for Paris, on my way to Switzerland, on the 5th of July. The S. Eastern rail-road company haves been kind enough to put a special train & boat at my service,[1] which will put us through from London to Paris in eight hours. I want, as you advise, to have it understood that for the present I will be in Paris this time simply in transitu and will make my visit of several weeks at a later period, probably about the middle or last of October.—My party will consist of Mrs. Grant & maid, Jesse & myself, and a courier who will look out for himself. Our stay will not exceed three days. You were kind enough to propose to engage apartments for us during our short stay! Will you be good enough to make them according to the above programme and advise me before my arrival.

    With kindest regards to yourself & family, I remain,

Very Truly Yours

U. S. Grant

ALS, IHi. On June 25, 1877, Elihu B. Washburne wrote to USG. "Please let me know in Season at what *hour* you will arrive here on the 5th July, so we can meet you at the depot. Our lease expiring, and intending to go home this Summer, we gave up our house last fall; otherwise we should have insisted upon you and your family as our guests while in Paris. We are now occupying, in awaiting our departure, a simple little *entresol* where we can pack up our 'duds.' I shall engage you nice quarters at an excellent hotel at a moderate price. Whenever we speak of your coming here, it will be merely as passing through, as you will want to avoid all demonstration. If you arrive Thursday night the 5th July, you will not, probably want to leave til the next Monday morning. If Mrs Grant wants to do any shopping while here, Mrs. Washburne will expect to place herself at her disposition. On Friday night we shall expect you to dine with us simply *en famille*. Mr Hitt, my Secretary of Legation, would be very glad to have you dine with him on Saturday and Genl. Torbert on Sunday, both *en famille*, the same as with me, for we all think it would not be well on this brief visit, to have any *formal* dinner. Should this be agreeable to you, it would be an answer to invitations to formal dinners that you might receive. I hope the weather here when you come will be as delightful as it is now, for then you can see Paris at its best—by far the most charming city in the world. I trust when you come for your visit in the fall, matters will be settled, but I confess that to me the outlook is very inquieting. Mrs. W. begs to join me again in kindest regards to Mrs. Grant and yourself." ALS (press), DLC-Elihu B. Washburne. On June 27, Adam Badeau, consul gen., London, wrote to Washburne. "Gen Grant wishes me to say that the programme of quiet dinners you have proposed for him in Paris will be very acceptable to him. He will as you suppose, probably leave Paris on Monday; and will advise you duly of the exact time of his departure from London and arrival in Paris. He has himself acknowledged the receipt of your letter to me, which of course I laid before him. He appreciated all you had to say, and I may add confidentially has been very much gratified at the kind interest you take in his visit." ALS, *ibid.* On the same day, Washburne wrote to Badeau. "Please call Genl Grants' attention to this letter and write me his wishes in regard of what Mr Byer says. Since the death of Mr. Upton at Geneva a few days ago, we now have only two consuls in Switzerland, and no minister. The consuls are at Zurich and Basle. Capt. Byers, who writes the letter, is a first rate consul and is the author of 'Sherman's march to the Sea.'" ALS (press), *ibid.*

    On June 30, Saturday, Washburne wrote to USG. "This will be handed to you on Monday morning by Genl Torbert, who will explain to you the object of it more fully than I can do in writing. He will express the opinion of all our friends here that it will be un-

wise for you to come to Paris at present, even *in transitu.* Though we have never spoken of
your coming, it has been announced in the Paris Journals that you are to be here next week.
It will be impossible for you to come here in anywise *incognito* and without having a demonstration, no matter how short a time you may stay. When it becomes known that you are
here, and if you do not call on the President, the Republican papers will say it is because
you are not in sympathy with his *Coup d'Etat,* and if you do call upon him the reactionary
papers will claim that it is to signify your approval of his action. Indeed, such is the excited
state of public feeling here that each party will want to play you off on the other, and there
is danger of much embarrassment following, and the effect of your visit at a later day will
be much impaired. I have talked with many of our best friends here on the subject and they
all concur in the view herein expressed. Mr. Boker is so impressed with it he asked me to
use his name with you. I need not tell you how greatly disappointed Mrs. Washburne and
myself will be not to see yourself and Mrs. Grant here, but knowing the situation of things,
I should be unjust to you, as well as the country which is so much interested in all that concerns your reception abroad, did I not speak frankly in the premises. By the time you will
want to come here in the fall I hope the political situation of the country, now so critical,
will be greatly ameliorated, when you will have a reception worthy of you and of our country. *Now,* it would be impossible. In going to Switzerland you would find it very pleasant
in going by Brussels and up the Rhine and passing a few days at Hamburg and Frankfort.
At the latter place you would have a very fine reception, for a large number of German
Americans are living there. Should you stay there any time I might have the pleasure of
meeting you when on my way to Carlsbad about the middle of July. But as I said, General
Torbert will explain to you fully the views we all take of this matter. I would have been
glad to run over to London and talk with you myself, but Mrs. Washburne is far from well
and we are all so busy every day of our lives in getting ready to go home." ALS, DLC-John
Russell Young. USG postponed his visit to Paris and instead went to Switzerland via Belgium and Germany.

On July 6, Edwards Pierrepont, U.S. minister, London, wrote to Washburne. "There
seems such a hitch about Paris that I showed Gen. Grant your letters as you desired &
which I at first did not intend to do as I wrote you—He assures me that he has no recollection of seeing the Herald Reporter and is sure that he did not say as reported—He
thinks he did not see the reporter at all—But if he has not done so before this reaches you
I do not doubt he will write—I told him that I should write you that I had shown him your
letters and that at first I had written you that I was unwilling to do so—He left yesterday
for Brussells He has been with Gen. Badeau since the 22 of June, 'till then he was at my
house. Shall you be in London this Summer & if so about when—" ALS, DLC-Elihu B.
Washburne. On July 6, a correspondent reported from Paris. "General Grant was originally expected to come to Paris from London, but the *Mémorial Politique* explains that he
resolved, on the advice of Mr. Washburne, the United States Ambassador, to defer his visit
here till after his tour in Northern Europe and Switzerland. It was feared that, 'in existing
circumstances, there would be endeavours to give to some of the demonstrations of which
he might be the object a character other than that of disinterested deference for an illustrious citizen who has held the chief magistracy of his country and is one of its mili[ta]ry
glories.' In other words there was a fear th[at] ex-President Grant would be played off
against P[re]sident MacMahon. General Grant re[ac]hed Brussels this evening." *The
Times* (London), July 7, 1877. See *New York Herald,* June 20, 29–30, July 4–5, 1877.

1. On June 27, 4:00 P.M., Charles Sheath, South Eastern Railway, had written to
Badeau. "Sir Edward Watkin—who has been in the North & is now leaving for Dover
wished me to say that he has now only got your note of the 25th—It will give him very

great pleasure to make all the necessary arrangements to ensure General Grant having a comfortable journey to Paris in daylight on Thursday the 5th July next—Sir Edward will send to you on Friday morning early a programme shewing the times of departure from London & arrival in Paris &c &c—and if necessary will see you personally—" ALS, DLC-USG, IB. See *The Times* (London), July 6, 1877.

To Edwards Pierrepont

June 27th /77

My Dear Judge.

I will not attend the Queen's Concert this evening[1] because I must be up early to-morrow morning to take the train for Liverpool where I am to attend a bBanquet at 7 O'Clock in the evening. After the Banquet my party go some six miles to the country for the night, and return to the city in the morning in time for the early train so as to be back in time to be present at a dinner party given to me in the evening.[2] I will make my apologies in the morning of course, but write you so that you may be able—if questions are asked—to make the explanation.

I explained this to the Duches of Wellington[3] while at Windsor Castle to-day or last evening.

Very Truly Yours
U. S. Grant

Hon. Edwards Pierrepont, Minister &c.

ALS, OHi. On June 27, 1877, Edwards Pierrepont, U.S. minister, London, wrote to Secretary of State William M. Evarts. "On the last day of May Ex-President Grant arrived in London and was my guest until the 22nd day of June. Learning of his proposed visit some twenty days before his arrival, I un-officially talked with Lord Derby the Minister of Foreign Affairs upon the subject and with others members of the Queen's Government. In a country like England where precedence and forms are of substance I deemed it important that one who had lately been the President of the United States should receive the same consideration as the Ex-Chief Ruler of a Kingdom or an Empire receives when he visits England. At first I was met with the objection that an Ex-President having no acknowledged rank or precedence in his own country could not have any here. I suggested that Louis Napoleon was an elected Ruler and not a hereditary Emperor and that as Ex-Emperor he had an acknowledged precedence in England. This was met by the remark 'Once an Emperor always an Emperor': to which I replied: 'then, once a President always a President, and as President all embarrassment about recognition would disappear.' Every disposition so to adjust the matter as to be most complimentary to our Country was every where manifested and the Queen, the Prince of Wales and every member of the British Government so far as I could see, have been most cordial in their reception of the Ex-President of the Great Republic and he has been received with all the honors accorded to an Ex-Emperor. The freedom of the City of London was bestowed upon the Ex-President with great ceremony at GuildHall, the Lord Mayor presiding. Yesterday General and Mrs Grant, the American Minister and Mrs Pierrepont were invited to dine with the Queen at Windsor Castle and to remain until to day, which we did and returned to London this forenoon. These courtesies as well as those of the Prince of Wales and of the Queen's Ministers of State were intended as friendly compliments to our Country and have their uses. Gen. Grant leaves London for Paris on the 5th of July." LS, DNA, RG 59, Diplomatic Despatches, Great Britain. *Foreign Relations, 1877*, pp. 261–62. On June 26, Edward H. Stanley, Earl of Derby, had attended the party at Windsor Castle and commented on USG. "He is certainly the roughest specimen we have yet had from the west. Any one who had seen him today would have said that his manners & intelligence were about on a par with those of a bulldog." John Vincent, ed., *A Selection from the Diaries of Edward Henry Stanley, . . .* (London, 1994), p. 412. For Queen Victoria's unflattering opinion of Julia Dent Grant and Jesse Root Grant, Jr., see Elizabeth Longford, *Queen Victoria: Born to Succeed* (New York, 1964), p. 420. See also *New York Herald*, June 27–28, 1877; *Daily Telegraph* (London), June 28, 1877; Wickham Hoffman to Hamilton Fish, Aug. 6, 1877, DLC-Hamilton Fish; *Julia Grant*, pp. 206–8; Jesse R. Grant, *In the Days of My Father General Grant* (New York, 1925), pp. 221–30; *Young*, I, 32–34.

On June 27, USG, London, wrote to Governor John F. Hartranft of Pa., Providence, R. I. "Grateful for telegram. Conveyed message to the Queen. Thank my old comrades." Herman Dieck, *Life and Public Services of General U. S. Grant* (Cincinnati, 1885), p. 461; Robert B. Beath, *History of the Grand Army of the Republic* (New York, 1889), p. 177. On June 26, Hartranft had telegraphed to USG. "Your comrades in National Encampment assembled in Providence Rhode-Island send heartiest greetings to their old commander and desire through Englands Queen to thank England for Grants reception—" Telegram received, DLC-USG, IB. USG endorsed this telegram. "Rec'd at Windsor Castle at 7.55 June 26th" AE (undated), *ibid.*

1. On June 21, Sir John Cowell, Master of the Queen's Household, Windsor Castle, had written to Adam Badeau, consul gen., London. "I have just telegraphed to you to say that, in consequence of the State Concert on the 27th The Queen will not expect general Grant or Mrs Grant to dinner here on that day.—I shall make known to The Queen the general's Engagement at Liverpool on the 28th—He could leave here as early as convenient to him any morning after dining with Her Majesty & when he does do so, this would be quite understood by The Queen.—" L, *ibid.* On the same day, Cowell telegraphed to Badeau on the same subject. Telegram recieved, *ibid.* See *The Times* (London), Aug. 30, 1894.

2. John Russell Young had invited journalists to a dinner for USG at Grosvenor Hotel, London. A menu and replies to Young's invitation from James Bryce, James Macdonell, Thomas Walker, Thomas J. Capel, Justin McCarthy, George C. Brodrick, William Stebbing, John Morley, and Henry W. Lucy are in DLC-John Russell Young. On June 29, Young wrote in his diary. ". . . Arose today nervous about my dinner to Grant. Despatch from Badeau asking me to ask Fairchild which I did. Then to see Smalley and we talked over the final arrangements. . . . To Badeau's & talked precedence with him, and to the Grosvenor early. Despatch from Conkling. Grant, & Badeau came early. . . . We had no speeches. Capel said grace, and Grant was in talkative mood. Conkling and Pierrepont

came in late on account of a blunder of Pierrepont. . . ." *Ibid.* See *ibid.*, June 15–17, 20–21, 28, 1877; Badeau to Young, June 17, 24, 25, 26, 1878, *ibid.*; *Young*, I, 35–40; McCarthy, *Reminiscences* (New York, 1899), I, 244–47; Moncure Daniel Conway, *Autobiography: Memories and Experiences* (Boston, 1904), II, 368–70.

    3. Elizabeth Hay married Arthur Richard Wellesley, the eventual second Duke of Wellington, in 1839 and served Queen Victoria as Mistress of the Robes. See *The Times* (London), Aug. 15, 1904.

Speech

                                                [*Liverpool, June 28, 1877*]

Throughout the land my reception has been far beyond anything that I could have expected to have been accorded to me. A soldier must die, and when a President's term of office expires he is but a dead soldier; but I have received an attention and a reception that would have done honour to any living person. I feel that that has been paid not to me, but to the country from which I hail. I feel that in this moment a good feeling and sentiment should exist between these two peoples above all others, and that they should be good friends. We are of one kindred, one blood, one language, and one civilization. In some particulars we believe that being younger we surpass you; but being older you have made improvments in the soil and the surface of the earth which we shall not take so long to do as it took you. That is our judgment. I have heard some military remarks which have impressed me not a little. You have got as many troops down at Aldershott as we have in the Army of the United States, and we have several thousand miles of frontier and hostile Indians to contend with; but if even it became necessary to raise an Army, we should get men from the volunteers and the reserves. General Fairchild[1] and myself are samples of the volunteers that spring up when the necessity arises. I will now propose his health along with that of the Mayor.[2]

The Times (London), June 29, 1877; variant text in *Young*, I, 34–35. On June 1, 1877, Mayor A. Barclay Walker of Liverpool wrote to USG. "I duly received your favor of the 29th ult. asking me to include General Badeau in my list of guests for the Banquet on the 28th inst and I have great pleasure in doing so. I am coming up to London next week for a few weeks and hope to have the pleasure of waiting upon you. I am glad to see the daily reports of your popularity in this country With kind regards to Mrs Grant . . ." ALS, DLC-USG, IB. On June 25, Walker wrote to Adam Badeau, consul gen., London. "I am in receipt of your favor of the 23rd inst. informing me that General Grant will leave London at 10 AM on Thursday the 28th inst that train I see reaches the Central Station here at 3.45. which will give General Grant and his party ample time to go out to my residence and rest and dress for the Dinner at The Town Hall at Seven of E and returning to Gateacre Grange to sleep for the night. I hope the General will accept my private hospitality as well as at The Town Hall but if it is not convenient for him to do so will you kindly favor me with line" ALS, *ibid.* On the same day, Elisa Walker, Gateacre Grange, wrote to Julia Dent Grant. "I hope you will feel able to come with General Grant on Friday. I would meet you at Edge Hill Station and we can go in to the Town Hall later in the evening if the General cannot come here to dress. It will be a great disappointment to me, and also to the Ladies of Liverpool were *you* not to be present at my husband's Banquet on Friday and I think *your husband* would like you to be there—Please write and say by return that you are coming and by what train, and if you can stay a day or two with us, I need not add that we should feel highly honoured. Liverpool being your *stepping stone* to England I think you will always have a warm heart to the Town. You have a deal of hard work to go through, and I hope your strength will keep up, to enable you to go through it all Will you kindly reply by return of post . . ." ALS, *ibid.* Julia Grant did not make this trip. See *Daily Telegraph* (London), June 29, 1877.

On June 22, Mayor Richard Nicholson of Southport had written to USG. "I understand from an invitation which I have received from The Worshipful the Mayor of Liverpool; that I am to have the honour of meeting you at dinner on the 28th Inst—It has therefore occured to me that you might be induced to visit for a few hours our 'Montpelier of the North', if so, I as The Chief Magistrate, as well as the Corporation of Southport, will feel honoured to receive you any time you may appoint, . . ." LS, DLC-USG, IB.

1. Lucius Fairchild served as col., 2nd Wis., receiving promotion to brig. gen., and as governor of Wis. (1866–72) before his appointment as consul, Liverpool. See *PUSG*, 19, 426; Sam Ross, *The Empty Sleeve: A Biography of Lucius Fairchild* (Madison, Wis., 1954), pp. 157–69.

On June 19, 1877, Fairchild wrote to USG, London. "I have just returned from my trip through the Mediteranean & I am sure I need not tell you how much I regret being absent when you arrived at Liverpool. . . ." ALS, DLC-USG, IB. On the same day, Fairchild wrote to Badeau. ". . . I love the General & will be most happy if I can contribute to the pleasure of the stay in England—I am glad to see that you are in attendance on him as I feel sure you can do so much towards making all concerned happy. And I hope we may have the pleasure of seeing you here. Mrs Fairchild joins me in kind regards" ALS, *ibid.*

2. After prospering as a brewer, Mayor Walker became an active Liverpool politician and benefactor. See *The Times* (London), Feb. 28, 1893.

To Ulysses S. Grant, Jr.

————

London July 2d *1877*

Dear Buck,

I have not written more frequently because the papers have kept you fully advised of our every movement. The labor has been hard to keep up with social requirements,[1] but it leaves a pleasant reflection behind. Every city of any prominence has sent me cordial invitations to visit them, and the local papers have been most complimentary in their allusions to both me and the country. The hard part with me has been the occasion to say something so often, and lacking the practice and the confidence to speak before an audience.

On the 5th of July we leave here to go to Switzerland. Our address will be Drexel, Harjis &co. Paris. I have stated to you before as much as I know of our line of travel for the present. We will be back in England the latter part of August to "do up Scotland and Ireland, and the cities in England not already visited. Jesse is now down with Nellie to stay until we start. He has not mailed his second letter to the Inter-Ocean, although he has written considerable, and done it very well.

We have not had a letter from Fred since we left home. Ida has written one letter.—I see Mr Childs has given the most of my letter to him to the press. There is nothing objectionable in it though I did not expect it to be published.[2] Give my regards to Mr. Drexel & Childs, to Judge Davies and to all the gentlemen in the office associated with you,[3] and do'nt forget our good friends Mr. Rodgers[4] and his family.

We are all very well and send much love to you. If Fred is not on the plains, blow him up for not writing.

Yours affectionately
U. S. Grant

U. S. Grant Jr.

ALS, CSmH.
    On July 18, 1877, Frederick Dent Grant, Chicago, wrote to Ulysses S. Grant, Jr., concerning a geometry problem. ALS, USG 3.

1. On June 23, Aaron Buzacott, secretary, Anti-Slavery Society, London, wrote to USG. "The Committee of the Anti Slavery Society have invited Mr William Lloyd Garrison, to meet several Members of Parliament, and other friends who have taken an active part in the Anti Slavery Movement to a breakfast at the Devonshire Street Hotel, on Tuesday morning next at quarter past ten oclock They would esteem it a great favour if you will favour them with your presence on this occasion I enclose a card of admission On behalf of the Committee, . . ." ALS, DLC-USG, IB. At this breakfast on June 26, Buzacott read apologies from USG and John Bright "containing warm expressions of respect for the veteran Abolitionist." *The Times* (London), June 27, 1877.

On June 23, Thomas B. Potter, Cobden Club, London, had written to USG. "I am requested by the Committee of the Cobden Club to ask you whether it would be agreeable to you to accept an invitation to dine with the Club at the annual dinner, to be held this year at the Ship Hotel Greenwich, on the 21st of July under the Presidency of the Marquis of Hartington. You know the objects of the Cobden Club—Peace & Free Trade—but it is possible that you may object to identify yourself with us. I therefore write this letter to you before sending a formal invitation" ALS, DLC-USG, IB. For Potter and the Cobden Club, see *The Times* (London), Nov. 8, 1898.

On June 28, William Sowerby, secretary, Royal Botanic Society, London, wrote to Adam Badeau, consul gen., London. "The Special Fête of the Season will take place in these Gardens on Wednesday next July 4th It is the only day during the whole year on which the Gardens are illuminated, and the Council thought it probable that General Grant or the Members of the General's Family might be pleased to honour the Society by visiting the Gardens on the occasion if even only for a short time The Gardens are open from 8 to 12 that evening—Should the General find it agreeable to visit the Gardens may I trouble you kindly to let me know the hour selected that the necessary arrangements may be made—" ALS, DLC-USG, IB. On June 4, Sowerby had invited USG to visit the gardens with his family whenever convenient. LS, *ibid.*

On June 29, Frederick A. Eaton, Royal Academy of Arts, London, wrote to USG. "I am directed by the President & Council of the Royal Academy to express to you their hope that they may be honoured by the presence of yourself & Mrs Grant & the members of your suite at the Annual Soirée of the Royal Academy on Wednesday July 4th" ALS, *ibid.*

On June 30, Francis H. Goldsmid, St. John's Lodge, London, wrote to Badeau. "If you think that Genl Grant & Mrs Grant would honor me by coming to the garden party on 12th July I will have great pleasure in sending you cards for them. I hope to see you at all events" ALS, *ibid.* See *The Times* (London), May 4, 1878.

2. See letter to George W. Childs, June 6, 1877.

3. Henry E. Davies, former judge, N. Y. Supreme Court and Court of Appeals, directed a law firm in New York City that included Ulysses S. Grant, Jr. For letterhead, see Davies to James A. Garfield, Nov. 10, 1880, DLC-James A. Garfield.

4. Charles H. Rogers.

Speech

[*London, July 3, 1877*]

GENTLEMEN—In the name of my country I thank you for the address which you have just presented to me. I feel that you are paying a compliment to the form of government which I represented, as well as to myself personally. Since my arrival on British soil I have received great attention, intended, I feel, in the same way—that is, for my country. I have received attentions and have had ovations and presentations from different classes, from the governing classes, and from the controlling authorities of your cities as well as from the general public; but there is no reception that I have met with which I am prouder of than this one to-day. I recognise the fact that, whatever there is of greatness in the United States, or indeed in any other country, is due to the labour performed, and to the labourer who is the author of all greatness and wealth, and without whom there would be no governing, no leading classes, nor anything worth the trouble of preserving. With us labour is regarded as highly respectable. When it is not so regarded it is where the man dishonours the labour. We recognise that labour dishonours no man; and, whatever a man's occupation, he is eligible for any post in the gift of the people, his calling being left out of consideration when it is a question of electing him as a law maker or an executor of the law. Now, gentlemen, all I can do in conclusion is to renew my thanks for your address, and to repeat that I have received nothing from any class since my arrival in England that has given me more pleasure.

Daily Telegraph (London), July 4, 1877; variant text in *The Times* (London), July 4, 1877, and *Young,* I, 40–41. On July 3, 1877, USG received a printed "Address of Welcome" from Daniel Guile *et al.* "The British Workmen feel that they cannot permit your visit to this Country to terminate, without expressing to you the pleasure it affords them of having this opportunity of paying their respects, and offering the gratitude of a liberty loving people, to one who happily possesses such distinguished claims to their esteem and admiration. We are lovers of Peace but in the noble struggle in which your genius and skill placed your name at the head of military commanders, and made it a household word in this Country, to be handed down from generation to generation, we looked upon your successes as our success. It was not difficult for us to understand that although the scene of conflict was confined to the American States, its results would affect the whole world; the interests of the entire Human family, of whatever colour or race, were at stake; it not only gave freedom to the slave, and consolidated the power of a great nation, but it enobled labour of all countries, and broadened the liberties of the free. The noble generosity of your country-men, in the midst of their life and death struggle, in sending food to the starving opera-tives of Lancashire, will never be forgotten by the British people, and will ever reflect to the Honour of the American Republic. We venture to say that your distinguished bravery in the field was only equalled by your magnanimity to the vanquished, and that your vic-tories were enlarged by the conditions made with the defeated. We earnestly hope that the exemplary peace then made, will never be broken in your Country, but that the prosperity which can only result from peaceful industry, will bless the nation which so amply vindi-cated the highest justice, and concluded its holy war without a stain on its fair escutcheon. The Working-men honour you as a representative Citizen of the American Republic, who has twice been called upon to fulfil the high office of Chief Magistrate of forty-millions of free people; and permit us to congratulate You upon the reasonable and just settlement during your term of office, of some apparent difficulties, which existed between your Coun-try and the British Government; a settlement which we feel convinced is destined to ex-ercise a civilizing and lasting influence on International Relations. We take this opportu-nity of assuring you of our sincere good wishes and deep regard for the welfare and progress of your Country in which British Workmen have ever found a kindly welcome and a peaceful home. We therefore assure you of our deep sense of the honour conferred upon us by this visit, and of our wish that your sojourn in Europe may be a pleasing one, your journey home, a safe one, and that your valued life may be for many years spared to your Country and your Family." D (58 names), Smithsonian Institution. On July 4, a cor-respondent reported from London. "A deputation of forty men, each representing a differ-ent trade, and representing altogether about one million English workingmen, waited on ex-President Grant, at Consul General Badeau's house yesterday, and presented him an address, welcoming him to England, and assuring him of their good wishes and deep re-gard for the welfare and progress of America, where British workmen had always found a welcome. Impromptu speeches were then made by various members of the deputation, all of which were extremely cordial." *New York Herald*, July 4, 1877.

On June 16, Henry Broadhurst, Labour Representation League, London, had written to USG. "Not having received a reply to my letter of the 5th inst asking of you the favour of a short interview for the purpose of ascertaining whether you would receive a deputa-tion from the Working men of London to bid you a welcome to this country, I fear the let-ter must have been overlooked. I may add to my former communication, that I write in the interest of the Metropolitian Workmen and not of a district only! The men at whos request I write were the foremost in promoting the large meetings held in this Country during the American War, and which did such good service in preventing this Country taking the part of the Southern States. I do not mention this to establish any special claims on their part, for distinctions but in order to assure you that the desire expressed in my Letter of the 5th inst was not written in a mere fit of enthusiasm, but arose from a thorough admi-ration of your great Services to the cause of Liberty and as a pledge of their unswerving friendship to the American Nation. Trusting that we may be honoured with a reply to this Letter." ALS, DLC-USG, IB. See Broadhurst, *Henry Broadhurst, M. P.: The Story of His Life from a Stonemason's Bench to the Treasury Bench* (1901; reprinted, New York, 1984), pp. 297–98; *The Times* (London), Oct. 12, 1911; A. W. Humphrey, *A History of Labour Representation* (London, 1912), pp. 31–48, 187–90.

On July 3, 7:30 P.M., the United Service Club honored USG at a banquet. Respond-ing to a toast, USG "alluded to the visit of the Prince of Wales to America, and said that he knew from all his friends, as well as his own personal knowledge, that he was received

as the son of England's Queen with the sincerest respect. He thanked the company for their hospitality—the most ineffaceable honour he had received during his visit to England."
Daily Telegraph (London), July 4, 1877.

Speech

[*Folkestone, July 5, 1877*]

I am much gratified, not only with the address which I have just heard, and the kind remarks of your Mayor, but with the whole of the reception I have had since I landed in England. I shall always retain pleasant memories of all I have seen and all I have heard, and all that has been done for me.[1] I thank you for what has been said in honour of my own great country. It has been a feeling of mine of many years' standing, that the United States and Great Britain should be the very best of friends. You have kindly alluded to my efforts as the Executive of the United States to settle questions that were existing between the two countries, and which were liable at any time to create a disturbance. Fortunately, however, these difficulties were settled in a manner creditable to both nations. There was no desire on my part, and I am sure there was none on the part of the thinking people of the United States, that England should be humiliated in any sense, and there was certainly a determination on our part that we should not be humiliated, but we wanted a settlement that should be honourable to both nations. That was my desire, at all events.

Daily Telegraph (London), July 6, 1877. On July 5, 1877, Mayor John Sherwood of Folkestone presented an address to USG. "... We express a hope that you have derived much enjoyment from your Visit to this Country, and may your life long be spared to witness, in your Country and in our own, increased amity and prosperity and may the Commercial relations of the two Nations be a blessing to both and the means of firmly cementing the friendly ties that exist between the Old Country and the New. ..." DS, Smithsonian Institution. On July 2, a secretary for John Shaw, gen. manager, South Eastern Railway, had written to Adam Badeau, consul gen., London. "Mr Shaw presents his compliments to General Badeau and hopes General Grant will have no objection to receive an address as he passes through Folkestone on Thursday next. ..." L, DLC-USG, IB. See Sherwood to Badeau, July 2, 1877, *ibid.* On July 3, USG replied that "he would be pleased to meet the Mayor and Common Council of Folkestone, but that his time would be too limited to permit of 'any extensive civilities.'" *New York Herald*, July 6, 1877.

Probably in late June, Edwards Pierrepont, U.S. minister, London, had written to USG. "I am convinced that a reception from 4 to 7 on the 4th of July with notice that you & Mrs Grant will be present prior to departure on the next day will be best—If you & Mrs Grant your son & General Badeau, will then take a quiet dinner without any change of dress that will I think be well   Senator Conkling will dine with us also   If you approve this please let Gen Badeau send a note—" ALS (undated), DLC-USG, IB. In an undated letter, USG wrote to "Judge," presumably Pierrepont. "If Mr. & Mrs. Crane, the American Consul at Manchester & Wife, have not been invited for this evening I would be pleased if they could be invited . . . The latter showed me much attention while in Manchester . . ." Robert F. Batchelder, Catalogue No. 56 [1986], no. 61. On July 7, Pierrepont wrote to Secretary of State William M. Evarts about the reception. LS, DNA, RG 59, Diplomatic Despatches, Great Britain. *Foreign Relations, 1877*, p. 262. See John Russell Young diary, July 4, 1877, DLC-John Russell Young; *New York Herald*, July 5, 1877; *Young*, I, 42–44.

On July 5, Daniel E. Sickles, London, wrote to Elihu B. Washburne. "I met Genl Grant yesterday at Pierreponts. They leave town for the Continent to-day but will not go to France before *October*—the General quite agreeing with your views respecting the relation of his visit to the French situation. . . ." ALS, DLC-Elihu B. Washburne. See letter to Elihu B. Washburne, June 22, 1877.

1. In June, a British reporter had interviewed USG. "'In the first place, the country is so beautiful everywhere that one never ceases to admire it. I have been to Bath and to Southampton, and driven a good deal in the neighborhood of London—to Richmond and other places—and everywhere it is the same. All the land is cultivated; one sees comparatively little wood, and it is difficult to imagine anything more beautiful than it all is. Yet, of course, one cannot but recollect how over-populated the country is. Here you can no longer produce enough food for your own people. In our country we could raise the means of support for 500,000,000, and to-day we have only about 2,000,000 more than England. We might not be able to buy anything whatever outside, and be cut off from all the rest of the world, but yet we could get enough out of the ground to live upon. What could England do if any disaster happened to cut her off from the rest of the world in a similar manner?' 'Mr. Disraeli said that in such a case the United States could begin "all over again,"—England could not.' 'I have met him, . . . and find him a very clever man, in your English sense. He seems to be thoroughly posted about our country. We were talking about Mexico last night, and he expressed a wish that we had kept Mexico after the close of our war with her. I said that there was a party in our country which had always opposed the annexation of Mexico, but that the Mexican people would welcome annexation, for it would more than double the value of their property, and give them a quiet and secure Government. . . . A clever man, I should think, is Lord Beaconsfield, though I should say a sufferer physically. He seems to me a man who could put up with any amount of insult or unpopularity if he were pursuing an end, and would patiently wait for the result. . . . your public men here get fair play. It is different with us. A man has only to be put into a public position to be a mark for every calumniator; the object on almost all sides is to destroy him. There has got to be a great change in that in our country some day. . . . As for the cities and large towns, I have never seen any so well managed. All that I have been to are governed on sensible principles. . . . What a contrast all this presents to the state of affairs in New-York! There money raised by taxation has been stolen by wholesale and now property will not sell for the value of the mortgages that are on it, and I declare I do not see what is to become of the City. The debt is enormous. See how well the paving and lighting are looked after here and how carefully the traffic is managed. The Police, too, seem to be excellent. . . . I have not noticed so many of the poor about London as I expected to see,

although I have been down Whitechapel and the Mile-end-road and other places. At Bath the people were most enthusiastic and I was much gratified with their kindness to me; they were very noisy and good-natured. . . . I cannot speak too warmly of the reception I have everywhere met with thus far. It was quite unlooked for. . . . I think good feeling has been increasing ever since the settlement of the Alabama claims. I was very glad they were settled; for if they had not been, undoubtedly a war would have arisen out of them some day; and the constant anticipation of that would have led to exasperation and ill-feeling. . . ." *New York Times*, July 9, 1877.

To Elihu B. Washburne

Frankfurt a/M., July 13th /77

MY DEAR MR. WASHBURNE;

Your letter expressing regret [th]at you could not be at the dinner [he]re last evening reached me in the after[no]on too late to answer until this a. m. [T]he dinner was a most pleasant affair, [an]d the grounds about where given surpass [any]thing I have ever seen for beauty and [exq]uisite taste horticulturally. I am sorry [you] could not be here but understand [ho]w impossible it ~~was~~ is under the circum[st]ances—having a family to move for the [su]mmer— to start off at [*a moment's*] notice. I must leave here on Monday next[1] to carry out my designs. I go direct from here to Luzerne, Switzerland, to commence the tour of that country. Having delayed so by the way I will have to be satisfied with a couple of weeks in Switzerland. It is my intention to visit Denmark, Norway & Sweeden so as to return to Scotland by the last week in ~~Scotland~~ August to do up that part of the Island of Great Bri[tain.] I will not be in Paris now before the middle to the last of October. I hope I may meet you there at that time.

If Mr. Davis, our Minister to Germa[ny] is with you please say to him for me that I received his very kind note at the same time I did yours. If he goes to Switzerland I shall hope to meet him there, and also Mrs. Davis. But I would not have him go to Berlin on my account. If there at all this Summer it will be but for a single day on m[y] [— — — — — — — —] to return this way and then to pay a longer visit to the German Capital. Possibly I may do so this fall after my visit to Scotland.

Please present Mrs. Grants and my best compliments to Mrs. Washbu[rne] and the children.

Truly Yours

U. S. GRANT

ALS (frayed), IHi. On July 11, 1877, Elihu B. Washburne wrote to USG. "I have just received a telegraphic despatch from Mr. Henry Seligman of Frankfort inviting me to be present at a dinner to be given to you to-morrow evening. The notice is so short that it is impossible for me to get away so as to be there in season. I shall leave here next Monday evening for Carlsbad and shall take Mrs. Washburne with me as far as Aix la Chappelle, where I leave her to take the waters, as she is far from well. I have thought you might stop a few days at Hambourg, to repose, after your campaign in England. If you would drop me a line to that effect, I will take Frankfort in my way to Carlsbad for the purpose of passing a day or two with you. I can reach F. next Tuesday p. m. With kindest regards to Mrs. Grant and Uncle Jesse. . . ." ALS (press), DLC-Elihu B. Washburne. On July 12, USG attended a dinner in Frankfurt, where he "thanked the citizens for the confidence they testified in the United States Government during the Civil War by investing in the Loan Act, from which they reaped no disadvantage." *The Times* (London), July 16, 1877. See Alfred E. Lee, *European Days and Ways* (Philadelphia, 1890), pp. 24–31.

On July 8, Grenville M. Dodge, Cologne, had written to USG. "I. regret. that my arrangements are such that I could not remain in Cologne, to meet you, and express my great satisfaction at the hearty and sponteneous reception you have received on this side of the 'Atlantic' I. beleive our people at home a portion of whom had begun to forget your services both military and civil will appreciate the attention awarded you; you say on behalf of our country perhaps partially so, but here where they perpetuate the distinguished services of their citizens under all circumstances, I beleive they weigh yours justly and award to you what they think is your due   While there is no doubt of its bringing about, a far better understanding between our country and these nations and cementing more solidly and lastingly their friendships, I hope it will cause those who seemingly, had forgot. many things of the past, to stop, to think and in the future give due weight and lasting credit to the services of their public men; On your return I am certain *they* and *the country will to you*   I assure you General no one can be more gratified than I at ~~the~~ your reception in this country, as a soldier and as a civilian I think I appreciate your services and I know I am greateful, for all you have done for me in the past   My family are with me sight seeing and enjoing this beautiful country—and join me in wishing you and your family a plesent visit and finally a safe return to 'America'   we trust that we may some place in our journeyings meet you and pay our respects—I saw, Mr Washburn in Paris who wished to be remembered if I met you—I think you did a very judicious thing in delaying your visit to Paris until the present political excitement is over—from here we go up the Rhine and into Switzerland" ALS, MiU-C. See Grenville M. Dodge, *Personal Recollections of President Abraham Lincoln, General Ulysses S. Grant and General William T. Sherman* (Council Bluffs, Iowa, 1914), pp. 107–8. On July 9, a correspondent reported USG's arrival at Cologne. *The Times* (London), June 12, 1877.

1. July 16.

To *Adolph E. Borie*

———

Luzerne, Switzerland,
July 19th 1877.

My Dear Mr. Borie,

We have been now at this beautiful place two days.[1] We have made the trip through the lakes, and back, and to-day,—if it clears up before 11.30 a. m.—we will ascend the Riga. This we can do with the facilities presented by the rail-road up the mountains,[2] built since you were here,—in a single afternoon. Mrs. Grant often regrets that you and Mrs. Borie are not along. To me it would have been a great relief so far, because then I would have had some one to make my speeches. As it has been I have been obliged to make them myself.

After making the tour of Switzerland—about three weeks more —we will visit Denmark, Sweeden & Norway so as to be back in Scotland by the last week in August. About the last of October we will go to Paris to spend the winter there; on the Medeteranean; and in Italy. The Sec. of the Navy has been kind enough to direct the commander of the fleet to put a vessel at my command to go where I wish.[3] I think we will spend five or six weeks on board vessel visiting the various ports on both sides of the Medeterian. If you were along you would be just in—or on—your element.

My visit thus far has been exceedingly pleasant. My reception everywhere has been flattering and cordial. But I have seen nothing to depreciate my own country or countrymen by comparison. Centuries of cultivation and improvements has made much to see which we cannot show. But we can improve more and do more in one year than any country on this side the water can in three.

Please present Mrs. Grant & my kindest regards to Mrs. Borie, and to all our friends in Phila

Yours Truly
U. S. Grant

P. S. I enclose a letter to Robeson which I wish you would forward. I do not know his address otherwise I should not trouble you

ALS, PHi.

1. Samuel H. M. Byers, consul, Zurich, accompanied USG in Lucerne. See Byers, *Twenty Years in Europe* (Chicago, 1900), pp. 128–32.
2. Railways completed in 1871 and 1875 allowed faster travel up the Rigi.
3. See letter to Richard W. Thompson, June 17, 1877.

To George M. Robeson

Luzerne, Switzerland,
July 19th /77

My Dear Ex-Sec.

You do not know how delighted I am to read in the American papers a full account of the banquet given to you in New Jersey, and of the speaches delivered and letters read. Judge Bradley expresses what I would like to say. No Cabinet officer has has been pursued, within my recollection, so unmercifully and so unfairly as you have been and with so little cause. I am glad to see your neighbors sustain you.[1]

An account of my trip ~~would be~~ is entirely unnecessary as the Herald seems to give a pretty full account of each days doings so that any one desirous of knowing my where-a-bouts can learn without waiting the delays of the mail. I will say however that we have had a delightful time though it has seemed long. I can scarsely realize that but two months have passed since we sailed down the Delaware. The Lakes of the Four Cantons, where we now are, present the grandest scenery immaginable from every point. Yesterday my party took a trip through the whole length of the Lakes, and back. On Saturday[2] we go to Interlocken, and on Monday to Geneva,[3] thence thence around to the east and back up North so as to visit Denmark, Sweeden and Norway in time to get back to Scotland by the last week in August. Please present Mrs. Grant's and my kindest regards to Mrs. Robeson, and believe me

yours Truly
U. S. Grant

Hon. Geo. M. Robison

ALS, ICarbS.

1. On July 2, 1877, former Secretary of the Navy George M. Robeson was honored at a dinner in Trenton, N. J., that also provided an occasion to acclaim USG. See *New York Herald,* July 3, 1877. On June 22, Joseph P. Bradley, U.S. Supreme Court, had written to the dinner committee. ". . . Mr. Robeson has been so persistently maligned by a reckless and dishonest press that his friends do well to show their continued confidence in him as a man and Jerseyman. I hope the gathering will be such as to make it a marked rebuke to the public slanders which have been heaped upon him." *Ibid.* See letter to George M. Robeson, March 2, 1876.

2. July 21. On July 24 and 25, USG visited Bern. See S. H. M. Byers, *Twenty Years in Europe* (Chicago, 1900), pp. 134–36.

3. On July 27, USG laid the cornerstone of the American Episcopal Church in Geneva. See *New York Herald,* July 28, 1877; *Young,* I, 48–49. At a reception that afternoon, USG spoke. "I have never felt myself more happy than among this assembly of fellow republicans of America and Switzerland. I have long had a desire to visit the city where the Alabama Claims were settled by arbitration without the effusion of blood, and where the principle of international arbitration was established, which I hope will be resorted to by other nations and be the means of continuing peace to all mankind." *Ibid.,* p. 50.

To Michael John Cramer

Ragatz, Switzerland,
August 13th, '77.

MY DEAR MR. CRAMER:

Before leaving England I had accepted invitations to visit cities and country houses in Scotland—and places in England not yet visited by me—to take up all the month of September and part of October. I thought there was time for me to visit this interesting country and to make a run through Denmark, Sweden and Norway and get back to Scotland in time to keep my engagements. But I have found so much of interest here, and the modes of conveyance so slow in reaching the points of greatest interest, that it is already too late to go even to Denmark, leaving out Norway and Sweden.[1] Already we have spent eight actual days in carriages in getting from point to point, exclusive of other modes of travel. We have visited most of the lakes and crossed the principal passes in Switzerland and Northern Italy.[2] It has all been exceedingly interesting to me, the greatest regret being that I had not more time. I intend yet to visit Denmark,[3] and the countries north of it, but whether this fall or next season is not yet

determined. Probably about next June. I am sorry not to be able to
see Mary before she returns to America.[4] I do not expect to return
there before next July a year, and possibly not so early.

All send love to Mary and the children with kindest regards for
yourself.

Yours truly,

U. S. Grant.

Dr. M. J. Cramer,
United States Minister,
Copenhagen, Denmark.

J. G. Cramer, pp. 130–31. On March 12, 1877, Abel R. Corbin, Elizabeth, N. J., wrote to
Secretary of the Treasury John Sherman. "After heartily expressing to you my congratulations upon your appointment to the Head of the most important Department of our Government, I wish to be permitted to say to you, an old friend of Gen. U. S. Grant, that his
youngest Sister, (Mrs. Cramer,) has written to her Sister (Mrs. Corbin,) saying that she
much desired the continuance of her husband, Hon. M. J. Cramer, in the Diplomatic Service. He is intrusted, at present, with a small place in the north of Europe—Chargé
at Copenhagen, and desires to be continued therein. Gen. Grant may have spoken to President Hayes relative to Mr. Cramer, who is very learned and very poor; if, from delicacy,
he has not, you will place me under great obligations to you if you will call his attention
to the only office held by any member of the family of Gen. Grant. Mr. Cramer has been in
the Diplomatic service ten or twelve years; is master of some Seven languages; is acceptable to the Court to which he is accredited; and is of unblemished reputation. Praying
to be excused for troubleing you with a personal matter, I cannot close without expressing a hope that Your Administration of the Treasury Department will be as successful and
as brilliant as those of Gallatin and Hamilton." ALS, DNA, RG 59, Applications and Recommendations, Hayes-Arthur. Sherman favorably endorsed this letter. AES (undated),
ibid. On March 7, Corbin had written to Charles Wolff, Cincinnati, on the same subject.
ALS, *ibid.* On Nov. 15, 1881, while on leave in Jersey City, Michael John Cramer wrote to
President Chester A. Arthur. "I take the liberty of addressing a few lines to you. You are
aware that I have the honor to be the Chargé d'Affaires of the United States at Berne,
Switzerland. I have also had the honor of being the Minister Resident of the United States
at Copenhagen, Denmark, from Nov. 1870, to Aug. 1876, when Congress saw fit to reduce
the rank of that position to that of a Chargé d'Affaires, and the Salary from $7500 to $5000
per annum. I held that position from August 1876 to August 1881, when the late President
Garfield transferred me to Berne. Having now been nearly eleven years in the diplomatic
service of the United States, I think that, according to the principles of civil Service reform, I deserve promotion. The records of the Department of State will show that I have
thus far discharged the duties of my two positions to the satisfaction of our own Government, as well as to that of the two Governments to which I have been accredited. I find that
the salary of my present position is insufficient for the adequate support of my family. I understand that the positions of Envoy Extraordinary and Minister Plenipotentiary at Vienna and St. Petersburg are, or will soon become vacant. I respectfully request you to have
the goodness to appoint me to one of these two positions; That at Vienna being preferable."
ALS, *ibid.* No appointment followed.

1. On May 29, 1877, Christopher C. Andrews, U.S. minister, Stockholm, had written to USG, London. "I read with much interest the news of your departure from the United States on a visit to Europe and trust I shall soon hear of your safe arrival at Liverpool. I now write to say that if it will be agreeable to you to visit this part of Europe it will afford Mrs. Andrews and myself great satisfaction to do every thing in our power to make you and your family welcome and to render your visit pleasant. Of course the summer is the preferable season for seeing Sweden and Norway, and if you purpose seeing the[m] at all perhaps they will make a better impression if seen before you have visited more opulent parts of the continent. If you should conclude to come it will afford us, I repeat, much happiness to be at your service." ALS (press), Andrews Papers, Minnesota Historical Society, St. Paul, Minn. On June 5, Adam Badeau, consul gen., London, wrote to Andrews. "General Grant directs me to express his thanks for your very kind note of the 29th of May, and to say that he certainly proposes to visit Norway & Sweden during the summer; he cannot how ever as yet determine the exact period, though he supposes it will be in the latter part of July or in August. Of that he will apprise you, and will be very happy to meet you again personally." ALS, *ibid.*

On July 2, Andrews wrote to USG. "I called at the Foreign Office a few days ago and told the Chief secretary (the Minister being absent at a Cabinet meeting) that it was your intention to visit Sweden and Norway and that I expected you would arrive here in the latter part of July or first part of August. He appeared gratified to hear this and said that the King would be glad to see you. He also said that the King, who is now at his chateau in the south of Sweden, would return here in the first week of August. Of course the more time you spend in Sweden and Norway and the more you go about to see the countries the more flattered will the inhabitants be. . . . I shall of course gladly accompany you in Norway if it should be your pleasure. It is important that you see some of the characteristic mountain scenery of Norway but to see the best would require a tour of about two weeks. However a trip of a day or two by rail and steamer north of Christiania will enable you to see a pretty part of the country; while a tour of three or four days South West of Christiania via Kongsburg, partly by carriage, would enable you to visit the celebrated *Rjukand* Falls and see some grand mountain scenery. I think you will be pleased to meet Mr. Stang the Prime Minister of Norway and other people at Christiania. I feel sure too you will be pleased at your reception by some of the principal & best men here. I trust that nothing will prevent your coming." ALS, DLC John Russell Young. On July 19, Badeau, Lucerne, wrote to Andrews. "General Grant desires me to express his thanks for your very kind letter of the 2d inst, to which he has until now delayed replying because of the indefiniteness of his plans. He is highly gratified with all that you propose doing for him, and nothing could give him greater pleasure than to be able to avail himself fully of all your courtesies. He cannot however promise himself more than a week in Sweden and Norway, and he has already arranged to be back in England by the 25 of August. He thinks that he can be at Stockholm during the second week of that month, or about that time; and on his return is anxious to stop only two days, one at the Hague and another at Antwerp; otherwise he will travel direct to London, only resting at night. He will be most happy to accept your kind offers of hospitality at Stockholm, and to have your company during his short trip to Norway; and would of course desire not to pass through Sweden without paying his respects to the King. He directs me to say however that he fears the dinner you are good enough to propose to give him will entail so much trouble on you, and necessitate engagements to be made so long in advance that it will be better not to undertake it. He cannot say, ten days in advance, that he will be at any particular place on a certain day, and while greatly obliged to you for the great compliment you suggest, he thinks on the whole he must decline it. He will apprise you again of his movements later; probably about the time when he leaves Switzerland. Mrs Grant desires me to add her thanks to those of the general for your marked politeness, . . ." ALS, Andrews Papers, Minnesota Historical Society, St. Paul, Minn. On Aug. 13, Badeau, Ragatz, wrote to Andrews. "General Grant directs me to inform you that he has been so much detained during his tour in Switzerland, that it will be impossible for him to visit Denmark Norway and Sweden this year, and be back in England at the time he has appointed. It is with great regret therefore that he feels himself obliged to withdraw his acceptance of your kind invitations, but he desires me to say that he hopes for the pleasure of seeing you at Stockholm next year." ALS, *ibid.*

2. On Aug. 9, a correspondent had reported from London on USG's welcome at Lake Maggiore, Italy, where USG said. "There is one Italian whose hand I wish especially to shake, and that man is General Garibaldi." *New York Herald*, Aug. 9, 1877.

3. On Jan. 2, Cramer, Copenhagen, had written to Secretary of State Hamilton Fish reporting an audience with Crown Prince Frederick. ". . . Among other things he said that he had read that the President contemplated visiting Europe soon after the expiration of his term of office, and if so, he hoped that he (the President) would visit Denmark; 'for' he added 'we all wish to see him.' I replied that at present I knew nothing definite of the President's plan respecting the President's contemplated visit; but that I would convey to him his (the Crown Prince's wish. I therefore respectfully request that the preceding be brought to the knowledge of the President. . . ." LS, DNA, RG 59, Diplomatic Despatches, Denmark. See Cramer to William M. Evarts, June 18, 1877, *ibid.*; letters to Michael John Cramer, June 3, 25, 29, 1878.

4. On Sept. 5, Mary Grant Cramer and her children sailed from Hamburg for New York City. See Cramer to Evarts, Sept. 29, Nov. 16, 1877, DNA, RG 59, Diplomatic Despatches, Denmark.

To Ulysses S. Grant, Jr.

————

Aug. 25th /77

DEAR BUCK,

We have just got back to London and will remain here until Wednesday next when we will start on our tour through Scotland.[1] The trip, as laid out, will take three weeks. I have accepted three engagements at private houses while there, one with the Duke of Southarland,[2] one with the Duke of Arguile[3] and one with a gentleman near Glasgow whom I have never met and whos name I can not give not having the invitation before me.[4] Our trip on the Continent was delightful. Switzerland we enjoyed, particularly in crossing the mountain passes in carriages.[5] The *Infant* however is not much of a traveler.[6] He would prefer settling down in one place, and I think has pretty much determined not to go with us through Scotland. Should he not go with us he will probably put in some time with Nellie, and

the balance at Brighton, or ~~som~~ some pleasant place, until our return. We found no letters awaiting here from the United States except one from Mr. Borie. I was expecting letters from Gov. Fish,
Don. Cameron and Ex. Sec. Robeson to all of whom I had written.
Should you meet them enquire if they received my letters. How is
Con. Va? The length of my stay abroad will have to depend in some
degree upon the length of time it continues to pay dividends, or the
price at which my stock in it sells. I hope you have passed a pleasant
summer and that practice flows in upon you.—I have not seen many
papers from the States recently and am consequently behind in the
news from there. But it is consoling to know that the country would
move on just the same with the loss of any one member of the large
family composing that community. My kind regards to your associates and all my friends, and much love from all of us to you.

Yours Affectionately

U. S. Grant

ALS, USG 3. Written on stationery of the Bristol Hotel, Burlington Gardens, London. On
Aug. 16, 1877, Drexel, Morgan & Co., New York City, wrote to Ulysses S. Grant, Jr., Deer
Park, Md., acknowledging that a $1,550.44 draft had been placed to his credit. D, *ibid.* On
Sept. 6, Drexel & Co., Philadelphia, wrote to Grant, Jr., New York City. "Yours of 5th inst
duly received with 2000.—for credit of U. S. Grant.—" D, *ibid.*

 1. On Aug. 29, USG, Julia Dent Grant, Jesse Root Grant, Jr., and William F. Cool-
baugh, a Chicago banker, departed for Edinburgh. See *The Scotsman* (Edinburgh), Aug. 30,
1877.
 On June 1, John T. Robeson, consul, Leith, had written to USG. "Allow me to tender
you my sincere congratulation on the safe arrival of your self and family in Britian. I trust
that you may visit Edinburgh before leaving the Kingdom. I consider it my duty and I
assure you it will afford me much pleasure to be of any service to you or any member of
your family during your stay in Great Britian or at any time" ALS, DLC-USG, IB. On
July 6 and Sept. 3, H. S. Roberts, Pullman Palace Car Co., wrote to Adam Badeau, consul
gen., London, concerning arrangements for USG's travel in Scotland. LS, *ibid.*, and ALS,
USG 3.
 2. George Granville William Sutherland Leveson-Gower, Duke of Sutherland,
known for his development of the Highland Railway, summered at Dunrobin Castle near
Inverness, Scotland. See *The Times* (London), Sept. 24, 1892; Jesse R. Grant, *In the Days of
My Father General Grant* (New York, 1925), pp. 245–46.
 On Sept. 3, the Elgin Town Council held a special meeting to consider honoring USG
with the freedom of the burgh. "The Provost also intimated that he had received a telegram from General Grant's secretary that morning, in which he expressed his pleasure
at the proposal, and asked the Council to wait on him at Dunrobin." *The Scotsman* (Edinburgh), Sept. 4, 1877. USG later telegraphed that he could not visit Elgin. *Glasgow Herald*, Sept. 8, 1877. In an undated printed letter, the Lord Provost of Elgin wrote to USG.
". . . We, the Provost, Magistrates, Town Council, and Community of Elgin, regret ex-

ceedingly that you are at this time unable to fulfil your intention of visiting our ancient city, whose streets your ancestors have no doubt often trod, and receiving at our hands the highest compliment we have it in our power to offer, but we trust that on some future occasion you will honour us by doing so." LS, Smithsonian Institution.

Traveling to Dunrobin on Sept. 4, USG "was welcomed at Nairn by Provost Leslie and the Magistrates, and was loudly cheered by the assemblage on the platform. A pleasing incident occurred. General Grant recognised and shook hands with an American lady, Mrs Donald Mackay, whose husband, a Scotchman, is in business in Nairn. During the war General Grant and his staff had long had their headquarters at Mrs Mackay's father's house, Clover Hill, Culpepper, Virginia, and the General remembered his worthy host's daughter at once." *Glasgow Herald,* Sept. 5, 1877.

On Sept. 5, 4:15 P.M., USG, Dunrobin, telegraphed to Gen. William T. Sherman, president, Society of the Army of the Tennessee. "Greeting to all comrades of the Army of the Tennessee." *Report of the Proceedings of the Society of the Army of the Tennessee at the Eleventh Annual Meeting . . .* (Cincinnati, 1885), p. 49. On Sept. 6, Manning F. Force, St. Paul, telegraphed to USG. "The Army of the Tennessee sends greeting to its first commander." *Ibid.,* p. 104.

3. George Douglas Campbell, Duke of Argyll, prominent Liberal party statesman and scientific writer, had supported the North during the Civil War. See *Glasgow Herald,* Sept. 18, 19, 1877; *The Times* (London), April 25, 1900; *Julia Grant,* pp. 215–16; Grant, *Days of My Father,* p. 246.

On Aug. 30, John Burns, Castle Wemyss, Scotland, wrote to USG. "I understand that you are going to visit the Duke of Argyll at Inverary & I shall be very glad if you and Mrs Grant and your party will stay with us either going or coming and you will find this a convenient half way house one of your sons paid us a visit some time ago accompanied by Col. McCook—we are not having company at present as I lost my Mother two months ago but you will meet Lord Shaftesbury & his family who stay with us in the autumn. I shall be glad to know that you can pay us a visit & the time at which are likely to come—A steamer leaves this every morning for Inverary at 9 a/m & leaves Inverary every day for this at 2 P M." ALS, DLC-USG, IB. On June 9, Burns, Carlsbad, Austria, had written to Grant, Jr., proposing a visit from USG. ALS, *ibid.* Burns was a manager of the Cunard Co.

4. Probably Lord Provost James Bain of Glasgow, who had prospered as an ironmaster. On Aug. 23, Bain wrote to USG. "At a meeting of the Town Council of Glasgow today I had the honour to propose and the motion was unanimously adopted that on the occasion of your approaching visit you should be presented with the freedom of the City 'in recognition of your distinguished abilities as a statesman your successful efforts in the noble work of emancipating your country from the horrors of slavery and for the great services you have rendered in promoting commerce and amity between the United States and Great Britain.'—That the necessary arrangements maybe made in good time it is of very great importance we should have early intimation of the days you shall be here.—Will you permit me to suggest a programme? Suppose you arrive in Glasgow in the afternoon of a day to be named by you,—yourself, Mrs Grant and your suite will dine with me and reside in my town house that night.—Next day,—receive an address from the corporation and the freedom of the City attend the corporation Banquet and remain over night with me.—Next day go down to Ayr a[nd] receive the freedom of that town,—visit Burns monument and the 'Banks and Braes o' bonnie Doon,'—dine at my country house Sundown and remain over night with me. I mean of course that Mrs Grant and your suite shall accompany you.—Next day remain with me or return to Glasgow or go any where as you may desire.—How will such arrangements do? Vary if you choose—so as to suit yourself;—but it will be very obliging and tend greatly to our comfort and that of the Citizens if you will

kindly cause to be made known to me *as soon as possible*—the day on which you will arrive in Glasgow and the hour,—also the numbers and names of your party.—Please excuse my anxiety in this matter.—I wish everything to go off well when we receive so esteemed a guest.—" ALS, USG 3. See Speech, [*Sept. 13, 1877*]; *The Times* (London), April 26, 1898.

    5. See *Julia Grant*, pp. 211–14.

    6. See Grant, *Days of My Father*, pp. 232–44.

To Commodore Daniel Ammen

—————

Bristol Hotel, Burlington Gardens, London, W.,

August [*26*], 1877.

My dear Commodore,—

I arrived here from the Continent yesterday, after a most pleasant visit of about seven weeks there, most of the time in Switzerland. There is no more beautiful scenery or climate for summer travel than Switzerland presents. The people are industrious and honest, simple and frugal in their habits, and would be very poor with all this, if it were not from the travel through their country. I wish their surplus population would emigrate to the United States. On our arrival here I found but few letters, but among them were yours and one from our mutual friend Borie. During my absence I will be glad to hear from you as often as you feel like writing. It is always interesting to me to get home news, and particularly from a friend. For the last eight weeks I have seen but few American papers, and am consequently behind in home news. The foreign papers, however, have been full of the great railroad strike, and no doubt exaggerated it, bad as it was. The United States should always be prepared to put down such demonstrations promptly and with severe consequences to the guilty.[1] I hope good may come out of this, in pointing out the necessity for having the proper remedy at hand in case of need. "An ounce of prevention is worth a pound of cure." One thing has struck me as a little queer. During my two terms of office the whole Democratic press, and the morbidly honest and "reformatory" portion of the Republican press, thought it horrible to keep U. S. troops stationed in the Southern States, and when they were called upon to protect the lives of negroes—as much citizens under the Constitution as if their skins were white—the country was scarcely large enough to hold the sound of indignation belched forth by them for some years. Now, however, there is no hesitation about exhausting the whole power of the government to suppress a strike on the slightest intimation that danger threatens. All parties agree that this is right, and so do I. If a negro insurrection should arise in South Carolina, Mississippi, or Louisiana, or if the negroes in either of these States—where they are in a large majority—should intimidate the whites from going to the polls, or from exercising any of the rights of American citizens, there would be no division of sentiment as to the duty of the President. It does seem the rule should work both ways.

How long my stay abroad may be prolonged is somewhat problematical. I shall remain on this side of the water, however, all of next winter, and will avail myself of the Secretary's kind offer of a naval vessel to visit the seaport towns on the Mediterranean. I received a letter from Admiral Worden[2] stating that he had received his orders in this respect,—giving me a copy of his instructions, which I had seen before,—to which I replied stating my plans. I wrote to the Secretary thanking him for the courtesy of his tender of a vessel, which letter I hope he received.[3]

During the strike you must have been compelled to stay in the city, leaving the little Ammens[4] to take care of themselves, or have resorted to private conveyance. In either case you have been taught the value of railroads to the country.

Mrs. Grant sends her love to Mrs. Ammen and the children, and asks me to say that she will miss you very much during our travels on board naval vessels.

Please present my kind regards to Mrs. Ammen and the children, and believe me,

Your sincere friend,
U. S. GRANT.

COMMODORE D. AMMEN, *U. S. Navy.*

Daniel Ammen, *The Old Navy and the New* (Philadelphia, 1891), pp. 537–38. For the date of this letter, see Ammen, "Recollections and Letters of Grant," *North American Review,* CXLI, cccxlvii (Oct., 1885), 372.

1. In July, 1877, a strike by Baltimore and Ohio Railroad workers to protest wage cuts quickly spread to other lines. President Rutherford B. Hayes responded by ordering U.S. troops to assist state authorities in efforts to protect property. See following letter; Robert V. Bruce, *1877: Year of Violence* (Indianapolis, 1959); Ari Hoogenboom, *Rutherford B. Hayes: Warrior and President* (Lawrence, Kan., 1995), pp. 326–35.

2. Rear Admiral John L. Worden, former commander of the *Monitor* and superintendent of the U.S. Naval Academy (1869–71), commanded the European Squadron.

3. See letter to Richard W. Thompson, June 17, 1877.

4. Commodore Daniel Ammen married for a second time in 1866 and had five children.

To Abel R. Corbin

BRISTOL HOTEL,
BURLINGTON GARDENS,
LONDON, W.
Aug. 26, '77.

MY DEAR MR. CORBIN:

We arrived here from the Continent yesterday, and found awaiting us your very acceptable letter. On Wednesday[1] we start again to visit Scotland where I have had many invitations from both corporations and from private gentlemen. We will take about three weeks for this trip, after which we will visit some portions of England not yet visited, and Nellie at her home, and get to Paris the latter part of October. The papers no doubt will keep you advised of our movements in advance of anything I could write to go by mail. Our visit has been most agreeable in every particular. People everywhere, both travellers and residents, did all they could to make everything pleasant for us. How long we will remain abroad is not yet determined, but I think for two years yet if the means to do so hold out.

During my visit to the Continent I saw but few American papers so that I am now somewhat behind in information as to what has been going on in the United States. All the foreign papers however have been full of the great strike which has taken place on our roads. It must have been serious but probably not so serious as it seemed at a distance. My judgment is that it should have been put down with a strong hand and so summarily as to prevent a like occurrence for a generation.

We have made a short visit to Nellie at her home.[2] She lives in a delightful part of the country.

All join me in love to Mother and Jennie as well as yourself. I will be glad to hear from you as often as you may feel like writing.

                              Yours truly,
                              U. S. GRANT.

We met Mrs. Clark and Roberts in Switzerland.[3] It was like being back home to meet old acquaintances. Except Senator Conkling[4] and some of our Government officials they are the only Americans I have met that I felt I knew very well. Please remember me to Senator Frelinghuysen and such other friends as you meet.

A. R. CORBIN, ESQ.,

ELIZABETH, N. J.

J. G. Cramer, pp. 132–33.

   1. Aug. 29, 1877.
   2. See letter to Adelaide Kemble Sartoris, June 2, 1877.
   3. Amos Clark, Jr., whom Abel R. Corbin and USG knew well, was friendly with William C. Roberts. USG probably met their wives Elizabeth H. Clark and Mary L. Roberts. See *PUSG*, 23, 248–49; Endorsement, June 28, 1876.
   4. U.S. Senator Roscoe Conkling of N. Y. visited Europe in June and July. See John Russell Young diary, July 5, 1877, DLC-John Russell Young; *New York Herald*, Aug. 11, 1877; Young, *Men and Memories* (New York, 1901), I, 225–31; David M. Jordan, *Roscoe Conkling of New York: Voice in the Senate* (Ithaca, 1971), pp. 274–75.

Interview

———

                              [*Aug. 29, 1877*]

I shall stay in Europe a year or more. I have special reasons for so doing. I am a private citizen now, and want nothing whatever to do with politics. If I were at home I would give Mr. Hayes and his policy all the support I could, because the object aimed at is a noble one, and I hope he will succeed.

. . . I have always of late years had an abiding faith in the success of the republican party at each election, not so much because it is always the strongest with the people as because always, just at the last moment, the democrats do some foolish thing and give the victory to the republicans. Now, mark my words, we will have a republican President in 1880, because the democracy cannot resist its general disposition to kick over the milk pail after it is filled. I told Judge Niblack,[1] of Indiana, so just before the last election, and he smilingly admitted the truth of what I said.

. . . I would like to see all Europe. But I propose to stay away till after the exciting scenes that will surround the test of Mr. Hayes' policy, for the reason that if I were at home I would be charged with having a hand in every kind of political manœuvring, whether I had or not, and I want to banish politics from my mind until everything settles down. I can say for one thing, however, that if I were at home I should exert my influence, as far as I could exert it, in aid of Mr. Hayes' plan of reconciliation.

What will be your course of travel?

To-morrow we shall leave Edinburgh for the castle of the Duke of Sutherland—Dunrobin Castle—away up in the far north of Scotland. We shall be in Glasgow on the 12th of September, thence to Ayr, Newcastle, York, Sheffield, Birmingham, Leamington and London. On the 20th of October we will go to Paris and stay six weeks; thence to Marsailles, Nice and Genoa. At Genoa we hope to take an American man-of-war to different ports in Spain, Turkey, Egypt, Malta, Sicily, &c., and the Grecian Archipelago. We will return to Naples about the 15th of February, stay there two weeks, proceed to Rome for a month, go to several large towns and return to Paris about the end of April, 1878. We will stay in Paris till about the end of May and then go to Denmark, Sweden, Norway, Russia, Austria, and return by the Stelveo Pass to Switzerland, where we expect to arrive September, 1878. I think the people of Europe have shown great honor to our country in their treatment of me. I look upon these grand receptions as a tribute of affection to an American because he is an ex-President, intended as a token of respect to our nation itself.

I notice as we pass stations these people hurrah and shake hands with you the same as our people do at home.

Yes; I was under the impression that there was no such custom here; but in England the habit is as strong as in America. I think handshaking a great nuisance, and it should be abolished. In 1865 it was awful with me; I thought I could hardly survive the task. It not only makes the right arm sore, but it shocks the whole system and unfits a man for writing or attending to other duties. It demoralizes the entire nervous and muscular system. None but a strong man could go through as much of it as I did in 1865. If Mr. Tilden, who, you know, is old and not very strong, had been elected, he would have been obliged to decline the handshaking business to a great extent, because I don't think his system would bear the strain of the amount of it that would have been expected of him. The most laborious and injurious handshaking is where you stand on an elevation and reach down. A man cannot stand much of that.

. . . I have been a good deal at sea during my life and generally got very seasick, but have not been troubled in these voyages. I say it is singular because from the 4th of March till the 17th of May I dined formally with friends, everyday lunched so, and sometimes took two lunches the same day. I thought I was a good subject for seasickness and expected the motion of the ship would turn me inside out, but I was not sick a minute. As a matter of fact I was disappointed.

I see a reference in a newspaper eulogy of Mr. Motley to your position toward that officer, and the intimation that your action was one of the remote causes of his death?

Yes, I have read it, and it does me a great injustice. Mr. Motley was certainly a very able, very honest gentleman, fit to hold any official position. But he knew long before he went out that he would have to go. When I was making these appointments Mr. Sumner came to me and asked me to appoint Mr. Motley as Minister to the Court of St. James. I t[ol]d him I would, and did. Soon after Mr. Sumner made that violent speech about the Alabama claims,[2] and the British government was greatly offended. Mr. Sumner was at the time chairman of the Committee on Foreign Affairs.

Mr. Motley had to be instructed. The instructions were prepared very carefully and after Governor Fish and I had gone over them

for the last time I wrote an addendum charging him that above all
things he should handle the subject of the Alabama claims with the
greatest delicacy. Mr. Motley, instead of obeying his explicit instructions, deliberately fell in line with Mr. Sumner and thus added
insult to the previous injury. As soon as I heard of it I went over to
the State Department and told Governor Fish to dismiss Motley at
once. I was very angry indeed and I have been sorry many a time
since that I did not stick to my first determination. Mr. Fish advised
delay because of Sumner's position in the Senate and attitude on the
treaty question. We did not want to stir him up again just then. We
despatched a note of severe censure to Motley at once, and ordered
him to abstain from any further connection with that question.[3] We
thereupon commenced negotiations with the British Minister at
Washington, and the result was the Joint High Commission and the
Geneva award. I supposed Mr. Motley would be manly enough to resign after that snub, but he kept on till he was removed.[4] Mr. Sumner promised me that he would vote for the treaty. But when it was
first before the Senate he did all he could to beat it.

I must tell you an incident about Mr. Sumner. The first time
I ever saw George William Curtis he called upon me to request on
behalf of a number of influential republicans the reinstatement of
Mr. Sumner as chairman of the Committee on Foreign Affairs.[5] I told
him that, if I should go to the Senate and dictate the organization
of the committees, I would be apt to hear something about the fellow who made a fortune by minding his own business. I said I certainly should suggest the idea to any part of the legislative branch
that should undertake to construct my Cabinet. I gave him distinctly
to understand that I did not propose to interfere in the matter at
all, even by advice to personal friends among the Senators, and that
I thought Mr. Sumner had not done his duty as chairman of the committee, because he had hampered the business of the State Department by pigeonholing treaties for months. Mr. Curtis said that was
impossible, for Mr. Sumner had only a short time before told him
that his successor would find a clean docket and made special claims
for the execution of the work of the committee. Knowing, as I did,
the adroit arguments used among Mr. Sumner's friends, I deter-

mined to test the matter of a clean docket. I told Mr. Curtis that I had proposed to prove to him that his friend Mr. Sumner had not told him the facts and that he made these statements knowing them to be falsehoods. Mr. Curtis was amazed at my offer, but I assured him that he had been frequently caught in similar misrepresentations. I told Mr. Curtis that there were nine or eleven treaties before the Senate from the State Department that had been there several months, and had been in Mr. Sumner's hands, but had never been laid before the committee. I wrote from the spot, Long Branch, to the State Department, and to my own surprise there proved to be more treaties than I had said that had been in Mr. Sumner's own hands for a longer time than I expected. That was the "clean docket." When I told Mr. Curtis about it and gave him the record, he was rather disappointed. He said it was remarkable[.] I told him my object in having the record searched was to show him that Mr. Sumner was not a truthful man, as others had found out before me, and as I had discovered on frequent occasions. The work of that committee when Mr. Cameron took charge was in a most deplorable state, due entirely to Mr. Sumner's persistent obstructiveness and dilatoriness.

I had nothing to do with his dismissal from the chairmanship of the Foreign Relations Committee, but I was glad when I heard that he was put off, because he stood in the way of even routine business, like ordinary treaties with small countries. I may be blamed for my opposition to Mr. Sumner's tactics, but I was not guided so much by reason of his personal hatred of myself as I was by a desire to protect our national interests in diplomatic affairs. It was a sad sight to find a Senate with the large majority of its members in sympathy with the administration, and with its chairman of the Foreign Committee in direct opposition to the foreign policy of the administration, in theory and detail. So I was glad when I heard of his successor's nomination as chairman of the committee. I shall never change my mind as to the wisdom of the policy that brought about the Washington Treaty with Great Britain, no matter how much the friends of Mr. Sumner and Mr. Motley may defend the indirect damage humbug.[6] We never could have procured the agreement of the British Commissioners or people to such a thing.

General, they are running civil service reform very strong just now?

So I see; but it will not work, because the theorists have disagreed among themselves as to its practical application. I do not attach much importance to that matter. I do not believe it will succeed, though I wish it could, in some practical way. Take Schurz, for instance. He is making a business of civil service reform. But he is a humbug, and Mr. Hayes will find him out before long. It is a good thing, but it is hard to apply in our country. It is all very well to say that the business of office seeking shall be abolished, but the office seeker cannot easily be abolished, and the more the theorists quarrel among themselves the further practical civil service reform seems to recede.

What do you think of the dissolution of republican State organizations in the South?

That is one of the usual violent effects of wise government after a scene of turmoil like we had last fall. For myself, I do not care for party. You can always depend upon the good sense of the people of the United States. They believe in the Republic. Their flag is to the fore, with strong arms behind it always, and they are sentimental, loyal and brave. They will never elect a high official except upon a common sense basis. For that reason I believe—the republican and democratic parties of late being so evenly divided—that the people will be compelled to vote in large majority for the republican candidate, no matter who he may be, because the democrats will do some silly thing that will drive the thinking people from their ranks at the last moment. The modern democracy always does it. It has made me smile frequently as I have thought of it; but there is some fatality at work in the premises.

New York Herald, Sept. 25, 1877. An editorial highlighted USG's remarks on U.S. Senator Charles Sumner of Mass., John Lothrop Motley, and Secretary of the Interior Carl Schurz. *Ibid.* William P. Copeland, an experienced journalist and friend of John Russell Young, interviewed USG and datelined the column, Sept. 11, Edinburgh. See letters to Hamilton Fish, Nov. 14, 1877; letters to John Russell Young, Nov. 21, 28, 1877; Interview, Jan. 17, 1878.

1. William E. Niblack, Democratic National Committee member (1864–72), served also as Ind. judge and U.S. Representative.

2. See *New York Times*, April 15, 1869; David Donald, *Charles Sumner and the Rights of Man* (New York, 1970), pp. 374–94.

3. See *ibid.*, pp. 396–413; Hamilton Fish to Motley, May 15, June 28, 1869, DNA, RG 59, Diplomatic Instructions; *SED*, 41-3-11.

4. See *PUSG*, 20, 183–88, 191–92.

5. Sumner's ouster as chairman occurred in March, 1871. After this date, USG communicated frequently with George William Curtis on Civil Service reform. See *ibid.*, 22, 297–300.

6. See second Speech, [*Sept. 13, 1877*].

Speech

———

[*Edinburgh, Aug. 31, 1877*]

My Lord Provost, Magistrates, and City Council, ladies and gentlemen,—I am so filled with emotion that I scarcely know how to thank you for the honour you have conferred upon me by making me a burgess of this ancient city of Edinburgh. I feel it as a very great compliment paid to me and to my country. Had I the proper eloquence, I might dwell somewhat upon the history of the great men you have produced, of the numerous citizens of this city and of Scotland that have gone to America and made their mark there. We are proud of Scotchmen as citizens of America. They make good citizens of our country, and they find it profitable to themselves. I will only say that I thank you sincerely for the honour you have this day conferred upon me.

The Scotsman (Edinburgh), Sept. 1, 1877. USG spoke in response to Lord Provost James Falshaw of Edinburgh. "... We feel proud of the occasion, and hail your arrival in our city with peculiar satisfaction, not only because of the honours you have achieved in your own country, but, also, claiming you by descent as one of our own—we hold out the right hand of fellowship and hail you as a brother Scot. . . ." *Ibid.* See *The Times* (London), June 15, 1889.

On May 31, 1877, Falshaw had written to Edward H. Stanley, Earl of Derby, London. "... If it were agreeable to General Grant, the Corporation would consider it an honour to confer the freedom of the City upon him. May I ask that your Lordship will be so good as cause this communication to be made to General Grant through the American Embassy or otherwise." Copy, DLC-USG, IB. On June 18, Falshaw wrote to USG, London. "I beg leave to subjoin copy of a letter which, on 31st ulto, I addressed to the Earl of Derby, Secretary of State for Foreign Affairs. Referring to that communication, and an interview which the Depute City Clerk had with the American Ambassador a few days ago, and which His Excellency was kind enough to promise to report to you, I now beg leave to ask if you will be good enough to inform me whether it will be agreeable and convenient for you to accept the proffer contained in the letter to Lord Derby, and, if so, about what time." LS, *ibid.* On July 26, William Skinner, town clerk, Edinburgh, wrote to USG. "Referring to the Lord Provost's letter to you of 18th June, I have now the honour to send you annexed Copy of the Resolution of The Lord Provost Magistrates, & Council, conferring upon you the Freedom of the City; and I shall be glad to be informed when it will be convenient for you to receive the Freedom in person." ALS, *ibid.* The testimonial dated July 9 is in the Smithsonian Institution. On Aug. 27, Skinner wrote to Adam Badeau, consul gen., London, concerning arrangements for the ceremony. LS, DLC-USG, IB.

On Aug. 30, William H. Logan, proprietor, Theatre Royal, Edinburgh, wrote to USG. "On this your visit to Edinburgh, as you may be desirous to see as many of the several sights of the City as your limited stay may admit of, the Lessees of this Theatre beg respectfully to say that, if it suits your convenience, they will feel honoured by your presence at the performances on the Evening of Friday next, and will be happy to place such accommodation at your disposal as you and your party may require. An early reply will be esteemed a favour" ALS, USG 3. On the same day, Robert Chambers, Edinburgh, wrote to [*USG*]. "Mr Robt Chambers begs the honour of General Grants' acceptance of a copy of TRADITIONS OF EDINBURGH, a work prepared by his late father. Mr Chambers trusts that General Grant's stay in Edinburgh and Scotland may be a pleasant one." N, *ibid.* Robert Chambers, *Traditions of Edinburgh* (London, 1868). For USG's activities while in Edinburgh, see *The Scotsman* (Edinburgh), Aug. 31, Sept. 1, 3–4, 1877.

On Sept. 1, USG visited the Tay Bridge at Dundee and replied to a toast at a luncheon. *Ibid.*, Sept. 3, 1877. On Sept. 3, a correspondent reported from Dundee. "General Grant has arranged to pay another visit to Dundee in the course of next week. . . ." *Daily Telegraph* (London), Sept. 4, 1877. On Sept. 5, Dundee officials decided to confer the freedom of the burgh on USG and telegraphed to find out the date of his visit. *Ibid.*, Sept. 6, 1877. On [*Sept. 6*], USG telegraphed to Dundee officials that other engagements prevented another visit "and that therefore he cannot be the recipient of the high compliment which the magistrates of the burgh contemplated paying him." *Glasgow Herald*, Sept. 7, 1877.

On Sept. 5, Francis A. Keith–Falconer, Earl of Kintore, Perth, had written to USG. "I beg to thank you fr yr. autograph—which you so courteously sent to me thro The Lord Provost of Edinburgh, & to say that on or after the 14th Inst—(for till then I am engaged) —it wd give me much pleasure to be able—to pay you, Mrs Grant & Party any little attention in Aberdeenshire that lays in my power—& with the offer of my best respects . . ." ALS, DLC-USG, IB. On Sept. 6, Thursday, Charles Gordon, Marquis of Huntly, Aboyne Castle, Aberdeenshire, wrote to USG. "I was informed by Mr Clark, whom you met at Dundee that you probably were to be in this part of Scotland on Tuesday or Wednesday next, & I ventured to send you a telegram this morning to say that we should be delighted if you paid us a visit here on either Tuesday or Wednesday next—The Aboyne Highland Games are on the latter day—We hope Mrs Grant & your son, will accompany you, if your arrangements permit of your honoring us with your presence for one or two nights." ALS, *ibid.* Also on Sept. 6, William Milligan, local secretary, National Association for the Promotion of Social Science, Aberdeen, wrote to USG. "The Executive Committee appointed to make preparations for the above Congress has been given to understand that it is the intention of the Town Council of Aberdeen to ask you to accept the well merited honour of the Freedom of the City. The Committee begs respectfully to express the hope that if you agree to accept the honour, and if not at variance with your other arrangements, you will do so at a time when it may be possible for you to be present at some of the meetings of the Congress. The Committee believes that the inhabitants of Aberdeen will be much gratified if you kindly assent to this proposal; and it is assured that, in that case, the Magistrates of the City will gladly make their arrangements so as to enable you to do so." ALS, *ibid.* USG did not visit Aberdeen.

To C. Stuart Patterson

> *Bristol hotel.*
> *Burlington Gardens.*
> *London, W.*
> Aug. 31st /77

My Dear Mr. Patterson,

Your favor of yesterday informing me that you sail for Phila on Wednesday next, and offering to convey anything I may have to transmit, and also asking for my autograph for Miss Gould, is just rec'd. I have nothing to send to America except my very best regards to all my friends there, and to desire to be specially remembered to your father and father-in-law. I hope you will have a smoother passage over than we had coming, and that Capt. Sargent—whom I shall always retain pleasant recollections of—will be relieved of the anxieties he experienced then.[1] My trip to the Continent was a most delightful one, and reading the American papers and seeing the trials of the President make me feel more than ever the relief of being again a *Sovreign.* I think I shall have no difficulty in containing myself, away from home, for a couple of years.

> Very Truly yours
> U. S. Grant.

ALS, DLC-George H. Stuart. C. Stuart Patterson graduated from the University of Pennsylvania (1860), served in the Civil War, and became a lawyer. His father was Joseph Patterson, Philadelphia banker; his father-in-law, George H. Stuart.

1. See letter to Ulysses S. Grant, Jr., May 26, 1877.

Speech

———

[*Inverness, Scotland, Sept. 8, 1877*]

I thank the citizens of this burgh for the honour they have conferred upon me by making me, as it were, a citizen eligible to perform the functions of a citizen, and to become a candidate for the high office of the Provost of this city. I am sorry not to be able to remain here long enough to go through a canvass for that high office—even if assured of election. But I assure you that I feel the honour which has been conferred upon me this evening very much. I shall always remember it, and shall carry to my own home the most pleasant recollections of what I have witnessed this evening. My visit to all points in Scotland to which I have gone has been most pleasant and agreeable. Since I landed on the shores of Great Britain I have received such attentions and kindness from the citizens, that I shall carry back no unpleasant recollections from any quarter of this great country. There has been an allusion made by the Provost to the settlement of a question that had been a cause of much irritation between our nation—which we believe to be great—and this nation, which we acknowledge is great, and you are sure of being great. I had occasion twice to say that it has always been a feeling of mine—which I expressed long before I had an opportunity to do anything towards the settlement of the question—that I thought it was due to ourselves and due to the world that the best of feelings should exist between the two great English-speaking nations. When I became President of the United States I set myself about the settlement of these questions, and I think they were fortunately settled in a manner honourable to both parties. I hope and trust that we may live long through the centuries to come the same good friends—friendship increasing—and I am sure that if we do, the effect of that friendship will be felt all the world over for the benefit of mankind and the advancement of civilisation. Mr Provost, ladies, and gentlemen, I again thank you.

The Scotsman (Edinburgh), Sept. 10, 1877; variant text in *Glasgow Herald*, Sept. 10, 1877. USG spoke in response to an address by Lord Provost Alexander Simpson of Inverness.

"We are here met to-night to bestow upon you the only distinction in our power to con-fer—the freedom of our ancient and Royal burgh. . . . It is not an unusual circumstance for us in the Highlands to claim kindred with successful men in all parts of the world; and we have a very great pleasure in having one of the famous clan Grant a President of the United States for eight years." *The Scotsman* (Edinburgh), Sept. 10, 1877. After Simpson proposed "three cheers for the youngest burgess," USG replied. "Permit me now, as the youngest burgess, to give three cheers for the senior burgess, the Provost, although he may not be the oldest." *Ibid.* The document presented to USG is in the Smithsonian Institution.

On Sept. 1, Simpson had written to USG, Edinburgh. "As Provost of the Burgh of In-verness,—the Capital of the Highlands—, I am desired by the Town Council to ask your acceptance of the freedom of the Burgh, on your journey to or from Dunrobin, as may best suit your convenience. We have many distinguished names on our Burgess-roll, and it will afford us sincere pleasure to have your honoured name added thereto." ALS, USG 3. In re-sponse to this letter, Simpson "received a telegram from the General's aide-de-camp stat-ing that the General felt much honoured by the proposal, but he was much pressed, and he could not wait longer than during the period he would be at the railway station." *The Scots-man* (Edinburgh), Sept. 4, 1877.

On Sept. 10, Stirling officials presented USG with a testimonial. DS, Smithsonian In-stitution. See *Glasgow Herald*, Sept. 11, 1877. On Sept. 11, USG, Glasgow, wrote to J. F. Crawford. "I take pleasure in acknowledging—as a souvenir of my visit to Sterling—the receipt of three volumes of books which you were kind enough to send for Mrs. Grant and my acceptance. In referring to them they will always serve as a reminder of a most pleasant, though brief, visit to the ancient burgh of Sterling." Kenneth W. Rendell, Inc., Catalogue 57 [1971], no. 77. A newspaper reported that Crawford had "presented the Gen-eral with a handsome copy of Scott's 'Lady of the Lake,' bound in oak and illustrated by photography, and Mrs Grant with the same work bound in Royal Stuart tartan, accom-panied by a book of views in same tartan. All the books bore the Royal arms, being the same as supplied to the Queen and various members of the Royal Family." *Glasgow Herald*, Sept. 12, 1877.

To Edward F. Beale

Sept. 9th /77

MY DEAR GENERAL:

I was delighted day before yesterday while visiting the very northermost part of Scotland by receiving your very acceptable fa-vor of the 15th of August. We have had a most delightful visit both in England & Scotland, and on the Continent. We will remain on this Island until about the 20th of October when we will go to Paris to remain some time. If the money holds out—it depends very much on Consolidated Va Silver Mining stock holding out—I will be able to stay abroad two years very pleasantly.

It has been very gratifying to me—though very irksome to one so little inclined to speaking—to see our country so respected as it is abroad, and as the people, of all classes, shew it on all occasions. The demonstrations on all the lines of railway, where the trains stop, are very much like they were immediately after the close of the re-bellion, in the Northern states, when any of the Army officers who were in high favor, were traveling. But the newspapers bore you enough with this subject without my inflicting anything further.

Traveling as I have I have not been very well able to keep up with affairs at home. Important matters like the great rail-road strike are fully reported—and duly exagerated of course—but little details I do not see as I would if receiving our own papers regularly. The progress of Civil Service reform—a very flexible reform, or hum-bug, that justifies whatever a few dissatisfied politicians want—comes by installments. There are two humbugs which Mr. Hayes will find out—for I believe he is an honest, sincere man, and pa-triot—one is Civil Service reform, the other reformers. This is my judgement. Let us see.

Soon after my arrival in England I had the pleasure of driving Kellogg. He came over in fine condition and is as good as ever. I hope Rockey may prove as good and that either Mrs. Beale or yourself will find enjoyment in using him. I left word before my departure that if Blossom was not in foal you could use her—on the turf or other-wise—as you choose. I will feel more at home back in Washington than any place els, and no place more than in visiting your farm with you. I also thank you and Mrs. Beale—Mrs. Grant joins me in this—for your kind invitatio[n] to your house. If we should conclude to remain there we will, of course, endeavor to have a house of our own. But we thank you all the same.

With kindest regards of Mrs. Grant & myself to Mrs. Beale and all your family I am, sincerely & truly,

your obt. svt.

U. S. GRANT

GEN. E. F. BEALE

ALS, DLC-Decatur House Papers. Written on stationery of Macdonald's Station Hotel, Inverness, Scotland. See *PUSG*, 26, 299–300; Gerald Thompson, *Edward F. Beale & The American West* (Albuquerque, 1983), pp. 208–12.

On March 8, 1877, Edward F. Beale, U.S. minister, Vienna, wrote to USG. "I congratulate you heartily on your retirement from the cares of official life. No man of whom History makes mention is more to be envied than you. In the very vigor and full maturity of life, and in the enjoyment of robust health, with every appetite left undisturbed either by age or excess, you will still live long to enjoy all that which makes life physically desirable, while the praises of a whole nation and the respect of the entire world will sweeten and satisfy every mental aspiration. Other men have reached great fame, but they have either outlived it or been taken off by death before the full completion of their affairs, or have come to it only in old age and when too feeble to appreciate or enjoy it, but you, having performed services to your country which have rendered you immortal in its history, have yet many years in which to receive the respect and honor from your fellow citizens to which your great actions so well entitle you. As party sentiment fades away, and the asperities of political life are smoothed out by time, you will stand as the great central figure of the age in which you have lived, and I consider it not among the least happy events of your life, that the last days of your administration of Public Affairs, mark the centennial year of our existence as a Nation and of our political liberties, and that, almost on that anniversary, you transmit the freedom you knew so well how to preserve intact and undiminished to your successor. As you have now passed into private life this cannot be considered the language of flattery, and can only be regarded as the expression of grateful friendship, and I trust the future has many days in store in which I may be permitted to enjoy the kind disposition you have heretofore displayed towards me." ALS, USG 3.

To Hamilton Fish

———

Inverness, Scotland,
Sept. 9th /77

MY DEAR GOVERNOR:

Your very acceptable letter of the 4th of Aug. only reached me three days ago while on a visit to Dunrobin castle, Scotland. It makes no mention of receiving a letter from me which I wrote but a short time after my arrival in London and while staying at the Pierreponts. There was nothing in the letter of importance even if it should have fallen into other hands.[1]

During my tour it would have been a great comfort if you and Mrs. Fish could have been along. On this island the receptions have been a little to much like our departure from Philadelphia to constitutute rest: but the welcom[e] has been hearty and gratifying[.] But on the continent it was very pleasant. My receptions while quiet were hospitable and agreeable. The lack of english speaking people was all that was required. In ascending and descending the beautiful mountain passes of Switzerland and Northern Italy Mrs. Grant always regretted she could not have some of her old friends like Mrs. Fish to help her enjoy the scenery. But, as you say in your letter, the papers have kept you fully advised of where we have been and wha[t] has been done, so nothing further on this subject is necessary from me.

I note what you say about the working of civil service reform, and the new Administration. I think Mr. Hayes is perfectly honest in his intentions; but, if so, I think he will find out that there are two great humbugs influencing him now: namely, reform & reformers. I might add reform directed by reformers. But I hope all will work out right and that three years hence the republican party will be united and triumphant.

We will leave for the Continent again about the 20th of Oct, and remain quiet for the Winter in Paris, on the Medeteranian and in Italy. My return to the States is as yet problematical, but I think not for a couple of years. It may be however much sooner.

I shall always be glad to hear from you and I know Mrs. Grant would be glad to get a letter from Mrs. Fish.

With kindest regards of Mrs. Grant & myself to both you & Mrs. Fish, and all the family, to the third generation, I am

yr. obt svt.
U. S. Grant

Hon. Hamilton Fish.

ALS, DLC-Hamilton Fish. On Aug. 4 and Nov. [13], 1877, Hamilton Fish, Garrison, N. Y., wrote to USG. "The public journals have kept us advised, almost daily, of your movements, & of the [—] tribute, so gratifying to all your friends, which is being paid to your character & to your services—many, who were not very friendly while you were in office manifest a certain amount of gratification in the complacent idea that as American Citizen, the honours paid to you are in part theirs. be it as it may, your reception abroad gives a universal satisfaction here—the popular demonstrations which you are receiving are hearty and sincere, & free from any suspicion of selfish purpose. You are doubtless fully advised as to the course, & the tendency of public affairs at home—The 'South' professes satisfaction with the course & policy of the Administration, but no Democrats in that section will make his satisfaction manifest by his a vote in support of the Republican party—At the South, the Democrats manage, without any expressed approval; while the Republicans, acquiesce, & with more or less of significant humiliation, in what they [—] not like, but cannot help. The Press, especially the Liberal Republican Press, and the mercenary, unprincipled Republican lick spittle press such as Murtagh, who always fawns where he hopes for favours, continue to talk of the 'Reforms' introduced & the improvements over the Corrupt ways of the last administration, [— — — — — — — — — —] As a general rule, While Civil Service is talked of, & is very admittedly good in the Abstract, from what so far as I can judge, the present Administration, like its predecessor, finds it easier to talk about, than to put in practice. There is however a very general conviction of the desire of the Administration, to harmonize all sectional feelings, & to conduct the Government economically & honestly. I wish that we were assured of the same inflexible purpose of resumption, & belief in solid hard money, ~~as~~ that marked ~~the last~~ your Administration—but John Sherman, never, while a Senator, shewed more than an Ohio-man's policy on that question— The disturbances arising from the 'Strikes,' are alarming, & pregnant of ~~future~~ grave questions in the future—the violence, & destruction of property by the strikers & by an idle & vicious mob (not really Labourers) have served to keep out of sight very many real wrongs, ~~both~~ against both their labourers & their stockholders, of many of the Rail Road Corporations, which need correction, if we are to hope for ~~quiet from the~~ peaceful relations between Labourers and Capital. But you get enough, & must be tired of such subjects, & I envy you, what the telegraph tells us you must be now enjoying—August & September in Switzerland are among my pleasant recollections of Europe—I hope that Nicholas may have the pleasure of seeing you—The Summer with us has been very pleasant—no excessive heat, & (what is rare, here) no cause, thus far, to complain of drought—Mrs Fish & I enjoy our retirement—friends, give kindly evidence, that they have not forgotten or deserted us—& in a quiet way, our Country home is cheered by the presence of children & grandchildren, & the frequent visits of valued friends—we are rarely quite alone, & never have more than we are delighted to have with us—I have been my own Gardener & farm & general Superintendent this year so you see that I have been sufficiently busy & occupied: he, whom I have had for more than thirteen years, has broken down in health, & his long & faithful service makes me reluctant to make a change; I have preferred assuming his labour: but I fear the change will be forced upon me—When you return, I shall hope to shew you what I may have done, notwithstanding that you always laughed at my farming & made amusing calculations of the cost of my hay & potatos—I fear that they still are rather expensive, but then ~~you~~ one must consider the feeling of '*independence*,' of raising all you need,!! (of hay & of potatos) but don't ask me about oats, & other grains. I am all right on apples—& in the matter of vegetables & small fruits, am in sufficient affluence to be a liberal dispenser to my neighbours—Mrs Fish, has been recruiting under the influence of summer saltair (which always gives service to her) at Newport—I went to bring her home, & enjoyed a few days there— ~~we returned two days since~~—She joins me in kindest & most affectionate regards to Mrs Grant & yourself . . ." "Your welcome letter of 9th Septr reached me, while I had a housefull of company staying with us. Nicholas and his wife, with his two children (whom we had never seen) had just arrived. A few days later I went to NewYork to attend the meeting of the Peabody trustees, where your absence was much regretted. We had a full quorum and very many kind things were said of you—thence I went to Boston to attend the triennial meeting of the Episcopal Church General Convention, and remaining there about three weeks, was summoned home to attend the funeral of my friend & relative Winthrop Chanler. I had a very pleasant visit to Boutwell, at Groton, & passed a night there. Many pleasant reminiscences were brought up—Boutwell was warmer in his expressions toward you, than he is generally on most subjects, but I was delighted with the enthusiasm with which his wife, daughter and son spoke of you & Mrs Grant, & of your Administration. Chief Justice Gray [—] & several others were equally earnest. I was satisfied that Boston is not 'all Sumner' nor very much 'Anti-Grant'. While I was in Boston Wendell Phillips delivered a lecture on Sumner, assailing you & denying the accuracy of your statements regarding Sumner, as reported by a Herald Correspondent, of his interview with you (I think) in Edinburgh. A correspondent of the Boston Transcript called on me, (whom Phillips had also attacked) and I confirmed the correctness of your Statements. A day or two after I had been summoned home, Mr Pierce, Sumner's Literary Executor, published his 'Inquiry' addressed to me, calling upon me for a 'specification' of the withheld Treaties &c, which, being published in a Boston Paper, which I rarely see, would not have been seen, but for the kindness of Robert C. Winthrop, who sent it to me. I addressed a letter to the Transcript answering Mr Pierce's 'Inquiry,' & giving, I think, a little more information than was expected. The public Press has very generally noticed it, & without an exception so far as I have seen seen, has considered your statement as fully substantiated—Phillips however, has returned to the charge, & repeated his 'Lecture' with additional false charges & vituperation of you & of me, in Philadelphia, on Thursday last, & in New York on Friday—you will find a report of it in the Herald, of 10th inst. I addressed a letter, on this lecture to the Herald, which will be the last notice that I shall feel called upon to take of any thing which that blackguard may say—I inclose copies, of the several articles—they may amuse a leisure ten minutes, if you have any such leisure. The acclaim extended to you wherever you go cannot fail to be highly gratifying, even though it must involve fatigue, & much inconvenience. I observe that you always accept these demonstrations as intended for your Country—in part, you are right—but, my dear General, (excusing your modesty) it would not be thus manifested, but for personal interest in, & admiration of the 'American private Citizen' whose presence calls it out—your replies have been [—] felicitous, and are universally commended—Robeson I fear, is to have trouble again this winter—Whitthorne is chairman of Naval Committee and threatens investigation and exposure, even talks of 'impeachment' and Thompson, Secr of Navy, *I hear*, talks very severely of Robeson, and charges misappropriation of moneys and other irregularities. The Elections this Autumn, have been about 'half & half'—'a good-deal mixed'—The Administration is sustained by the votes of Democrats, in both houses —the Republicans are divided—while confidence is very general, in the integrity of character & of purpose of the President, it is very slight, & diminishing, in the *practical* wisdom, & political soundness of his Cabinet, & of himself—There is less tendency than there was to make invidious contrasts of the preceding Administration, & men & public journals who were praising to the skies, the present, & denouncing the preceding Administration are now freely criticising the present, & remembering *some* good of the former—Time, is apt to work out justice. We have had a pleasant Autumn as yet, very little cold. Nicholas & his family sail day after tomorrow on his return to his post. I hope that he may have the pleasure of seeing you—Mrs Fish desires to be most affectionately remembered to you & to Mrs Grant, to whom I beg you to present my very kindest, & sincere regards— ... P S. your letter reminds [m]e that I must have failed to acknowledge a previous one. I had received it with great pleasure." ALS (press), *ibid.* See *New York Times*, October 4, 5, 1877; *Boston Evening Transcript*, Oct. 19, 22, 26, 1877; Fish to Sevellon A. Brown, Oct. 25, 1877, Fish to Robert C. Winthrop, Oct. 26, 29, 1877, Fish to Henry B. Anthony, Nov. 9, 1877, Fish to editor, *New York Herald*, Nov. 10, 1877, DLC-Hamilton Fish; letters to Hamilton Fish, Nov. 14, 1877.

    1. See letter to Hamilton Fish, June 22, 1877.

To William Rae

Glasgow.
Sept. 11th /77

DEAR SIR:

Please accept my thanks for your remembrance of my request for a copy of the address with which you presented to me the freedom of the Burgh of Wick. It came duly to hand on Sunday morning, the 9th inst. while I was in Inverness spending the day. Your kind words will be preserved by me as a remembrance of a most pleasant visit to the North of Scotland.

With high regards for yourself, the town authorities and the people of Wick, I am, with great respect,

your obt. svt.
U. S. GRANT

THE PROVOST OF WICK

ALS, Gallery of History, Las Vegas, Nev. On Sept. 7, 1877, USG spoke at Wick after an address by Provost William Rae. "I am happy to say that during the eight years of my Presidency it was a hope of mine, which was, I am glad to say, realised, that all differences between the two nations should be healed in a manner honourable to both. All the questions, I am glad to say, were so settled—and in my desire for that result, it was my aim to do what was right, irrespective of any other consideration whatever. During all the negotiations I felt the importance of maintaining these friendly relations between the great English speaking peoples of this country and the United States, which I believe to be essential to the maintenance of peace principles, and I felt confident that by the continuance of those relations the two countries will exercise a vast influence in promoting peace and civilisation throughout the world." *Glasgow Herald*, Sept. 8, 1877. On Sept. 5, Wick officials had designated USG as a burgess. DS, DLC-USG, IB.

En route to Wick on Sept. 7, USG responded to a welcome from officials and citizens in Thurso. DS, *ibid.*; *Glasgow Herald* and *The Scotsman* (Edinburgh), Sept. 8, 1877.

Speech

[*Glasgow, Sept. 13, 1877*]

I rise to thank you for the great honour that has been conferred upon me this day by making me a free burgess of this great city of Glasgow. The honour is one that I shall cherish, and I shall always remember this day. When I am back in my own country, I will be able to refer with pride not only to my visit to Glasgow, but to all the different towns in this kingdom that I have had the pleasure and the honour of visiting. I find that I am being made so much a citizen of Scotland that it will become a serious question where I shall go to vote. You have railroads and other facilities for getting from one place to another, and I might vote frequently in Scotland by starting early. I do not know how you punish that crime of illegal voting over here; it is a crime that is very often practised by people who come to our country and become citizens there by adoption. In fact, I think they give the majority of the votes. I do not refer to Scotchmen particularly, but to naturalised citizens. But to speak more seriously, I feel the honour of this occasion, and I beg to thank you, ladies and gentlemen of this city of Glasgow, for the kind words of your Lord Provost, and for the kind expression of this audience.

Glasgow Herald, Sept. 14, 1877. USG spoke in response to a speech by Lord Provost James Bain of Glasgow. ". . . I think the example shown by the American people in the forgiveness of injuries, and in their desire to live amicably with those who had been their enemies, presents the greatest triumph of Christian principle and practice the world has ever seen. In other countries, what crimes of vengeance have followed on revolutionary wars! The scaffold, the galleys, the fetid swamps of Cayenne, or the frozen deserts of Siberia, have been the fate of misguided patriots; but no such thing happened in America when the war closed. Not a drop of blood was spilt in vengeance. North and South shook hands, agreed to decorate together the graves of their dead, and to go on as one nation—a united and a free people. This great end has been attained by the wisdom and prudence of General Grant—for though he loved the North much, he loved the whole United States more. . . ." *Ibid.* After Bain proposed "three hearty cheers for the youngest burgess," USG replied. "Ladies and Gentlemen,—I am sure you will give a willing response to what I now ask you to do, and that is to give three hearty cheers in honour of the Senior Magistrate, the Lord Provost of Glasgow." *Ibid.* A document given to USG is in the Smithsonian Institution.

On Sept. 12, Greenock officials telegraphed an invitation to USG, who answered. "Many regrets that my time will not permit of acceptance of your kind invitation to visit Greenock." *Glasgow Herald*, Sept. 13, 1877.

Speech

[*Glasgow, Sept. 13, 1877*]

I am called a man of war, but I never was a man of war. Though I entered the army at an early age, I got out of it whenever I found a chance to do so creditably. I was always a man of peace, and I shall always continue of that mind. Though I may not live to see the general settlement of national disputes by arbitration, it will not be very many years before that system of settlement will be adopted, and the immense standing armies that are depressing Europe by their great expense will be disbanded, and the arts of war almost forgotten in the general devotion of the people to the development of peaceful industries. I want to see, and I believe I will, Great Britain, the United States and Canada, joined with common purpose in the advance of civilization, an invincible community of English speaking nations that all the world beside could not conquer. . . . There was one point in connection with that matter that I was glad we yielded—that was the indirect damage claim. I was always opposed to it, because I feared the future consequences of such a demand. In any future arbitration we would have been placed at a great disadvantage by its allowance. After that was settled we made our other demands, you made yours. It was a long time before the Joint High Commission came together, but each side yielded here a bit and there a bit, until about as good a treaty as we could expect to get was completed. Mr. Anderson says many of the people of Great Britain believe we got the best of the bargain. I can assure you that we did not come out of the discussion as much benefited as we should have been. Many of our people were quite incensed and fought the confirmation of the treaty, claiming that its terms were not broad enough to cover the losses of local interests, but a very large majority determined to stand by it in the interests of peace and manly dealing with friends. We yielded more than we intended to yield, but had got so far into the business of doing what we advocated that nine-tenths of our people had no desire to recede. We did not want war, or even a new arbitration. We had been satisfied with the former, and the latter meant delay. We wanted the question settled peacefully, at once and forever.

As to the $8,000,000 surplus, Mr. Anderson mentions, I will explain that briefly. After the $15,500,000 awarded at Geneva, was paid by Great Britain the matter of its distribution was presented to Congress. It became necessary to distribute it under the terms of the treaty, and it was found that if the insurance companies which had received war premiums were admitted to participation in the sum it

would not be large enough to go around. So they and other parties
were excluded. Congress will legislate further in the matter, and the
money will be distributed to rightful claimants, so that it will not be
necessary to discuss the question of returning it to Great Britain.

New York Herald, Oct. 1, 1877. USG spoke at an evening banquet in response to George
Anderson, member of Parliament, who charged "that the United States had gained a victory over Great Britain in the creation of the Geneva arbitration. However, he said, Great
Britain had agreed to the Washington treaty, and while disappointed with the result at
Geneva, had stood manfully by it. In view of this, and the fact that the United States had
completed the distribution of the award and had some $8,000,000 left after all claims had
been satisfied, he would be pleased to see the government return that amount in the interests of concord and thorough amity." *Ibid.*

Speech

[*Ayr, Scotland, Sept. 14, 1877*]

MR PROVOST AND MAGISTRATES, LADIES AND GENTLEMEN—I accept the honour which you have conferred upon me to-day with great
pride and satisfaction. It affords me great pleasure to meet the people
of Scotland, and to meet them so pleasantly as I have done. At every
place I have visited I have felt quite at home with you, as my ancestors did eight or nine generations back. I have been made a burgess
of a good number of burghs in Scotland, but it affords me special
pleasure to be made a citizen of the burgh and the home of Burns. I
have to thank you all for the great honour conferred on me.

Glasgow Herald, Sept. 15, 1877. USG spoke in response to an address by Provost Thomas
Steele of Ayr. The document designating USG as a burgess of Ayr is in the Smithsonian
Institution. At a reception, USG again spoke. "I have been travelling through your country, and have had the honour conferred on me of being made burgess of a number of cities;
but this is the first occasion on which I have felt embarrassed. Why I should have been so,
I cannot say. It was impossible for me this morning to thank the citizens of Ayr as I could
have liked for the honour they have done me. It was a feeling that just came over me at the
moment. I never was a public speaker, but I never was so embarrassed in the few words I
had to say. I have to say now that I disagree with the Provost altogether that this is a small
matter to me. It is a very big matter, and a very great honour you have conferred upon me
and upon my country. Your Provost is generally a correct man, but in this statement I must
take issue with him. I thank you heartily for the compliment, and I now beg to propose
'The Health of the Senior Burgess of Ayr,' your worthy Provost." *Glasgow Herald*, Sept. 15,
1877.

On July 7, 1877, John Pollock, town clerk, had written to USG. "At a recent meeting of the Town Council of the Royal Burgh of Ayr it was stated you are to visit Glasgow, and to be the guest of the Lord Provost of that City, whose residence is in the County of Ayr— the 'Land of Burns.' The Council thereupon unanimously resolved to ask you to honour the town by accepting the Freedom of the Burgh, & they trust it will be consistent with your arrangements to accede to their wish." ALS, USG 3.

To Charles Ratcliff

Inveraray
Sept. 17th 1877

My Dear Colonel;

Your favor of the 15th inst. inviting me to be your guest during my stay in Birmingham is received. It will afford me much pleasure to accept should I visit Birmingham, which I now fear will not be my privilege at the present time. It is my desire to be in the South of England before the close of Sept. and the date for my visit to Birmingham has been fixed for some time in Oct. Should I be able to go to Birmingham however I will inform you of the time as soon as known to myself. With many thanks to Mrs. Ratcliff and yourself for your kind invitation, I remain,

> Very Truly
> your obt. svt.
> U. S. Grant

Col. Charles Ratcliff

ALS, WHi. Birmingham banker Charles Ratcliff served as lt. col., 1st Warwickshire Rifle Vols. (1867–71), and was named honorary col. in another unit (1877). See *The Times* (London), Sept. 4, 1885.

Speech

[Newcastle, Sept. 22, 1877]

Mr. Burt and Workingmen: Through you, I will return thanks to the workingmen of Tyneside for the very acceptable welcome address which you have just read. I accept from that class of people the reception which they have accorded me, as among the most honorable. We all know that but for labor we would have very little that is worth fighting for, and when wars do come, they fall upon the many, the producing class, who are the sufferers. They not only have to furnish the means largely, but they have, by their labor and industry, to produce the means for those who are engaged in destroying and not in producing. I was always a man of peace, and I have always advocated peace, although educated a soldier. I never willingly, although I have gone through two wars, of my own accord advocated war. I advocated what I believed to be right, and I have fought for it to the best of my ability in order that an honorable peace might be secured. You have been pleased to allude to the friendly relations existing between the two great nations on both sides of the Atlantic. They are now most friendly, and the friendship has been increasing. Our interests are so identified, we are so much related to each other, that it is my sincere hope, and it has been the sincere hope of my life, and especially of my official life, to maintain that friendship. I entertain views of the progress to be made in the future by the union and friendship of the great English-speaking people, for I believe that it will result in the spread of our language, our civilization, and our industry, and be for the benefit of mankind generally. I do not know, Mr. Burt, that there is anything more for me to say, except that I would like to communicate to the people whom I see assembled before me here this day how greatly I feel the honor which they have conferred upon me.

Young, I, 94–95. USG spoke in response to Thomas Burt, member of Parliament. "In the name of the working classes of Northumberland and Durham, we welcome you to Tyneside, and we are proud of the opportunity afforded us of expressing to you our admiration for the noble deeds which have made you famous in the history of your country, and the welcome guest of Englishmen. . . . Though you are skilled in the art of war, we are pleased to regard you as a man of peace; but the peace which commands your sympathy must be founded on the eternal laws of equity and justice. The rough scenes of war have no charms for you; but we believe if duty called you would be ready to strike again for the consecration of noble principles. . . ." *Ibid.*, pp. 92–94. See *Daily Telegraph* (London), Sept. 24, 1877.

On Sept. 21, 1877, USG spoke at Newcastle. "The president in his remarks has alluded to the personal friendship existing between the two nations—I will not say the two peoples, because we are one people but we are two nations having a common destiny, and that destiny will be brilliant in proportion to the friendship and co-operation of the brethren on the two sides of the water. During my eight years of Presidency, it was my study to heal up all the sores that were existing between us. That healing was accomplished in a manner honorable to the nations. From that day to this feelings of amity have been constantly growing, as I think; I know it has been so on our side, and I believe never to be disturbed again. These are two nations which ought to be at peace with each other. We ought to strive to keep at peace with all the world besides and by our example stop those wars which have devastated our own countries, and are now devastating some countries in Europe." *Young*, I, 86–87. USG spoke after receiving an address from the Newcastle and Gateshead Incorporated Chamber of Commerce detailing the commercial and industrial growth of the area "since this Country adopted the wise and sound policy of Freetrade, a policy which we regret has not been more generally followed, by other nations recognising as we do to the fullest extent that commerce draws nations together and promotes 'peace and goodwill amongst men.'" D (undated), DLC-USG, IB.

On Sept. 22, Mayor John O. Scott of Newcastle toasted USG at an evening banquet. USG replied. "Mr. Mayor and Corporation of Newcastle: I scarcely know how to respond to what has been said by the Mayor. I have a very vivid recollection that immediately upon my arrival upon these shores the Mayor invited me up here, and we have been carrying on a correspondence, directly and indirectly, ever since as to the time when I should be here. But as to my saying anything after I came, such a thing never occurred to me. I will say that the entertainment by your worthy Mayor has exceeded my expectations. I have had no better reception in any place, nor do I think it possible to have a better. All I have seen since I have been on the Tyne has been to me most gratifying as an individual, and I think when I go back to my own country I will find that it has been very gratifying to my countrymen to hear of it. It has been gratifying all along the Tyne to Tynemouth. It has been gratifying ever since my landing upon English soil. It has been gratifying because I have seen that which is extremely pleasant, namely the good relationship existing, that should always exist, between English-speaking people. I think that is a matter of the vastest importance, because I believe that we have the blessing of civilization to extend. I do not want to detract from other civilizations; but I believe that we possess the highest civilization. There is the strongest bond of union between the English-speaking people, and that bond should and will serve to extend the greatest good to the greatest number. That will always be my delight." *Young*, I, 101.

On Sept. 20, William G. Armstrong, Newcastle, had written to Scott. "Hearing that General Grant is coming to Newcastle at a much earlier hour than was expected I beg that you will inform him that I shall feel much honoured & gratified if he & his suite will accompany you to day to the dinner which I am giving to the Iron & Steel Institute & the Corporation of Newcastle at my Banquet Hall. . . ." ALS, DLC-USG, IB. USG attended Armstrong's dinner. See *The Scotsman* (Edinburgh), Sept. 21, 1877.

On Sept. 21, USG received addresses from officials in Tynemouth and Jarrow. DS, Smithsonian Institution. The North Shields Shipowners Society also presented an undated testimonial to USG. DS, *ibid.* In response to speeches at Tynemouth, USG expressed thanks for the "great and unexpected reception of him that day. He said it struck him as a circumstance of no ordinary interest that 150,000 (as had been estimated) mostly working people had made so great a sacrifice as to keep holyday to receive him as the representative of American institutions in the extremely enthusiastic manner they had done." *The Times* (London), Sept. 22, 1877. USG had been invited to visit Middlesbrough on the same day. See William Hanson to Adam Badeau, Sept. 11, 1877, DLC-USG, IB.

On Sept. 22, Gateshead officials welcomed USG. DS, Smithsonian Institution. USG "said that he felt it a great honour to receive addresses from the different cities in the North of England. He had already expressed his sentiments with regard to the amity existing between the two English-speaking peoples, and was glad to say that this feeling was warmer than it has ever been before." *Daily Telegraph* (London), Sept. 24, 1877. See *Young*, I, 106.

To Ulysses S. Grant, Jr.

———

Hesleyside,
Bellingham,
Northumberland.
Sept. 23d /77

DEAR BUCK.

Since you have had a letter from either your Ma or I we have rec'd two from you. I hope you will continue to write often because when your Ma is a week without letters from her worthless children she grows uneasy. The Cub has left us and gone to Paris where I suppose he is vagebondising to his hearts content.[1] We had a most delightful visit through Scotland, and most enthusiastic receptions everywhere. In Glasgow we were the guests of Lord Provost Bain who, with his daughter, seem to remember you most pleasantly. They are very pleasant people, and I much regret that we did not have the pleasure of entertaining them when they were in America. My reception at all points has been most gratifying but it is getting wearisome. Before we went to the Continent I had invitations to visit every important town in England & Scotland. Some I accepted positively and others conditionally. This week will close up all the positive engagements and I shall accept no more.[2] Next Sunday[3] we will spend quietly at Leamington and the next day go down to see Nellie and lay off there, and at Mr Jessup's,[4] Torque, until about the time to start for Paris.—Yesterday and the day before I received no less than six addresses from corporations, Merchants Exchange, working men &c. to all of which I had to reply, without the slightest idea beforehand of what I was to hear, or what I should say. It being very well understood that I am no speaker makes the task much easyer than it otherwise would be, but even as it is I would rather be kicked—in a friendly way—than to make these replies. Remember me to Judge Davies, Mr. Tremain,[5] your partners in business, Messers Alexander & Green and to Miss Gaither[6] when you write. Miss G. is a very nice girl and I see you think so too.

Affectionately yours
U. S. GRANT

ALS, USG 3.

On Oct. 15, 1877, a correspondent reported from Washington, D. C. "Ex-President Grant, in a letter just received by a relative, states that he has found the labor of accepting the hospitality of his English friends more arduous than the cares of State. It had, in fact, become so great a tax upon his health that from the 1st of October he had determined to retire to private life and that the first thing he should do would be to avail himself of the courtesy extended by the Secretary of the Navy to visit the Mediterranean in one of the vessels of the European squadron and spend some time in the waters of Italy. He does not expect to return to the United States until December of next year." *New York Herald,* Oct. 16, 1877. See letter to Richard W. Thompson, June 17, 1877.

1. On Sept. 9, Jesse Root Grant, Jr., had left Edinburgh. *The Scotsman* (Edinburgh), Sept. 10, 1877. His memoirs inaccurately portray him as continuing to tour with his parents. See Jesse R. Grant, *In the Days of My Father General Grant* (New York, 1925), pp. 246–50.

2. On Sept. 23, Mayor John J. Nason of Stratford upon Avon wrote to Adam Badeau, consul gen., London, welcoming USG. ALS, DLC-USG, IB. On Sept. 28, USG received an address from Stratford upon Avon officials encased "in a Casket made out of Shakespeare's Mulberry Tree." DS, Smithsonian Institution. In response to a toast, USG "said it afforded him the greatest pleasure to visit the birthplace and home of so distinguished a citizen of the world as Shakespeare. That name was regarded with as much reverence and honour in America as in this country. He should not have considered himself a true American if he had neglected to visit Stratford-on-Avon." *Daily Telegraph* (London), Sept. 29, 1877. Also on Sept. 28, J. Scott James, Congregational minister, and three other ministers, Stratford upon Avon, wrote to USG. "We write to express the deep interest with which we regard your visit to this ancient & classic town. We should not like this occasion to pass without intimating to you the deep interest & admiration with which we have regarded your public career, & our knowledge—of the wide-spread sympathy which pervaded the religious bodies with which we are connected during the progress of that momentous struggle in which you bore so conspicuous & noble a part Our devout hope is that the outcome of that struggle will be the lasting consolidation & signal prosperity of the great Commonwealth over which it was your lot to preside Trusting that you may long be spared to render valuable service in the councils of your country, & that Almighty God may ever hold you in in his gracious keeping . . ." LS, Smithsonian Institution.

3. Sept. 30.

4. Alfred D. Jessup, retired Philadelphia paper manufacturer and wealthy investor, maintained a residence in England. See *New York Tribune,* July 6, 1881; *Julia Grant,* p. 216.

5. Probably Lyman Tremain, noted N. Y. lawyer, former county judge, and U.S. Representative (1873–75). See letter to Ulysses S. Grant, Jr., Oct. 27, 1877; *New York Times,* Dec. 1, 1878.

6. Possibly the daughter of Alfred Gaither, western superintendent, Adams Express Co. See *ibid.,* Nov. 26, 1880.

Speech

[Sunderland, England, Sept. 24, 1877]

I wish to return my thanks to the Trades Union and the friendly societies who have honored me with this address this morning. I wish you to say to these societies that I regard it as a very great honor. The language of the address which has just been read has shown so much friendliness, not only for me personally, but to my country, that it gives me great cause for pride. I shall preserve this with many other addresses I have received while on these shores, and I shall hand them down to my family to be revered by them, no doubt, as long as our generations last.

Young, I, 106–7. USG received an address from John Jeffrey, president, Trade and Friendly Societies, Sunderland, and fourteen others. ". . . We noted with feelings of gratification your expression of goodwill towards our fellow workmen in the South of England and the way in which you spoke of labour, when you said it was held in such high esteem in your Country, that there was no public office, but that it could aspire to—. . . We would now General ask you to exercise your great influence in advancing Free Trade, the removal of unjust tariffs and other obstructions to Commercial intercourse between your Country and ours and that you will ever continue to encourage all measures productive of peace that give security to Nations. . . ." D, Smithsonian Institution. See Speech, *[July 3, 1877]*.

On Sept. 1, 1877, Mayor Samuel Strong of Sunderland wrote to Adam Badeau, consul gen., London, concerning USG's visit. ALS, USG 3. On Sept. 17, Henry Martin, vicar of St. John's, Sunderland, had written to USG. "Before the honour of your visit to Sunderland was contemplated, arrangements were in progress for having a large public meeting on the evening of Sept. 24th in connexion with the Church of England Temperance Society. Sermons are to be preached in all the Church of England Churches in the town on the previous day. I do not know what arrangements are intended for you for the evening of that day & whatever they may be I do not wish to interfere with them, or to trespass on your time or Kindness, but if you can come for a few moments to our meeting and address it in a few words, you would help forward a great and important cause in the town, and give great pleasure and encouragement to many. . . ." ALS, DLC-USG, IB. On Sept. 22, William Snowball, town clerk, wrote to Badeau completing USG's arrangements. ALS, *ibid.* On Sept. 24, Sunderland officials welcomed USG. D, Smithsonian Institution. At a luncheon, USG spoke. "I know the best feeling exists in the United States towards the people of Great Britain. We feel that it is a matter of the greatest importance, not only to ourselves, but [al]so to the civilised world, to move together. With one language, with one energy, with one interest, I may say in all that goes to advance civilisation, we are destined as friends to take a big figure in the civilised world. Therefore it is my sincere hope that the friendship that exists now may continue and increase." *Daily Telegraph* (London), Sept. 25, 1877; variant text in *Young*, I, 107–8.

Speech

—

[*Sheffield, England, Sept. 26, 1877*]

It affords me singular pleasure to visit a city the name of which has been familiar to me from my earliest childhood. The name of your industrial city has been familiar not only in the States, but, I suppose, throughout the civilized world; your city has been distinguished for its industry, its invention, and its progress. If our commerce with you has not increased so much as you might wish, yet it has increased, I think, with Sheffield since the days of which I speak—when we had no cutlery except that marked "Sheffield"—for it must be very much larger to-day than it was then. We are learning to make some of these goods ourselves, and I believe occasionally now we put our own stamp upon them. But Sheffield cutlery still has a high place in the markets of the world. I assure you that it affords me very great pleasure to receive the welcome you have given me to-day, and I shall carry away with me pleasant recollections of all I have seen in Sheffield.

The Times (London), Sept. 28, 1877; variant text in *Young*, I, 108–9. USG spoke after a welcome by Sheffield officials and a formal address. ". . . We hope that your visit to Sheffield may afford you gratification, and may enable you to ascertain the means whereby the Trade and Manufactures between the United States and this Country may be encouraged." DS, Smithsonian Institution.

On June 28, 1877, Mayor George Bassett of Sheffield had written to USG. "I am requested by the Council of this Borough to present to you the annexed Resolution passed by them at a Special Meeting held this morning, inviting you to honor Sheffield with a visit, which I hope you will be able to do on your return from the Continent." LS, DLC-USG, IB. The resolution is *ibid.* On Sept. 20, John Yeomans, town clerk, wrote to USG, Newcastle, concerning his visit. LS, *ibid.* On July 4 and Sept. 17, Yeomans had written to Adam Badeau, consul gen., London, on the same subject. ALS, USG 3; DLC-USG, IB.

On Sept. 21, Claudius B. Webster, consul, Sheffield, wrote to Badeau. "I think it proper to consult you in regard to a wish I have to invite the American Merchants of Sheffield to meet Gen. Grant for an hour at a convenient time and place, during his visit. The Shippers of goods to the U. S. from Shefd are an important body of men, and such an attention would be *very* gratifying to them, and would promote good feeling, at this time when they are feeling so much the loss of their trade. . . ." ALS, *ibid.* See Webster to Badeau, Sept. 22, 1877, *ibid.*

Speech

[*Sheffield, England, Sept. 26, 1877*]

I feel highly gratified with the reception that you have this day given to me. In the matter of free trade that you refer to, I would hardly be able to speak without some preparation. It must be recollected, however, that the country which I have the honour of representing has gone through a great war. It contracted a great debt in suppressing the rebellion, and this has rendered it necessary to raise large means to support the remaining expenses of the Government, and to pay the interest of the debt, and it is impossible to raise those revenues from internal resources. Revenue from imports is now regarded as one of the means of raising the necessary money to pay the interest upon the national debt, and the other expenses incident to the carrying on of the Government, and if we were to abolish all revenues from imports the foreign bondholders would very soon be crying out against us, because we failed to pay the interest upon the bonds which they hold. But we will get on rapidly enough, and will compete with you in your own manufactures in the markets of the world.

The Scotsman (Edinburgh), Sept. 27, 1877; variant texts in *The Times* (London), Sept. 28, 1877, and *Young*, I, 109. USG spoke in response to an address by David Ward, master cutler, that "referred expressly to the extensive trade that was carried on between Sheffield and America, and expressed a hope that the effect of General Grant's visit to England would be to assist in removing the very high import duties which now pressed very severely upon Sheffield manufacturers trading with America." *The Scotsman* (Edinburgh), Sept. 27, 1877. Ward also presented USG with a testimonial dated Sept. 21, 1877. DS, Smithsonian Institution.

On Sept. 26, the Sheffield Chamber of Commerce presented USG with an address. DS, *ibid.* USG replied. "It is scarcely necessary I should add anything to what I have already said in acknowledgment of my reception in Sheffield. In regard to your merchants and mechanics who have gone to our country and have helped to build up our manufactures, I can only say we received them with open arms. The more of you who go the better we will like it, and I hope it will be to their advantage. Business with us at this time is a little depressed, as it is all over the civilized world; but the day is not far distant, in my judgment—certainly I hope it is not far distant—when trade and commerce will revive, and when we shall see more of you and your sons and daughters over there; see them succeed, see them make pleasant homes and become good citizens and law-makers with us, and see them, when they are qualified, office-holders. I can assure you nothing gives us more pleasure than to see the emigration of the industry and intelligence of this community. We have room for all, and a hearty welcome for all, and if you only come among us we will try to treat you as you have treated me today." *Young*, I, 109–10.

Speech

———

[*Sheffield, England, Sept. 27, 1877*]

MR. MAYOR, AND LADIES AND GENTLEMEN OF SHEFFIELD: It makes my heart feel glad when I hear these sentiments uttered in regard to my own country, and to the friendship which should exist between the two nations. As I have had occasion to say frequently, it has always been a cherished view of mine that we should be the best of friends. I am sure, as an official in a position that gave me some little power of healing the little grievance that was caused between the two nations, I exercised all the influence I had to bring about a settlement that would be a final settlement, as I believed— and I believe now that it is a final settlement. It was not a question of whether we should get this or that, it was simply a question of whether we should agree; it was not a matter of dollars and cents —they were entirely unnamed as compared with the question of a settlement. Our wish was simply to have a settlement—that both parties should agree and settle the matter. We have agreed upon terms, and I believe that this is the beginning of a long series of years —I hope centuries—of friendly and honorable rivalry between the two great English-speaking nations and the advancement of each. Whatever tends to the advancement of one in some way or other will tend to the advancement of the other.

Young, I, 114. USG spoke at a banquet in response to speeches, including one by Anthony J. Mundella, member of Parliament. *Ibid.*, pp. 112–13.

Speech

———

[*Leamington, England, Sept. 29, 1877*]

I know the feeling of friendship between the two great English-speaking nations is strengthening day by day and year by year. I have no doubt that in the future, all our differences having been amicably and fairly adjusted, we shall go along hand in hand, as honourable rivals in producing what is necessary for the comfort and the support of man, and that our united efforts will be felt throughout the civilized world, and will have the beneficial effect of carrying there a better civilization than I fear is now existing in some of those nations that are regarded as civilized. I hope that, through our influence, we may be able, at some future day, to settle questions of difference that may spring up among nations without resorting to arms. Although it has been my misfortune to have been engaged in as many battles as it was possible for an American to have been engaged in, I never was for war, but always preferred to see questions of difference settled by arbitration. But in our great conflict there was the institution of slavery, which was not a conflict between two nations, but a family quarrel, and there was no other way of settling it. Every honourable effort was made on the part of the North to avoid war. One thing that possibly is not generally known—at all events, it is not generally spoken of—is that our lamented and martyred President, when he said that the conflict was inevitable, proposed to the South that the planters should be paid for their slaves, if they would surrender them, and return into the family circle. This the South refused, and the result, as you are all aware, was the loss of this species of property without compensation. I thank you heartily for the kind reception which you have given me.

The Times (London), Oct. 1, 1877; variant text in *Young*, I, 116–17. USG spoke after receiving an address from Mayor Henry Bright of Leamington. "... It was a memorable day for your Country, and a great day for humanity at large when by the efforts of Abraham Lincoln and yourself, aided by the enlightenment of the American people, Slavery was for ever abolished from your Land—We are proud to honor and welcome you to-day as one who completed that great work. ..." DS, Smithsonian Institution. On Sept. 24 and 25, 1877, Bright had written to Adam Badeau, consul gen., London, concerning arrangements for USG's visit. LS, DLC-USG, IB.

To Adam Badeau

———

Wars-Ash House
Titchfield Hants
Oct. 3d /77

DEAR GENERAL:

I am in receipt of your letter enclosing Mr. Jessups invitation and your two replies. It is ofcourse always pleasant for me to have you with me but as I do not intend to have any public demonstrations it is not necessary if your public duties require you at home. I have written to Southampton declining the banquet but saying [that, if agreeable to the Mayor and Corporation, I would drive over there on Friday or Saturday by 12 M., and would pay my respects to them at any place they might designate, and return here not later than at five,—starting time—in the evening.[1]

I am surprised at Alvord's letter.[2] Does he explain the change come over his views since his former letter advising you of the decision of the Atty Genl? There are but two officers—you and Sickles —affected by the decision, and as you had made no claim for Army pay while] in other Govt. employment, and as Sickles is now out of the public service—active—it would look as though he had raised the question and got a decision in his favor.

I shall probably go to Torquay on Monday next. If you feel like going, and that you can do so without detriment to the public service, my sending your letter ~~of~~ declining need not interfere.

I will telegraph you the exact day when I will be in London as soon as possible, and also the day when I will go to Birmingham.

Yours Truly
U. S. GRANT

GEN. A. BADEAU

ALS (incomplete), Munson-Williams-Proctor Institute, Utica, N. Y.; *Badeau*, p. 482.
On Aug. 29, 1877, Adam Badeau, consul gen., London, wrote to Orville E. Babcock. "You know what a life one leads travelling with General Grant, and how little time is left for writing letters; you will not think I have forgotten to write, or that I neglected to do so. All that you and I saw with him the first year after the war has been repeated here, and is still going on. I am amazed beyond what I can tell you, at his reception every where—

not only in England but Belgium, Germany Switzerland—Italy. He did not enter a single town where some extraordinary attention was not paid him. And now that he is back on this island, the invitations from cities and great Individuals are coming in daily by scores. You can imagine how delightful it is to me to be by his side again, and to witness all this honor paid him after enduring for years the sight of the efforts to injure and malign our old chief. He often talks of you, and always with the profoundest sympathy and kindness. He repeats to me all that Porter said of his entire confidence in you, and of his detestation of those who so cruelly sought to wound him through you. He expresses the same opinion of the one detestable viper whom we all warmed in our bosoms, and who turned upon each one of us to sting us; but whose venom was more particularly spent in his attacks on you. The wretch I certainly think the worst man alive. I never read or heard of inquity like his. I dont know that I have any news for you beyond what I suppose you have seen in the newspapers. I find the General just what he always was, as simple and natural as it is pos- sible to imagine amid all these newer honors; and more affectionate, kinder, more confiding than ever. I find him grown in character, in head, and heart; or rather I should say devel- opped, not grown. He told me that he had spoken twice to Mr. Hayes who promised him twice that I should not be disturbed; so your good offices last spring were not in vain. I thank you again, my friend; and hope sometime I may repay them. Give my best and kind- est wishes to Mrs Babcock and the boys, . . ." ALS, ICN.

1. On Oct. 6, Saturday, USG visited Southampton and received memorials from lo- cal officials. D (Oct. 4) and LS (Oct. 6), Smithsonian Institution. USG then "said that the warmth of the reception he had met with on all hands since his arrival in this country from all classes of the people of Great Britain was very gratifying to him as an individual, and especially so as in some measure representing officially the people of the United States. It always afforded him great pleasure, as far as lay in his power, to cultivate the feelings of union between the two nations, which should always be strong friends and allies in the spread of commerce and civilization. He begged sincerely to thank the Mayor and author- ities of Southampton for the kindness of that day's welcome." *The Times* (London), Oct. 8, 1877.

On June 7, R. J. Pearce, town clerk, Southampton, had written to USG, London, invit- ing him to "a Municipal Banquet." ALS, USG 3. On June 9, Pearce wrote to Badeau ex- pressing regret that USG declined this invitation. ALS, *ibid.*

2. On July 2, Brig. Gen. Benjamin Alvord, paymaster gen., Washington, D. C., wrote to Badeau concerning retirement pay from the army while on the State Dept. payroll. Copy, ICN. See Babcock to Badeau, Oct. 7, 1877, DLC-Adam Badeau. On Dec. 11, Attorney Gen. Charles Devens wrote to Secretary of War George W. McCrary that Badeau "has ceased to be a retired officer of the Army . . . and, in direct answer to the question submitted by you, I have the honor to state that, in my opinion, his name cannot therefore be now legally continued on the retired list." *Official Opinions of the Attorney General,* XV, 407–10.

To Adam Badeau

———

Wars-Ash
Oct. 5th /77

DEAR GEN.

I enclose you two cards of invitation to the Merchant Taylors[1] feast which you may accept formally. I have already informed them informally, in reply to a note sent to ascertain if I could attend, that I would be in London on the 18th of Oct.

My plans from now until we go to the Continent are about complete, and if you will be kind enough you may arrange accordingly. On Monday the 15th we will be in London; on Wednesday, the 17th, I would like to go to Birmingham to return the next day evening. On Saturday—the 20th—we go to Brighton to be the guests of Capt. Ashbury[2] until the following tuesday. We then return to London and will go to Paris on the 24th

I am amased at what you say about Pierrepont, but are you sure he has made any such statements as you quote? Every thing I have said in his presence—or elswhere—disproves his statements if he has made them. You have been of incalculable help to me, and your presence has been most acceptable to our whole party. When I see Pierrepont I will take occasion to put in a few words that he will feel if he has been talking as you suspect.[3]

Very Truly Yours
U. S. GRANT

GEN. A. BADEAU

ALS, Munson-Williams-Proctor Institute, Utica, N. Y.

1. A London guild co. chartered in 1327.
2. James L. Ashbury, railroad manager and champion yachtsman, had represented Brighton in Parliament since 1874.
3. According to Badeau, "[t]he last part of this letter refers to the assertion made by a prominent American that I had not been authorized or invited to accompany General Grant on his tour, but had thrust myself upon him." *Badeau*, p. 483.

To Adam Badeau

Wars-Ash
Titchfield
Oct. 8th /77

DEAR GENERAL:

I enclose you a letter which has just been returned to me. I wish you would drop a note to Mr. Walter [1] making the explanation.

I was under the impression that I wrote you that we would go to Birmingham on Wednesday, and telegraphed to correct the date. From your last letter however I see you wrote to the Mayor [2] that we would be there on tuesday, which is right. [3]

We start in a few minuets for Torquay.

AL (signature clipped), Munson-Williams-Proctor Institute, Utica, N. Y.

1. John Walter followed his grandfather and father as chief proprietor of *The Times* (London). See Samuel Smiles, *Men of Invention and Industry* (New York, 1885), pp. 180–204.
2. On June 20, 1877, Mayor George Baker of Birmingham invited USG to "visit and to dine with the Burgesses in the Town Hall." LS, USG 3. On Aug. 30, Baker wrote to Adam Badeau, consul gen., London, that USG had postponed acceptance of this invitation until autumn. Copy, DLC-USG, IB. On Sept. 15, Baker wrote to USG to ascertain the date of his visit. ". . . I have to apologise for your having been troubled so frequently on this point but as many official & other appointments are dependent on your reply I shall be glad to be favored with it as early as may be convenient to yourself In a communication made to General Badeau a period between the 5th & 13th October was suggested, but any day after the 4th of that month will be equally convenient for your reception in Birmingham— . . ." LS, *ibid.*
3. USG arrived in Birmingham on Tuesday, Oct. 16.

To Adam Badeau

Torquay
Oct. 9th /77

DEAR GENERAL:

I shall leave London for Paris on the 24th. The Saturday [1] preceding we go to Brighton to remain until the following tuesday. You see by a letter returned to me—and which I sent to you—that I answered Mr. Walter promptly. I also wrote, the first day after my arrival at Wars-ash, to every one who had entertained me—including the Mayor of Leamington[2]—whom I had not previously written to. We will go to London on Monday next. I will telegraph you the station at which we will arrive, and the hour in time.

yours Truly
U. S. GRANT

GEN. A. BADEAU

ALS, Munson-Williams-Proctor Institute, Utica, N. Y.

Probably in Oct., 1877, a *London World* reporter questioned USG's reputation for taciturnity. "I know at least that he kept a friend of mine by the button hole for two hours at a stretch the other day while discussing a variety of topics and getting through three cigars. Among other things, he said that the deep current of English sympathy for America, as evinced by the reception he had received, had made a great impression on the American people. He gathered this from the numerous letters that had reached him, as well as from the spirit of the press in America. He appeared to take a lively interest in India and all relating to it, and mentioned his intention of visiting that country on his way back to America. He thought we need have no fear about our silver currency, as America could provide now more than enough for the whole world's use. Comparing the Indian mutiny with the rebellion of the South, he said that they had to contend against one factor which we in England seemed never to have taken into account. During the war they had 4,000,000 of traitors in the North itself, who required constant watching, and were an ever present element of danger. With regard to the present war, he said that at first America was with Russia, as her old ally; but that since the war commenced opinion had undergone a great change, and it was now pretty equally divided on the subject. Mr. Vanderbilt., who died the other day worth £18,000,000, he said, could neither read nor write; yet he was, to look at, a most polished gentleman. His chief pleasures were trotting horses and whist. He would think nothing of staking £500 or £1,000 on a rubber, as he said, 'just to keep away the boys.' His son, who has inherited this colossal fortune, is a comparative miser. Leaving him out, the four wealthiest men in America at the present day are Irishmen and Roman Catholics; they have got all the silver mines in their hands, and no one can tell the amount of their money. The ex-President declared he would have made very short work of the railway strike, by a wave of his hand indicating he would have brought the sabre into play at an early stage, and so have nipped it in the bud." *New York Herald*, Oct. 15, 1877. On Nov. 2, USG discredited this report as "absolutely false" and "gave expression to his feelings in very strong language." *Ibid.*, Nov. 3, 1877.

    1. Oct. 20.
    2. See Speech, [*Sept. 29, 1877*].

Speech

[*Birmingham, Oct. 16, 1877*]

Mr Mayor, ladies and gentlemen, it is with great pleasure I find myself in Birmingham, a city that was so well-known in my country during the trying periods that have been referred to by your worthy Mayor. The name of your distinguished representative who has represented you so long,[1] is as familiar in my own country as in his own home, and I can promise that if he should ever visit the United States, and I hope he will, he will receive as hearty a welcome as it has been my privilege and pleasure to receive at the hands of the English community whilst I have been among you. The connection between this city and the United States has been as intimate as that between the States and any other city of the same population. There is a warm feeling of fellowship between our citizens and the citizens of Birmingham. That feeling existed when the feeling was not good between the United States and all parts of Great Britain—I mean to say that that feeling has existed as far back as I know. I believe the feeling between the citizens of the United States and the citizens of this great Empire is good, is increasing, and is what it should be.

Glasgow Herald, Oct. 17, 1877; variant text in *Young*, I, 118. USG spoke in response to an address by Mayor George Baker of Birmingham.

1. John Bright, political reformer and noted orator, first won election to Parliament from Birmingham in 1857. Unable to attend a banquet for USG, Bright sent a letter. ". . . I do not doubt that you will give to General Grant a reception which will show how much Birmingham has been in sympathy with himself and his country." *The Times* (London), Oct. 18, 1877.

Speech

[*Birmingham, Oct. 16, 1877*]

Workingmen of Birmingham: I have just heard your address with great interest. I have had occasion twice before, I believe, since I have been in England, to receive addresses from the workingmen

of Great Britain—once in London and once in Newcastle-on-Tyne.[1]
In my response, on both occasions, I expressed what I thought was
due to the workingmen, not only of my country and of Great Britain, but to the workingmen all over the world. I said that we in our
country strove to make labor respectable. There is no class of labor
that disqualifies a man from any position, either in society or in official life. Labor disgraces no man; unfortunately you occasionally find
men disgrace labor. Your Mayor has alluded to the fact that the population of Birmingham had tripled itself in fifty years. I would ask
the Mayor whether, if Birmingham had been deprived of its handi-
craft laborers, it would have seen any such increase? It is due to the
labor and to the manufacture of articles which are turned out by the
means of labor, that you have grown in population and in wealth. In
response to the kindly feelings which exist between the workingmen
of Birmingham and those of the United States, and the compliments
you have paid to me for the efforts I have made in the cause of freedom and the North, I thank you most heartily.

Young, I, 118–19. USG spoke in response to an address by George Hanson, a jeweller who
represented "the working classes of Birmingham." *The Times* (London), Oct. 17, 1877.

1. See Speeches, [*July 3, 1877*] and [*Sept. 22, 1877*].

Speech

————

[*Birmingham, Oct. 16, 1877*]
MEMBERS OF THE MIDLAND INTERNATIONAL ARBITRATION UNION:
I thank you for your address. It is one that gives me very little to
reply to, more than to express my thanks. Though I have followed a
military life for the better part of my years, there was never a day of
my life when I was not in favor of peace on any terms that were honorable. It has been my misfortune to be engaged in more battles than
any other general on the other side of the Atlantic; but there was
never a time during my command when I would not have gladly chosen some settlement by reason rather than by the sword. I am conscientiously, and have been from the beginning, an advocate of what

the society represented by you, gentlemen, is seeking to carry out; and nothing would afford me greater happiness than to know, as I believe will be the case, that, at some future day, the nations of the earth will agree upon some sort of congress, which shall take cognizance of international questions of difficulty, and whose decisions will be as binding as the decision of our Supreme Court is binding on us. It is a dream of mine that some such solution may be found for all questions of difficulty that may arise between different nations. In one of the addresses, I have forgotten which, reference was made to the dismissal of the army to the pursuits of peaceful industry. I would gladly see the millions of men who are now supported by the industry of the nations return to industrial pursuits, and thus become self-sustaining, and take off the tax upon labor which is now levied for their support.

Young, I, 120. USG spoke in response to an address by Arthur G. O'Neill commending his policies on arbitration, Indians, and blacks. *Ibid.*, p. 119. For O'Neill, see *The Times* (London), May 15, 1896.

Speech

———

[*Birmingham, Oct. 17, 1877*]

Mr Mayor, ladies, and gentlemen of Birmingham, I scarcely know how to respond to a toast which has been presented in such eloquent language, and in terms so complimentary to myself and to the nation to which I belong, and in which I have had the honour of holding public positions. There were some few points, however, alluded to by your Parliamentary representative to which I will refer. He alluded to the great merit of retiring a large army at the close of a great war, but if he had been in my position for four years, and undergone the anxiety and care that I had undergone in the management of that large army, he would appreciate how happy I was to be able to see that it could be dispensed with. I disclaim all credit or praise for doing that one thing. I knew that I was doomed to become a citizen of the United States, and so far as my personal means went, to contribute my share to any expenses that had been borne for the support of the large standing army. We Americans, however, claim to be so much Englishmen, and to have so much general intelligence, so much personal independence, and so much individuality, that I don't quite believe it is possible for any one man to assume any more right and authority than the constitution and the laws give to him. Amongst the English-speaking people we don't think such things possible. We can fight amongst ourselves and abuse each other, but we will not allow ourselves to be abused outside, nor will those who look on at our own little personal quarrels in our own midst permit us to interfere with their rights. Now, there is one subject that has been referred to here that I don't know that I should refer to, and that is the great advantage that would accrue to the United States if Free Trade could only be established. I have a sort of recollection from reading that England herself had a Protective tariff until she had had her manufactories established. I think we are rapidly progressing in the way of our manufactures, and I believe we are becoming one of the greatest free trade nations on the face of the earth. When we both get to be free traders I think it is probable all other nations had better stand aside and not contend with us at all. If I had been accustomed to public speaking I would have said more, but I never spoke in public in my life until I came to England. I think it will be better policy for me, however, to content myself with simply thanking you, not only for the toast and for the language in which it has been presented, but for the very gratifying reception I have had personally in Birmingham.

Glasgow Herald, Oct. 18, 1877; variant texts in *The Times* (London), Oct. 18, 1877, and *Young*, I, 122–23. USG spoke in response to a toast by Joseph Chamberlain, member of Parliament.

To Adam Badeau

London, Oct. 18th *1877*

DEAR GENERAL,

I just returned this a. m. from Birmingham. The reception there was extremely flattering, and the speaches showed not only present

warmth of sentiment for America but that it had been the same during the trying days when many other communities in England felt
and spoke quite differently.—I regret that I shall not be able to get
out to your house—probably—during my stay in London. Hope
however that you will be able to get to Bristol Hotel.

Yours Truly
U. S. Grant

P. S. Will you be kind enough to let me know if Sir __ Watkins
has made arrangements for our departure on Wednesday next?[1] and
if so at what hour we will start, what hour arrive in Paris, and at
what depot we will arrive.

ALS, ICN.

1. On Friday, Oct. 19, 1877, USG, London, wrote to Sir Edward Watkin concerning
travel to Paris. ". . . The hour suits very well and I feel under many obligations for your
kindness. My party consists of Mrs. Grant, self and son, and two servants. I may avail myself of your invitation to invite friends to accompany me as far as . . . Bologna, but I think
not beyond three or four persons. If I do invite any I will inform you of the names and
number." Kenneth W. Rendell, Inc., *Autographs and Manuscripts: The American Civil War*,
Catalogue No. 98, 1974, no. 120. For Watkin, see *The Times* (London), April 15, 1901.

To Adam Badeau

Brighton,
Oct. 22d /77

Dear General:

We leave here at 11 am to morrow; will be at Victoria Stan at
12 30. It will not be necessary for you to send your carriage however
unless you are recovered sufficiently to go yourself. We have a Lan-
dau to meet us. I hope you will be able to go to Bologne on the following day. I have not availed myself of Sir Edward Watkin's invitation to take other guests with me, but if you will write a note to
Russell Young saying that I would be pleased with his company I will
be obliged.[1] If the weather should be rough he might stop in Folk-
stone until the boat returns. I wish you would write a letter for me
to the commander of the Med. Squadron saying that about the first
of Dec. I will go to Spain[2] and if he can have a vessel at Lisbon I will

join him at that port about ten days later. If preferable to meet me at some Medeteranean port I would be glad to have the Comdr inform me, to the care of Drexel Harjes & Co. Paris.

As the time approaches I am anxious to get off to the Continent, though I have no idea that I shall enjoy my visit there half so much as in England. With kind regards of myself & family, I am,

Truly Yours

U. S. GRANT

GN. A. BADEAU
U. S. CONSUL GN.

ALS, Munson-Williams-Proctor Institute, Utica, N. Y.

1. On Oct. 23, 1877, John Russell Young wrote in his diary. "... Letter from Badeau that Gen Grant wants me to go to Folkestone with him.—Call on the Gen. at Hotel Bristol and meet him as he comes in from Brighton in a heavy pouring rain.—See Smalley who thinks it very nervy to have printed the interview about Sumner in which I do not agree" DLC-John Russell Young. See *ibid.*, Oct. 21, 1877; following letter; first letter to Hamilton Fish, Nov. 14, 1877.
2. See letter to Ellen Grant Sartoris, Nov. 22, 1877.

Speech

————

[*Brighton, Oct. 22, 1877*]

MR. MAYOR AND GENTLEMEN: I have to rise here in answer to a toast that has made it embarrassing to me, by the very complimentary terms in which it has been proposed. But I can say to you all, gentlemen, that since my arrival in England, I have had the most agreeable receptions everywhere; and I enjoy yours exceedingly. In a word, I will say that Brighton has advantages which very few places have, in consequence of its proximity to the greatest city in the world. There you can go and transact your business, and return in the evening. If I were an Englishman, I think I should select Brighton as a place where I should live, and I am very sure you could not meet a jollier and better people anywhere. But I would say one word in regard to a toast which preceded, and that is in regard to your Forces. I must say one word for the Volunteers, or Reserve

Forces, as I believe you call them. They are what the English-speaking people are to rely on in the future. I believe that wherever there is a great war between one civilized nation and another, it will be these Forces in which they will have to place their confidence. We English-speaking people keep up the public schools in order to maintain and advance the intelligence of our country, and, in time, fit our people for volunteer service, and for higher training; and you will always find the men among them who are equal to any occasion.[1] I have forgotten a good deal our Mayor has said that I would like to respond to, but I can say, that since I landed in Liverpool, my reception has been most gratifying to me. I regard that reception as an evidence of the kindest of feeling toward my country, and I can assure you, if we go on as good friends and good neighbors, that the English-speaking people are going to be the greatest people in the world. Our language is spreading with greater rapidity than the language of any other nation ever did, and we are becoming the commercial people of the world.

Young, I, 124. USG spoke in response to remarks by Mayor John Mayall of Brighton.
    On June 15, 1877, G. Reeves Smith, gen. manager, Brighton Aquarium Co., wrote to USG. "I am desired by my Directors to express the hope that you will honor the Brighton Aquarium by a visit during your stay in this Country—I need scarcely say that your wishes as to the details, would be strictly adhered to. I shall be obliged by the favor of an early reply." LS, DLC-USG, IB.

    1. A variant text adds: "In the course of my experience I went out as a Volunteer, and I had occasion to build a bridge 2,000ft. long across a very rapid stream; and I found that the Volunteers were capable of doing the work. It was during the Vicksburg campaign, and the success of my scheme was due to that. I always find this among Volunteers, but never among Regulars. We don't find that intelligence in the rank and file of the Regulars. They can do manual labour; but among the Volunteers you find that you have mechanics and men of every profession and capacity, so that with them I built 2,000ft. of bridge where there was great depth of water and great swiftness of stream, and that, too, with very little delay. That is where the Volunteers come in and play the most active part, and the ablest part." *The Times* (London), Oct. 25, 1877.

To Abel R. Corbin

————

HOTEL BRISTOL
5 PLACE VENDÔME.
Paris,
Oct. 25th, '77.

MY DEAR MR. CORBIN:

Our trip has been a most agreeable one though the time seems long. I can scarcely realize that but little more than five months have passed since we sailed from Philadelphia. But we have received nothing but kindness wherever we have been. In England, as you may have seen, our reception has been as enthusiastic as anything in the States directly after the war. We are now in Paris for the first time. As yet I have seen but little of it, though enough to know that it is a most beautiful city. We shall probably remain here over a month, and then make a trip through Spain and Portugal, and up the Mediterranean, in a naval vessel, stopping at all points of interest on both sides. Mrs. Grant finds she has brought too much baggage with her and proposes to send two or three trunks back, clothing brought from the States, and wants to send them either to Jennie or Mrs. Sharp to keep until our return. If they are sent to you I will advise you when they are shipped.

We were disappointed in not getting to Copenhagen while Mary was there. But Switzerland was so agreeable, and there were so many points of interest to visit that I found it impossible to get there and return to Scotland at the time I had promised. It is now very doubtful whether we will not have to abandon the idea of going there altogether.[1] That will depend however upon whether we remain over another year. This winter we propose to go up the Nile, and may keep on east and return by San Francisco. But if we return we will stop in Italy until the weather begins to get warm in the Spring and then go north through Austria, North Germany, Russia, Sweden, Norway and back by Denmark and Holland, spend the latter part of the summer again in Switzerland, and go east the following winter. Jesse will hardly go with us unless we go through this winter. He does not wish to leave another year before beginning the battle of life.

Give Mrs. Grant's, Jesse's and my love to Mother and Jennie, and
Mary if she is with you.

I keep very little track of political matters at home, knowing
from experience the trouble a "new hand at the bellows" has. I hope
all will be smooth and satisfactory before my return. I have not yet
experienced any discomfort from lack of employment after sixteen
years of continuous care and responsibilities. I may however feel it
when I once settle down, though I think not.

Very truly yours,
U. S. Grant.

P. S. Direct letters to the care of Drexel, Harjes, & Co., Bankers,
Paris, France.

J. G. Cramer, pp. 134–36. On Oct. 24, 1877, USG, Julia Dent Grant, Jesse Root Grant, Jr.,
and John Russell Young traveled from London to Paris. See Young diary, Oct. 24, 25, 1878,
DLC-John Russell Young; *The Times* (London) and *New York Herald*, Oct. 25, 1877.

  1. See letter to Michael John Cramer, Aug. 13, 1877.

To Ulysses S. Grant, Jr.

Paris, France
Oct. 27th /77

Dear Buck,

We came over here on Wednesday, the 24th, and are staying at
the Hotel Bristol. Departments the finest in the city, and terms moderate considering their ordinary charges. I am not prepared yet to
say whether I shall like Paris or not, but I have seen enough to say
that it is a most beautiful city. We have called on Pres. McMahon,[1]
and dine with him on the 6th of Nov. We now have engagement
for three evenings in in the week up to the 10th of Nov. I intend to
have a more quiet time than when in England. We had Nellie with us
the last three weeks in England. She is very well but a little thin. I
see by the New York Herald that Con. Va. was up to—and above—
the limit which I had fixed for its sale! Has it been sold? If it has not
I will state to you my directions in the matter. I fixed Forty-two dollars pr. share as the price before dividends were resumed, and a re-

duction of $1.50 pr. s. after each dividend. Afterwards I directed Seligman to hold 300 shares for your Ma from sale until specially directed. These orders hold good now if the stock has not been sold. There has been now—I think—six dividends declared which brings the limit down to 33. My recollection is that dividends commenced in May. If so I am right in my statement. If not until June then the present limit is 34 50 or 50 cts. above the limit. I wish you would look after this matter for me.[2] Jesse does not seem well, and is very anxious to return, but his mother is not willing. He will return however in time to enter Columbia Law School next Autumn.

Give my kindest remembrance to Judge Davies, Judge Tremain and to each member of your firm. All join in love to you.

Yours Affectionately
U. S. GRANT

U. S. GRANT, JR.

ALS, USG 3.
    On Oct. 10, 1877, Frederick Dent Grant, Chicago, wrote to Ulysses S. Grant, Jr. "... I have received several news papers from Mother & they are haveing a time (not pleasant) but very complimentary) . . ." ALS, *ibid.*

    1. Maurice de MacMahon attained the rank of field marshal in the French army (1859) and succeeded Louis Adolphe Thiers as president (1873). On Oct. 26, 1877, a correspondent reported from Paris. "General Grant paid a visit to the Élysée yesterday. The Marshal expressed his pleasure at making the acquaintance of so distinguished a soldier, and offered him every facility for examining the military establishments in Paris and the Provinces in which he might be interested. Mr. Vignaud, Secretary of the American Legation, acted as interpreter. Madame MacMahon, who speaks English with fluency, also conversed with General Grant. . . ." *The Times* (London), Oct. 27, 1877. Interviewed by a French reporter, USG commented on meeting the MacMahons, the excellence of French railroads, and his travels in England. *Le Figaro*, Oct. 27, 1877; *New York Herald*, Nov. 15, 1877. See also *ibid.*, Oct. 26, 30, 1877; *Glasgow Herald*, Oct. 27–30, 1877; *The Scotsman* (Edinburgh), Oct. 29, 1877.
    On Oct. 26, 27, and 28, John Russell Young wrote in his diary. ". . . This evening walked with the General. . . . Talked a good deal about the operations of the armies before Richmond. . . ." ". . . In the morning after breakfast the General went to Healy's studio & gave a sitting for a portrait. . . ." "spent the afternoon with Mr. Bennett. . . . While walking on the boulevard with Mr. B. we run against Gen. Grant with whom Mr. B. goes into a long conversation on the Indian question,—the General giving Mr. B. an idea about Sitting Bull which I send to N. Y. . . ." DLC-John Russell Young. See *ibid.*, Oct. 29–31, 1877.
    2. On Nov. 10 and 22, Anthony J. Drexel, Philadelphia, wrote to Grant, Jr. "Yours of 8th recd. I enclose the statements of your Fathers' & mother's accounts by which you will see that the only balance available for investment is that of your mother. Your Father's is drawing on his currency balance for his travelling expenses & it will be soon exhausted. If the Consolidated Stock should go to a price to be able to sell at his limit it would give a

balance in his favor, but in that case that had better be reserved to meet his drawings on us for his expenses unless he has other revenue or income coming in which you intend depositing. I think this explains the position of affairs will be plain to you . . ." "I telegraphed you to day that your mother has drawn a check on us for $3950 *Gold* dated Paris 2d November and to make the check good it is necessary for you to put back the $3000 you drew the other day Please remit it . . . P S. Have just recd your telegram of deposite of $3000 I enclose receipt" ALS, USG 3. The receipt is *ibid.* On Nov. 13, Drexel & Co., Philadelphia, had written to Grant, Jr., New York City. "Your favor of yesterday received with check of $1000 on Drexel Morgan Co. New York which we post to the credit of your father's Currency account as advised. Our charge 77 Oct 4. Should read £150 instead of £50; it is a clerical Error in copying the account which please kindly Excuse—" L, *ibid.*

To Edward F. Beale

————

hôtel Bristol.
Paris.
Nov. 4th, 77

DEAR GENERAL:

I am just in receipt of your letter of the 19th of Oct. I want you to do with "Bob Akers" just as you would if he was your own. Breed him to just as many mares as you think proper. If I should ever want him I will send for him. If not you keep him. It is most likely that when I settled down I shall want a pair to drive, and if he proves fast may want him. In the mean time there will be an opportunity of seeing his colts.

We have been now ten days in Paris, and I have seen pretty well the outside of it.[1] But I have seen nothing here that would make me want to live in Paris, or elsewhere out side of the United States. My preference would be for England of all the countries abroad I have yet seen. It has been a mystery to me how so many Americans can content themselves here, year after year, with nothing to do. Houses are not so comfortable as with us; living is not so good, Society is confined—almost—to the colony temporarily residing here, and the only thing I see to commend Paris to foreigners is that everybody minds their own business and do not interfere with their neighbors—if they pay their bills. We have seen Mamie and have promised to dine with her and husband,[2] quietly, if we get through other engagements in time before leaving. She is very well and appears very contented.—I note what you say about the administration. I hope all will turn out right, and if it does not that the democracy will do some foolish thing in time to consolidate the republicans by the time of the next presidential election.

Poor Morton is dead![3] He is a great loss to the country. His patriotism never deserted him, and the party had no abler expounder of its principles in the Senate. I hope his friends will see that his family do not want.

Please present Mrs. Grant & my kindest regards to Mrs. Beale and Miss Emma.[4]

yours Truly
U. S. Grant

Gen. E. F. Beale

ALS, DLC-Decatur House Papers.

1. On Oct. 26 and Nov. 2, 1877, Edward F. Noyes, U.S. minister, Paris, wrote to Secretary of State William M. Evarts reporting USG's reception in Paris. LS, DNA, RG 59, Diplomatic Despatches, France. See also *The Times* (London), Oct. 30, 1877; *New York Herald*, Oct. 31, Nov. 2, 1877.

2. Edward F. Beale's daughter Mary, called Mamie, had married Russian diplomat George Bakhméteff on Feb. 11. See Gerald Thompson, *Edward F. Beale & The American West* (Albuquerque, 1983), pp. 207–8.

3. See following letter.

4. Beale's daughter Emily, the model for a vivacious character in Henry Adams, *Democracy*. See Thompson, p. 219.

To Lucinda B. Morton

———

Paris, France,
Nov. 5th /77

My Dear Mrs. Morton;

The painful news of your bereavement, and the Nations great loss, in the death of your great husband reaches us here by telegraph. While I was reading from the latest papers of his rapid recovery this sad news comes. His services as Governor of Indiana in the most trying times the Nation has ever passed through, and his counsils and services in the Senate since, and during such an eventful period, will rank him with America's greatest patriots and statesmen. You have the sympathy of all good citizens in your great bereavement, and none I know sympatize more sincerely than Mrs. Grant and myself.

                                    Very Truly & sincerly
                                    your obt. svt.
                                    U. S. GRANT

ALS, InHi. U.S. Senator Oliver P. Morton of Ind. died on Nov. 1, 1877. See William Dudley Foulke, *Life of Oliver P. Morton* (1899; reprinted, New York, 1974), II, 494–506.

On Nov. 5, John Russell Young wrote in his diary. ". . . Walked about an hour with Gen Grant this morning, mainly in the direction of the Arch. Talked about the offer of the C. Justice to Morton and Conkling, and Howe.—Said he never thought of giving it to Stanley Matthews. The story of the offer to R. C. is one that does both the Pres. & R. C. great honor. . . ." DLC-John Russell Young. See *PUSG*, 24, 253–56.

Speech

                                    [*Paris, Nov. 6, 1877*]

LADIES AND GENTLEMEN: After your flattering reception and the compliments of Gov. Noyes I am embarrassed to thank you as I should wish. During the five and a half months I have been in Europe my reception has been very gratifying, not only to me, but also, above all, to my country and countrymen, who were honored by it. I thank the American Colony of Paris. I hope its members will enjoy their visit here as I am doing and hope to do for some weeks yet. I hope when you return home you will find you realized the benefits predicted by our Minister.

New York Times, Nov. 7, 1877. USG spoke at a banquet given "by the American residents of Paris" under the chairmanship of Edward F. Noyes, U.S. minister. *Ibid.* See John Russell Young diary, Nov. 6, 1877, DLC-John Russell Young; *New York Herald* and *Le Figaro*, Nov. 7, 1877. Former col., 39th Ohio, Noyes served as governor of Ohio (1872–74), nominated Rutherford B. Hayes for president at the 1876 Republican convention, and investigated the disputed vote in Fla. See *HMD*, 45-3-31, 495–509.

To Adam Badeau

Paris, Nov. 9th 77

DEAR GENERAL:

In answer to your letter of the 5th inst. I cannot give you definite information as to dates when Mrs. Grant visited me at City Point. She went there however soon after my Hd Qrs. were established there. She returned to Burlington, N. J. after a short visit to arrange for the childrens schooling and went back to City Point where she remained—with the exception of one or two short visits to N. J.—until Lee's surrender and my return to the National Capitol. Mrs. Grant made a short visit to me—the first time after leaving Cairo—at Corinth, next at Jackson, Tenn. then at Memphis where I left her when I went to Youngs Point, at Youngs Point one or two days before running the Vicksburgh Batteries, and at Vicksburgh after the surrender. She again visited me at Nashville.

On leaving Ragatz we traveled to Bale, Switzerland, layover Sunday there; thence to Strasburg where we stopped five or six hours, visiting the Cathedral, fortifications &c. thence to Metz for the night. The next day, until late in the afternoon, was spent in visiting points of interest in and about Metz, and in the evening we went on a few hours travel to a little town—I have forgotten the name of it—near the border of Belgium. This was to save a too early start from Metz. The following day to Antwerp where we spent two days—Thence by steamer to London.

I do not now think I sha[ll] visit Portugal. I have had some correspondence with Adm.l Le Roy [1]—who has taken Wordens place—in regard to the route. He advises against sending a vessel to Lisbon at this season of the year on account of the insufficiency of the Harbor for large vessels, making it necessary to anchor outside. My route will probably be through Madr[id] to Cadiz, thence up the Mediteranean[.] I will write a letter soon to Ge[n.] Sherman, and will take pains to say a word in the direction you mention, and will also remind him of the Presidents promise to me.[2]

We are all very well. I have seen all I want of Paris and bu[t] for engagements ahead[3] would leave without much delay.

With kind regards,

yours Truly

U. S. GRANT

GEN. A. BADEAU

ALS, Munson-Williams-Proctor Institute, Utica, N. Y.

1. Rear Admiral William E. Le Roy. See letter to Commodore Daniel Ammen, Aug. 26, 1877; *New York Times*, Dec. 11, 1888.

2. See letter to Gen. William T. Sherman, Nov. 17, 1877.

3. On Nov. 11, 1877, USG wrote to Emile de Girardin. "Genl Grant accepts with pleasure the invitation of M. Emile de Girardin to dinner on the 27th of November at 7 o'-clock." D (facsimile), eBay, Aug. 24, 1999. On Nov. 17, Robert R. Hitt, secretary of legation, Paris, wrote to USG. "General Noyes on yesterday, calling at Mrs. Sickles house, arranged with her that her dinner to you and Mrs. Grant should be on *Saturday the 24th*; and subsequently at the house of Mr Emile de Girardin who desired to give you a dinner, arranged that it should be on the *27th Tuesday*. Mr. Girardin; who is the leading editor of Paris (La France), and has been recognised for 20 years as one of the ablest friends of Republicanism, will invite Mr. Gambetta and several other leading Republicans to meet you—also the gentlemen of this Legation; and I feel sure that you will find the entertainment at his elegant house an interesting occasion. Please indicate if this meets with your approbation. The Girardin dinner is for *gentlemen* only We now understand your engagements to be for the 17th (tonight) Monday, 19, afternoon at M. Meniers; then dinners on the 20th MacKays, 22nd Talleyrands, 23rd Laugels, 24th Sickles and 27th Girardins" ALS (press), DLC-Robert R. Hitt. At the Girardin dinner on Nov. 27, USG "drank to the prosperity of the French Republic, saying he hoped it would attain the result which Americans had endeavored to attain, namely, a *régime* of liberty accessible to everybody." *New York Herald*, Nov. 28, 1877. See *ibid.*, Nov. 22, 26, 1877; Oscar Lewis, *Silver Kings: The Lives and Times of Mackay, Fair, Flood, and O'Brien, Lords of the Nevada Comstock Lode* (New York, 1947), pp. 70–80, 86–89.

On May 30, 1878, Elizabeth Bates Laugel, Paris, wrote to Elihu B. Washburne. "... In the Autumn we had the great pleasure of seeing General Grant, and the honor of receiving him under our own roof. It was the first time I had ever seen the General; as I was not with my husband when he stayed with General Grant at his camp before Richmond. I need not tell you how much we all liked him and how much we were impressd by the dignity and perfect simplicity of his manner. We asked the Comte de Paris to meet him, and a few friends the Corcelles, and others, who knew and felt a real interest in our country. The General was most interesting and by no means silent,—for he told many most curious things of his own experiences during the war and after he and the Comte de Paris had a very long conversation to which all listened with very great pleasure. . . ." ALS, DLC-Elihu B. Washburne. See Auguste Laugel, "A Frenchman's Diary in our Civil-War Time," *The Nation*, 75, No. 1936 (Aug. 7, 1902), 108.

To Adam Badeau

---

hôtel Bristol.
Paris.
Nov. 11th /77

DEAR GENERAL.

Lest you may want Porter's letter [1] I return it. I wrote to Porter but did not tell him that you had submitted it to Pierrepont before sending it to me. I have nothing new to say to you only that the Count d Paris [2] called on me soon after my arrival here. I was out at the time so I did not see him. But I called at his house soon after— within a day or two—and found that he was living in the country about six hours, by rail, from Paris. I am to meet him at dinner on the 23d [3] when he comes in for the night.

Very Truly yours
U. S. GRANT

GEN. A. BADEAU

ALS, Munson-Williams-Proctor Institute, Utica, N. Y.

1. Horace Porter had made "some political suggestions" concerning USG. *Badeau*, p. 488.
2. Louis Philippe Albert d'Orléans, Comte de Paris, the oldest grandson of Louis XVI, spent 1848 to 1871 in exile and served on Maj. Gen. George B. McClellan's staff during the Civil War. See *PUSG*, 25, 427; *New York Times*, Sept. 9, 1894.
3. See previous letter, note 3.

To Hamilton Fish

Hotel Bristol, Paris,
Nov. 14th /77

MY DEAR GOVERNOR;

I have just received the Herald of the 1st of Nov. containing your most admirable statements in reply to Phillips characteristic scolding of both you and myself. [1] I have not had the opportunity of reading Philips speech,[2] but have seen a number of notices of it. It, and much else I have seen, would leave the impression that I had voluntarily come out to a reporter to injure the posthumous fa[me] of the dead.[3] To disabuse any such impression you might have I now write. The fact is Mr. Sumner's & Mr. Motley's frien[ds] might have extolled their heroes to the skies and I should have never said a word to dim their fame if their overzealous friends had n[ot] found it necessary to abuse th[e] living to magnify public respect for the subjects of their speeches a[nd] writing. But reading Mr. Jay's address to the New York Historical Society—or some society[4]—and Mr. Smaley's eulogy of Motley in the N. Y. Tribune,[5] I did take occasion to state carefully all the facts of differences between the departed statesmen, and the departed Historian, and myself and the the members of the Administration. In both these publications—Mr. Jay's & Mr. Smalley's—either ingnorance of facts were shewn, or else intentional misrepresentations. My statement was made while traveling from London to Edenburg, while the train was traveling at the rate of forty-five miles an hour, and was written out by the correspondent—from memory—afterwards.[6] I never saw his statement until it had been printed in the United States, and the paper in which it was published come to England. It was an undoubted effort to give what I said fully and with accuracy. But it was defective both by omissions and by commissions, all of which I could have corrected if the opportunity had occurred. One important error of commission was in making me pronounce Mr. Sumner so emphatically a lyiar. I stated specifically what I had said to Mr. Curtis about Mr. Sumners misrepresentations; that I did not regard him as an ordinary falsifyer of the truth because he was so egotistical, so infalible in his own estimation, that he believed what he said, and would try to force his statements upon the credulity of those who knew better; instancing his claim to Mr. Boutwell of the authorship,—and the influence to put through Congress—a House Bill which originated in the Committee of which B. was then Chairman, and which he prepared, and wrote himself. Mr. Sumner insisted to Gov. Boutwell that he had written every line of that bill and had forced it through. I stated in regard to Mr. Motley that I regarded him as a gentleman, a scholar and a man of ability, fully capable of representing his government in any capacity, but that he had made a mistake when he was first appointed by me, to England, and explained what that mistake was. Smalley charges me with having been instrumental in producing his death. Six years after his removal—I understand—his health was as good as it ever had been. There was not half the cruelty in his removal,—if it had been made without cause—that there is in this charge of slow murder. Nothing would have been said by me about the true facts in the case but for this and other eq[ua]lly erronious statements published.

Mr. Phillips charges "afterthought" ~~for~~ in bringing charges against Mr. Sumner of neglecting to bring treaties ~~promptly~~ promptly before the Senate! This is so grossly untrue that it contains all the wickedness of a falshood. He either knew better or should have informed himself on the subject. If Geo. William Curtis was as ready to defend me as he is Sumner or Motley, or as he is to abuse me, he could correct this statement.[7] In the course of my conversation with Mr. Curtis about the restoration of Mr. Sumner to the Chairmanship of the Foreign Relations Committee Mr. C. stated that when Mr. S. was removed from that Committee all the work before it was complete, that S. had told him so. I said there were 7, 9, or 11 treaties not acted upon and expressed gratification that when there was a question of veracity between ~~me~~Mr. S. and myself I was glad that it should be on a point so easily settled as to which was right. I sent at once to the State Dept. to get a list of all the treaties before the Committee at the time of Mr. Cameron's elevation to the chairmanship and in a short time Bankroft Davis—you being away from Washington at the time—answered giving full details of all the ~~bills~~ treaties before that Com. at the time referred to, their nature, dates when submitted, &c. and my recollection is now that the number was twelve, not seven, nine or eleven, as I thought. Much with Mr. Sumner must have been afterthought. I never addressed him as Mr. Chairman in my life. I always addressed him as Senator, Mr. Senator or Mr. Sumner. He and his friends claiming that you tried to bribe him to favor the San Doming treaty is an afterthought too that was very unfortunate. I did not ride to Mr. S. house when I went to speak to him about the treaty, but walked. I had not a scrap of paper about me referring to the treaty, but told him the substance of it. He seemed pleased with it and expressed the desire to see it, and asked me to send Gen. Babcock—who had been to San Domingo— to see him with the draft. Gen. Babcock did shew such a draft to him, and he again expressed his approval, pointing out some slight changes,—of language only I believe—that ought to be made. After talking of the treaty Mr. S. turned upon me about his friend Ashly[8] who he hoped I would do something for. It never occurred to me that he tried to purchase a commission for Ashley by giving his support to the San Doming treaty. But in the light of his subsequent conduct, and the readiness of his friends to impute improper motives to you and I, it is a much fairer inference to impute such motives to him. I do not however. Mr. Sumner could never have been bribed but in one way. That would be by flattery.

I have written this off hastily to inform you more particularly as to why I happened to mention this subject in such a way as to get into print. It is probably well however that it has seen the light. The living will die someday, and the friends of Mr. Sumner would have sent false history of them to future generations but for this. I shall be very glad to hear from you.

yours Truly
U. S. Grant

ALS, DLC-Hamilton Fish. See letter to Hamilton Fish, Sept. 9, 1877.

1. On Oct. 29, 1877, Hamilton Fish, Garrison, N. Y., wrote at length to the editor, *Boston Evening Transcript*, concerning differences between U.S. Senator Charles Sumner of Mass. and the Grant administration. ALS (press), DLC-Hamilton Fish. Fish included a list of nine treaties delayed in Sumner's committee. See *Boston Evening Transcript*, Oct. 31, 1877. On Nov. 1, Fish wrote to the editor, *Boston Evening Transcript*, correcting an inadvertent misdating in his original letter. ALS (press), DLC-Hamilton Fish. For letters to Fish supporting his views, see Nathan Appleton (Nov. 2), Timothy O. Howe (Nov. 8), and Henry O'Connor (Nov. 11), *ibid.* See also Fish to Roscoe Conkling and Fish to Sevellon A. Brown, Nov. 28, 1877, *ibid.*, Nevins, *Fish*, pp. 890–93.
2. On Oct. 18, Wendell Phillips, renowned abolitionist and social reformer, had presented a revised lecture on Sumner to the Young Men's Christian Association, Newton, Mass., that "replied to the charge recently made by General Grant, in Scotland, that Senator Sumner was removed from the chairmanship of the Committee on Foreign Relations because he impeded the business of the State Department by neglecting the consideration

of treaties." *Boston Evening Transcript*, Oct. 19, 1877. Phillips also alleged that Fish and USG mistreated John Lothrop Motley. For Fish's response, see *New York Herald*, Oct. 20, 1877. See also *ibid.*, Nov. 10–12, 17, 1877.

3. See Interview, [*Aug. 29, 1877*].

4. To publicize the decision of the New-York Historical Society to reject his tribute to Motley in favor of one that omitted controversial references, John Jay published "Motley's Appeal to History," *International Review*, IV (Nov., 1877), 838–54. Jay especially regretted "that the society should have taken such a step just after General Grant himself had made the opportune and interesting disclosures touching his dismissal, which confirm Mr. Motley's conviction that the coincidence of dates which he placed on record was not accidental, but that his removal was connected with the position of Mr. Sumner in the Senate on the San Domingo treaty." *Ibid.*, p. 839. See *New York Herald*, June 15, Oct. 28, 1877.

5. George W. Smalley graduated from Yale (1853) and Harvard Law School (1855), practiced law in Boston (1855–61), and then began a career as correspondent for the *New York Tribune*. On June 1, 1877, Smalley eulogized Motley, who had died on May 29, and attributed the end of his tenure as minister to Great Britain to "a fit of political ill-temper in Gen. Grant." *New York Tribune*, June 16, 1877. See *ibid.*, Oct. 29, 1877; Smalley, *Anglo-American Memories* (London, 1911); *PUSG*, 20, 183–88.

6. On Aug. 29, 10:00 A.M., USG left London for Edinburgh, arriving that night. *The Times* (London), Aug. 30, 1877.

7. See following letter.

8. James M. Ashley, U.S. Representative from Ohio (1859–69), was among the instigators of President Andrew Johnson's impeachment. After his ouster as governor of Montana Territory, Ashley joined the Liberal Republicans in opposition to USG. On Nov. 12, 1877, George S. Boutwell, Boston, wrote a memorandum. "Accidentally I called at Senator Sumner's house when he was with President Grant and engaged in conversation upon the San Domingo Treaty. . . . When conversation was resumed the President said to Senator Sumner 'I will send the papers over to you in the morning by Gen. Babcock'. Mr. Sumner merely said that he would examine them and he then immediately introduced the subject of the removal of Gov. Ashley from the office of Governor of Montana. He spoke of Ashley's early and faithful service in the anti slavery cause and of his claims upon the republican party. The President was annoyed, evidently, and as far as I recollect he made no answer to Mr. Sumner's remarks. When there was a pause in Mr Sumners observations the President rose, moved toward the door and repeated his remark that he would send the papers in the morning by Gen. Babcock. Mr Sumner then said, after thanking the President, 'I expect Mr President to support the measures of your administration.'" DS, DLC-Hamilton Fish. See Ben: Perley Poore to Henry B. Anthony, Nov. 9, 1877, Fish to Poore, Nov. 21, 1877, Fish to Boutwell, Nov. 22, Dec. 1, 1877, Boutwell to Fish, Nov. 28, Dec. 4, 1877, Fish to Timothy O. Howe, Dec. 1, 2, 1877, Howe to Fish, Dec. 22, 1877, *ibid.*; *PUSG*, 19, 369–71.

To Hamilton Fish

Paris, France,
Nov. 14th /77

DEAR GOVERNOR:

This evening, having read your very interesting reply to Statements made by Mr. Wendel Phillips, in relation to Sumner Motley
matters, I hastily wrote, and mailed, a letter to you while Mrs. Grant
was dressing for a dinner party which I had also to dress for in time
to accompany her. Having returned from the party it occurs to to me
that I neglected to state that as soon as I received Bancroft Davis' reply I forwarded it to Mr. Curtis. He recollects the matter I know, for
he afterwards told me so, remarking that it was astounding. I should
probably have left out of my letter the words, "or if as ready to defend as to assail me" in the sentence in which I stated that Mr. Curtis could have corrected the statement that it was an afterthought
to charge Mr. Sumner with deliquency in presenting matters before
his Committee to the Senate. I keep no copies of letters, hence do
not quote, verbatum, the sentence referred to, and probably not the
words in quotation.

Please remember Mrs. Grant and myself to Mrs. Fish and to all
the members of your family.

Very Truly Yours
U. S. GRANT

GOV. HAMILTON FISH.

ALS, DLC-Hamilton Fish. See previous letter.

On March 8, 1878, J. C. Bancroft Davis, Washington, D. C., wrote to Hamilton Fish.
"I saw today a letter from Gen. Stone to Gen. Sherman, written from Cairo, in which he
says 'Gen Grant told me as he was leaving that since he left America he had enjoyed his
stay in no country so much as he had that in Egypt. He received here the newspapers containing Bancroft Davis' demolishment of Sumner, and I think that had something to do
with his enjoyment of Egypt. I need hardly state that I thoroughly sympathised with him
in his satisfaction at seeing that empty idol of New England shown up as Mr Davis did
it.'. . ." ALS, DLC-Hamilton Fish. For Davis on Charles Sumner, see *New York Herald*,
Jan. 4, 1878, reprinted as *Mr. Sumner, the Alabama Claims, and their Settlement* (New York,
1878). See also *New York Herald*, Jan. 9, 12, 1878; *New York Times*, Jan. 9, 1878; Davis to
Hamilton Fish, Jan. 13, 15, 1878, DLC-Hamilton Fish.

To Frederick Dent Grant

———

hôtel Bristol.
Paris.
Nov. 16th /77

DEAR FRED.

Your last letter was rec'd, and, strange to say, there was not one word in it about little Julia. We always like to hear of her if she is a little nuisance. No doubt she will grow entirely out of our knowledge by the time we return to America—unless the bottom should entirely fall out of Con. Va Stock. In that case we will have to return *without delay.*—We have now been in Paris over three weeks. It is a beautiful city, but I cannot see what keeps Americans here except those engaged in business. We are engaged out three or four evenings in each week, but it is always at the houses of Americans temporarily residing here, and the people who we meet on all such occasions are Americans. Of course when I first arrived I was invited to a dinner given by the President, at which his Cabinet was present.[1] But except that it has been American. I do not see that our people have any society except what they furnish among themselves. This is however a very exciting, ~~ploitically~~ time, politically, among the french people. There is just now a bitter struggle between the republicans and the Monarchists, or Conservatives as they call themselves.[2] What the upshot of it all will be is hard to foretell. But I do not give myself any trouble about these matters, nor do I watch home matters as closely as I supposed I would. I have an abiding faith in the good sence of our own people and believe that no matter how uncomfortable appearances may be, at times, all will end well.—I am not certain now that we will not give up our proposed trip through Spain. Every one tells me that the travel is very unpleasant, and particularly when there is a lady in the party, and that the climate is disagreeable at this season of the year. If we do not go by the way of Spain we will probably linger a little longer than we intended in the South of France. Jesse is more reconciled to his travels than he was, but is still anxious to go back and graduate with his class at Cornell.³—All are well and send much love to you all, and kisses to little Chatterbox.

Yours Affectionately

U. S. GRANT

ALS, USG 3.

On Tuesday, Nov. 13, 1877, a correspondent in London transmitted a report sent from Paris the previous night. "General Grant passed an hour this morning (Monday) at the HERALD office, 61 Avenue de l'Opera, reading the American and French newspapers. He expressed himself as highly amused at an article in the *Gaulois* filled with personal abuse of himself and with surprise that the French people should show him so much attention. The *Gaulois*, assuming the leadership of the anti-American crusade, says that our women dress like bar maids and that the men dress like anything but gentlemen. General Grant laughed heartily over both the assaults upon himself and upon the character of the American people. This evening General Grant dined with Mr. Healy, the artist, and attended a reception given by M. Gambetta at a later hour." *New York Herald*, Nov. 13, 1877. See George P. A. Healy, *Reminiscences of a Portrait Painter* (Chicago, 1894), pp. 193–95; Laura E. Richards and Maud Howe Elliott, *Julia Ward Howe 1819–1910* (Boston, 1916), II, 25–26.

1. See *Le Figaro* and *The Times* (London), Nov. 3, 1877.

2. On Dec. 14, 1879, at Pittsburgh, USG spoke at length to reporters and others gathered in his hotel parlor. "When I was in Paris I was visited only by Monarchists of the determined sort. I never saw a Republican at the Elysee. From President MacMahon's conversations with me I was quite certain that his wish to reëstablish the monarchy again for the good of the people, was due wholly to the requirements and influences of the rabid Monarchists who were his only companions. I am convinced that Marshal MacMahon was a loyal Republican at heart and was acting with the best of intentions toward the people, who, his Monarchist counsellors told him, had established a republic in hot blood and after a disastrous war; and they would be very much better off if the monarchy were reinstated. The Marshal was easily influenced by the advisers, and, believing that he was acting for the best, he dismissed every Republican prefect and placed Royalists in their stead. When he issued orders to the army to adopt every fair measure on election day to secure a majority for the Monarchist candidates, Gambetta was thrown on MacMahon's side, and his wonderful Republican speeches before the Chamber of Deputies frightened the President's counsellors, who then persuaded him to take advantage of the power invested in his office of adjourning the legislative body until after election day. Gambetta was thus suppressed, but he advised his Republican friends to adopt no extreme measures, but to vote their ticket quietly. It was then that I arrived in Paris, and I think now that the French people barely escaped another revolution. Marshal MacMahon ordered provincial troops to concentrate on Paris, while all the city barracks were crowded with armed soldiers, waiting the result of the election. It was a great Republican victory at the polls, you know, and, after what he had done, Marshal MacMahon had no alternative but to resign. I am satisfied, however, that his efforts to restore the monarchy were disinterested and loyal to the people; but I am also sure that the French people are Republicans to the heart, and that the present Republic is sure to live, unless the Red Republican Radicals obtain sway." USG then "described his own meetings with President MacMahon, and for more than an hour had the conversation all his own way." *Philadelphia Press*, Dec. 15, 1879.

3. See Jesse R. Grant, *In the Days of My Father General Grant* (New York, 1925), pp. 251–53.

To Edwards Pierrepont

Paris, France,
Nov. 16th /77

MY DEAR JUDGE;

I am in receipt of your letter yesterday, asking me for Mr. B. F. Stevens[1] to set for a Photograph to put in a book which is writing. He probably wants the negative? If he does not most excellent ones can be obtained from Theodore Humblot,[2] whose place is near the Grand Opera House, Paris. As some six or eight negatives were taken it might be one of them could be   If however this will not do I will set again, but would like to have the direction to the Artist sent to me, leaving the name—of the Artist—blank. I ask this because I have promised to set for another Photograph and have forgotten the name of the photographer.

My present plan is to leave here about the 1st of Dec. to go through Spain, coming out at Cadiz about the 15th. From there I shall go up the Mediterranean on one of our Men of War, stopping at all points of interest on both sides the sea. Before spring we expect to go up the Nile.

Please present Mrs. Grant's and my kindest regards to Mrs. Pierrepont, and accept for yourself our acknowledgments for your kindness and hospitality while we were in England.

Very Truly, yr. obt. svt.
U. S. GRANT

HON. EDWARDS PIERREPONT
U. S. MINISTER &c.

ALS, OHi.

1. Benjamin F. Stevens, U.S. dispatch agent, London, also worked extensively in the book trade. See letter to Adam Badeau, Nov. 27, 1877; G. Manville Fenn, *Memoir of Benjamin Franklin Stevens* (London, 1903).
2. French photographer active during the 1870s. See John Russell Young diary, Nov. 7, 1877, DLC-John Russell Young.

To Gen. William T. Sherman

---

hôtel Bristol. Paris.
Nov. 17th /77

DEAR GENERAL:

Ever since I heard that you were on your return home from what must have been a most interesting trip through the far West, I have been thinking of writing to you, though I have but little to say. I read one of your interesting letters to the Sec. of War with great interest.[1] Miles[2] has done good work since, which, with what he had done before, must rank him high with our young officers.

My visit to this side of the water has been enjoyable though not without fatigue and embarrassments. In England everything was pleasant except the necessity of keeping time to engagements that had necessarily to be made in advance. Here in Paris different reasons exist to make my visit at least not independent. France has been for some time in the midst of a political revolution. There seems to be as much estrangement among the members of the different parties as there was between Unionests and secessionests in our border cities during the rebellion. At dinners, receptions &c. you do not meet the two parties mingling. I have nothing to do with their party differences of course, but their papers keep a watch, and attack, no matter where I go in a public way. I am indifferent as to what they say of me, but I do not like to be the cause of attack upon others.

I have not kept well posted on home affairs, but from what I do see I suppose Mr. Hayes is having trials inevitable to his position. In his foreign appointments, and removals, I regreted the removal of Birney, from the Hague,[3] and quite as much the appointment of Goodloe[4] who has all the selfishness common to too many. But it took me some time to find that out. I see it rumored almost every week that Badeau is to be removed from the Consulate Generalship of London! I hardly credit the rumor however because Mr. Hayes told me he would not be,—except for cause, of course—[w]hich means that the mere wanting the place for some one else would not be sufficient reason for his removal.

I shall leave here in a couple of weeks and go up the Mediterranean on a Naval Vessel, stopping at all points of interest on both sides. If you should write to me, a letter directed to the care of Drexel, Harjes, &co. Bankers, Paris, would reach me.

Please present Mrs. Grant's and my kindest regards to Mrs. Sherman and the children, and believe me,

Very Truly yours,
U. S. GRANT

GEN. WM T. SHERMAN

ALS, DLC-William T. Sherman.

1. While on an inspection tour, Gen. William T. Sherman wrote letters to Secretary of War George W. McCrary describing army operations, the Indian situation, and the Yellowstone country. See *New York Herald,* Oct. 13, 1877; *Reports of Inspection Made in the Summer of 1877 by Generals P. H. Sheridan and W. T. Sherman of Country North of the Union Pacific Railroad* (Washington, 1878), pp. 27–58.

2. Col. Nelson A. Miles, married to Sherman's niece, led successful campaigns against the Sioux and Nez Perce in 1877. See Jerome A. Greene, *Yellowstone Command: Colonel Nelson A. Miles and the Great Sioux War, 1876–1877* (Lincoln, Neb., 1991); Peter R. DeMontravel, *A Hero to His Fighting Men: Nelson A. Miles, 1839–1925* (Kent, Ohio, 1998), pp. 81–136.

3. President Rutherford B. Hayes did not remove James Birney, former Mich. lt. gov. and judge, as minister to the Netherlands. See *PUSG,* 26, 193–95.

4. A lawyer who had helped to organize the Republican party in Ky., William C. Goodloe initially advocated the nomination of Benjamin H. Bristow for president but then supported Hayes and was appointed minister to Belgium.

To Adam Badeau

hôtel Bristol.
Paris.
Nov. 17th /77

DEAR GENERAL,

Your letter of yesterday reminds me that I neglected to answer yours about Sheridan. As you may remember—or have data to show—I ordered first one then the second Div. of Sheridans Cavalry Corps to the department commanded by Gen. Hunter. About the time the second division was going I visited General Hunter at Monocacy, where I found his army encamped promiscuously around over the fields in the neighborhood, and a very large amount of rail-road rolling stock concentrated about there. I asked Gen Hunter where the enemy was. He sa[id] he did not know, his orders kept coming so rapidly from Washing[ton] directing him to move here and there to keep between the enem[y] and the National Capital tha[t] he could do nothing towards locati[ng] or pursuing the enemy. I told him that I would find out where he was, and put the whole army rail-road trains and all, in motion for the valley of Va knowing full well—no matter where the enemy might be at the time—that when the rich storehou[se] of the Valley of Va was threatened the enemy would be in the front of our Army to defend it. I then wrote out at Gen. Hunter's table, his instructions. After reading them to him I told him that Gen. Sheridan was in Washington and that I would order him up at once, and advised Gen. Hunter to put Sheridan in Command of the Army "in the field," and to select Dept. Hd Qrs. for himself whereever he liked, and retain general command himself. He said he thought I had better relieve him altogether because Gen. Halleck did not seem to repose the confidence in him he should have in a Dept. Commander. I then telegraphed Sheridan to go to Monocacy at once where I would remain to meet him. When he arrived I was at the station with the orders written out for, and addressed to, Gen. Hunter. The whole country about—which had been filled but a few hou[rs] before with troops and trains of cars—was then entirely clear from all appeara[nce] of warlike preparations. In a short time Sheridan started for his new command and I back to Washington[.] I believe this is all the information called for in your letter, which I have not now got.

I sent all the addresses, boxes &c. I had—excepting the box given by the city of London—to the U. S. before leaving London.[1] The latter I deposited at the bank of Morton Rose &c. I wish, when you are ready to do so, you would box up all the boxes, addresses, albums &c. you have for me, have my name marked outside, and deposite them at the same place.

Very Truly yours
U. S. GRANT

GEN. A. BADEAU

ALS, Munson-Williams-Proctor Institute, Utica, N. Y. See *PUSG*, 11, 358–60, 376–81.

1. See Speech, [*June 15, 1877*]; *Philadelphia Record,* May 1, 1878.

To Adolph E. Borie

Hotel Bristol, Paris.
Nov. 19th /77

MY DEAR MR. BORIE:

We have now been in Paris for nearly four weeks. I know the city "like a native," and Mrs. Grant is quite well acquainted with the places we most hear of: Worths',[1] Bon Marche, the Louvre,[2] fashionable dress & bonnet makers, &c. It is a beautiful city, but I am quite ready to leave. We cannot do so however, before the 1st of Dec. because we have accepted invitations to dinners up to the 29th of Nov. There is a very excited state of public feeling here—as you no doubt see by the papers—and how matters are to terminate is hard to fortell. It looks very much though as if the President might have to retire. I have not seen much of the French people so far, no doubt because of the troubled condition of affairs. But every thing has been pleasant. I called, of course, on the President immediately upon my arrival; the call was returned promptly, and I, with Mrs. Grant & Jesse, were invited to a dinner to meet the family and Cabinet. They were all very agreeable, the [—] speaking most excellent english, as [*do*] several of the gentlemen and ladies of the Cabinet. All seemed inclined to make our stay in this Capital as pleasant as possible, but finding from the press that I was the instrument of attacking—or through whom to attack—others, I have kept as much as possible with foreigners,—to France—mostly Americans.

When we leave here it will be to take a Naval Vessel to go up the Mediterranean. I am getting to be a good sailor like yourself. I wish you could be along, with two other good fellows to play Boston[3] while off of land. We will stop at all places of interest, on both sides of the sea, and probably run up the Nile before we come back. It is possible that on our return from up the Nile we may keep on east, coming out through China, Japan & San Francisco. If so I may stay in the latter place for some time. You and Mrs. Borie must join us there in that case.

Give our love to Mrs. Borie and all our Phila friends, and write to me without waiting as long as I have to answer your letter.

Yours Truly
U. S. GRANT

ALS, PHi.

1. English-born dressmaker Charles F. Worth and his sons sold expensive clothing in Paris. See *The Times* (London), March 12, 1895.

2. Bon Marché and Grands Magasins du Louvre were large clothing stores.

3. A popular card game.

To Ulysses S. Grant, Jr.

Paris, France,
Nov. 21st /77

DEAR BUCK:

Your Ma has purchased two opera cloaks, exactly alike, one for herself and one for a wedding present to Fanny Drexel.[1] The latter I will ship to-morrow, to your address, care of the Collector of the port. The cost of each was four hundred franks, but this is retail price, so I would allow it to be appraised and pay duties on it accordingly. Pay the duties and send it—or take it—to Miss Fanny with your Mas & my compliments, and wish for both of us prosperity and happiness for the young couple.

We have given up the idea of going through Spain this Winter. Every one tells me this will be a most disagreeable season of the year to go there. We may go in the Spring, but even that is by no means certain. On the 1st of Dec. we will leave here for the south of France, and will take a Naval Vessel soon after to coast up the Mediterranean.

I am sorry my Con. Va has not been sold, but I do not doubt but the limit I wrote you will yet be attained.—Some of us have written so often since our arrival in Paris that I have nothing new to write about from here. I have walked over the city so thoroughly that the streets are quite familiar to me. The city is beautiful, but I do not see the inducements for so many Americans remaining here year after year who are not engaged in business. I certainly should prefer any of our large cities as a residence. When you go to Chicago—if you should go—I hope you will run down to St. Louis, at my expense. When you go you will see Judge Long, of course. I want you in addition to call on Mr. Robert Campbell, Gen. Harney, Mrs. Beverly Allen,[2] Mr. & Mrs. Bott (the father & mother of the Mrs. Allen you met at the White House with your cousin Ilie Reese) Mrs. Parsons[3] and Mrs. John O'Fallon, and her sons.[4] Say to Mrs. O'Fallon that you mMa sees a great deal of her daughter, Mrs. Pope,[5] and family, here. They are very well. Judge Long can give you the directions to find all these people, and to see them all will give you a few very pleasant days in St. Louis. I might add to this list Mr. & Mrs. Gerard Allen,[6] who always call on us when we go to St. Louis. Say that we met their daughter—Mrs. Crane in Liverpool, Manchester & London, and became quite well acquainted, and with Mr. Crane, her husband also.[7] All send love.

Yours Affectionately
U. S. GRANT

ALS, USG 3.

1. Frances C. Drexel, daughter of Anthony J. Drexel, married James W. Paul, Jr. See *New York Times*, Sept. 26, 1908.

2. Penelope Pope Allen, widow of a St. Louis lawyer who died in 1845, and a sister of Maj. Gen. John Pope.

3. Possibly Martha P. Parsons, whose husband, Charles, served as asst. q. m. (1862–64) and became a St. Louis banker. See J. Thomas Scharf, *History of Saint Louis City and County:* . . . (Philadelphia, 1883), II, 1398.

4. Caroline S. O'Fallon was her husband's second wife. A son, John J., born in 1840, worked as a realtor. See *PUSG*, 1, 342; John W. Leonard, ed., *The Book of St. Louisans:* . . . (St. Louis, 1906), pp. 441–42.

5. Julia Dent Grant's girlhood friend Caroline O'Fallon had married Charles A. Pope. See *PUSG*, 20, 255–56.

6. Born in 1813 in Cork, Ireland, Gerard B. Allen conducted several businesses in St. Louis. He and his second wife, Eugenia, were both widowed when they married in 1873. See *St. Louis Globe-Democrat*, July 22, 1887.

7. Newton Crane, consul, Manchester, and former managing editor, *St. Louis Globe-Democrat*, had married Mary Frances Allen. See *PUSG*, 25, 320–21; *The Times* (London), May 7, 1927.

To Édouard Laboulaye

[*Paris, Nov. 21, 1877*]

HON: EDWARD LABOULAYE
PRESIDENT OF THE COMMITTEE OF THE FRANCO-AMERICAN UNION.
SIR

I have visited with great interest the work now in progris at the atelier of Mr Bartholdi.[1] The Statue of Liberty promises to be in every way worthy of its purpose and will fitly express the friendship, of the two nations—

The action of the French people in this matter is appreciated by Americans who all regard France with the Kindest Sentiments.

Trusting that this great work will Soon be completed

I am with Sentiments of highest regards

very Respectfully

yours very obdent Servant

[*U. S. GRANT*]

Copy (embedded in Jacques Hartog to John Russell Young, Nov. 20, 1877), DLC-John Russell Young; in French, *Notice sur l'Union Franco-Américaine inauguration de l'exposition des lots de la loterie Franco-Américaine . . .* (Paris, [*1879*]), p. 27. Hartog served as USG's courier. See *Young*, I, 220–24. On Nov. 22, 1877, Édouard Laboulaye, Paris, wrote to USG acknowledging his visit. Walter D. Gray, *Interpreting American Democracy in France: The Career of Édouard Laboulaye, 1811–1883* (Newark, Del., 1994), p. 132; in French, *Notice sur l'Union Franco-Américaine*, p. 28. Laboulaye, French senator and college professor, led the movement to present the Statue of Liberty to the U.S. See Gray, pp. 128–33; message to Congress, Feb. 9, 1877.

1. Born in 1833 in Colmar, France, Frédéric Auguste Bartholdi was known for his colossal statuary. See *New York Herald*, Nov. 1, 1877; Bartholdi, *The Statue of Liberty Enlightening the World* (1885; reprinted, New York, 1984); Marvin Trachtenberg, *The Statue of Liberty* (New York, 1976), pp. 41–61.

To John Russell Young

———

Paris, France,
Nov. 21st /77

MY DEAR MR. YOUNG:

I am in receipt of your note of the 17th inst. inclosing a portion of a letter to you from your brother[1] in Washington. I fear, from all I hear and read, that there are many of his way of thinking. But I trust to the democratic party—by showing their hands in time—to bring~~ing~~ us all out right. I thank you for your courticy in sending me this note, and for your many other courticies. Please say to Mr. Bennet also that I received his note with latest dispatches from his Washington correspondent, and thank him for me.[2]

I enclose you a clipping from Golignani's Messenger.[3] The same thing has come to me before in some of our own papers. It does seem to me that Mr. Sumners friends should be more cautious lest they should convict him of intentional misrepresentation, or themselves of worse. I did not ask Mr. Sumner to support the San Domingo treaty. When the subject of annexation was first proposed by the authorities of San Doming I found they had negociated a conditional loan, on very unfavorable terms, with Hartman [*Hartmont*] Brothers.[4] By the time of the loan they were bound to issue bonds to the extent of fifty ~~million~~ thousand pounds, with high interest, for every thirty-eight thousand pounds of money delivered, up to the following 1st of Jan.y, the total amount of the loan being seven hundred & fifty thousand pounds sterling. Knowing that the U. S. would be bound for this if annexation took place, and that the money would probably be furnished if there was a reasonable prospect of its success, and if not, not, I kept the whole matter a profound secret— from the public—until the time mentioned had expired. As soon as it had I called on Mr. Sumner, not thinking the treaty would be objected to by him, or any one, but because he was the chairman of the Committee on Foreign Relations. A man who had advocated the annexations of islands extending nearly to Asia, so vehemently as Mr. Sumner had done, I did not suppose would oppose the acquisition of fertile lands so near our own shores and masses of population. Mr. Sumner seemed very much interested in my recital of what had been done; the description of the country; its resources, &c. and Mr. Forney—who was present,—said; Senator, you will support that. His reply was prompt and satisfactory, to the effect that he would.[5] He then said he would like to see the treaty. I told him that Gen. Babcock—who had been twice to San Domingo—had a rough draft of it, and, if he desired, I would send him over with it. He said he wished I would. Not before the next day, but within a day or or two, Gen. B. did take the treaty—draft—to Mr. Sumner, who again expressed his approval of it, except in some phrasiology, or minor matters. The treaty, by its terms, expired in four months if not acted upon within that time. Nearly four months expired and it had not been brought before the Senate, when I urged upon other Senators the necessity of taking some action upon the matter; and to secure time, had to get an extension of the treaty for two months. My recollection is that a further extension became necessary before the matter was disposed of.

As soon as the talk ceased about San Doming at the time of my interview with Mr. Sumner, he commenced, abruptly, to talk about his friend Ashley whom he hoped I would do something for. Ashley had been barely confirmed for the Governorship of Montana, and I had removed him for good reasons, and thought of doing so before he ever joined his post. I could not appoint him, under the circumstances, to a new position.

I never thought Mr. Sumner meant the apt. of Ashley as a condition of his support. But I do believe the favor would have been appreciated by him to a considerable extent.

There is no likelyhood that Mr. S. spoke to Mr. Schurtz, at the time mentioned in the enclosed article, about what was said by him or me in the interview which took place. Nothing had occurred, at that time, to bring the subject up. It was weeks afterward before Mr. Sumner manifested any opposition to the measure. The fact is he got at outs with both Gov.r Fish and myself about some matters, without blame on the part of either of us, and became so angered that he was scarsely responsible for his sayings. As many persons, now living can bear witness, on the mere mention of my name, in his presence, he would utter the most outrageous slanders upon me, and say things, even if true, he could [have] known nothing about. I do not want you to publish this; but as I was writing to thank you for favors, and having just read the enclosed slip, I state this for your information.[6]

With great respect,
your obt. svt.
U. S. GRANT

ALS, DLC-John Russell Young. USG mailed this letter in an envelope addressed to John Russell Young in London. AD, *ibid.*

1. James R. Young, chief clerk, U.S. Senate, and former correspondent for the *New York Tribune* (1866–70).

2. James Gordon Bennett, owner of the *New York Herald*, moved to Europe in 1877.

3. An enclosed undated clipping from *Galignani's Messenger*, an English-language Paris newspaper, summarized an interview with Carl Schurz in which he defended Charles Sumner's course during consideration of the proposed treaty to annex Santo Domingo. ". . . Nobody could ever accuse Mr. Sumner of any act of untruthfulness or duplicity in this or any other matter." *Ibid.* For the complete interview, see *New York Herald*, Oct. 29, 1877.

4. Edward H. Hartmont did not act with brothers. See *PUSG*, 20, 122–23, 159; Charles Callan Tansill, *The United States and Santo Domingo, 1798–1873* (Baltimore, 1938), pp. 347–50.

5. Probably in early Oct., 1877, John W. Forney had corroborated USG's recollection of this conversation with Sumner but added qualifications. ". . . There was no bad faith about Sumner's course. I thought, with the President, that he had agreed to support the St. Domingo acquisition, but Mr. Sumner took the ground that he had only consented to consider the subject. With a little more moderation on both sides the two men could have been reconciled; but they were controlled, especially General Grant, by some politicians, who wanted to produce a rupture between the President and the Senator. I tried to compose the trouble, but failed—the quarrel had gone too far. It is not pleasant to reopen these wounds, now that the grave has closed over the illustrious Senator; but I solemnly believe that there never lived a purer, better or more truthful man than Charles Sumner. He had his faults, but he never violated a promise, deserted a friend or uttered a falsehood." *New York Herald*, Oct. 5, 1877; reprinted from *Philadelphia Press*, Oct. 3, 1877.

6. See first letter to Hamilton Fish, Nov. 14, 1877.

To Ellen Grant Sartoris

———

Hotel Bristol, Paris.
Nov. 22d /77

DEAR DAUGHTER:

I received a very nice letter from you day before yesterday, which we were all glad to receive. We like to hear from you just as often as you will write. The only point to answer specially is in regard to the sale of your Adams & Co. Express stock, and converting it into Pullman. If Buck has done so you may be sure it is right. He is where he sees, and knows.[1] It may be that Adams is about to reduce the dividend from 8 to 6 pr. ct. Pullman pays the latter, and is bought for 75 cts.—or thereabouts—on the dollar, while the latter sells for one hundred. I have trusted Buck with a pPower of Attorney for me in all I have.

We have abandoned all idea of going to Spain from here. Every one tells me that it is an unpropitious season of the year, and that the travel would be most uncomfortable, specially for a lady. We will leave here for Nice on Saturday week, the 1st of Dec. and will probably remain in the South of France for as much as ten days. From Nice we will take a *Man of War*—a United States Vesel—and sail along the Mediterranean, stopping at all points of interest, going up to Constantinople, possibly, and certainly going up to the Nile, and up that—but not in the Man of War. We will no doubt meet you in Italy on our return from the Nile.

Your Ma and I will express to you to-morrow a cloak as a New Year's present—a little early, but we do not know that an opportunity will present itself later.

To night we go out to dine with the Marquis d Taillerand.[2] It will be our first dinner with,—exclusively,—French people, since we have been here, except the dinner immediately after our arrival, given by the President, at which his Cabinet was present. We have accepted invitations for every evening but two up to the close of the month. Otherwise I should insist on leaving here earlyer.[3]

Give our love to Algy and the babe, to Mr. & Mrs. Sartoris, and write just as often as you can to some one of us.

Yours Affectionately

U. S. GRANT

ALS, ICHi. Probably in 1877, USG wrote to Ellen Grant Sartoris. "All well and send much love to you Algie & the babe. Your box was sent last tuesday. Your Ma says she will write to-morrow." AN (initialed, undated), *ibid.* See letter to Adelaide Kemble Sartoris, June 2, 1877.

1. On Oct. 26, Adams & McHarg, New York City bankers, wrote to Ulysses S. Grant, Jr., concerning his sale of Adams Express stock. L, USG 3.

2. Napoléon Louis de Talleyrand-Périgord held the title first given to French diplomat Charles Maurice de Talleyrand-Périgord. See *The Times* (London), March 22, 1898.

3. On Nov. 23, Friday, USG's courier Jacques Hartog, Paris, wrote to John Russell Young. ". . . The Dinner yesterday at the Marquis de Taillerand was a splendid affair. I think the best one, the Gen had, althought he is not a great eater, this evening they dine at Mr Augel [*Laugel*], where the Conte de Paris will be: and on Sunday the General take lunch with Mr de Bakhmeteff Secretary to the Russia Ambassy, Prince Orloff has been invited, to lunch with the General. Whe are going this morning to visit the manufactory of Silks, and the Gobbelen Tapistery; I think this will interest the General very much. . . ." ALS, DLC-John Russell Young. For the Gobelins manufactory, see K. Baedeker, *Paris and Environs* . . . (Leipsig, 1888), pp. 257–59.

To Edmund Sturge

hôtel Bristol. Paris.
Nov. 26th /77

MY DEAR SIR:

Your letter of the 21st of this month reminding me of our interview of the 19th of Oct. at the Bristol Hotel, London, and of my promise to acknowledge the receipt of an address from the Society of Friends, to be forwarded to the care of the U. S. Minister to this Capital was received several days since. Although I had received no such address I could not answer your letter more promptly because having received large packages of letters, pamphlets, &c. through our Minister, on my arrival here, I was not sure but the address of which you speak may have been among them, and escaped my attention. But I find that it has not been received. My courier, who packed away my papers, assures me this is the case. I regret it, although I do not know the purport of the Address. But I do know that the Society of Friends, in the United States sustained me through my eight years of the Presidency, in my Peace policy towards the Indians of North America, and in all my efforts to settle, without resort to Arms, all questions between our country and all foreign powers. I most highly appreciate their services in this regard, and shall feel proud to be able to retain the respect and confidence of that society at home and abroad.

Very Truly, Your obt. svt.

U. S. GRANT

EDMD STURGE.

FOR THE SOCIETY OF FRIENDS LONDON

ALS, The Library, Friends House, London, England. Edmund Sturge was a leading member of the British and Foreign Anti-Slavery Society. See *The Times* (London), June 29, 1893. George Stacey Gibson, clerk, Society of Friends, London, signed an address to USG adopted at a meeting on Aug. 3, 1877. "It is with feelings of respect and gratitude that we take the opportunity, afforded by thy visit to this country, of conveying to thee our satisfaction at the cordial support given during thy late Presidency to a general Policy of Justice and Conciliation towards the Indian tribes. Our religious Society, as is well known, always felt the great debt of responsibility which civilized and professedly Christian nations owe to those that are less civilized and enlightened; and we have rejoiced at the opportunity which was afforded, under thy administration, to our brethren in America, of putting their Christian principles to a practical test by sharing with other religious bodies the duty of watching over the interests of the Indians on behalf of your government. . . ." DS, Smithsonian Institution. On Nov. 30, USG, Paris, wrote to Gibson. "I am in receipt of the copy of an Address, the original of which was mailed on the 22nd of September, from the Society of Friends in London, to me, supporting the policy which I adopted during my term of office towards the Indian savages of the West. I thank your Society for their kind expressions, and approval of my course, and assure them—the Friends—that I ever had the unanimous support of their brethren in America in this policy." *Extracts from the Minutes and Proceedings of the Yearly Meeting of Friends, Held in London, 1878* (London, n. d.), p. 67; copy (printed), Earlham College, Richmond, Ind.

To Adam Badeau

———

Paris, France,

Nov. 27th /77

DEAR BADEAU.

I met Mr. Lincoln at Ft. Monroe the day after the Mine explosion.[1] I do not think anything was said about putting Sheridan in command of "the Army in the Field" under Hunter. Having sent the majority of Sheridans command North I sent him also. He did not join it however until I telegraphed him from Monocacy, to Washington, to join me there. I remember distinctly requesting that Sheridan should be put in command of the forces in the field, and of receiving a reply to the effect that it was feared he was too young for so important a command. The Magnanimous action of Gen. Hunter enabled me to give him the command while I was upon the field from which he started.

I do not recollect anything that was talked about while in Washington on my return from Monocacy.

I wrote Pierrepont a letter in reply to one from him containing a request from the publishers of "Men of Mark,"[2] asking me to set for a photograph for their work, adding my thanks for his hospitalities while at at his house.—I wrote to Sherman as I told you I would do, speaking of your services to me, and of the Presidents promise that you should not be disturbed.[3]

Your statement is correct that I was not on the field when Warren carried the Weldon road nor at his Reams Station battle.

I have given up my visit to Spain for this Winter. On Saturday of this week[4] we start for Niece, stopping over sunday at Lyons, and over tuesday at Marsailes. From Niece we will take the Vandalia[5]— Naval Vessel—and sail along the Mediterranean. Just our stopping places will be determined after we go aboard.

All my family are well and join in best regards to you, and wishes for your health and prosperity. Whether Jesse goes with us will depend upon a letter he hopes to receive from Cornell University. I rather think however his mother will insist upon his going.[6]

yours Truly

U. S. GRANT

ALS, RPB. See letter to Adam Badeau, Nov. 17, 1877.

1. July 31, 1864. See *PUSG*, 11, 356–57.
2. Possibly correspondence related to *Men of Mark: A Gallery of Contemporary Portraits . . .* (London, 1876–83), a series that never published an entry for USG. See letter to Edwards Pierrepont, Nov. 16, 1877.
3. See letter to Gen. William T. Sherman, Nov. 17, 1877.

4. Dec. 1, 1877.

5. On Nov. 30 and Dec. 20, Lt. Commander Albert G. Caldwell, U.S.S. *Vandalia*, wrote to his family. ". . . We are to take the great ring-master about the mediterranean it has cost me much annoyance & trouble already and Im in hopes that his money will give out before he gets to Cadiz where we are to pick him up—I hear that it costs him nothing to travel gets special trains & steamers, hotel men struggle to get him into their houses free & in fact I think he travels cheaper than I can do it without family. Cruising on the Mediterranean in winter is no fun—I hope we will get heavy gale on his first visit & then he will leave for good & all. We have a lot of his wine aboard & Govt has ordered certain expenses to be paid—(It comes out of contingent fund) . . ." ". . . The party consists of Genl & Mrs Grant—young Jesse, a lad of 19 summers with promise of a beard & mustache: a maid servant; a courier; and Mr J. Russell Young—Asst Editor of the Herald. Genl Grant is bluff & hearty weighs about 180 lbs—looks grim & does not talk when strangers are about but is quite chatty with us on board   I think he is a very capable man—bright & witty when he wants to be but diffident as a young girl in company & silent as a post before the world.—is full of anecdotes about Mexican war & men of the times—some of his remarks are very terse & epigrammatical. Mrs Grant is about the height of Mama—not of graceful or Sylph like figure—must weigh as much as the Genl: has a pleasant motherly face—expects a good deal of attention—is not well up in history & geography—very cross eyed: always kind & pleasant. Jesse is a good deal like his father—quiet but desires to be a swell—has been much flattered but on the whole is a nice young fellow—smart enough—always gentlemanly & gives no trouble. The maid is large enough for two maids—towers away above all the family is an old family servant & seems to be a good one—The Courier speaks all the tongues under the sun—is rather forward & has to be set back now & then—quite a good looking fellow & the best dressed man on board. Mr Young is a brick full of fun—just like a boy off for a holiday which indeed it is to him. I like him very much—is a Philadelphian by birth—lives in New York—5 ft 8 high—blue eyes brown hair an open countenance—red English whiskers—is full of information & is the confidant & personal friend of the Genl   There you have the whole party . . ." ALS, InHi. On Jan. 10, 1878, Caldwell again wrote to his family. ". . . my opinion of old USG has changed wonderfully—he is as pleasant & jolly as can be & I can see now how he had friends who stuck to him through thick & thin—One thing that makes me like the whole party is the affection existing between all them   the Boss & Jesse are as kind and attentive to the mother as if she were a sweet girl of 18 summers—she must have been a good mother & wife to have held on to their affection so strongly through all the temptations of their high life & that too against odds for she is very cross eyed. We had a picture taken of Officers & the Grant party—. . ." ALS, *ibid.*

6. See Jesse Root Grant, *In the Days of My Father General Grant* (New York, 1925), pp. 257–67.

To Michael John Cramer

Paris France,
Nov. 27th, '77.

MY DEAR MR. CRAMER:

I am just in receipt of your letter of the 21st inst. enclosing one from the Portuguese Minister to Denmark recounting the cause of his brother-in-law's removal from the diplomatic service. I know Baron de S—,[1] and the Baroness very well and esteem them very highly. There was never any difficulty with him and the State Department, or with any official at Washington that I have any recollection of. I am very sure that no cause of complaint could have existed on our part without my knowing it. It would afford me the greatest pleasure to meet the Baron and his wife during my European tour, but I fear I shall not be able to do so. My trip through Spain and Portugal has been put off, or at least postponed, for this year.[2] On Saturday[3] we leave here for the South of France, from there to take a naval vessel to visit all points of interest on the Mediterranean. We shall probably go up the Nile, and spend the winter in a warm climate, to be ready for our northern tour in the spring. It is barely possible that when we return from up the Nile we may go on East, through China and Japan to San Francisco. But this is not probable for another year. This will probably be the last opportunity I shall ever have of visiting Europe, and there is much to see that I have not seen, and cannot see this winter.

I hear from home occasionally, but not as often, probably, as you do. All were well by the last advices received two days ago from Orville.

Please assure your colleague that I have no recollection of other than the most pleasant relations between U. S. officials and the Baron de S.

With kind regards of Mrs. Grant, Jesse and myself, I am,

Very truly,
U. S. GRANT.

J. G. Cramer, pp. 137–38.

1. Baron de Sant' Anna's differences with Portuguese commissioners to the Centennial Exhibition contributed to his removal as minister to the U.S. See Benjamin Moran to Hamilton Fish, Nov. 13, 1876, DNA, RG 59, Diplomatic Despatches, Portugal.

2. On Dec. 11, 1877, Benjamin Moran, U.S. minister, Lisbon, wrote to Secretary of State William M. Evarts reporting that Portuguese officials felt "the greatest gratitude towards ex-President Grant for his just decision in the affair of the Island of Bolama" and would be disappointed if he did not visit their country. LS, *ibid. Foreign Relations, 1878,* p. 736. See letter to Adam Badeau, Oct. 27, 1878; *Documentos Relativos á Questão dos Direitos de Portugal á Soberania da Ilha de Bolama . . .* (Lisbon, 1870); António dos Mártires Lopes, *A Questão de Bolama: Pendência entre Portugal e Inglaterra* (Lisbon, 1970).

3. Dec. 1.

To John Russell Young

hôtel Bristol. Paris.
Nov. 28th /77

MY DEAR MR. YOUNG:

Your last letter, and enclosures, were duly received. Please accept my thanks. I had seen, and read, all except the card of Curtis.[1] It is hardly worth while to reply to any thing he states because he shows that if he could conscienciously contradict any statement of mine he would willingly do so. Please do not publish anything I have written to you. It will tend only to keep open a strife where those who have papers at the controll, and dead men for their subjects, have greatly the advantage.

But for Jay's attack on Gov. Fish & myself, and Smalley's very unjust statements in his notice of Mr. Motleys death, I would never have given my statement to the papers.

Very Truly Yours,
U. S. GRANT

ALS, DLC-John Russell Young. See letters to Hamilton Fish, Nov. 14, 1877; John Russell Young diary, Nov. 13, 26, 1877, DLC-John Russell Young; Edward L. Pierce, "A Senator's Fidelity Vindicated," *North American Review,* CXXVII, CCLXIII (July–Aug., 1878), 61–80.

1. On Nov. 12, 1877, George William Curtis, West New Brighton, N. Y., wrote "To THE EDITOR OF THE HERALD:——In your issue of to-day, referring to the Sumner controversy, you say:——'In these circumstances it is hardly credible that Mr. Curtis would remain silent if there were anything he could say in vindication of Mr. Sumner. This silence has the air of an admission that he knows General Grant's charges to be true.' I cannot allow that con-

struction to be put upon my silence. General Grant said to your reporter in Scotland that he had undertaken to prove to me that Mr. Sumner had made statements 'knowing them to be falsehoods.' The facts are these:—In a conversation with General Grant, which I have always considered as confidential, I mentioned as evidence of Mr. Sumner's peculiar fitness for the chairmanship of the Committee of Foreign Affairs that he had said to me that upon leaving the committee he had left a clean docket. General Grant replied that this was untrue, for there were several treaties upon which Mr. Sumner had not reported, and he added that he would send me a list of them. Subsequently I received from him the list which Mr. Fish has recently published. I was naturally surprised, but never for a moment did I suppose that Mr. Sumner meant to deceive me. My confidence in his truthfulness was not in the least disturbed. My conviction was then and is now that I had misunderstood what he intended to express by the phrase he used, and having learned the hopelessness of any effort to effect a good understanding between him and General Grant I never mentioned the subject to him again. But whatever the misunderstanding may have been, I do not believe, nor did I ever give General Grant reason to suppose, that I believed that Mr. Sumner, as General Grant asserts, stated what he knew to be a falsehood." *New York Herald,* Nov. 13, 1877. See *ibid.,* Nov. 10–12, 28, 1877; *Harper's Weekly,* XXI, 1089 (Nov. 10, 1877), 878–79.

Earlier, Curtis had upset USG by charging the Prince of Wales with disrespectful treatment of USG at a dinner. See *Harper's New Monthly Magazine,* LV, cccxxvii (Sept., 1877), 622–23; *New York Herald,* Oct. 1, 1877.

To Adam Badeau

———

hôtel Bristol. Paris.
Nov. 30th /77

DEAR GENERAL:

Your letters of the 28th, with enclosures, were received this morning. I took time to read your chapter of history with which I am much pleased, and find nothing to correct. Being my last day in Paris—for the present—I had much to do, calls to return, &c. and to dine out this evening.[1] I could not answer until now—nearly midnight.

The cattle raid took place [while I was away from City Point.[2] I cannot call to memory the time of my visit to Burlington to see after the children's schooling;[3] but Mrs. Grant never went with me there before the night of Mr. Lincoln's assassination.[4]

The present Atty. Gen. Devens was, I think, the Cavalry Gen.[5] Gen. Torbert can answer that question, and it is too late for me to ask him. He goes with me in the morning however and I will ask him then.

I believe this answers all your questions in your last letters. For the next fifteen days my address will be Nice, France. After that anything directed to Drexel, Paris will reach me. But it is likely you will have my directions.

I told you in a former letter that I had written to Sherman as I stated I would.[6] I also wrote to Porter, but nothing affecting your status in your present position. Porter received my letter I know because Buck says in one of his last that it was shown to him.[7]

I hope you will persevere in your work, and if "four-in-hand" goes slower than a "single team" that you will come down to the faster method of driving] one at a time.

With kindest regards,
your obt. svt.
U. S. GRANT

GEN. A. BADEAU

ALS (incomplete), Munson-Williams-Proctor Institute, Utica, N. Y.; *Badeau*, pp. 492–93.

1. Prominent banker John H. Harjes gave a farewell banquet for USG. *New York Herald*, Dec. 1, 1877.

2. C.S.A. cav. raided the army cattle herd at Coggins' Point, Va., on Sept. 16, 1864. See *PUSG*, 12, 168–71.

3. USG went to Burlington, N. J., on Sept. 17–18. See *ibid.*, pp. 171–72.

4. See *Julia Grant*, pp. 154–56.

5. USG confused Charles Devens with Brig. Gen. Henry E. Davies, Jr. For Devens, see *PUSG*, 10, 324; *ibid.*, 24, 141–42.

6. See letter to Gen. William T. Sherman, Nov. 17, 1877.

7. See letter to Adam Badeau, Nov. 11, 1877.

To Commodore Daniel Ammen

HÔTEL DE FRANCE, NICE, December 10, 1877.

MY DEAR ADMIRAL,—On Thursday afternoon[1] we go aboard the Vandalia to make our excursion of the Mediterranean.[2] How much I wish you were in command to unfurl, for the first time, your Admiral's flag![3] We breakfasted the other day with Admiral Le Roy, and saw all of the officers then in port here. They seem to be a nice set of youngsters. They were not all at the breakfast, of course, but they came on board of the flag-ship, and I had the pleasure of meeting them. It would be pleasant to you to hear how they all spoke of you. There was quite an expression of opinion among them, placing you in the highest place in the profession. Of course I told them that I owed you an old grudge as being responsible for the many trials and difficulties I had passed through in the last half a century; for nearly that length of time ago you rescued me from a watery grave.[4] I am of a forgiving nature, however, and forgive you,—but is the feeling universal? If the Democrats get into full power, may they not hold you responsible? But, as you are about retiring, I hope no harm will come to you for any act of kindness done to me.

Our trip thus far has been most agreeable. The weather in Paris was most atrocious, but I got to see most of the people. My opinion of their capacity for self-government has materially changed since seeing for myself. Before coming here I did not believe the French people capable of self-government. Now I believe them perfectly capable, and they will be satisfied with nothing less. They are patient "and of long suffering," but there will not be entire peace and quiet until a form of government is established in which all the people have a full voice. It will be more republican than anything they have yet had under the name of a republic.

Give all our love to Mrs. Ammen and all the children; write to me often, and don't be disappointed if I do not answer each of your letters as received.

Yours faithfully,

U. S. GRANT.

Daniel Ammen, *The Old Navy and the New* (Philadelphia, 1891), p. 17. Since leaving Paris on Dec. 1, 1877, USG had traveled to Lyons and Marseilles.

1. On Dec. 13, John Russell Young wrote in his diary. ". . . Went on board the U. S. S. Vandalia, with Gen. Grant & family,—and was received with very great cordiality.—Sailed at five for Genoa—The sea calm and the weather cold." DLC-John Russell Young. Young had resigned as manager of the *Herald* London office and procured leave from James Gordon Bennett to travel with USG. See *ibid.*, Dec. 4–6, 8, 10–12, 14–15, 1877.

2. See letter to Adam Badeau, Nov. 27, 1877, note 5.

3. Commodore Daniel Ammen's promotion to rear admiral dated from Dec. 11.
4. See Ammen, p. 16.

To Adam Badeau

Naples, Dec. 18th /77

My Dear General:

Your letter and enclosed chapter of history were received here on our arrival yesterday. I have read the chapter and find no comments to make. It is no doubt as correct as history can be written "except when you speak about me." I am glad to see you are progressing so well. Hope Vol 2 will soon be complete, and that the book will find large sale. No doubt but Gov. Fish will take great pleasure in aiding you in your next book. He has all the data so far as his own dept. was concerned. It was his habit to sum up the proceedings of each day, before leaving his office, and to keep that information for his private journal.

To-day we ascend Mt. Vissuv[ius] to-morrow visit Pompeii & Herculaniu[m.] [1] About Saturday, the 22d, start for Palermo,[2] thence to Malta where we will probably spend the 25th.[3] From there we go to Alexandria and up the Nile. That is about as far as I have definitely planned, but think, on our return from the Nile, we will go to Joppa and visit Jerusalem from there, possibly Damascus and other points of interest also and take the ship again at Beyrout. The next point will be Smyrna, then Constantinople. I am begining to enjoy traveling and if the money holds out, or if Consolidated Va Mining stock does, I will not be back to the eastern states for two years yet. Should they—the stocks—run down on my hands, and stop dividends, I should be compelled to get home the nearest way.

Jesse is entirely well and himself again, and enjoys his travels under thes changed conditions, very much. I wrote a letter to Porter a good while ago but have received no answer yet.[4]

Very Truly yours,
U. S. Grant

ALS, Munson-Williams-Proctor Institute, Utica, N. Y.
      On Dec. 16, 1877, John Russell Young wrote in his diary. "Sailing all day on the Me-
diaterranean, and as we had a rough sea, I felt quite ill. . . ." DLC-John Russell Young. USG
reached Naples on Dec. 17. See *ibid.*, Dec. 17–18, 20–22, 1877.

      1. See *ibid.*, Dec. 19, 1877; *New York Herald* and *The Times* (London), Dec. 27, 1877;
Young, I, 165–96; *Julia Grant*, p. 218.
      2. USG arrived in Palermo on Dec. 23. See Young diary, Dec. 23, 25–26, 1877, DLC-
John Russell Young.
      3. After spending Christmas in Palermo, USG reached Malta on Dec. 28. On Dec.
30, USG, Julia Dent Grant, and Jesse Root Grant, Jr., "lunched with the Duke and Duchess
of Edinburgh, and in the evening dined with the Governor. At night there was a gala performance at the opera in honour of the distinguished visitor." *The Times* (London), Dec. 31,
1877. Alfred Ernest Albert, Duke of Edinburgh, Queen Victoria's second son, was an
officer in the Royal Navy; he had married Marie Alexandrovna, the only daughter of Tsar
Alexander II. See *ibid.*, Aug. 1, 1900; Young diary, Dec. 28–30, 1877, DLC-John Russell
Young; *Young*, I, 197–216; *Julia Grant*, pp. 218–20.
      4. See letter to Adam Badeau, Nov. 11, 1877.

To Ulysses S. Grant, Jr.

———

Alexandria, Egypt.
Jan. 7th /78

DEAR BUCK:

My last letter was from Malta. We left there on the 31st of Dec.
and were five days on the way here, a little more than one day exceedingly rough.[1] We have done up this place very thoroughly[2] and
leave in the morning for Cairo. The authorities have been exceeding
kind and attentive. Immediately on our arrival we were waited on by
all the official dignitaries, and by our Consul General[3] with a message from the Kedive[4] placing a palace at my disposal, for occupancy,
during our stay in Cairo, and a special boat to carry us up the Nile.
We will occupy the palace for six days, from to-morrow. A visit to
the Levant is disappointing, so far. All the romance given to Orien-
tal splendor in novels and guide books is disipated by witnessing the
real thing. Innate uglyness, slovenlyness, filth and indolence witnessed here is only equaled, in my experience, by seeing the lowest
class of Digger Indians found on the Pacific Coast. There is nothing
wild or threatning in the appearance of the people.

I have nothing special to say—because I do not intend to write discriptions—but I will continue to drop you a line occasionally to let you know how we are.

All send love to you, and much disappointment that we found no letters here from either you or Fred. or indeed from any one at home. Our letters have been coming from Paris here now for more than three weeks.

Affectionately yours

U. S. Grant

U. S. Grant Jr.

ALS, USG 3.
    On Dec. 11, 1877, Frederick Dent Grant, Chicago, wrote to Ulysses S. Grant, Jr. "I have just returned from a trip up the Missouri river looking after some 14.000 or 15.000 government pets (Indians) and did not get your letters until I returned, ⊕Of course Julia is a fat as a little pig. If you think Elevated R. R. a good thing you can take the 100 shs & I will take part of them with you All send love to you & expect to see you on the 20th of this month . . . P. S. I dont think Ida wants anything" ALS, *ibid.*

    1. John Russell Young noted winds and rain on Jan. 2, 1878. Young diary, Jan. 2, 1878, DLC-John Russell Young. For the voyage from Malta to Alexandria, see *ibid.*, Dec. 31, 1877, Jan. 1, 3, 1878; *Young,* I, 216–18, 224–29; *Julia Grant,* p. 220.
    2. See Young diary, Jan. 5–7, 1878, DLC-John Russell Young; *Young,* I, 230–33.
    3. Elbert E. Farman, agent and consul gen., Cairo, had graduated from Amherst College (1855) and practiced law in western N. Y. See *PUSG,* 25, 126; Farman, *Along the Nile with General Grant* (New York, 1904), pp. 4–7, 11–14.
    4. Isma'il Pasha, ruler of Egypt since 1863. See *The Times* (London), March 4, 1895.

To Abel R. Corbin

————

Cairo, Egypt,
Jan'y 13th, '78.

My dear Mr. Corbin:

I am in receipt of your letter of December '77 at this remote, but historically interesting quarter of the globe. We have been in Cairo since last Tuesday. This is Sunday. I have seen the city very thoroughly; visited the pyramids; the Virgin Mary's tree where she took shelter some twenty centuries ago; the spring which became sweet from being saline, on her quenching her thirst from it, and which re-

mains sweet to this day,—while I was there water was being pumped
from it, by ox power, with a revolving wheel, to irrigate the neighboring ground—; Heliopolis, the great seat of learning in the days
of Moses, and where he was taught, and where the father-in-law of
Joseph was a teacher. The tree and the well are at Heliopolis, about
six miles from here.[1]

On Tuesday we start up the Nile on a special steamer provided
by the Khedive.[2] We expect to go as far as to the first rapids stopping
at all the points of interest on the way. This will probably take three
weeks. On our return we expect to go to Suez, thence by Canal to
Port Said, and then take our steamer again. From Port Said we will
go to Joppa and out to Jerusalem. Returning to Joppa we will go to
Beirout, and out to Damascus—possibly diverging to visit Baalbec,
thence to Smyrna from which we will visit Ephesus, thence to Constantinople. Returning we will stop a few days at Athens, thence to
old Syracuse on the island of Sicily, then to some convenient point
on the Italian coast from which to reach Rome. We will remain in
Rome for several weeks. Should you write me any time within six
weeks from this directed to the care of our Minister at Rome,[3] the
letter will reach me.

Altogether we have had a most pleasant visit. Our return to
America during this year depends somewhat on circumstances,
principally the means to stay away longer. It is likely this will be the
last opportunity I shall ever have of travelling abroad and I am desirous of making the most of the pleasant opportunity.—Give our
love to Mother, Jennie and Mary, and accept my thanks for your kind
offers.

Very truly yours,

U. S. GRANT.

J. G. Cramer, pp. 139–40.

On Jan. 10, 1878, Elbert E. Farman, consul gen., Cairo, invited John Russell Young
to a dinner honoring USG. D (in French), DLC-John Russell Young. On Jan. 12, a correspondent in Cairo reported USG's speech at this dinner. "He said to the Consul-General
and the ladies and gentlemen present that from the bottom of his heart he thanked one and
all for the cordial reception he was receiving here, and for the general manifestation of
kindness which he and his were receiving in the country. The exalted terms in which he
was spoken of by the Consul, he said, made him feel that there was a blush upon his cheek,
(and here he turns his head shortly around toward some friends just to his right, as much
as to say, is it not so?) but he would say that after 55 years of life, in which he had labored

to find some ease, a time for recreation, he was able to say that he had finally found it, and in its enjoyment here he could say that he would carry away with him from Egypt recollections as pleasant as those—yes, second to none, he said—from countries he had already visited, and believed he would carry away from countries he intended yet to visit. I thank you again, sincerely he said." *New York Times,* Feb. 6, 1878.

1. USG traveled from Alexandria to Cairo in Isma'il Pasha's private railroad car. See *Young,* I, 233–37; *Julia Grant,* pp. 221–22; Farman, *Along the Nile with General Grant* (New York, 1904), pp. 15–47, 66–68; Jesse R. Grant, *In the Days of My Father General Grant* (New York, 1925), pp. 267–72.

2. USG began this trip on Wednesday.

3. George P. Marsh, U.S. minister to Italy since 1861. See *PUSG,* 20, 280–81.

Interview

CAIRO, Jan. 17, 1878.

This article is most unjust and does not reflect credit upon the reputation of Mr. Curtis for honesty and fairness. It is assumed by Mr. Curtis and other defenders of Mr. Sumner that I, in some way, wantonly attacked the reputation of Mr. Sumner and Mr. Motley. Now here are the facts. When Mr. Motley died I was in England. Two articles came to my attention: one from the pen of John Jay, and the other from that of Mr. Smalley, of the *Tribune.* Both of these articles did myself, and especially Governor Fish, great injustice, saying, among other things, that we had killed Mr. Motley, although he left his mission in 1870 and died in 1877. Some time after I was travelling from London to Edinburgh and I met Mr. Copeland on the train, who was representing the NEW YORK HERALD. I took occasion to speak to Mr. Copeland of the articles of Mr. Jay and Mr. Smalley, and of their injustice, and to state the real facts as I remembered them. The train was travelling about forty-five miles an hour at the time and no notes were taken. My statement was written out afterward by Mr. Copeland from memory, and sent to the HERALD without my seeing it. When the paper containing the article reached me I saw plainly that the author had endeavored to state the conversation with accuracy; but there were some errors both of omission and of commission, as was most natural under the circumstances. It has been so long since I read the articles that I cannot specify what these errors were.

But I never said that Mr. Sumner, in stating "that when he was removed from the chairmanship of the Senate Committee on Foreign Relations he left a clean docket, Mr. Sumner asserted what he knew to be a falsehood." The fact is, "clean docket" is a term that has been introduced by Mr. Sumner's overzealous admirers to give this uncalled for controversy a turn that would enable them to contradict my statement successfully. What I said was entirely in relation to what had passed between Mr. Curtis and myself in a conversation at Long Branch when he asked me to use my influence to have Mr. Sumner restored to his former position on the Foreign Relations Committee. Mr. Curtis should remember that I told him that I had nothing to do with the formation of the Senate committees, and that if I had I would not regard Mr. Sumner as a proper man for that committee under the administration, because he had put himself out of relations between the Secretary of State and myself, and without any reason, so far as either Mr. Fish or myself were concerned. I told Mr. Curtis that the chairman of that committee above all others should be on good terms at least with the Secretary of State. I said also to Mr. Curtis that Mr. Sumner had a most unfortunate temper for any business transactions. He was dogmatic, opinionated, infallible in his own estimation—the be all and do all in any matter in which he took part; of a temper that made business with him almost impossible. In proof of this I stated that when Mr. Sumner was relieved from the chairmanship of his committee there were several treaties before him—seven, nine or eleven—not acted upon. I told Mr. Curtis that some of these treaties had been before the committee for about sixteen months, and that although I did not know the fact I would venture the assertion that the other members of the committee did not even know of their existence. Mr. Curtis replied that this could not be true, as Mr. Sumner had told him that, when he was displaced, the work before his committee was finished, and there was nothing for his successor to do. I told Mr. Curtis that I was very glad that in any question of veracity between Mr. Sumner and myself it should be upon a point so easily determined, and that he should be convinced I was right. I at once wrote to the State Department for a list of the treaties and conventions before the Committee on Foreign Relations at the time of Mr. Sumner's removal, their nature, the time they had been under consideration by the committee and their final disposition. The reply from the State Department showed that there were, as far as I can recollect now, twelve treaties and conventions, and that of these twelve two had been before the committee for about sixteen months. I see that Governor Fish says there were nine; but my recollection is that number was twelve. I sent the list that came from the State Department to Mr. Curtis. He can answer whether I was right or not, and if he cannot then the Hon. J. C. Bancroft Davis can. Mr. Davis was acting Secretary of State at the time and answered my letter.

I said to Mr. Curtis at the time—I said specifically that I did not accuse Mr. Sumner of knowingly and intentionally falsifying the facts. I say so now. That is too grave an imputation to be made against any man unless upon indubitable evidence of an intent to deceive. But what I said then and what I say now is that Mr. Sumner's temper and nature were such that he believed his own illusions without regard to the facts. It really almost amounted to a mental delusion, and, so far as his feelings toward Governor Fish and myself were concerned, it is most charitable to feel that it was a mental delusion. Thus, in the later years of his life, whenever my name was mentioned in Mr. Sumner's presence, he would lose all control of himself and say things about me of the severest and most outrageous nature—things of which he could not by any possibility have had a knowledge, even if they had been true. I told Mr. Curtis of one incident showing how Mr. Sumner's temper and nature were affected. This is an incident which can also be verified. A House bill had passed Congress during reconstruction times. This bill was popular with the admirers of Mr. Sumner, and it originated in the committee of which Mr. Boutwell was chairman. It happened that Mr. Boutwell, who, you will remember, took a leading part in the legislation upon reconstruction, was almost if not altogether the author of this bill, and had written it out without consulting any one, except, perhaps, another member of his committee. Notwithstanding this Mr. Sumner told Mr. Boutwell that he (Mr. Sumner) had prepared that bill, every word and every line, himself, and had passed it through Congress.[1] Now, this is not the conduct of a liar, but that of a man whose mind, by sorrow or suffering or some visitation of Providence, had become distempered; and I have always so interpreted the conduct of Mr. Sumner toward me. I have no animosity toward him nor his memory; but his admirers, or people who now pretend to be his admirers, use his name and memory to attack me.

Here is Mr. Jay among the admirers and defenders of Mr. Sumner. Now Mr. Jay, as no one knows so well as Governor Fish and myself, makes a pretext of eulogizing the dead to attack Governor Fish. If any one hated Mr. Sumner it was Mr. Jay at the time of the appointment of Mr. Motley as Minister to England. Mr. Jay wanted to go to England, and was sorely disappointed that a change would not be made in his favor, even after Mr. Motley had been fully assured of his appointment. Mr. Jay most probably forgave Mr. Sumner before the Senator's death, but he blamed him for his failure to go to London.

I have no disposition for controversy, and particularly would I abstain from anything that seemed like unfavorable reflections upon the dead. But something is due to truth in history, and my whole object in making my statement to Mr. Copeland was to correct grossly unjust and untrue statements in regard to facts—statements which reflect upon the living. I had no ill will toward Mr. Motley. Mr. Copeland will no doubt recollect that in the conversation I had with him I said I regarded Mr. Motley as a gentleman of culture and ability and in every way qualified to fill any position within the gift of the President or the people. I said that the best people—even men as accomplished and estimable as Mr. Motley—made mistakes, and that Mr. Motley had made a mistake which made him an improper person to hold office under me. I was then and I am now absolutely without any unkindness of feeling toward Mr. Motley. I was sorry for the necessity which compelled me to replace him, and if called upon to speak of him I should pay a high tribute to his character and qualifications.

The pretext that I disliked Mr. Motley, is a pretext invented by people some of whom, like Mr. Jay, hated him when living, and now only use him, when dead, to wound Governor Fish and myself. Other friends of Mr. Sumner seem to regard him as made of different material from other men. It is proper enough for Mr. Sumner, when living, and his admirers, when dead, to attack Governor Fish and myself—to fill the air with maledictions and execrations. But when one word of defence is made against abuse it is not to be tolerated. It is proper to say of me that I killed Mr. Motley, or that I made war upon Mr. Sumner for not supporting the annexation of St. Domingo. But if I dare to answer that I removed Mr. Motley from the highest considerations of duty as an Executive, if I presume to say that he made a mistake in his office which made him no longer useful to the country, if Governor Fish has the temerity to hint that Mr. Sumner's temper was so unfortunate that business relations with him became impossible, we are slandering the dead. If respect is due to the dead, truth and justice are due to the living, and I only spoke in self-defence, and after many years of silent submission to assaults from Mr. Sumner and his friends, only in the interest of truth and justice.

It is possible that but for Mr. Sumner's opposition to the St. Domingo treaty he would never have been removed from the chairmanship of the Committee on Foreign Relations. But if that opposition had anything to do with the estrangement of Mr. Sumner and myself the fault was his and not mine. I made no question with Senators who opposed St. Domingo. I recognized on that question, as I did always, that a Senator had his independent duty and responsibility, the same as an Executive. Some Senators, like Mr. Edmunds, whom I rank among my best friends and for whom I have never ceased to feel the highest admiration and respect, opposed the St. Domingo treaty as vehemently but not as abusively as Mr. Sumner. It is one thing to oppose the measures of an Executive and another to express that opposition in terms of contumely and attributing the basest motives, as were attributed to me in the St. Domingo business. My relations with Mr. Edmunds and his colleague, with Mr. Wilson and numerous other Senators who opposed the St. Domingo treaty, and whose names can be found in the *Congressional Record*, were never disturbed for a moment.

There is another misapprehension. It is said that I made my visit to Mr. Sumner about January 1, 1870, to try and induce him to support the St. Domingo treaty. I never thought of such a thing. I had no idea that the treaty would meet with opposition from him or any one else. I called simply out of respect to the position Mr. Sumner held as the head of the Committee on Foreign Relations, and to explain why the fact of such a treaty being negotiated should have been kept from the public and from Congress until that time, and to explain to him also the reports brought back by the agents of the government who had visited the island as to the resources of St. Domingo, its soil, the character of the people, their wishes in regard to annexation and other points. The question as to whether or not he would support the treaty was asked by Colonel Forney, who happened to be present. You see I called as Mr. Sumner was finishing his dinner, and Colonel Forney was one of the guests. He rose to leave when I entered, but I asked him to remain. When I had finished my statement Colonel Forney said:—"Of course, Mr. Sumner, you will support this treaty," or some such thing, I don't remember the words. If I had any doubts as to the course of Mr. Sumner in relation to the treaty the answer would have been very satisfactory.[2] I may as well say that during this conversation, after I had finished what I came to say about St. Domingo, Mr. Sumner opened about his "friend Ashley" as he called him, and asked me if I could not do something for him. It would be quite as proper for me to charge that Mr. Sumner's subsequent opposition to the treaty was due to his disappointment in not procuring a good position for his friend as it is for the admirers of Mr. Sumner to make charges against Governor Fish and myself of improper motives in our difference with the Senator. The charge would be much more susceptible of proof without changing facts to accommodate argument. But I do not charge improper motives in this matter, and sincerely believe that I would do the memory of Mr. Sumner great injustice if I did.

New York Herald, Feb. 22, 1878. John Russell Young interviewed USG after showing him "an important article from the pen of George William Curtis on the Sumner controversy." *Ibid.* In this unsigned editorial, Curtis criticized USG for charging U.S. Senator Charles Sumner of Mass. with deception and asserted that Sumner's support for Santo Domingo's annexation would have mollified USG. Young sent his dispatch on Jan. 31, 1878. See "Mr. Sumner and General Grant," *Harper's Weekly*, XXI, 1093 (Dec. 8, 1877), 959; Young diary, Jan. 30–31, Feb. 1, 19, 1878, DLC-John Russell Young; Interview, [*Aug. 29, 1877*];

letters to Hamilton Fish, Nov. 14, 1877; letters to John Russell Young, Nov. 21, 28, 1877; *Young*, II, 263–64, 279–81.

1. On Feb. 22, 1878, a correspondent reported from Washington, D. C. "Ex-Senator Boutwell, of Massachusetts, says that General Grant is essentially correct in his statements relative to ex-Senator Sumner as made in the interview had with him by the HERALD correspondent at Cairo. The legislation referred to, however, did not pertain to reconstruction, but was a resolution in a reference to a section of the law passed March 2, 1867, providing that the headquarters of the General of the Army should be at Washington, and not removed unless with the sanction of Congress. . . ." *New York Herald*, Feb. 23, 1878.

2. See *PUSG*, 20, 163–64.

To Frederick Dent Grant

Jan.y 25th /78
On Steamer above Thebes.

DEAR FRED.

We have just left ancient Thebes where we spent two days in viewing the ruins of many ages. One day more is necessary to see all of them, but as we are all fatigued we concluded to ascend the river and spend a day here (at Thebes) on our return. I have seen more in Egypt to interest me than in all my other travels. Some day I may write it up, but at present I shall say but little. One thing however is certain: the ancient Egyptian was a cultivated man, but governed— sole and body—by a ruler. Without a thorough command of all the strength, muscle and mind of the inhabitants such structures could never have been built. Without talent, learning and training the inscriptions could not have been made; and without Mechanical teaching the large blocks of granite and sand stone could never have been taken from the quarries to their present resting place, nor dressed as they are. We will get to the first falls of the Nile day after to-morrow. I have written you our proposed route after that. The coming fall we will probably go home—to see little Julia.

One thing I forgot to mention: your Ma balances on a donkey very well when she has an Arab on each side to hold her, and one to lead the donkey. Yesterday however she got a little out of balance twice, but claims that the saddle turned. Of course it did. How could it have done otherwise with 185 lbs. in a stirrup on on[e] side and the donkey only weighing 125 pounds. But she rides a donkey verry well on the whole. I wish Ida was along to keep her company.

Mr Young, of the New York Herald, is with us and no doubt keeps you posted as to where we are all the time, and as to our doings. In Egypt—as every where else—we have received the kindest reception and the greatest hospitality. I wish Egypt was free from debt and the iron heal of her creditors.

Give our love to Ida and Julia, and kindest regards to Mr. & Mrs. Honoré, Mr. and Mrs. Palmer,[1] and to all my friends in Chicago.

Yours Affectionately

U. S. GRANT

P. S. Tell Gen. Sheridan that I have been expecting a letter from him for some time. I wrote to him some time ago and no doubt but he received my letter. If you write promptly on the receipt of this direct to our Consul Gen. at Rome.[2]

ALS, USG 3. For accounts of USG's Nile River trip, see *Young,* I, 238–319; *Julia Grant,* pp. 222–24, 227–30; Elbert E. Farman, *Along the Nile with General Grant* (New York, 1904), pp. 69–84, 90–179, 189–246, 255–308, 328–29; Jesse R. Grant, *In the Days of My Father General Grant* (New York, 1925), pp. 272–78.

On Jan. 19, USG visited Assiut and attended a dinner where the son of his host delivered a speech. "It is with much pleasure that we rise to express the feelings of joy and delight with which we welcome to Egypt and especially to Assiout, our distinguished gest His Excellency General Grant, along with the friends who accompany him; and we beg that he will give us the liberty to try as much as possible to express in few words, the feelings of our hearts towards himself personally, and towards the great country which he so honorably represents. Hence we say: Long have we heard and wondered at the strange progress which America has made during this last century, by which she has taken the first position among the most civilized nations. She has so quickly improved in science, morals and arts, that the world stands amazed at this extraordinary progress which surpasses the swiftness of lightning. It is to the hard work of her great and wise men that all this advance is imputed, those who have shown to the world what wise, courageous, patriotic men can do. Let all the world look then to America and follow her example, that nation which has taken as the basis of her laws, and the object of her undertakings, to maintain freedom and equality among her own people and secure them for others, avoiding all ambitious schemes, which would draw her into bloody and disastrous wars, and trying by all means to maintain peace internally and externally. The only two great wars in which she has engaged were entered upon for pure and just purposes, the first for releasing herself from the english yoke and erecting her independence, and the other for stopping slavery, and strengthening the union of the states, and well know that it was sip sim mainly under God, to the talent, courage and wisdom of his excellency Gen. Grant that the latter of the two

~~entrepr~~ enteprises was brought to a successful issue. But while thus improving the condition of her own people, America has not been forgetful of other less favoured lands, but has stretched out her benificent hand to other less favoured places particularly to the east, where she has established schools and colleges, in S Turkey, Syria, and Egypt, our own town also having been favoured by the establishment in its midst of two academies, one for boys and one for girls. . . ." D, DLC-John Russell Young. USG responded "that nothing in his whole trip had so impressed him as this unexpected, this generous welcome in the heart of Egypt. He had anticipated great pleasure in his visit to Egypt, and the anticipation had been more than realized." *Young*, I, 258.

 1. Bertha Honoré, sister of Frederick Dent Grant's wife, had married Chicago entrepreneur Potter Palmer in 1870. See Ishbel Ross, *Silhouette in Diamonds: The Life of Mrs. Potter Palmer* (New York, 1960).
 2. Charles McMillan.

To Ulysses S. Grant, Jr.

On the Nile above Thebes, Jan. 25th, 1878.

Dear Buck

 . . . Have just left ancient Thebes where we have spent 2 days viewing ruins that have been standing—as ruins—some of them, for many ages before the beginning of the Christian era. . . . Egypt has interested me more than any other portion of my travels . . . your Ma has become quite an expert in donkey riding? it is true that she keeps an Arab on each side to hold her on and one to hold the donkey. . . . I am glad to hear that you are getting something to do on your own account. Stick to it and you will do well in the end. Persiverence is the only thing that succeeds in this world, added to thorough integrity.

 All send love to you, and wish that you would keep up your weekly letters, . . . Tell Gen Porter that I am disappointed at not receiving a letter from him before this.

Yours Affectionately
U. S. Grant

U. S. Grant Jr.

ALS (partial facsimile), Historical Collectibles Auctions, June, 2000, no. 660.
 On Jan. 31, [*1878*], Anthony J. Drexel wrote to Ulysses S. Grant, Jr. "There is due Drexel & Co on stocks $2020.19 gold & there is acy balance of $1218.23 due US Grant,

which I suppose you will draw for from Europe You better deposit $2020 19 gold & square that ac I have written you & sent acs by mail" Copy, USG 3.

To Adam Badeau

Cairo, Egypt
Feb.y 4th /78

DEAR GENERAL;

Your letter of the 3d of Jan.y enclosing a chapter of your book, and a letter from Babcock reached me some five or six days up the Nile from here. There was no use in answering earlyer becaus the reply could not do better than to come by the boat I did. Our trip has been a most enjoyable one and the sights exceed in collossal grandeur the guide book discriptions. One is kept in constant wonder how any people could have [mo]ved such immense blocks, in such huge numbers, for so great a distance as most of them ha[d] to be moved, and put them in their places. The Khedive gave m[e] a special boat, and sent with m[e] one of his household, Sami Bey, an educated Egyptian who speaks English well—in fact he was educated in England—and a German Egyptolog[ist][1] who has been a long time a student here, and who reads all the inscript[ions] in the Temples & Tomb with facility. His presence added much to the value of the journey.

I have read the last chapter of your book over carefully and see nothing to correct except as to one little matter of fact. My recollection is that I recommended Sherman Sheridan and Hancock for [promotion] precisely as you say. Sherman and Hancock's names were promptly sent to the Senate, and they were confirmed, but some one at Washington had failed up to that time to appreciate Sheridan as I did, and withheld his name. He was not nominated until I urged his promotion a second time. It is possible that he was given the same date when appointed that he would have had if appointed when first recommended.[2]

We leave here on the 7th to take up our travels again.[3] I have given you our proposed route in a previous letter I believe. When you write to Babcock give him and his family my kindest regards. All my family [join] me in desiring to be kindly remembered to you.

Yours Truly
U. S. GRANT

GEN. A. BADEAU.

ALS (torn), Munson-Williams-Proctor Institute, Utica, N. Y.; *Badeau*, pp. 494–95.

On Jan. 20, 1878, Adam Badeau, consul gen., London, wrote to Orville E. Babcock. "I enclose you the proofs of the Reams Station & Weldon road fights, and of Sherman's Atlanta campaign, and shall be very glad of any corrections or suggestions you will be good enough to make; also to receive any remarks in advance—in regard to what is yet to come;—notably Sherman's march, Thomas's delay at Nashville, and—all the details especially personal incidents, and matter not likely to be in the official reports—about the Five Forks and Dinwiddie fights, the capture of the Petersburg works, entrance into the town, and the pursuit of Lee. I want to make the final chapter as graphic and *personal* as possible. I also propose to describe Grant personally at City Point—his cares; and anxieties, and habits during that last winter; our long talks around the campfires at night—his sleep lessness until the small hours—the sentryship you suggested for staff officers &c . . ." AL (incomplete), ICN. On Jan. 28 and 31, Badeau again wrote to Babcock. ". . . The General is up the Nile, wont be back at Cairo for two or three weeks.—It looks very warlike here.— From this point of view, it looks as if the financial question would be the issue in the next Presidential election; and we know whose record is right on that point. . . ." "I enclose you two slips of proof—one to add on to my general discussion of the Wilderness campaign, which you may remember; the other to conclude the comments on Sherman. I am now doing engineers work—trying to describe the works—rebel and our own—in front of both Richmond and Petersburg; and shall send you the sketch for correction and revision, before long. . . . Yesterday Col. Forney, who is staying in London, told me he had heard from the editor of a paper published here, and called 'The Anglo-American'—that my place (Consul Genl) was in danger. Col Forney offered to write direct to Mr. Hayes about it, and tho I think my strength is altogether on Gen Grants name—I thought it would do no harm to let the President know I have other friends. Do you hear anything unfavorable? I am daily expecting a letter from Gen Grant, but he can yet hardly have returned from the Nile. . . . Pierrepont goes home on the 15th of Feby; says he will visit Washington; and I have no sort of doubt will do and say all in his power to injure me. He got horribly jealous of Gen Grants kindness to me and told innumerable falsehoods; said I was a self appointed ADC—did not belong to the Genl's party &c—. . ." ALS and AL (initialed), *ibid.* On Feb. 4, Badeau wrote to Gen. William T. Sherman. ". . . I have written to Genl Grant and told him of your kindness, and also that you had been so good as to see the President in person, and remind him of his promise to retain me in my civil office. There is never a month, and hardly a week that I do not hear that I am to be removed; but now I shall rest safe in the promise and personal honor of the President. I did not suggest to Gen Grant to make the request he did of you. I told him that Mr. Pierrepont had said I was a self-appointed aide dc camp, and given out generally that I had thrust myself on Genl Grant, (you know Mr P's reputation for veracity) and I begged him, if he was writing to you to say that my applications for a leave, and to attend him both had his sanction (he insisted on *paying*—for both telegrams); and he was kind enough to write as you say, which I did not know till your letter informed me. . . ." ALS, DLC-William T. Sherman.

On Jan. 21, Babcock, St. John's River, Fla., had written to Badeau. "*Personal* . . . Just before leaving W. for a business trip here I received your letter enclosing one to Sherman—I went and saw Sherman, who was very pleasant—said he would do what he could, but said it had all been done without his knowledge—He said there evidently was a press to get your place, and asked me why it was—I told him I did not know—I told him what President Hayes had promised Genl Grant—He said he knew it—and that he had spoken to Mr Hayes—on receipt of a letter from Genl Grant, on the matter He said Hoffman, from St Petersburgh—wants to go to Paris—and came to get his recommendation—saying there was a pressure to get Badeau out—and if Tolbot [*Torbert*] could be transferred to London in Badeaus place. H he thought he could get Tolbots place. He said he asked Hoffman why they pressed for Badeau's place—and H said he was told Badeaus habits were bad. I denied it to Sherman—and told him I knew all about it and there was nothing in it, and beside that no consulate was in better order than yours. Sherman said, 'I suppose Evarts wants the place. He dont care.' Tell Badeau, I am his friend &c—I saw Barnes— and posted him also. Now when we get Sangers Certificate we will follow it up, and make them correct the matter. I read the manuscript you sent to Porter hurriedly, I like it—I left all well at home. I am looking after a little orange grove I have down here, and hope to find it a good thing. I have to scramble home to save something from the wreck. I do not suppose Sherman would like to have what he said of Evarts repeated. I feel sure he is your friend. I am glad to see how splendidly the Genl is received everywhere. I hope he will not think of returning for two years at least." ALS, Gallery of History, Las Vegas, Nev.

1. Heinrich Karl Brugsch. See *The Times* (London), Sept. 11, 1894.
2. See *PUSG*, 11, 400–401, 427; *ibid.*, 12, 175; *Senate Executive Journal*, XIV, part 1, p. 21.
3. The Egyptian Railway Administration supplied a timetable for the special train taking USG from Cairo to Suez. D, DLC-USG, IB. See *Foreign Relations, 1878*, pp. 915–16; *Young*, I, 319–26; *Julia Grant*, pp. 230–33; Jesse R. Grant, *In the Days of My Father General Grant* (New York, 1925), pp. 279–80.

To Adam Badeau

Smyrna, Asia Minor
Feb.y 22d /78

My Dear General:

On our arrival here this a. m. I found a mail and with it your letter and the enclosed chapter. I have read it carefully and see no word to change. I am glad you have submitted it to Sherman. He must feel pleased with the way you have treated his Atlanta Campaign, and if there is any error, in fact, he will correct it. He is at Washington where he has access to all the records and if there is any mistake in minor details he will be able to inform you. You no doubt received back the former chapter sent from Cairo, Egypt? I am almost afraid to send any matter of importance, by mail, from this wretchedly governed country, and will keep this until a steamer is going to some more civilized part, or until I get to Athens[.] We go from here to Constantinople first.

Our visit to Jerusalem was a very unpleasant one. The roads are bad and it rained, blew and snowed all the time. We left snow six inches deep in Jerusalem.¹

I wrote to Porter several months ago but have received no reply from him. He got my letter I know because Bucky wrote me that Porter showed it to him.

AL (signature clipped), Munson-Williams-Proctor Institute, Utica, N. Y. See Jesse R. Grant, *In the Days of My Father General Grant* (New York, 1925), pp. 285–88.

1. On Feb. 18, 1878, Joseph G. Willson, consul, Jerusalem, wrote to William Hunter, 2nd asst. secretary of state, describing USG's visit. ALS, DNA, RG 59, Consular Despatches, Jerusalem. On May 30, 1876, U.S. Senator George G. Wright of Iowa and eight others had written to USG. "We the undersigned members of the Iowa delegation in Congress respectfully recommend the appointment of J. G. Willson of Fort Madison Iowa, to the position of *Consul at Hokodadi Japan*, or to some other not less important position in the foreign service of the government. . . ." LS (misfiled under J. Greenwood Wilson), *ibid.*, Applications and Recommendations, Hayes-Arthur. Related papers are *ibid.*, filed under J. Greenwood Wilson and Willson.

On Tuesday, Feb. 19, 1878, H. Z. Sneersohn and two others, Jerusalem, wrote "To THE EDITOR OF THE HERALD." "It will doubtless be interesting to your readers to learn that General Grant has paid a visit to the Holy City. He appeared in the gates of Zion on Monday, and every manifestation of respect possible was shown him by the local authorities and by the representatives of the different European governments. He dined at the Governor's residence on Thursday last. Among those who waited upon him were the undersigned. A committee for distributing relief to American Jewish citizens here under the superintendence of Colonel J. G. Willson, United States Consul, were also honored with an interview. The deplorable condition of our community was made known to the General, and he kindly promised to inform some of his friends, leaders of Israel in America, of the facts. He left Jerusalem on Saturday last, and the best wishes of all our community for his safe journey, the prolongation of his life and continued prosperity followed him. . . ." *New York Herald*, March 18, 1878. See *Young*, I, 326–45; *Julia Grant*, pp. 233–36; Grant, *Days of My Father*, pp. 280–85.

On Feb. 17, USG, Jerusalem, had written to Rolla Floyd. "Before leaving Jerusalem allow me to thank you for myself and entire party with me for the great assistance you have rendered us in our visit to all points of interest in and about the Holy City. Your thorough knowledge of Bible references, History & Tradition of all points of interest in the Holy Land and your clear and concise explanation of the same has very much added to the interest and pleasure of our visit." Reed M. Holmes, *The Forerunners* (Independence, Mo., 1981), p. 254. See Helen Palmer Parsons, ed., *Letters from Palestine: 1868–1912* (n. p., n. d.), p. 36; Floyd to Hamilton Fish, Sept. 13, 1872, DNA, RG 59, Letters of Application and Recommendation.

In [*April, 1876*], Lucy A. Fernald, Farmington, N. H., had written to USG. "Pardon me for taking permission to address upon a subject which may not interest you,—Yet I sincerely hope it will I have a sister and her husband and three children liveing in Jaffa Syria that would like to come home to America—but has not the means to come. Perhaps I ought to mention how they come out there My sister and her husband and five children went from Rochester New Hampshire with the Colony that went out there nine or ten years ago. They sailed from Jones Port main[e.] Her husbands name was George W. Clark He went out there as a contracter for the colony every thing was mis represented he was disappointd and was taken with the Syrian feve and and died soon after they arived there —then two of her children died she was almost heartbroken Adams the leader of the colony swindled them out of most of their property The American consul offered to send her home—but in her deep grief she thought she could not leave the remains of her husband and children out there—others of the colony prevailed on her to stay (she did not act wisely) but that cannot be helped . . ." ALS (docketed April 29), *ibid.*, Miscellaneous Letters. See Holmes, *Forerunners*, pp. 165–69, 207, 235, 257–60.

To Elizabeth King

Smyrna, Asia Minor,
Feb.y 22d 1878

MY DEAR MRS. KING.

We arrived at this Ancient city of the East to-day, and found a Mail, and in it your very welcome letter. I hasten to answer it. Probably the papers have kept you fully advised of all my journyings; but I will say that the winter has passed most pleasantly with me and mine. After spending five weeks in in Paris we come east to the Mediterranean, at Nice, and took an American Man of War on which we have traversed all this end of the sea. Our first stopping place was Genoa,—the birth place of Christopher Columbus; the next Naples—from which we visited Mount Vissuvious and Pompeii—, then Palermo, on the island of Sicily; then Malta, where St. Paul was shipwrecked; then Alexandria, Cairo, and up the Nile, examining old ruins of cities, temples and tombs, built many centuries before the begining of the Christian era, then the Red Sea; Joppa—where Jonah was swallo[wed] by the Whale—Jerusalem; the garden of Bethsemane; the Mount of Olives—from which you look down on the Dead Sea and the Valley of the Jordan—; Bethlehem and the stable where Christ was born; and all the points of interest about Jerusalem. We will go out to Ephisus—about two hours by rail from here—in a day or two. From here we go to Constantinople, thence to Athens, Greece, then to Rome, and after that, when the weather begins to get warm, to Russia, Sweeden and Norway. By fall I think of returning home. Where to live when I get there is not determined. I have no home.

I was much interested to hear from all my old friends in Georgetown, but extremely sorry to hear of the misfortunes of your son and son-in-law.[1] I hope they may yet come up, and only wish it was in my power to be of service to them. Mrs. Grant joins me in wishing to be kindly remembered to all our friends in Georgetown, and to you and Mr. King[2] personally we send our affectionate regards.

Yours Very Truly

U. S. GRANT

ALS, provided by Candace Scott, Victorville, Calif. See *PUSG*, 26, 245–46.

1. Elizabeth King's family owned a Georgetown, Ohio, bank that failed in 1878. She was the mother of several children. See Carl N. Thompson, ed., *Historical Collections of Brown County, Ohio* (Ripley, Ohio, 1969), pp. 842–43, 1112.
2. Born in 1797 in Gettysburg, Pa., George W. King married Elizabeth Wills in Ripley, Ohio, and settled in Georgetown to practice law.

To John F. Long

Smyrna, Asia Minor

Feb.y 22d /78

MY DEAR JUDGE:

Since my last letter to you I have had a most interesting visit to the Ancient places on the Mediterranean and up the Nile. You have probably seen from the papers my general route, and much better descriptions than I could give in the limits of a letter. I get the papers from the states now with much more regularity than for the first few months after my departure, and that they not only follow up my lines of travel and what I do from day to day, very closely, but some of them speculate upon my designs I see. They may know them, but if they do I do not. I have been under the impression that

I was carrying out a long cherished desire to travel and see as much of the old world as possible before settling down in a home where to spend the remainder of my days in quiet. But if I was where I was one year ago, and for the previous seven years, I would put a most determined veto upon the repudiation bill—called Silver bill—if it should receive the vote of Congress. I fear it has passed,[1] but hope, if so, all business men in the country will work to defeat its opperation by refusing to make contracts except to be paid in gold coin.

I see Ulysses has been in St. Louis twice since Christmas.[2] You saw him no doubt. He gives me but little news from there and says nothing about the revival of business. I hope there will be a change for the better soon. On my return to the states I must sell off at least a portion of my [——] to invest in something [————] income, I [————] next fall. It is my desire to visit Austri[a,] Prussia, Russia, Sweeden, Norway and Denmark before returning; and as I do not wish to visit either of these countries until warm weather it will probably be Octob[er] before I do go back.

I am always pleased [to] hear from you and [*hope*] you will write often.

Please remember me to all your associates in the Custom House, and Mrs. Grant & myself to Mrs. Long and your family.

AL (signature clipped), CSmH.

1. On Feb. 28, 1878, an act to remonetize silver, commonly called the Bland-Allison Act, became law over President Rutherford B. Hayes' veto. *U.S. Statutes at Large*, XX, 25–26. See letter to Edward F. Beale, March 6, 1878; letter to Gen. William T. Sherman, March 21, 1878; letter to Anthony J. Drexel, March 22, 1878; Ari Hoogenboom, *Rutherford B. Hayes: Warrior and President* (Lawrence, Kan., 1995), pp. 356–60.
2. See letter to Ulysses S. Grant, Jr., Nov. 21, 1877.

To Michael John Cramer

Constantinople
March 5th /78

MY DEAR MR. CRAMER:

On my arrival here I found your letter specially enquiring about the time I expect to be in Copenhagen. My plan is to be in Sweeden by the middle of June, and after visiting that country and Norway, to return by way of Copenhagen. It is not likely that I will be there before the fifth to the 10th of July, and it may be that I will like the northern country so well that my visit to Copenhagen will be postponed even a month longer.

We have had a delightful Winter. Over a month was spent in Egypt, visiting the old ruins of that country under the most favorable circumstances. Leaving Cairo we visited Suez and passed through the Suez Canal to Port Said. From the latter place we went to Joppa and out to Jerusalem. Since then we visited Smyrna, and Ephesus and are now here. The Russians are outside of the city but do not come in. A stranger would not detect, from appearances, that an enemy was so near. In fact I think the Turks now regard the Russians as about the only people in Europe from whom they can expect any thing.[1]

When you write home give my love to Mother, Mary and children and Jennie.

I will inform you later, when I know definitely, about the time to expect me in Copenhagen.

Very Truly Yours
U. S. GRANT

ALS, deCoppet Collection, NjP. For USG in Constantinople, see *The Times* (London), March 25, 1878; *Young*, I, 346–54; *Julia Grant*, pp. 237–39; Jesse R. Grant, *In the Days of My Father General Grant* (New York, 1925), pp. 290–94.

1. After a war lasting nearly one year, negotiators from Russia and Turkey concluded a peace agreement on March 3, 1878. See following letter.

To Edward F. Beale

Constantinople,
March 6th /78

MY DEAR GENERAL:

After a delightful trip through Egypt; up the Nile to the first falls; back to Cairo; to Suez and through the Suez Canal to Port Said; to Joppa and Jerusalem; to Smyrna and Epesus, we are now at this historically interesting place. We have been here five days, and leave this evening for Athens.[1] The city is very quiet, but in government circles one discovers a deep gloom. The Russians are but a few miles out side of the city and can come in when they please. But as terms have been signed, and the Russian Minister ~~to~~ to Turkey[2] is now in this city, they may abstain from coming in altogether. I feel a great desire to visit the Russian camp, but as the Turks have been very hospitable, and might look upon such a visit with suspicion, I shall refrain.

I was invited to an audience with the Sultain[3] the other day, and to visit his private stable of thorough bred Arabian horses. A Turkish Admiral who was educated in England, and speaks perfect English, acted as interpreter.[4] After we had left the Sultain he sent for the Admiral, who, on returning, said that "His Highness" would send to the ship on the following day one of the horses and equipments. I thanked him very kindly but declined on the ground that the ship was not coming directly to the United States, that I should not go back soon myself, &c. But in visiting the stables—where there are sixty or seventy of these horses; it may be more—I found the officers were anxious to get my views as to which were the best. There were three, one a beautiful dappled grey, one a blood bay and one a sorrel which I designated as very beautiful. Dining last night with the Minister of War[5]—at which the Cabinet and many other officials and others were present—I was told that the Sultain would think hard of it if I should decline to receive the horse, and that he would be sent to Marseilles for me. If he is I shall make arrangements to have him sent to Liverpool, to the care of our Consul, Gen. Fairchild to be shipped by him to Phila to your care. If he goes I hope you will take him and use him—for breeding purposes or otherwise—as your own until I call for him, which may not be for a year or two. These horses, I am told, have their pedigrees kept for one or two hundred years back, and are of the purest blood. It may be of some value to breeders in the United States to get some of this blood, and if so I will be amply repaid. I will make arrangements for the payment of all expenses in getting the horse to Phila, and when I return will pay all other expenses.[6]

It is more than probable now that I will return to the U. States next fall. But, if so, I shall not go to housekeeping—except at Long Branch in the summer—until the fall of /79, and where, I have not yet determined. Washington is my choice, but this I will leave to be determined after my return.

I received your very welcome letter at Smyrna, and one at the same time from Adm.l Ammen. I get the home papers now with much regularity, and regret to see politics at home in such a troubled condition. We learn that the silver bill—which I regard as dishonest and very destructive to the interest of the country—has passed both houses by a large majority. I hope the President will veto it, and that his veto will prevail. Should it pass I look to the best interests of the country rendering it nugatory by refusing to make contracts except on a gold basis. The double standard I regard as wholly impracticable. The currency of lesser value will drive the better out of market. Gold would simply become an article of Merchandise, being bought and sold at so much premium. The Supreme Court will no doubt decide that part of the law which makes silver a legal tender in payment of principle & interest on the public debt as unconstitutional—ex post facto.[7]

Mrs. Grant joins me in desiring to be kindly remembered to Mrs. Beale and your family. If you should write to me within a few days of the receipt of this, directed to Rome, I will no doubt get it there. Later direct to the care of Drexel, Harjes &co, Paris.

Very Truly yours,
U. S. GRANT

ALS, DLC-Decatur House Papers.

1. On March 7, 1878, Horace Maynard, U.S. minister, Constantinople, wrote to Secretary of State William M. Evarts discussing USG's six-day visit and enclosing newspaper accounts. LS and enclosures, DNA, RG 59, Diplomatic Despatches, Turkey. *Foreign Relations, 1878*, pp. 861–64.

2. Nicolas P. Ignatieff. See *The Times* (London), July 6, 1908.

3. Abdul Hamid II, Sultan of Turkey.

4. Possibly former British naval officer Augustus Charles Hobart-Hampden, known as Hobart Pasha. See *ibid.*, June 21, 1886.

5. Raouf Pasha, Turkish minister of war.

6. On March 4, Lt. Commander Albert G. Caldwell, U.S.S. *Vandalia*, Constantinople, wrote to his mother. "... Tonight the British Minister Mr Layard gives Genl Grant a re-

ception to which I expect to go. . . . Dont mention anything I say about Grant as it would be a breach of trust on my part—the old man talking freely to us beleiving that we are not going to give him away—caution Ben & Charley also not to let my statements leak into the papers. . . . Mar 5. Went ashore today with Genl Grant to see the Sultan's horses—40 of them, purest of the pure Arab—five of the sacred breed have never been backed except by Sultans—all beauties it takes as much ceremony to see them as to see the Sultan himself—all stallions, colors from pure white to the blackest coal. intelligent almost human eyes & such legs it is a sight to see them walk—they pick up their feet like a cat & so quickly that one can scarcely follow their motions. The stable covers four acres, all under one roof, has a large place for exercising like a Circus ring only larger—horses very affectionate, come up to be petted, gentle & full of action—Sultan gave Genl Grant one but I think he will not receive him—price if sold about 30000 dollars—not a horse in the stable worth less than 25.000 dollars— . . . Grant was more interested than I've ever seen him before—would go back & look again at horses & ask opinions about them—got quite enthusiastic over them. picked out one 'if he took any' a dappled grey with beautiful head about 18½ hands high, ears so small that you could put a lady's kid glove on them. . . ." ALS, InHi. See following letter; letter to Randolph Huntington, July 28, 1882; [Randolph Huntington], *History in Brief of "Leopard" and "Linden," General Grant's Arabian Stallions, Presented to Him by the Sultan of Turkey* . . . (Philadelphia, 1885).

    7. See letter to John F. Long, Feb. 22, 1878.

To Alfred T. A. Torbert

———

[*Athens, March 9, 1878*]

After a most pleasant visit up the Nile, back through the Suez Canal, then to J[o]ppa and out to Jerusalem, up to Smyrna and from there to Constantinople . . . we have reached this City on a way to a different civilization. I found the authorities in Constantinople looking and feeling very gloomy, but the appearance of a successful foe immediately outside the gates of the city did not seem to effect the population generally. But the sight is wretched enough. In a small portion of the city is stored away in the Mosques and public buildings probably more than a hundred thousand refugees, men women and children, who have fled to the Capitol before a conquering Army. They are fed entirely by charity and mostly by foreigners. What is to become of them is sad to think of. Beside these many tens of thousands have been shipped to places in Asia Minor and turned loose upon the inhabitants. . . . My reception however, notwithstanding these surroundings, was cordial. I was invited to an interview with the Sultan and to visit his stable of blooded Arabian horses. After the interview, when I retired, the Sultan sent for the Turkish Admiral who had acted as interpreter who, on returning, said that *His Highness* wished to present me with one of his best horses, and that he would send him to the ship the following day. I thanked him for his kindness but declined the proffer. On dining with the Minister of Marines[1] after . . . I learned that my declination had not been communicated to the Sultan, and was informed that he would feel very badly if his offer was declined. If the horse is sent—I hope he will not be—he will be sent to Marsailles, care of our Consul there. I shall not be back in Paris before May and I want to ask you if you will be kind enough, if the horse goes to Marsailles, to have him taken charge of and forwarded carefully to Gen. Fairchild, Consul at Liverpool. . . .

Paul C. Richards, Catalogue No. 225 [1987], no. 119. See previous letter; letter to Frederick Dent Grant, March 22, 1878; letter to Rear Admiral Daniel Ammen, March 25, 1878; *Young,* I, 354–60; *Julia Grant,* pp. 239–40; Jesse R. Grant, *In the Days of My Father General Grant* (New York, 1925), pp. 296–97.

On March 9, 1878, John Meredith Read, Jr., U.S. chargé d'affaires, Athens, wrote to Secretary of State William M. Evarts. "General Grant arrived at the Piraeus in The Vandalia yesterday at 3.30 P. M. from Constantinople, . . . The Mayor of the Piraeus, M. Mitzopoulos, advanced to the steps and addressed General Grant . . . General Grant replied thanking the Mayor and the city for his hearty reception; expressed his joy on account of the progress of Modern Greece, and hoped that she might be permitted to continue to advance in glory and take that high position among the nations of the earth to which she is justly entitled. . . . Upon the arrival at Athens the Mayor of the city, the Prefect of Attica and Boeotia and the Municipal Council surrounded by a great and enthusiastic crowd welcomed General Grant. The Mayor addressed him as follows: 'The city of Athens receives with profound respect the late President of the glorious American Confederation. Seizing this occasion Greece manifests in the strongest manner her undying gratitude towards the great American Nation for the aid and sympathy which it copiously granted to her in her great struggle for independence. She feels moreover grateful for the interest which the United States manifests in behalf of the progress and future of Greece and she is delighted to welcome the illustrious ruler and captain.' General Grant replied with great emphasis: 'I am glad to find that the sentiments of both peoples are mutual. I sincerely wish that Greece may enjoy every species of prosperity, and I think that she should be allowed to take that enlarged position to which her ancient achievements and her modern progress clearly entitle her.'" LS, DNA, RG 59, Diplomatic Despatches, Greece. *Foreign Relations, 1878,* pp. 366–68. On March 11, 12, 13, 14, and 15, Read, Jr., wrote to Evarts concerning USG's stay in Athens. LS, DNA, RG 59, Diplomatic Despatches, Greece. *Foreign Relations, 1878,* pp. 368–70. See Read, Jr., to Hamilton Fish, March 22, 1878, DLC-Hamilton Fish.

1. Said Pasha, Turkish minister of marine. See following letter.

To Gen. William T. Sherman

——————

Rome, Italy,
March 21st /78

MY DEAR GENERAL:

Your very prompt and very welcome answer to my first letter to you reached me at Smyrna. Your second reached me at Athens. I was delighted to receive them as I always am to hear from you. You say that having been over the ground—most of it—that I have been ~~following~~ traveling, you can follow me with interest.[1] I have very much enjoyed all my travels on this side the Atlantic, but nothing has equaled in interest the trip up the Nile and in the Levant. The courticy of the Khedive added much to the interest of the former. But things are different with him from what they were when you were in Egypt. His debts, private and public, have accumulated to such an extent that the resources of the state cannot possibly meet the interest. This indebtedness is mostly held in England and the English Govt. have appointed agents—with big salaries paid out of the resources of Egypt—to collect and pay out all the revenues to bond holders. This leaves nothing for the Khedive to use in payment of current expenses of Govt. Throughout the Turkish Empire things are worse. Syria & Asia Minor are rich in soil and climate beyond anything in the U. States, but under their Govt. there is no encouragement for its developement. The state is bankrupt without the costs of a disastrous war being added to former indebtedness. Except they pay in real estate, and disappear from the Continent of Europe, the Archipelago (islands of) and some of Asia Minor, or Syria, it seems to me their creditors will go unpaid. With the Naval Officers on the Vandalia—some of whom accompanied me always when I left the ship—there was no durth of agreeable company at all times. But if I could have had you, with a few others of my old associates, it would have added much to the interest.—The accounts you have read in the papers show you that we visited Joppa and Jerusalem; Smyrna & Epesus; Constantinople & Athens. The effects of the war have no doubt materially changed the high official[s] of the Govt.

and saddened them very much. But in going through the city you
could not discover from the manner of the people that anything unusual had taken place although there was an invading army within
eight miles of the city, and nothing to keep them out, and all the
Mosques filled with refugees—propably not less than fifty thousand
of them—being fed by charity. They are a queer people and probably not capable of anything above supporting a few leaders sumptu-
ously and licentiously. With the ch[a]stening they have had they
may do better in the future.

I have not yet made up my mind when I will go home. Possibly
however next fall. But if I should meet a few pleasant acquaintances
willing to go up the Nile next winter I think I would go back again,
taking a sail instead of steam vessel, and spend three or four months
on the trip.

I have received the American papers much more consecutively
this winter than before, and have watched home affairs with great interest. I have been supremely disgusted with many things I have seen
in the way of legislation and of proposed legislation. Nothing however has disappointed me more than the passage of the "Silver Bill"
over the Presidents veto.[2] The country, and country's credit, has not
received so severe a blow since the attempt of the Southern states to
secede. A great deal of the sting was taken out of the measure by the
Senate Amendments; but we stand more or less disgraced nevertheless. Our credit abroad was so high before that, in my opinion, there
would have been no difficulty in placing all the 4 pr. ct. bonds but for
the measure. Now we must go on paying the present rate of interest
unless the same wise legislators should conclude to repudiate the
whole. The crime would be about the same as that already committed except it would be another crime, and nine times as large. I presume we would think better of a highway man who stops us on the
road and only takes one tenth of our money than if he takes the
whole. But in this instance we take the tenth from the creditor and
continue a burden upon the taxpayer by making him continue to pay
a high instead of a low rate of interest. If I was in John Sherman's
place I would carry out the law as slowly as possible, and after the
first coinage of silver dollars I would refuse to give money for the

payment of Congressmen, and employees about Congress, in any other money than these same silver dollars. All other payments I would make in currency,—as long as it holds out—until all the sub-treasuries in the Country were filled and new buildings, with good guards, were necessary for its accommodation. and security. A million of silver, I believe, weighs thirty tons. A member of Congress could not carry three months pay from the house to his boarding house.

While I was in Constantinople Said Pasha, Minister of Marines, requested me to furnish him with a list of the studies at the Military and Naval Academies. I promised him that I would do so, and would send him a complete copy of all the text books. The Minister was educated at Edinborough, and afterwards graduated at the Artillery school in England. He speaks English therefore perfectly. I wish you would ask the Sec. of War and the Sec. of the Navy if they will not furnish a complete copy—leaving out the French & Spanish books, but state that these languages are taught—of these books, and you forward them with a short note stating how it has been done. If they cannot do so I wish you would purchase them—and forward in my name, and draw o[n] U. S. Grant, Jr. 120 Broadway New York City, for the cost. I am sorry to put you to this much trouble, but the request was made of me while I was in the Palace of the Sultain and I made the promise.

The address would be, His Excely Said Pasha Ministre de la Marine, L'Amiranté Imperiale Ottomane, Constantinople.[3]

Mrs. Grant joins me in kindest regards to yourself and family.

Yours very Truly

U. S. GRANT

GEN. W. T. SHERMAN,

COMD.G U. S. ARMY.

P. S. All the blots on these sheets have been made since I wrote them, and I am to lazy to re-write or even correct.

ALS, DLC-William T. Sherman. From Athens, USG went to Naples and then to Rome. See Jesse R. Grant, *In the Days of My Father General Grant* (New York, 1925), pp. 297–302, 306–9.

Probably while visiting Rome, USG wrote to Caroline C. Marsh, wife of the U.S. minister to Italy. "Mrs. Grant wishes me to say that we have not received notice of any entertainment to be given by the Court for tuesday next, or any other day." ALS (undated), University of Vermont, Burlington, Vt. On March 25, 1878, George P. Marsh "gave a grand dinner and soirée" for USG. *New York Times*, March 26, 1878. On April 11, George Marsh, Rome, wrote to Secretary of State William M. Evarts concerning expenses incurred entertaining USG. ALS, DNA, RG 59, Diplomatic Despatches, Italy. On April 17, Marsh wrote to Evarts detailing protocol issues that complicated USG's visit. LS, *ibid.*

    1. See *PUSG*, 22, 356–58; *ibid.*, 23, 82–85.
    2. See letter to John F. Long, Feb. 22, 1878; *John Sherman's Recollections of Forty Years* . . . (Chicago, 1895), II, 603–26.
    3. On April 8, Gen. William T. Sherman, Washington, D. C., wrote to Maj. Gen. John M. Schofield, superintendent, USMA. ". . . I Enclose you an Extract of a letter from General Grant received this morning, dated Rome March 21, in which is Embraced a Request that I ask you to comply with as far as the Military Academy is concerned—. . ." ALS, CSmH. See Said Pasha to Sherman, May 29, 1878, DLC-William T. Sherman.

To Adam Badeau

———

Rome, Italy.
March 22d /78

MY DEAR GENERAL:

On arrival here I found a large Mail, and in it yours enclosing a Chapter of your book with letters from Sherman, Porter & Babcock. I return the whole without comment, seeing nothing absolutely to correct or change. I also return two little slips previously received— at Athens I believe—which seem to me proper addendums.

I observe from Porter's letter that he has made marginal notes on previous chapters! Of course I cannot tell what those notes were, but knowing that you have done Sherman justice, and nothing more, I suggest that you change nothing that relates to him or his movements. Young left this morning for London. He will be there about the time you receive this and will give you a graphic account of all we have seen. I will only state that my trip up the Nile, and in the Levant—all of my travels out of the beaten track—have been the most pleasant of my life. I should like to do the same thing over again next Winter. Most every letter I get from the states—like Porter's to you—ask me to remain absent. They have designs for me which I do not contemplate for myself. It is probable that I ~~shall~~ will return to the United States either in the fall or early next spring.

Sherman did not say in hi[s] letter to me what the President replied when he notified him of my desire for your retention, and of his
previous promise to me in the matter[.] I have no doubt but it is all
right, and that you have been retained to this time solely on account
of that promise. You know there has been a terrible pressure by reformers for your place.[1]

Mrs. Grant and Jesse desire to be most kindly remembered
to you.

Very Truly Yours
U. S. GRANT

GEN. A. BADEAU
CONSUL GEN. OF THE U. S.

ALS, Munson-Williams-Proctor Institute, Utica, N. Y.

1. See letter to Adam Badeau, Feb. 4, 1878.

To Anthony J. Drexel

Rome, Italy,
March 22d /78

MY DEAR MR. DREXEL:

Your last letter was received during our visit to Athens. I was
glad to hear from you again as I always am from my Phila friends.
Since my last letter to you we have had the most interesting travels
of my—our—life. A winter on the Nile cannot be surpassed for
lovelyness of climate, and no part of the world can show more to see.
The letters published in the Herald give a more minute description
than I would want to give in the space of a letter, and gives it better
than I could if I should try. But suffice it to say that both Mrs. Grant
and I often spoke of how delightful it would have been if we could
have had you, Mr. Childs and Mr. Borie, with your wives, with us to
help us enjoy it. We would have wanted one more to fill out the Boston table while Mr. Childs would have entertained the ladies. Our
visit through the Levant was also interesting. I have seen the home
papers much more consecutively during the Winter than before, and

since the meeting of Congress have felt quite sad over the legislation, and proposed legislation of that August body. It has looked to me as though we were fast drifting to the point where loyalty to the Union was to be a degridation, and disloyalty was to be rewarded and respected as just the thing. The passage of the silver Bill too I look upon as a national disgrace.[1] It was so amended in the senate that it may work no great harm; but it discredits us all the same nevertheless. It shows a willingness on the part of a Majority to repudiate a percentage of their indebtedness, and people who will do that are capable of repudiating the whole. The man who would steal a lamb would not be safe to trust with a sheep. I trust there will be a reaction and that we will get back to an honest currency, and to a point, where the ex rebel will admit that the Union man has equal rights with himself in the government of the country.

We will probably spend three or four weeks here and then work up North so as to be in Sweeden & Norway during June, and get back to the Paris exposition in July. We will meet Mr. & Mrs. Childs there I see by the papers.[2] If you and Mr. Borie will come over, and lay aside the cares of business for a season, we will all go up the Nile next Winter.

Present Mrs. Grant's and my kindest regards to Mrs. Drexel & the children, and to all our Phila friends.

yours Very Truly
U. S. GRANT

Nellie is here spending the winter, she and her little boy both very well. We expect her to be with us ~~also~~ in Paris.

ALS, MHi. For USG's contacts with Anthony J. Drexel in Paris during May and June, 1878, see John Russell Young diary, DLC-John Russell Young.

1. See letter to John F. Long, Feb. 22, 1878.

2. Appointed an honorary commissioner to the Paris Universal Exposition, scheduled to open May 1, George W. Childs did not travel to Paris. See *Reports of the United States Commissioners to the Paris Universal Exposition, 1878* (Washington, 1880), I, 54.

To Frederick Dent Grant

———

Rome, Italy,
March 22d /78

DEAR FRED,

Since my last we have visited Constantinople for five days and Athens, Greece for five days. We saw Constantinople at a historically interesting time, but a very unfavorable time for seeing the Turks in their glory. They were very hospitable however notwithstanding their embarrassing situation. The Russian Army was but eight miles outside and the road entirely open from the city to the Russian camp. I was anxious to visit their camp, but having received the hospitalities of the Turkish officials I doubted the propriety of such a visit, and therefore abstained.

I differ from you in regard to the Greeks. They seem to me to be a very energetic and advancing people. Athens, which had not a single house forty-five years ago, is now one of the most beautiful, cleanest and best paved cities in Europe, containing a population of about 45000 people. The houses are substantial and present a fine architectural appearance, the people, high & low, are well and comfortably clad and every thing indicates prosperity. I am inclined to think that if they could regain their former territory, or a good part of it, with the addition of the Greek population this would give them, they would become a very respectible Nation. The Turco-Russian war may yet end in this. My visit through the Turkish Empire does not impress me favorably with their power to develope the resources of a country.

We have seen nothing but the outside of places of interest here as yet, but will commence to-morrow to make a regular inspection taking American studios in the fore noon and the churches and other places in the afternoon. I think we can put in a month here very pleasantly.

Nellie is here and is looking very well. She will leave about the same time we do and may travel with us. Jess will go home during the Summer to commence his preparations for the battle of life.[1] He has the ability for success if he has the energy. I hope he will not be found deficient in that. We received, on our arrival here, a letter from each Ida & yourself. I hope we may be able to meet Mr. & Mrs. Palmer, who you say are coming to Europe during the Summer, but, unless they go up North to Sweeden & Norway it is not likely we will meet until late in the season. We will be at the Paris exposition late in the Summer, and may be in Switzerland before the summer closes. All send love & kisses to you, Ida & little Julia and kindest regards to Gen. & Mrs. Sheridan, Mr. & Mrs. Honoré and all our friends in Chicago.

Yours Affectionately
U. S. GRANT

ALS, USG 3.

  1. See Jesse R. Grant, *In the Days of My Father General Grant* (New York, 1925), p. 312.

To Rear Admiral Daniel Ammen

ROME, ITALY, March 25th, 1878.

MY DEAR ADMIRAL,—

I have received three interesting letters from you since my last to you. You must excuse this, and continue to write, because I am always glad to receive your letters, as are all the family,—and they all read them; and then I am writing to so many persons that I cannot be prompt in my replies.

The winter's trip has been the most pleasant of my life. It has been entirely out of the usual course of travellers abroad, and has opened a new field. My whole family—or at least those with me— are such sailors that a home on shipboard was as comfortable as if on land, even when it was rough weather. The officers, without exception, were agreeable and did all they could to make us feel at home. Captain Robeson,[1] the commander, was most attentive both to his guests and to his duties. I judge a more safe commander to a ship could not be found. The second officer, Lieutenant Caldwell,[2] is a very superior man in education and acquirements, and especially so in all scientific subjects, and professional ones too. He is very much such a man as Comstock, who served on my staff, and whom you remember. If you do not remember him, you do his horse at least.[3] The other officers are nice fellows, and some of them I think would make their mark if occasion presents itself. The third officer, Lieutenant Strong,[4] is from the volunteers, and commands the respect of all others, from the captain down. It would be hard to convince any of them that a more thorough navigator is to be found in or out of the service.

Mr. Young, of the New York *Herald*, accompanied us during our naval experience, and to this place, and wrote very good and very descriptive letters. You have no doubt read them, so that I will leave out all account of places. But my impression of peoples are that in the East they have a form of government and a civilization that will always repress progress and development. Syria and Asia Minor are as rich of soil as the great Northwest in our own country, and are blessed with a climate far more suitable to production. The people would be industrious if they had encouragement, but they are treated as slaves, and all they produce is taken from them for the benefit of the governing classes and to maintain them in a luxurious and licentious life. Women are degraded even beneath a slave. They have no more rights than the brute. In fact, the donkey is their superior in privileges.

I was in Constantinople at a very interesting time historically. The Russian army was but a few miles outside, and there was no barrier to their entrance. But the stolidity of the people is such that in the five days I spent in Constantinople I should never have discovered from the manner of the people, outside of the Sultan and a few of the high officials, that anything unusual had happened.

We spent five days in Athens on our way here. It is a beautiful city now. It is well built, well paved, and very clean. Considering that there was not a house where the present city stands, forty-five years ago, and that the opposition of the Turks has kept them from communication with the balance of Europe except by sea, they have certainly made wonderful progress. I hope they may have their territory increased as one of the effects of the present war, so as to give them more Greek population, more space, and a full chance to develop. It seems to me England, and the balance of Europe, except Russia, is

interested in seeing such a consummation. But I am much more interested in home affairs. I have read the home papers much more attentively this winter than during the earlier part of my travels. Since
the meeting of Congress I have felt almost discouraged at times. The
legislation and the proposed legislation almost convinces me that, if
the North does not rally, we who were so *unfortunate* as to serve on
the Union side, *from a false sense of right,* might yet be required to get
one of Andy Johnson's pardons to relieve us from responsibility as
murderers, robbers, and illegal and unjustifiable invaders of the sacred soil of the South. I believe there is a settled determination to destroy the army and navy, and to reorganize it so as to bring back,
with their lost rank, those who saw better than we did the right, and
quit the service to follow it. Poor fellows! what a pity they were not
successful! They would have such an opportunity now of showing
their chivalry—by putting us all in State's prison.

The passage of the silver bill is very discouraging.[5] It is dishonest in the extreme, although practically it may not work the harm
contemplated by its main supporters. But it shows a willingness on
the part of a majority of our present legislators to repudiate a portion of public and private indebtedness. The crime would be only
greater in magnitude if they should repudiate the whole. The man
who would steal your lamb would not be a safe custodian of the old
sheep. But let us hope that wiser counsels will prevail. Mr. Hayes, it
seems to me, exercises but little influence with the legislation. This
I suppose is partly due to the very slight majority he had in the Electoral College, and more to the Utopian ideas he got, *from reformers,*
of running a government without a party. The Democrats have deceived him. I hope he will return to those who elected him. I believe
he is a perfectly sincere man, purely patriotic, and a good Republican. But he has been wofully mistaken,—or I am, from a distant
point of view. Give Mrs. Grant's love to Mrs. Ammen and the children, and mine too if you will, and write to me often. My address is
Drexel, Harjes & Co., Paris.

Yours very truly,
U. S. GRANT.

ADMIRAL D. AMMEN, *U. S. Navy.*

Daniel Ammen, *The Old Navy and the New* (Philadelphia, 1891), pp. 539–41.

1. Henry B. Robeson graduated from the U.S. Naval Academy (1860), served along the coasts of N. C. and S. C. during the Civil War, and received promotions until made commander (1874). He became capt. of the U.S.S. *Vandalia* in 1876.

2. Albert G. Caldwell graduated from the U.S. Naval Academy (1864) and advanced in rank to lt. commander (1869). On March 19, 1878, Caldwell, U.S.S. *Vandalia*, Naples, wrote to his mother. ". . . We had vicissitudes at Piraeus—Genl & party went off as soon as the anchor was down—stopped with Reed at Athens—he is wealthy & I think didnt let the Genl spend a cent—old friends . . . Genl leaves us tomorrow for Rome—special car— invited me to go—couldnt— . . . I'm sorry Grant is going away   he is chock full of infor- mation & good ideas He says about the silver bill 'If I were (*was*, he said) President now I'd make $2000.000 in silver a month and lock it up as reserve & issue greenbacks instead. It's the worst thing since the war & will be worse for the working man than for capitalists that its aimed at. President Haye's veto will make him very popular in two years.' That is sound talk. Grant knows what it costs to make a yard of cotton south or in Providence— the bushels of grain exported for years—the fluctuations of exchange—the Army & Navy ration to an ounce & all such information & he is *never* wrong about a figure or a date. He has taken rather a fancy to me because I play a good game of whist—says he never saw anyone play better—we play Boston every night—learn it—its the best game I ever saw . . ." ALS, InHi. See Caldwell to his sister, March 9, 1878, *ibid.*

3. "The quiet humor of the general is seen in his allusion to Comstock's horse, which I rode on a visit to Mr. Blair at Silver Spring, and my experience with which was a subject of far more merriment to others than it was to me during the actual time of the riding." Ammen, p. 541. See Ammen, "Recollections and Letters of Grant," *North American Review,* CXLI, cccxlviii (Nov., 1885), 421.

4. Born in 1840 in Ipswich, Mass., Edward T. Strong joined the merchant marine (1857), entered the navy as mate (1862), was commissioned ensign (1868), and promoted to lt. (1870).

5. See letter to John F. Long, Feb. 22, 1878.

To Ulysses S. Grant, Jr.

———

Rome, March 25th /78

DEAR BUCK:

I have made no allusion in my two last letters to what you say about running over here, and joining us, for your f vacation: If you have two full months you could do so and have quite a pleasant visit besides on this side the water. You had better do so by all means. I do not know at what time your vacation commences, but probably in time to enable you to reach Liverpool or Havre early in July. If you come—and you must come if you can—join us where ever we may be. My present plan is to work north from here, by way of Florence,

Venice, Vienna, Berlin and St. Petersburgh so as to get into Sweeden by the 10th of June, or thereabout. After seeing a little of Sweeden & Norway to come back to Copenhagen and stay about a week there if your Aunt Mary is there, which seems unlikely now because of proposed legislative action abolishing the mission to Denmark.[1] If she and Mr. Cramer are not there we will stop but a couple of days and about the same time at the Hague. We will go directly from there to Paris and try to get apartments and keep house for a month or two. You would of course stay with us whereever we might be. All are very well. We see a great deal of Nellie. She is looking very well and will probably be with us in Paris.

All send love.

Affectionately yours
U. S. GRANT

U. S. GRANT JR.

ALS, ICarbS.

On March 4, 1878, Ulysses S. Grant, Jr., New York City, wrote to Adolph E. Borie. "I am just in receipt of your letter, *all* of which I have read. When in California I heard of nothing that tended to shake my believef in the mine of that name. Every thing seemed most prosperous that was connected with it. I sold out fathers interests because he directed me to do so when he could get out square. I have no fear but that California will pay dividends for months yet. . . ." ALS, PHi.

1. The House of Representatives eliminated the appropriation for the chargé d'affaires to Denmark from the diplomatic service bill; the Senate restored the position. See *CR*, 45–2, 1612, 1699, 2068–69.

To Abel R. Corbin

Rome, Italy,
March 29th, '78.

MY DEAR MR. CORBIN:

Mr. Young, of the New York *Herald*, has been with us from the time we went on shipboard until we arrived here. His letters published in the papers are all good,[1] and save me writing descriptive letters. Presuming that you have read them I will say nothing further than that my winter travels, in the Mediterranean, on the Nile, and in the Levant generally have been the pleasantest of my life. I should enjoy doing it over again next winter. We have been in Rome eight days. It is a city of great interest. But one should visit it before making the Nile trip. Here you see modern and comparatively insignificant ruins, not dating back many centuries before the beginning of the Christian era. On the Nile one sees grand ruins, with the inscriptions as plain and distinct as when they were first made, that antedate Moses by many centuries.[2]

It was our plan on leaving Suez to go to Florence, Venice, Vienna, Berlin, Dresden, St. Petersburgh, through Sweden, Norway, back to Denmark, through Holland to Paris, reaching the latter place about the middle of July, and to spend six or eight weeks there to see the Exposition and the people that will fill the city. I think now I will change my plan and go from Venice, by easy stages, to Paris, reaching there early in May, and make my visit while the weather is pleasant. I will then go north in the summer, taking Holland first, Denmark next, and Sweden and Norway in August. I fear from present indications that Mr. Cramer and Mary will not be there.[3]

It looks to me that unless the North rallies by 1880 the Government will be in the hands of those who tried so hard fourteen—seventeen—years ago to destroy it. B——[4] is evidently paving a way for re-organizing an army favorable to such a change.

I think now we will not return to the States until about a year from May. I have no idea where we will live on our return, and if we should go back in the fall we would have to determine the question without delay. We can go back in May and occupy our Long Branch house and have all summer to prepare for the winter.

I was getting some little mosaics—specialties of Rome—to-day and I bought, among other things, what I think a very pretty pin and earrings for Jennie. I have also got bracelets for Clara Cramer and Jennie Grant. If I see an opportunity of sending them home before going myself I will send them. I have written to Buck to come over and spend his vacation with us. I can send them with him.

Give our love to Mother, Jennie, Mary and the children.

Yours very truly,

U. S. Grant.

P. S. It is very kind in Mr. Clark,[5] and the gentlemen associated with him, to send the message you convey from them; but they must recollect that I had the harness on for sixteen years and feel no inclination to wear it again. I sincerely hope that the North will so thoroughly rally by next election as to bury the last remnant of secession proclivities, and put in the Executive chair a firm and steady hand, free from Utopian ideas purifying the party electing him out of existence.

J. G. Cramer, pp. 143–45.
   Probably in early Nov., 1878, a reporter interviewed Abel R. Corbin, covering Orvil L. Grant's insanity and subjects related to USG. ". . . General Grant never was a tanner, never worked at the tanners's trade. Strictly speaking, neither did his brothers. Their father, however, carried on a tannery at Galena, Ill., and made a great deal of money. He set up in business the General's two brothers, putting in about $100,000. The business was that of leather dealing, shoe findings, &c. . . . I have no authority to speak for General Grant, but I am sure he thinks, as others think, that he has had his full share of official honors. Whether he will take any part in the next Presidential canvass or not I cannot say, though I think it certain that whoever it is that gets the nomination of his party will have the General's hearty support. If such a state of things should arise—if such a contingency should present itself, which, let me say right here I do not consider even remotely probable, but on the contrary most improbable—as that the great republican party should, after due and ample deliberation, deem it best to pass by all its other worthy and deserving leaders and nominate General Grant, I feel certain that the General would, for the sake of his party and the country, yield to the desires expressed by the highest party councils. . . ." *New York Herald*, Nov. 11, 1878. For another interview with Corbin on USG's political future, see *ibid.*, Dec. 4, 1878.

   1. For John Russell Young's columns on USG's travels dated Dec. 28, 1877, Jan. 10, 25, 26, 30, 31, Feb. 3, 14, 1878, see *ibid.*, Jan. 20, Feb. 15, March 2–5, 18, 1878.
   2. See letter to Frederick Dent Grant, Jan. 25, 1878.
   3. See previous letter.
   4. U.S. Representative Henry B. Banning of Ohio influenced army organization as chairman, Committee on Military Affairs. A former officer in the Ohio vols., and bvt. maj. gen., Banning entered Congress in 1873 as a Liberal Republican and won two more terms as a Democrat.
   5. Probably Amos Clark, Jr.

To Adam Badeau

———

Rome, Italy,
March 30th /78

DEAR GENERAL:

I have your letter of yesterday. I will instruct Hartog to execute your commission at once. I have written to you since my arrival here, and returned the last of your Manuscript.

We leave here two weeks from to-day to go to Florence for a week, thence to Venice for about the same time, then to Milan and on to Paris where we expect to arrive on the 10th of May. We will remain there until about the middle of July and make our journey north, to ~~Sweeden~~ Sweden & Norway, after that. As I shall see you so soon I will say nothing of what we have seen, or of the recent news from home.

Yours Truly
U. S. GRANT

GEN. A. BADEAU

ALS, Munson-Williams-Proctor Institute, Utica, N. Y. See *Badeau*, p. 497.

To Adam Badeau

———

[*March–April, 1878*]

To GENL A. BADEAU
U S CONSUL GENERAL
LONDON ENG

I return Pemberton's letter. Your ~~letter~~ statement of the circumstances attending the Vicksburgh Surrender are as absolutely correct as it can well be made. I presume Bowen did ask the interview between P & myself without authority. I did not propose or submit to the settlement of terms by a refferrence to Commissioners. Finding that we were about to separate without coming to an agreement Bowens—who seemed very anxious about an agreement—

proposed that he and others of the Reb. Army, and Gen. A. J. Smith and some others of our Army who were present at the time, should consult and see if they could not agree upon terms which Pemberton and I would accept. I declined that and the terms were finally arranged between us through a correspondence which extended late into the night of the 3d of July /63.

U. S. Grant

ALS (undated), Gallery of History, Las Vegas, Nev. Written on a letter of Jan. 21, 1878, from Orville E. Babcock to Adam Badeau. See *Badeau*, p. 498; letter to Adam Badeau, Feb. 4, 1878; *PUSG*, 8, 455–58.

On May 11, Louis Philippe Albert d'Orléans, Comte de Paris, wrote to Badeau. "I thank you very much for your letter of April 21st, and for the most valuable information which you have given me. I had, of course, the greatest doubts about the accuracy of General Pemberton's statement, as it was so much at variance with your own account; but coming from such high authority I could not put it aside without mentioning it to you. I am very grateful to General Grant for the trouble he took to answer himself, and to give such a detailed account of what happened between him and General Pemberton. I regret very much not to be able to go myself to Paris to thank him; but the Countess de Paris having given birth to a daughter four days ago only, I cannot leave her presently." *Badeau*, pp. 587–88. Comte de Paris, who served on Maj. Gen. George B. McClellan's staff, wrote *Histoire de la Guerre Civile en Amérique* (Paris, 1874–90), also published in English (Philadelphia, 1875–88). See letter to Adam Badeau, May 19, 1878; *The Times* (London), Sept. 10, 1894.

To John Russell Young

Rome, Italy,
Apl. 7th /78

My Dear Mr. Young:

Your letter of _____ was received three days ago. I have not got it before me having given it to Badeau to read and return, the latter of which requests he has not yet complied with. The only point I recollect requiring a special answer is in regard to authority to deny Dick Taylor's statement in regard to war matters.

The Atlantic Monthly which you speak of sending did not come. Hence I have not read what you kindly propose to contradict. But, as you remember, I saw the newspapers synopsis of Taylors statements and expressed to you my denial of them, and gave you the facts as to whad did occur between the President, Sec. of War and myself, seeing them separately. They never asked me for my plans nor to follow any proposed by themselves. I would be very glad to have you make the contradiction in your own way. When Badeau returns he will give you any facts you want, from actual records, or if you will write him a letter making enquiries as to what you want he will answer.[1]

I have seen Rome very thoroughly spending about five hours each day in sight seeing, and have repeated on nothing. We leave for Florence on the 13th next Saturday. The Saturday following we go to Venice, the Saturday following that to Milan, and will go from there to reach Paris on the 10th of May.

Mrs. Grant was much pleased with your letter to her, and wishes to be specially remembered to Mrs. Young and yourself.

Very Truly yours
U. S. GRANT

ALS, DLC-John Russell Young. On April 10, 1878, John Russell Young, London, received this letter from USG and responded with a letter of his own. Young diary, DLC-John Russell Young. On March 23, Young had left the Grants in Rome to visit his wife and newborn daughter. *Ibid.* See *ibid.*, March 31, April 1, 3, 1878; *New York Times*, Jan. 5, 1881.

1. In an article critical of USG's generalship during the Va. campaign, Gideon Welles, former secretary of the navy, assailed former C.S.A. Lt. Gen. Richard Taylor's published assertion that President Abraham Lincoln and Secretary of War Edwin M. Stanton compelled USG to advance overland on Richmond, characterizing the charge as "an afterthought to cast from the shoulders of General Grant the responsibility of the 'bloody march' and place it upon the kind-hearted president." Welles, "The Opposition to Lincoln in 1864," *Atlantic Monthly*, XLI, ccxlv (March, 1878), 366–76. See Taylor, "Reminiscences of the Civil War," *North American Review*, CXXVI, cclx (Jan.-Feb., 1878), 95–96, and *Destruction and Reconstruction: Personal Experiences of the Late War* (New York, 1879), pp. 33–34; Interview, May 9, 1878.

To Frederick Dent Grant

Rome, Italy,
Apl. 9th 1878

DEAR FRED.

We have now been in Rome nearly three weeks and have seen about all there is to see. It is a city of great interest to the traveler, as you know, but to enjoy the ruins one should come here before going up the Nile. The ruins here seem modern in comparison and insignificant in size, finish and structure. But the city—and Italy generally—has improved very much since you were here.[1] In the cities beggars have almost wholly disappeared. Going outside the gates a few are encountered, but they are neither so numerous nor so importunate as in Egypt, or as they are said to have been here a few years ago. We leave on Monday next[2] for Florence, ~~Naples~~ Venice, Milan & Paris, reaching the latter place—intending to—by the 10th of May. We will probably remain in Paris ten weeks. I have written Buck to come over and spend his vacation with us.[3] I wish you and Ida could do the same thing, leaving little Julia behind. Jesse left yesterday for Paris with the intention of going home soon. I hope however he will remain there until we arrive, and conclude to stay with us until August. He could then return home in time to commence his studies. Nellie will be with us, and if you & Ida could come over we would have all the family together. It would not involve a very heavy outlay, and if you could not bear it very well I will help you as much as the extra expence would amount to.

I sometimes get homesick for America, but I shall not return before next Spring, in time to go to our Long Branch house. Should I go back this fall we would have to determine, at once, where we are to live and prepare for it. By waiting until the next season we can go to our Long Branch house and have the summer to prepare our winter quarters.

I have never heard from Gn. Sheridan since coming abroad! I wrote to him I do not know how long ago. Give my kindes[t] regards to him and his numerous but small family.[4]—Your Ma sends love and kisses to Ida and Chatterbox.

Yours affectionately,
U. S. Grant

ALS, USG 3. See *Young*, I, 361–66; *Julia Grant*, pp. 210–12; *New York Times*, March 31, 1878.

    1. See *PUSG*, 22, 357–58.
    2. April 15, 1878.

3. See letter to Ulysses S. Grant, Jr., March 25, 1878.
    4. Lt. Gen. Philip H. Sheridan's family included three daughters born since his marriage in 1875.

To James Gordon Bennett

Florence, Italy.
Apl 20, 1878.

MY DEAR MR. BENNETT.

During my winter wanderings, on board the U. S. Steamer Vandalia, I met many accomplished & efficient officers connected with Uncle Sam's Maritime service.—While I would not like to make invidious distinctions among gentlemen who generally bore themselves so well, there was one, who I several times spoke of to the Captain of the Vandalia[1] and to Mr Young as a man I should select to do anything that required daring, judgement and the other qualities of success. His name is Dannenhauer, a graduate of the US. Naval Academy of a few years since, and an officer, now of the *Vandalia.* Mr Young writes me that Dannenhauer would like to go on your Polar Expedition. I feel no hesitation in saying that my judgment would be in favor of this young naval officer if the leave of absence can be obtained for him, and that although he might be too young to assign to the command of the expedition, yet if anything should happen by death or accident to throw him in command he would be abundantly capable of the position.

Very Truly Yours,
U. S. GRANT.

J. G. BENNETT, EQ.,

Copy, DLC-John Russell Young. John W. Danenhower, U.S. Naval Academy (1870), received promotion to master (1873) and joined the U.S.S. *Vandalia* after recovering from a mental breakdown. For Danenhower and the tragic polar expedition sponsored by James Gordon Bennett, see Danenhower to John Russell Young, June 13, 1878, Jan. 1, Aug. 19, 1879, *ibid.*; *HED*, 47-2-108; *HMD*, 48-1-66; *New York Times*, April 21, 1887; Leonard F. Guttridge, *Icebound: The* Jeannette *Expedition's Quest for the North Pole* (Annapolis, 1986).

    1. Commander Henry B. Robeson.

To John Russell Young

———

Florence, Italy,
Apl. 20th /78

My Dear Commodore:

Your telegram of yesterday asking for a note from me, in favor of Danenhaur for a position on the Polar Expedition, is received. I give the letter consciensciously believing that a better person could not be selected for second or third officer. I send the letter, open, to you so that you can use your discretion about sending it to Mr. Bennett.[1]

Your previous note does not say whether you sent Badeau's reply to Ex. Sec. Welles to the Herald or not? I hope you did because it was carefully prepared, and has data. Badeau fortunately had with him the advance sheets of his second Volume from which to get his data.[2]

Yours Very Truly
U. S. Grant

P. S. Your friend, Mr. Huntington,[3] is a guest here in the house—of Mrs. Graham[4]—with us. Of course I see much of him and like him very much. He desires to be specially remembered. We start on Monday for Venice.[5] Will probably start on the following saturday for Milan.

ALS, DLC-John Russell Young. John Russell Young was then in Paris. See Young diary, April 19, 22, 1878, DLC-John Russell Young.

1. See preceding letter.
2. See letter to John Russell Young, April 7, 1878; Adam Badeau, *Military History of Ulysses S. Grant*, . . . (New York, 1881–82), II, 12–14.
3. USG met both Henry G. Huntington, vice consul, Florence, and William H. Huntington, *New York Tribune* correspondent and art collector. See Henry G. Huntington, *Memories: Personages, People, Places* (London, 1911), pp. 299–304; *New York Tribune*, Oct. 4, 1885; *New York Times*, Nov. 21, 1926.
4. Louisa Graham, widow of the former U.S. consul, Florence. See *PUSG*, 19, 411–12; Huntington, *Memories*, p. 300.
5. On Monday, April 22, 1878, Jacques Hartog, Venice, wrote to John Russell Young describing USG's reception. ALS, DLC-John Russell Young. On April 16 and 18, Hartog, Florence, had written to Young concerning USG's plans and activities. ALS, *ibid*. See *Young*, I, 366–75; *Julia Grant*, pp. 242–43.

To Charles D. Miller

MILAN, ITALY, April 27, 1878.
Major Charles D. Miller, Secretary of the Society of Soldiers and Sailors
of Licking County, Ohio:

DEAR MAJOR: Your cordial invitation for me to attend a general
Re-union of the Veterans of Ohio, to be held under the auspices of the
Society of the Soldiers and Sailors of Licking County, at Newark, on
the 22d of July, is this day received.[1] It always affords me pleasure to
attend at the gatherings of the soldiers and sailors who patriotically
risked their lives for the preservation of the country, and it would afford me special pleasure to meet with those hailing from my native
State.

But the Atlantic will be between us at the time of your proposed
re-union. This is the first opportunity of my life to visit Europe, and
will likely be my last. There is much here to see which I have not
seen, and I desire to remain to partly accomplish the tour which I
had marked out for myself. I trust the Veterans of Ohio will have a
most auspicious re-union on the coming occasion and that none of
them will ever feel a disposition to apologize for the part they took
in the late struggle for national existence, nor for the cause for which
they fought.

With great respect, your old companion,

U. S. GRANT.

Charles D. Miller, *Report of the Great Re-Union of the Veteran Soldiers and Sailors of Ohio*
(Newark, Ohio, 1879), pp. 36–37. On April 12, 1878, Charles D. Miller, former capt., 76th
Ohio, and bvt. maj., Newark, wrote to USG. "You are cordially invited to attend a general
Soldiers' Re-union of the Veterans of Ohio, to be held under the auspices of the 'Society of
the Soldiers and Sailors of Licking County,' in this city, on the 22d day of July, next. Should
your sojourn in Europe prevent you from being present with us on that day, permit us to
express the deep loss we shall feel in the absence of our beloved commander, and be assured that the hearts of American soldiers are with you wherever you may be in foreign
lands. As you pass through France you may observe the reverence yet cherished for the
deeds of the great Napoleon. Such will ever be the devotion in the hearts of America's Sons
who followed your victorious standards. We would be pleased to hear from you and to
know that you think of us. Please accept our best wishes for your health and happiness."
Ibid., p. 36.

1. On April 27, USG arrived in Milan. See *Young*, I, 375–77.

To J. Schuyler Crosby

[*April, 1878*]
Venice, Italy.

MY DEAR COLONEL,

We are in receipt of your two letters and enclosures and thank you not only for the trouble you have taken in executing commissions but for your courtesy and attention during our stay in Florence and which contributed so largely to the pleasure and profit of the visit. I have written to Col. Mc Millan saying how much I regretted the unpleasantness created by his reception at the Florence's station, that I was sure from your subsequent manner that you regretted it also, and that nothing of the kind was contemplated, much less meditated. The notice of our arrival in Florence, in which the Consul General's name was omitted, I accounted for on the theory that no information was given to the press after our arrival, and up to that time it was not known that either he or Mrs. Dinsmore [1] were of the party. . . .

Mrs. Grant wants to thank you for the photograph you send. Did I give you mine while in Florence? If not I will send it from Milan.

Always truly yours
U. S. GRANT

COL. J. SCHUYLER CROSBY U S CONSUL

Copy (ellipsis in original), DNA, RG 59, Applications and Recommendations, Hayes-Arthur. Born into a wealthy N. Y. family, J. Schuyler Crosby served in the 1st Art. and as a staff officer (1861–70) and then worked as an engineer until his appointment as consul, Florence, where he received the Grants upon their arrival on April 15, 1878. In Florence through April 21, USG visited art galleries, attended religious services on Holy Saturday, and participated in a banquet. USG left for Venice on April 22 and stayed there until April 27. See letter to Ministers and Consuls, May 13, 1876; *New York Herald*, April 16, 21, 24, 1878.

On April 19, Crosby had written confidentially to George P. Marsh, U.S. minister, Rome, on USG's reception in Florence and the grievance of Charles McMillan, consul gen., Rome. ". . . I dined at the house of Mrs. Graham with the Grants & after dinner about 10 o'ck Gen. Grant & I took a walk around the hills, by the Piazza Michelangelo & only got back at 12.15 midnight. I then went home & found a letter from one of the Gentlemen (American) who was at the Depôt, saying that 'General' Mac Millan had stepped up to him and said that 'I had insulted him, had treated him with the greatest disrespect, that I had shown him no attention and had introduced him as "DOCTOR" Mc Millan instead of "Gen-

eral"—Then he abused me & said 'I had done it on purpose—& that he had never been
placed in a position so disagreeable in all his experience, having had all the charge and duties put upon him since General Grant came to Rome & Naples in regard to his reception
& management, he had had no trouble & difficulty & had been properly recognized, until
he reached Florence, & that he should at once return to Rome & not remain a day longer
in this city.' Wishing to avoid any complication & really having had not the slightest intention of doing any thing to render Mr. Mc Millan's position disagreeable, I sat down at
once and wrote him a *nice* friendly note, commencing it 'Dear Mc Millan,' repeating what
I had heard by note, naming my authority—telling him that in the hurry of Gen. Grants
arrival & the number of persons there, that I had no recollection of what title I had given
him in introducing him to the Authorities saying that he ought to know that I had no desire to treat him with disrespect, but at the same time I really was the one to complain, in
finding that *he* should misjudge me, by thinking I desired to insult him &. The next morning I left a card in person at his hotel on him. He never returned my card, took especial
pains to tell every one whom he saw, that I had insulted & treated him with the greatest
disrespect and *officially* told my Vice Consul Mr. Huntington the same. He then (that
night) returned to Rome!!! He also *wrote a note to Gen. Grant* saying I had acted so discour-
teously to him & & that he could not remain in Florence & . . ." Copy (second ellipsis in
original), DNA, RG 59, Applications and Recommendations, Hayes-Arthur. See Crosby to
McMillan, April 22, 1878, *ibid.*

    1. Probably Augusta S. Dinsmore, whose husband, William B., was president of the
Adams Express Co. See *PUSG*, 24, 12.

Interview

PARIS, May 9, 1878.

So far as Mr. Welles is concerned, he is dead, and any resentment
one might feel at his extraordinary misstatements would now be out
of place. It is unfortunate for Mr. Welles' fame that he should have
spent his last years in striving to belittle the very administration
in which he held a prominent place.[1] But the real reason is that
Mr. Welles never was a republican. He blundered into Lincoln's Cabinet. He remained as quiet as a mouse so long as he held a high office
under the republicans and drew a large salary. As soon as Mr. Johnson made his advances toward the democrats he became a loud and
earnest supporter of his administration. From that time to the end of
his life Mr. Welles was in perfect sympathy with the men who tried
to break down the government, and it is only natural that he should
belittle and defame those who did their best to save the government,
men who, whether they did much or little, did all in their power.

Mr. Welles was never so sincere in anything in his life as in his democracy, and nothing that he has written against myself or others
for what we tried to do in the war would cause me the least surprise
or vexation. My only sorrow is that a gentleman who had been Secretary of the Navy during the rebellion should devote his powers to
defame men who did all they could to suppress the rebellion. I cannot conceive a more painful and humiliating position. As to General
Taylor's assault on Mr. Lincoln I am not surprised. General Taylor
fought on the other side, drew pay on the other side and writes on
the other side. Taylor, unlike Welles, is loyal to his cause, and if
he can destroy the reputation of Mr. Lincoln, and those who served
Mr Lincoln, why, of course, he has a right to do so. That's what the
Southern Confeder[a]cy tried to do for many years. So far as Taylor
and I are concerned we are friends, and have maintained the best
relations.[2] I am quite sure he would not do me any unkindness, as I
would not do him. Taylor is one of the most agreeable of men, who
talks well and talks a great deal, and, like men of that kind, often gets
his facts blended with fiction. I mean by that that if Taylor said about
me a positive untruth, as he does in this article, it would be a misfortune on his part or an inadvertence—not any wilful error. He
would speak in all seriousness without knowing any better.

I have no doubt there are some true things in the article; but
the part which refers to me is wholly false, utterly false, without a
shadow of foundation.[3] General Taylor says that in a conference between President Lincoln, Secretary Stanton and myself, in 1864, the
approaching campaign in Virginia was discussed. No such conference was ever held, and no such campaign was ever discussed. General Taylor says that I insisted upon advancing my whole army
against Richmond by the James River. I never said a word to the
President or Secretary of War, or any one else in authority, as to how
I would advance. General Taylor reports Mr. Lincoln as saying that
the government required the interposition of an army between Lee
and Washington. Mr. Lincoln never said a word resembling this, or
anything at all on the subject. General Taylor reports me as saying that any change of route from my own by the James to another
would cost 100,000 men. This is a pure fiction, as, indeed, the whole

story is a pure fiction. General Taylor says that the story comes to him well authenticated, and he has no doubt of his correctness. There are only three persons who could authenticate such a story— Mr. Lincoln, Mr. Stanton and myself. Lincoln and Stanton are dead, and I say the whole story is a fabrication, and whoever vouched for it to General Taylor vouched for a fiction.[4] I feel it due to the memory of these great men, apart from any sentiment of self-vindication, to make this denial as emphatic and clear as possible.

I remember very well my first interview with Stanton. You know I did not come to Washington until I came in relation to an order to assume command of the armies.[5] I had once been there as a young man, but otherwise it was my first trip. I found Stanton cordial and willing to do anything, so we suppressed the rebellion. Nothing could have been more earnest and hearty than his treatment of me. "Now," says he, "General, I do not want to know your plans. Tell me what you need to carry them out. That is all I care to know. And when you go to see Mr. Lincoln you will do well to observe the same discretion. Mr. Lincoln may not want to know any more of your plans than I do, but I can understand how you might naturally seek the confidence of the President. Now Mr. Lincoln is of a gentle and tender nature, apt to confide in many people, and what you tell him about military movements he may tell to the next Senator with whom he has an intimate conversation." I saw Lincoln. He was as cordial and hearty as Stanton, if possible more so, because he was a man of more affable and gracious manners. When Lincoln and I were alone the President began the conversation by repeating a story from an article by Orpheus C. Kerr—a comic article satirizing the conduct of the war. It was, as I remember, a story about Captain Bob Shorty and the Mackerel Brigade, and the anaconda policy, something about generals in the field being hampered by a flood of orders.[6] When he had finished Lincoln said very much what Stanton had said—that he did not care to know what I was to do, only to know what I wanted; that I should have all I required. He wished me to beat Lee, how I did it was my own duty. He said he did not wish to know my plans or to exercise any scrutiny over my plans; so long as I beat the rebel army he was satisfied. He spoke of a plan he had long thought over and took down a map. He drew an imaginary line between two of the Virginia creeks or rivers, the names of which have escaped me, and said that I might move on that line and have the streams for supplies. I looked at the plan and saw in a moment that if I put my army on such a line I would be in much the same position as the army of the James. I would be powerless; I could do no g[o]od to our side and no harm to the other. I would be locked up. I told Mr. Lincoln I would consider the plan and that was the last of it. The route was an impossible route, and was never mentioned again by Mr. Lincoln. That is, as far as I remember, the exact story of the conference between Mr. Lincoln, Mr. Stanton and myself when I took command of the army. The question of my plans and their wisdom and unwisdom was never afterward a subject of conversation or correspondence. If there were blunders in that campaign the blunders were mine and not those of Lincoln or Stanton.[7] They did everything in the world to assure my success. Upon me and upon me alone must the whole responsibility fall.

Yes, as history goes on we shall discover that the North were fighting windmills, that the South had no troops, that in time we discovered the absence of any enemy and stepped in and claimed victories. I sometimes ask where were all these able-bodied men of the South during the war? If we are to believe history not many of them were in battle. It always struck me that I saw enough of them in every engagement, and that I had but little advantage in force—none if you consider the fact that the Southern men were always on the defensive. In these articles of Welles and Taylor you note that they not only assume that the true and proper way to have attacked Lee was by way of the James River, but that this also was my opinion. If the whole of my command had gon[e] by the way of the James River I certainly would have found enough of Lee's force to have retarded my progress and to fight me, and possibly enough would have been spared to have threatened the national capital. As it was I confronted Lee, and held him and all his hosts far from Richmond and the James, while I sent, the same day of my advance across the Rapidan, a force by the James River sufficient, as I thought, to have captured all south of Richmond to Petersburg and hold it. I believe now that if General Butler had had two corps commanders such as I might have selected had I known the material of the entire army as well as I did afterward, he would have done so, and would have threatened Richmond itself, so as materially to have aided me further to the North.[8]

There is another point that these historians omit. It is said that we overwhelmed the South. In foreign journals and foreign assemblies it is put this way, that we overran the South with the scum of the world—with hirelings and Hessians. No one would do more honor to the foreigners who came into our ranks than myself. They were brave men and earned our gratitude. But so far from our armies being foreign I question if more than three per cent were aliens. Yet I have no doubt many well informed authors will tell you that there were only three per cent Americans. This is the way public opinion was made during the war, and this is the way history is made now. We never overwhelmed the South, and I am only sorry we could not have done so and ended the war and its miseries. What we won from the South we won by hard fighting, and the odds, when there were odds, were never decisive. We had to fight the Southern States. They were a unit and we were divided. Every able-bodied male in the South from fourteen to sixty was in the army, or was supposed to be there. We had to depend upon volunteers and the conscription. The South had 4,000,000 of negroes. These negroes kept the farms, protected the families, supported the armies, and were really a reserve force, a most important reserve force in a fighting nation. Those 4,000,000 of negroes did a work that white men would have been compelled to do. Yet they are never counted in any summary of the forces of the South. They are forgotten as if they never had existed, and yet they kept the acres green and the harvests growing while the white men were in the war. Men, women and children went into the fields. The South was really an organized army. During the war in the South all progress, all industry came to a halt and nothing was allowed to interfere with the war. Even now the South suffers from war stagnation, from war paralysis. In the North industry was never more brisk; all the arts of peace were cherished; society moved on; inventions were discovered; the genius of the country was as keen as

ever. We supported an army and a blockading fleet. We never flagged
in our industry. We kept our place as a manufacturing commercial
power. Cities like Chicago, New York, San Francisco grew and grew,
while Savannah and New Orleans and Charleston languished. We
not only sustained our part in the war, but all that was required for
peace. In spite of all the drain upon the resources of the North we
were more prosperous, more powerful, more respected and feared by
the nations than when the war broke out. Remember, as I have said,
that we had by no means a united North, while the South was a unit.
We had to send troops to suppress riots in New York; we had enemies in our midst. In every Northern State there was a strong party
against the war; always rejoicing over disaster, always voting to par-
alyze our forces; ready for any concession or surrender. This party
was strong in every State—strong enough to carry States like Indiana, Pennsylvania and New York during the war. Nothing but Morton's courage saved it from making Indiana a rebel State, like Kentucky. This was the party that voted the war was a failure at the time
Sherman was setting out on his march to the sea, at the very time
when that great General and his great army were about to cover our
arms with imperishable renown. You can imagine the effect such a
resolution must have had upon the enthusiasm of an army, for it is
a mistake to imagine that such things did not affect an army. They
did affect it as I know well. During our war there was scarcely a
wind that came from the North, from our own homes, that did not
come laden with calumny and disparagement. The Southern generals were models of chivalry and valor—our generals were venal, in-
competent, coarse. I am speaking now of our own people, of writers
and speakers who were loyal and to a certain extent republican.
Everything that our armies did was wrong, could have been done so
much better. Everything that our opponents did was perfect. Lee was
a demigod, Jackson was a demigod, while our generals were brutal
butchers. So it was in Europe. With a few exceptions here and there
the public opinion of the world was against the North, and our own
friends at home would often grow nervous and fault-finding with the
army. You cannot read a file of journals in England of that time that
did not contain some horrible calumny about men in the army, and

copied from our own journals. If we won a battle like Shiloh, for instance—one of the most useful victories of the war, one of the most
important in its results—our own papers set to work to belittle the
victory and give the enemy as much advantage as possible. These
were essential elements in a war like ours—the war of a free people.
I do not recite these things to complain especially. I have nothing to
complain about. The more foes we conquered the more important
was our victory. Having conquered it is not for us to say anything
unkind or in disparagement of our enemies. That is not my purpose.
I merely mention these points in a general way, as points which our
historians overlook and which show that the North and South were
not as unequal in force as alleged—that the South had advantages
which we never possessed—and that, if we had a larger population
than the South to draw from, there were probably as many living under our protection whose hearts were with the rebellion as there
were in the Confederacy itself.

New York Herald, May 27, 1878. John Russell Young introduced USG's remarks. "Your correspondent took occasion to bring to the General's attention the publication in the *North
American Review* from General Richard Taylor, saying in effect that General Grant had
fought his campaign in Virginia against his own judgment, and in doing so had thrown
away the lives of a hundred thousand men. Your correspondent also called the attention of
the General to the article in the *Atlantic Monthly* from the pen of the late Gideon Welles,
in which Mr. Welles arraigned General Grant, upon the authority of General Taylor, for
having insulted Lincoln's memory by attempting to throw upon Lincoln his own fault in
the Wilderness and other campaigns. The result of this was an interesting conversation
with General Grant, some of the points of which I will rescue from oblivion for their historical value." *Ibid.* On May 12, 1878, Young, Paris, wrote in his diary that he met USG
and "walked with him to the baths on Rue St Amand. Bathed.—Then wrote out an interview about the war, Welles, Taylor &c. Showed it to the General who said it was most
splendid." DLC-John Russell Young. On May 13 and 15, Young again wrote in his diary.
"Called on General Grant, and saw Mrs. Grant. Did some work in the arranging and
despatching of my interview.—Sent it off to Badeau, & told him by wire to expect it." "Gen.
Grant came in. . . . Letter from Badeau about the interview, & I [t]elegraph him—send it
on—a course which Gen. Grant approves." *Ibid.* See *ibid.,* April 15, 1878; letters to John
Russell Young, April 7, 20, 1878; letters to Adam Badeau, May 14, 19, June 16, 1878; Interview, July 6, 1878.

On June 28, Edgar T. Welles, Hartford, wrote "To the Editor of the Herald:—I
was pained to read the article in your issue of the 27th ult. under the title, 'A Chapter of
History,' but not surprised. The silence observed by General Grant concerning my father
has been studied, and now, while the sod is yet fresh upon his grave, the venom and malice nourished for the past ten years begin to break forth. The whole article—and I refer
to the interview and General Badeau's letter as one, for both are published as a statement

of General Grant—as far as my father is concerned, is a deliberate attempt at calumny and misrepresentation—a tissue of falsehoods cunningly interwoven and called 'history.' The public position General Grant has occupied is my only reason for noticing the slanderous utterances. . . ." *New York Herald*, July 1, 1878. Gideon Welles had died on Feb. 11.

1. See John Niven, *Gideon Welles: Lincoln's Secretary of the Navy* (New York, 1973), pp. 569–70, 575–77.

2. See Richard Taylor, *Destruction and Reconstruction: Personal Experiences of the Late War* (New York, 1879), pp. 242, 256, 259, 261–62, 264–67.

3. Young queried whether "this article is not altogether true?" *New York Herald*, May 27, 1878. For former C.S.A. Lt. Gen. Richard Taylor's historical accuracy, see T. Michael Parrish, *Richard Taylor: Soldier Prince of Dixie* (Chapel Hill, 1992), pp. 490–94.

4. On June 6, a correspondent in Winchester, Va., interviewed Taylor, who identified deceased Maj. Gen. Henry W. Halleck and former C.S.A. Gen. Joseph E. Johnston as the sources for his statements on USG's Va. campaign. *New York Herald*, June 7, 1878. When asked by a correspondent in Richmond on June 8, Johnston refused to name his informant. See *ibid.*, June 10, 1878.

5. See *PUSG*, 10, 195; *Memoirs*, II, 114–16.

6. Capt. Bob Shorty and the Mackerel Brigade appeared in comic Civil War stories published by Orpheus C. Kerr, pen-name for Robert H. Newell, a New York City humorist. See *Orpheus C. Kerr Papers* (New York, 1862–65); *New York Tribune*, July 13, 1901.

7. See *Memoirs*, II, 122–23, 536–37; *Young*, II, 358–59.

8. A fragmentary letter from USG to Young, dated April 9 from internal evidence, contains this language, suggesting that USG supplied some comments in writing. "have done so, and would have so threatened Richmond itself as to have materially aided me further to the North. Badeau will see you as soon as he gets back to London and will talk the matter over with you. . . . Jesse left yesterday for Paris expecting to go home soon. He will ~~Send~~ see you as he passes through London if you are there." ALS (incomplete), DLC-John Russell Young. Probably in reference to this letter, USG wrote an undated note to Adam Badeau, consul gen., London. "Read this and mail if you approve. If not, retain until to-morrow and make your suggestions to me. Add a not if you choose to ~~y~~Yound and send with mine." AN (initialed), Munson-Williams-Proctor Institute, Utica, N. Y. Badeau wrote on the bottom. "Written in Rome 1878 while I was there, and sent to me at my rooms" AN (initialed, undated), *ibid.* On May 6, Badeau wrote "To THE EDITOR OF THE HERALD" refuting the arguments of Taylor and Welles upon USG's authority. *New York Herald*, May 27, 1878. An editorial largely favorable to USG and Badeau is *ibid.*

To Adam Badeau

Paris, France
May 14th /78

MY DEAR GENERAL:

Your letter written in answer to the despatch of Mr. Rice,[1] of the North American Review, just reached me to-day. Your reasons for not writing the article for his Review ~~that~~ as he requested are exactly the reasons I gave why I could not write such an article, even if I had the material before me, and was disposed to write it. I thought however you might do so, and possibly with good effect. But on reflection I think you are right, and that your reasons are good for not writing it. I said so to Mr. Rice. He is still very anxious ~~yet~~ that some one who has served with me should write an article for the review ~~who has served with me~~, and one who can reply to some of the statements published, and wanted to know from me who would be the next best person to apply to. I told him Horace Porter. I presume he has written to Porter to-day. If Porter can take the time to it, and do it in his own way, there is no man who could write a more scathing review of the history our rebel friends are trying to hand down to posterity than he can. Your letter to the Herald, and my interview with Young, both of which will appear in the Herald of next Sunday week will serve to freshen his memory on many facts. I hope Porter will try to do the thing unless his business relations makes it unadvisable. In that case he should not write the article.[2]

We are all very well and having what you might call a pleasant time.[3] I have not ceased to enjoy *Vagabondizing* yet but may become tired of it after a while.

Kindest regard,

U. S. Grant

ALS, Horace Porter Mende, Zurich, Switzerland.

1. Allen Thorndike Rice purchased and began to edit the *North American Review* in 1876.

2. Horace Porter published reminiscences of USG only after USG's death.

On April 25 and May 27, 1878, Adam Badeau, consul gen., London, wrote to Orville E. Babcock. ". . . I saw the Genl at Rome; gave him your letter which he read to me. He and Mrs Grant seemed much interested to hear of you. On my return, I found another from you which I at once forwarded. He expects to return to Paris on the 5th of May, which I very much regret. I dont want him to go *twice* to any place; but he means to stay six or eight weeks in Paris; he says he may return home in the autumn, but certainly in the spring. I did my best to combat this determination. Mrs Grant, however, is tired of travelling. The Genl says his friends have desires for him in which he does not share. I wrote a reply to the articles of Dick Taylor and Gideon Welles, while I was at Rome, which will probably appear in the N. Y. Herald. It was of course submitted to him, indeed suggested by the Genl. . . ." ". . . I shall send your letters to Genl Grant who is still at Paris. He tells me he has written in answer to your last. He will spend the summer travelling in Germany and the North of Europe, including Russia, and then he says look out for 'Winter quarters;' I understand,—abroad. I suppose before this reaches you—Young's Interview and my letter will have appeared, in the N. Y. Herald. As soon as I saw the ~~text~~ ms of the Interview, I wanted to withhold my letter, but the General was very determined it must appear; so I had no option but to yield. I thought it would look better for only one to be given to the world. The two—make the General appear too anxious; I thought I was not with him when the interview was written, nor have I seen him since. I hope he will not be inter viewed again; but I cannot say so, lest I should seem jealous. Young is a devoted faithful friend of the General; but of course he wants all he can get for his newspaper, and perhaps over rates the effect. However, tis a matter of judgment. This is strictly confidential. I said it to Porter but to no one else.—I tried to stick to plain statement and proof of facts in my letter—without comment, or opinion of my own. . . ." AL (initialed), ICN. See following letter; *Badeau*, p. 499.

3. On May 10, Young had reported on USG's arrival in Paris. ". . . He is accompanied by his daughter, Mrs. Sartoris, and his youngest son, J. R. Grant. He hoped to have a visit from his other sons, and a kind of family reunion in Paris, but it does not seem feasible. Jesse R. will return home to enter upon the study of law in New York with his brother. Whether the General will return to America or not this year is a question. The trip has been an immense rest. He would like to go to India, China and Japan, and return by way of California, so as to reach America in June, 1879. He was so much pleased with his visit to Egypt and his hurried trip on the Nile that he thinks of taking a dahabeah and going as far as the second cataract. 'I regard,' said the General, 'the few weeks I spent on the Nile as among the happiest in my life.' . . ." *New York Herald*, May 30, 1878. On May 11, USG officially visited the Paris Universal Exposition. See *ibid.*, May 12, 1878; *Young*, I, 378–80; *Julia Grant*, pp. 243–44; Jesse R. Grant, *In the Days of My Father General Grant* (New York, 1925), pp. 312–14.

On May 9 and 10, Young had written in his diary. "Wrote Childs an important letter about the General & his trip to the east. If the matter can be in any way arranged I may see India, & in seeing that wind up my traveling life.—Gen. Grant came in and we walked as far as the Boulevard Sabastopol, & up & down the boulevards.—Gen. thinks the Communism at home is taking rapid strides, & should require severe treatment—" "Mr. Bennett sent me mail to invite Gen. Grant to the Polo.—Grant accepts.—At four Mrs. Gurney & I join the Gen. at the Liverpool.—We meet Gen. & Mrs. Beale. Mr Bennett met the Gen. on the grounds. . . ." DLC-John Russell Young. For more details on USG in Paris, see *ibid.*, May 7–8, 11, 18, 20, 23, 26–27, June 4–8, 12–13, 1878.

To Adam Badeau

Paris, France
May 19th /78

MY DEAR GENERAL:

I return you Porters & the Count de Paris letters and the part of chapter of your book. I feel very sure you have the Vicksburgh surrender right,[1] and see nothing wrong in the printed matter you send.[2] If there is anything it is in not showing the failure of Warren more distinctly. But that I think you did in the chapter of which this is to form a part—or a correction.

I am very glad you sent on your letter to the Herald in answer to Taylor & Welles. Young's without yours, would not have much point. I become responsible for yours and I can very well afford it because Taylor's was a deadly attack upon two now dead—Lincoln & Stanton—and Welles upon two dead persons—Stanton & Halleck—all untrue—the attacks—and I feel it a duty to relieve all three of aspersions so unjust to their memories.[3]

We are going all the time and I am becoming very tired of it. Think we will leave several weeks earlier than we expected. Our contemplated route, as you know, is to The Hague, Copenhagen, through Sweden Norway, then back to St. Petersburgh, through Prussia & Austria to quarters for next winter.

All send regards to you. I shall write to Babcock in a few days.

Yours Truly
U. S. GRANT

ALS, Munson-Williams-Proctor Institute, Utica, N. Y.

1. See letter to Adam Badeau, [*March-April, 1878*].
2. USG commented on the battle of the Crater. *Badeau*, p. 499.
3. See letters to John Russell Young, April 7, 20, 1878.

To John Russell Young

Paris France.
May 22d /78

J. R. YOUNG, ESQ.
DEAR SIR:

On my return to this hotel last evening I found your note enclosing two letters from Mr. McHenry offering me the presidency of the A. & G. W. rail-road. I have thought the matter over and have come to the conclusion that I must decline the offer,—as flattering & tempting as it is—for the present. After my return to the United

States however if the offer should be reniewed I would investigate the affairs of the road, and if I should feel that I could earn the salary allowed I would then accept.

Please convey this decission to Mr. McHenry, and thank him for me for his offer.

Very Truly yours
U. S. GRANT

ALS, DLC-John Russell Young. James McHenry prospered as a merchant in Liverpool and London before experiencing an uneven career as promoter of the Atlantic and Great Western Railroad in association with Jay Gould. On April 16 and 25, 1878, John Russell Young, Paris, wrote in his diary. "Call on McHenry and talk railways & write to Gen Grant what may be to him an important letter." "Important letter from Gen. Grant about the Erie R. W. which may have an important influence upon events. . . . Saw Mr McH. & pass him Gen. Grant's letter." DLC-John Russell Young. See *ibid.*, May 22, 1878; *New York Times,* May 2, June 9, July 20, 1874, Aug. 16, 1879, Nov. 13–14, 1883, March 17, 1885, Dec. 18, 1886, May 27, July 1–3, 1891; *New York Herald,* Aug. 19–20, 1879; Julius Grodinsky, *Jay Gould: His Business Career 1867–1892* (Philadelphia, 1957), pp. 30–31, 58–59, 67, 96–104; Maury Klein, *The Life and Legend of Jay Gould* (Baltimore, 1986), pp. 116–25.

To Frederick Dent Grant

Paris, France.
May 24th /78

DEAR FRED.

Your last letter is received. I think your determination not to come over here, under the circumstances, is the right. We would all be rejoiced to see you & Ida but it would be for so short a time. Then too we now propose to leave here in about three weeks. Jesse & Nellie will leave next week, and Buck has about abandoned the idea of coming. But the best reason of all is the one you give: that you do not want another to do your duties for you.[1]

Jesse will sail from Liverpool on the 4th of June with Gen. Beale[2] & family. Whether he will go to Cornell, or whether he will commence the study of law at once I do not know, but judge the latter.[3]— I am getting quite homesick to get back to the states. But as this will probably be my last opportunity to visit this side of the water, and there are yet many places that I want to see that I have not yet seen,

I shall not return before next year. Then too if I should go back this fall I would have no place to go to. In the spring we can go to our Long Branch house and make arrangements during the summer for our winter home.—All send much love to you, Ida and the babe, and desire to be specially remembered to Mr. & Mrs. Honoré.—Tell Gen. Sheridan that I was much pleased to receive his letter[4] and will write to him soon. I am getting very lazy however about writing and have failed to answer some letters that I should not have neglected.

Yours Affectionately
U. S. GRANT

LT. COL. F. D. GRANT

ALS, USG 3. See letter to Frederick Dent Grant, April 9, 1878.

1. Frederick Dent Grant inspected western army posts. See *New York Times*, June 12, 1878.

2. On May 20, 1878, USG wrote to Edward F. Beale. "Mrs. Grant and I, will have to postpone our visit to the *Horse Oppera* until another day to enable us to return some calls which should not have been delayed so long. We have not yet returned the calls of the President, the American Ministers &c. & others and want to attend to that duty to-day." ALS, DLC-Decatur House Papers.

3. Jesse Root Grant, Jr., studied law at Columbia. See letter to Michael John Cramer, June 3, 1878; *New York Times*, June 9, 1934.

4. On April 28, Lt. Gen. Philip H. Sheridan, Chicago, had written to USG. "I am ashamed to attempt to offer an excuse for not writing to you long ago, and ~~will simply~~ can only beg pardon, and promise to do better here after. There is no one in the world who has been more gratified than ~~my self~~ I have been by the kindly, & brilliant & well merited receptions given to you by the people accross the waters, and I have followed your journey everywhere with delight   Fred and his charming little wife with Julia are getting along nicely. ~~Fred~~ You can tell Mrs Grant that Fred is everything she could desire ~~of him.~~ I said to him that if he desired to accept your your proposition to go over to meet you in Paris he could do so; but I doubt if Ida will leave the baby. If Fred does not go over I will send him out with some of the expeditions during the Summer, . . ." ADf (incomplete), DLC-Philip H. Sheridan.

To Rear Admiral Daniel Ammen

PARIS, FRANCE, May 25th, 1878.

MY DEAR ADMIRAL,—

Since my last letter to you I have received two or three from you, the last one containing a copy of your reply to the two French gentlemen in regard to Inter-Oceanic Canal matters. I have been pestered, or rather refused to be pestered, by adventurers who desire to get me interested with them in an enterprise to build such a canal. Before I left Washington I called on Mr. Evarts specially to interest him in the matter of a canal by the Nicaragua route. I was in hopes he would take the matter up. I told him all about the surveys that had been made, the reports upon the surveys, how he could get access to them, etc., and that he could get fuller information at any time by sending for you. I advise that you call on the Secretary and bring the subject up. Edmunds is the only Senator that I know of who takes an interest in the subject. But he would interest others if the subject could be brought up in a tangible shape.

We have now been here for three weeks, will remain about three weeks more, and then go north through Holland, Denmark, Norway, and Sweden, back east to St. Petersburg, Moscow, and Vienna, then visit Berlin and a few other Prussian places, and then find winter quarters either here, at Nice, or in Southern Italy. In June of next year I shall be in my Long Branch house, if spared to that time, when we will hope to have a visit from you and Mrs. Ammen.

I have visited the Exposition several times. It is quite a success, but, I think, no improvement on our Centennial show. The buildings and grounds are far inferior to ours. Jesse sails for home on the 4th of June. Mrs. Grant joins me in love to Mrs. Ammen and the children.

Very truly yours,
U. S. GRANT.

ADMIRAL D. AMMEN.

Daniel Ammen, *The Old Navy and the New* (Philadelphia, 1891), pp. 541–42. See Speeches, [*March 21, 1876*], [*Oct. 31, 1876*]; letter to Daniel Ammen, June 6, 1879.

To James Birney

———

Hotel Liverpool, Paris
May 25th /78

Hon. Judge Birney,
U. S. Minister,
Dear Sir:

It is my present purpose to leave Paris for the Hague either Saturday—three weeks from to-day—or on the tuesday following. It is my recollection that when we met last you asked me to inform you of the time of my proposed visit to your post and I do it with pleasure. My stay will probably be but for a few days—three or four—and I will then go to Copenhagen. If you should be on leave of absence at this time, or desire to be away at that particular time, I beg that you will not make any change in your plans on my account.

With assurances of my best respects

I am, very truly,
U. S. Grant

P. S. My party will consist only of Mrs. Grant & myself. My son sails from Liverpool for home on the 4th of June.

ALS, Keya Galleries, New York, N. Y. See letter to Adam Badeau, June 16, 1878.

To Michael John Cramer

———

Hotel Liverpool, Paris
May 25th /78

My Dear Mr. Cramer:

I am now for the first time able to fix, approximately, the time of my visit to Copenhagen. We will leave here on Saturday, three weeks from to-day, or on the following tuesday. We will stop at the Hague three or four days. Jesse leave for home so as to take the Steamer of the 4th of June from Liverpool. Our party therefore will consist only of Mrs Grant—with her Maid [1]—and myself. If your arrangements are made to be away from Copenhagen at the time mentioned above I beg that you will not change your plans. Should you be there we will probably remain over about one week. Should you be away we will stop only a couple of days.

I have not heard directly from Elizabeth for some time; probably my own fault for Mr. Corbin is very prompt in answering every lette[r.] But Buckey writes regularly every week from New York, so I hear indirectly. When you write home give my love to all of them at Elizabeth.

Very Truly yours
U. S. Grant

P. S. I go from Copenhagen directly to Stockholm. I am not personally acquainted with our present Minister there though I once appointed him to a South American Mission.[2]

U. S. G.

ALS, deCoppet Collection, NjP. See letter to Michael John Cramer, June 3, 1878.

1. See *Young*, I, 301.
2. John L. Stevens, minister to Sweden and Norway, had been minister to Uruguay and Paraguay (1870–73). See *PUSG*, 20, 144.

To Adam Badeau

Paris, France
May 29th /78

My Dear General:

I am just in receipt of your letter of the 27th,—with enclosures,—and hasten to answer so as to return the papers you want without loss. I am certain you need not feel alarmed about your position on the retired list.[1] But I should not trouble myself about Townsend. He is badly beaten as the matter stands. I wrote to Babcock since my arrival in Paris. My correspondence is large, and delays occur sometimes; but when I set to it I bring up all arrears— that I intend to bring up. I get letters from persons with whom I have never corresponded, desiring answers, but whos letters I do not answer. B's was not one of that class.

I wrote the Duke of Argyll a letter of condolence the very moment I heard of the death of the Duchess—day before yesterday I think.[2]

We leave here on the 15th of June for our northern trip. Jesse, you know, goes back. He & Nellie leave on Friday—day after to morrow—for London. He will sail on the 4th of June from Liverpool.

With kindest regards of all, I am, as ever, very Truly yours,

U. S. GRANT

GN. A. BADEAU.

ALS, Munson-Williams-Proctor Institute, Utica, N. Y. See *Badeau*, p. 500.

1. Badeau remained on the U.S. Army's retired list. See Badeau to Gen. William T. Sherman, July 23, 1878, DLC-William T. Sherman.
2. The Duchess of Argyll died on May 25, 1878. See *The Times* (London), May 25, June 4, 1878; letter to Ulysses S. Grant, Jr., Aug. 25, 1877.

To James Birney

31, *Boulevard Haussmann.*
Paris. May 29th *1878.*

MY DEAR JUDGE:

Mrs. Grant & myself accept with pleasure your and & Mrs. Birney's invitation to be your guests during our sojourn at the Hague. We will leave here on Saturday, the 15th of June, and go directly through, arriving at the Capital of Holland about 8 in the evening. Should there be any change of day or hour of arrival I will inform you either by letter or telegraph.

Our stay at the Hague will probably be until the following thursday.

Please present the compliments of Mrs. Grant & myself to Mrs. Birney and your daughter, and believe me, with great respect,

your obt. svt.

U. S. GRANT

HON. JAS. BIRNEY, U S M[INISTER]

ALS (torn), NHi. James Birney, minister to the Netherlands, and his wife, Amanda M., had married in 1841. For USG's visit, see letter to Adam Badeau, June 16, 1878.

To Adam Badeau

————

Paris, France.
June 1st /78

MY DEAR GENERAL:

I am much obliged for your kind invitation for Mrs. Grant & I to visit you but we will not be able to accept. In two weeks we start on our northern trip and will not return until the Autumn. We will then probably visit Spain and settle down about Nov. for the Winter. Where I have not yet determined, but either here Nice or southern Italy.

You must keep up your courage. There is no reason why you may not have many years before you yet. I return Porters letter which I have read with pleasure; & one from Babcock which I find on my table.

Yours as ever,
U. S. GRANT

GN. A. BADEAU.

ALS, Munson-Williams-Proctor Institute, Utica, N. Y. See *Badeau*, p. 501.

To Michael John Cramer

————

Paris, France
June 3d /78

MY DEAR MR. CRAMER:

Your letter of the 31st of May is just received. I should have written to you within a day or two to inform you of a slight change of plan, which will bring me into Copenhage from ten days to two weeks later than ~~my~~ I wrote you I would be there even if I had not received your letter. To save retracing my steps, as I should be obliged to do by the routes laid out in my last letter, I now intend to go from the Hague to Berlin and visit a few of the German Cities before going to Denmark. From Copenhagen I shall go by water to Norway, thence to Sweeden, St. Petersburg, Moscow and to Vienna[.] I shall be very glad indeed to see Mary and the children and hope they may be back by by the time I reach Copenhagen, about from the 5th to the 10th of July.

Jesse sails from Liverpool to-morrow for home. He has been very homesick for some time.[1]

With best regards of Mrs Grant & myself, I am, Very Truly.

U. S. GRANT

ALS, deCoppet Collection, NjP. See letters to Michael John Cramer, May 25, June 25, 1878.

1. On June 13, 1878, upon his arrival in New York City from Europe, Jesse Root Grant, Jr., spoke to a reporter about his early return. "I had enough of it; I got tired of these foreign countries. To tell you the truth, I was very homesick. . . . I am happy that I am once more among our own people. We had a very pleasant trip. . . . I left [USG] at Paris in good health, enjoying the Exhibition and its attendant festivities. He likes foreign travel more than I do. . . . He has arranged matters so that he will evade either too warm or too cold weather. He will go to Denmark, Sweden, Norway and Russia during the warm summer months, and after visiting Holland, Belgium and other places on his return will manage to spend the winter months in the South of Europe, very likely in Spain. He will remain there long enough to avoid the inclement winter weather of the North, will then return to Paris in the beginning of spring and thence to this country. . . . He takes a very deep interest in all that transpires here. He is posted as to everything going on. To tell you the truth, he does not read an English newspaper at all. The British papers have, apparently, not much in their columns that interests him. He does go for the American papers, however. . . . I can tell you that he regards the Potter investigation as a useless, foolish piece of business. He thinks that President Hayes is duly and legally elected, and that this Congressional investigation business is arrant nonsense." *New York Herald*, June 14, 1878. On June 14, Grant, Jr., gave a second interview. *New York World*, June 15, 1878. See Jesse R. Grant, *In the Days of My Father General Grant* (New York, 1925), p. 321; *HMD*, 45-3-31; Ari Hoogenboom, *Rutherford B. Hayes: Warrior & President* (Lawrence, Kan., 1995), pp. 365–68.

To Adam Badeau

Paris, France,
June 7th /78

My Dear General:

I return your last chapter, or part of chapter, without comment. It seems to me to be very good, and calculate[d] to call to the minds of some of the Northern gushers of to day for peace and fraternity between the sections, of the terms we might have expected had the south been successful.

I am getting tired of Paris and feel almost impatient for the day—the 14th of June—of our departure to arrive.

Mrs Grant joins me in best regards to you, and in wishing you good health & happiness.

Very Truly Yours
U. S. Grant

Gen. A. Badeau.

ALS, Munson-Williams-Proctor Institute, Utica, N. Y. See *Badeau*, p. 502.

In early June, 1878, Grenville M. Dodge wrote to his brother from Paris about a conversation with USG. "... He gives no uncertain sound as to the future of the United States, is outspoken in the belief that loyal men must still control our Government, and has no faith in the promises of unrepentant rebels. He put it tersely when he said that 'Wade Hampton, as great a traitor as ever lived, praised President Hayes without stint to his Southern friends, but at the same time told them that in another year no Republican Party would exist in South Carolina.' Such friends, the General thinks, are no benefit to any President or country. He doesn't believe that treason can be made respectable, even if it should be successful. For the President he had kind words to say, but hoped he would see it for his interest to bring to his advice tried Republicans, and to his support a strong party, and seemed to think that was what was just now lacking...." *New York Times*, July 5, 1878.

In July, a reporter interviewed a friend of USG in Philadelphia. "General Grant does not desire to be President again, ... I have received a number of letters from the General, but he does not discuss the question in any form. He has given me to understand that he does not desire to be President again, because he is tired of public life and desires to settle down again into the seclusion of private citizenship. The General believes that eight years as a President and almost that term as a soldier entitle him to that quietude which a man who has acquired such great honors should enjoy...." *Philadelphia Record*, July 20, 1878. While in Paris, USG expressed similar views to James N. Tyner, asst. postmaster gen. See *New York Times*, Aug. 3, 20, 1878. For the views of George M. Robeson, see *Philadelphia Record*, July 13, 1878.

On July 24, John S. Mosby spoke to a reporter acknowledging "a long letter" he had received from USG "about a month ago" and sharing his views on USG's potential as a presidential candidate. ". . . I have no doubt of his nomination by acclamation. . . . I believe he will be overwhelmingly elected. . . . I believe that he can carry all the states that Hayes carried, and several that he didn't carry. . . . Southern men will dare more and risk more to support Gen. Grant than anybody else. Southern men remember this fact; that he always stood by the Southern men who stood by him, and he did more for the relief of the Southern people than any other man could have done. . . . For example, when Grant was inaugurated the first time, the whole South was under military government, and nearly the entire white population of the South was under the disabilities of the fourteenth amendment and the iron-clad oath. When Grant retired from the Presidency, the Southern people had all been relieved of their political disabilities, and the men who had fought to destroy the Union were in a perfect equality with the men who had fought to uphold it. Of course, Grant would have done and could have done a great deal more for the Southern people, but for the fact that they kept up a continual fire upon him during the whole time he was President. The Southern people have encouraged Hayes, and have given him credit for all the good he has done for them, but they never gave Grant credit for anything he did for them, although it was through his influence that they were relieved from military government, and were restored to civil government. . . . Grant came into the Presidency when the country was red-hot with the passions of war, and in order to effect any good for the Southern people he had to move slowly and not too far in advance of the Northern sentiment; but, to my knowledge, he was always far in advance of any man of the North, of either political party, in liberality towards the Southern people. I'll say this: that whenever he used the military arm of the Government in the South it was not to subvert civil authority, but to support it. He never used soldiers to overturn the laws, but simply to aid in executing them. . . . It's the natural desire of the American people to see a great man at the helm of the government, and those who desire to see the national credit upheld against repudiators are for him; those who regard the rights of property as sacred, are for him, because they believe the Government needs a strong man to protect the rights of property against the assaults of the communists. Gen. Grant will be sustained by the conservative sentiment of the country at the next election. . . . And be elected." *Washington Post*, July 25, 1878.

On Aug. 14, a Chicago reporter interviewed John P. Newman, Methodist pastor, concerning news from USG. "A letter reached me about two weeks ago, . . . He was on the eve of leaving Paris for the north. He gave me a description of his journey up the Nile, and his reception by the Khedive of Egypt. I had been over the ground twice myself, and could judge of the accuracy of his statements. . . . He told every point of the route, and all the Egyptian and Arabic names were spelled with the utmost accuracy. I had told him that when he reached Joppa he had better go up to Jerusalem, but to prepare his mind for what he would see: I told him he would be disappointed, but that he must forget the present, and think of the past; to go up and sit on the Mount of Olives, and contemplate its history. He wrote me that he had done as I advised, and he could not help thinking that the country looked like a land that had been decaying for two thousand years. The point I wish to make is that General Grant is traveling around the world, making the closet observation, and, when he returns, will be the best informed man in America upon the manners, institutions, geography, topography, populations, and, above all, the resources of all the peoples of the globe. This nation has never appreciated the intellectual greatness of the man. His mind is not one of ratiocination, but of intuition. He grasps a thing instantly and unerringly. . . . I wrote him that every one was asking me about his sentiments regarding the third term. He replied that he had been through the trials and labors of sixteen years of public life, and was taking a rest. . . . But General Grant is supremely honest, entirely conscientious, and should an emergency arise where the American people demanded his services again, I know he would not refuse. He would regard it as a call of Providence. He has an unwavering belief in Providence, and he has often related to me various instances wherein he has pointed out the providential events of his life. He will never do the slightest thing to bring it about, but if the people, with spontaneity, should elect him, he would give his services to the country again. . . ." *Chicago Inter-Ocean*, Aug. 15, 1878.

On Sept. 20, Andrew D. White spoke upon his return from Europe to a reporter in New York City. "I met General Grant several times, but did not find him especially elated over his brilliant receptions in Europe. He seems to take great delight in talking about his Egyptian trip. As for a third term, he thought little about it. . . ." *New York Herald*, Sept. 21, 1878. Alexander R. Shepherd, Pinckney B. S. Pinchback, and Wendell Phillips also expressed views on USG as a presidential candidate in 1880. See *ibid.*, Oct. 7, 20, Nov. 9, 1878.

On Dec. 6, a correspondent in Washington, D. C., interviewed U.S. Senator Blanche K. Bruce of Miss., who had spoken with USG in Paris during the summer. ". . . I called his attention to the popular feeling looking to his nomination for the Presidency in 1880. I cannot recall the precise language he used in reply, but he left the impression upon me that he was really happy in the freedom from official care which had come with the close of his Presiden[t]ial service, and that he was content with the honors that had already been conferred upon him by his countrymen. I do not believe that the Presidency is either a matter of personal desire or anxiety with Gen. Grant; yet, if a general demand for his services should be expressed by the American people, and the matter should be presented in the light of a duty to the country, I have no doubt he would accept the nomination. . . . The four names most familiar to the colored people of the South, among all our public men, are those of Lincoln, Sumner, Morton, and Grant. The most ignorant voter in that section knew these men, and attributed the possession and enjoyment of their political freedom and personal rights largely to their influence and efforts. Unless public sentiment has undergone a great change during the last four months, Gen. Grant would be the first choice for the Presidency of nine-tenths of the colored voters of the South. . . . Among the most satisfactory interviews I had with Gen. Grant at Paris was one in which he declared that he had no apprehensions relative to the success of the colored people as citizens of the United States. He cited notable instances of success among this class in various departments of life, and he especially dwelt upon the name of Frederick Douglass. He affirmed that observation of the colored people, both from military and civil experience with them, convinced him that their emancipation and enfranchisement was not a mistake, but a wise and beneficent measure, which the future history of the race would vindicate." *New York Times*, Dec. 7, 1878.

To Adam Badeau

Legation of the United States.
At the Hague
June 16th /78

DEAR GENERAL:

Your letter of the 12th, with enclosures, was received before my departure from Paris. But I had no time to do more than read your letter before leaving, so brought the whole here to examine and approve or otherwise. I have made marginal notes in pencil of all I have to say. I do not think there is anything to strike out, nor anything to add except what you can get from the notes referred to. You may recollect that when I visited Sheridan, at Charles town, I had a plan of battle with me to give him. But I found him so ready to move—plans and all—that I gave him no order whatever except the authority to move.[1] He is entitled to all the credit of his great victory, and it established him in the confidence of the President & Sec. of War as a commander to be trusted with the fullest discretion in the management all the troops under him. Before that, while they highly appreciated him as a commander to execute they felt a little nervous about giving him too much discretion.

We leave here on thursday for Amsterdam; Saturday for Hanover, Monday following for Berlin. How long I will stay in Berlin I cannot say but probably until the following Saturday.[2] We will then go to Copenhagen, breaking the journey at Hamburg. You might send anything you have for me, direct according to this programme. We will stay in Copenhagen for several days and then go direct to Norway, thence to Sweden.

I am glad to see that you are getting on so well with Vol. II. It looks now as if it might be out the coming fall.

Your letter to the Herald, and the interview, have been copied everywhere in the states much to the gratification of friends and the confusion of enemies. I think you will have no cause of regret for writing your letter.[3]

With Mrs. Grant's and my kindest regards,

yours Truly
U. S. GRANT

P. S. Remember both of us to Mrs Robeson[4] if she is still in London. Mrs. Grant & I regret that we did not meet her before our trip north

ALS, Munson-Williams-Proctor Institute, Utica, N. Y.

   On Sunday, June 23, 1878, an unnamed person, possibly James Birney, U.S. minister, The Hague, wrote a private letter from Amsterdam about USG's visit first published in the *Detroit Post.* ". . . At Amsterdam there was a large dinner party on his account. Upon the Republic of the United States being toasted, the General was called out and made a very happy speech, and one which received enthusiastic applause. Among other things he assured them that there was plenty of room in the United States for good Dutchmen, and they could become citizens in five years, and jocularly said they could vote earlier if they preferred the Democratic ticket. Something having been said about the losses of Holland in American railroad securities, he told them they might rely upon everything offered by the Federal Government as perfectly safe; that it would redeem its pledges and maintain its credit. . . . When allusion was made in his presence to the clamor about fraud in the late Presidential election, he remarked that the assertion that the popular vote showed a Democratic majority was a palpable absurdity when the figures were examined; that the real fraud was in a dishonest count of the vote on their side. 'Look, for example,' said he, 'at New-York. The entire vote of that State in 1868 was 849,766. In 1872 it was only 827,838, out of which the Republican ticket had a majority of 53,420, yet in 1876 the entire vote was raised to 1,011,156, an increase of 183,318, and by no means warranted by the growth of population. Out of this the Democratic ticket was counted as having 134,670 more votes than it had at the preceding election, and this, too, although the Republican ticket gained 49 000 votes. Can anybody,' he said, 'believe this to have been an honest count? And yet it has been tolerated and conceded by the Republican Party. Or,' said he, 'take the facts in regard to Mississippi. In 1872 the entire Presidential vote was 129,107, of which the Democratic ticket had only 47,191, but yet in 1876 the entire vote was 164,778 out of which were counted for the Democrats 112,173, giving their candidate a majority of 59,468. No one,' said he, 'who is well informed in regard to the situation of that State can believe that such a count was an exposition of the preference of the electors. Also, of South Carolina. In 1872 the entire vote was 95,193, of which the Democrats only claimed 22,903, yet in 1876 the entire vote is run up to 183,521, and the Democratic vote to 91,440. Can any one believe,' said he, 'that there was neither fraud nor intimidation in securing such a result? No, the real fraud has been perpetrated by those who are raising the cry of fraud.' The General seemed perfectly familiar with the figures and the results. He appears to have studied the Southern question very thoroughly. During all his conversation, not a word was heard from him expressive of any desire to be again in office. A gentlemen introduced to him having remarked that when he went back to his country he might be again a candidate for the Presidency, he at once replied, 'If I thought that, I would not go back at all.' No one can be in the company with the General long without being impressed with the conviction that he is thoroughly a man of peace. He has no fondness for conflict, no fondness for the trappings of war. He often expressed his surprise that the Governments of Europe still tolerated the maintenance of such large bodies of troops at the expense of the people. When allusion was made to his keeping his plans to himself while Commander-in-Chief, he replied: 'It is true that I did not talk over my intended movements even with my staff officers. I learned all the facts I could upon which to base my judgment, then I wrote out my orders, and had them copied or put in type, delivered without delay to the proper officers, when they were to be obeyed and not discussed.' When his attention was called to a recent New-York paper, in which was given an interview with a prominent politician who was bemoaning the bad management of the Government at home. 'Well,' said he, 'I wish he could be employed to run it a while, to see how he would bring it out.' To-day a paper arrived which contained an alleged interview by the correspondent of a Philadelphia paper with Orville Grant at San Francisco. When the General looked at it he said: 'It is impossible that my brother could have said some of these things. There are statements in it that I know to be without the slightest foundation in fact, and if they had occurred, they could not have been known to him. It is for the most part a sheer fabrication. When my brother sees it, he will deny it.' The General appears in good health, . . . He is very fond of travel, and inquires into everything that will add to his stock of useful information. He inquired very particularly into the canal and drainage system of Holland, visited the wind-mills to see them in operation. Passing one evening near a large café garden, he was asked whether he would look in. 'Certainly,' said he; 'I am traveling to see the people and to learn what I can.' He appeared much pleased with the attentions he received in the Netherlands, admired the neatness and thorough drill of the soldiers, and, when taken into the art gallery, he was enthusiastic in his admiration of the celebrated picture known as 'Paul Potter's Bull.' I have never seen it stated, though it is a fact, that, in his earlier years, the General was himself given to the culture of art. He painted a number of pictures, one of which is now preserved in the library of ex-Secretary Borie, of Philadelphia." *New York Times,* July 21, 1878. On June 25, Birney, The Hague, wrote to Secretary of State William M. Evarts describing USG's visit. *Foreign Relations, 1878,* pp. 701–2. See David Eckstein to Francis W. Seward, June 25, 1878, DNA, RG 59, Consular Despatches, Amsterdam; *Young,* I, 381–94; *Julia Grant,* pp. 244–45.

A Pittsburgh newspaper correspondent in San Francisco interviewed Orvil L. Grant. "Upon my honor, my brother left Washington a comparatively poor man. Although he has a little more property than I he cannot be said to be as well fixed in this world's goods. He has a house in Chicago and one in the East; he also has the now celebrated farm which the newspapers took such delight in describing, but these three properties are hardly worth the owning. The houses yield a little rent over and above the taxes, insurance, repairs, &c., but this is more than swallowed up by the almost unavoidable expense of the farm. . . . All his fancy horses and stock on his farm, which the newspapers made famous, he has sold off much below their value, and, in some cases, cost, in order to save the expense of feeding them. . . . Don't understand me that he has no income. He had a few thousand dollars saved up at the time he stepped out of the White House, and then he sold the fancy stock above referred to; but this fund, if invested in any of the Eastern securities that were considered safe, would not yield him sufficient to live on. He could not expect over ten per cent would yield him a living. Having devoted himself to military and public affairs for so long, he did not feel that he could succeed in business, and he had not the inclination to try. . . . He invested all the money he had in the 'Bonanza stocks' controlled by Flood & O'Brien. . . . On this he has been able to live comfortably. . . . Well, the fact of the matter is my brother's trip to Europe and his long sojourn there was not of his own choosing. I venture to say that he would gladly return to his farm and remain there if he could, but his advisers here decreed otherwise. . . . Before my brother went to Europe a number of republican politicians of national reputation held a meeting. There were at least two well known Western journalists present, one being from Chicago and the other from Cincinnati. I think two other newspaper men, from New York and Boston also attended, but I am not certain. At all events, they were made parties to the arrangement, as were journalists from St. Louis and, I think, Evansville. The object of this meeting was to prepare for what they believed to be inevitable before or at the expiration of Rutherford B. Hayes' term of office—this was nothing more nor less than revolution! . . . No man on this continent would be so enthusiastically welcomed home in such an emergency as my brother. No man could so speedily or so thoroughly rally about him an army of the Boys in Blue as General Grant. . . . Even if revolution is avoided (which the recent action of Congress would not seem to indicate), the republican leaders still need a man capable of cementing the party together again. While Hayes is no doubt honest and sincere in his 'policies,' the inevitable result of such policies, if long continued, is to shatter the republican party and allow it to fall to pieces, as a barrel would when you cut the hoops. . . . Indeed, I am as certain that U. S. Grant will be the next President of the United States as I am that I live." *New York Herald,* June 6, 1878. For Orvil Grant's financial and mental health problems, see *New York Times* and *New York Herald*, Sept. 5, 1878. In late May, Congress had authorized an investigation into the legitimacy of the vote that elected President Rutherford B. Hayes.

On July 24, Adam Badeau, consul gen., London, wrote to Orville E. Babcock. ". . . Genl. G. is in the north of Europe The last he wrote to me, he meant to go from Copenhagen to Sweden & Norway, then to Russia, so South by Austria, and winter at Nice or Rome. The newspapers say that he has taken a heavy cold, and in consequence will not go to Russia; but (confidentially) I think Stoughton said something to him, which might interfere with Russia more than a cold. My last letter was from the Hague, two or three weeks ago. I don't beleive he will return home before the nominations, though he has never actually said to me that he would not. I urge him, especially if he is determined not to run, to remain away; as nothing will persuade the Democrats that he is not dangerous, and if he goes home, he must incur all the abuse of an actual candidate. Why do this, when, after the nominations, if he is not a candidate the whole country will welcome him. I am sure from what every human being from America tells me, that no other Republican can be elected; but can *he*? I shouldn't want him to be defeated, now. I see the rumors of my being removed are started again, but I dont beleive them. Doubtless plenty of people want my place, and but for Mr Hayes's promise to the General, I should certainly have been removed long ago, but I dont think that personal promise will be broken. If I should be removed, I should stay here till I finish Vol II.—Vol III must be written in America, or partly at Gen Grants side. . . ." AL (initialed), ICN.

1. See *Memoirs*, II, 327–28; *Personal Memoirs of P. H. Sheridan* (New York, 1888), II, 1–10.
2. See letter to Michael John Cramer, June 29, 1878.
3. See letter to John Russell Young, April 7, 1878; Interview, May 9, 1878.
4. Mary Robeson, wife of the former secretary of the navy.

To Michael John Cramer

———

Hannover, Germany
June 25th /78

MY DEAR MR. CRAMER:

Mrs. Grant & I are now here on our way to the German Capital. We will probably remain in Berlin until Monday, the 1st of July. We will stop over by the way from Berlin to Copenhagen—particularly at Hamburg—so as to reach Copenhagen about the 5th of July. If you will drop me a line to the Keiser-hof hotel, Berlin, to let me know if Mary will be home at the time designated I will be obliged. If she is not to be at home I may change my plan and go direct to Sweed[en] thence Norway and return South by Denmark.

Mrs. Grant & I are both well and send much love to Mary & the children

Very Truly Yours
U. S. GRANT

ALS, Hagley Museum and Library, Wilmington, Del. See letter to Michael John Cramer, June 3, 1878.

To Michael John Cramer

—————

BERLIN, GERMANY, June 29, 1878.
MY DEAR MR. CRAMER: I have received your last letter, and am sorry to learn that Mary and the children will not be in Copenhagen at the time I propose being there. We will go on, however, as previously proposed, leaving here on Tuesday, the 3d of July,[1] remain over the 4th, and possibly the 5th at Hamburg, reaching Copenhagen the same day. I will telegraph you from Hamburg the day and the hour of our departure and the line by which we will travel.

Very truly yours,
U. S. GRANT.

M. J. Cramer, *Ulysses S. Grant: Conversations and Unpublished Letters* (New York, 1897), p. 145. On July 3, 1878, USG, Hamburg, wrote to Michael John Cramer, U.S. chargé d'affaires, Copenhagen. "On friday, the 5th of July, Mrs. Grant and I will leave here for Copenhagen by way of ~~Keil~~ Lubec. The boat will arrive in Copenhagen some time in the morning of saturday, but at what hour I am not informed. . . . I have just learned that the boat arrives at 8 a. m. in Copenhagen" ALS, IHi. See letter to Edward F. Beale, July 7, 1878.

1. USG left Berlin on Tuesday, July 2.

To Ulysses S. Grant, Jr.

—————

[*Berlin, June 29, 1878*]
. . . Owing to the condition of the Emperor[1] there are no festivities here . . . I have received marked attention and kindness from all the authorities . . . your Ma and I dined . . . with the Crown Prince[2] at

his castle at Pottsdam. This Monday we dine with Prince Bismarck[3] ... I have bought 2000 shares of Yellow Jacket Mining stock[4] ... If you and Fred feel like buying 100 shares each ... you will have an opportunity of loosing your investment or of quadrupling it ...

Alexander Autographs, Inc., Nov. 25, 1005, no. 473.

1. Emperor William I of Germany had been wounded during an assassination attempt, the second within a few weeks. He escaped the first unscathed.
2. Crown Prince Frederick William of Germany, born in 1831, had distinguished himself as an army commander.
3. Chancellor Otto von Bismarck of Germany gave a dinner for the Grants on July 1, 1878. John Russell Young described the conversation between USG and Bismarck after the meal. *New York Herald*, July 20, 1878. See *Young*, I, 422–28.
4. See Grant H. Smith, *The History of the Comstock Lode 1850–1920* (Reno, Nev., 1943), pp. 90–94; letter to Ulysses S. Grant, Jr., [*Sept. 14, 1878*].

Conversation with Otto von Bismarck

[*Berlin, June 30, 1878*]

"I regard Sheridan as not only one of the great soldiers of our war, but one of the great soldiers of the world—as a man who is fit for the highest commands. No better General ever lived than Sheridan."

. . .

The General made a reference to the deliberations of the Congress[1] and hoped that there would a peaceful result.

. . .

"His Majesty," said the Prince, "has been expecting you, and has the greatest interest in your character and history and in your visit to Germany. He commands me to say that nothing but his doctor's orders that he shall see no one prevents his seeing you."

The General said, "I am sorry that I cannot have that honor, but I am far more sorry for the cause and hope the Emperor is recovering."[2]

"All the indications are of the best," answered the Prince, "for the Emperor has a fine constitution and great courage and endurance, but you know he is a very old man."

"That," said the General, "adds to the horror one feels for the crime."

"It is so strange, so strange and so sad," answered the Prince, with marked feeling. "Here is an old man—one of the kindest old gentlemen in the world—and yet they must try and shoot him! . . . I should have supposed that the Emperor could have walked alone all over the Empire without harm, and yet they must try and shoot him."

The General said that it was a horrible thing, and referred to Lincoln—a man of the kindest and gentlest nature—killed by an assassin.

. . .

The General answered that the influence which aimed at the Emperor's life was an influence that would destroy all government, all order, all society, republics and empires.

"In America," he said, "some of our people are, as I see from the papers, anxious about it. There is only one way to deal with it, and that is by the severest methods. I don't see why a man who commits a crime like this, a crime that not only aims at an old man's life, a ruler's life, but shocks the world, should not meet with the severest punishment. In fact," continued the General, "although at home there is a strong sentiment against the death penalty, and it is a sentiment which one naturally respects, I am not sure but it should be made more severe rather than less severe. Something is due to the offended as well as the offender, especially where the offended is slain."

. . .

"All you can do with such people," said the General quietly, "is to kill them."

"Precisely so," answered the Prince.

. . .

The General said that he had accepted the Crown Prince's invitation to a review for next morning,[3] but with a smile continued:— "The truth is I am more of a farmer than a soldier. I take little or no interest in military affairs, and, although I entered the army thirty-

five years ago and have been in two wars, in Mexico as a young lieutenant, and later, I never went into the army without regret and
never retired without pleasure."

"You are so happily placed," said the Prince, "in America that you
need fear no wars. What always seemed so sad to me about your last
great war was that you were fighting your own people. That is always so terrible in wars, so very hard."

"But it had to be done," said the General.

"Yes," said the Prince, "you had to save the Union just as we had
to save Germany."[4]

"Not only save the Union, but destroy slavery," answered the
General.

"I suppose, however, the Union was the real sentiment, the dominant sentiment," said the Prince.

"In the beginning, yes," said the General; "but as soon as slavery
fired upon the flag it was felt, we all felt, even those who did not object to slaves, that slavery must be destroyed. We felt that it was a
stain to the Union that men should be bought and sold like cattle."

. . .

"I suppose if you had had a large army at the beginning of the
war it would have ended in a much shorter time."

"We might have had no war at all," said the General, "but we cannot tell. Our war had many strange features—many things which
seemed odd enough at the time, but which now seem providential. If
we had had a large regular army, as it was then constituted, it might
have gone with the South. In fact the Southern feeling in the army
among high officers was so strong that when the war broke out the
army dissolved. We had no army—then we had to organize one. A
great commander like Sherman or Sheridan even then might have
organized an army and put down the rebellion in six months or a
year, or, at the furthest, two years. But that would have saved slavery,
perhaps, and slavery meant the germs of new rebellion. There had to
be an end of slavery. Then we were fighting an enemy with whom we
could not make a peace. We had to destroy him. No convention, no
treaty was possible—only destruction."

"It was a long war," said the Prince "and a great work well done—and I suppose it means a long peace."

"I believe so," said the General.

. . .

The Prince and the General walked side by side to the door, and after shaking hands the General passed into the square. The guard presented arms and the General lit a fresh cigar and slowly strolled home.

New York Herald, July 20, 1878. John Russell Young reported USG's conversation with Chancellor Otto von Bismarck of Germany in a column dated Berlin, July 2, 1878. The conversation lasted about thirty minutes. See *Young*, I, 410–18; Young diary, June 30, July 3–5, 1878, DLC-John Russell Young.

Bayard Taylor, U.S. minister, Berlin, had written several letters to his wife before USG's arrival concerning arrangements. Marie Hansen Taylor, *On Two Continents: Memories of Half a Century* (New York, 1905), pp. 282–89. On July 1, Taylor wrote to Secretary of State William M. Evarts discussing USG's visit. LS, DNA, RG 59, Diplomatic Despatches, Germany. *Foreign Relations, 1878*, pp. 223–25. See Young, *Men and Memories* (New York, 1901), I, 20–22.

1. A diplomatic congress was in session at Berlin to settle issues arising from the recent war between Russia and Turkey. In late Nov., 1879, at Galena, USG spoke to a reporter about his observations abroad. "He particularly took up the Turkish Government and went over with great perspicuity its internal systems of military and civil affairs. He showed himself entirely conversant with its abominable system of taxation and declared that the Government itself ought not to exist and that the great Christian powers, instead of sitting in deliberation of plans for its continuance, should have rather debated measures for its annihilation, subdivision, and distribution—making Constantinople a free city." *Milwaukee Sentinel*, Dec. 25, 1879.

2. Both men who attempted to assassinate Emperor William I of Germany advocated Socialism. See preceding letter.

3. Despite driving rain and a severe cold, USG reviewed Prussian army units on the morning of July 1, 1878. Young reported that USG "complimented the movement of the troops highly, but said he questioned very much whether in modern war the sabre or the bayonet were of use. 'What I mean,' said the General, 'is this; anything that adds to the burdens carried by the soldier is a weakness to the army. Every ounce he carries should tell in his efficiency. The bayonet is heavy, and if it were removed, or if its weight in food or ammunition were added in its place, the army would be stronger. As for the bayonet as a weapon, if soldiers come near enough to use it they can do as much good with the club end of their muskets. The same is true as to sabres. I would take away the bayonet and give the soldiers pistols in place of sabres. A sabre is always an awkward thing to carry.'" Responding to a Prussian officer's rejoinder, USG "said no doubt war showed instances when the bayonet was effective, but those instances were so few that he did not think they would pay for the heavy burden imposed upon an army by the carrying of the bayonet. In any army he commanded he would feel like taking away the bayonet, and telling the men to trust to the butt ends of their muskets. . . ." After inspecting a cav. regt., USG "observed

that the mare was more used in the Prussian than in the American cavalry service, which he said, 'I think to be an advantage.' He thought the soldiers in their exercises used the spur too much. After inspection there was a quiet mess room lunch and a good deal of military talk, which showed that the General had not forgotten his trade. The General, at the close of the lunch, asked permission to propose the prosperity of the regiment and the health of the colonel. It was a regiment of which any army would be proud, and he hoped a day of trial would never come; but if it did he was sure it would do its part to maintain the ancient success of the Prussian army. He also desired to express his thanks to the Crown Prince for the pains that have been taken to show him this sample of his magnificent army. . . ." *New York Herald*, July 20, 1878. See *Young*, I, 419–22.

4. See *PUSG*, 21, 163–67, 219–21.

To Maj. Culver C. Sniffen

Berlin, Germany,
July 1st /78

My Dear Major:

The several letters you have written me, with all their inclosures, have come regularly to hand, and have been received with great pleasure. I have been negligent about answering, but you must forgive that.—We are now on our way north through Denmark, Norway, Sweden & Russia. In the fall we expect to visit Spain & Portugal and then settle down for the winter at some pleasant place, probably the south of Italy. In the spring I shall go back to the United states and settle down for life. Where, it is not yet determined. My whole trip abroad has been exceedingly pleasant. As yet not a single unpleasant incident has occurred. Every place, in every nation, and by all classes of society, from rulers to the working people the greatist civility has been shown me, and the profoundest respect expressed for our country and countrymen. As pleasant as everything has been however I long for the time to come when I am to return home. I would go back after visiting Spain & Portugal in the fall—I will then have visited every country in Europe, Egypt in Africa, Syria & Asia Minor in Asia—only that I have no place to go to. By waiting until spring I can go to my Long Branch home and have the summer for preparing a winter home.

Please present Mrs. Grant's and my kindest regards to Mrs. Sniffen. I shall always be pleased to hear from you though I cannot promise to be very punctual in answering.

Truly yours

U. S. GRANT

MAJ. C. C. SNIFFEN U. S. ARMY.

P. S. Jesse left us several weeks since for the United States.

ALS, ICarbS. On March 3, 1877, USG nominated Culver C. Sniffen, his secretary, as a maj., paymaster. Sniffen was stationed at San Francisco during 1878. See DNA, RG 94, ACP, 1208 1877; *New York Times*, March 2, 1925; *Washington Post*, July 29, 1930.

Speech

———

[*Near Hamburg, July 4, 1878*]

MR. CONSUL AND FRIENDS—I am much obliged to you for the kind manner in which you drink my health. I share with you in all the pleasure and gratitude which Americans so far from home should feel on this anniversary. But I must dissent from one remark of our Consul, to the effect that I saved the country during the recent war. If our country could be saved or ruined by the efforts of any one man we should not have a country, and we should not be now celebrating our Fourth of July. There are many men who would have done far better than I did under the circumstances in which I found myself during the war. If I had never held command; if I had fallen; if all our generals had fallen, there were ten thousand behind us who would have done our work just as well, who would have followed the contest to the end and never surrendered the Union. Therefore, it is a mistake and a reflection upon the people to attribute to me, or to any number of us who held high commands, the salvation of the Union. We did our work as well as we could, and so did hundreds of thousands of others. We deserve no credit for it, for we should have been unworthy of our country and of the American name if we had not made every sacrifice to save the Union. What saved the Union was the coming forward of the young men of the nation. They came from their homes and fields, as they did in the time of the Revolution, giving everything to the country. To their devotion we owe the salvation of the Union. The humblest soldier who carried a musket is entitled to as much credit for the results of the war as those who were in command. So long as our young men are animated by this spirit there will be no fear for the Union.

New York Herald, July 24, 1878. John M. Wilson, consul, Hamburg, presided over "a dinner at a country hotel" for "about thirty Americans, ladies and gentlemen." *Ibid.* USG had arrived in Hamburg on July 2, 1878. See *Young*, I, 430–46; *Julia Grant*, p. 246; *PUSG*, 24, 399; *ibid.*, 26, 182.

Interview

HAMBURG, July 6, 1878

Such a movement would have involved moving my army from the Rapidan to Lynchburg.[1] I considered the plan with great care before I made the Wilderness move. I thought of massing the Army of the Potomac in movable columns, giving the men twelve days' rations, and throwing myself between Lee and his communications.[2] If I had made this movement successfully—if I had been as fortunate as I was when I threw my army between Pemberton and Joe Johnston the war would have been over a year sooner. I am not sure that it was not the best thing to have done; it certainly was the plan I should have preferred. If I had failed, however, it would have been very serious for the country, and I did not dare the risk. What deterred me, however, was the fact that I was new to the army, did not have it in hand and did not know what I could do with the generals or men. If it had been six months later, when I had the army in hand, and knew what a splendid army it was and what officers and men were capable of doing, and I could have had Sherman and Sheridan to assist in the movement, I would not have hesitated for a moment.[3]

By the way, there is one point about the campaign in the Wilderness worth remembering. My critics say that I threw away 100,000 men in that campaign. This has been repeated so often that it will soon be history. Now, my total losses were about thirty-nine thousand, all told. Badeau's book will have the figures,[4] but that is about the figure; and those losses do not mean killed, but the number of effective men taken from my army by death, wounds, capture and desertion. That movement cost me 39,000 men, but do not forget what it cost Lee. Remember that Lee had to fight as much as I did. He had the advantage of being on the defensive, which is always an advantage, and I had to attack and attack, but every blow I struck weakened him, and when at last he was forced into Richmond it was a far different army from that which menaced Washington and invaded Maryland and Pennsylvania. It was no longer an invading army. The Wilderness campaign was necessary to the destruction of the Southern Confederacy.

I have always regretted the censure that unwittingly came upon Butler in that campaign, and my report was the cause. I said that the General was bottled up, and used the phrase without meaning to annoy the General or give his enemies a weapon.[5] I like Butler and have always found him not only as all the world knows a man of great ability, but a patriotic man, and a man of courage, honor and sincere convictions. Butler lacked the technical experience of a military education, and it is very possible to be a man of high parts and not be a great general. Butler as a general was full of enterprise and resources and a brave man. If I had given him two corps commanders like Adelbert Ames, or Schofield, or Mackenzie, or a dozen I could mention, he would have made a fine campaign on the James and helped materially in my plans. I have always been sorry I did not do so. Butler is a man it is a fashion to abuse, but he is a man who has done the country great service and who is worthy of its gratitude.

The night before Lee surrendered, I had a wretched headache— headaches to which I have been subject—nervous prostration, intense personal suffering. But, suffer or not, I had to keep moving.[6] I saw clearly, especially after Sheridan had cut off the escape to Danville, that Lee must surrender or break and run into the mountains —break in all directions and leave us a dozen guerilla bands to fight. My campaign was not Richmond, not the defeat of Lee in actual fight, but to remove him and his army out of the contest and, if possible, to have him use his influence in inducing the surrender of Johnston and the other isolated armies. You see the war was an enormous strain upon the country. Rich as we were I do not now see how we could have endured it another year even from a financial point of view. So with these views I wrote Lee, and opened the correspondence with which the world is familiar.[7] Lee does not appear well in that correspondence—not nearly so well as he did in our subsequent interviews, where his whole bearing was that of a patriotic and gallant soldier, concerned alone for the welfare of his army and his State. I received word that Lee would meet me at a point within our lines near Sheridan's headquarters. I had to ride quite a distance through a muddy country. I remember now that I was concerned about my personal appearance. I had an old suit on, without my sword, and without any distinguishing mark of rank, except the shoulder straps of a Lieutenant General on a woollen blouse. I was splashed with mud in my long ride. I was afraid Lee might think I meant to show him studied discourtesy by so coming—at least I thought so. But I had no other clothes within reach, as Lee's letter found me away from my base of supplies. I kept on riding until I met Sheridan. The General, who was one of the heroes of the campaign, and whose pursuit of Lee was perfect in its generalship and energy, told me where to find Lee. I remember that Sheridan was impatient when I met him—anxious and suspicious about the whole business, feared there might be a plan to escape, that he had Lee at his feet, and wanted to end the business by going in and forcing an absolute surrender by capture. In fact, he had his troops ready for such an assault when Lee's white flag came within his lines.[8] I went up to the house where Lee was waiting. I found him in a fine, new, splendid uniform, which only recalled my anxiety as to my own clothes while on my way to meet him. I expressed my regret that I was compelled to meet him in so unceremonious a manner, and he replied that the only suit he had available was one which had been sent him by some admirers in Baltimore and which he then wore for the first time. We spoke of old friends in the army. I remembered having seen Lee in Mexico. He was so much higher in rank than myself at the time that I supposed he had no recollection of me. But he said he remembered me very well. We talked of old times and exchanged inquiries about friends. Lee then broached the subject of our meeting. I told him my terms, and Lee, listening attentively, asked me to write them down. I took out my manifold order book and pencil and wrote them down. General Lee put on his glasses and read them over The conditions gave the officers their side arms, private horses and personal baggage. I said to Lee that I hoped and believed this would be the close of the war. That it was most important that the men should go home and go to work, and the government would not throw any obstacles in the way. Lee answered that it would have a most happy effect and accepted the terms. I handed over my pencilled memorandum to an aide to put into ink[9] and we resumed our conversation about old times and friends in the armies. Various officers came in—Longstreet, Gordon, Pickett, from the South; Sheridan, Ord and others from our side. Some were old friends; Longstreet and myself,[10] for instance, and we had a general talk. Lee no doubt expected me to ask for his sword, but I did not want his sword. It would only have gone to the Patent Office to be worshipped by the Washington rebels. There was another pause when he said that most of the animals in his cavalry and artillery were owned by the privates and he would like to know, under the terms, whether they would be regarded as private property or the property of the government. I said under the terms of surrender they belonged to the government. General Lee read over the letter and said that was so. I then said to the General that I believed and hoped this was the last battle of the war, and I saw the wisdom of these men getting home and to work as soon as possible, and that I would give orders to allow any soldier or officer claiming a horse or a mule to take it. General Lee showed some emotion at this—a feeling which I also shared—and said it would have a most happy effect. The interview ended, and I gave orders for rationing his troops. The next day I met Lee on horseback and we had a long talk. In that conversation I urged upon Lee the wisdom of ending the war by the surrender of the other armies. I asked him to use his influence with the people of the South—an influence that was supreme—to bring the war to the end. General Lee said that his campaign in Virginia was the last organized resistance which the South was capable of making—that I might have to march a good deal and encounter isolated commands here and there; but there was no longer any army which could make a stand. I told Lee that this fact only made his responsibility greater, and any further war would be a crime. I asked him to go among the Southern people and use his influence to have all men under arms surrender on the same terms given to the army of Northern Virginia. He replied he could not do so without consultation with President Davis. I was sorry. I saw that the Confederacy had gone beyond the reach of President Davis, and that there was nothing that could be done except what Lee could do to benefit the Southern people.[11] I was anxious to get them home and have our armies go to their homes and fields. But Lee would not move without Davis, and, as a matter of fact at that time, or soon after, Davis was a fugitive in the woods.

I never thought so.[12] Davis did his best, did all that any man could do, to save the Confederacy. This argument is like some of the arguments current in history, that the war was a war against windmills, and that if one man or another had been in authority the result would have been different; that some more placable man than Davis could have made a better fight. This is not true. The war was a tremendous war, and no one knows better than those who were in it. Davis did all he could and all any man could for the South. The South was beaten from the beginning. There was no victory possible for any government resting upon the platform of the Southern Confederacy. Just as soon as the war united and aroused the young men of the North and called out the national feeling there was no end but the end that came. Davis did all he could for his side, and how much he did no one knows better than those who were in the field.

I had a letter from Mosby, some time ago, deprecating some attack I had made upon Stonewall Jackson. I wrote him there must be some mistake, as I had never attacked Jackson.

I knew Stonewall Jackson at West Point and in Mexico.[13] At West Point he came into the school at an older age than the average and began with a low grade. But he had so much courage and energy, worked so hard and governed his life by a discipline so stern that he steadily worked his way along and rose far above others who had more advantages. Stonewall Jackson, at West Point, was in a state of constant improvement. He was a religious man then, and some of us regarded him as a fanatic. Some times his religion took strange forms—hypochondria—fancies that an evil spirit had taken possession of him. But he never relaxed in his studies or his Christian duties. I knew him in Mexico. He was always a brave and trustworthy officer, none more so in the army. I never knew him or encountered him in the rebellion. I question whether his campaigns in Virginia justify his reputation as a great commander. He was killed too soon, and before his rank allowed him a great command. It would have been a test of generalship if Jackson had met Sheridan in the Valley instead of some of the men he did meet. From all I know of Jackson and all I see of his campaigns I have little doubt of the result. If Jackson had attempted on Sheridan the tactics he attempted so successfully upon others he would not only have been beaten but destroyed. Sudden, daring raids, under a fine general like Jackson, might do against raw troops and inexperienced commanders, such as we had in the beginning of the war, but not against drilled troops and a commander like Sheridan. The tactics for which Jackson is famous and which achieved such remarkable results belonged entirely to the beginning of the war and to the peculiar conditions under which the earlier battles were fought. They would have ensured destruction to any commander who tried them upon Sherman, Thomas, Sheridan Meade, or, in fact, any of our great generals. Consequently Jackson's fame as a general depends upon achievements gained before his generalship was tested, before he had a chance of matching himself with a really great commander. No doubt so able and patient a man as Jackson, who worked so hard at anything he attempted, would have adapted himself to new conditions and risen with them. He died before his opportunity. I always respected Jackson personally and esteemed his sincere and manly character. He impressed me always as a man of the Cromwell stamp, a Puritan—much more of a New Englander than the Virginian. If any man believed in the rebellion he did. And his nature was such that whatever he believed in became a deep religious duty, a duty he would discharge at any cost. It is a mistake to suppose that I ever had any feeling for Stonewall Jackson but respect. Personally, we were always good friends; his character had rare points of merit, and although he made the mistake of fighting against his country if ever a man did so conscientiously he was the man.

I never ranked Lee as high as some others of the army, that is to say, I never had as much anxiety when he was in my front as when Joe Johnston was in front.[14] Lee was a good man, a fair commander, who had everything in his favor. He was a man who needed sunshine. He was supported by the unanimous voice of the South; he was supported by a large party in the North; he had the support and sympathy of the outside world. All this is of an immense advantage to a general. Lee had this in a remarkable degree. Everything he did was right. He was treated like a demi-god. Our generals had a hostile press, lukewarm friends and a public opinion outside. The cry was in the air that the North only won by brute force; that the generalship and valor were with the South. This has gone into history, with so many other illusions that are historical. Lee was of a slow, conservative, cautious nature, without imagination or humor, always the same, with grave dignity. I never could see in his achievements what justifies his reputation. The illusion that nothing but heavy odds beat him will not stand the ultimate light of history. I know it is not true.

The South and North were more nearly matched than you would suppose. The whole population were in the war. The 4,000,000 of negroes were the same as soldiers because they did the work in the fields which white men would have to do. I believe the South had as many men under arms as the North.[15] What defeated the Southern arms was Northern courage and skill, and this, too, with d[i]straction all around. You cannot imagine how disheartening it was at the time, not only to officers but men.

Take the battle of Shiloh, for instance, the correspondents and papers at the time all said that Shiloh was a surprise—that our men were killed over their coffee, and so on. There was no surprise about it, except, perhaps to the newspaper correspondents.[16] We had been skirmishing for two days before we were attacked. At night, before Buell's army came up, I was so well satisfied with the result and so certain that I would beat Beauregard, even without Buell's aid, that I went in person to each division commander and ordered an advance along the line at four in the morning. Shiloh was one of the most important battles in the war. It was there that our Western soldiers met the enemy in a pitched battle. From that day they never feared to fight the enemy and never went into action without feeling sure they [w]ould win. Shiloh broke the prestige of the Southern Confederacy so far as our Western army was concerned.[17] Sherman was the hero of Shiloh. He really commanded two divisions—his own and Mc-Clernand's—and proved himself to be a consummate soldier. Nothing could be finer than his work at Shiloh,[18] and yet Shiloh was belittled by our Northern people so that many people look at it as a defeat. The same may be said of Fort Donelson. People think that Donelson was captured by pouring men into it ten to one, or some such odds. The truth is our army, a new army, invested a fortified place and compelled a surrender of a force much larger than our own. A large number of the rebels escaped under Floyd and Pillow, but as it was I took more prisoners than I had men under my command for the first two days of my investment. After the investment we were reinforced, so that at the surrender there were 26,000 Union troops, about 4,000 of which were sent back to guard the road to where the steamers lay with our supplies. There were 22,000 effective men in Donelson at the beginning of the siege. Of course there was a risk in attacking Donelson as I did, but I knew the men who commanded it.[19] I knew some of them in Mexico. Knowledge of that kind goes far toward determining a movement like this.

If Longstreet or Jackson or even if Buckner had been in command I would have made a different campaign. In the beginning we all did things more rashly than later, just as Jackson did in his earlier campaigns. The Mexican war made the officers of the old regular armies more or less acquainted, and when we knew the name of the general opposing we knew enough about him to make our plans accordingly. What determined my attack on Donelson was as much the knowledge I had gained of its commanders in Mexico as anything else. But as the war progressed and each side kept improving its army these experiments were not possible. Then it became hard, earnest war, and neither side could depend upon any chance with the other. Neither side dared to make a mistake. It was steady, hard pounding, and the result could only be ruin to the defeated party. That was a peculiarity in our war that we were not fighting for a peace, but to destroy our adversary. That made it so hard for both sides, and especially for the South.

Yes, Mr. Johnson had made up his mind to arrest Lee and the leading Southern officers.[20] It was in the beginning of his administration when he was making speeches saying he had resolved to make all treason odious. He was addressing delegations on the subject and offering rewards for Jeff Davis and others. Upon Lee's arrest he had decided. I protested again and again. It would come up in Cabinet, and the only Minister who supported my views openly was Seward. I always said that the parole of Lee protected him as long as he observed it. On one occasion Mr. Johnson spoke of Lee and wanted to know why any military commander had a right to protect an arch-traitor from the laws. I was angry at this, and I spoke earnestly and plainly to the President. I said that as General it was none of my business what he or Congress did with General Lee or his other commanders. He might do as he pleased about civil rights, confiscation of property and so on. That did not come in my province. But a general commanding troops has certain responsibilities and duties and power, which are supreme. He must deal with the enemy in front of him so as to destroy him. He may either kill him, capture him or parole him. His engagements are sacred so far as they lead to the destruction of the foe. I made certain terms with Lee— the best and only terms. If I had told him and his army that their liberty would be invaded, that they would be open to arrest, trial and execution for treason, Lee would never have surrendered, and we should have lost many lives in destroying him. Now my terms of surrender were according to military law, to the instructions of Mr. Lincoln and Mr. Stanton, and so long as Lee was observing his parole I would never consent to his arrest. Mr. Seward nodded approval. I remember feeling very strongly on the subject. The matter was allowed to die out. I should have resigned the command of the army rather than have carried out any order directing me to arrest Lee or any of his commanders who obeyed the laws.[21] By the way, one reason why Mosby became such a friend of mine was because as General I gave him a safe conduct to allow him to practise law and earn a living.[22] Our officers in Virginia used to arrest leading Confederates whenever they moved out of their homes. Mrs. Mosby went to Mr. Johnson and asked that her husband might be allowed to earn his living. But the President was in a furious mood, and told her treason must be made odious, and so on. She came to me in distress, and I gave the order to allow Mosby to pass and repass freely. I had no recollection of this until Mosby called it to my attention. By the way, Mosby deserves great credit for his sacrifices in the cause of the Union. He is an honest, brave, conscientious man, and has suffered severely for daring to vote as he pleased among people who hailed him as a hero and in whose behalf he risked his life.

There were a few men when the war broke out, to whom we who had been in the army looked for success and high rank—among them Rosecrans, Buckner, McClellan, Stone, McDowell, Buell.[23] I felt sure that each of these men would gain the highest commands. Rosecrans was a great disappointment to us all—to me especially. Stone's case was always a mystery, and I think a great wrong was committed.

I knew Stone at school. I have always regarded him as very good, a very able and a perfectly loyal man, but a man who has had three or four severe and surprising reverses of fortune. After the arrest of Stone and his treatment his military career in our war was destroyed. I believe if Stone had had a chance he would have made his mark in the war.[24] McDowell was also the victim of what I suppose we should call ill luck. You will remember people called him a drunkard and a traitor. Well, he never drank a drop of liquor in his life, and a more loyal man never lived. I have the greatest respect for McDowell's accomplishments and character, and I was glad to make him major general.[25] The country owed him that, if only as an atonement for its injustice toward him. But McDowell never was what you would call a popular man. He was never so in the army nor at West Point. Yet I could never understand it, for no one could know McDowell without liking him. His career is one of the surprising things in the war. So is Buell's. Buell does not like me, I am afraid, but I have always borne my testimony to his perfect loyalty and his ability.

Buell is a man who would have carried out loyally every order he received, and I think he had genius enough for the highest commands;
but, somehow, he fell under a cloud.[26]

The trouble with many of our generals in the beginning was that
they did not believe in the war.[27] I mean they did not have that complete assurance in success which belongs to good generalship. They
had views about slavery, protecting rebel property, State rights—
political views that interfered with their judgment. Now I do not
mean to say they were disloyal. A soldier had as good a right to his
opinions as any other citizen, and these men were as loyal as any
men in the Union—would have died for the Union—but their opinions made them lukewarm, and many failures came from that. In
some cases it was temperament. There is Warren, whose case may be
regarded as a hard one. Warren had risen to one of the highest commands in the army, and was removed on the field of battle and in the
last battle of the war. Yet it could not be helped. Warren is a good
soldier and a good man, trained in the art of war. But, as a general, if
you give him an order he would not act until he knew what the other
corps would do, instead of obeying—and knowing that the power
which was guiding him would guide the others—he would hesitate and inquire and want to debate. It was this quality which led to
our disaster at the mine explosion before Petersburg. If Warren
had obeyed orders we would have broken Lee's army in two and
taken Petersburg. But when he should have been in the works he was
worrying over what other corps would do, so the chance was lost.
I should have relieved Warren then, but I did not like to injure an
officer of so high rank for what was an error of judgment. But at Five
Forks it was different. There was no time to think of rank or persons' feelings, and I told Sheridan to relieve Warren if he at all failed
him. Sheridan did so, and no one regretted the necessity more than
I did.[28]

So far as the war is concerned, I think history will more than approve the places given to Sherman and Sheridan. Sherman I have
known for thirty-five years. During that time there never was but
one cloud over our friendship, and that lasted about three weeks.
When Sherman's book came out, Mr. Boynton, the correspondent,

printed some letters about it. In these Sherman was made to disparage his comrades, and to disparage me especially. I cannot tell you
how much I was shocked. But there were the letters and the extracts.
I could not believe it in Sherman, the man whom I had always found
so true and knightly, more anxious to honor others than win honor
for himself. But there were the letters and the extracts. So I sent for
the book and resolved to read it over, with paper and pencil, and
make careful notes, and in justice to my comrades and myself prepare a reply. I do not think I ever ventured upon a more painful duty.
I was some time about it. I was moving to Long Branch. I had official
duties, and I am a slow reader. Then I missed the books when I
reached the Branch and had to send for them. So it was three weeks
before I was through. During these weeks, I did not see Sherman,
and I am glad I did not. My mind was so set by Boynton's extracts
that I should certainly have been cold to him. But when I finished the
book I found that I approved every word—that it was a true book,
an honorable book—creditable to Sherman, just to his companions
—to myself particularly so—just such a book as I expected Sherman
would write. Then it was accurate, because Sherman keeps a diary,
and he compiled the book from notes made at the time. Then he is a
very accurate man. You cannot imagine how pleased I was, for my respect and affection for Sherman were so great that I look on these
three weeks as among the most painful in my remembrance. I wrote
Sherman my opinion of the book. I told him the only points I objected to were his criticisms upon some of our civil soldiers, like Logan and Blair. As a matter of fact there were in the army no two men
more loyal than John A. Logan and Frank Blair. I knew that Sherman did not mean to disparage either of them, and that he wrote
hastily. Logan did a great work for the Union in bringing Egypt out
of the Confederacy, which he did; and he was an admirable soldier,
and is, as he always has been, an honorable, true man—a perfectly
just and fair man, whose record in the army was brilliant.[29] Blair also
did a work in the war entitling him to the gratitude of every Northern man and the respect of every soldier.[30] But with these two exceptions I approved of every line of Sherman's book and think it of
great value as a history.[31]

Sherman is not only a great soldier, but a great man. He is one of the very great men in our country's history. He is a many-sided man. He is an orator with few superiors. As a writer he is among the first. As a general I know of no man I would put above him. Above all, he has a fine character—so frank, so sincere, so outspoken, so genuine. There is not a false line in Sherman's character—nothing to regret. As a soldier, I know his valor. I know what he was before Vicksburg. You see, we had two lines to maintain. On one side was Pemberton, his army and his works. That I was watching. On our rear was Joe Johnston, who might come at any time and try and raise the siege. I set Sherman to keep that line and watch him. I never had a moment's care while Sherman was there. I don't think Sherman ever went to bed with his clothes off during that campaign or allowed a night to pass without visiting his pickets two or three times in person. His industry was prodigious. He worked all the time, and with an enthusiasm, a patience and a good humor that gave him great power with his army. There is no man living for whose character I have a higher respect than for that of Sherman. He is not only one of the best men living, but one of the greatest we have had in our history.

As for Sheridan, I have only known him since we met during the war. He joined my regiment—the Tenth [*Fourth*] Infantry—after I left it, and so I did not see him. Then he is a much younger man than Sherman or myself and did not serve in Mexico. The first time I remember meeting Sheridan was when he was the Colonel of a Michigan regiment. We met at a railway station. He was about to move his regiment to join some other general—I think Gordon Granger. I knew I had sent a regiment, but had not indicated that of Sheridan, and really did not wish it to leave. I spoke to Sheridan, and he said he would rather go than stay, or some such answer, which was brusque and rough and annoyed me. I don't think Sheridan could have said anything to have made a worse impression on me.[32] But I watched his career and saw how much there was in him. So when I came East and took command I looked around for a cavalry commander. I was standing in front of the White House, talking to Mr. Lincoln and General Halleck. I said, "I wanted the best man I could find for the cavalry." "Then," said Halleck, "why not take Phil Sheridan?" "Well,"

I said, "I was just going to say Phil Sheridan." So Sheridan was sent for and he came very much disgusted. He was just about to have a corps, and he did not know why we wanted him East, whether it was to discipline him or not.[33] But he came, and took the command, and came out of the war with a record that entitled him to his rank. As a soldier, as a commander of troops, as a man capable of doing all that is possible with any number of men, there is no man living greater than Sheridan. He belongs to the very first rank of soldiers, not only of our country, but of the world. No man ever had such a faculty of finding out things as Sheridan, of knowing all about the enemy. He was always the best informed man in his command as to the enemy. Then he had that magnetic quality of swaying men which I wish I had—a rare quality in a general. I don't think any one can give Sheridan too high praise. When I made him lieutenant general there was some criticism. Why not Thomas or Meade? I have the utmost respect for those generals, no one has more; but when the task of selection came I could not put any man ahead of Sheridan. He ranked Thomas. He had waived his rank to Meade, and I did not think his magnanimity in waiving rank to Meade should operate against him when the time came for awarding the higher honors of the war. It was no desire on my part to withhold honor from Thomas or Meade,[34] but to do justice to a man whom I regarded then, as I regard him now, not only as one of the great soldiers of America, but as one of the greatest soldiers of the world, worthy to stand in the very highest rank.

I was very fond of MacPherson, and his death was a great affliction.[35] He was on my staff, and there I learned his merit. He would have come out of the war had he lived with the highest rank. When I look for brave, noble characters in our war, men whom death has surrounded with romance, I see them in characters like MacPherson, and not only in the Southern armies. Meade was a fine soldier and a loyal, good man. He has been criticised for not having destroyed Lee after Gettysburg, and the country seemed to share that disappointment after the battle. I have never thought it a fair criticism. Meade was new to his army, and did not feel it in his hand. If he could have fought Lee six months later, when he had the army in his hand, or if

Sherman or Sheridan had commanded at Gettysburg, I think Lee would have been destroyed. But if Meade made any mistake, if he did not satisfy the wishes of the country who hoped for Lee's destruction, he made a mistake which any one would have made under the circumstances. He was new to the chief command. He did not know how it felt toward him, and, having rolled back the tide of invasion, he felt that any further movement would be a risk. Meade served with me, served in command, and to my perfect satisfaction. His memory deserves to be honored among the heroes of the war.[36] Hancock is a fine soldier. At the time he was named Major General we were not very good friends, and I had personal preferences for Schofield, but I felt Hancock had earned the promotion and gave his name to Stanton. He wrote me a beautiful letter on the subject, and our relations have always remained on the most cordial footing. I have great respect for Hancock as a man and a soldier.[37] We had a good many men in the war who were buried in the staff and did not rise. There is Ingalls, for instance. Ingalls remained Quartermaster of the Army of the Potomac during all commands, and did a great work. Yet you never heard his name mentioned as a general. And yet Ingalls in command of troops would in my opinion have become a great and famous general. If the command of the army of the Potomac had ever become vacant I would have given it to Ingalls.[38] Horace Porter was lost in the staff. Like Ingalls he was too useful to be spared. But as a commander of troops Porter would have risen, in my opinion, to a very high command. Young Mackenzie at the close of the war was a most promising soldier He is an officer, I think, fitted for the highest commands.[39] I have no doubt there are many others in the army, for we had really a fine army. These are names that occur in the hurry of conversation. You never can tell what makes a general. So many circumstances enter into success. Our war and all wars are surprises in that respect. But what saved us in the North was not generalship so much as the people.

I knew Albert Sidney Johnston before the war. When he was sent to Utah I had a high opinion of his talents. When the war broke out he was regarded as the coming man of the Confederacy. I shared that opinion, because I knew and esteemed him and because I felt as we all did in the old army, where there was a public opinion among the officers as to who would come out ahead. In many cases, in most cases, our public opinion was in error.[40] Bragg had a great reputation in the South. Bragg was the most contentious of men, and there was a story in Mexico that he put every one in arrest under him and then put himself in arrest.[41] Albert Sidney Johnston might have risen in fame, and we all had confidence in his doing so, but he died too soon, as Stonewall Jackson died, too soon for us to say what he would have done under the later and altered conditions of the war. The Southern army had many good generals. Lee, of course, was a good soldier, and so was Longstreet, but I do not know that there was any better than Joe Johnston. I have had nearly all of the Southern generals in high command in front of me, and Johnston gave me more anxiety than any of the others. I was never half so anxious about Lee. By the way, I saw in Joe Johnston's book that when I was asking Pemberton to surrender Vicksburg he was on his way to raise the siege.[42] I was very sorry. If I had known Johnston was coming I would have told Pemberton to wait in Vicksburg until I wanted him, awaited Johnston's advance and given him battle. He could never have beaten that Vicksburg army, and thus I would have destroyed two armies perhaps. Pemberton's was already gone, and I was quite sure of Johnston's. I was sorry I did not know Johnston was coming until it was too late. Take it all in all, the South, in my opinion, had no better soldier than Joe Johnston—none at least that gave me more trouble.

I never held a council of war in my life. I never heard of Sherman or Sheridan doing so. Of course I heard all that every one had to say, and in headquarters there is an interesting and constant stream of talk. But I always made up my mind to act, and the first that even my staff knew of any movement was when I wrote it out in rough and gave it to be copied off.

The battle of Lookout Mountain is one of the romances of the war. There was no such battle and no action even worthy to be called a battle on Lookout Mountain. It is all poetry.[43]

I was never more delighted at anything than the close of the war. I never liked service in the army—not as a young officer. I did not want to go to West Point. My appointment was an accident, and my

father had to use his authority to make me go.[44] I never went into a
battle willingly or with enthusiasm. I was always glad when a battle
was over. I never want to command another army. I take no interest
in armies. When the Duke of Cambridge asked me to review his
troops at Aldershott I told His Royal Highness that the one thing I
never wanted to see again was a military parade. When I resigned
from the army and went to a farm I was happy.[45] When the rebellion
came I returned to the service because it was a duty. I had no thought
of rank; all I did was to try and make myself useful.[46] My first commission as brigadier came in the unanimous indorsement of the delegation from Illinois. I do not think I knew any of the members but
Washburne, and I did not know him very well.[47] It was only after
Donelson that I began to see how important was the work that Providence devolved upon me. And yet after Donelson I was in disgrace
and under arrest, and practically without a command because of
some misunderstanding on the part of Halleck. I do not know what
would have come of that had not the country interfered. You see
Donelson was our first clear victory, and you will remember the enthusiasm that came with it. The country saved me from Halleck's
displeasure.[48] When other commands came I always regretted them.
When the bill creating the grade of lieutenant general was proposed,
with my name as the lieutenant general, I wrote Mr. Washburne opposing it. I did not want it.[49] I found that the bill was right and I was
wrong, when I came to command the Army of the Potomac—that a
head was needed to the army. I did not want the Presidency, and have
never quite forgiven myself for resigning the command of the army
to accept it; but it could not be helped. I owed my honors and op-
portunities to the republican party, and if my name could aid it I was
bound to accept. The second nomination was almost due to me—if
I may use the phrase—because of the bitterness of political and personal opponents. My re-election was a great gratification, because it
showed me how the country felt. Then came all the discussions
about the third term. I gave my views on that in my letters to Senator White, of Pennsylvania.[50] It is not known, however, how strongly
I was pressed to enter the canvass as a candidate. I was waited upon
formally by a distinguished man, representing the influences that

would have controlled the republicans in the South, and asked to allow my name to be used. This request was supported by men in the Northern States whose position and character are unquestioned. I said then that under no circumstances would I become a candidate. Even if a nomination and an election were assured I would not run. The nomination if I ran would be after a struggle and before it had been unanimous. The election, if I should win, would be after a struggle, and the result would be far different from what it was before. If I succeeded and tried to do my best, my very best, I should still have a crippled administration. This was the public view. Personally I was weary of office. I never wanted to get out of a place as much as I did to get out of the Presidency. For sixteen years, from the opening of the war, it had been a constant strain upon me. So when the third term was seriously presented to me I peremptorily declined it.

Speaking of St. Domingo, it is strange how impressions have gone abroad as to my connection with that whole business. I did not seek the annexation of St. Domingo. The project had never occurred to me, nor, indeed, had any project of annexation. The important things to be done when I became President were the consolidation of our finances, the reduction of the debt and of the taxes that came with the debt, and the pacification of the South. So far as the South was concerned I had the ideas that prompted my conversations with Lee, that what the country wanted was peace, and peace would come with concord. No one knew as well what the war cost as we who were responsible for its management. So when the proposition for the annexation of St. Domingo came I was opposed to it. I did not want to entertain it. But i[t] came from a people, and in such a form that I could not, as Executive, refuse to consider it. I found when I entered into the question that my experiences were like those of President White, of Cornell, and Dr. Howe, of Boston. The more I thought of it the more I saw it was for the advantage of the country. There was no wrong, no spoliation implied, no war, as in the case of Texas and Mexico. It was the will of the people of St. Domingo, as I knew from incontestable proof. I still refused to consider the proposition which came from the President of the Republic until I sent my own agents into the island. They went, caring, as I did, nothing about it, hoping, perhaps, as I certainly did, that there would be no reasons for annexation. They brought back their report. I made the treaty. I submitted it to Mr. Sumner in the first place, not, as has been falsely said, because I wanted him to support it, but because Mr. Sumner was chairman of the Committee of Foreign Relations, and I wished as a matter of courtesy to him to tell him why the treaty had been made in secret. The reason was to prevent certain jobbers from speculating in the debt of the island. Mr. Sumner did not oppose the treaty in the Senate, but tried to smother it. You see treaties have a limit, and Mr. Sumner's idea was to allow the limit to pass. I did not think that was frank with St. Domingo, and I pressed the Senate to say something.[51] Under this pressure the opposition developed. Seeing that it embraced not only Mr. Sumner and Mr. Schurz, who had resolved to oppose me, no matter what I did, but good, honorable men like Edmunds, with whom I was friendly, seeing that even friends like Conkling and Cameron were lukewarm, I then appointed a commission. I selected two men who were opposed to St. Domingo—President Andrew White, of Cornell University, and Dr. Samuel G. Howe. I also sent Senator Wade, who was probably as lukewarm as Mr. Cameron, who felt perhaps as I did in the beginning—that we probably had as much as we wanted in the way of land—and who, however he might feel, would of all men living be sure to make an honest report. I also sent Frederick Douglass. And when Wendell Phillips speaks of "the treachery to the black race" involved in the treaty he might do me the justice to add that Mr. Douglass was among the most enthusiastic supporters of the treaty, and that he is perhaps as good a friend of the black man and as jealous of his rights as Mr. Phillips or myself. I gave these men no instructions as to their report. If I had been mean enough to do so they certainly were not degraded enough to have gone. Dr. Howe was Mr. Sumner's lifelong friend. When they returned they were unanimous in favor of the annexation. I then turned over the whole matter to Congress in a special message, and from that time I have had nothing to do with with St. Domingo.[52] I used no pressure about the treaty. I had honestly tried to do my duty in the matter, not only to my own country but toward St. Domingo. So long as Dr. Howe lived he labored for the annexation. He visited the country, he wrote about it, and never ceased to agitate. I think now, looking over the whole subject, that it would have been a great gain to the United States to have annexed St. Domingo. It would have settled many problems that now disturb us. It would have rendered the Cuban question more easy of solution. It would have given a new home for the blacks, who were and as I hear are still oppressed in the South. If two or three hundred thousand blacks were to emigrate to St. Domingo under our Republic the Southern people would learn the crime of Ku Kluxism, because they would see how necessary the black man is to their own prosperity. It would have settled several questions of political economy. We should have grown our own coffee and sugar, our own hard woods and spices. We should have become an exporter, as we are now an importer of coffee. There would have been a new field for American capital and commerce. You remember how large a portion of the West Indian trade used to come to us, how, in fact, so large a portion of our trade was West Indian. All this would have revived. We should have made of St. Domingo a new Texas or a new California, with sources of strength or national prosperity even greater in some respects than those possessed by Texas or California.

That could not very well have been, as he supported the annexation of Alaska, and was anxious to confirm Mr. Seward's treaty for St. Thomas.[53] We paid Russia $7,000,000 for Alaska, and he wanted us to pay $7,000,000, I think, for St. Thomas. I suppose one of his reasons for wishing Alaska was that it might annoy England—for at that time he was severe upon England. But I never shared that feelin[g]. I do not speak of Alaska to demur to its annexation, but only to say that if it was worth $7,000,000 St. Domingo was certainly worth taking for a trifle. If St. Domingo had come we should have had Hayti. A Power like ours in St. Domingo makes us masters of the Gulf of Mexico. If the democrats ever gain power at home they will revive this question. I suppose if the treaty had been confirmed we should have made St. Domingo a territory under a military government at the outset. In that case I should most probably have appointed General Schofield or General Terry its governor.

New York Herald, July 24, 1878. John Russell Young explained his "interview" method. "I have some memoranda of odds and ends of conversations in idle moments while wandering about these old towns, and it seems to me that I can do no better service to the historian than to throw these memoranda into some shape. There are few men more willing to converse on any subject which he knows than the General, and although his fame is that of a silent man those who know him at all know that in reality we have few better talkers in America. The charm of the General's talk is that it is never about anything he does not know, and what he does know he knows well. He is never vindictive and never gossips, and when referring to men and things in the great events of his career he is as passionless and just as a historian. He never refers to the war unless you put the subject to him directly. I am afraid I have been curious on this point, not that I ever wanted to trouble General Grant, but because the judgments and opinions of such a man belong to history. I hope, therefore, that what I gather up and send you from various table talk memoranda will have a value to the historian. I do not hope to give you the General's exact words, although as far as memory serves I do so." *Ibid.* On Aug. 8, 1878, Young, London, wrote in his diary. "Wrote General Grant this morning about many things. . . . Think the General will not in any way disapprove the additions I made to my interview: Seems to have been an immense sensation." DLC-John Russell Young. See letter to Daniel Ammen, Aug. 13, 1878; letter to Adam Badeau, Aug. 22, 1878; letter to John Russell Young, Aug. 28, 1878; Young diary, July 8, 12, Aug. 27, 1878, DLC-John Russell Young; Wendell Phillips to Young, Aug. 18, 1878, *ibid.*; *Young*, II, 151–53, 210–13, 288–93, 296–98, 300–301, 304–7, 450–53, 455–63, 468–70.

On July 30, John McDonald spoke to a reporter in Dartford, Wis., concerning USG's published remarks. "They are the first utterances of his that I have seen in a long while that sounded like Grant's talk, . . . Have you noticed the difference in tone between these talks and the little speeches he made when he first went over to the other side? At first, whenever he made a speech, no matter if it was only to a street crowd that hurr[a]hed him as he passed, he would take off his hat and thank them for the expression of friendship to 'his country'—never to himself? I tell you, those first little speeches were as much advertisements as these last long ones are. It's an open secret now, and has been for some time that he is in training for a third race. There are very few people in this country know the general. He's pretty much all for Grant. If he had it in his power to become emperor of this country to-day, by seizing the reins of government as Napoleon did, he'd do it quick as turning his hand over. . . . Gen. Grant is very much the result of circumstances. He is one of the most remarkably favored men by fortune that I have ever heard of. But no man could remain on top for a period of between fifteen and twenty years by force of circumstances alone. People have never found him out. Now, I know that an idea prevails to a considerable extent that he is a dull and stupid man. It is a wrong idea. Gen. Grant graduated from West Point when he was a young man. He has told me that he was forced into West Point by his father, very much against his own will. But he went through there, and came out with a certain culture that he had to acquire whether he liked or not. Then he has had considerable experience of men and things. And he has a wonderful amount of 'horse sense,' and he's as full of cunning and tricks as an egg is full of meat. But the great secret of Grant's success is in his way of finding out things and keeping them until he can use them. He don't forget anything about anyone, and he never tells what he knows. Knowledge is power with him, literally. Very few people become well acquainted with him. He meets a stranger with as few words as he can get along with; but among those he knows well he is as talkative as anyone. He'll let himself out, and be as lively as the liveliest of them. . . ." *Chicago Times*, Aug. 2, 1878. See letter to Alphonso Taft, Nov. 8, 1876.

1. Young asked USG to explain "why he had not invested Richmond as he had invested Vicksburg and starved out Lee." *New York Herald*, July 24, 1878.

2. See *Memoirs*, II, 134–37.

3. On Dec. 16, 1877, Young had written in his diary. "In the evening talked with the General about a good many things. Said he thought one time of getting between Lee & Lynchburg. He was afraid he could not trust his commanders and a defeat would have been most destructive,—If Sheridan & Sherman had been with him would have done so." DLC-John Russell Young.

4. See Adam Badeau, *Military History of Ulysses S. Grant, . . .* (New York, 1881–82), II, 323–24, 329–32.

5. See *PUSG*, 15, 172; *Memoirs*, II, 150–52; *Butler's Book* (Boston, 1892), pp. 853–61.

6. See *Memoirs*, II, 483–85; Horace Porter, *Campaigning With Grant* (New York, 1897), pp. 462–64.

7. See *PUSG*, 14, 361, 367, 371–73.

8. See *Memoirs*, II, 486; *Personal Memoirs of P. H. Sheridan* (New York, 1888), II, 194–202.

9. See *PUSG*, 14, 373–75.

10. See James Longstreet, *From Manassas to Appomattox* (Philadelphia, 1896), p. 630.

11. See *Memoirs*, II, 488–97.

12. USG commented on "the feeling in the South that Davis was an injury to the Confederacy and did not do his best." *New York Herald*, July 24, 1878.

13. Young asked USG "how he ranked Jackson among soldiers." *Ibid.*

14. Young introduced USG's comments: "This led to a remark as to the great and universal fame of Lee—especially in Europe—a reputation which seemed to grow every day." *Ibid.*

15. See *Memoirs*, II, 500–504.

16. See *PUSG*, 5, 73–74, 78; *Memoirs*, I, 340–42.

17. See *ibid.*, I, 355–57.

18. See *ibid.*, I, 343.

19. See *ibid.*, I, 294–95, 308–15.

20. Young "recalled a rumor current at the time about the intention of Johnson to arrest Lee." *New York Herald*, July 24, 1878.

21. See *PUSG*, 15, 149–51, 210–12.

22. See *ibid.*, 16, 450.

23. Young noted: "We were talking of the various commanders in our war and how surprising were the changes of fortune in the way of reputation and so on." *New York Herald*, July 24, 1878.

24. See *PUSG*, 9, 93.

25. See *ibid.*, 23, 280–81.

26. See *ibid.*, 11, 28; Stephen D. Engle, *Don Carlos Buell: Most Promising of All* (Chapel Hill, 1999), pp. 318–42.

27. Young explained: "This conversation about the failures of the war took a wider and more personal range than would be suitable for a journal; but I will venture to glean a few observations that may interest you." *New York Herald*, July 24, 1878.

28. On July 25, 1878, Maj. Gouverneur K. Warren, Newport, R. I., replied to USG's criticisms. ". . . If I could believe that General Grant would acknowledge as his own the charges made against me about the 'mine explosion' at Petersburg I would refute them at length. But it is enough now to say that there was a court of inquiry, of which Major General Hancock was president, immediately after that event, and the finding of that court charged no part of that 'disaster' to me. At the battle of Five Forks I was not relieved till

after the battle had ceased. Thousands of soldiers in the Fifth army corps and many in the ranks of our foes can testify that I led the final attack that completed that victory. There was no cause to take me away for any misconduct, and General Grant would never allow me a court of inquiry, because thereby I could have shown there was no cause. I claim the honors of that day are mine. The portrait the correspondent gives us of General Grant in his idle moments, repeating a calumny to be spread broadcast over the world against one whom he is made to say 'is a good soldier and a good man trained in the art of war,' whose command won all the vantage ground in the siege of Petersburg from the place of the mine explosion to Five Forks—the portrait, I say, is not that of the magnanimous man we would have our children believe him." *Ibid.*, July 27, 1878. See Testimony, [*Oct. 23, 1880*]; *Memoirs*, II, 442–45; *Personal Memoirs of P. H. Sheridan*, II, 155–70.

29. See James P. Jones, *"Black Jack:" John A. Logan and Southern Illinois in the Civil War Era* (Tallahassee, 1967).

30. See *Memoirs*, I, 573–74; William E. Parrish, *Frank Blair: Lincoln's Conservative* (Columbia, Mo., 1998).

31. Young observed. "The General told his story of the three weeks' cloud as though the recollection amused him." *New York Herald*, July 24, 1878. See letter to Gen. William T. Sherman, [*Jan. 29, 1876*]; Harry James Brown and Frederick D. Williams, eds., *The Diary of James A. Garfield* (East Lansing, Mich., 1967–81), III, 216–17.

32. See *Personal Memoirs of P. H. Sheridan*, I, 181–82.

33. See *PUSG*, 10, 217; *Memoirs*, II, 133; *Personal Memoirs of P. H. Sheridan*, I, 339–43.

34. On July 27, George Meade, Philadelphia, future biographer of his father, wrote "To the Editor of the Herald:—In the interview or series of interviews with General Grant, published in your edition of July 24, in the paragraph under the heading 'Grant's Estimate of Sheridan,' I find what purports to be an explanation of the precedence over General Meade given General Sheridan when he was appointed lieutenant general. General Grant is represented there as saying:—'He (General Sheridan) had waived his rank to Meade, and I did not think that his magnanimity in waiving rank to Meade should operate against him when the time came for awarding the higher honors of the war.' I was astonished at seeing the above statement published as coming from General Grant, who of all men living is familiar with the facts of the case, although I had heard before the same statement emanating from other sources and attributed to General Grant. I believe that a statement of facts will disabuse the minds of any persons desiring to know the merits of the case of the idea that there is any foundation whatever in truth for the assertion, and will show that it is unfair to the memory of General Meade and undignified in those that offer it. At the beginning of the campaign, in the summer of 1864, General Meade held a commission as brigadier general in the regular army, dated July 3, 1863, and General Sherman the same, dated July 4, 1863, the former thus ranking the latter. General Sheridan at this time was not even a brigadier general in the regular army. . . . In August, 1864, General Sherman was appointed a major general and General Sheridan a brigadier general in the regular army. General Meade's name was not acted upon. In explanation of this General Grant stated to General Meade that it was his act; that he had asked for the immediate appointment of the others, but not for his, for the reason that if Meade and Sherman had been appointed on the same day the former would have ranked the latter, and he desired Sherman to rank Meade. He further stated that neither his opinion nor that of the President or Secretary of War had changed with regard to him; that he still had their entire confidence, and assured him that it was a settled thing that he was to have the vacant major generalcy. Early in November, 1864, General Sheridan's appointment in the regular army was announced, to fill the vacancy caused by the resignation of General McClellan.

General Meade, upon hearing of this, at once sought General Grant, and in very decided terms expressed his opinion of the injustice to himself by this appointment. He said the action of the government was unjust, not only to himself, but to the army he commanded. Moreover, that any censure of him at this time was a virtual censure of General Grant, for he had simply obeyed his orders in everything that he had done in this campaign. He demanded that either he should be sustained or else relieved from command of the army. General Grant admitted the justice of these remonstrances and disclaimed any agency in General Sheridan's appointment, acknowledged that General Meade was entitled to it before and ought now to be appointed his senior, and promised to use all his influence to have justice done. He expressed regret at not having insisted on General Meade's appointment when General Sherman was appointed, and assured General Meade on his word of honor that he had never entertained nor expressed any but the strongest feelings in his behalf, whether in speech or writing. General Grant went to Washington and brought the matter to the attention of the President. He informed General Meade that as soon as he spoke to the President the latter acknowledged the justice of his statements, and said that he had hesitated when appointing General Sheridan on the very ground of its seeming injustice to General Meade. He at once, at the suggestion of General Grant, ordered the Secretary of War to make out General Meade's appointment as major general in the regular army, to date from August 19, 1864, the day of the capture of the Weldon Railroad. General Sheridan's appointment to the same rank had been dated November 3, 1864. It was evident that General Sheridan's appointment was made on the spur of the moment, in order that General McClellan's resignation should appear in greater contrast to Sheridan returning covered with laurels from his success in the Valley. General Grant virtually admitted this, and also that if General Meade's name had not, owing to these circumstances, been overlooked for the moment, he would certainly have been appointed a few days in advance. . . . It is evident, then, that there was no waiving of rank on the part of General Sheridan, but rather that an act of admitted injustice to General Meade had been rectified, and that principally through the efforts of General Grant. I have felt it my duty to make the above statement to put at rest an erroneous impression, which by your reported interview has now received the sanction of General Grant, and I have done this without any intention of detracting from the merit of General Sheridan's services to his country. But it was unnecessary to attempt to enhance the value of these services by detracting from the merits of another. . . . In the selection of the one who should hold the Lieutenant Generalcy there was allowed to enter no question of record, no question of service, no question of a previous waiving of rank. It was simply an act of personal favoritism, and it had better be placed on that ground, where it properly belongs. It was an act of gross injustice and saddened the last days of a worthy officer, who deserved fairer treatment from his goverment and from one who so well knew and had so often testified to the important services he had rendered his country." *New York Herald,* July 31, 1878. USG answered Meade's letter. "His statements and citations are correct, but he makes a mistake in his inferences if he supposes that I could in any way reflect on his father. It was not my fault, nor General Meade's, that Sheridan was confirmed before him as major-general. I did all I could to have Meade appointed so as to antedate Sheridan. At the same time, when the permission of Sheridan was asked, he gave it in a handsome manner. When the nomination for lieutenant-general became necessary, I would have liked to appoint Meade. If there had been enough to go around, there were others I would have promoted with the greatest pleasure. But there was only one place, and Sheridan was the man who had earned the place. I never could have felt comfortable if I had promoted any one over Sheridan, and when the fact that Meade ranked him was advanced as a reason, I was bound to remember the manner in which Sheridan had agreed to my wish that Meade should take from him a rank that the Senate had given him, and see that it did not count against him. . . ." *Young*, II, 298–99. See *PUSG*, 10, 434, 469–71; *ibid.*, 13, 299–300; *ibid.*, 19, 143; Freeman Cleaves, *Meade of Gettysburg* (Norman, 1960), pp. 304, 347–48.

35. See *PUSG*, 11, 397–98; *Memoirs*, II, 169.

36. See *PUSG*, 23, 279–80; *Memoirs*, II, 538–39.

37. See letter to Adam Badeau, Feb. 4, 1878; Interview, [*Sept. 21, 1880*]; *Memoirs*, II, 539–40; David M. Jordan, *Winfield Scott Hancock: A Soldier's Life* (Bloomington, Ind., 1988), pp. 157–58, 213–14, 229, 235.

38. See *PUSG*, 10, 131–32; *ibid.*, 12, 399–400; *ibid.*, 15, 322–23; *ibid.*, 16, 207–8, 415; *ibid.*, 25, 146–47; letter to Rutherford B. Hayes, April 27, 1877.

39. See *PUSG*, 14, 151–52; letter to Col. Benjamin H. Grierson, Oct. 10, 1882; Michael D. Pierce, *The Most Promising Young Officer: A Life of Ranald Slidell Mackenzie* (Norman, 1993).

40. See *Memoirs*, I, 360–62; Charles P. Roland, *Albert Sidney Johnston: Soldier of Three Republics* (Austin, 1964), pp. 258–61, 347–49.

41. See *Memoirs*, II, 86–87; Grady McWhiney, *Braxton Bragg and Confederate Defeat* (New York, 1969), pp. 31–34.

42. See Joseph E. Johnston, *Narrative of Military Operations*, . . . (New York, 1874), pp. 202–4; *Memoirs*, I, 548–49.

43. Young remembered "another question as to the poetic effect of such a battle as that of Lookout Mountain, the battle above the clouds." *New York Herald*, July 24, 1878.

On Aug. 17, retired Maj. Gen. Joseph Hooker, Martha's Vineyard, Mass., wrote "*To the Editor of The Tribune*" concerning USG's dismissal of the battle of Lookout Mountain as a romance. ". . . General Grant has thought proper to open with me and my command in regard to the fight. The interview said to have been held with that gentleman by a correspondent of *The Herald* I have always seriously doubted, and shall continue to do so until more fully confirmed respecting it. Interviewers have of late displayed so much cunning and mischief-making in the practice of their pursuits that I think my incredulity will not appear strange to you. General Grant has held such high positions that I am unwilling to believe that he will voluntarily go back on himself, or on the troops that served him with all the ardor and devotion of their natures, as he seems to have done, and which I can account for in no other way than that he was in his cups, or that the prospect of a third term had crazed his brain. Of course, General Grant will never be charged with having written or spoken the substance of the interview as reported to us, for that is foreign to his style, as any one who has either read or listened to him can readily discover. I strongly suspect that the interviewer was 'coached' by another officer of the army, of high rank, whose peculiar mode of warfare for some time past has been of this covert character. . . . General Grant, as well as some other officers high in rank, is famous for after-thoughts, as you will find on critical examination. We had, and I presume still have, rings in the army as well as out of it. I have not written so much about the fight at Lookout since the war as I now have, as I am anxious that you should know all the facts. My fight at Lookout might have equalled General Grant's in the Wilderness had I chosen to advance in front on the enemy behind their entrenchments, which seemed to be his favorite mode, but which his whole army revolted at at Cold Harbor. But I had no particular desire to be considered a butcher in my mode of making war. Sometime I do hope that a committee of intelligent and fearless Congressmen may be appointed to investigate this subject, and to report not only on this battle but Shiloh, the losses in the Wilderness, etc., etc., as in no other way can the truth of history be made out. General Ingalls, Grant's own Quartermaster, informed me that he furnished transportation for ninety thousand men to go north between the Rapidan and the James Rivers, and, of course, this number could not embrace all the casualties.

If General Grant expects to reach the third term by the circulation of such imposing and abominable statements, I am inclined to think that he will find it rough travelling before he reaches half way there. But you may feel assured that these are not his statements. Some one is 'bulldozing' him, the same as was the case among the politicians while he was administering the Government as President. . . ." *New York Tribune*, Aug. 22, 1878. See *New York Herald*, Oct. 12, 1878; *Brooklyn Eagle*, Oct. 20, 1878; *Memoirs*, II, 69–73.

    44. See *ibid.*, I, 32–34.
    45. See *PUSG*, 1, 334–35; *Richardson*, pp. 139–47; *Memoirs*, I, 210–11.
    46. See *PUSG*, 2, 6–8.
    47. See *ibid.*, pp. 81–82, 182–83.
    48. See *ibid.*, 4, 317–21, 331, 334–35, 412–16, 443–44; *Memoirs*, I, 316–28.
    49. See *PUSG*, 9, 521–23.
    50. See *ibid.*, 26, 132–35.
    51. See *ibid.*, 20, 121–23, 153–59.
    52. See *ibid.*, 21, 39, 78–83, 85–90, 122–27, 132–39, 145–49, 237–41, 281–301.
    53. Young "ventured to suggest that Mr. Sumner may have had a conscientious opposition to annexation—a feeling prevalent in New England." *New York Herald*, July 24, 1878.

To Gen. William T. Sherman

———

Copenhagen, Denmark.
July 7th 1878

MY DEAR GENERAL:

On leaving Paris and packing up and destroying letters I found one that I had written to you—but not completed—that I thought had been sent. But as there was nothing important in it I did not send it. There is nothing special to write about now only to elicit a further letter from you. Since my my departure from Paris I have visited Holland & North Germany. Holland is the most interesting country—and people—that I have yet seen. The people look prosperous, free and happy, and entertain an exalted opinion of our country and countrymen. I visited the three principle cities, The Hague, Rotterdam & Amsterdam and a few minor places. You have been through this country I think.—Since you were in Berlin[1] the city has improved and grown very much. It numbers now nearly one Million inhabitants. Much of the city looks modern. The Peace Congress being in session the city is very full of people although, so far as I could see, the latest news of its proceedings were obtained from the papers

from other Capitols, particularly London. Our new ~~m~~Minister[2] I
think will prove very popular but he will miss his second Secretary—Chapman Coleman—very much. Taylor told me that he did
not know how he was to get along without Coleman.[3] He is a thorough German & French scholar, has been with the legation a long
time and is acquainted with the duties and has studied law ~~law~~ which
fits him for duties which the legation has so much of in a country
where there are so many people living who claim American citizenship and retain yet property in, and business relations with, the
United States.

I arrived here this morning and have not yet been out of the
house to see anything of the city. On friday[4] I shall start for Christiania and after seeing something of Norway will visit Sweden, then
pass through St Petersburgh & Moscow, go through some of the
principle cities of Austria and then go to Spain. After that I will be
ready to settle down some place until it is time for me to go to my
Long Branch home—the only home I have—next Spring.

Very Truly yours
U. S. GRANT

GN. W. T. SHERMAN

ALS, DLC-William T. Sherman.

1. See *PUSG*, 23, 82–83.
2. Bayard Taylor, noted poet and author, assumed office as minister to Germany in
May. See letter to Michael John Cramer, June 29, 1878.
3. Chapman Coleman faced removal as 2nd secretary of legation, Berlin, because of
congressional budget cuts. For USG's interest in his family, see *PUSG*, 26, 156–58.
4. July 12.

To Edward F. Beale

Copenhagen, July 7th /78

MY DEAR GENERAL.

We arrived here this a m and found a mail for us, and with it your
welcome letter written after your return home.[1] I wish I could be
with you long enough to visit the farm and the colts. I look forward

to my return to the states with more pleasure than I do upon any visits yet proposed to countries I have not yet visited. Since seeing you
I have done up Holland and North Germany very thoroughly. The
Hollanders are a great people, good looking, industrious, free and
rich. North Germany is better than I expected to find, that is, more
productive. The people of course we know all about. We have them
by the tens of thousands at home. On friday we leave here to go
through Norway where I hope to do some fishing. After that we will
go through Sweden, Russia & Austria; after which we will take a run
through spain and then settle down for the winter, some place. In the
spring we will go home in time to be an early settler at our Long
Branch home—the only one we have.

Now that Congress has adjourned it is to be hoped that business
will revive, harmony prevail, and the newspapers become stupid for
the want of exciting, or sensational topics to write upon. I note what
you say about the prospects for /80, and hear the same thing from
other sources—letters and papers.[2] But with the revival of business
all this will be forgotten, and I am very sure it will be gratifying to
me. I have had all the honors, and would like to avoid the vexations
of political life for the future. Although not sensitive to abuse of opponents—who slander without regard to facts,—I do not care to be
a constant antagonist. I have children—and childrens children, in a
small way—who may be effected by these things, and I want to spare
them. I am very glad Phelps[3] has been continued as one of the Commissioners for the District. I know a more competant nor honest
officer could not have been selected. Then he is acquainted with the
duties. He has too, large executive duties abilities; with the strictest
integrity behind—qualities inculcated by both the Military & Naval
service. I received a letter from Phelps some time ago—more than a
month—which I am ashamed to say I have not answered. Give him
my kindest regards and say that I had got into a sort of rut in the way
of writing to a few persons,—ten or a dozen outside of my own family—and that while I intended writing to him I have always found
that when I do set down to write I have more letters to answer than
I can get through with.

Remember me to my Washington friends—and Long Branch

ones too, where I suppose this will find you—and give Mrs. Grant's love to Mrs. Beale & to Miss Emily, and my kindest regards.

Very Truly Yours

U. S. GRANT

GEN. E. F. BEALE.

ALS, DLC-Decatur House Papers. The Grants left Hamburg for Copenhagen on July 6, 1878. See Michael John Cramer to Secretary of State William M. Evarts, July 13, 1878, DNA, RG 59, Diplomatic Despatches, Denmark; *Pall Mall Gazette*, July 12, 16, 1878; *Young*, I, 436–40; *Julia Grant*, pp. 246–47.

1. See letter to Frederick Dent Grant, May 24, 1878; Gerald Thompson, *Edward F. Beale & The American West* (Albuquerque, 1983), p. 212.

2. See letter to Adam Badeau, June 7, 1878. On July 11, a correspondent had reported from Philadelphia. "Already, although the Presidential election is two years off, events are shaping for it, and a great deal of what the politicians are doing has that event in view. . . . On the Republican side, while President Hayes has the usual willingness to accept a second term which accompanies Presidential service in a first term, and Sherman, Blaine, Conkling, and others are hoping that the mantle may fall upon them, there is nothing more likely than that General Grant will be the candidate. His absence from the office has taught the public something. When he was there they were accustomed to some mistakes, but to a firm and honourable policy. They hated to have the 'third term,' for it was a violation of loved tradition in the Presidential office; but they some time ago began thinking that various things they were enduring might be worse even than a 'third term,' and that the country during the past two years has not presented a very creditable appearance to foreign observers, or in some respects a very comfortable condition for people at home. This feeling, without any particularly special encouragement, has been gradually growing, until it has assumed among the Republicans a pronounced form, which finds vent in every gathering of the party, and has made General Grant to-day the most popular American, and, if the Republican nominating convention for 1880 were now to meet, would give him the nomination in spite of the 'third term,' or any other objection that might be urged. Another strong point in Grant's favour is that he seems the only man under whom the party has any prospect of victory; and this to politicians is the chief essential in a candidate. In fact, the politicians already recognising this, appear to be preparing the way for his nomination, and there are outgivings in many quarters pointing to a concerted movement, when the time comes, for Grant's nomination. But his election is another matter, and though Tilden and Grant may oppose each other as the candidates of the two great parties, it is too soon now to predict the success of either. . . ." *The Times* (London), July 25, 1878. A related editorial analyzed congressional investigation of the 1876 presidential election and asserted widespread disillusionment with political leaders. ". . . In this state of feeling it is scarcely surprising that the name of General GRANT should be again brought forward prominently as the champion of the Republican party. The late PRESIDENT lost ground mainly because he refused to believe in the practicability of breaking down the convention and patronage systems. His successor was expressly chosen to break down those systems. But President HAYES can hardly be regarded as a reforming President, and the Republicans may well turn back upon the thought that they abandoned General GRANT without much advantage of any kind either to their party or their country. . . ." *Ibid.*, July 27, 1878. On July 27, Adam Badeau, consul gen., London, wrote to Gen. William T. Sherman characterizing this edi-

torial's remarks on USG as "far from agreeable to me. I cant see why having had all the honor, power, and consideration that the Presidency can give—the General should desire to return to politics, and submit once more to be the target of abuse and calumny. He says him self to me that his friends or some of them 'have designs for him that he does not share.' And I am sure he is sincere." ALS, DLC-William T. Sherman. Badeau had been trying to influence British press coverage. See Badeau to Sherman, July 23, 1878, *ibid.*

3. S. Ledyard Phelps. See *PUSG*, 25, 134–35; Alan Lessoff, *The Nation and Its City: Politics, "Corruption," and Progress in Washington, D. C., 1861–1902* (Baltimore, 1994), pp. 126–27.

To John A. Kasson

Copenhagen July 12th *1878*

HON. JOHN A. KASSON, U. S. MIN. PLEN. &C.

VIENNA, AUSTRIA,

DEAR SIR:

You were kind enough, during my visit to Rome early in the spring, to make enquiry about the probable time of my arrival in Vienna. Our Minister to Italy, Mr. Marsh, replied by letter, I believe, and I did by telegraph to the effect that I should make this Northern tour before going to Vienna, and that it would probably be late in the summer before I should reach there, but that I would let you know at as early a date as possible. I cannot give anything definite now about it, only state in general terms that my plan is to go from here to Christiania, spend a week or ten days in Norway, go from there to Stockholm and pass a week in Sweden, thence to St. Petersburgh & Moscow, stopping over a few days—say three—at each plance, thence proceeding to Vienna with probably a stop at Prague & Dresden on the way. If you should be absent from the Austrian Capitol at the time this programme would take me there I beg that you will not throw up a day of your leave on my account. On the contrary if you will drop me a line to any of the places I have mentioned as in the line of my travels, saying that you will be away, and about the time of your probable return I will make my visit to Vienna conform to your movements. It is my intention anyway to spend a few weeks quietly at some watering place in Southern Germany or in Switzerland when I get through this Northern trip and I could do it just as well before going to Vienna as afterwards.

I shall be very much pleased to hear from you at Christiania or Stockholm.

Very Truly yours
U. S. Grant

ALS, IaHA. See *PUSG*, 24, 299.

On July 16, 1878, a correspondent condensed an interview USG gave a Norwegian reporter concerning his travels. "The Prince Imperial was at Copenhagen at the same time as I was there, but I did not feel inclined to call upon the heir of the Bonapartes. I don't like the family. No doubt I admire the genius of Napoleon I.; but as for Napoleon III., I think he abused in a shameful manner the confidence placed in him by the French people when they elected him to be the President of the Republic and he founded the Empire; and, later, his unnecessary wars brought shame and ruin on his country." Evaluating U.S. politics, USG observed. "Some months ago it looked rather black, as the Socialist elements then apparently enjoyed a strong and dangerous organization, to oppose which one wanted the necessary armed force; but as all the classes who are better off have now united against the agitation, it will result in the failure of the agitators, who are mostly composed of Germans, French, and Irishmen, while the real Yankee population hold aloof from the movement. . . ." *Pall Mall Gazette*, July 19, 1878.

To Adam Badeau

———

St. Petersburg,
~~Ju~~ Aug. 4th /78

My Dear General.

I have your letters of July the 25th & 29th with Porters enclosed. I am sorry that the Harpers are not willing to take your book. Porter is probably the best man to manage the affair, and to see that it is got out by the best publishers, whether the Appletons, now that they have it, or other parties.[1]

I have but little to say only that my receptions everywhere since leaving Paris have been very flattering. Through Norway,[2] Sweden[3] & Finland[4] it was by all the people and as hearty, with as much cheering, as you ever saw in the states or in England. Here, to my surprise somewhat, I have been received by the officials not only with courticy but with warmth. Before my arrival Gottchicow—

who is at his country place near the Emperor—requested our Minister[5] to inform him the moment I arrived. He did so and received a reply within a few hours saying that the Emperor would receive me on the following friday,[6] at 1 pm. At the Station on friday we found the royal rooms thrown open for us to pass through to the track, an elegant Salon car in reserve for us—the Minister and myself—and at the close of the rail-road journey the same attention so far as rooms at the station are concerned, and two imperial carriages awaiting us to take us to the palace. At the interview the Emperor met me at the door, or near to it, and took me by the hand in the most cordial manner, and showed me to a seat. We had a conversation in the most familiar style of near half an hour.[7] I mention this because, you know, we had intimations before that such would not be my reception. Everything has been most agreeable and you will probably read fuller particulars hereafter.

I go from here to Moscow on wednesday next,[8] and from there to Austria where my address will be with the legation for a month.

yours Truly
U. S. GRANT

ALS, Horace Porter Mende, Zurich, Switzerland. On Aug. 18, 1878, Adam Badeau, consul gen., London, wrote to Horace Porter and enclosed USG's letter. AL (initialed), ICN.

1. D. Appleton & Co. had published Volume I of Badeau's *Military History of Ulysses S. Grant* and also published the two concluding volumes. See *PUSG*, 24, 169–70.

2. A Chicago newspaper translated a Norwegian reporter's account of USG's arrival in Norway on July 13. "Having been notified of the ex-President's expected arrival, the American Consul at Christiania, Mr. Gerhard Gade, went down the fiord to meet the distinguished guest. . . . Having exchanged courtesies, the Consul introduced Mr. Balling to Gen. and Mrs. Grant. The General grasped Mr. Balling by the hand, and shook it cordially, and then said: 'I don't know if I've met you before; still your face seems familiar.' Having been made acquainted with the fact that Mr. Balling was with him during the War, the General was still more pleased, and expressed great satisfaction at the unexpected meeting. The journey from Horten to Christiania lasted but a few hours. The General and wife were both on deck, . . . Several newspaper-men boarded the steamer Christiania upon its arrival at Horten, and 'interviewed' the General. They found him very pleasant and communicative. He praised the Norwegian people, whom, he stated, he had lived among and associated with a number of years. There were thousands and thousands of them in the Northwestern States. They were thrifty and enterprising, and a very honest people. . . ." *Chicago Tribune*, Aug. 11, 1878. See *Young*, I, 441–57; *Julia Grant*, pp. 247–49; Gerhard Gade to Secretary of State Hamilton Fish, May 28, 1869, and related papers, DNA, RG 59, Letters of Application and Recommendation; Gade, "General Grant in Norway," *The American-Scandinavian Review*, XXI, 5 (May, 1933), 233–40. For Ole Peter Hansen Balling, see *PUSG*, 24, 443–44.

Another newspaper reported on a letter from USG to a Philadelphia friend, dated Christiania, Norway, July 15, and received Aug. 8. ". . . The epistle is characteristic of the writer in its brevity. It covers but three pages of small note paper, and contains a vast deal of information as to the General's movements. In the letter the ex-President details his movements in the cities of Hamburg and the other places which the cable has notified us that he had visited. Then it goes on to say that the party arrived at Christiana on the 13th of July, and that nearly a week had been spent in Copenhagen. Holland is spoken of as a beautiful country. One week from the 15th of July the General was to proceed to Stockholm, thence to St. Petersburg, passing into Austria about the 5th of August. From this country he desires to proceed to some watering place where he will meet a prominent Philadelphia gentleman, now sojourning in Europe, and will spend four or five weeks at the place the latter selects. . . . The Record is at liberty to state that Ex-President Grant will, if he adheres to his present resolution, make a tour of the world before he returns to America, and that the winter months will be spent in India and China. Private letters state that the General's idea is to learn the methods and manners of all the people on the face of the globe. . . ." *Philadelphia Record,* Aug. 9, 1878.

3. On July 29, John L. Stevens, U.S. minister, Stockholm, reported to Secretary of State William M. Evarts on USG's visit. ALS, DNA, RG 59, Diplomatic Despatches, Sweden and Norway. *Foreign Relations, 1878,* pp. 823–24. See *Young,* I, 457–64.

4. On July 27, USG left Stockholm on a steamer for St. Petersburg and stopped briefly at Helsinki. See *ibid.,* pp. 465–67; *Julia Grant,* pp. 249–51.

5. Edwin W. Stoughton, New York City lawyer and Republican stalwart during the 1876 presidential controversy, reluctantly accepted appointment as minister to Russia. Stoughton wanted to be minister to Great Britain, an appointment USG had considered late in his presidency. See Note, May 22, 1876; Stoughton to James A. Garfield, March 12, Oct. 13, 1877, DLC-James A. Garfield.

6. Aug. 2, 1878.

7. Tsar Alexander II of Russia commented on USG's long tour and asked many questions about Indian policy and warfare. See *New York Herald,* Aug. 18, 1878; *Young,* I, 468.

8. Aug. 7.

To Ulysses S. Grant, Jr.

———

St. Petersburg, Russia
August 4th /78

Dear Buck,

We have now been here five days. The weather has been beautiful and I have seen St Petersburg very thoroughly. It is a beautiful city. My reception by the Emperor, and all the authorities, has been most cordial and agreeable. The Emperor makes the impression of being a very superior man, and one who will look to the best intersts of his people. Through the Scandinavian countries,—Denmark,[1]

Norway, Sweden and Finland—my reception by the people was much like what you have seen at home soon after the war. It was by the people at every place and was most enthusiastic, with loud cheering &c.

We go from here to Moscow on the 8th and will be in, or near, Vienna about the 15th. We will rest there for a month and go on to Spain & Portugal. After that we will settle down for the winter in the south of France or Italy, or go eastward until we get home.

If you think it advisable you may sell my elevated rail-road stock. But do not do so without consulting Porter or Pullman o[r] both. It may be very fine stock.[2] Watch my Yellow Jacket stock[3] but do not sell that unless they strike rich ore and begin to pay dividends. In such case it will probably go up to a high figure which would justify realizing without waiting.

Look after Jesse and see that he attends to his studies[4] and that he lives within his $150 00 pr. month, which is all that I can afford, and until I can realize on real estate or my mining stock ~~and~~ I cannot do for him what I did for Fred and you.

Tell Gov. Fish that I have received his very welcome letter and will write to him as soon as I reach Vienna.[5] We met Ham. Fish[6] in Christiania. He seemed to be enjoying his Northern trip very much, and was looking very well.

Affectionatily yours
U. S. GRANT

U. S. GRANT JR.

ALS, Austin B. McLogan, Flint, Mich. See previous letter.

1. See letter to Edward F. Beale, July 7, 1878.
2. See letter to Ulysses S. Grant, Jr., April 11, 1877.
3. See letter to Ulysses S. Grant, Jr., [*June 29, 1878*].
4. Jesse Root Grant, Jr., studied law with his brother in New York City.
5. See letter to Hamilton Fish, Aug. 22, 1878.
6. Born in 1849, Hamilton Fish, Jr., served as his father's private secretary (1869–71), graduated from Columbia Law School (1873), and entered the N. Y. assembly (1874).

To Pierson H. Bristow et al.

St. Petersburg, Russia, Aug. 5. [*1878*]
P. H. Bristow, G. L. Godfrey and E. R. Hutchins, Committee: Dear
Sirs—I am just in receipt of your invitation for the 4th, 5th, and 6th
of September, to attend a Soldiers and Sailors' Reunion, to be held in
Des Moines on those dates. While it is only a county organization,
as your invitation states, it would be none the less pleasant for me
to attend if I were in a region round about there at the time. But
my present plans will separate us at the time of the Reunion wider
than the remotest States are from each other. It is not my purpose
to return home until next year. But with a lively recollection of a
Soldiers' Reunion in Des Moines, a few years since,[1] I hope you will
have a more pleasant gathering and that in reciting the past you will
have nothing to regret, either in the conduct of Iowa troops during the years of trials they went through, nor of their compatriots
from other States, who enlisted in the same cause. They suffered in
a sacred cause and the fruits of their sufferings must never be lost.
Regretting that I cannot be with you in September next, and repeating the wish that you will have a pleasant reunion, I am, with great
respect, your obedient servant,

U. S. Grant.

Iowa State Register (Des Moines), Sept. 7, 1878. Pierson H. Bristow, born in 1846, served
as corporal, 45th Iowa. George L. Godfrey served as 2nd lt., 2nd Iowa, and lt. col., 1st Ala.
Cav. After practicing law in Des Moines, he received appointments as land office receiver
(1869–76) and asst. district attorney. Edward R. Hutchins studied at Williams College
and served as both an army and navy surgeon. After practicing medicine in Philadelphia (1866–70), he moved to Iowa. See Hutchins, comp., *The War of the 'Sixties* (New York,
1912). On July 17, 1878, Bristow *et al.*, Des Moines, issued a circular. "The Soldiers and
Sailors' Association of Polk County hold their annual reunion September 4th, 5th and 6th.
It belongs not simply to this county, but it is hoped that from all over the State those that
fought for the Nation's honor when it was in peril will pitch their tents with us again, and
that these days of encampment may be those in which old ties may be more strongly ce-
mented, new ones formed, and the reminiscences of sabre and cutlass, of musket and cannon, of land and sea, shall be happily freshened in our minds. The last Congress passed a
bill by which ample lodging in tents will be afforded for all that come. We expect to have
a grand good time, and want you to be with us. We promise you a soldierly welcome: Will
you not come?" *Iowa State Register* (Des Moines), July 17, 1878.

1. See *PUSG*, 26, 342–51.

To Daniel Ammen

———

ST. PETERSBURG, RUSSIA, Aug. 13th, 1878.

MY DEAR ADMIRAL,—

After spending two days at this place I went to Moscow, where I stayed five days,[1] and returned this noon. On arrival found a large mail, in which was one from you, enclosing a paragraph about Murphy's bankruptcy[2] and my losses in real estate. So far as I am concerned, there is not one word of truth in the statement. I never owned or purchased a piece of real estate in New York City in my life. I never owned any property in New Jersey—except the two houses at Long Branch which I now own—in my life. I never held a piece of property in my life, that I remember of, on which I owed anything. What I have—not much—is paid for. I have sold nothing to pay up debts. My farming experience in Missouri, while so far away myself, was expensive, and I sold out, and gave away stock, and rented the farm. That was several years ago.[3] Had I gone out of office at the end of four years, when my salary was twenty-five thousand dollars a year, I would have been compelled to sell something—quite an amount—to have carried me out of Washington. But with my private income and increased salary,[4] I came out at the end of eight years free from debt and without having incurred any loss anywhere in speculation. I am very sorry to hear what you say about ____. I always thought well of him. In fact, I could never bear to think illy of any one whom I had selected for responsible positions, unless proven guilty. Calumny has been so rife since the war that it is unsafe to be prejudiced by what you see in partisan papers. But we will talk this matter over within a year.

I do not remember where my last letter to you was from. Since leaving Paris, however, I have travelled through Holland, North Germany, Denmark, Sweden, Finland, and a portion of Russia. The New York *Herald*, which comes by the same mail as your letter, gives an account of a portion of my visit to Germany. The statement is given very correctly, though from accounts I see in other papers the correspondent has fallen into some errors in regard to what I said

about military matters.[5] I never said, for instance, that my losses
from the Rapidan to the James River, including killed, wounded, and
missing, was less than forty thousand; that thirty-nine thousand
would cover the whole. What I did say was that since Taylor's and
Welles' letters,[6] the public seem to have fallen into the idea that I lost
one hundred thousand men in getting to the south side of the James,
where I could have gone by boat, without loss, and ignore the fact
that Lee sustained any loss; that while the returns given after battle,
when every captain, colonel, and brigade commander would like
to see our aggregate loss as small as possible, he did not wish to diminish his importance in the fray by reducing his own losses: in fact,
the greater his "killed and wounded and missing," the more his command might have been considered to have been hotly engaged. In
this way every man not at the first roll-call after an engagement was
reported in one of the above categories. In this way many men have
been reported wounded two, three, or four times, in different engagements, but never lost a day, and now live to tell this honorable
experience. In the same way many men are missing after an engagement, some turning up afterwards for duty and some as prisoners in
the hands of the enemy. We captured and buried more of their men
than they claim to have lost. I stated as my recollection that our actual losses before crossing the James River in actual killed or totally
disabled was less than forty thousand,—probably thirty-nine thousand would cover it, but that Badeau's forthcoming book, which was
taken from actual records, would show the figures with the greatest
attainable accuracy. But it is only just to the *Herald* correspondent to
say that I have not seen his letter, but only the criticisms in the New
York *World*.[7] Possibly he has been correct in his statement. I have
seen his Berlin letter—sent, I think, from Hamburg—giving an account of the receptions, dinners, reviews, Bismark conference, etc.,
and they are correctly stated.[8] There might be a question about the
propriety of some things stated, but they are nevertheless correct so
far as my memory could verify them. I hope I will find the other letter equally correct.

I have been very much pleased with the people of Holland, Denmark, Norway, Sweden, and Finland. They are a free, intelligent,

honest, and industrious people. My reception among them was the most cordial, as indeed it has been everywhere. Here, in Russia, I have been surprised at the cordiality; though there has always existed a traditional friendship between the two countries.

To-morrow we start for Warsaw; from thence to Vienna. We will rest in Austria until about the right season for visiting Spain and Portugal. These latter states "done up," I will have been in every country in Europe, in Egypt, and Africa, and a little bit of Syria and Asia Minor, in Asia; not much for an "old tar," but a good deal for a "landsman."

I am glad that Mrs. Ammen is to keep you at home for the future. I believe your determination to retire was a wise one. If you had been an "old fogy," with a family of children all over thirty, I can see why you might want to be retained on the active list. But with five young children,—no telling how many to follow,—and the retirement being entirely voluntary, I look upon your course in the matter as entirely wise.[9] I have had a number of letters from you since my last, and am always glad to receive them. Mrs. Grant sends her love to Mrs. Ammen and the children. Please present my regards also.

Yours very truly,

U. S. GRANT.

I forgot that I wrote to you from here before going to Moscow.

Daniel Ammen, *The Old Navy and the New* (Philadelphia, 1891), pp. 542–43.

1. See *Young*, I, 482–93; *Julia Grant*, pp. 253–54.
2. In June, 1878, Thomas Murphy, former collector of customs, New York City, assigned his assets to satisfy creditors. On Aug. 30, he registered for voluntary bankruptcy, declaring $726,000 in liabilities. See *New York Herald*, Aug. 31, 1878; *St. Louis Globe-Democrat*, Sept. 6, 1878.
3. See *PUSG*, 26, 299, 301.
4. See *ibid.*, 24, 10–12.
5. See Interview, July 6, 1878.
6. See letter to John Russell Young, April 7, 1878.
7. On July 25, this newspaper editorialized that "we doubt the propriety of publishing all the careless gossip of a man whose lightest word of censure may affect the reputation of others when he speaks of the events of the war in which he commanded. That he is capable of error where he ought to be surest is shown in his own account of how easily he was taken in by a newspaper correspondent's criticism of General Sherman's Memoirs, when, through the skilful manipulation of a few documents, he lost confidence in his friend and comrade and became confused in his memory of the events which he was supposed to

have controlled. In his narrative of incidents, and in his statement of figures especially, if not in his estimate of men, he is liable to be mistaken, removed as he is from books of reference and from the companionship of those whose recollection might serve to test the accuracy of his own. . . ." *New York World*, July 25, 1878. This editorial specifically criticized USG's remarks on Fort Donelson, Maj. Gen. Gouverneur K. Warren at the battle of the Crater, casualties in the Va. campaign, and the relative strength of the Union and Confederate armies. Subsequent editorials denounced USG's high estimate of Joseph E. Johnston's generalship, attacked USG's statements on Gen. William T. Sherman's memoirs, and questioned the decision to promote Maj. Gen. Philip H. Sheridan to lt. gen. over Maj. Gen. George G. Meade. *Ibid.*, July 27, Aug. 2, 1878.

8. See *New York Herald*, July 20, 1878; conversation with Otto von Bismarck, [*June 30, 1878*].

9. Rear Admiral Daniel Ammen had retired as of June 4. See letter to Daniel Ammen, Aug. [26], 1877.

To Adam Badeau

Vienna, Austria.
Aug. 22d 1878.

My Dear General.

I have your letter of the 17th with chapter enclosed, which I have read and have no comments to make upon. it.—I agree with you in the impropriety of the publication of my "table talk," upon Military or other matters. There is not a word I said which was intended for publication or even to be taken down. But traveling together as long as Young & I did conversation naturally covered a good many subjects Civil & Military. Many things I said explained matters—or put a new light upon them—to Young, so that he noted them down. He wrote them out afterward and gave me the manuscript to read—about twice as much as is published. I put it in my trunk and forgot it for several months. I afterwards read it and found it in the main correct errasing however all relating to Civil Administration.[1] Young makes an error in stating my losses from the Rapid Ann to the James river which I did not notice in the Manuscript. I did not say that about 39.000 would cover my losses in killed, wounded & missin[g.] What I did say was that Welle[s,] Taylor &c. would soon have it pass into history that we had a 100 000 men killed in getting to the James river, where we could have gone by boat, without loss, and ignoring the fact that Lee sustained any loss whatever. ~~But that your~~ That 40.000, I thought about 39.000,—would cover such losses, but that the reports from time to time would show a much greater loss. I explained that after a battle every Capt. Col. & Brigade commander liked to show his own losses as large as possible. Consequently we had a full report of every man who had a scratch as wounded. Many men would be reported before we got to the end of the Campaign, in that category, two, three or more times, yet never lost any time. In the same way many men would be reported missing who would afterward turn up. Others had fallen into the hands of the enemy, unhurt, and would be exchanged for. I made a full statement of how these reports were made up. Young though[t] he was doing right in this publication, and thinks now that he has done me good service. I do not think it will do any harm, but I wil[l] caution him for the future[.] I have no idea now of making the tour around the world, but will go back home in the spring. We will stay in Austria through September and then go to Spain and probably Portugal. I will then have seen every country in Europe and wil[l] be ready to set down for the Winter. Mrs Grant joins me in kindes[t] regards.

Very Truly yours
U. S. GRANT

GN. A. BADEAU.

ALS, Munson-Williams-Proctor Institute, Utica, N. Y.

1. See Interview, July 6, 1878. On Feb. 1 (touring the Nile) and June 9 (in Paris), 1878, John Russell Young wrote in his diary. ". . . Have a long talk with the General who does not retire until about midnight.—He tells me many stories about the war, and says he will read my interview at sea, and if he can approve it and allow me to print." ". . . Called & saw the Gen. He returned me my *MSS.* interview but not all of it. Marked out many parts as not discreet. Received *Herald* with my interview sent May 13.—Gen. said it was admirable.—He read me a letter from Sherman saying the same thing. . . ." DLC-John Russell Young. See *ibid.,* Jan. 30, Feb. 19, 1878; following letter; Interview, May 9, 1878.

To Hamilton Fish

Vienna Austria,
Aug. 22d 1878

MY DEAR GOVERNOR:

Your very welcome letter of the 12th of July reached me in St. Petersburg, where I enjoyed a visit of about two weeks,[1] very much. While in Berlin Gortchacoff expressed a great desire to see me, but his physical condition was such at the time—from goute—that he could not walk. I went therefore to see him, and had a long pleasant talk. He asked me about my proposed visit to Russia, and seemed to regret that he would n[ot] be there when I arrived;—I expecte[d] at that time to reach St. Peters[burg] some three weeks early than I did—but said I would meet with a most hearty reception. Whether felt or not the reception was mos[t] cordial in appearance. Our Ministe[r] was requested days before my arrival to notify the Prime Minister the very moment I got there. He did so an[d] in two hours after—although the Minister, Gortchacoff, lived some twenty miles o[ut] by rail—an answer was sent fixing the time for an audience with t[he] Emperor. When I called the Emper[or] approached me and taking me by the hand led me to a seat after which we had a talk of some twen[ty] minuets or more. I know thi[s] is an uninteresting subject to write about, but I tell you because we both had serious apprehensions that the case would be quite different. There is no doubt but that the United States stands very high in the estimation of the Russians, from the Emperor down. They fully expect some day to have their aid in the settlement of European matters, which they think further from a satisfactory and peace inspiring solution than before the Berlin Congress met.

I read all the New York papers regularly and get slips from papers from all parts of the U. States, good & bad, abusive & commenditory. I am very sorry Young published what he calls our table talk.[2] There is not one word in it which was said with a view of its publication or even of its being taken down. Mr. Young traveled with us up the Nile & on the Mediterranean and during so many weeks much was said upon war matters &c. He told me afterwards that he was so much interested in many things I said that he had taken them down from time to time, with as much accuracy as he could, for future reference though he did not know that he should ever publish it. He handed me the manuscript—enough of it to fill two pages of the Herald—to read. I put it in my trunk and forgot all about it for several months, until after Jesse had gone back to the United States. I then looked for it but could not find it. I supposed it had been packed in Jesse's trunk. But further searc[h] produced the documents, which I read over hurriedly and struck off a large part relating more particularly to my civil administration.[3] The balance was substantially correct except in relation to looses in the Campaign from the Rapid Ann to the James river. I said that Welles & Taylor, and other writers would soon have it pass into history that we had a 100000 men killed in that Campaign to reach a point which could have been easily reached, by boat, without loss, and ignoring the fact that Lee sustained any losses during this time; that 40.000—I thought about 39000—would cover such losses; but that Badeau's book would give the facts with the greatest attainable accuracy. I said our reports from time to time of killed, wounded & missing would show a much greater loss. But of the missing reported many would turn up in a day or two, many again would be found in the hands of the enemy and ~~were~~ would afterward be exchanged for, and many again were slightly wounded but not disabled from duty. It would often happen that the same man would be reported in different engagements, wounded two, three and sometimes as much as six times yet lives to tell of his honorable scars.

I met Hamilton the day before my audience with the King of Sweden & Norway. The King spoke of hearing that he was in Christiania and desired to have him meet me at dinner at the Palace on the following day. But Hamilton & his companions had gone on their excursion. I know it must have been pleasant. The four days excursion I took in Norway was very enjoyable. It is a picturesque country and there are no finer, more honest and simple people than the Norwegian; infact you might include all the Scandinavians. We have now been several days in Vienna. My audience & dinner with the Emperor is over. We are the guests of our Minister, Mr Kasson.[4] Early next week we will go some place in the mountains and take a months rest. After that we go to spain & Portugal. I will then have visited every country in Europe and will be ready to go home. Having no winter quarters in the United States however, I will defer my departure until time to go to my Long Branch house next Summer. I can then fix winter quarters—probably my Galena house—by the end of the season.

Mrs. Grant sends much love to Mrs. Fish, and promises me that she will write to her soon. please present my kindest regards also.

Very Truly Yours

U. S. Grant

Hon. Hamilton Fish

P. S. I am quite ready to believe that you have been working quite hard as a "farm laborer" and that some days you may earn as much as 25 cts. by your labor, and that your hands are blistered, your face bronzed &c. but it taxes my credulity to much when you say you would not *swop* your present position even for a place in Mr. Hayes Cabinet. You express your contentment with your present lot however very forcibly and I take it the expression means that and nothing more. Do you suppose either Schurz or Evart would fully credit your statement? But I shall keep it a profound secret. I too am entirely content with my present lot. But I do not know what the offer of such a position as you speak of might effect. The President declining to give me the Berlin Mission which Halstead, of the Cincinnati Commercial, urged so strongly upon him might prevent me from accepting any other position under this administration.[5] Then too I should object to association with Schurz. I make up my mind the position will not be offered to either of us, and it is an easy matter to decline what we know we cannot have.

ALS, DLC-Hamilton Fish. On July 12, 1878, Hamilton Fish wrote to USG. "I need not confess that I am a bad Correspondent, for, as the Frenchmen say, 'that goes without telling'—but I have been quiet,—out of the world, had nothing to tell, that you did not know—& had two pretty bad turns of illness during the winter & spring, of some three or four weeks each, & for the last two months [*now*] (since I have been here in the Country) have been looking after my farm playing farmer (dont laugh) & here in 'hay-time' have got my hands pretty well blistered, & my skin burnt, with *actual* work in the fields—pretty well, this you will say for an old fellur! but notwithstanding the smarting & the inconvenience of thumbs, fingers, & palms of the hands being blistered & stiff, so even as to keep me awake at nights. I am well, & enjoy the exercise, & would not exchange for a place in Mr Hayes Cabinet—There may be a profundity of wisdom in the present Administration, that is beyond the capacity of my plumb & line to fathom—but, so far as my limited vision can reach, the best that can be said of it, is that it may be governed by that kind of 'intentions' with which a certain very hot & undesirable place, is said to be paved—If there be any thing further to be done to weaken & to distract the Republican party, it is safe to assume that the Administration will do it—To day we hear of the removal of Arthur & Cornell from the N. Y. Custom House. The blow is aimed, ostensibly (though not avowedly) at Conklin & through him at Grant. It will make Conklins friends more earnest, but will render less easy, any union within the Republican ranks, on the Choice of Senator—Potters investigation, was tending to the conciliation of the Republicans: & just at that point, with the blundring that has marred its whole career, the Administration drives in this wedge of discord. If the power & patronage of the N. Y. Custom House be not now used to control the nominations, & elections to the NY Assembly this Autumn, it will not be, for want of desire, & intent: & it will be the first occasion of the kind under this Administration— where profession & practice have been in accord—The Administration may secure the Election of a Democratic Senator from New York—it may be able to defeat Conklins re- election—it will be powerless to elect or to aid in the election of a Republican other than Conklin unless with Conklins assent & this is not likely to be had—They found fault with you, for what they called *'personal'* appointments—but Hayes would give you ten & beat you—The interference of Senators & Members of Congress with the appointments of Govt was the cardinal point of objection in the professed creed of this Administration; & it has been more faithfully carried out than any other of ~~their~~ its declaredations ~~doctrines~~, for they do exclude from influence, all real Republicans, but Aleck Stephens (who lives in the *Newspapers*) & Gordon, & Democratic Senators & Representatives have the ear of the appointing power, & get ~~what~~ all that they ~~all~~ ask. Consistency, & gratitude, & fidelity to friends, no doubt, are virtues—probably they are theoretically recognized as such by all men, but practically Govr Hayes & his f[ri]ends (I do not know that he has friends) his toadies, & tuft-hunters subordinate them, to the declared intention, of 'reforming the many abuses of the last Administration.' Poor Hayes, has (I believe without knowing how he did it, & probably without, yet, even, knowing that he has done it,) given himself up, 'body & breeches' to the control of the most embittered hostility, of the most disappointed of the 'Liberals' toward 'Grant' & 'Grantism'—he is amiable, I believe, but weak as dish water, & that, when ['——']. It is delightful to your friends to observe the dignity, & *reticence*, which, under many provocations, you observe toward this Administration—It was only yesterday that I was in one of the neighboring [—] Counties, to the north of this, & heard from some, who at times, were a little critical of your Administration, warm contrasts in its favour, coupled with hopes for its restoration, & admiration of your generous abstinence from comment, or complaint—My Dear General, while you have reason to be gratified with your receptions abroad, ~~you are not forgotten by friends~~ you have as much fuller affection with which you are remembered & spoken of at home, ~~in fact,~~ your friends I think ~~they~~ are more numerous today, than when you left. I suppose you now to be in Denmark, or Sweden, & envy you the Cool weather which I hope ~~that~~ you are enjoying— We have had nearly three weeks of *excessively* ~~hot~~ heat ~~weather~~. May I venture to express the hope that you will not go to Russia, unless *specially* invited, in the name of the Emperor. Gortchacoff, has not forgiven the dismissal of his pet, that scamp Catacazy, & he persuades the Emperor to believe, that you did not sufficienty appreciate the visit, of the Grand Duke Alexis & will not lose the opportunity of doing something disagreeable, either by omission, or commission, if you go within his jurisdiction. I imagine that you may find it agreeable & convenient to prolong your visit, for another winter, although we shall all be glad to welcome your return, there may [be] reasons why your prolonged absence, may be compensated, by its consequences. We had a visit, a short time since from Ulysses, who is looking well, & is the same gentle generous unaffected character that he has always been. Judge Taft & wife passed a day with us, on their way to New Haven, to the Commencement, where his son graduated with high honours. His other son (who was married & visited Washington a couple of years since) has been unfortunately affected, with a mental derangement. The Judge writes to me however, that he exhibits marked evidence of improvement, & he entertains strong hopes of his restoration. Whitehorne, & the Administration have again been after Robeson, who, h[owever,] boldly defies them, & declares his readiness, & ability, to meet all their charges and to justify all that they ~~charg~~ complain of. Chandler (Zach) seems to be putting himself in the field, for the Senatorial contest in Michigan, & to be fully hopeful. He is full of fight, & of pluck, & is true to his friends. Pierrepont writes me from London of the honours conferred upon him at Oxford, & is evidently much pleased with the 'Scarlet gown' & the 'Doctorate of Laws'—Sumner's literary Executor (Pierce) has an article in the last North American, ostensibly defending Sumner, but really abusing me—he is too wise to direct his abuse directly against you, it is safer to assail me—Possibly I may reply to him. My son Hamilton left us about a fortnight since, to visit Denmark & Sweden. I hope that he may be fortunate enough to meet you— Pray present my very kindest regards to Mrs Grant, to whom as to you, my wife desires to be most affectionately rembered." AL (press), *ibid.* See *PUSG,* 22, 130–33, 147–52.

On July 20, Fish, Sea Girt, N. J., spoke to a reporter concerning USG's presidential ambitions. ". . . I know—nobody could know it better, for to no one did he speak on the subject more unreservedly and intimately—that when Grant's second nomination was broached he did not desire it. He wanted to go back to St. Louis, on his farm. . . . The newspapers and the men who started the movement wanted to drive Grant into declaring that he would not accept what had never been offered to him, and General Grant is not a man to be driven into anything. He would not be driven—that was all. He did not desire his third nomination, as he had not wished his second. . . . I am in constant correspondence with General Grant, and only a few weeks ago I received a letter from him in which he tells me how much more he is enjoying the latter part of his trip, in which he has not been delayed so much with answering speeches in non-English speaking countries. I know, from all his letters, that he has never taken these attentions in any other light than as a compliment to his country. He knows that they are meant not so much for himself as for the country he represents. . . . Grant is no fool, and he who takes him for one makes a sad mistake. . . ." *New York Herald,* July 22, 1878. See letter to Adam Badeau, June 7, 1878.

1. See letter to Adam Badeau, Aug. 4, 1878; *Young,* I, 467 82; *Julia Grant,* pp. 251–53.
2. See Interview, July 6, 1878.
3. See preceding letter.
4. On Aug. 27, John A. Kasson, U.S. minister, Vienna, wrote to Secretary of State William M. Evarts reporting USG's visit, including his cordial reception by Emperor Francis Joseph I of Austria and the unwillingness of ambassadors "to yield precedence to an Ex-President of the United States,—a fact which, at a dinner given in his honor at a Legation of the United States, necessarily deprived both himself and them of the pleasure of meeting on that occasion." LS, DNA, RG 59, Diplomatic Despatches, Austria. *Foreign Relations, 1878,* p. 52. In 1885, Kasson recalled USG's conversational remarks. "I entered the White House as President without any previous experience either in civil or political life. I thought I could run the government of the United States, as I did the staff of my

army. It was my mistake, and it led me into other mistakes." Praised for his "veto of the Inflation bill" in 1874, USG observed. "I will tell you about that. I had watched the progress of the debate, but declined whenever it was a subject of conversation to express any opinion upon the merits of the bill. After it was passed and came to my hands, many influential members of the Senate and House came to me to discuss it and to urge my approval of it. So also many Senators and members on the other side opposed it, and hoped for its disapproval. I told none of them what my inclination on the subject was, nor did I bring it to the attention of the Cabinet for several days. Final action had to be taken within the constitutional period. I believed at first that I could approve the bill upon the construction that I gave to its terms. I thought it admitted of a construction which would obviate the evil effects which were apprehended from its passing, and that my approval could be accompanied by a message to Congress giving the grounds of that approval upon the interpretation of the bill to which I have referred. After finishing the draft of this message I read it over, and then said to myself, 'That is not my real, honest opinion. I am not convinced of the rightfulness of this view; it is not sincere.' I took the draft, tore it in pieces, and threw it in the waste basket. I then sat down and wrote the veto message to which you have referred, and the next morning, for the first time, read it to my Cabinet, and let them know what my action was on the subject." Kasson also discussed USG's meeting with Emperor William I and Chancellor Otto von Bismarck of Germany. *New York Tribune*, Sept. 20, 1885. See *PUSG*, 25, 65–81; letter to Julia Dent Grant, Sept. 11, 1878; Jacques Hartog to John Russell Young, Aug. 24, 1878, DLC-John Russell Young; *New York Herald*, Aug. 25, 1878; *Young*, I, 496–500; *Julia Grant*, p. 254; Egon Caesar Conte Corti, *Mensch und Herrscher: Wege und Schicksale Kaiser Franz Josephs I.* . . . (Graz, Austria, 1952), p. 537; Edward Younger, *John A. Kasson: Politics and Diplomacy from Lincoln to McKinley* (Iowa City, 1955), pp. 280–81.

5. After an unprofitable alliance with the Liberal Republicans in 1872, Murat Halstead, influential editor of the *Cincinnati Commercial*, supported Rutherford B. Hayes and emerged as an important presidential advisor.

Probably in early Jan., 1879, Halstead spoke to a reporter concerning USG's political career, starting at the close of the Civil War, when "at once the politicians and the managers of the party began coquetting and flattering him in order to gain control of him and use him for their own purposes. Grant was not much of a politician then; he is a better one now; and the result was that he fell into their hands. They were thus enabled to make use of him to carry out their schemes, and thus help to make themselves money. . . . I saw the way he was being run by these men was subversive of good government, and for that reason I opposed his re-election,   Grant is not a thief, but the ring of whiskey thieves and the other corrupt rings that surrounded him brought him into disrepute. . . . That ring influence was traceable through both of Grant's administrations, though in his second term he had learned more of politicians, and was consequently better able to control it and keep it under. Still it continued to exist, and when Grant's second term was about to expire I used what influence I had to help Bristow as being the one who, most of all men in that party, had shown a determination to fight these influences and stand up for honesty in the government. . . . I can say of my own personal knowledge that he does'nt want to be President again. I consider it doubtful if he could be if he wanted to, but I know he does not want it. I was in Paris last summer while he was there, and when Marshal MacMahon addressed him as the Field Marshal of the United States he struck a chord in Grant's vanity, or ambition rather. If Congress would pass a law by which he could be made Field Marshal, giving him a salary of $50,000, and then allow him to retire on half pay with the honorary title and $25,000 a year, the summit of his ambition would be reached. There are members of his family who want him to be President again, and many of his adherents, his old personal friends, believe that he should be in order to give us what they call a strong government. And this brings me to speak of some of Grant's friends who are not associated with these ring movements I first alluded to. Not all his friends are corrupt. He has many in Philadelphia and New York, bankers and men of great wealth, who, out of the personal regard they hold for him, desire him to receive this further honor." Halstead then identified George W. Childs and Anthony J. Drexel and also "the Seligmans and other capitalists whose connections are largely in Europe. They are abroad a great deal, and, being close observers of events there, they think they forsee the cloud of Communism threatening our own country. This leads them to ask for a strong government and naturally to look to Grant for it; so that their fears are added to their kind feelings towards him in wishing his re-election. This class, which is not large, added to the other, which embraces the old office-holders and ring managers, make up, in my opinion, the Grant movement at this time. . . ." *New York Herald*, Jan. 14, 1879.

To Frederick Dent Grant

———

Vienna, Austria
Aug. 22d 1878

Dear Fred.

I do not remember where my last letter to you was written from, but I think St. Petersburg. My visit there was agreeable and my reception by the Authorities and people cordial. We staid some eight or nine days in St. Petersburg, then went to Moscow where we staid four more days & returned to St. Petersburg and stopped over two days more. We then came to Warsaw where we stopped for two days more.[1] There is but little in Russia to interest the traveler—as you know[2]—outside of the three cities named, and possibly a little on the Black Sea. We have now been in Vienna four days. My audience & dinner with the Emperor is over. The reception by the Authorities has been very cordial. I do not know whether you visited Vienna or not. It is one of the most beautiful cities in Europe if not the most beautiful. The people too compare, in appearance, very favorably with any others. We will remain here until next Monday[3] or tuesday and then go to the country to remain quiet for about a month. After that we will go to Spain and Portugal after which nothing will be left but to spend a quiet Winter and go home in the Spring.

your Ma sais to tell Ida that she is distressed that she—Ida—does not get her letters. Your Ma has written to Ida a number of times, twice from Stockholm. She is always delighted when she gets letters from Ida because they always contain so much news, then too she loves her so much.

When we last heard you were still out on the plains:[4] I hope you have escaped the terrible heated turn, which I see from the papers, has visited the states generally. We have not felt a warm day this summer. Your Ma is now out shopping and it is less than an hour to the time when we are to be at a dinner party, and she has to dress after her return. Ladies never do take notice of time. I get the New York City papers regularly, and slips by the hundred from papers from all parts of the states, good and bad, complimentary & abusive. I see Young's letter over "table talk"[5] has created quite a sensation. None of the talk was ever intended for publication, but he thought— and still thinks—it all right. I would rather however that such things should not be published, and will tell him to be cautious in the future.

I do not like to write about European politics, particularly as I have been received so well everywhere. But it looks to me as if the Berlin Congress has by no means settled affairs even for a short time. I hope I am mistaken, but ~~it looks~~ I feel that there is more danger now of a general war than there was at any time during the conflict between Russia & Turkey. Do not express this as my view.

Your Ma joins me in love and kisses to you, Ida & Julia.

Yours Affectionately
U. S. GRANT

COL. F. D. GRANT

ALS, USG 3.

1. See *Young*, I, 493–96; *Julia Grant*, p. 254.
2. Frederick Dent Grant toured Russia while overseas with Gen. William T. Sherman. See *PUSG*, 23, 82–85.
3. Aug. 26, 1878.
4. After Frederick Grant completed an army inspection tour in early Aug., he spoke to a reporter in Chicago. ". . . He says the stories set afloat that the bones of Custer's braves are bleaching in the sun, and that they have not received decent interment, are in the main false and sensational. The ground is covered with the bones of animals, but, with the exception of a few skeletonic reminders of the massacre in the shape of human bones which had recently been washed out of the sand, the field presented no such ghastly spectacle as has been pictured. He learned that relic-hunters had dug up some of the bones and carried

them away. . . ." *Chicago Times,* Aug. 9, 1878. See letter to Frederick Dent Grant, May 24, 1878.

    5. See Interview, July 6, 1878.

To Ulysses S. Grant, Jr.

                                        Ischl, Austria,
                                     Aug. 28th /78

Dear Buck:

    My last letter was from Vienna, and to the infant. We come to this beautiful mountain watering place last evening. Will probably remain two weeks and then go to Salzburg for the same length of stay. The excursions from this place are said to be beautiful. If the weather is favorable we will make all of them. I shall enjoy the rest, hot baths and fishing at all events. After Salzburg our next resting place will be Paris, but not for a long time before our departure for Spain and Portugal. We think now that we will make our winter stay in Paris. After all one sees more Americans there than any place else in Europe, and I find it pleasant abroad exactly in proportion to the number of Americans one finds to talk to. The fact is no American would stay in Paris if he found himself the only one of his country-men there. Washington City ought to superscede Paris as a resort for our people who think they must go away from home.—I have no business matter to write about and your Ma has, so I will leave the balance of this sheet for her.[1]

                            yours affectionately
                            U. S. Grant

ALS, Austin B. McLogan, Flint, Mich.

    1. Julia Dent Grant wrote to Ulysses S. Grant, Jr. "Dear Buckie your nice long let-ters to your Papa & me are all ways receeved with pleasure. I hope you have enjoyed your holiday & that you have been to see Fred & [. . . .] baby Has Jesse been yet? I am quite dis-gusted at the way The Elizabeth friends receeved Jesse I should not bother about them any more By the way you ask if the 5 five pieces of mosiac 2 two brass candle sticks & 2 two agate saucers were all I sent in the box you receeved from Rome. I sent in that box 5 pieces of fine Roman Mosaic 2 brass candle sticks 1 one beautiful Photograph Album bound in white velum, & filled with fine Photographs of scenes around & in Rome 3 or 4

Agate plates or saucers, & two agate paper waits one with a Lizard on it & a snail made of agate on the other. Also severa[l] books of value one book of Poems written by Mr Charlton. of England Let me know if you receeved all of these things—" ANS (undated), *ibid.*

To John Russell Young

———

Ischl, Austria
Aug. 28th /78

MY DEAR COMMODORE:

All your letters to Mrs. Grant and myself, with the slips enclosed, have come regularly. Mrs. Grant is always glad to get your letters, but when she reads the unfavorable comments she think the publication of "table talks" was unwise. When she reads the favorable comments she thinks otherwise. There was but one special mistake that I see in your letter further than it does not give explanations as fully as I probably give them in conversation. If your letter had it would have filled all the pages of the Herald with a rambling incoherent mass of matter that would not have been read through by any body. The mistake you make is in saying that 39000 would about cover my losses in killed, wounded & missing, from the Rapid Ann to the James. You will probably remember that what I did say was about this: "That Taylor, Welles and other writers would soon have it pass into history that in that Campaign we had a 100.000 men killed in reaching a point which we could have reached, by boat, without loss, and ignore the fact that Lee sustained any loss during the same time; that infact has the 40.000, I thought 39.000, would cover such loss, but that Badeaus book would contain the best attainable data on that subject." I then stated how our losses were made up after each battle. No officer commanding a company, regiment or brigade wanted to belittle his own services by failing to report his full list of killed, wounded & missing. In that way losses are made to appear large. Many of the wounded reported would be so slightly so as not to keep them from duty a single day. Many a man has been reported wounded—and actually wounded—two, three and some times as much as six times during all those battles, and still live to tell the story of his honorable scars. So too with the missing: Many turn up within a day or two, and many fall into the hands of the enemy to be exchanged for later. I see they have got Lee's losses down to about 20.000 in the engagements where mine was 100000! I think history will show that we captured and sent North more than that number.

I do not think the publication of your letter has done any harm. At all events it is too late now to help it if it has. It will at least bring out some writers on the Union side.

Very Truly Yours,
U. S. Grant

ALS, DLC-John Russell Young. On Aug. 30 and Sept. 5, 1878, John Russell Young, Paris, wrote in his diary. ". . . I see the newspapers at home are having [a] lively time over my interview—[w]ish was I had made it twice [a]s long, and interesting—. . ." ". . . Two letters from the General. He approves my interview, all but one statement about the number of Lee's troops—. . ." *Ibid.* See *ibid.*, July 31, Aug. 1–2, 12, 14, 20, 1878; Interview, July 6, 1878; letter to John Russell Young, Sept. 3, 1878. Young's "table talk memoranda" provoked widespread comment and controversy. For editorial assessments, see *New York Herald*, July 26, 31, Aug. 3, 1878.

To Adam Badeau

Ischl, Austria
Aug. 29th /78

My Dear General:

Your letter of the 22d of August—herewith returned—reached me just before leaving Vienna. The outline you propose for your history of "the March to the Sea" is exactly right. Follow it and give all the letters and dispatches in the body of the narative. When you have it in type send a copy to Sherman. You have certainly divided the honors of the Campaign correctly. The particular Campaign made was Shermans conception and execution. Supposing that I was to remain in the West, in command, I had conceived earlier a different Campaign,[1] leading practically to the same result. Subsequent events would have modified that plan beyond doubt even had I remained. Events shaped Sherman's Campaign.

Your book will necessarily be criticised, but criticism will do no harm so long as your facts are right. My opinion is that Young's publication of "table talks"[2] will add many thousands to the number of readers of your book. People will look to that as the authentic views which I entertain. The others will be looked upon as hastily noted recollections of what was said in conversation without the data at hand to speak with entire accuracy.

I shall remain here some eight days more and then in Salzburg for ten days or more. My next address after that will be in Paris though but for a short time.

I wrote Washburne a letter telling him the outrageous stories Wilson had told me about him. I said also that he had told you, Porter and Babcock—old Staff associates—the same things.[3]

Very Truly yours
U. S. Grant

Gn. A. Badeau.

ALS, Munson-Williams-Proctor Institute, Utica, N. Y. See letter to Adam Badeau, Aug. 22, 1878. On Sept. 7, 1878, Adam Badeau, consul gen., London, wrote to Orville E. Babcock. ". . . The Genl writes me he will go to Spain and Portugal this month or next, and then settle down somewhere for the winter. He says he will not go to India, but return home in the Spring. What a row Young has raised. I saw it stated positively that I was the author of the Interviews, and Young offered to telegraph my denial. I hope he did so, as I at once wrote it out, and sent him; but I have heard nothing more. On the general's account and on mine that lie should be nailed at once. Young was very anxious too about his laurels as an interviewer. Will write, whenever I have any thing of interest about the General to tell you. I hope to see in less than a month. He proposes to be in Paris for a few days." ALS, ICN. Badeau's disclaimer telegram, dated Aug. 27, provoked editorial comment. ". . . We make the correction with the same promptness and pleasure with which we always do an act of justice. The Herald did not originate the statement which General Badeau denies. We merely republished without comment an article in the *Sun* containing it. . . ." *New York Herald*, Aug. 28, 1878.

1. USG contemplated striking Mobile. See *PUSG*, 10, 16–18; *Memoirs*, II, 351–52.
2. See Interview, July 6, 1878.
3. See letter to James H. Wilson, [*Sept. 8, 1878*].

To James E. Montgomery

————

Ischl, Austria.
Aug. 29th /78

Gen. J. E. Montgomery,
U. S. Consul
Dear ~~Sir~~Gen.

Your kind invitation of the 19th of this month, for me to visit Geneva after following me to St. Petersburg, Russia, thence to Vienna has at last reached me at the secluded Mountain resort. I wrote Mr. Fish, in answer to an invitation from him to visit the Capitol of Switzerland, that before returning to the United States next Spring I should try to do so. I do not know whether this would take me through Geneva—where I have already spent about one week—without going much out of my way or not. Should I be passing Geneva again however I will be glad to stop there ~~again~~ for a few days.

Whether I do or not I am under the same obligation to you for your polite invitation, and will inform you as soon as I know the fact.

Very Truly Yours
U. S. Grant

ALS, Heirlooms of History, Northboro, Mass. James E. Montgomery, consul, Geneva, graduated from Princeton (1845), worked as a Pennsylvania Railroad engineer (1847–51), and served as asst. AG (1861–66). For USG's travels in Switzerland, see letter to George M. Robeson, July 19, 1877; letter to William T. Sherman, Sept. 21, 1878.

On April 5, 1869, Montgomery, New York City, wrote to USG. "I have the honor to apply for an appointment to one of the first class Consulates in Europe and in support of my claim for such position, to inform you that I was among the first to enter the Army in the spring of 1861—at the breaking out of the rebellion and that I remained in the service for nearly six years during which time I was twice wounded, once almost mortally, and suffered severely upon the field—. . ." ALS, DNA, RG 59, Applications and Recommendations, Hayes-Arthur. On Dec. 9, 1874, George H. Sharpe, surveyor of customs, New York City, wrote to USG. "I learn that application has been made by Major James E. Montgomery, of this city, to be appointed to the mission at Ecquador, South America. Major Montgomery is the brother of the late Revd Dr. Montgomery, a distinguished and eloquent minister of this city, and is connected, socially and otherwise, with many of the leading gentlemen of New York. His service in the War was distinguished; so much so as to invite his selection to accompany the late Admiral Farragut during his long tour abroad, when he was received by nearly all the crowned heads of Europe. I believe that by birth, temperament, education and instinct he is fitted for the Diplomatic Service, and that his representation of our country and its interests would be able and high-toned." ALS, *ibid.*

On Dec. 12, 1876, Montgomery wrote to USG. *"Personal—* . . . Recalling the assurance given at our last interview, that you would not overlook my claims for a position under your Administration, I have the honor herewith to renew my application for the same, and to express the hope you may find it convenient to bestow it. . . ." ALS, *ibid.* Related papers are *ibid.* On Jan. 30, 1877, USG wrote a note. "Jas. E. Montgomery asks for Prague. Mr. Hale asks this for him." AN, Columbia University, New York, N. Y. No appointment followed.

To William W. Smith

Ischl, Austria
Sept. 1st /78

Dear Smith:

I do not recollect to have received a letter from your, or to have written you one, since my departure for Europe. We have now been over fifteen months abroad, and have had as pleasant a time, and have seen as much country, and under as advantageous circumstances as any one probably ever has in the same length of time. Home papers have kept the public very well informed of all my movements—and a great deal more about me that is entirely unnecessary—ever since I left. Where we are now staying for a short time is in the Austrian Alps, among beautiful mountain scenery, with lakes and fine running streams of water.[1] This section, for many miles around, is a great resort for people of the Austrian cities who are able to leave their homes for the summer. But you see no gaiety at European watering places as you do in America. In this one particular—I know no other—they are more sensible than our people. Summer life, either in the country or at a watering place, is with them a season of entire rest. With us it is the gay season over intensified. But I miss English speaking people. I find that I enjoy european travel just in proportion as I find Americans to associate with. I do not believe there would be a duller place on earth for Americans than Paris if they did not have a large colony of their own countrymen to go with.

In a few weeks we go to Spain and Portugal, after which we will settle quietly for the Winter. We will then have visited every country in Europe and a little of Africa and Asia. My most pleasant recollections of travels will be that in Egypt. It is the only country where I have been where the reality exceeds the expectations, or the descriptions. Any guide book of the country describes what there is to be seen better than I can, but will fail to give a realizing idea of all. I have seen nothing however, any where, that makes me want to live elsewhere than in my own country. I often get homesick to get back to it, but I started to spend two years, and shall do so unless something unforeseen turns up to take me back earlyer.

Remember Mrs. Grant & I to Judge & Mrs. McKennan, and the family and our kindest regards to Emsy and the children. My address is always Drexel Harjes & Co. Bankers, Paris, France.

Yours Truly
U. S. GRANT

ALS, Washington County Historical Society, Washington, Pa.

1. See *Julia Grant*, p. 254.

To John Russell Young

Ischl, Austria
Sept. 3d /78

DEAR COMMODORE;

Your letter of the 29th of August only came to hand last evening. If I should go home by the east I should be delighted to have you with me. Will always be glad to have you along, when it is convenient to you, in my travels. But I shall not go home by the east, this winter at least. There is so much water communication and so little to see that I am rather deterred from making the journey. We will be in Paris, on our way to Spain, about the 25th of this month.

Our kindest regards to Mrs. Young.

yours Truly
U. S. GRANT

J. R. YOUNG, ESQ.

ALS, DLC-John Russell Young. John Russell Young received this letter from USG, and another one with travel plans, on Sept. 19 and 22, 1878. Young, Edward F. Noyes, U.S.

minister, Lucius Fairchild, consul gen., and others, greeted USG upon his arrival in Paris on Sept. 25. Young diary, Sept. 19, 22, 25, 1878, *ibid.* See letter to John Russell Young, Aug. 28, 1878; letter to Edward F. Beale, Oct. 6, 1878.

To James H. Wilson

[*Salzburg, Austria, Sept. 8, 1878*]

GEN. J. H. WILSON, SIR: Your letter of Aug. 17 reached me a few days since at Ischl, Austria. I was surprised to receive it and am surprised that you cannot conjure up reasons why I should distrust you and feel hard towards you. The quotation you give from Mr. Young's statements of what I said are probably correct. It expresses at all events what I feel that I have undoubted proof of. You stood high in my estimation. When you told me anything I believed it, only making allowances for your prejudices which I knew to be strong, and for your enthusiasm which might carry you further in censure or praise than the exact facts might warrant. When you told me that you knew a thing of your own knowledge I implicitly relied on your statements. You told me many things about Porter to his discredit which I did not fully believe but credited you with believing. . . . At the very time you were making statements to me to the discredit of Porter you were a frequent visitor at his house, often taking dinner, sometimes staying over night and occasionally borrowing money from him. After your return from Europe[1] you told me of scandals about Washburne—the best friend I had in Congress during the war—with the view of effecting his removal. You characterized him as a disgrace to the country. Since saying these things to me you have been accepting Washburne's hospitalities and dining at his house. What, I ask you, ought to be my feelings towards a man once enjoying my entire confidence who could be guilty of these things?. . . I am sorry of these things and that you should have given me cause to distrust you. But so it is and must remain until what I have stated here is disproved. Even then the fact remains that you were carrying stories for the purpose of injuring a man whose hospitalities you were accepting at the very time and to whom you were indebted for the very place which was giving you support. You have also been accepting hospitalities of a man whose reputation you tried to blast after a most honorable public career of twenty years. Explain these things if you can and I will listen impartially to the explanation.

U. S. GRANT.

P. S. You remember our interview during the session of '76, '77. It was just before your brother began his testimony before a Congressional Committee and after the Sec. of the Treasury had prohibited his carrying off papers from the Dept. without inspection. You called to get my order for them on the ground that it was a degradation to have them examined when he asserted that there were none but private papers among them. The examination had to be made and I have the authority of Sec. Morrill for saying that out of some seven hundred papers packed to take out of the Dept. more than one half were papers belonging to the files of the office. I never saw you afterward though you wrote me a note saying you would call if I wanted to see you, and said that the one paper particularly wanted had been found—and that it was the only one not private—making a very lame excuse for its being there[2]

Typescript (ellipses in original), Culver C. Sniffen Papers, PCarlA. USG sent the original letter to Ulysses S. Grant, Jr., from Salzburg, Austria, on Sept. 8, 1878. See *ibid.*; letter to Elihu B. Washburne, Oct. 7, 1878. On Dec. 15, James H. Wilson, St. Louis, wrote to USG, Paris. "Although I am without reply to my letter of Aug. 17th, addressed to you as above, I have received information through another source of such character as to leave but little doubt that you have spoken of me substantially as indicated in the letter just referred to. In order that there shall be no ground for further misunderstanding on your part, I quote from a letter addressed to me by a friend (whose name is not material to this correspondence) as follows: 'On Saturday last the 19th of October, Gen. A. T. A. Torbert, in the course of a conversation with me on the train on the Delaware RR. told me of a conversation between him and Gen. Grant in Paris, in which the latter charged you with treachery to him and other friends worse than any since Judas Iscariot, and particularly that you had while he was President told him that Gen. Horace Porter had a contract with Capt. Eads, by which Porter was to receive one fourth of all Capt. Eads should receive from the Government on his Mississippi River contract. That Gen. Grant at this information felt that his confidence had been abused by Gen. Porter and treated him coldly when they next met, without however informing Gen. Porter of the cause of his displeasure; that Gen. Porter heard of the matter from some friend of his in New York to whom you had told it, and went at once to Gen. Grant to inquire about it. Gen. Grant told Gen. Porter fully what you had said, whereupon Gen. Porter laid before Gen. Grant the evidence which showed that so far from he (Porter) being guilty of the charge, that he had introduced you to Capt. Eads, by which Eads employed you as an engineer in preparing his papers, that you yourself got from Eads some sum (not mentioned) for this service, that having become embarrassed in your circumstances, you wished to transfer this consideration received by you from Eads to Mrs. Wilson, which transfer in writing with your acknowledgment before a notary, Gen. Porter laid before Gen. Grant, or in other words that you being on terms of great friendship with Generals Grant and Porter, and under obligations to him for many acts of kindness, requited it by falsely charging Gen. Porter with a grave act and one of baseness on his part to Gen. Grant, when in fact Porter was innocent of it, and you yourself were guilty.' From the context of the foregoing, I thought it possible that Gen. Torbert had confused a part of what you had told him with what Gen. Porter might have told him, and hence I wrote at once to Gen. Torbert asking him to put in writing just what he told my friend whether it came from you or Gen. Porter. To this, Gen. Torbert after some delay replied that he do so with pleasure if I could meet him in New York, which it was impossible for me to do at the date named, and I so notified him again urging him as a friend to 'write me just what either you or Gen. Porter may have told him about my relations with either of you or with public affairs.' To this last letter I have as yet received no reply, Gen. Torbert being absent in California as I am informed. This explains why I have not written to you sooner. I had hoped to get a specific statement from Gen. Torbert and thus eliminate all uncertainty as to his authority for what he had told my friend. Having waited a reasonable length of time without receiving his further reply, I now write to you for the purpose of saying in the most emphatic manner that if Gen. Porter ever undertook to do what the foregoing report of his conversation with Gen. Torbert says he did, he has deceived you again and added forgery to falsehood. In justice to myself as well as to you, I propose to convince you of that fact before I consent to let the matter drop. While I am somewhat surprised at the curious and somewhat ingenious perversion of the real facts in this case and of the entire omission of important circumstances connected with it, and might perhaps interest you by directing your attention to them, I purpose only to refresh your memory in reference to the essentials of what I really did tell you in Febry. 1876, about Gen. Porter's connection with Capt. Eads, and what followed subsequently between myself and Eads. You seem to have forgotten that during the conversation which I held with you on the subject of Porter and Babcock['s] conduct towards you. I told you I had a *profound suspicion* that Gens. Porter and Babcock were the men who had betrayed you, and that at your request I explained the grounds of my suspicion. In doing this I called your attention to their connection with the Black Friday conspiracy, the facts of which, their couns[el] Gen. Sharpe had related to me, and afterwards as he informed me and others, laid fully before you together with such supporting documents as had remained in his possession. At the same time I told you of my efforts some time previous to convince Porter that Babcock had become a source of injury to you, and should vacate his place near your person in favor of your son, that Porter had combatted this suggestion on the ground that your son could not leave his studies, or had not the ability to fill the place of private secretary properly and besides that you had made him (Porter) promise when he left that Babcock 'should remain with you through to the end.' I told you of my willingness to resign my position as Chief Engineer of the Metropolitan Elevated Railway and help to elect Babcock to the vacancy, and that this had also been declined. I also related to you that I had introduced Eads to Porter as a person who could help him secure favorable legislation from Congress in behalf of his plans for improving the mouth of the Mississippi, which I believed to be good and in accordance with the principles of correct engineering; that Porter was then as I recollect it in civil life and had a perfect right to help Eads or anybody else who would pay him for it; that Eads had offered to divide with me & Porter; that in due time Congress had authorized a contract to be made with Eads, and that nearly a year thereafter, when I had ceased to give Eads or his enterprise any serious thought, Porter had told me Eads had in writing assigned him a one-quarter interest in his contract, one half of which (or one-eighth) he would reserve for me and himself, and the other half of which he 'had placed with a man whose name he would no more tell me than he would tell mine to him.' As I afterwards learned this assignment was made before Congress authorized the acceptance of Eads' proposition. I called your attention to the fact that I had shortly after this conversation with Porter written him a letter informing him that after reflection I had decided that I could not 'have or accept any part or parcel' in his contract with Eads,' and that he 'must therefore count me absolutely out of the enterprise, that Porter never notified Eads, and that afterwards I told Eads in person of my decision and of my letter making it known to Porter. Finally I informed him that this withdrawal on my part was based upon the fact that my suspicions were aroused by Porter's proposition to put me into a concern having a secret partner or partners, and not by any doubt of the propriety of either of us having an interest in Ead's contract. I now reiterate all this, and declare that it contains the whole truth and nothing but the truth so far as I know it, except what I shall relate hereafter about the Ead's contract. It is not true that Porter introduced me to Eads, but the fact is, I introduced Eads to Porter. It is not true that Eads ever paid me a cent of money or a share of stock in his Jetty Company, or in any other Company, for services rendered to him in connection with any of his enterprises, in any of their stages, or in connection with the preparation of any of his plans ~~for improving the Mouth of the Mississippi River~~ or papers, or for any other service or purpose whatsoever. It is true that when he first approached me about his plans for improving the Mouth of the Missippi River which must have been in 1874 or 75, he did say if I would help him get the legislation he required from Congress he would 'divide with me.' It is also true that I told Gen. Porter when I spoke to him several months later about Eads' plans, that Eads would 'divide' with us, and that I thought a great deal of money might be legitimately made out of the enterprise. It is not true that Gen. Porter ever held any stock of any kind as trustee for Mrs. Wilson or myself, least of all did he ever hold any in the Jetty Company for either of us as before stated, as soon as I was apprised of the fact that he had reserved an eighth interest for himself and me, and another eighth for a man whose name he would not give, I notified him in writing that I could not have or accept any part or parcel in his contract with Eads. It cannot therefore be true, and in fact it is not true, that Gen. Porter or anybody else ever laid before you a transfer in writing of any such stock from me to himself, with my 'acknowledgment before a notary.' It is true however that if he or any one else laid before you anything purporting to be such a transfer, he has added forgery to falsehood. It is not true that I charged Gen. Porter with 'a grave act' or 'one of baseness on his part toward you' in connection with the Eads' contract, but it is true that I charged him with an effort to place me in business relations with a secret partner, and that this was one of a series of circumstances which aroused my profound suspicion that he and Babcock had betrayed your confidence and scandalized your administration. It is entirely susceptible of proof that there has never been a share of Jetty stock, or of any other stock controlled by Eads, or by the Jetty Company, in my name on the books of that company, and I hope to show that there has never been a dollar of that stock transferred by anybody else to Porter for me or Mrs. Wilson, or for any of my name or connection near or remote. If anybody has shown you any such stock, assignment or transfer, it is certainly a forgery, or at least was made without my knowledge or consent. There is yet another chapter in the Eads matter, with which you are perhaps not acquainted, and now that we are on that subject, it had better be narrated. You may remember that after I told you about Porter's contract, you said: 'Well, there's one thing certain, Eads will not get a cent of money from the Government so long as I am President unless that contract is destroyed;' whereupon I called your attention to the fact that so far as I knew, there was not the slightest reason why Porter should not be interested with Capt. Eads but that I could not consent to be a party to an arrangement in which there was a secret partner, and besides that I had not rendered Eads any service for which I was willing to lay him under contribution. It so happened that as I was returning to New York, after my last interview with you, I met Eads on the train, and after asking him if Porter had ever mentioned my letter declining to have any interest in the Jetty contract, and receiving an assurance that he never had, I told Ead of my conversation with you and your declaration that he should not be paid any money on his work till the contract with Porter had been destroyed. I gave this information to Eads because nothing could have been further from my desire than to injure him or his undertaking, and because I did not know what course you would find it necessary to take to discover the secret partner or to protect the Government's interests, nor in case of investigation how much he might be injured, through my communication to you. The same or the next day I wrote Capt. Eads a letter reciting the fact that I had written to Porter nearly a year before, declining to have any interest in the contract between him and Porter, and reiterating my determination from the date of my letter to Porter to have nothing whatever to do with his enterprise. Eads called at my office the next day and asked me to withdraw my letter which I declined to do. He then said he should have to reply to it, and in a manner which might not be pleasant to me, whereupon I assured him that if he stated in his reply nothing but the truth, I could take no exception to it. He then said he would have to assert that I had 'solicited an interest,' in his enterprise. I replied that I had not solicited an interest, but had been willing to have an interest on proper terms and he might so state it. He then proposed that I should destroy the press copy of my letter to him and he would destroy the original and (as I recollect it) also the contract with Porter. This I also declined. Eads then said that he might be greatly injured by my communication to you and that he would consider it a great personal favor if I would consent to his proposition, which I finally did upon the condition that he would show me the original contract between himself and Porter. This, after some hesitation, he consented to do. I read the paper, which was in the handwriting of Eads and not of Porter, and was dated eight or nine months previous, and several months previous to the passage of the Act of Congress authorizing the contract with Eads. It was addressed to 'Gen. Horace Porter, New York,' and 'for services rendered and to be rendered,' conveyed to him a clear unembarrassed one quarter interest in the enterprise, without [assessments or limitations.] It contained nothing in the nature of, or suggesting a trust, and did not mention my name nor that of anybody connected with me. This assignment was endorsed across the back with the signature of 'Horace Porter.' Again calling Eads' attention to the fact that I had no interest in it, I declared that I did not wish in any way to terminate or interfere with the relations between him and Porter in reference to this or any other matter. During the conversation, Eads expressed the idea that the assignment had been made originally as much on my account as on Porter's, that he was sorry I had decided not to avail myself of it, and that he had supposed without knowing anything about it, the arrangement was for the benefit of Mrs. Wilson and had been entered into because of certain financial embarrassments in which my late firm was then involved. I repelled this gratuitous supposition with indignation and thought I had satisfied him of its falsity. That this was an afterthought of Porter's or his will be apparent when I remind you of the fact that in telling me of the assignment or contract, Porter told me also that he had placed one-eighth with a man whose name he would not tell me. Will it be supposed for one moment that he or any other prudent business man could thus dispose of a trust or any part of it? To any one who knows Porter the mere suggestion is preposterous. When you remember he did not even mention to me the existence of the contract with Eads till it was nearly a year old, that I [at once re]nounced all part or parcel in it, and that he did not mention this renunciation to Eads till Eads told him I had brought the whole affair to your attention, the absurdity of the trust theory in reference to this assignment or contract will be apparent. The simple truth is that while he may have accepted that assignment intending to divide the benefits of it with me he retained it from the time he mentioned its existence to me (immediately after which as before stated, I peremptorily and emphatically declined to have any part or parcel of it) solely for his own benefit and that of the secret partner whose name he would not give. To any dispassionate mind his action subsequent to my decision to have nothing to do with it, is a more suspicious circumstance than his giving an eighth to a person whose name he would not mention, and leaves me now no doubt that he had a corrupt association with that secret partner and feared exposure and detection. As there never has been any stock or money paid to me or to anybody else for me, there never could have been and in fact never was any held by Gen. Porter in trust for me, or anybody connected with me, the whole trust theory falls to the ground and never had any foundation in truth or in fact, and this must be apparent to you as well as to every one else who may inquire into the matter. The fact is, General, that Porter is an adroit liar and scoundrel whom both you and I have trusted to our sore cost, and whom neither of us suspected or found out a day too soon. More than one of your best friends is now convinced of this and can give you irrefutable proof of it if so disposed. If you have further interest in the question you need not go out of Pennsylvania to satisfy yourself in reference to it. A few words more, and I leave this letter and the subject of it for your calm consideration. I am not unmindful of, nor I trust ungrateful for, your many acts of personal and official friendship to me, but great as they have been I feel that they have been worthily bestowed and worthily requited. I may add without egotism that I have been in my sphere quite as good a friend to you as you ever were to me, and have as fully as possible repaid you and the country for all benefits received, by faithful and honest service, at all times and in all places. I claim furthermore that I could not with loyalty to the truth and my conception of your character have pursued any other course than the one I did pursue, not only in reference to Porter but toward everybody else personally or officially connected with you. Had I acted otherwise, I should indeed have been faithless, and in my own eyes, at least, unworthy of your continued confidence and respect. I am not willing to submit in silence to the grave charges against me, which are report[ed] from various sources as having been made and repeated by you, and for this reason, I have stated the facts of the case in question fully and frankly, not doubt[ing] that your own sense of [justice] and fair dealing will prompt you to set me right, and that I shall be spared the unpleasant necessity of meeting the unfounded charges against me in any other way. Strong in the belief that you cannot want to do me any injustice, I leave the matter for the present for such thoughtful and I trust friendly action as you may think proper to take. Meanwhile if Gen. Porter or any one else concerned feels aggrieved by my course, or wants an investigation, or other satisfaction he can have it, so far as I am concerned or can give it to him. As a matter of course, you are at liberty to make such use of this letter as you may think best." Copies (press), DLC-Philip H. Sheridan; (illegible), DLC-James H. Wilson; typescript, WyU. On Jan. 28, 1879, Lt. Gen. Philip H. Sheridan, Chicago, wrote to Wilson. ". . . I met Gen. Torbert here a short time ago, but he made no remarks on the subject of your letter, and I never had heard a word on the subject from any one. . . ." Copy (press), DLC-Philip H. Sheridan. See *PUSG*, 26, 255−58; LeGrand B. Cannon to Wilson, July 28, 1878, Benjamin H. Bristow to Wilson, Dec. 22, 1878, Emory Upton to Wilson, Jan. 13, 1879, Wy-Ar; Wilson, *Under the Old Flag* (New York, 1912), II, 388−89; Elsie Porter Mende, *An American Soldier and Diplomat: Horace Porter* (New York, 1927), p. 138.

On Jan. 29, Wilson wrote to Alfred T. A. Torbert, Milford, Del. "Having waited patiently for some time for a reply to my last letter to you and not having heard from you, I have written to Genl Grant and now beg to hand you herewith a copy of my letter, to which I invite your careful attention, which I think you will find to contain a complete answer to all the points mentioned by you to Mr Higgins. If it does not & you will kindly indicate wherein it falls short, I shall have much pleasure, in writing to Genl Grant, or any one else who may chance to be concerned, still further. You are at liberty to retain the copy herewith or to make such other use of it as you may think proper in the cause of justice and truth   I do not intend to rest quietly under any such imputations as those contained in your communication to Mr Higgins, and shall meet all such no matter from whom they come, from time to time, as circumstances may seem to require." ALS (press), DLC-James H. Wilson.

Wilson later asked Gen. William T. Sherman to act as an intermediary in his dispute with USG. On Dec. 24, Sherman wrote to Wilson. ". . . I saw Gnl Grant at Chicago & also at Phila—but did not touch on any personal matters, as on both occasions he was all the time surrounded by others, and had hardly time to take a quiet meal or Smoke He looks as natural & well as I ever Saw him—When at Chicago Fred Grant came to see me at my Room at the Grand Pacific, and with him I had a two hours talk—mostly of his own observations in India, China & Japan—I did ask him how his father felt towards you, and he answered with his usual frankness that his feelings were not friendly, to your brother & you—I dont think he associated you both with Bristow—for whom he feels real animosity—but I do know that Fred Grant said his father was not friendly to you, and your brother Bluford. . . ." ALS, Wy-Ar. Wilson never reconciled with USG. See Sherman to Wilson, July 11, Oct. 18, 1879, Jan. 9, 1880, *ibid.*; Wilson to Sherman, July 13, Oct. 24, Dec. 22, 1879, Jan. 6, 20, 1880, DLC-William T. Sherman; Ross A. Webb, *Benjamin Helm Bristow: Border State Politician* (Lexington, Ky., 1969), pp. 285–86.

1. Between 1871 and 1873, Wilson had courted investors in Europe as a railroad official. In late 1874, Wilson went to Europe as George M. Pullman's business agent. In 1875 and 1876, he worked for elevated railroads in New York City and resigned over differences with Horace Porter, Pullman's vice president. See *PUSG*, 21, 187–89; Wilson, *Under the Old Flag*, II, 394–95, 399–400; Edward G. Longacre, *From Union Stars to Top Hat: A Biography of the Extraordinary General James Harrison Wilson* (Harrisburg, Pa., 1972), pp. 238–42; Paul Clayton Pehrson, "James Harrison Wilson: The Post-War Years, 1865–1925," Ph.D. Dissertation, University of Wisconsin, 1993, pp. 125–33.

2. See letter to Lot M. Morrill, July 19, 1876; Longacre, *Union Stars to Top Hat*, pp. 243–45.

To Julia Dent Grant

———

Willbad Gastein,
Sept. 11th /78

Dear Julia;

We arrived here at 6 O'Clock last evening after a pleasant railroad excursion of three hours, through a picturesque mountain region, and a drive of four & a half hours through the same sort of scenery. The weather has been pleasant, without rain, though cloudy. The Emperor has fixed 2 O'Clock this afternoon for an audience, too late to return to Salzburg to-night. We return as early as we can to-morrow, reaching Salzburg, I think, five or six in the afternoon. You have not missed much by not coming here. The scenery is good, but much of a kind—not so good—with what you saw day-before-yesterday, visiting Konigsee Lake. The hotels—there are not many buildings besides the hotels—are in a mountain gorge where to go from one to another, or to take a walk, one has to go up and down stairs or steep inclined plains.

With much love, and a very poor hotel pen,

Affectionately
U. S. GRANT

ALS, DLC-USG. See *Julia Grant*, pp. 254–55.

On Sept. 7 and 12, 1878, Jacques Hartog (USG's courier), Salzburg, Austria, wrote to John Russell Young on USG's meeting at Gastein with Emperor William I and Chancellor Otto von Bismarck of Germany. ALS, DLC-John Russell Young. See conversation with Otto von Bismarck, [*June 30, 1878*]; letter to Hamilton Fish, Aug. 22, 1878.

To Ulysses S. Grant, Jr.

———

[*Munich, Sept. 14, 1878*]

. . . your ma and I are very well . . . I have fallen off twenty-five pounds and feel much better for it; that I can walk now like a boy—of sixty . . . Yellow Jacket[1] was up to $20. My 2,000 shares cost $8.00 . . . I want you to subscribe $500.00 for me to the Yellow fund.[2] If I have not got the money in bank, you can sell a bond to pay it . . . I shall be very glad to get home again and settle down in a home of my own . . .

Alexander Autographs, Inc., April 25, 1996, no. 561.

On June 19, 1878, Ulysses S. Grant, Jr., New York City, wrote to Orville E. Babcock. "I scarcely know how to reply to your friendly letter just received, I think of so many things I might say. I thought that you personally had little interest in the prosecution of the claim against Mrs Dent, that Mr Cooke was pushing matters intending to follow up success with many more such proceedings. I used the language I did hoping to get an explanation of how the case really stood. Judge Dent and some other relatives have had little trouble in incurring many debts; and though the creditors have a right to collect these debts if they can, it is scarcely to be expected that father should settle them all. However I will enclose your letter to him. I would like very much to see you if you come to New York." ALS, ICN. On June 21, Babcock, Baltimore, wrote to Grant, Jr. "I am in receipt of your favor of the 19th—I am glad you received my letter in the really friendly spirit I meant it—Now as to Col Cook I have never heard him mention a claim against your uncles estate and I am satisfied he has none except the one I turned over to him—I know of no other claim in the world against the estate—I am glad you referred my letter to your father for I want him to know what I have done—and if you imagine either Col Cook or I even wish to have your father pay the claim you are very much mistaken And I assure you now as I shall him should he offer such a thing, that I shall never accept his money to pay that claim—I will if in my power do anything to help him make money but *never* take his money to pay any other mans debts—If the estate of Louis Dent has not money to pay the claim it will never be paid . . . P. S. As you sent my other letter to your father please to send this" ADf (initialed), *ibid.* On June 22, Grant, Jr., wrote to Babcock. "Your first letter had not yet been sent when your second one arrived as I had not written to father since its arrival. I enclosed them both without any remarks to day in my weekly letter . . ." ALS, *ibid.*

    1. See letter to Ulysses S. Grant, Jr., [*June 29, 1878*].
    2. In early Oct., Grant, Jr., called upon Mayor Smith Ely, Jr., of New York City "and informed him that his father had given directions to hand in a check for $500 for the benefit of the yellow fever sufferers." *New York Herald,* Oct. 4, 1878. See J. P. Dromgoole, *Yellow Fever: Heroes, Honors, and Horrors of 1878* (Louisville, 1879).

To Alphonso Taft

———

Munich, Bavaria,
Sept. 14th /78

MY DEAR JUDGE:

Your very welcome letter reached me some two weeks since while in Ischl, Austria, a pleasant Alpine watering place, where Mrs. Grant and I spent a short time most pleasantly. Our travels abroad have been very enjoyable, but I often feel homesick to get back to the United States. We will stay however until next Spring. From here we go to Paris on our way to Spain & Portugal. Having visited those two countries I will have been in every country in Europe beside a little in Africa & Asia. The rest has been most grateful to me. While in the most perfect health all the time I have reduced in weight twenty-five pounds, bringing me down, if not to fighting weight at least to comfortable weight for locomotion.

I receive home papers regularly, and read them closely, and confess that I do not get all the comfort from them I should like. What between Kearneyism,[1] inflationism,—when we are already back to resumption substantially—and the late action of South Carolina in holding U. S. revenue officers, or threatning it,[2] does not look encouraging. But it is encouraging to think that the present Congress has but a short session before it, and that they probably can do but little harm during their short tenure, and that before another Congress meets the Country may have settled the disturbing issues so as to take the dangerous ones out of politics. Let us hope so.

Mrs. Grant joins me in kindest regards to Mrs. Taft, yourself and family.[3] Please remember me also to all my friends in Cincinnati, and say to Mr. McLean that Gen. & Mrs. Hazen[4] are here with us, both very well.

Very Truly Yours
U. S. GRANT

HON. A. TAFT.

ALS, DLC-William H. Taft. See *Young*, I, 501–2.

1. Born in 1847 in Ireland, Denis Kearney, a labor leader in San Francisco, agitated against industrialists and Chinese immigration as president of a new Workingmen's party. In Aug. and Sept., 1878, he spoke in Boston, Chicago, Washington, D. C., Philadelphia, and New York City. See *New York Times*, Aug. 6, 19, 21, 30–31, Sept. 3–4, 7–8, 1878.

2. U.S. revenue officers had killed a man in S. C. while attempting to arrest a whiskey tax violator. Challenging the constitutionality of U.S. revenue laws, a state judge denied removal of the homicide case to a U.S. court. This defiance of federal authority concerned President Rutherford B. Hayes as well as USG. See *ibid.*, July 27, Aug. 9–10, 16, 20, 1878, April 15, 1881, April 5, 1882; Charles Richard Williams, ed., *Diary and Letters of Rutherford Birchard Hayes* (Columbus, 1922–26), III, 492–93.

3. Alphonso Taft married Louise Torrey in 1853, the year after his first wife's death. Six children from his marriages survived to adulthood.

4. Col. William B. Hazen had gone to Europe as a military attaché to observe the war between Russia and Turkey. His wife, Mildred, was the daughter of Washington McLean. See *PUSG*, 9, 568; letter to Ulysses S. Grant, Jr., March 26, 1877; letter to Hamilton Fish, April 1, 1877.

To Adam Badeau

Ragaz, Switzerland
Sept. 18th /78

MY DEAR GENERAL;

Your letter of the 12th of Sept. reached me at this place last evening. I have no recollection whatever of the dispatches you speak of between Sherman and myself about the 4th of October /64 and my subsequent dispatch saying that his movement should be independent of mine.[1] I remember that I sent a shipload of provisions to meet him on the Seacoast wherever he might come out.

I will be in Paris, at the hotel Liverpool, on the 25th of this month to remain there until about the 10th of Oct. when I expect to start for Spain. Expecting to see you so soon I will write no more except to say that I have lost twenty five pounds weight, while in perfect health, and without doing any thing to bring about such a result. It makes me feel much more comfortable

yours Truly
U. S. GRANT

GN. A. BADEAU.

ALS, Munson-Williams-Proctor Institute, Utica, N. Y.
On Sept. 12, 1878, Adam Badeau, consul gen., London, wrote to Orville E. Babcock. ". . . I think I told you that the Genl will be in Paris about the 25th of this month. I shall run over for a day or two to see him, I think. He goes then to Spain and Portugal: then settles down for the winter; in the Spring he now says he will go home, *not by India.*" ALS, ICN.

1. See *PUSG*, 12, 289–91.

To Gen. William T. Sherman

Ragaz, Switzerland,
Sept. 21st /78

DEAR GENERAL.

I do not remember where my last letter to you was from, but I do not think I have written since the receipt of a letter from you while I was in St. Petersburg. My visit through Norway, Sweden & Finland was delightful. The weather was very fine, the scenery grand and the people I regard as very superior, and very fond of America and Americans. Our Manufactures are getting quite a foothold in those countries—in fact they are more or less so all over Europe—and there seems to be no prejudice against them or jealousy towards us. I wonder that more Americans do not spend their

Summers in those countries instead of in the old beaten track more in the Southern part of the continant.

Youngs publication of "Table Talk"[1] has given me something of the experience you had after the publication of your book. I believe I have stated to you that I said nothing intended for publication. I was not even aware until afterwards that anything I had said was noted down. Young told me however afterward that he was much interested in many things I said; that it had explained or cleared up many things that he had not understood or had misunderstood before, &c. and that he had noted them down for future reference, though he did not know that he should ever publish it. He gave the paper to me to read, which I did, hastily, a long time after, striking out a large part.[2] What was published was substantially correct except in two or three particulars, but it was not as full as I had expressed myself. For instance there could have been no just criticism of what I said about Lookout if all I said had been published. So with much of the matter.

I deeply sympathize with you General in your disappointment about your son. But there is great consotation in the fact that he has [n]ot gone as too many young men do, into a life of disipation and general worthlessness. There was no danger of Tom, in that way however, and where ever he is he will be an ornament and a credit to his profession. I am sorry his inclination did not keep him in the profession you had chosen for him, or he had chosen first for himself.[3]

We are all very well and are longing for the time to go back to America. We leave here for Paris, on our way to Spain and Portugal, next Monday.[4] That visit over we will have seen something of every country in Europe, and a little of Asia & Africa. I have no idea of going round the world. If I was alone I might, but there is to much sea travel and to little to see Without hardships to great for a lady.

Mrs. Grant joins me in kindest regards to Mrs. Sherman and the young ladies.[5]

Very Truly Yours
U. S. GRANT

GEN. W. T. SHERMAN

ALS, DLC-William T. Sherman. On Oct. 30, 1878, Gen. William T. Sherman read USG's letter to the Society of the Army of the Tennessee reunion in Indianapolis. *New York Her-*

ald, Oct. 31, 1878. On Oct. 13, Sherman, Washington, D. C., had written to Lt. Gen. Philip H. Sheridan. ". . . I have a most friendly letter from General Grant, which Convinces me that Spite his association with the public Civilians, his thoughts and feelings revert to his Old Army Comrades. No man of Either Party, Seems to rise above Mediocrity, or to Command public Confidence. If this Continues two years More Grant may again be President, and though he does not manifest the wish, being out of employmt, and too vigorous to remain idle he cannot well refuse. He writes me that he has given up his purpose to return home by way of India, China, Japan & California as at one time contemplated, but that after doing Spain & Portugal, he will have seen All of Europe & some of Asia & Africa, and he will then Come home. The papers add the same & that he will Spend the Winter in Paris—When I was in California, the Poeple counted on his 'coming that way' and will be much disappointed. I wrote him as much, and if he Contemplates another tour of the White House, I am sure it would be to his interest to Come back by that route   Still his reasons, were that Such a journey required more Sea travel than was agreable to Mrs Grant—who must be tired, and wants to get rest. . . ." ALS, DLC-Philip H. Sheridan. On Oct. 29, Sheridan, Chicago, wrote to Sherman. ". . . I think as you do, that general Grant should go to California. The people out there, were greatly disappointed at his not going out ~~there~~ when he was at Salt Lake some three years ago—and he ought to make himself good. He has grown wonderfuly in public confidence as an able and strong man, and it would not surprise me a bit, if he was called upon to again go to the White House. There would certainly be no doubt about it, if the election was to take place this fall, but the political Wheel is e[rrati]c in its revolutions & sometimes great changes happen inside of two years—. . ." ALS, DLC-William T. Sherman. See letter to Gen. William T. Sherman, Dec. 8, 1878.

In early Oct., a reporter interviewed George W. Childs, who had received a letter from USG "last week." "He was preparing for his journey to the East. . . . He anticipates a very interesting trip through the Eastern countries. In several places great preparations are making to receive him." *New York Herald*, Oct. 6, 1878.

1. See Interview, July 6, 1878.
2. See letter to Adam Badeau, Aug. 22, 1878.
3. After graduating from Yale and intending to become a lawyer, Thomas E. Sherman joined the Jesuits to prepare for the priesthood. See Joseph T. Durkin, *General Sherman's Son* (New York, 1959).
4. On [*Sept. 20*], Friday, USG had telegraphed to Samuel H. M. Byers, consul, Zurich. "I accept your invitation for Monday." Byers, *Twenty Years in Europe* (Chicago, 1900), p. 148. Byers arranged a dinner at which USG "expressed a deep sense of pleasure and honor at meeting such distinguished Swiss gentlemen. He thanked the citizens of Zurich, through their Mayor, for their cordial reception, which he regarded as a symbol of the good feeling existing between the two countries. The General concluded by proposing the health of the President of the Federal Council and nation and the prosperity of the city of Zurich." *New York Herald*, Sept. 25, 1878. On Sept. 24, USG left for Paris. See Byers, *Twenty Years in Europe*, pp. 148–52; Nicholas Fish to William M. Evarts, Sept. 25, 1878, DNA, RG 59, Diplomatic Despatches, Switzerland. *Foreign Relations, 1878*, pp. 839–41.
5. Sherman's three youngest daughters, born between 1852 and 1861.

Calendar

1876, Nov. 2.   USG endorsement. "Referred to the Sec. of the Treas. The brother of Mr. Dapray—now Stenographer in the Supervising Architects office—is willing to resign if his brother—a Stenographic writer also—can have his place. Both brothers are described as being earnest republicans."—AES, DNA, RG 56, Applications. Written on papers concerning St. Julien B. Dapray, phonographer, Treasury Dept. Thomas B. Dapray later clerked in the Post Office and War Depts.

1876, Nov. 3.   USG note. "Will Mr. Marshall, Act. Postmaster Gen. please see Mr. John West of Alexandria who is anxious to obtain a position in the department? If anything can be done for Mr West please do it."—ANS, CSmH.

1876, Nov. 3.   Robert Ward and eleven others, Great Nemaha Agency, Nohart, Neb., to USG. "We, your children would ask your attention to the following statement. Our Agent M. B. Kent has removed one of our Chiefs without giving us any reason for doing so and as we believe without just cause. We are members of the Iowa tribe of Indians and have been at peace with our white brothers for more than Thirty years. sometimes we have had good aAgents and sometimes bad Agents. Our present Agent is bad, he does not explain our business to us and we know nothing about our affairs, and now Our Great Father we want you to restore our Chief that the Great spirit made for us to his place as Chief"—DS (by mark), DNA, RG 75, Letters Received, Montana Superintendency. See *HED*, 44-2-1, part 5, I, 498–501, 45-2-1, part 5, I, 537–39.

1876, Nov. 6.   USG note. "The Act. Sec. of the Int. ~~promis~~ said he would notify Mrs. Stevens that her position in the Dept. would be permanent. I therefore return the inclosed papers."—ANS, DLC-USG, IB. Widow of Walter H. Stevens, USMA 1848, and sister of Paul O. Hébert, both brig. gen., C.S. Army, Ernestine H. Stevens had worked as a copyist in the patent office. See Stevens to James A. Garfield, June 21, Oct. 19, 1880, DLC-James A. Garfield; Frances E. Willard and Mary A. Livermore, eds., *A Woman of the Century* (1893; reprinted, Detroit, 1967), p. 685.

1876, Nov. 6.   Horatio King, Washington, D. C., to USG. "I understand that the Hon. Mr. Rublee has resigned, or is about to resign the position of *Chargé d'Affaires* at Berne, and I beg to recommend my friend (and *yours*,) Hon. Charles H. Upton, U. S. Consul at Geneva, to succeed him. . . ." —ALS, DNA, RG 59, Letters of Application and Recommendation. Related papers are *ibid.* Charles H. Upton continued as consul, Geneva. See *New York Times*, July 9, 1877.

1876, Nov. 6.   Anne E. Rothschild, "Taunton Insane Asylum," Mass., to USG. "For more than two years, I have been an inmate of this Hospital, unjustly deprived of my liberty. My Father is a native born free citizen of the Common Wealth of Massachusetts. As his child I am entitled to all the rights and priviledges accorded by The Constitution of Said State These have been denied me. I have used every effort possible to obtain a public hearing. I now Appeal to you, to restore to me the liberty guaranteed by The Constitution of the United

States of America. Given this day from Hall Number nine, . . ."—ALS, DNA, RG
60, Letters from the President.

1876, Nov. 14.   Samuel S. Smoot, president, Southern Maryland Rail Road Co.,
Washington, D. C., to USG. "I was at the Executive Mansion to day and waited
some time to see you—but found you so much occupied that I could not have
that pleasure—the object of my visit was to request you to assist me in getting
the Secretary of the Navy to call the attention of Congress to the report of the
Board of Naval Officers appointed under Resolution of Congress looking to the
establishment of a Naval Coaling Station at the St Marys River—. . ." —ALS,
DNA, RG 45, Letters Received from the President. An enclosure urging an appropriation of up to $10,000 for a coaling station at "the harbor of the Saint
Marys River Maryland" is *ibid.* See *HED,* 43-2-108; *HRC,* 43-2-271.

1876, Nov. 16.   Governor Henry Lippitt of R. I. to USG. "I have the honor to
request that you will appoint as a Board Advisory to the Harbor Commissioners of this State, the Chief of Engineers, U. S. A; the Superintendent of the U. S.
Coast Survey; and the Chief of the Bureau of Navigation of the Navy Department."—LS, DNA, RG 45, Letters Received from the President. On Dec. 26,
Secretary of War James D. Cameron wrote to USG. ". . . The Chief of Engineers,
to whom this letter was referred, recommends that, in view of the extended
duties now devolved upon him, and the number of Boards of which he is a member—the Engineer officer stationed in Newport, Brevet Major General G. K.
Warren, be substituted for the Chief of Engineers in the proposed Advisory
Board."—LS, *ibid.* On the same day, Culver C. Sniffen endorsed this letter to
Cameron. "Genl. Warren may be substituted for the Chief of Engineers—"
—AES, *ibid.* Related papers are *ibid.* On Dec. 30, Sniffen wrote to Secretary of
the Navy George M. Robeson. "The President directs me to request the return
to him by bearer of the papers referred to you yesterday afternoon relative to
the designation of Commodore Ammen to act as one of the advisory Board to
the R. I. harbor Commission"—ALS, *ibid.*

1876, Nov. 18.   Charles C. Brown, Willow Dale, Iowa, to USG. "I write you in
reguard to certain lands lying in North western Iowa in the Council Bluffs &
Sioux City districts under the Homestead acts. . . . Now it appears that a rumor
began to Spread over this country about the first of April 1874 that the Cedar
rappids & Missourri R R Co or more commonly called the Northwesten R R Co
claimed all the lands that was and had been homsteaded. People did not take
much notice of the rumor then, but of late it is creating quite a Sensation. One
of their agents told me not more than two months ago that the company intended to take possession of said lands in less than 2 years and tried to induce
me to buy the companies claim on my land or they would dispossess me of the
property. Now the question is does the Government consider my *Homestead
Pattent Vallid* or *Void* . . ."—ALS, DNA, RG 60, Letters from the President.

1876, Nov. 20.   Almon M. Clapp, public printer, Washington, D. C., to USG.
"I enclose a letter to you, which has been received by an assistant foreman in

this office, and which tells its own tale. I have written Hon. A. B. Cornell of New York soliciting his kind offices in the case, and now transmit the letter to you, thinking perhaps you may be able to facilitate relief through the Department of Justice. The man is poor, but industrious and worthy and I am convinced has not violated the law in exercising the right of suffrage by voting where he has voted consecutively for many years. His offence is that he voted a Republican ticket in a democratic neighborhood. he has been employed in this office for ab[o]ut a year, and has a family here dependant upon his daily toil for bread. They must become objects of charity or submit to starvation if he is to be incarcerated until Feby awaiting the action of the Grand Jury. With this statement of the case I submit it to you, trusting that you may find it consistent with your sense of duty to interpose in some way in the line of relief."—ALS, DNA, RG 60, Letters from the President. The enclosure is a letter of Nov. 15 from J. D. Boyce, "New City—Rockland Co. N. Y. Court-House Prison," to "Friend Norton." "I arrived at my old neighborhood (about six miles south of this) on the afternoon of the 6th and at about 10 a. m. on the 7th voted. At midnight of the latter day was dragged from my warm bed on a warrant of arrest on a *charge of illegal* voting—and taken, in the face of a cold northeast storm, six miles, to Nyack, and locked up in a cell 3 x 8 ft. where I had to lie upon a bunch of straw and 2 damp blankets the balance of the night—at 9 a. m. the 8th, was taken to a justice's court, but did not get a hearing till 8 p. m.—The justice, was half drunk, and a rotten democrat, dyed in the wool of old rotten Tammany, then committed me to wait the action of the grand jury at the General sessions, in February next, just 3 months hence. I was then put in a waggon and arrived at 11. o'clock the same night—handed over to the sheriff, who put me imediately in a fellan's cell 7 x 8, in which is a mattress and 2 filthy blankets with their usual accompaniment, lice. I have 2 meals a day, differing not more than 3 per cent. from bread and water. . . ." —ALS, *ibid.*

1876, Nov. 23.   Culver C. Sniffen to Secretary of the Treasury Lot M. Morrill. "The President directs me to ask whether you have heard anything from the Collector of the Port of Richmond with reference to the nomination of R. P. W. Garnett as Deputy Collector—?"—Copy, DLC-USG, II, 3. On Dec. 1, 1st Lt. Francis V. Greene wrote to Maj. William P. Craighill, Baltimore. "The President desires to have appointed in the Treasury Department, Mr. R. P. W. Garnett, who has been employed by you, but objection is made on the ground that his habits are bad,—intoxication, &c., The Secretary therefore directs me to write you a private letter and ascertain if this is a fact,—as far as your knowledge goes."—Copy, DNA, RG 107, Letters Sent, Military Affairs. No appointment followed.

1876, Nov. 23.   Thomas Van Zandt, Paris, to USG. "Permit me to return you my sincere thanks for the honor you have done me in sending me your Photograph & signature, through my son-in law, Alexr J. P. Garesché of St Louis— This affords me an opportunity I have long desired of expressing to you personally my admiration & gratitude, for the inestimable services you have rendered to our beloved country, only equalled by the immortal Washington— These sentiments, General,—whatever political adversaries & office seekers

may say—vibrate in the hearts of every true & loyal American in the Union—"
—ALS, USG 3.

1876, Nov. 24. USG note. "Will the Sec. of the Treas. please see Mrs. Mills,
the widow of Surgeon Madison Mills of the Army whos daughter I earnestly
desire should have an appointment."—ANS, DNA, RG 56, Applications. On
July 31, Clara Mills, Mount Vernon, N. Y., had written to USG for assistance in
finding employment.—ALS, *ibid.* Related papers are *ibid.* On Nov. 28, Mills received appointment as a laborer in the Treasury Dept. See *PUSG*, 9, 11–12;
ibid., 15, 253–56.

1876, Nov. 25. USG endorsement. "Referred to the Sec. of State. If this position is not accepted by the party recommended by Senator West for a Consulate—I see no objection to this appointment."—AES, DNA, RG 59, Letters of Application and Recommendation. Written on a letter of Nov. 24 from
John T. M. Orendorf, Washington, D. C., to USG. "I most respectfully ask of
you to appoint me as Consul to Santiago-de-Cuba."—ALS, *ibid.* No appointment followed.
    On Nov. 15, 1880, USG, New York City, wrote to Secretary of State William
M. Evarts. "This will present Mr. J. T. M. Orendorf, of Md, who I have personally known for a number of years as a republican. Mr Orendorf will make known
his wishes himself, and can no doubt bring abundant testimonials of his fitness for what he may ask."—Copy, *ibid.*, Applications and Recommendations,
Hayes-Arthur. On the same day, Orendorf, New York City, wrote to Evarts. "I
am an applicant for the vacant Consulship at Pernambuco, Brazil. I am indorsed
by the leading Coffie importers of my native City, Baltimore Md. and by many
prominent merchants of this Metropolis, to whom I am personally known. . . ."
—Copy, *ibid.* Related papers are *ibid.* On Feb. 8, 1881, President Rutherford B.
Hayes nominated Orendorf as consul, Manzanillo.

1876, Nov. 25. USG endorsement. "Referred to the Sec. of State with approval
of this nomination if not already tendered to another."—AES, DNA, RG 59,
Letters of Application and Recommendation. Written on a letter of the same
day from James W. Siler, Washington, D. C., to USG. "Resting under the belief
that a vacancy in the U. S. sconsular service now exists at Tampico, Mexico, I
would respectfully solicit the appointment to fill the place. As to the merits
upon which this application is based, I have the honor to state that at the age of
17 years I entered the army, (12th Ills. Vol. Infty,) under the first call for troops
for the late war, and served through the entire period of the contest. I afterward
entered the Army of the Republic of Mexico, and and served against Maximi-
lan until his final overthrow. In the early part of 1867, I established a 'Reconstruction' news paper in Arkansas, which I continued to edit till March 1871,
when I had the honor to receive from your Excellency the Commission as U. S.
Consul at Santa-Cruz, Danish West Indies. This position I continued to fill up
to the date of the passage of the Consular and Diplomatic appropriation Bill, by
the last session of Congress, which, by its provisions, abolished my post. I flat-
ter myself that, owing to my knowledge of the customs and language of the

Mexican people, I might serve this Government to advantage, if assigned to a consular post in that Republic. I would respectfully invite your attention to the accompanying letters from Senators Dorsey, Spencer, Clayton and Morton; these gentlemen being personally acquainted with my past record, I dare believe that their testimonials will meet with the consideration which they merit."—ALS, *ibid.* Related papers are *ibid.* On Jan. 18, 1877, USG nominated Siler as consul, St. Helena.

1876, Nov. 25. USG endorsement. "Referred to the Sec. of the Treas. with the request that the solicitor of the Treas. examine into this matter and see that no injustice is done the surities of Postmaster Chism."—AES, DNA, RG 206, Letters Received from the President. Written on an undated letter from Wendell Phillips to USG. "My friend, Dr D. K. Hitchcock, the bearer of this, was, four or five years ago, surety, with others, for the Postmaster at Newton, where he lives. Funds were stolen from this officer, which his death soon after prevented his repaying. There was no criminal default, only an accident. Mr Banfield, then representing the Treasury, after examining the affair, assured Dr Hitchcock that He should not be be called on to respond. The present agents of the Treasury are taking measures to collect what remains due of Dr Hitchcock; who alone of the bondsmen is able to pay, unless *one* other should. If you should see it to be consistent with the public service to give my friend your countenance & aid in having this obligation cancelled, I should esteem it a great personal favor"—ALS, *ibid.*

1876, Nov. 27. USG commutation "to imprisonment at hard labor for life" for Johanna Turbin, a black woman sentenced to be hanged for murder in Washington, D. C.—Copy, DNA, RG 59, General Records. On Oct. 31, a newspaper reported the judge's comments at Turbin's sentencing. "'I do not know that it has ever fallen to the lot of a judicial officer in this District to pronounce sentence of death on one of your sex. This may be accounted for by the fact that women observe the law better than men. The crime of which you have been convicted is a most atrocious and revolting one, and perhaps there never was one committed by either sex which surpasses it in atrocity. The victim was your husband, and after inflicting the fatal blow you mutilated the body in the most barbarous manner. If there ever was a case in which capital punishment is deserved this is the case.' Judge MacArthur continued, remarking that the jury had a repulsion to the execution of a woman, and they had petitioned for the intervention of executive clemency, and after passing the sentence he would sign a paper which would give her her life. He advised her that her life would be passed in prison; that she need entertain no hope of ever escaping therefrom, for he was assured that executive clemency would grant her no further boon than her life, . . ."—*Washington Evening Star,* Oct. 31, 1876. See *ibid.,* July 7–8, Oct. 25–28, 30, 1876.

1876, Nov. 30. To John F. Long, surveyor of customs, St. Louis. "I should be very glad indeed if you can find a position in your office for Mr. C. C. Fouke, who is the son of Col. Fouke, an old comrade and personal friend, very recently de-

ceased, and whose pecuniary affairs were left in such an embarrassed condition
as to leave his widow in dependent circumstances."—Copies, MoSHi; DLC-
USG, II, 3. On the same day, USG wrote similarly to Chauncey I. Filley, postmaster, St. Louis.—Copy, *ibid.* Probably on Dec. 14, Culver C. Sniffen wrote on
the copy meant for Long. "Mrs Fouke informs the President that her son has
not received the following letter & the President directs that this copy of the
original be again forwarded to Mr Fouke for delivery to you—"—AN (initialed), MoSHi. Philip B. Fouke, former U.S. Representative and col., 30th Ill.,
had died on Oct. 3.

1876, DEC. 1.   Robert Campbell, St. Louis, to USG. "My friend W. E Burr
President of the National Bank of Saint Louis is very desirous of obtaining an
appointmet for his son as Cadet at West Point and desires me to write to you on
the Subject   The young gentleman is now Seventeen years of age, and has the
highest testimonials from the Professors of the Washington University where
he has been educated   I am satisfied that if you shoul[d] confer upon him an appointment you will find that he will do honor to the profession, and, confer a
great favor upon me, as his father is a valued friend"—ALS, DLC-Edward Burr.
On Dec. 2, Albert G. Edwards, USMA 1832, asst. treasurer, St. Louis, wrote to
USG on the same subject.—ALS, *ibid.* Related papers are *ibid.* Edward Burr
graduated USMA in 1882, first in his class.

1876, DEC. 2.   USG endorsement. "I cheerfully endorse Senator Anthonys rec-
ommendation and desire, that Miss Getty should be restored to to place in the
Treas."—Copy, DNA, RG 56, Applications. Written on a letter of Oct. 27 from
U.S. Senator Henry B. Anthony of R. I. to Secretary of the Treasury Lot M.
Morrill recommending Addie E. Getty, "grand niece of President Harrison."
—Copy, *ibid.* USG also wrote an undated note. "See Sec. of the Treas. in behalf
of Miss Addie Getty, long in the Treas. but recently ~~furloughed~~ discharged. Desires to get back. Was aptd. originally on recommendation of Mr. Orth. Is from
Ia. Has a mother to support."—AN, *ibid.* Related papers are *ibid.*
     On Oct. 12, 1871, USG had endorsed a recommendation for Alonzo F. Getty.
"Respectfully refered to the Com. of Agriculture. Can not Mr. Getty be appointed to some other position in the Ag. Bureau?"—AES, *ibid.* On March 12,
1872, Addie Getty, Washington, D. C., wrote to USG. ". . . When I called upon
you some ten days ago and asked you to aid me in procuring my Brother A. F.
Getty a situation of some kind, you were very kind in telling me then that *you*
would see Secretary Boutwell, in *person. . . .*" —ALS, *ibid.* Alonzo Getty had
failed the required examination. On April 23, Addie Getty wrote to USG appealing again for her brother. ". . . I could support my ever dear mother.
brother. and self. too willingly would I do it, but my slender means. $75.00. will
not enable a little girl only 17 years old to do it. . . ." —ALS, *ibid.*

1876, DEC. 11.   USG endorsement. "The report of the Secretary of War is approved."—Copy, DNA, RG 107, Letters Sent, Military Affairs. Written on a
letter of Dec. 8 from Secretary of War James D. Cameron to USG opposing the
reinstatement of former 1st Lt. Francis S. Davidson, 9th Cav., dismissed in 1875
for gambling with enlisted men.—Copy, *ibid.*

1876, DEC. 12.   Robert Hasson, Jacksonville, Ala., to USG. "Some years ago I
wrote you asking an appointment in United States secret service and was answered your Chief officer of that service who notified me that my application
had been placed on file. I have not sence heard from it. and would say to you now
there has been one of the wost crimes on record ~~in~~ that ever occured in this
county in 2 white men trying to fource a freedman to live with them. they
whiped or beat him so severely he died in about (7) seven hours afterwards—&
the best citizens of ~~thate~~ neighborhood in which they the (2) two men lived as
soon as the could went to work and arrested the parties and worked hard to secure all the proof necessary to convict them and would have done the officer in
charge (a constable) I think was bribed and let the priseners make their escape
and have fled to parts unknown. and if you will now give me the appointment I
will go to work and finde out where they are and have them arrested again and
land safly in gail at Huntsville if you wish or at Jacksonville (this place) which
ever you may think best—for it is an offense against the constitution of the
United States & I think should be tried by their court. I can work up the case
and not only but many others. & will do it if you will give me the appoinment
and the salery asked. But cannot do it without pay—and as the Poor negros are
here recognized as citizens I am for giving them full protection though I am a
mamed soldier of the lost cause but in every case I am in for jestice to all and if
appointed I want no one here to know it. . . ." —ALS, DNA, RG 60, Letters from
the President.

1876, DEC. 16.   USG endorsement. "Referred to the Sec. of War. This is an application for restoration to the Army from which Lt. Macklin was dismised during the past Summer."—AES, DNA, RG 94, ACP, 6746 1876. Written on a letter of Dec. 15 from Col. David S. Stanley, 22nd Inf., New York City, to USG. "I
have the honor to state to your Excellency, that James E. Macklin late a 2nd
Lieut in my regiment served continuously under my command from 1870 until last July—during that time I never had occasion to find any fault with his
conduct, official, or social,—In regard to sobriety he was a *teetotelar*, and was
much relied upon by me, when an enterprizing officer was needed—"—ALS,
ibid. On Dec. 27, Secretary of War James D. Cameron endorsed papers in the
case of former 2nd Lt. James E. Macklin, court-martialed for drunkenness during the campaign against the Sioux in Aug. "Respectfully submitted to the President, recommending the reappointment of Mr. Macklin, who appears to have
been dismissed for a single offense—not of the most aggravated character—after his service with a highly creditable record, from the commencement of the
rebellion."—ES, *ibid.* On Dec. 28, USG approved Cameron's recommendation.—AES, *ibid.* On Jan. 2, 1877, USG nominated Macklin as 2nd lt., 11th Inf.
See *SRC*, 45-3-547, 3; *HRC*, 48-1-621, 2.

1876, DEC. 19.   USG pardon for Madison Doom, sentenced Oct. 18 to four
months in prison in Augusta County, Va., for violating the 1875 civil rights
act.—Copy, DNA, RG 59, General Records.

1876, DEC. 19.   Lt. Gen. Philip H. Sheridan, Chicago, to USG. "It gives me
pleasure to recommend to your kind consideration, for appointment in the

Army as Second Lieutenant, A. C. Macomb. He is reported to me as in every
way fitted for the service mentally and physically. His father, Col. J. W. Macomb,
of the Engineer Corps is well known to you as of long service and distinguished
merit. Should a vacancy exist and you can give the appointment it will give
great gratification to his numerous friends."—Copy, DLC-Philip H. Sheridan.
Augustus C. Macomb, a naval cadet from 1872 to June, 1876, was appointed 2nd
lt. in 1878.

1876, DEC. 19.   J. Newton Crittenton, Chicago, to USG. "Owing to Nervous
Prostration, one of my Physicians recommends me to go to the Sea Shore for
Six weeks or two months. I have tried to arrange a Transfer from Chicago to
Washington for three or four months intending to take half of the time for Resting and Recuperation But Mr Whitney Manager W U Telegraph Office at
Washington says it is impracticable for him to favor me as his force have to be
ready for duty at all times. I would therefore respectfully ask if you cannot ar-
range to make me one of your Private Secretaries until March 4th and allow me
the privilege of absence Sundays and, if consistent one or two other days of the
week. A short Sea Voyage would benefit me. My association with you in the
South as a military Telegraph Operator and my ability as a moderate Short
Hand writer emboldens me to make this request."—ALS, DLC-USG, IB. No
appointment followed. Crittenton had served as 1st lt., 1st Mich. Engineers.
See William R. Plum, *The Military Telegraph During the Civil War in the United
States,* ... (1882; reprinted, New York, 1974), I, 208, 210, 283–84, 291.

1876, DEC. 20.   USG note. "Will The Sec. of the Treas. please see Miss
Greene, formerly from Me. for a few moments."—ANS, DNA, RG 56, Applications. In an undated letter, Chestina S. Greene, Washington, D. C., wrote to
USG requesting reinstatement as a treasury clerk. ". . . My friends from Va have
been repeatedly to the Secretary and to the Appointment Clerk but to no avail
so far—The Secretary in my presence requested the Appointment clerk to appoint me and the latter promised, and still promises, to do but he adds those du-
bious words 'as soon as possible' The effort now seems to be to put off the matter until the Presidential question is settled, and it is known whether the
Treasury Dept. will remain in the hands of the present party another four years.
But I am extremely anxious to get my appointment before the 4th of March for
several reasons. In the first place I can not but feel that from your successor,
even if he be the Republican candidate,—I may not meet with the kind reception which I have been so fortunate as to meet with from you.—Again, even
though Mr Tilden is inaugurated, if I already was reinstated, I should have some
faint hopes of retaining my position although of such well known Republican
antecedents, through personal friends amongst Democrats. . . ." —ALS, *ibid.*
On Sept. 25, former U.S. Representative James H. Platt, Jr., of Va., Norfolk, had
written to Secretary of the Treasury Lot M. Morrill supporting Greene because of her family connections.—ALS, *ibid.* No appointment followed.

1876, DEC. 20.   USG note. "Will the Com.r of Agriculture please see
Mrs. [E. S.] Waterhouse, Sister of the wife of the Mexican Minister, who will

state her application better than I could do."—ANS (bracketed material in another hand), Gallery of History, Las Vegas, Nev. The back of the card is marked
"Essex. Conn."—E, *ibid.*

1876, Dec. 20.   Hannah L. Chadbourne, Eastport, Maine, to USG. "I take the
liberty from the circumstance that you were a class-mate of my son Lincoln at
West Point—to ask a favor of you—I have a grand-son George Wallingford
Chadbourne—who is very anxious to be admitted to the West Point Academy—His Father is dead—and he has no friends of sufficient influence to procure an appointment for him—He is fifteen years old, tall—well-built, and vigorous, and a good scholar—He is now in the High school here—He would like
to enter the Academy in a year from June next—It will gratify me much if you
can consistently aid my grand-son in obtaining the appointment he so much desires—As to the character and standing of my grand-son I can refer you to Mr
N. B. Nutt, collector of customs at this port—"—ALS, DNA, RG 94, Unsuccessful Cadet Applications. Theodore L. Chadbourne, USMA 1843, was killed
May 9, 1846, at the battle of Resaca de la Palma.

1876, Dec. 20.   Jacob R. Riblett, Shawneetown, Ill., to USG. "Having served
under you in the Vicksburg campaign as a soldier in the 108th Ill. Vol. and having there learned the deep, kind interest you took in the welfare of every man
under your noble guidance, I at this time appeal to you as I would to my own
father were he living. I have the dearest little wife in the world and a bright little
son 3 years of age, and all three of our lives are being made miserable by the
influence of her family and relatives. In 1872, just after my graduation from
West Point, we were married, my wife was heir to some thousands of dollars'
worth of realty, that will not come into her possession until 1878. I had nothing but my commission in the army and a good fair name, as I always was a poor
boy. Ours was a love-match and it was very happy, our life together, until we
came here among her family. They did all in their power to keep us from mar-
rying, failing in that they have since been doing all in their power to render our
life miserable. When our child was born the strain upon her system affected
h[er] mind, and she has never been mentally sound since,   this makes her an
easier subject for th[eir] influence, which is used to destroy our happiness. In
1873, I resigned from the army on account of [my] father's death,   they prevailed on us to move here and ever since then we have had much to contend
against. . . ." —ALS, DNA, RG 94, ACP, 1634 1873. No reinstatement followed.

1876, Dec. 21.   George Sauer, London, to USG. "I have the honor to transmit
herewith a copy of a little work entitled 'Handbook of European Commerce'
published by me a short time ago.—I have to request that you will do me the
honor to accept of the same"—ALS, USG 3.

1876, Dec. 23.   Charles Rhind, New York City, to USG concerning his brother,
Commodore Alexander C. Rhind, removed from duty as lighthouse inspector.
". . . Commodore Rhind made personal application to the Secrty for a revocation
of the order—The Secrty remarked: 'You are a bachelor, etc;' to which the Com-

modore replied: 'I think my pecuniary responsibilities are as great as his,' i. e. his successor's. It may be proper to state that the Commodore's sisters reside with, and are dependent on him. Commodore Rhind's record during the war will bear the most rigid scrutiny. He was always stationed where there were *hard knocks, and no prize money*—The unusual circumstance of his being detached, without cause, when only about one third of the customary period of duty had expired, has excited no little comment in naval circles; and, when generally known, may warrant the imputation of private and sinister motives . . ." —ALS, DNA, RG 45, ZB File. A similar letter, dated Dec. 30, is in DLC-Hamilton Fish. See Hamilton Fish to Rhind, Jan. 3, 1877, *ibid.* Commodore Rhind resumed lighthouse duty in March, 1877.

1876, DEC. 26.   Col. James H. Simpson, St. Louis, to USG appealing for intervention in the case of Janet C. Gabaudan, former Treasury Dept. clerk "discharged, as she thinks, without a proper regard to her ability & deserts."—ALS, DNA, RG 56, Applications. On Dec. 7, Gabaudan, New Brunswick, N. J., had written to Simpson. ". . . Provision was I heard made last year for the relatives of those who died in their Country's service, my son served his Country from the age of 15 until he died in his 26th year—Admirel F. wrote my ~~son~~ husband at the taking of Port Hudson 'Ed & I did it'—had he not taken the despatches to Gen Grant Vicksburgh might not have been taken, . . ." —ALS, *ibid.* On April 8, 1875, USG had endorsed a letter of the same day from Matilde G. Frelinghuysen, Washington, D. C., to Crawford C. Adams, principal clerk, currency div., concerning an earlier discharge of Gabaudan from a temporary position. "I   hope   the   Sec.   of   [the]   Treas.   will   be   able   to   retain   Mrs. Gabaudan—the mother of the Private Sec. to Adml Farragut during the war—in the Treas."—AES, *ibid.* Related papers are *ibid.*

1876, DEC. 27.   USG note. "Will the Sec. of the Treas. please see Mrs. Garvey, the wife of a soldier who lost a leg, and his health, in the service."—ANS, DNA, RG 56, Applications. On Dec. 19, Catherine Garvey, Washington, D. C., had written to Secretary of the Treasury Lot M. Morrill. "Having been discharged from the Bureau of Engraving and Printing on the 16th inst where I have been employed for the last twelve months at a salary of $1.50. per day (in Mr Morgans counting room.) I would most respectfully request a reconsideration of the above action, my case being one of peculiar hardship My husband (James Garvey) has served in the Volunteer Army of the U. S. (18th N. Y. Infantry) during the late rebellion, lost his leg in the service and has by reason of said disability and severe illness (consumption) been unable to earn a cent during the last 18 months; he and our two children have therefor alltogether depended upon ~~the~~ my earnings for their daily bread. With this last dependence gone starvation stares us all in the face. In concluding my humble request for re-instatement Mr Secretary I would beg to state that out of 2 families, on my own & my husbands side, no less than 6 male members have stood to the Country in its hour of need, and out of those 2 families there is not one member to day holding a position of any kind under the government. Hoping that you will believe my case to be one meriting your kind consideration . . ."—ALS, *ibid.* Garvey returned as a counter to the Bureau of Printing and Engraving.

1876, DEC. 27.   Edward Hamilton, Portland, Ore., to USG. "I respectfully ask the appointment of Visiter to the West Point Military academy for the ensuing summer. The interest I have in the Institution since my grand son E H Brooke has been a Cadet there induces a wish to be present at the examinations, and inspections of the Board. I will deem it a high compliment coming from you, and a recognition, arising out of events most memorable and agreeable to us both: It has not been in my way to be at Washington, at any time since my coming to Oregon in 1850. That you have not probably heard my name mentioned during your residence there, may be owing to the fact of my having been entirely out of public life, and from choice not at any time serving in that grand army of office beggars by whom I imagine you have been surrounded. Allow me to add, that I avoid the routine mode of all such applications because I prefer being under obligations to you, rather than to any other who would be likely to suggest or solicit it. It so happens that I am rich in personal and political friends around you in the various departments, who will cheerfully concur in approving your action in this matter"—ALS, DNA, RG 94, Correspondence, USMA. No appointment followed for Hamilton, former secretary, Oregon Territory (1850–53). Admitted in 1875, Edward H. Brooke left USMA in June, 1877; he was appointed 2nd lt. in 1879.

1876, DEC. 30.   Postmaster Gen. James N. Tyner to USG concerning post office appointments.—Paul C. Richards Autographs, Catalogue No. 22, no. 876.

[*1876, Dec.*].   Olive J. Ennis, Cincinnati, to USG. ". . . I am the widow of an officer of the 3d U. S. Cavalry—1st Lieut. J. J. Ennis—a man not unkwon to Gen'l Dent and others of your family—He has been dead seven years and during that time I have supported my self and one little son: the most of the time being employed ein the Enquirer. My salary is not enough now that my boy is growing larger—he is now ten years old—and I have dared to hope that your all powerful influence might be exerted in my behalf in procuring some position that would enable me to be more comfortably situated. Your old friend Col Barnard of St Louis in the years gone by knew both my husband and myself and I think will tell you that I am not without intelligence, education and energy. In the old days, we were warm friends. Another, whom I knew intimately was Mrs John Dent. These friends of yours, will, I am sure vouch for my ability to fill any position an average woman could take. I do not wish to go into any of the Departments, the tenure is too uncertain, the remuneration too little, but I would very much like some position in the military branch of the government, where I would receive enough to live upon and have the opportunity to give my boy the education he is fitted for, a soldier's . . ."—ALS (docketed Dec. 20), DNA, RG 107, Appointment Papers. No appointment followed.

[*1876, Dec.-Jan., 1877*].   James Millward to USG. "The undersigned would respectfully solicit the appointment of United States Consul at some port in Great Britain or elsewhere, and respectfully refers to the following named gentlemen"—LS (undated, docketed Jan. 9, 1877), DNA, RG 59, Letters of Application and Recommendation. Chester A. Arthur, collector of customs, New York City, Thomas Murphy, and five others, favorably endorsed this letter.—ES, *ibid.*

Letters recommending Millward from Abram J. Dittenhoefer and Arthur to U.S. Senator Roscoe Conkling of N. Y. are *ibid.* On Jan. 11, 1877, USG nominated Millward as consul, Ghent. See *New York Times,* Aug. 31, 1892.

[*1876*].   USG note. "Apt Capt. S. L. Phelps Member of Board of Visitors to Naval Academy Sec. of the Navy,"—AN (undated), Wayde Chrismer, Bel Air, Md. S. Ledyard Phelps served on the board of visitors, U.S. Naval Academy, in June, 1876.

[*1876*].   USG note. "The statement that Clark was appointed postmaster of Mattoon, Ill. vice Lynn removed is incorrect. Clark is postmaster and was removed & Lynn aptd but the question was reconsidered ~~and commission withheld from Lynn,~~ and no removal made"—AN, OHi. On Sept. 22, 1873, USG had suspended James H. Clark as postmaster, Mattoon; on Nov. 18, USG suspended George W. Lynn. Clark continued as postmaster.

1877, JAN. 3.   USG endorsement. "Referred to the Sec. of War. The Military order referred to does practically relieve Indian Agt. Cravens of all powers as an agt. and should be modified."—AES, DNA, RG 94, Letters Received, 4163 1876. Written on a letter of Dec. 28, 1876, from John Q. Smith, commissioner of Indian Affairs, to Secretary of the Interior Zachariah Chandler complaining that 2nd Lt. Ralph W. Hoyt had usurped the duties of James T. Cravens, Cheyenne River Agency, Dakota Territory.—Copy, *ibid.* On Jan. 5, 1877, Gen. William T. Sherman endorsed these papers. "Respectfully returned to the Hon Secretary of War, requesting that he hold these papers till Monday next Jan 8 when Genl Sheridan will be here. The language of Mr Chandler Secretary of the Interior was that pending the Sioux War, the Commanding officers of the garrisons at the Several Agencies including that at Cheyenne might Exercise '*absolute*' control over the Agencies, especially to control issues. I beg that the President will not insist on a modification of this order. There should be but one Commanding officer at Cheyenne, and he should not be the Indian agent" —AES, *ibid.* On Jan. 10, Lt. Gen. Philip H. Sheridan endorsed these papers. "Respectfully returned to the General of the Army requesting from the Hon. Secretary of the Interior and Commissioner of Indian Affairs a continuance of the Military supervision at the Cheyenne Agency. Lieut Colonel Buell, the officer in Command at the Agency, is a very careful officer and I am sure will not do anything but what is proper and necessary, and his desire to have a full knowledge of the amount of food issued to Indians, is in my opinion, correct. It is well known that before the issues were supervised by the Comdg officers that large amounts of food were conveyed to the hostile camps, this is true of Standing Rock and Red Cloud. We do not wish to exercise the supervision a moment longer than necessary but it is too soon to withdraw it yet."—ES, *ibid.* On Jan. 12, Secretary of War James D. Cameron wrote to Chandler approving Sheridan's views.—LS (press), *ibid.* See *HED,* 45-2-1, part 5, I, 447–50.

1877, JAN. 8.   USG endorsement. "Referred to the Sec. of the Int. The enclosed endorsements of Mr. Strohm are very strong and I hope he may get one of the vacancies in the Patent Office."—AES, deCoppet Collection, NjP. Probably in reference to Isaac Strohm, former engrossing clerk, House of Representatives. See Strohm to James A. Garfield, Sept. 14, 1880, DLC-James A. Garfield.

1877, JAN. 11.   USG endorsement. "Referred to the Sec. of the Treas. I am disposed to think Mr. Lee should be removed."—AES, DNA, RG 56, Letters Received from the President. Written on a petition of Jan. 8 from Rusha Denise *et al.,* Norfolk, to USG. "We the undesigned citizens of Norfolk city Norfolk county and vicinity state of Virginia, Earnestly request that Luther Lee Esq collector of customs for the ports of Norfolk and Portsmouth Va. may be removed from said collectorship and some suitable person appointed in his stead. We ask the removal for the following reasons—1st That Mr Lee has held the office nearly seven years and during that time has never personally discharged the duties of his office but has entrusted the duties and responsibilities of the sane entirely to the Deputy collector—2nd That Mr Lee does not possess that exalted char[a]cter and intelligence necessary to inspire the confidence or respect of the community in which he resides or of the republican party of the 2nd congressional District of Va—3rd That Mr Lee in the spring of 1875, basely betrayed the republican party in Norfolk county the county in which he resides, and allied him self with the conservative party of said county And by speech, official influence and act defeated the republican party of said county in an important county election, and thereby demoralized the republican party to such an extent that a county heretofore casting a republican majority of 1200. has been turned over to the conservative party—4th That Mr Lee owns no property in the state of Va either real or personal, and is in no way identified with the interests of the community or state in which he resides—5 That we believe that the interests of the republican party of the 2nd Congressional District will be materially enhanced by the removal of Mr Lee and the appointment of a gentleman of character and ability who will be identified with the interests of the state, and whose public and private Character will tend to elevate the standing of the republican party in said Congressional District"—DS (4 signatures), *ibid.* Joseph E. Segar endorsed this document. "The above signers to this letter are prominent and most worthy citizens of the second Congressional district of Va, well known to me. They are incapable of making any but a reliable statement about any person or thing, and in the statements set forth in the foregoing letter I am sure they are strictly accurate. And I concur in opinion with them that the removal of Mr Lee will greatly advance the character, respectability, and success of the Republican party in the District and in the state. I was the Republican Candidate for Congress in that district in the late election." —AES (undated), *ibid.* On Jan. 26, Lewis W. Webb and two others, Norfolk, telegraphed to USG. "at a mass meeting of the republicans of Norfolk Norfolk County Portsmouth & Vicinity held this Evening resolutions were adopted protesting against the appointment of Either Jno S Braxton or Jas D Brady as Collector of this port Vice Lee Deceased & Recommending that no appointment be made for interval between this & fourth March next but that present deputy Collector act and fees and Emoluments go to family of late Collector and a Committee was appointed to present resolutions in person by Order of meeting"—Telegram received (at 10:49 P.M.), DLC-USG, IB. See *New York Times,* Jan. 22, 1877.

On Dec. 2, 1869, Mayor George Chahoon of Richmond had written to USG. "I affords me great pleasure to state that I have been acquained with Capt Luther Lee, Jr. for several years and can confidently recommend him as an honorable, upright man and a true hard working republican. He was a faithful soldier during the late war and has been of great service to the republican party since the war terminated"—ALS, DNA, RG 56, Collector of Customs Applications. Related papers are *ibid.* On Sept. 9, 1867, Luther Lee, Jr., Norfolk, had written to USG seeking bvt. promotion.—ALS, *ibid.*, RG 94, ACP, 513L CB 1867. On Jan. 21, 1870, USG nominated Lee, Jr., as collector of customs, Norfolk and Portsmouth; on Jan. 12, 1874, USG renominated Lee, Jr. On Jan. 14, George W. Dawley, Norfolk, wrote to USG. "If you will give us Mr A L Hill as our next Collector of Customs the coloured people will be much obliged to you Mr Lee has had it 4 years and Mr Hill is a good honest man"—ALS, *ibid.*, RG 56, Collector of Customs Applications.

On July 31, 1875, Judge Robert W. Hughes, Norfolk, wrote to USG. "I learn that the consulship at Montevideo is vacant or about to be, and as Virginia has lost the Portuguese mission, I hope some compensation may be made to her by minor appointments. I therefore would respectfully request the appointment of John S. Braxton of Tappahannock Va He is a man of excellent standing, and his family are amongst the most reputable people of the state; his grandfather was a signer of the Declaration of Independence. He has been a Republican from the close of the war, and has several times been a candidate of the party with little hope of election, for the sake of the cause. He has been once or twice in the legislature, and stands high in the community. His object in asking this office, is in order to make some means for the education of his children, who are of the age when that must be done if at all. I sincerely trust you can see the propriety of giving him this appointment"—ALS, DNA, RG 59, Letters of Application and Recommendation. Related papers are *ibid.* On May 16, 1876, USG nominated John S. Braxton as consul, Montevideo; on Jan. 26, 1877, USG nominated Braxton as collector of customs, Norfolk and Portsmouth.

1877, JAN. 12. Judge William McKennan, 3rd U.S. Circuit, Washington, Pa., to USG. "I beg to introduce to you Mr. Walter C. Childs of Pittsburgh, who wishes to confer with you in furtherance of his desire to be appointed to a Consulship at some French port. I have but a slight personal acquaintance with Mr. Childs, but I know that he belongs to a most respectable family. . . ." —ALS, DNA, RG 59, Applications and Recommendations, Hayes-Arthur. On Jan. 22, Walter C. Childs, Pittsburgh, wrote to Secretary of State Hamilton Fish. "I would hereby make application for an appointment to one of the French consulates—my preference being for Rheims or Bordeaux. On the 18th inst., the President received my letter of recommendation, and informed me that he would refer it to the Department of State."—ALS, *ibid.* No appointment followed. See *New York Times,* July 19, 1934.

1877, JAN. 15. USG endorsement. "Referred to the Sec. of the Int. This is from a Mich. Indian woman whose complaint I gave the Sec. some week or ten days since."—AES, DNA, RG 75, Letters Received, Mackinac Agency. Written on a letter of Jan. 7 from Margaret Ogabegijigokwe, Little Traverse, Mich., to USG.

"A poor child went a great long way to see her great Father to the poor Children returning home with greater grieve no satisfaction answer from the great Father to his poor Child, I went there to ask you to give these few familys who never had any Lands from the great Father who ought have had the Lands, that was my intention of undertaking that long bitter journey, many times most throwing me out of Cars because I had not money enought to pay ful fare, and after all not obtaining anything, we do not want take the Lands as homestead, because we are oblige to cut down trees and clear the Land but we want preserve our Trees from cuting down to make Sugar for we use greatdeal of Sugar, this is the object of your poor Children by sending me to go see their great Father personally, to hear him from his own word and when they saw me coming home they all rush in haste to the house asking what the great Father had said, all most ashame to tell them that the man who toke me to see the great Father did not give me no time to hear any answer or obtain even a spool of thread from the Father of poor Children O! great Father who is ful power to do any thing all but creat another world, do please have compassion and pity your Children for we are your poor Indian Children, for I was weeping all way coming home, Such bitter long journey for a poor old woman of sixty years like me, please excuse and pardon me a poor child went so far to see her great Father to talk to him personally as a child to his own Father . . . Please Excuse my poor writing I was told by some of those men in the office that the great Father did not wish to see his Children, poor me, going so far purpose to see the Father, I do not see why a Father does not wish to see his poor Child, coming to him, from so long way, and not let her see him only half minute, O! tears tears all way home, and the same time, of me going so far, trying to sell our Indian work to get money by, to pay our Taxes these Whites here who are with us they Tax us so high, so that we cannot no way get money to pay for tax, and then they buy our Lands for tax, this is why they do it to take our Lands away from us poor Indians do great Father of all send some one here to stay with us right here to protect & defend for us poor Indians, we always thought & our fore fathers told us, that the great Spirit created us & gave us this part of world to be our living Lands all this your poor child would tell you, but no time giving to her to talk to her Father poor me"—ALS, *ibid.*

1877, JAN. 15. USG veto. "For the reasons set forth in the accompanying communication addressed to the Secretary of the Interior by the Commissioner of the General Land Office, I have the honor to return herewith without my signature House bill No. 2041, entitled 'An Act to amend section twenty-two hundred and ninety-one of the Revised Statutes of the United States in relation to proof required in homestead entries'"—DS, DNA, RG 233, 44A-D1. *SMD,* 49-2-53, 405. On Jan. 11, James A. Williamson, commissioner of the General Land Office, had written to Secretary of the Interior Zachariah Chandler. ". . . The purpose of the act is to enable parties seeking title under the homestead law to make final proof before a Judge or Clerk of Court in the county or district where the lands are situated. Its provisions are in conformity with the views and recommendations of this office and I see no objection to them in so far as relates to the taking of the testimony. I observe, however, that the second section provides that the proofs, affidavits and oaths shall be filed in the office of the Register and

no provision is made for the transmission of either the original papers or dupli-
cate to this office, in order that patents may properly issue thereon—the provisions relating to certification for the purposes of evidence seeming to require
that they shall remain on file in the district office. There is therefore no opportunity for the supervisory control of the Commissioner over entries so made
to be exercised under the Statutes, . . ."—LS, DNA, RG 48, Miscellaneous
Div., Letters Received. On Jan. 12, Chandler wrote to USG concurring in
Williamson's views.—LS, *ibid.,* RG 233, 44A-D1. See *CR,* 44–1, 1518–20,
5335–36, 44–2, 426. On March 3, USG approved a revised homestead entry
bill. See *U.S. Statutes at Large,* XIX, 403–4; *CR,* 44–2, 1548–49, 1854, 2137.

1877, JAN. 19. USG endorsement. "Referred to the Sec. of War who will please
have the Commander of the troops in the states referred to instructed to give
all the aid necessary to enable the Rev. Officials to perform their duties, and to
arrest the violaters of the Rev. laws."—AES, DNA, RG 94, Letters Received,
3681 1876. Written on the docket of a letter dated Jan. 18 from Green B. Raum,
commissioner of Internal Revenue, to Secretary of the Treasury Lot M. Morrill. "I have the honor to invite your attention to the increase of frauds upon the
revenue by the illicit distillation of spirits, and to the difficulty of enforcing the
internal revenue laws in several of the Southern States. . . . In North Carolina,
South Carolina and Georgia, a considerable number of persons were arrested.
These active operations and arrests seem not to have at all deterred the viola-
tors of the law. They are now more bold and defiant than ever, especially in
North Carolina, South Carolina and Georgia. They have combined together to
resist the execution of the laws, and they boast that they will resist to the end
and meet force with force. A few weeks since a party under the charge of Revenue Agent Wagner, searching for illicit stills, were attacked at about daylight
by a force of 20 armed men, and fired upon. On the 12th inst. Deputy Collector
Barton of the South Carolina district, and his assistant Hendricks, were both
wounded by a distiller they were attempting to arrest. Hendricks was fatally
shot. It is impossible to execute the laws in these States with the force now at
my command, or with any force that I can employ under the present appropriation. . . ." —LS, *ibid.* Related papers are *ibid.*

1877, JAN. 19. To House of Representatives. "At the request of the Attorney
General, I have the honor to transmit herewith a report in answer to resolution
of the House adopted on the 1st of August, 1876. relative to certain matters oc-
curring in the administration of the provisional government of the District of
Columbia. and chiefly affects the Commissioners and the late Board of Audit—"
—Copy, DNA, RG 130, Messages to Congress. *HED,* 44-2-26. On Jan. 14,
Samuel F. Phillips, solicitor gen., had written to USG evaluating the conduct of
the D. C. commissioners and board of audit.—Copy, DNA, RG 60, Opinions.
HED, 44-2-26, 1–5. See *CR,* 44–1, 5051; *HMD,* 44-1-103; *HRC,* 44-1-702.

On July 6, 1876, William Dennison, John H. Ketcham, and S. Ledyard
Phelps, D. C. commissioners, had written to USG. "We have the honor to send
you a copy of the Congressional Record of this date, and will thank you at your
leisure to read the speech of Hon. George W. Hendee on District affairs, as being a fair statement of the results of the Investigation of the Commissioners'

administration of the District government."—LS, DLC-USG, IB. See *CR*, 44–1, Appendix, 162–70.

1877, JAN. 19.   John Welsh, Philadelphia, to USG. "I presume an invitation has been received by you from the French Govt for the UStates to take part in the Exhibition of 1878 at Paris. As a republican movement it would be most uncivil for our Govt to decline, but, that question aside, it is for our interest that we should, and being so, there is little enough time for preparation. It might seem to be an unfit moment to communicate with Congress on the subject, but a matter outside of politics might be a relief to them. It is however of the utmost importance that we should take part with the French, & that we should do so creditably, and this cannot be done without the time and the means. I hope the selection of the Chief Commissioner may be with you and, if so, that A. T. Goshorn, who has distinguished himself so greatly as our Director General, may be your choice. He is a man of integrity, capacity, good temper & good judgment, whose management in his present office has shewn his eminent fitness for the suggested position. The Chief Commissioner should be absolute. In every instance where that was so, in our Exhibition, there was harmony, and the reverse, where it was not. Pardon me for these suggestions. Disinterested suggestions are often valuable as aids. . . . I am very glad to see that hopes are entertained for the adoption by Congress of the report of the joint committees. The plan meets with great favor on the part of all thoughtful people. I rejoice in it myself, and should it pass, no one ought to be congratulated more heartily than yourself, for then the close of your Administration will be of such a character as to allow the more readily of that appreciation of it which must come when prejudice and passion have passed away."—ALS, DNA, RG 59, Miscellaneous Letters. On Feb. 27, H. de Mareil, *Messager Franco-Americain,* New York City, wrote to USG urging coordination with Congress to ensure U.S. participation in the Paris exhibition. ". . . I will not intrude on your valuable time by stating in detail the numerous reasons why the United States should not be absent from the Universal Exhibition next year. It is obviously true that, at this time, when the foreign trade of the country is growing, the public interest requires a large representation of the American manufacturers at the World's fair. No one understands this better that the manufacturers themselves, and they will, no doubt, take a large part in the Exhibition, if not debarred from doing so by the non-action of Congress. It may also be said that the French have some little right to expect this participation, after having themselves contributed to the success of the Philadelphia Exhibition. . . ." —LS, *ibid.* On Feb. 9, Culver C. Sniffen had written to de Mareil. "The President tells me that he did to-day deliver to the Members of the Cabinet to whom they were addressed, the communications you left—"—Copy, DLC-USG, II, 3. See *SMD,* 44-1-109; *Foreign Relations, 1877,* pp. 135–37.

  On Dec. 9, 1876, Secretary of State Hamilton Fish had written to Welsh. "I think that you mentioned to me that a Son of yours was in Europe, or was about to proceed thither The Consulate at Prague, is vacant, in mentioning it to the President I remembered, (or thought that I remembered) what you had said, and named your Son to him. He replied 'there is no man in the United States, whom I should be more glad to recognize by such an appointment than

Mr John Welsh—write to him & offer the appointment to his Son' Pray let me
know if I misapprehended you, or if I did wrong in Saying any thing to the President—If your son would like the place, let me know his *full* name, & he will
be nominated at once—Prague is regarded as one of the most pleasant of the
Consulates—the emoluments are at least twenty five hundred dollars, a year,
although, that possibly is a secondary consideration"—ALS (press), DLC-
Hamilton Fish. Health considerations prevented Welsh's son from accepting the consulship at Prague. See Welsh to Fish, Dec. 11, 1876, *ibid.*; Welsh to
John L. Cadwalader, Aug. 25, 1876, DNA, RG 59, Letters of Application and
Recommendation.

On Jan. 24, 1877, Ulysses S. Grant, Jr., wrote to Fish. "The President says
that Mr Quarles claims to speak and write the French language with the same
facility that he does English, and in addition speaks German, Spanish and Italian—the latter too he writes—Mr Quarles asks to go to Prague even if he
should have to return with the incoming aAdministration. His family and effects
are now in Europe. The President thinks it would be well to make the appointment"—ALS, DLC-Hamilton Fish. Papers concerning John F. Quarles are in
DNA, RG 59, Applications and Recommendations, Hayes-Arthur. See *PUSG*,
24, 314.

On Feb. 13, Fish recorded in his diary. "The President spoke of Charles A.
Phelps of Mass whom he said he wished appointed to some position—I suggested the Consulate at Prague. It meets the Presidents approval, so the nomination is made out there, and sent to the Senate."—DLC-Hamilton Fish. See
Charles A. Phelps, *Life and Public Services of General Ulysses S. Grant, . . .* (Boston, 1868; revised 1872).

1877, JAN. 19.   Julian T. Wright, "a Union man, and a friend to the Government of the United States," Lynchburg, Va., to USG asking the removal of
Warren S. Lurty, U.S. attorney, Western District, Va., for malfeasance and
drunkenness.—LS, DNA, RG 60, Letters from the President. Lurty, former art.
officer, C.S. Army, remained in office.

1877, JAN. 20.   USG pardon for Frank L. Taintor upon recommendations from
"a large number of the citizens of the City of New York, Bankers, Merchants,
and lawyers, of high respectability."—Copy, DNA, RG 59, General Records. On
Nov. 29, 1873, Taintor had been sentenced to seven years in prison for embez-
zlement from the Atlantic National Bank of New York City. See *New York Times*,
April 27, 30, Oct. 30, Nov. 30, 1873.

1877, JAN. 20.   To Congress. "Herewith I transmit a Report from the Secretary
of State with accompanying papers relating to the Court of Commissioners of
Alabama Claims.—"—Copies, DNA, RG 59, Reports to the President and Congress; *ibid.*, RG 130, Messages to Congress. *SED*, 44-2-21. On the same day,
Secretary of State Hamilton Fish had written to USG. "I have the honor to
transmit herewith a report from the Clerk of the Court of Commissioners of Alabama Claims together with several of the Opinions of the Judges of the Court,
delivered in the more important cases submitted to that Body. The Court having examined and decided all claims submitted to it in accordance with the sev-

eral Acts of Congress prescribing its jurisdiction, adjourned on the 29th ultimo."—Copy, DNA, RG 59, Reports to the President and Congress. *SED*, 44-2-21.

In a letter docketed Jan. 30, Frederick M. Shaw wrote to USG. "Refering to suggestions said to have been made by you as to the disposition of the Geneva Award; permit me to say; I hold the idea a sound one to devote the remaining amount to rebuilding our merchant Marine. Having expended many years and a fortune in perfecting ways and means for rendering the cost of transport of by sea of passengers & freights merely nominal; I am deeply interested in the rehabilitation of our own Merchant Navy. Please find enclosed a circular that mentions my plans. My mode—although thoroughy tested is not patented—" —ALS (undated), DNA, RG 56, Letters Received from the President. An enclosure outlining the organization and goals of "The Southern California Sanitary Hotel, & Industrial College Association" is *ibid.*

1877, JAN. 22. USG pardon for John Ryan, sentenced to imprisonment at Fort Smith, Ark., and fined $1,200 and costs for "selling at retail, spirituous liquors in the Choctaw Nation, Indian Territory, without having paid the special tax required by law."—Copy, DNA, RG 59, General Records. See *HED*, 44-2-1, part 5, p. 467.

1877, JAN. 23. To Senate. "I transmit in answer to a resolution of the Senate of the 16th instant, a Report of the Secretary of State with its accompanying papers."—Copies, DNA, RG 59, Reports to the President and Congress; *ibid.*, RG 130, Messages to Congress. *SED*, 44-2-24. On the same day, Secretary of State Hamilton Fish had written to USG transmitting diplomatic correspondence concerning Turkey.—Copy, DNA, RG 59, Reports to the President and Congress. *SED*, 44-2-24.

1877, JAN. 23. U.S. Senator John Sherman of Ohio to USG. "Please delay all action on appointment of Pension Agent at Columbus until I can see you"— Telegram received, DNA, RG 107, Telegrams Collected (Bound). On Jan. 30, USG nominated Allen T. Wikoff as pension agent, Columbus.

On Jan. 26, Sherman had telegraphed to USG. "Genl Keifer Member of Congress Elect residing at Springfield Ohio strongly urges the appointment of Shipman Postmaster at that place. Please determine it. Two good applications but think Keifer best able to make choice between them."—Telegram received, *ibid.* On Jan. 27, USG nominated John A. Shipman as postmaster, Springfield.

1877, JAN. 24. USG endorsement. "Referred to the Sec. of the Treas. This applicant seems to have unusual claims upon the Govt. and is from a state having but few employees in the Departments."—AES, DNA, RG 56, Applications. Written on a letter of Jan. 22 from William A. Austin, Washington, D. C., to USG. "I served as a private soldier for three years in Battery A. First Middle Tennesee Light Artillery, in the Union Army, during the late war, and was honorably discharged I have a wound in my head, both legs were broken by a shell, a wound in my wrist and a sabre cut in the abdomen I am poor and out of employment and have no means of support for my self and family I earnestly beg your Excellency to give me a letter of recommendation to the Secry of the Treasury, for an appointment as a watchman"—ALS, *ibid.*

1877, JAN. 24.   USG endorsement. "Respectfully referred to the Atty. Gen."—AES, DNA, RG 60, Letters from the President. Written on a letter of the same day from Secretary of the Treasury Lot M. Morrill to USG. "I have the honor to return herewith the bill (H. R. 231) for the relief of Robert Irwin and to state that the object of the bill being to confer jurisdiction on the Court of Claims over claims of said Irwin for proceeds of captured property, which claims are now barred by statute, and the defence of the Government in such cases being in the charge of the Attorney General I respectfully suggest that the bill be referred to him for his views thereon."—LS, *ibid.* On Feb. 1, U.S. Senator John B. Gordon of Ga. wrote to USG. "I am confined to my bed with, illness, or I should have done myself the honor of calling upon you and stating to you personally, what I am now compelled to put on paper. Mr Robert Erwin of Savannah Georgia, a well known and responsible Merchant in that city, has a Bill now pending before you, for your signature, and I learn it is feared it may be drawn into a hurtful precedent.—I desire then, to call your attention to the exceptional and isolated character of Mr Erwins case, and would remark, that it was this together with the great hardship of his case, which secured a unanimous vote, of both houses of Congress. . . ." —ALS, *ibid.* On Feb. 5, this bill giving jurisdiction over Robert Erwin's cotton case to the Court of Claims became law without USG's signature. See *U.S. Statutes at Large (Private Laws)*, XIX, 95; *CR*, 44-2, 616–18; *HRC*, 44-1-6, 46-1-30; *SRC*, 44-1-430; *SMD*, 46-1-22.

1877, JAN. 26.   USG veto. "I have the honor to return herewith, without my approval, Senate Bill No 685—entitled 'An Act to place the name of Daniel H. Kelly upon the Muster-roll of Company F—Second Tennessee Infantry—The reasons for with holding my signature to this bill may be found in the accompanying report received from the Secretary of War.—"—Copy, DNA, RG 130, Messages to Congress. *SMD*, 49-2-53, 408. On Jan. 24, Secretary of War James D. Cameron had written to USG transmitting a report from AG Edward D. Townsend. ". . . 'The enclosed act directs the Secretary of War to place the name of Daniel H. Kelly upon the muster roll of Co. F. 2d Tennessee Infantry. to date December 1. 1861. There is no record of enlistment service or death of this man on file in this office, and if this Act becomes a law, as it now reads it will be of no benefit to the heirs.'"—Copy, DNA, RG 107, Letters Sent, Military Affairs. *SMD*, 49-2-53, 408. Delilah Kelly sought this recognition for her husband, who had died in a Richmond prison. See *SRC*, 44-1-220; *U.S. Statutes at Large*, XX, 571.

1877, JAN. 26.   To Samuel M. Shoemaker, Baltimore. "Myself five of the cabinet and Private secretary will go up."—Telegram received, Maryland Historical Society, Baltimore, Md. On Jan. 27, USG, Frederick Dent Grant, Secretary of War James D. Cameron, Secretary of the Navy George M. Robeson, Secretary of the Interior Zachariah Chandler, and Postmaster Gen. James N. Tyner attended a reception at Shoemaker's home. See *Washington Evening Star* and *Baltimore American and Commercial Advertiser*, Jan. 29, 1877.

1877, JAN. 29.   To Congress. "I hav[e] the honor to transmit herewith the proceedings of the Commission appointed to examine 'the whole subject of reform and reorganization of the Army of the United States' under the provisions of the Act of Congress, approved July 24. 1876—The Commission report that, so fully has their time been occupied by other important duties—that they are not at this time prepared to submit a plan or make proper recommendations.—" —Copy, DNA, RG 130, Messages to Congress. *SED*, 44-2-26. See *U.S. Statutes at Large*, XIX, 101; DNA, RG 94, ACP, 1316 1877.

1877, JAN. 29.   Jesse Wimberly, former sgt., C.S. Army, Waynesboro, Ga., to USG. ". . . Although I am the only white republican in this (Burke Co) and have supported you in the elections of 1868 & 1872—for the Presidency, I have never asked you for an office of profit. The position of Collector of Customs at Augusta for which I applyied two years ago pays nothing. I only wanted it because it *was at my home.* Those who opposed my appointment at Augusta, failed in the late National Canvass to give their support to Gen'l Hayes for the Presidency. These men are now holding Office under an administation that they refuse to support, while others who have breasted the political storms, are out in the cold. I beg of you to investigate the matter."—ALS, DNA, RG 56, Collector of Customs Applications. See Wimberly to James A. Garfield, Jan. 24, 1881, DLC-James A. Garfield.

1877, JAN. 30.   Lt. Governor Thomas L. Young of Ohio to USG. "Having learned that the Hon. Warner M. Bateman U. S. Dist. Attorney for the Southern District of Ohio is about to tender his resignation of that Office, which for many years he has filled with marked ability I take the liberty of addressing you to recommend as his successor Channing Richards Esq of Cincinnati. Mr. Richards has for some years occupied the position of first Assistant to Mr. Bateman and hence he is perfectly familiar with the duties of the Office and the condition of every cause now pending in the Circuit and District Courts in which the United States has any interest. . . ." —ALS, DLC-William H. Taft. On Jan. 31, Warner M. Bateman, Washington, D. C., wrote to USG resigning as U.S. attorney.—ALS, DNA, RG 60, Letters from the President. On Feb. 2, USG nominated Channing Richards to replace Bateman.

[*1877, Jan.-Feb.*].   USG note. "Will Mr Conant please see Mrs. Anthony, of R. I. the lady of whom I spoke yesterday desiring that she might be able to get some"—AN (incomplete), Goodspeed's Book Shop, Inc., Boston, Mass. On Feb. 2, 1877, Nora V. Anthony, Washington, D. C., wrote to USG. "I presented the card you gave me to the U S Treasurer   he tells me he can do nothing for me. I am here without a cent to leave the city with or even buy a loaf of bread and I only ask for work that I may live   I know I have no claims upon you beyond the assurance of my dead friend who told me to call on you in my hour of need. that you had promised her to aid her or a friend sent by her. Will you please give me a *Strong* card to the Secretary of the Treasury or some other department that will get me a place which will enable me to Support two little children   I do not know what to do unless you will aid me   I can not see my little ones suffer.   my husband as I told you and all his people were Rhode Islanders and I lived there

a while. by aiding me you will add another to the many acts of kindness which
has marked your carreer through life. Gen Burnside & Sen Anthony have given
me there aid but they had so many to take care of before I went to them that
they have not been able to do any thing for me yet. they knew my husbands
family well by aiding me you will perhap save a life."—ALS, DNA, RG 56, Applications. Starting in Nov., 1875, Anthony had clerked temporarily in the
Treasury Dept.—*Ibid.*

1877, FEB. 2.   USG endorsement. "Referred to the ~~See. of the Int.~~ Atty. Gen.
With the concurrence of Senator Hitchcock—on whos recommendation the
present Marshal of Wyoming Ter. was appointed—I approve this change."—
AES, DNA, RG 60, Letters from the President. Written on an undated letter
from U.S. Senators-elect Jerome B. Chaffee and Henry M. Teller and U.S. Rep-
resentative-elect James B. Belford of Colo. to USG. "We respectfully ask the appointment of Charles H Phelps of Colorado to the position of U. S. Marshal for
the Territory of Wyoming. He is a man well fitted for the position in every respect."—LS, *ibid.* On Feb. 7, USG nominated Charles H. Phelps as marshal,
Wyoming Territory, in place of William S. Sweezy. On Feb. 8, U.S. Senator Algernon S. Paddock of Neb. telegraphed to USG. "On behalf of Senator Elis
Saunders of my state & myself I ask you to withdraw nomination of Phelps for
Marshall Wyoming Territory, removing Sweeney of Nebraska. Please answer"
—Telegram received (at 2:00 P.M.), *ibid.* On Feb. 9, Governor John M. Thayer
of Wyoming Territory wrote to Paddock. "I am very much surprised at the removal of Sweezey I can conceive of no reason for it, as there can be no charges
against him, or, at least, I never heard of any. He ~~has~~ has made an excellent Marshal, and his Republicanism is unquestioned, and he is an earnest friend of the
President. I understand Hitchcock returned to Washington declaring he would
have Sweezy's head, because Maj Balcombe, ~~went~~ his deputy, went to Lincoln
and worked against Hitchcock's re-election. It seems hard that Sweesy should
suffer for that. I fear the President has been deceived. Will you not go with
Sweesey to the President? Would he not withdraw the nomination?"—ALS,
ibid. On Feb. 15, Paddock again telegraphed to USG. "By an irregular proceeding without notice to myself on the ninth Phelps was confirmed Marshal of
Wyoming Sweeney removed. I urgently request you withhold your signature
until I can see you. I denominate confirmation a trick"—Telegram received,
ibid., RG 107, Telegrams Collected (Bound). On Feb. 27, the Senate reconsidered its confirmation of Phelps and recommitted his nomination to committee.

1877, FEB. 3.   George W. Childs, Philadelphia, to USG. "I have just received
the enclosed memorandum from Paymaster Pettit and would be glad if you
would ask the Secretary of the Navy to send Mr. Arthur Peterson to be *examined* for position of Ast. Paymaster U. S. N. Mr. Borie is awfully depressed, and
we all feel that his proposed visit to you will be of great service to him.
Mr. Drexel & Mae are much improved by their trip. With kind regards to
all, . . ."—ALS, DNA, RG 45, ZB File. On Feb. 15, Childs wrote to Ulysses S.
Grant, Jr. "I enclose a letter I received from an old friend in regard to Pay Director Watmough & can add my testimony in his behalf also. Mr. Borie has re-

turned much better for his visit. He expects your Father & Mother to make them a visit next month. We shall all be glad to see them here. I want you always to look to me as a friend. Mr. Peterson has not yet heard from the Navy Dept."—ALS, *ibid.*, Subject File, Div. NI. On the same day, Robert Pettit, Philadelphia, wrote to Childs. "As a friend from his boyhood, and during his whole career in the Navy of Pay Director *Jas. H. Watmough,* I beg of you the strength of your great influence with the President to the end of his appointment as Paymaster General, the nomination being likely to be made any day within the present week; . . ."—ALS, *ibid.* Also on Feb. 15, Hugh J. Hastings, *New York Commercial Advertiser,* wrote to USG. "I have set my heart on the nomination of my friend *Watmough* for Pay Master General of the Navy It would make me feel very unhappy if he should fail. I have served your administration faithfully and well and have asked no favors from it. I would feel under great obligation if I could be *gratified in this one particular.*"—ALS, *ibid.* On Feb. 20, Culver C. Sniffen wrote to Secretary of the Navy George M. Robeson. "The President directs me to say that he will be pleased to receive the nomination of Watmough to be Paymaster General of the Navy in time to be sent to the Senate to-day. The President thinks it should be worded 'to take effect on the 22d [23d] instant.'"—ALS (bracketed material in another hand), *ibid.* On Feb. 23, USG nominated Arthur Peterson as asst. paymaster, U.S. Navy.

1877, FEB. 3.   Augustus R. Grote, director, Buffalo Society of Natural Sciences, to USG proposing an "International Scientific Service," supported by member governments, which "would provide for explorations and observations at all points deemed advisable and would recommend to the different Governments occasions for increased or particular outlays. It should establish posts of observation at different points and provide for their service and maintenance under the protection of international law. It seems to me that it would be greatly to the credit of our country to assume the initiative in this matter and to your Administration to appoint the first Commissioners to act on the part of the United States and negotiate to secure the cooperation of foreign Powers. . . ." —ALS, DNA, RG 59, Miscellaneous Letters.

1877, FEB. 3.   George Schloetzer, Middle Village, Mich., to USG. "As a Surgeon with Rank as Major I served the United States for the preservation of our Union in the 82nd Regt. Ills. Vols. (Colns. Hecker and Salomon). For the glory of our old Chief and of his administration I went 1871 to Varzin from Washington Territory, as a self constituted diplomat to see Bismarck about the Island of San Juan in Puget Sound and by my explanations of the real facts and the right of the United States I was successful in so far as Emperor William's decision restituted the Island to the United States As the English never before under any other administration made a cession of territory to the United States I believe this success was a great triumph of your Excellency's administration. . . . Being sick and very weak—I lost fifty pounds in a few months—I made application for increase of my pension and I allow me respectfully to ask your Excellency for recommendation of my application; or perhaps you will please recommend me to the favors of the Secretary of State, he may have some funds to recompense such secret diplomatic services although not asked for."—ALS, DNA, RG 59, Miscellaneous Letters.

1877, FEB. 7. USG endorsement. "I commend the appointment asked for by Mr Brown"—Copy, DNA, RG 56, Applications. Written on papers including an undated letter from James W. Brown, Washington, D. C., to Secretary of the Treasury Lot M. Morrill. "Owing to severe wounds incurred in the late war, and adverse circumstances, I am compelled to apply to you for a position in your department. Hoping the attached endorsements, are sufficiently influential to procure the same. . . ." —Copy, *ibid.* U.S. Senator Oliver P. Morton of Ind. and others favorably endorsed Brown's application.—Copies, *ibid.* No appointment followed.

1877, FEB. 7. USG note. "The Sec. of War may detail Lt. Paul, 3d U. S. Cavalry to the Artillery School at Fort Monroe if two officers will be left with his company thereafter."—ANS, NN. On March 12, 1869, 2nd Lt. Augustus C. Paul, 3rd Cav., had written to Secretary of State Hamilton Fish seeking appointment as consul, Dundee.—ALS, DNA, RG 59, Letters of Application and Recommendation. Lewis Dent, U.S. Senator Carl Schurz of Mo., and others favorably endorsed this letter.—AES, *ibid.* No appointment followed. On Jan. 7, 1873, USG nominated Paul as 1st lt.

1877, FEB. 7. Culver C. Sniffen to U.S. Senator Thomas W. Ferry of Mich., president *pro tem.* "The President will be pleased to receive tickets of admission for his family to-day."—ALS (telegram sent), DNA, RG 107, Telegrams Collected (Bound).

1877, FEB. 7. Secretary of State Hamilton Fish to USG. "In accordance with your request of yesterday, I have the honor to return herewith the papers relative to the East Florida cases referred on the 15th January to this Department."—Copy, DNA, RG 59, Domestic Letters. See Fish diary, Feb. 16, 1877, DLC-Hamilton Fish; *HRC,* 43-1-816, 46-3-227; *SED,* 46-2-101, 46-2-205.

1877, FEB. 7. Clinton B. Fisk *et al.,* Board of Indian Commissioners, Washington, D. C., to USG. ". . . The commission has uniformly during the eight years of its existence, steadily and emphatically labored to uplift the Indian by all the institutions of civilization and religion. They believe the Indians are the wards of the Government, and in no sense should they be regarded or treated as independent sovereignties; that they should, so far as practicable, be consolidated upon few reservations, and provided with *permanent individual homes;* that the tribal relation should be abolished; that lands should be allotted in severalty, and not held or occupied in common; that the Indians should become citizens of the United States speedily, that they may enjoy the protection of law, and be required to yield obedience thereto; and that it is the duty of the Government to afford them all reasonable aid in their preparation for citizenship, by educating them in industry and the arts of civilization, and to so disburse appropriations for their benefit as to discourage idleness and vice. . . . We would, if possible, have the public conscience aroused to a full comprehension of the utter want of good faith, the oft-repeated violations of the most sacred promises and agreements, which have characterized the intercourse of this nation with its helpless wards. Let us hope, for the sake of our common humanity, for the honor of the nineteenth century, the credit of Christianity, and our boasted civilization, that a better day is about to dawn upon this unfortunate race, and that justice, tardy though it be, is to be recognized in our future dealings with them. . . . From various causes some tribes show a far higher condition of improvement than others. This is due, among other things, to the possession of a better soil for agricultural purposes, a more genial climate, isolation and non-intercourse with uncivilized whites, and more intelligent and successful management on the part of agents and teachers. The policy now earnestly recommended is, to remove those occupying comparatively small tracts and showing little progress, to the large reservations, where they would have the example of their brethren, who are more advanced in the arts of industry, for their encouragement, and where they may learn by daily observation that thrift, enterprise, and energy do always produce their legitimate fruits of civilization and self-dependence. The encouragement afforded by such intercourse and examples would not fail to produce wholesome and practical results. Under this arrangement where large numbers were collected a system of law could be more successfully introduced, which with the early allotment of lands in severalty under a regulation forbidding their alienation for two or three generations, would speedily result in the breaking up of its tribal relations and go far toward the successful solution of the Indian problem, which has so long perplexed our nation, puzzled our statesmen, and disturbed our philanthropists. . . . Among the most important measures that ought to receive immediate attention are the following, to many of which the consideration of the Government has heretofore been repeatedly invited: 1. Immediate compliance on the part of the Government with terms of existing treaties with all the Indians. 2. Appropriations for consolidating agencies. 3. Generous appropriations for educational purposes. 4. Discontinuance of tribal relations. 5. Extension of law for protection of life and property. 6. Allotments of land. 7. Establishment of industrial and agricultural boarding-schools, compelling attendance of all between seven and seventeen years of age. 8. Issues of supplies to be made to heads of families. 9. Increase in salaries of Indian agents. All of which is respectfully submitted."—*Eighth Annual Report of the Board of Indian Commissioners . . .* (Washington, 1877), pp. 4–6, 10.

On Feb. 27, John D. Lang, Vassalboro, Maine, wrote to USG. "At the late meeting of the Board of Indian Commissioners, a document was presented & approved of, from the Representatives of different religious denominations commending thy peace policy & its good fruits. But I shall feel best satisfied to add my own humble testimony before the close of thy administration, to its wise & merciful dealings with an oppressed portion of our fellow beings. Having now served on this Commission seven years, & being the only one remaining of those appointed at that time, & having been interested about forty years (of my seventy eight) & undergone the toil & fatigue & suffering of travelling over 100,000 miles on behalf of the Indians—permit me to say, that while the Administrations, from Washington to the present, have generally recommended kind treatment of the Aborigines, yet none have upheld a policy, so wise, humane & fruitful of good as the present one. I have seldom heard a voice raised against it from any party or sect. Thy determination to adhere to it, & thy kindness & assistance to the Commissioners, has given confidence & encouragement to the true friends of the Indian. The work, in my humble belief, originated from a higher power than man, & its faithful execution must partake of the promise, 'Blessed is the man that considereth the poor; the Lord will deliver him in times of trouble.' May the rich ~~promise~~ blessing continue to rest on thee & thy beloved family is the sincere desire of thy attached friend"—ALS, USG 3.

1877, FEB. 8.   U.S. Senator George F. Edmunds of Vt. to USG. "Personal . . . Unable to call personally, I take the liberty to write what I wish to say. 1st. Gen Miles has recommended, I learn, that my brotherinlaw Capt. Wyllys Lyman 5th infantry, be ordered before a retiring board. Capt Lyman does *not* wish to be retired, & hopes to be well again. . . . Second. I shall be glad if you can appoint young Mr Woodbridge a paymaster in place of Col Halsey who is to be retired I am told. It is the only paymaster ship Vt has."—ALS, DNA, RG 94, ACP, 779 1877. Capt. Wyllys Lyman retained his commission. See *PUSG*, 18, 555. On Feb. 12, USG nominated John B. Keefer as maj., paymaster, in place of Maj. Thomas H. Halsey, retired.

1877, FEB. 10.   Isaac F. Quinby, U.S. marshal, Rochester, N. Y., to USG. "Yesterday P. M in response to a telegram from Gen'l C. D. Mac Dougall M. C I sent one to you, placing in your hands my resignation as Marshal of this district. This office I have now held for nearly eight years and with the incoming Administration of whichever political party I could not expect to hold it much longer. If Hayes is your successor, and it is my earnest prayer that he may be, Mac Dougall may be able to retain the office for the next four years You have loaded me with substantial evidences of your friendship and I do not believe that you doubt the heavy debt of gratitude that I feel for it all: It does not seem as if it would ever be in my power to express my sense of this except in words: will you believe that they come from the depths of a loving heart."—ALS, DNA, RG 60, Letters from the President. On Feb. 13, USG nominated Clinton D. MacDougall as marshal, Northern District, N. Y. On Feb. 14, Quinby again wrote to USG. "It was reputed among my friends that you had demanded my resignation as might be inferred from the injudicious wording of General Ma Dougall's despatch 'The President directs you to tender your resignation by telegraph.' This in some manner got out, certainly not through me, and you see what sinister interpretation could be, and was, placed upon the language. Thanking you for your telegram of today . . ."—ALS, *ibid.* On Feb. 15, Charles C. Barton, Rochester, wrote to [USG]. "Through fraud, chicanery and misrepresentation, Gen. I. F. Quinby, you friend and mine, was induced to tender his resignation as U. S. Marshal, believing that it was your wish. I know that he now regrets it, and I know also that both he and his family need that he should retain the position so long as possible. You may not remember the writer by his signature, but you will remember the hero of the practical joke of the 'bewitching widow' who lived near the 'Tallahatchie' on the Oxford road."—ALS, *ibid.* See letter to Rutherford B. Hayes, Jan. 21, 1881.

On Sept. 3, 1876, Quinby, New York City, had telegraphed to USG "or His Secy." "Will the President be at his Cottage tomorrow answer to thirty three East seventeenth st"—Telegram received (at 7:00 P.M.), DLC-USG, IB.

1877, FEB. 12. USG note. "The Sec. of War may place the name of Oliver T. Morton, son of Senator O. P. Morton, on the list of cadet appointments, for June next, below those already named. It may be that failures enough will occur among the apts. 'At Large' to admit him."—ANS, DNA, RG 94, Correspondence, USMA. A clerk noted on the docket. "Failed to report."—E, *ibid.*

[*1877, Feb. 12*]. To [*Culver C. Sniffen*]. "Submit to the Sec. of War whether the unexpired sentence of Capt. Morgan might not now be remitt[ed.] Would like answer to-day as the Sec. of War leaves in the morning to be absent for several days."—AN (undated), Wayde Chrismer, Bel Air, Md. On the same day, Secretary of War James D. Cameron wrote to USG that he had remitted the sentence of Capt. Morgan L. Ogden.—Copy, DNA, RG 107, Letters Sent, Military Affairs.

1877, FEB. 12. Maj. Thomas A. McParlin, Santa Fé, to USG. "First Lieutenant Granville Lewis fifth infantry acting Assistant Commissary subsistency fort Leavenworth wounded in Knee by indians seventy five Campaign on Genl Miles is Somewhat lame Can ride Any distance Walk without Cane do any kind garrison duty will improve in time Can recommend him as highly Competent & meritorious & believe generals PALL and Miles will Corroborate his fitness for Captaincy in quartermaster or Commissary Department to retire him would be great injustice to him & the service Commend him to your most favorable Consideration and trust you will recommend to your successor—"—Telegram received (at 7:40 P.M.), DNA, RG 94, Applications for Positions in War Dept. 1st Lt. Granville Lewis retained his commission. ·
On Oct. 31, 1866, Maj. Gen. Philip H. Sheridan, New Orleans, had written to USG. "As the cholera and yellow fever have nearly disappeared from among the troops of my command I deem it my duty to notify the General in Chief of the valuable services rendered by Brevet Colonel and Surgeon T. A. McParlin U. S. A. Medical Director Department of the Gulf. . . ." —Copy, *ibid.*, ACP, S1330 CB 1866. On Nov. 15, USG favorably endorsed this recommendation.—Copy, *ibid.*, RG 108, Register of Letters Received. McParlin was appointed bvt. brig. gen. to date from Nov. 26.

1877, FEB. 13. USG veto. "I have the honor to return herewith, without my approval, H. R. No 3367. entitled 'An Act to remove the charge of Desertion from the Military record of Alfred Rouland.'—The reasons for withholding my signature may be found in the accompanying report received from the Secretary of War—"—Copy, DNA, RG 130, Messages to Congress. *HED*, 44-2-39; *SMD*, 49-2-53, 409. Ill with fever, Alfred Rouland had left the 28th Mich. without leave in April, 1866; the regt. mustered out before he could rejoin.

1877, FEB. 13. Henry J. Scudder *et al.*, New York City, to USG. "On behalf of the Bar of this City we respectfully ask that no change be made in the office of

Marshal until the present incumbent and his friends have at least a chance of being heard."—Printed copy, DNA, RG 56, Applications. On Feb. 23, USG nominated Louis F. Payn as marshal, Southern District, N. Y., in place of Oliver Fiske.

In Feb., 1873, Noah Davis and ten others had written to USG recommending Fiske as marshal.—Printed copy, *ibid.* On March 14, USG nominated Fiske. Related papers are *ibid.*

1877, FEB. 14.   USG veto of an act to amend the Revised Statutes, citing a provision to compel executive depts. and U.S. courts "to publish all their advertisements in newspapers selected by the Clerk of the House of Representatives."—Copy, DNA, RG 130, Messages to Congress. *SMD*, 49-2-53, 409–10. On Feb. 27, USG approved a version of the bill omitting that provision. See *CR*, 44–2, 1614.

[*1877, Feb. 14*].   Levi P. Morton to USG. ". . . Mr. Hess is a German; has long been an active influential supporter of the Republican cause, and enjoys the confidence of the community. He is a very popular man amongst the Germans especially, and if you can see your way clear to give him the position, I shall be much gratified"—LS (partial facsimile), eBay, Sept. 24, 1999. In Nov., Jacob Hess, a New York City Republican, lost his bid for county register.

1877, FEB. 15.   To Senate transmitting a statement of State Dept. appropriations and expenditures from 1789 to 1876.—Copies, RG 59, Reports to the President and Congress; *ibid.*, RG 130, Messages to Congress. *SED*, 44-2-38.

1877, FEB. 16.   Washakie and three others, Big Wind River, Wyoming Territory, to USG. "We the undersigned, Chief, Head-men, and men of the Shoshone Indians, (Eastern Band) in council assembled this 16th day of Febry, 1877, beg to be permitted to inform you, that we have heard with sorrowing hearts, that our good Agent, Dr Irwin, is about to be called away from us, to assume other duties. We fear that our Great Father intends to send some stranger here, to be our Agent; one whom we do not know—and who does not know us, nor understand Indians. We do not like to have a stranger for our Agent   He might not like Indians. We might not like him. He might be quick to get angry with us. The Shoshones all know James I. Patten our former teacher   He taught our children for a long while. They all know him. He talks good Shoshone. He knows all of our people. He has never lied to us. We believe he will give us all the goods the Great Father sends to the Shoshones. We want Mr. Patten for our Agent. He was with our old Agent and knows how he treated us, how he managed our affairs. Because he has been with us a long time he knows our wants better than any stranger could, and will be able to let the Great Father know what is best for us   He can induce our men to continue to farm and to improve themselves better than one whom we do not know and in whom we would have no confidence   He is our friend—"—LS (by mark), DNA, RG 48, Appointment Papers, Wyoming Territory. Washakie endorsed this letter. "I hereby certify that the other chiefs of the band are away—But we know that they will all heartily endorse our action in the above"—ES (by mark), *ibid.* On March 29, James I. Patten replaced James Irwin as agent, Shoshone and Bannock Agency.

On Oct. 21, 1869, USG had authorized the proclamation of a treaty concluded Oct. 1, 1863, with western Shoshone bands.—DS (facsimile), eBay, Nov., 2001. See *PUSG*, 19, 548.

1877, Feb. 19.   U.S. Representative Elias W. Leavenworth of N. Y. to USG. "I have the honor to present to you the accompanying application, the commend it to your favorable consideration."—ALS, OFH.

1877, Feb. 20.   USG endorsement. "I would nominate Gen: Jas A. Williamson to be Commissioner—"—Copy, DNA, RG 59, Letters of Resignation and Declination. On Feb. 21, Admiral David D. Porter *et al.* petitioned USG. "The undersigned, residents of Washington City, having learned that a vacancy is about to occur in the Commission for the Government of the District of Columbia, beg leave to recommend for appointment to such vacancy, Mr Archibald Campbell of Washington, a resident of the city for thirty years past, whose well known integrity and experience in public affairs eminently qualify him for a position of such trust."—DS (12 signatures), *ibid.*, RG 60, Records Relating to Appointments. On Feb. 26, U.S. Representative John M. Davy of N. Y. telegraphed to USG. "I have just been informed that Williamson will not accept the commission ship of the District of Columbia in place of Ketchum resigned it would be very gratifying to me to receive the appointment if agreeable to your wishes   I will call and see you in the morning in reference to the matter"—Telegram received, *ibid.*, RG 107, Telegrams Collected (Bound). On March 2, Ulysses S. Grant, Jr., wrote to Sevellon A. Brown, chief clerk, State Dept. "The President wishes to withdraw the resignation of Genl Ketcham as Com. of Dist. of Columbia so that he can go on with some important work on hand. Will you please send it over by messenger and have the records corrected so that there will appear no intermission in his office as Commissioner"—ALS, *ibid.*, RG 59, Letters of Resignation and Declination. See *Washington Evening Star*, Feb. 26, 1877.

1877, Feb. 22.   Ulysses S. Grant, Jr., to Attorney Gen. Alphonso Taft. "The President asks that you will consider the question of the propriety of pardoning all the political prisoners now confined"—ALS, DLC-William H. Taft. On Feb. 23, Secretary of State Hamilton Fish recorded in his diary. ". . . I ask what is meant by Political Prisoners, he says 'the Ku Klux Klan' who have now been in prison, for some two or three years."—DLC-Hamilton Fish. See *PUSG*, 23, 228–32.

1877, Feb. 23.   To Congress transmitting the report of a commission to determine the U.S.-Canada boundary "from the Northwest angle of the Lake of the Woods, to the summit of the Rocky Mountains."—Copies, DNA, RG 59, Reports to the President and Congress; *ibid.*, RG 130, Messages to Congress. *SED*, 44-2-41.

1877, FEB. 23.   Joseph Henry, Washington, D. C., to USG. "In behalf of the National Academy of Sciences, I beg leave respectfully to nominate for the position of Superintendent of the National Observatory, left vacant by the death of Admiral Davis, Mr Simon Newcomb, a Professor in the Navy and now First Assistant in the Observatory. . . ." —LS (press), Smithsonian Institution Archives. John W. Draper, New York University, and Frederick A. P. Barnard, Columbia College, wrote to USG on the same subject.—Copies, *ibid.* Rear Admiral John Rodgers succeeded Charles H. Davis as superintendent, Naval Observatory.

[*1877, Feb. 24*].   USG note. "I wish the Sec. of War would designate an officer of the War Dept. to hear and examine fully the case and application of Lt. Romey, 5th Inf.y and ~~extend his leave of absence~~ [give him authority to delay rejoining his regiment—] to cover the time necessary for this. He should also have orders to proceed to Ft. Gibson to attend the pr[oce]edings of the board of survey to convene there March 1st if his statement warrats such order."—AN (bracketed phrase not in USG's hand), Wayde Chrismer, Bel Air, Md. On March 1, Judge Advocate Gen. William M. Dunn wrote to Inspector Gen. Randolph B. Marcy concerning the case of 1st Lt. Henry Romeyn, court-martialed in 1875 for neglect of duty in the loss of more than sixty tons of forage. Dunn ruled that the army could not continue to stop Romeyn's pay.—Copy, DNA, RG 94, Letters Received, 2966 1875. Related papers are *ibid.*

1877, FEB. 24.   Postmaster Gen. James N. Tyner to USG. "I have notice of the sudden death this morning of A. W. Denison, postmaster at Baltimore, Md. In accordance with the law, I have passed the office over to the only surviving surety on his bond. It would be well to promptly nominate a successor. Do you know whom it should be? If so, please notify me, that I may make up the papers."—*Washington Evening Star*, March 1, 1877. On the same day, Culver C. Sniffen wrote to John A. J. Creswell, Washington, D. C. "The President directs me to forward the enclosed letter from the Postmaster General, for your perusal, and to ask you to name the best man, in your judgment, for the place—" —Copy, DLC-USG, II, 3. On March 1, Creswell wrote to the editor, *Evening Star*, that he saw USG twice and on his second visit concurred with others who had recommended John B. Askew.—*Evening Star*, March 1, 1877. On Feb. 27, USG had nominated Askew as postmaster, Baltimore; the Senate did not confirm this nomination.

1877, FEB. 25.   Thomas C. Fletcher, Washington, D. C., to USG. "Milo Blair Esqr of Boonville, Missouri, will be named by his friends, to you for some appointment. I am not advised what they will ask for him. I desire to say that Mr Blair is a man of integrity & high character and standing. He is Editor & proprietor of one of the leading Republican papers in central Missouri and has been for a number of years an active and prominent man in the management of party affairs in Mo I know of no man in all the state more deserving of your confidence or by his services better entitled to favor at the hands of the party."— ALS, NNP. No appointment followed.

1877, FEB. 26.   USG pardon for Edgar R. Pierce, indicted in Nev. "for stealing money-letters from the mails, while engaged in the Postal service, upon which indictment no trial has been had."—Copy, DNA, RG 59, General Records. On April 26, 1876, Culver C. Sniffen had written to Attorney Gen. Edwards Pierrepont "that from the verbal statements of Senator Jones," USG opposed indictment in this case.—Copy, DLC-USG, II, 3.

1877, FEB. 26.   To Senate. "I have the honor to return herewith Senate Bill. No 234. entitled 'An Act to allow a pension of thirty-seven dollars per month to soldiers who have lost both, an arm and a leg'—Under existing law soldiers who have lost both an arm and a leg, are entitled to draw a monthly pension of eighteen dollars—As the object of this bill is to allow them eighteen dollars per month for each of these disabilities—or thirty-six dollars in all, it is returned simply for an amendment of title which shall agree with its provisions—When this shall have been done, I will very gladly give it my immediate approval—" —Copy, DNA, RG 130, Messages to Congress. On Feb. 28, USG approved a corrected bill.

1877, FEB. 26.   Solomon R. Devinney, Mays Landing, N. J., to USG seeking aid in obtaining the discharge of his son Walter, who had enlisted in the British army.—DS, DNA, RG 59, Miscellaneous Letters. Related papers are *ibid.*

1877, FEB. 28.   USG veto. "I have the honor to return herewith without my approval Senate Bill No 691 entitled 'An Act for the relief of Edward A. Leland' The reasons for withholding my approval may be found in the accompanying communications received from the Secretary of the Interior—"—Copy, DNA, RG 130, Messages to Congress. Edward A. Leland's patent for a paint can had expired in 1874; the bill to extend the patent failed to indemnify subsequent users. See *CR*, 44–2, 2069; *SRC*, 44-1-456.

[*1877, Feb.*].   USG endorsement. "Referred to the Postmaster General, hoping that he may be able to give a position to Mr. Fisk."—Robert F. Batchelder, Catalog 9, no. 155; Charles Hamilton Auction No. 53, Oct. 21, 1971, no. 174. Written on a Feb. letter from James Redpath to Postmaster Gen. James N. Tyner, favorably endorsed by U.S. Representative Nathaniel P. Banks of Mass., recommending Henry C. Fisk, former col., 65th N. Y., and bvt. brig. gen. No appointment followed.

[*1877, Feb.*].   USG note. "Bring up the papers in the application for pardon of Jas. M. Rothrock for purling letters from—Balt P. O. Served as a soldier: took no money: has served 14 months out of 3 years."—AN (undated), Mrs. Paul E. Ruestow, Jacksonville, Fla. In Dec., 1875, Joseph M. Rothrock, former 1st lt., 5th Md., and Baltimore postal clerk, had been arrested "on suspicion of purloining letters containing money."—*Baltimore American and Commercial Advertiser*, Dec. 22, 1875.

[*1877, Feb.*]. USG note. "Miss Loughborough asks to be appointed in the Light House Board. See the Sec. of the Treas. in her behalf."—AN (undated), DNA, RG 56, Applications. Filed with a letter of Feb. 8 from Margaret A. Loughborough, Washington, D. C., to USG. "Owing to the illness of the Secretary of the Treasury I have not been able to have an interview with him since I saw you and I have been advised by Captain Walker, of the Light House Board, to obtain a card from you recommending me to the Assistant Secretary of the Treasury for an appointment. If I am not trespassing too much on your kindness, I will be so much indebted to you if you will give me the card to the Assistant Secretary at your earliest convenience, . . ."—L, *ibid.* Related papers are *ibid.* On Feb. 23, Loughborough was appointed writer, Lighthouse Board.

[*1877, Feb.*]. To [*Culver C. Sniffen*]. "Notify Ch. Com. on public lands—Oglesby—that I withdraw request to hold nomination of land officer at New Ulm, Minn."—AN (undated), Wayde Chrismer, Bel Air, Md. On Feb. 8, Sniffen had written to U.S. Senator Richard J. Oglesby of Ill. "The President desires me to ask you to please take no action on the nomination of Charles C Goodenow, whose name was sent to the Senate yesterday for the office of Receiver, at Ulm Minn."—Copy, DLC-USG, II, 3. On Feb. 23, the Senate confirmed this nomination.

[*1877, Feb.-March*]. USG endorsement. "Referred to the Sec. of War. Lieut. Birnie graduated No 1 in his Class at West Point and has since been examined for admittance into the Ordnance Corps, passing a satisfactory examination. Had there been a vacancy in that Corps occurring after his examination during my term of office he would have been appointed to it. I commend him as in every way worthy and capable."—AES (undated), DNA, RG 94, ACP, 1373 1874. Written on an undated letter from 1st Lt. Rogers Birnie, Jr., Washington, D. C., to USG. "Pursuant to your Verbal directions to me on the 31st of July 1876, that in the event of a vacancy in the Ordnance Department of the Army, I should write you personally of it, and you would appoint me to that vacancy, as I have already passed the examination required by law, Such a vacancy having occurred I have taken the liberty to address you."—ALS, *ibid.* Related papers are *ibid.* Birnie, Jr., USMA 1872, transferred from the 13th Inf. to the Ordnance Dept. as of June 13, 1878.

1877, MARCH 2. USG proclamation convening the Senate at noon on March 5 "to receive and act upon such communications as may be made to it on the part of the Executive."—DS, DNA, RG 130, Presidential Proclamations. See George F. Edmunds to Hamilton Fish, Dec. 26, 1876, and Fish to Edmunds, Jan. 27, 1877, DLC-Hamilton Fish.

On March 3, Saturday, Culver C. Sniffen wrote to Secretary of State Hamilton Fish. "The President directs me to say that he thinks an Executive Order should be issued closing the Departments on Monday next—If you agree with the President in this view, you are authorized to issue the order—"—Copy, DLC-USG, II, 3. On the same day, Fish wrote to USG. "I understand that it has not been the custom to issue an Executive Order closing the Departments on the Inauguration Day; but that each of the Departments has been *practically* closed, so far as any business is concerned, having only some one or more to of the officers or Clerks on hand, to meet any Emergency that may arise."—ALS (press), DLC-Hamilton Fish. Also on March 3, Sniffen wrote to cabinet secretaries that USG had authorized executive depts. to close on March 5.—ALS, DNA, RG 45, Letters Received from the President; *ibid.*, RG 56, Letters Received from the President.

1877, MARCH 2.   U.S. Senator John B. Gordon of Ga. and U.S. Representative Lucius Q. C. Lamar of Miss. to USG. "Can we have very brief interview with you to-day on matter of public interest and at what hour"—Telegram received, DNA, RG 107, Telegrams Collected (Bound).

1877, MARCH 3.   USG order designating Commodore Robert W. Shufeldt, John W. Hunter, and John W. Coe as a commission to oversee the sale or exchange of U.S. land in Wallabout Bay, N. Y., to Brooklyn.—DS, DNA, RG 45, Letters Received from the President. See *CR*, 44–1, 3834–36; *SRC*, 44-2-658; *HRC*, 45-2-932; *U.S. Statutes at Large*, XIX, 239; *New York Times*, Jan. 19, 1890, April 18, 1900.

1877, MARCH 3.   USG pardon. "Whereas, John A. Lant, having been convicted of transmitting unlawful matter through the Mail, in the District Court of the United States for the Southern District of New York, was by the said Court sentenced, on the 30th. day of December, 1875, to imprisonment for eighteen months in the Penitentiary at Albany in the State of New York; And whereas, he has served more than three-fourths of the said term, and his pardon is prayed for by many respectable citizens; and inasmuch as he has a wife and young family needing his assistance, and deeming that the ends of justice do not require his longer imprisonment: . . ."—Copy, DNA, RG 59, General Records. Anthony Comstock, special postal agent, had pressed the charges. See *New York Times*, Aug. 25, Dec. 11, 1875.

[*1869–1877*].   USG note. "The mourning drapery about the house may be taken down"—AN, Wayde Chrismer, Bel Air, Md.

[*1869–1877*].   USG note. "Send notice to members of the Cabinet that there will be a Cabinet meeting at 11 a. m. to-morrow."—AN, Ulysses Grant Dietz, Maplewood, N. J.

[*1869–1877*].   USG note. "Refer to Atty. Gen. and recommend that he have this printed so that copies may be sent to Congress"—AN, Wayde Chrismer, Bel Air, Md.

[*1869–1877*].   USG note. "Ask Atty. Gen. to make his recommendation in the Georgia cases as soon at his earlyest convenience."—AN, Wayde Chrismer, Bel Air, Md. Culver C. Sniffen endorsed this note. "Apl. 29. endorsement on brief"—AE (initialed), *ibid.*

1877, MARCH 8.   USG endorsement. "I hope the Sec. of War will take the same action in the case of Gn. Reynolds that was taken in the case of Maj. Moore."— AES, DNA, RG 94, Letters Received, 2440 1876. Col. Joseph J. Reynolds and Capt. Alexander Moore had been court-martialed after an unsuccessful attack in March, 1876, on a Sioux village near the Little Powder River, Montana Territory. See *PUSG*, 16, 577–78.

On April 6, 1876, Culver C. Sniffen had written to U.S. Senator Oliver P. Morton of Ind. "The President directs me to acknowledge the receipt of your letter of todays date, enclosing telegram from Genl. Reynolds, and in reply to say that no charges against Genl. Reynolds have reached him. Due time will be given the General before any action will be taken here against him."—Copy, DLC-USG, II, 3. On Feb. 22, 1877, Reynolds, Lafayette, Ind., telegraphed to Ulysses S. Grant, Jr. "Please ask president Send for record and act on my Case"—Telegram received (at 11:24 A.M.), OFH.

On March 4, 1877, Gen. William T. Sherman wrote to Lt. Gen. Philip H. Sheridan. ". . . A new Board was Called here yesterday, Reynolds was on hand, and the Board pronounced him incapacitated for Service—But meantime I hear, (am not certain) that Gnl Grant desirous to provide for his Secretary Sniffen—retired a Paymaster, & appointed Sniffen to the place, thus using the only vacancy in the Retired list & Shutting out Reynolds. If another vacancy happens very soon I will endeavor to have the new Regime put in Reynolds for with you I agree that of all things we need young Colonels of Cavalry—. . ."—ALS, DLC-Philip H. Sheridan. Reynolds was retired as of June 25. See letter to Maj. Culver C. Sniffen, July 1, 1878.

1877, MARCH 16.   Sampson P. Bayly, "Hayes Elector Va," Washington, D. C., to USG. "The order you made on the 28th of Feb—to appoint Wm H. Mosby Special Agt—of Customs, and put Chamberlin, back in the Internal Revenue department has not been carried out. Mr Conant made out Mosbys commission and signed it, but orderd the appointment Clerk to hold the commission untill Chamberlin was appointed by Gen—Raum,   Please give me your card to the Secretary of the Treasuary and I will see him upon the Subject,"—ALS, USG 3. See Bayly to James A. Garfield, Jan. 24, 1881, DLC-James A. Garfield.

1877, MARCH 23.   To William H. Lowdermilk. "I can give you but little information in the direction asked in your letter of the 20th inst. except that Mr. Dent was born in Cumberland, Md. in 1787—October or Nov.—, moved to Pittsburgh Pa in early life, and to Mo. in 1817."—ALS, H. Bartholomew Cox, Oxen Hill, Md. See Lowdermilk, *History of Cumberland, (Maryland) from the Time of the Indian Town,* . . . (Washington, 1878), pp. 262–63.

1877, MARCH 26.   Joseph Henry, Smithsonian Institution, to USG. "I hereby certify that the Smithsonian Institution has received from General U. S. Grant, for exhibition in the National Museum of the United States, a Wire Bust of himself presented to him through the Peruvian Commn to the Int. Ex. of 1876."—DS (press), Smithsonian Institution.

1877, APRIL 13.   Reuben E. Fenton, Jamestown, N. Y., to Secretary of State William M. Evarts. "Hon S J Bowen of Washington, whom I beg to introduce, is aggrieved to find that your understanding of the matter of difference grow-ing out of the sale of property by Genl Grant to him in the winter of 1869 was arranged on the basis of a control of the Dist-patronage. Pardon me, but I hardly think this ~~is so~~ was the case, at least my knowledge of the affair tends to a different conclusion. Hon E B Washburne & myself learning, a few days sub-sequent to the 4th of Mch 69, of the sale & resale by Genl Grant, were anxious as to what might be said prejudicial to him & after conferring together, it was determined that I should see Mr Bowen & urge an abandonment of his claim. I did so—& upon my appeal to him, without reference to patronage or office for himself or others, he finally consented to release the property. I cannot say what followed between the parties, but have always supposed that Mr B—was moved by my entreaty to cancel the contract & let the matter drop, upon repayment of the sum advanced. Commending Mr Bowen to your regard, . . ."—ALS, DLC-William M. Evarts. See *PUSG*, 19, 118–25, 128–29.

1877, JUNE 4.   Benjamin W. Richardson and two others, Royal Historical Soci-ety, London, to USG announcing his election as an honorary member.—DS, Smithsonian Institution.

1877, Nov. 24.   To President Rutherford B. Hayes. "Please extend leave of Lieutt Rice army to Covet time for Return to Regiment."—Telegram received (at 1:25 P.M.), DNA, RG 94, ACP, 5066 1877. On the same day, Secretary of War George W. McCrary endorsed this telegram. "The President directs that this request be granted and that Gen Grant be advised by cable"—AES, *ibid.* Also on Nov. 24, McCrary telegraphed to USG, Paris. "Extension Granted Rice." —ANS (telegram sent), *ibid.*, RG 107, Telegrams Collected (Bound). On Nov. 27, Gen. William T. Sherman endorsed papers concerning 1st Lt. Edmund Rice, 5th Inf. "No man knows better than General Grant how damaging it is to discipline to permit an officer to ignore all authority and do what he pleases— The President moved by high courtesy had no alternative but comply with General Grants request—This leave is merely to cover the time necessary to enable Lt Rice to reach his Regiment"—AES, *ibid.*, RG 94, ACP, 5066 1877. During 1877, Rice observed European armies. See *Brigadier-General Edmund Rice, U. S. A.* (n. p., [*1907*]), p. 6.

1877, Nov. 26.   To Achille Vogue, Guînes, France. "Your request for my auto-graph, attached to my own hand writing, was received some time since. I take pleasure in replying to your request."—ALS, Munson-Williams-Proctor Insti-tute, Utica, N. Y.

[*1877?*].   USG note. "Please telegraph reply. Tell Fred to send me six or eight of my Photograph, & oblige . . . Please mail enclosed letters also."—AN (ini-tialed), DLC-USG, IB.

1878, JAN. 30.   Orvil L. Grant, San Francisco, to U.S. Representative James A. Garfield of Ohio. "The Post master here is a personal friend of my brother who has deep Interest in his Welfare   prevent any adverse action until I Communicate With You   his retention desired by persons here"—Telegram received, DLC-James A. Garfield. On Jan. 31, Grant wrote to Garfield defending James Coey, postmaster, San Francisco, and former maj., 147th N. Y. ". . . If you will lay these facts before the President I know my Brother will appreciate it even more than I do. I feel that I will make a success here in my business"—ALS, *ibid.* On April 11 and June [10], Grant wrote to Garfield seeking political assistance for a struggling business venture.—ALS, *ibid.*

On May 14, 1870, Coey, San Francisco, had written to Columbus Delano, commissioner of Internal Revenue. "I learn by telegraph of the Presidents withdrawal of my name as Postmaster. I am now compelled by circumstances to request from you some appointment in the Revenue Department. . . ." —ALS, DNA, RG 56, Applications. Appointed assessor of Internal Revenue, Utah Territory, Coey resigned as of Feb. 1, 1872. See *PUSG,* 23, 340–41. On March 10, 1874, USG nominated Coey as postmaster, San Francisco.

Index

All letters written by USG of which the text was available for use in this volume are indexed under the names of the recipients. The dates of these letters are included in the index as an indication of the existence of text. Abbreviations used in the index are explained on pp. xvii–xxii. Individual regts. are indexed under the names of the states in which they originated.

Grant, Ulysses S. (*cont.*)
316, 362, 368*n*, 389, 440, 461; issues
pardons, 13, 13*n*–17*n*, 139*n*, 487, 489,
500, 501, 513, 515; third term for, 13*n*,
168*n*, 361, 371 and *n*, 399*n*–401*n*, 403*n*,
404*n*, 405*n*, 429–30, 433*n*, 437*n*, 438*n*,
440, 441*n*–42*n*, 456*n*, 457*n*, 458*n*–59*n*,
480*n*; administers army, 17, 17*n*–19*n*,
19–20, 20*n*, 36–37, 37*n*, 78*n*, 122–23,
123–28, 123*n*, 158 and *n*, 422, 426,
436*n*–37*n*, 488, 489, 498, 506, 508, 512,
514, 516; confronts electoral crisis, 17
and *n*, 18*n*–19*n*, 19–20, 20*n*, 21, 30,
31*n*–32*n*, 32, 32*n*–33*n*, 33, 34*n*, 36–37,
37*n*, 38, 38*n*–39*n*, 44 and *n*, 51*n*, 52*n*, 75,
78, 78*n*–82*n*, 95, 131*n*–32*n*, 143–45,
145*n*–46*n*, 148*n*–49*n*, 150*n*, 158–59;
disparaged, 18*n*, 175 and *n*, 321–22,
374*n*, 386*n*–87*n*, 437*n*; threatened with
assassination, 23*n*, 24*n*–25*n*, 27*n*, 30*n*,
34*n*, 35*n*, 36*n*, 135*n*–36*n*, 150*n*; relations with friends, 39, 94–95, 96, 192–
93, 194 and *n*, 331–32, 345, 347*n*, 350–
52, 362–63, 375, 388 and *n*, 392, 395,
397, 423–25, 438, 439–41, 439*n*, 443,
448–50, 450*n*–51*n*, 453–55, 455*n*–57*n*,
464, 468–69, 469*n*–74*n*, 476–77, 478–
79, 479*n*–80*n*, 487–88, 508, 516, 518;
annual message, 40, 48, 62–69, 69*n*–
73*n*, 89; family visits, 40, 88–89; during
Civil War, 41*n*–42*n*, 215*n*, 226, 250*n*,
303*n*, 347*n*, 464*n*, 490, 508; staff officers,
43*n*, 464; intervenes in S.C., 49 and *n*,
50*n*, 53–54, 56*n*–58*n*, 58, 59 and *n*, 60–
61, 60*n*, 73, 74*n*, 79*n*–80*n*, 81*n*–82*n*,
82–84, 87*n*, 88*n*, 89; personal reflections, 62–64, 67, 69, 71*n*, 78*n*–79*n*, 94–
95, 158–59, 202, 243, 297, 304 and *n*,
334, 366, 391–92, 408–9; administers
Indian policy, 64–65, 94, 97, 97*n*–98*n*,
99*n*, 325 and *n*, 494, 496–97, 506–8,
511; promotes education, 67; assesses
U.S. politics, 67, 184*n*, 240*n*, 254–55,
259, 265, 267, 271, 292, 313, 320, 351–
52, 355, 359–60, 362–63, 367, 368*n*,
370, 371, 389*n*, 403*n*, 440, 443*n*, 476–
77; interested in Santo Domingo, 68–
69, 162, 162*n*–64*n*, 306–7, 308*n*, 320–
21, 322*n*, 341–42, 342*n*, 430–32; racial
views, 71*n*, 251–52, 401*n*, 431, 432; pur-
sues extradition cases, 100–103, 103*n*–
5*n*; confronts Miss. unrest, 105; con-
cludes presidency, 106 and *n*, 160 and *n*,
161, 167, 266*n*, 285*n*, 514–15; intervenes in La., 106–7, 107*n*, 109*n*, 110*n*,
112*n*, 114, 116*n*–19*n*, 121*n*, 164–65,
165*n*–66*n*; intervenes at USMA, 113
and *n*; overhauls D.C. police commis-

sioners, 137–38, 138*n*–41*n*; vetoes bills,
137–38, 168*n*, 458*n*, 497, 502, 509, 510,
513; personal finances, 142, 142*n*–43*n*,
159, 174–75, 175*n*, 179, 179*n*–80*n*, 183,
184*n*–85*n*, 185, 186–87, 186*n*, 187*n*,
188*n*, 195*n*, 205, 214, 249 and *n*, 253,
264, 297–98, 298*n*–99*n*, 310, 317–18,
323, 324*n*, 336, 345*n*–46*n*, 352, 369*n*,
375, 404*n*, 407, 446, 448, 475, 475*n*–
76*n*; ponders future residence, 142, 265,
355, 370, 375, 392, 411, 455; visits Baltimore, 145*n*, 502; favors specie resumption, 152–53, 153*n*, 154–56, 154*n*, 156*n*;
promotes Statue of Liberty, 156 and *n*,
157*n*, 319; private secretaries, 164,
470*n*, 490; supplies autographs, 168*n*,
261*n*, 262, 485, 517; recommends appointments, 170, 171 and *n*, 175, 176
and *n*, 190, 486; manages cabinet, 172–
73, 173*n*–74*n*, 515; smokes cigars, 175*n*,
288*n*, 410; recalls Civil War, 177–78,
203, 206*n*, 283, 288*n*, 289, 291–92, 295,
298*n*, 314–15, 325–26, 330–31, 372–
73, 373–74, 373*n*, 381–86, 386*n*, 387*n*,
402, 403*n*, 409–10, 412–29, 433*n*, 434*n*,
449, 450*n*–51*n*, 451–52, 452*n*, 453–54,
462–63, 477–78, 479; as artistic subject, 178–79, 179*n*, 298*n*, 516; in Cincinnati, 179; in St. Louis, 180, 181, 183,
183*n*–84*n*, 221*n*; interested in veterans,
180, 193 and *n*, 232*n*, 250*n*, 378, 447;
visits Ohio, 181, 182*n*; visits Pa., 181,
182*n*–83*n*, 189 and *n*, 311*n*; recalls
presidency, 181, 239, 241*n*, 251–52,
256–58, 259*n*, 263, 270*n*, 272–73, 275
and *n*, 282, 301*n*, 304–7, 307*n*–8*n*, 309,
320–22, 325, 337–42, 342*n*–43*n*, 429–
32, 438*n*, 451, 454, 457*n*–58*n*, 469; in
Chicago, 182*n*, 185–87, 186*n*, 187*n*,
188, 195 and *n*, 202*n*, 474*n*; assessed,
182*n*, 212*n*–13*n*, 232*n*, 327*n*, 368*n*,
400*n*–401*n*, 433*n*, 434*n*–36*n*, 437*n*–
38*n*, 457*n*, 458*n*–59*n*; contemplates
memoirs, 183*n*–84*n*; in Galena, 186,
186*n*–87*n*, 195*n*, 410*n*; visits Washington, D.C., 192, 193, 194; early life, 192,
227*n*, 271, 280, 327*n*, 332, 351, 371*n*,
382, 404*n*, 415, 417–18, 420, 422, 427,
428–29, 433*n*, 491, 493; visits N.J., 196,
197 and *n*, 198 and *n*; visits Philadelphia,
196–97, 196*n*, 197*n*, 199 and *n*, 200–
201, 200*n*, 201*n*, 202 and *n*, 203 and *n*,
210, 266, 474*n*; as Rawlins trustee, 198–
99, 199*n*; advises sons, 199 and *n*, 201,
219, 368–69, 370, 375, 391, 407; sails
for Europe, 203 and *n*, 204–5, 204*n*,
205*n*, 210, 262; tours Europe, 205*n*–
480*n* passim, 517; advocates interna-

Virginia (*cont.*)
Republicans in, 22*n*; assassination threats from, 25*n*; blacks in, 28*n*–29*n*; during electoral crisis, 30*n*; political intimidation in, 89–90, 90*n*–93*n*, 124, 125; before Civil War, 127; patronage involving, 161, 161*n*–62*n*, 490, 495–96, 516; Reconstruction in, 421–22; civil rights enforced in, 489; Unionist in, 500; mentioned, 130*n*
Virginia, University of, Charlottesville, Va.: documents in, 89–90, 92*n*–93*n*
Vizzolo, Angelo (of Monkton, Md.), 131*n*
Vogue, Achille (of Guînes, France): letter to, Nov. 26, 1877, 517
Voorhees, Daniel W. (attorney), 14*n*

Waco, Tex., 29*n*
Wade, Benjamin F. (U.S. Senator), 431
Wadesborough, N.C., 129*n*
Wagner, Jacob (revenue agent), 498
Wagoner, Henry O. (of Denver), 72*n*
Wales, 210, 220
Walker, A. Barclay (Mayor of Liverpool), 208*n*, 210, 233, 233*n*–34*n*
Walker, Elisa (wife of A. Barclay Walker), 234*n*
Walker, John G. (U.S. Navy), 514
Walker, Samuel (Kan. militia), 146*n*
Walker, Thomas (British journalist), 232*n*
Walkerton, Ind., 25*n*
Wallabout Bay, N.Y., 515
Wallace, Lewis, 48*n*
Wallace, William H. (S.C. representative), 52*n*, 54*n*, 61*n*, 78*n*, 84*n*
Walter, John (*The Times* [London]), 206*n*–7*n*, 287 and *n*, 288
Wanderers' Club (London), 228*n*
Ward, David (master cutler), 281*n*
Ward, Robert (Iowa), 483
Ware, H. R. (of Miss.), 28*n*
Warmoth, Henry C. (Gov. of La.), 120*n*
Warren, Gouverneur K. (U.S. Army), 326, 390, 423, 434*n*–35*n*, 451*n*, 484
Warren, James H. (of San Francisco), 169*n*
Warsaw, 450, 459
Washakie (Shoshone), 510–11
Washburne, Adèle G. (wife of Elihu B. Washburne), 214, 215*n*, 218, 219*n*, 229*n*, 230*n*, 242 and *n*
Washburne, Elihu B. (minister to France): addresses protocol breach, 8*n*, 9*n*; in Chicago, 187*n*; disparaged, 213*n*, 464, 468, 469; letter to, June 9, 1877, 214; anticipates USG's visit, 214, 214*n*–15*n*, 216, 218, 219*n*, 228–29, 229*n*–30*n*; let-

ter to, June 11, 1877, 216; letter to, June 16, 1877, 218; letter to, June 22, 1877, 228–29; learns USG's plans, 240*n*, 241–42, 242*n*; letter to, July 13, 1877, 241–42; French friends of, 303*n*; during Civil War, 429; involved in USG's home sale, 517
Washburne, Hempstead (son of Elihu B. Washburne), 187*n*
Washington, George (U.S. President), 5*n*, 62, 127, 147*n*, 148*n*, 174*n*, 182*n*, 212*n*, 485, 507–8
Washington, D.C.: during electoral crisis, 36*n*, 37*n*, 150*n*; officials, 66, 164*n*, 440, 511; newspaper, 121*n*; reform school, 122–23, 123*n*; police commissioners, 137–38, 138*n*–41*n*; blacks in, 138*n*, 139*n*, 140*n*–41*n*, 487; in USG's travel plans, 180, 185–86, 188; as possible USG residence, 181, 265, 355; USG's properties in, 185, 186*n*, 517; bank in, 187*n*; USG visits, 189 and *n*, 190, 192, 193, 194, 202*n*; navy yard, 191*n*; as army hd. qrs., 343*n*; USG commends, 461; labor agitator in, 477*n*; murder in, 487; governed, 498–99
Washington, Miss., 28*n*
Washington, Pa., 40, 182*n*, 183, 186, 188, 189 and *n*, 496
Washington County Historical Society, Washington, Pa.: documents in, 189, 189*n* (2), 466–67
Washington Evening Star (newspaper), 110*n*
Washington Territory, 505
Washington University, St. Louis, Mo., 488
Waterhouse, Mrs. (sister-in-law of Ignacio Mariscal), 490–91
Waterman, Alfred (Ill. gauger), 17*n*
Waterman, John L. (U.S. commissioner), 92*n*
Watertown Arsenal, Watertown, Mass., 151
Watkin, Edward (South Eastern Railway): arranges USG's travel, 230*n*–31*n*, 293 and *n*; letter to, Oct. 19, 1877, 293*n*
Watmough, James H. (U.S. Navy), 504, 505
Watts, Frederick (Commissioner of Agriculture): submits report, 65; endorsement to, Oct. 12, 1871, 488; involved in appointments, 488; note to, Dec. 20, 1876, 490–91; administers dept., 490–91
Waynesboro, Ga., 503
Webb, Lewis W. (of Norfolk), 495
Webb, Sydney (Trinity House), 222*n*